Computational and Mathematical Modeling

Computational and Mathematical Modeling

Edited by Paul Cooper

CLANRYE
INTERNATIONAL
www.clanryeinternational.com

Clanrye International,
750 Third Avenue, 9th Floor,
New York, NY 10017, USA

ISBN: 978-1-63240-701-6

Cataloging-in-Publication Data

Computational and mathematical modeling / edited by Paul Cooper.
p. cm.
Includes bibliographical references and index.
ISBN 978-1-63240-701-6
1. Computer simulation. 2. Mathematical models. I. Cooper, Paul.
QA76.9.C65 C66 2018
003.3--dc23

For information on all Clanrye International publications
visit our website at www.clanryeinternational.com

CLANRYE INTERNATIONAL

Contents

Preface

Mathematical modeling uses mathematical models to represent ideas derived from the real world in order to make computable and analyzable data. Models can be divided according to results such as deterministic models and stochastic models and the level of details of data of a model, such as mechanistic and empirical models. Mathematical modeling allows users to make informed decisions and develop a scientific understanding. This book is a valuable compilation of topics, ranging from the basic to the most complex advancements in the field of mathematical modeling. It will help the readers in keeping pace with the rapid changes in this field.

All of the data presented henceforth, was collaborated in the wake of recent advancements in the field. The aim of this book is to present the diversified developments from across the globe in a comprehensible manner. The opinions expressed in each chapter belong solely to the contributing authors. Their interpretations of the topics are the integral part of this book, which I have carefully compiled for a better understanding of the readers.

At the end, I would like to thank all those who dedicated their time and efforts for the successful completion of this book. I also wish to convey my gratitude towards my friends and family who supported me at every step.

Editor

1

A combination of genetic algorithm and particle swarm optimization method for solving traveling salesman problem

Keivan Borna[1*] and Razieh Khezri[2]
*Corresponding author: Keivan Borna, Faculty of Mathematics and Computer Science, Kharazmi University, Tehran, Iran
E-mail: borna@khu.ac.ir

Reviewing editor: Cedric K.F. Yiu, Hong Kong Polytechnic University, Hong Kong

Abstract: Traveling salesman problem (TSP) is a well-established NP-complete problem and many evolutionary techniques like particle swarm optimization (PSO) are used to optimize existing solutions for that. PSO is a method inspired by the social behavior of birds. In PSO, each member will change its position in the search space, according to personal or social experience of the whole society. In this paper, we combine the principles of PSO and crossover operator of genetic algorithm to propose a heuristic algorithm for solving the TSP more efficiently. Finally, some experimental results on our algorithm are applied in some instances in TSPLIB to demonstrate the effectiveness of our methods which also show that our algorithm can achieve better results than other approaches.

Subjects: Algorithms & Complexity; Applied Mathematics; Computer Mathematics; Computer Science; Linear Programming; Mathematics & Statistics; Science; Technology

Keywords: traveling salesman problem; particle swarm optimization; genetic algorithm; optimization

1. Related works

The origins of the traveling salesman problem (TSP) are unclear. A handbook for traveling salesmen from 1832 mentions the problem and includes example tours through Germany and Switzerland, but contains no mathematical treatment.

Mathematical problems related to the TSP were treated in the 1800s by the Irish mathematician W. R. Hamilton and by the British mathematician Thomas Kirkman. Hamiltons Icosian Game was a

ABOUT THE AUTHORS

Keivan Borna joined the Department of Computer Science at the Faculty of Mathematics and Computer Science of Kharazmi University as an Assistant Professor in 2008. He earned his PhD in Computational Commutative Algebra from the Department of Mathematics, Statistics and Computer Science of the University of Tehran. His research interests include Computer Algebra, Cryptography, Approximation Algorithms, and Computational Geometry. He is the author of the "Advanced Programming in JAVA" (in Persian) and is a life member of "Elite National Foundation of Iran".

Razieh Khezri was graduated from Faculty of Engineering at Kharazmi University, Tehran, Iran. Her research interests include evolutionary computations.

PUBLIC INTEREST STATEMENT

This paper was benefited from a clean idea of combining two important methods in the famous "Traveling Salesman Problem":

Genetic Algorithm + Particle Swarm Optimization

This study enables us to make use of capabilities of both approaches. The practical results also admit the improvement of our approach.

recreational puzzle based on ending a Hamiltonian cycle. The general form of the TSP appears to have been first studied by mathematicians during the 1930s in Vienna and at Harvard, notably by Karl Menger, who defines the problem, considers the obvious brute-force algorithm, and observes the non-optimality of the nearest neighbor heuristic (Pang, Wang, Zhou, & Dong, 2004; Zhang, Guan, & Liu, 2007).

A salesman spends his time visiting *n* cities (or nodes) cyclically. In one tour, he visits each city just once, and finishes up where he started. The aim of the problem is to minimize the distance traveled (Lin & Kernighan, 1973).

Several techniques to obtain the optimal solution for the TSP have been provided by researchers, such as genetic algorithms (GAs), ant colony optimization (ACO), simulated annealing, neural networks, particle swarm optimization (PSO), evolutionary algorithms, mimetic computing, etc. Among them, PSO has gained much attention and been successfully applied in a variety of fields mainly for optimization problems (Zhang et al., 2007).

In Xu, Cheng, Yang, Yang, and Wang (2013), the concepts of mobile operators and mobile sequence are introduced, with which it reddened the rate of PSO algorithm and the formula of position updating. In Liao, Yau, and Chen (2012), the improved version of the PSO approach to solve TSP, which uses Fuzzy C-Means clustering, a rule-based route permutation, a random swap strategy and a cluster merge procedure is introduced. In Pang et al. (2004), fuzzy matrices were used to represent the position and velocity of the particles in PSO. In elsewhere, a discrete PSO is presented to solve TSP on a set of benchmark instances. The discrete PSO algorithm exploited the basic features of its continuous counterpart (Tasgetiren, Suganthan, & Pan, 2007). In another study, the generalized TSP by employing the generalized chromosome is solved. The subtraction operator between two particle positions is modified and a discrete PSO method is constructed for the TSP (Shi, Liang, Lee, Lu, & Wang, 2007). In Yan et al. (2012), the authors proposed an improved PSO by using a self-organizing construction mechanism and dynamic programming algorithm; their optimized model for the balanced multiple-salesman problem with time and capacity constraints is presented. It requires that a salesman visits each vertex at least once and returns to the starting vertex within given time. In Pang, Li, Dai, and Yu (2013), the traveling salesman problem was solved using GA approach.

More precisely, the system starts from a matrix of the calculated Euclidean distances between the cities to be visited by the traveling salesman and randomly chosen city order as the initial population. Then new generations are created repeatedly until the proper path is reached upon reaching a stopping criterion. In Gupta and Panwar (2013), the recent TSP-based re-indexing technique with PSO was enhanced. In this study, the color re-indexing is done by solving the problem as a TSP using PSO. In this paper, we combine the capability of PSO algorithm and heuristic crossover operator of GA to gain more efficiency.

2. A brief introduction to PSO

PSO is an approach to problems whose solutions can be represented as a point in an n-dimensional solution space. A number of particles are randomly set into motion through this space. At each iteration, they observe the "fitness" of themselves and their neighbors and "emulate" successful neighbors (those whose current position represents a better solution to the problem than theirs) by moving towards them. Various schemes for grouping particles into competing, semi-independent flocks can be used, or all the particles can belong to a single global flock. This extremely simple approach has been surprisingly effective across a variety of problem domains. PSO was developed by James Kennedy and Russell Eberhart in 1995 after being inspired by the study of bird flocking behavior by biologist Frank Heppner. It is related to evolution-inspired problem-solving techniques such as GAs (see Ai & Kachitvichyanukul, 2008; Arumugam & Rao, 2008; Chen et al., 2010; Hu, 2006; Kennedy & Eberhart, 1995, 2001; Labed, Gherboudj, & Chikhi, 2012; Li & Zhang, 2007; Liao et al., 2012, for more details and some recent advances using PSO).

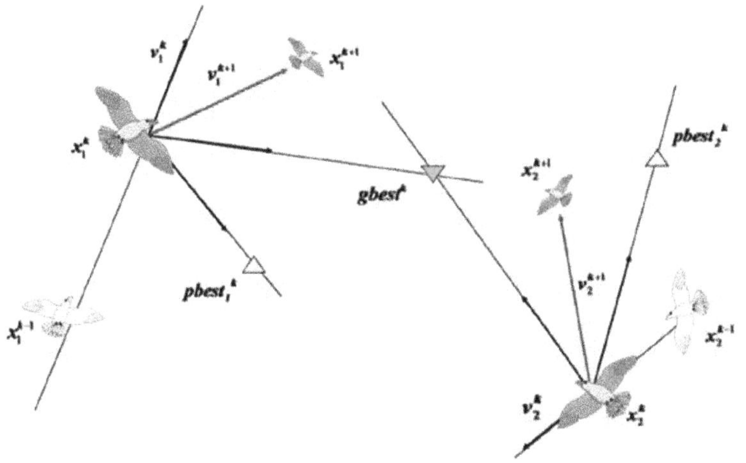

Figure 1. What is the best strategy to find the food?

PSO simulates the behaviors of bird flocking (Figure 1). Suppose the following scenario: a group of birds are randomly searching food in an area. There is only one piece of food in the area being searched. All the birds do not know where the food is. So what's the best strategy to find the food? The effective one is to follow the bird which is nearest to the food.

PSO learned from the scenario and used it to solve the optimization problems. In PSO, each single solution is a "bird" in the search space. We call it "particle". All of particles have fitness values which are evaluated by the fitness function to be optimized, and have velocities which direct the flying of the particles. The particles fly through the problem space by following the current optimum particles. PSO is initialized with a group of random particles (solutions) and then searches for optima by updating generations. At each iteration, each particle is updated by the following two values: the first one is the best solution (fitness) it has achieved so far, which is called *pbest*. Another value that is tracked by the particle swarm optimizer is the best value obtained so far by any particle in the population. This best value is a global best and called *gbest*. When a particle takes part of the population as its topological neighbors, the best value is a local best and is called *lbest*. After finding the two best values, the particle updates its velocity and positions with following Equation 1 and 2.

For each $1 \leq i \leq s$, where *s* is the size of swarm:

$$v[i] = v[i] + c1 \times rand() \times (pbest[i] - \text{present}[i]) + c2 \times rand() \times (gbest[i] - \text{present}[i]) \quad (1)$$

$$\text{present}[i] = \text{present}[i] + v[i] \quad (2)$$

where v[i] is the *i*th particle velocity, present[*i*] is *i*th particle solution, *pbest*[*i*] and *gbest*[*i*] are defined as stated before, and *rand*() is a random number in range [0; 1). c1, c2 are learning factors usually c1 = c2 = 2.

Particles' velocities on each dimension are clamped to a maximum velocity. If the sum of accelerations would cause the velocity on that dimension to exceed V_{max} which is a parameter specified by the user. Then the velocity on that dimension is limited to V_{max} (see Hu, 2006, for more details.

Algorithm 1*: Pseudo code for PSO*

1. ***Initialization***

Parameters and size of the swarm (S)

Randomly initialize particles positions and velocities

For each *particle, let pbest = x*

Calculate f(x) of each particle

Calculate gbest

2. ***While*** *(termination criterion is not met)*

For *i = 1 to S*

Calculate the new velocity using equation (1)

Calculate the new position using equation (2)

Calculate f(x) of each particle

If *(f(x) < f(pbest)) pbest = x*

If *(f(pbest) < f(gbest)) gbest = pbest*

3. ***Show*** *the best solution found gbest*

3. A comparisons between GA and PSO

According to Kachitvichyanukul (2012) and van Hook, Sahin, and Arnavut (2008), most of evolutionary techniques have the following procedure:

(1) Random generation of an initial population.

(2) Reckoning of a fitness value for each subject. It will directly depend on the distance to the optimum.

(3) Reproduction of the population based on fitness values.

(4) If requirements are met, then stop. Otherwise go back to 2.

From the procedure, we can learn that PSO shares many common points with GA. Both algorithms start with a group of a randomly generated population, both have fitness values to evaluate the population. Both update the population and search for the optimum with random techniques. Both systems do not guarantee success.

However, PSO does not have genetic operators like crossover and mutation. Particles update themselves with the internal velocity. They also have memory, which is important to the algorithm.

Compared with GA, the information sharing mechanism in PSO is significantly different. In GAs, chromosomes share information with each other. So the whole population moves like a one group towards an optimal area. In PSO, only *gbest* gives out the information to others. It is a one-way information sharing mechanism. The evolution only looks for the best solution. Compared with GA, all the particles tend to converge to the best solution quickly even in the local version in most cases.

4. Crossover operation

In optimization, *k*-opt is a simple local search algorithm first proposed by Cores in 1958 for solving the TSP (Labed et al., 2012). The main idea behind it is to take a route that crosses over itself and reorder it so that it does not.

The 2-opt is one of the models of *k*-opt. The 2-opt operator will have to be slightly modified in order to be used in multi-objective TSP. A simple way to apply the 2-opt operator would be to randomly apply it either to the first objective, or the second objective, and so on, with equal probabilities. Let's call this method A.

But this yields an uneven non-dominated set, with a majority of the points flying at the extremities. An alternative would be to sum up the objective function and use $d(x; y)$ as the sum of the individual costs or distances between the cities x and y. Let's call this method B. This method results in a dense midsection in the non-dominated set, but values do not reach extreme values of the objectives.

During the improvement process, the algorithm examines whether the exchange of two edges produces a shorter tour. The algorithm continues until no improvement is possible Figure 2. The steps of the algorithm are presented below:

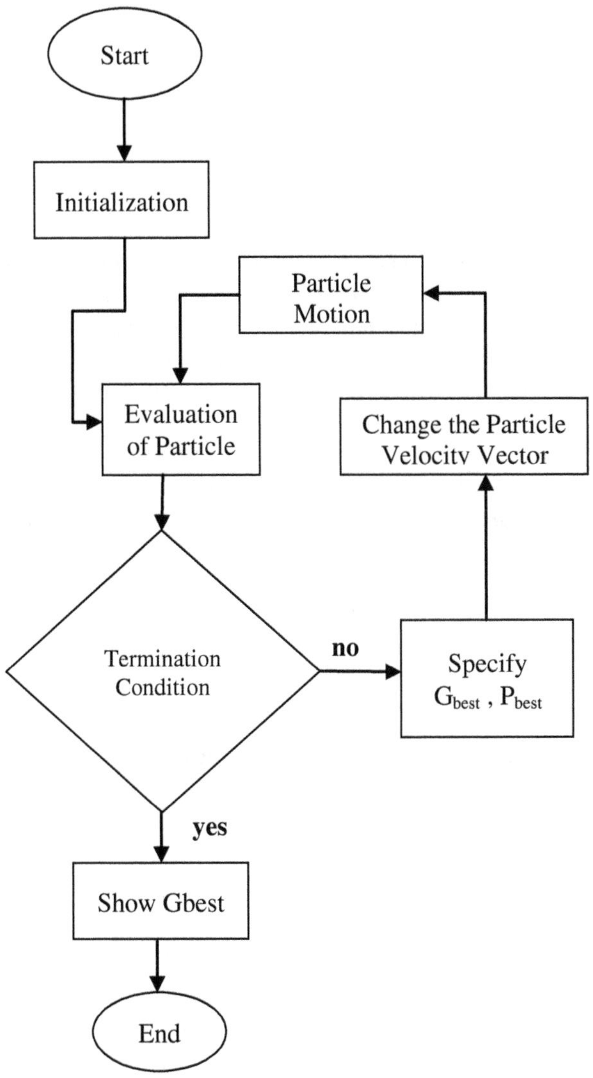

Figure 2. The diagram of PSO algorithm.

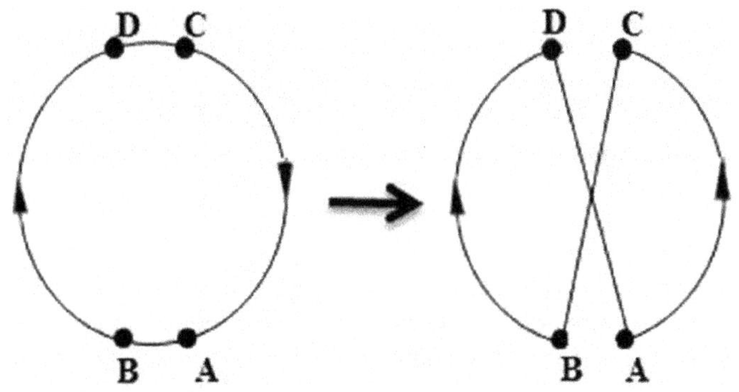

Figure 3. The 2-opt operator.

(1) Take two pairs of consecutive nodes, pairs (A, B) and (C, D) from a tour (see Figure 3).
(2) Check if the distance (AB + CD) is higher than (AD + BC).
(3) If that is the case, swap A and C, resulting in reversing the tour between the two nodes.
(4) If improvement of the tour, then go to 1, otherwise stop (see Labed et al., 2012).

The time complexity for the 2-opt algorithm is $O(n^2)$.

For the ease of reader and also for the sake of completeness, we have include an explanation of the Crossover Operation mainly from Genetic Server and Genetic Library (NeuroDimension: www.nd.com/products/genetic.htm) in the next section.

5. Crossover operation

Crossover is a genetic operator that combines (mates) two chromosomes (parents) to produce a new chromosome (offspring). The idea behind crossover is that the new chromosome may be better than both of the parents if it takes the best characteristics from each of the parents. Crossover occurs during evolution according to a user-definable crossover probability. In our proposed algorithm, we have introduced the crossover operator in the aim to produce a new population.

5.1. Types of crossover

1. One Point: A crossover operator that randomly selects a crossover point within a chromosome then interchanges the two parent chromosomes at this point to produce two new offspring. Consider the following two parents which have been selected for crossover. The symbol | indicates the randomly chosen crossover point.

Parent 1: 11001|010

Parent 2: 00100|111

After interchanging the parent chromosomes at the crossover point, the following offspring are produced:

Offspring 1: 11001|111

Offspring 2: 00100|010

2. Two Point: A crossover operator that randomly selects two crossover points within a chromosome then interchanges the two parent chromosomes between these points to produce two new offspring. Consider the following two parents which have been selected for crossover.

Parent 1: 110|010|10

Parent 2: 001|001|11

After interchanging the parent chromosomes between the crossover points, the following offspring are produced:

Offspring 1: 110|001|10

Offspring 2: 001|010|11

5.2. Uniform

A crossover operator decides (with some probability known as the mixing ratio) which parent will contribute each of the gene values in the offspring chromosomes. This allows the parent chromosomes to be mixed at the gene level rather than the segment level (as with one and two point crossover). For some problems, this additional flexibility outweighs the disadvantage of destroying building blocks. Single and multi-point crossovers define cross points as places between loci where a individual can be split. Uniform crossover generalizes this scheme to make every locus a potential crossover point. A crossover mask, the same length as the individual structure, is created at random and the parity of the bits in the mask indicates which parent will supply the offspring with which bits.

Consider the following two parents which have been selected for crossover:

Parent 1: 01110011010
Parent 2: 10101100101

For each variable, the parent who contributes its variable to the offspring is chosen randomly with equal probability. Here, the offspring 1 is produced by taking the bit from parent 1 if the corresponding mask bit is 1 or the bit from parent 2 if the corresponding mask bit is 0. Offspring 2 is created using the inverse of the mask, usually.

Offspring 1: 111/011/1111
Offspring 2: 001/100/0000

Uniform crossover, like multi-point crossover, has been claimed to reduce the bias associated with the length of the binary representation used and the particular coding for a given parameter set. This helps to overcome the bias in single-point crossover towards short substrings without requiring precise understanding of the significance of the individual bits in the individual's representation. It is known how uniform crossover may be parameterized by applying a probability to the swapping of bits. This extra parameter can be used to control the amount of disruption during recombination without introducing a bias towards the length of the representation used.

5.3. Arithmetic

A crossover operator that linearly combines two parent chromosome vectors to produce two new offspring according to the following equations:

$$\text{Offspring 1} = a \times \text{Parent1} + (1 - a) \times \text{Parent2}$$
$$\text{Offspring 2} = (1 - a) \times \text{Parent1} + a \times \text{Parent2}$$

where a is a random weighting factor (chosen before each crossover operation).

Consider the following two parents (each consisting of four oat genes) which have been selected for crossover:

Parent 1: (0:3)(1:4)(0:2)(7:4)
Parent 2: (0:5)(4:5)(0:1)(5:6)

If $a = 0.7$, the following two offspring would be produced:

Offspring 1: (0:36)(2:33)(0:17)(6:86)
Offspring 2: (0:402)(2:981)(0:149)(6:842)

5.4. Heuristic

A crossover operator that uses the fitness values of the two parent chromosomes to determine the direction of the search. The offspring are created according to the following equations:

$$\text{Offspring 1} = \text{BestParent} + r \times (\text{BestParent} - \text{WorstParent})$$
$$\text{Offspring 2} = \text{BestParent}$$

where *r* is a random number between 0 and 1. It is possible that offspring 1 will not be feasible. This can happen if *r* is chosen such that one or more of its genes fall outside of the allowable upper or lower bounds. For this reason, heuristic crossover has a user settable parameter *n* for the number of times to try and find results in a feasible chromosome. If a feasible chromosome is not produced after *n* tries, the worst parent is returned as offspring 1.

6. Our algorithm for TSP using PSO

The famous TSP is a typical combination optimization problem, which is often used to assess the performance of the metahuristic algorithms. Currently, metahuristic algorithm mainly consists of GA, ACO algorithm and PSO algorithm. Each of these algorithms for solving TSP has advantages and disadvantages. For example, the GA may spend a lot of time to search for the optimal solution. The ACO spends less time but the ACO falls in local optimum easily. PSO is a relatively simple procedure due to the lack of these problems and has attracted researchers from various fields. TSP can be formulated such that we assume *n* is the number of cities we shall pass through them, and $D = (dij)$ is the distance matrix between each city *i* and *j* where $i, j = 1, 2, 3, \ldots, n$ (see Figure 4 for an example).

In our proposed algorithm for TSP, we use heuristic crossover (HC), which as we can see in the next section, will improve the performance of our algorithm.

Algorithm 2: *Pseudo code for* heuristic crossover (HC),
Input: Two solutions ***x1*** *and* ***x2***
Output: One solution ***x***
Steps:
Choose a random city ***v***
Move the city ***v*** *in the beginning of* ***x1*** *and* ***x2***
Initialize ***x*** *by* ***v***
i = 2; j = 2
While *[(i & j) <= n]*
  If *(x1(i) & x2(j) ∈ x))*
    i = i + 1
    j = j + 1
  Else If *(x1(i) ∈ x)*
    Concatenate x2(j) to x
    j = j + 1
  Else If *(x2(j) ∈ x)*
    Concatenate x1(i) to x
    i = i + 1
  Else
    Let ***u*** *be the last city in* ***x***

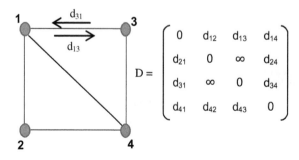

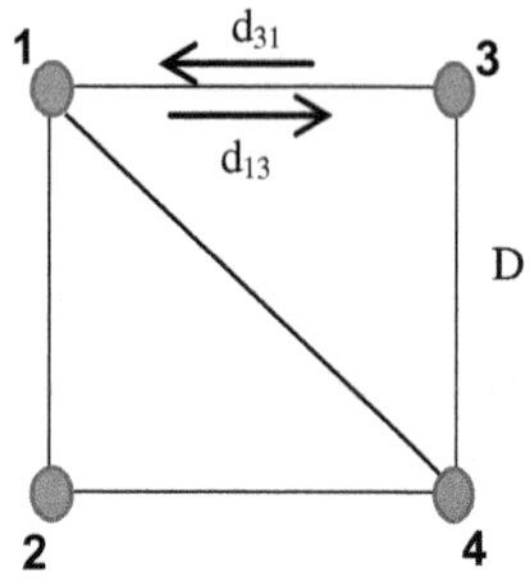

$$D = \begin{pmatrix} 0 & d_{12} & d_{13} & d_{14} \\ d_{21} & 0 & \infty & d_{24} \\ d_{31} & \infty & 0 & d_{34} \\ d_{41} & d_{42} & d_{43} & 0 \end{pmatrix}$$

Figure 4. A simple graph and its adjacency matrix as the input for TSP.

If (*distance [u, x1(i)]) < (distance[u, x2(j)])*
  concatenate x1(i) to x
  i = i + 1
Else
  concatenate x2(j) to x
  j = j + 1

In this method, HC first chooses a random starting city such as *v*, then compares the two edges emanating from this city in two parents (*x*1, *x*2) and selects the shorter edge. We moved between them to obtain a new position.

The city on the other end of the selected edge becomes the starting city and the process is repeated, again, a random edge is introduced to avoid a cycle. Our modification of HC uses the following two rules:

- If the shorter of the two edges causes a cycle, then try to take the latter edge.
- If the longer edge also causes a cycle, then choose the shortest of the q randomly selected edges.

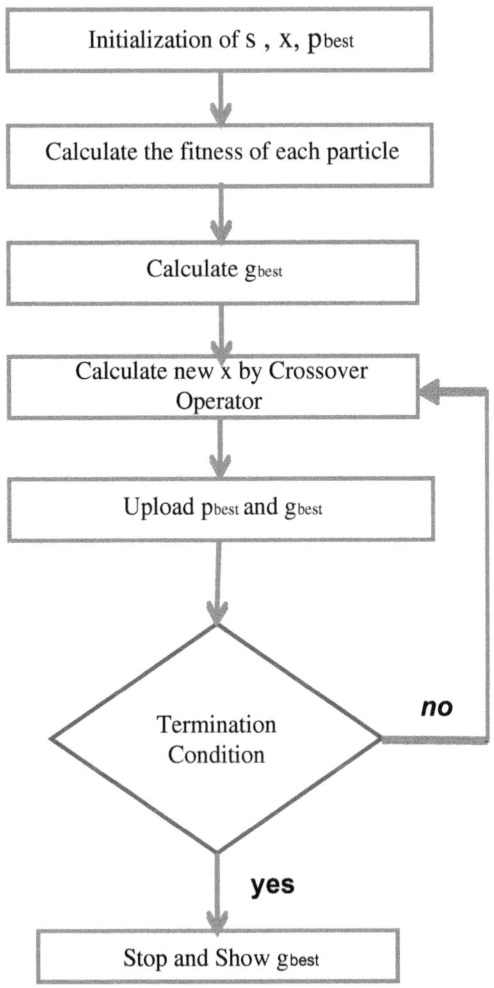

Figure 5. The diagram of our proposed algorithm.

This heuristic tries to combine short sub-paths from the parents. It may leave undesirable crossings of edges.

Algorithm 3: *Steps of our proposed algorithm (MPSO) (see also Figure 5)*

Step 1.

Initialize a swarm of size s

Random position of each particle

For each particle, pbest = x

Step 2.

Calculate the fitness of each particle

Step 3.

Calculate gbest

Step 4.

For each particle, calculate new position:

x = (pbest) © *(gbest)*

//© is the crossover operator (HC) and **x**

computes the best position (offspring).

Step 5.

Update pbest and gbest:

If (f (x) < f(pbest)) pbest = x;

If (f (pbest) < f (gbest)) gbest = pbest;

Step 6.

Stop iterations if stop condition is verified. Otherwise go to Step 4.

In this algorithm, we first initialize a swarm of size s. Next, randomly one position is set for each particle. Then, according to the pbest value, we compute fitness and *gbest* values for each particle. Next, in order to obtain new positions, each particle uses crossover operator which crosses between *gbest* and pbest values. Then for obtaining less distance and to modify *gbest* and pbest, we compare fitness function with *x* and pbest values. The Stop condition occurs when we achieve maximum iterations or the minimum error criterion is attained. Otherwise the algorithm continues to calculate new positions.

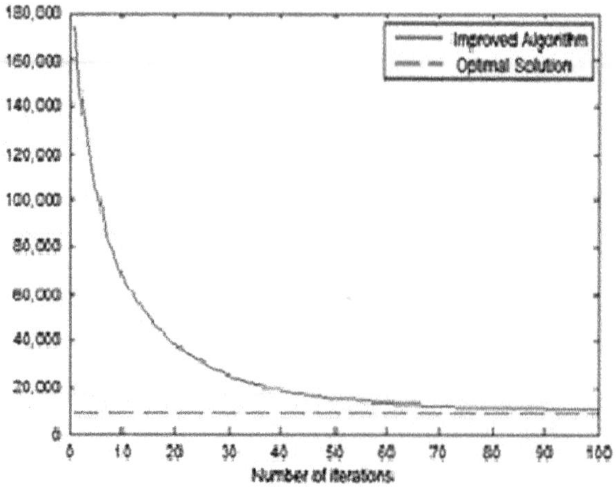

Figure 6. Algorithm converges after about 50 iterations.

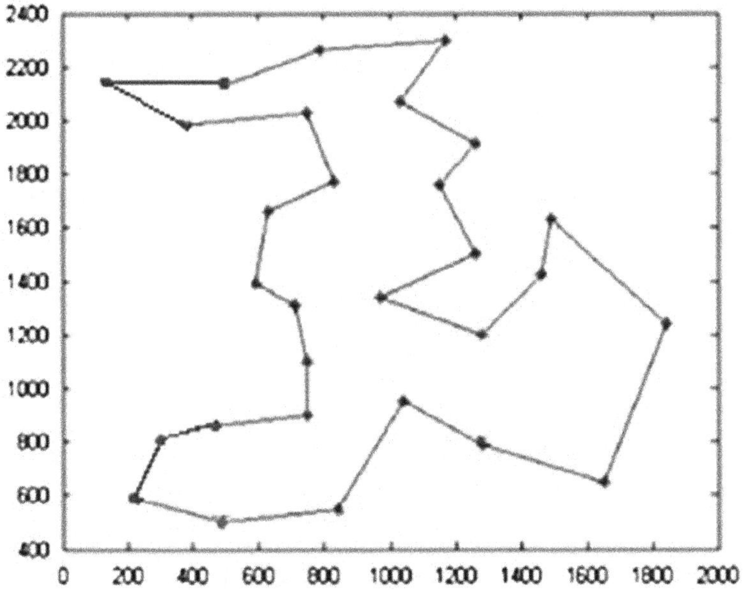

Figure 7. Output for Bays29 instance.

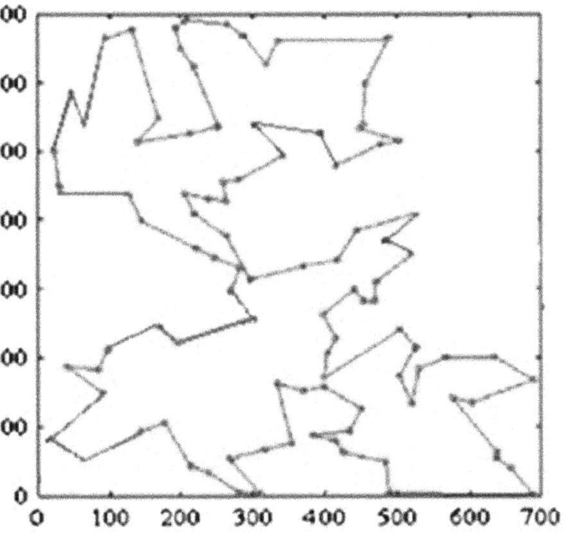

Figure 8. The obtained route from our proposed algorithm.

Table 1. MPSO results

Instance	Instance problem size	Best known TSPLIB	MPSO result
Bays29	29	2,020	2,020
Berlin52	52	7,542	7,540
Dantzig42	42	699	698
Rat99	99	1,211	1,210
Eli76	76	538	538
Pr124	124	59,030	59,028
Fri26	26	937	637

7. Conclusions and experimental results

In this paper, we used a heuristic algorithm based on the PSO method for solving the TSP.

Our algorithm to solve the problem has been inspired by PSO and the crossover operator of GAs. The proposed algorithm is described due to its simplicity and good balance between exploitation and exploration in the search space. The algorithm for solving the problem needs to set some parameters. In this section, our goal is to test and demonstrate the efficiency of our proposed algorithm to deal with other algorithms for TSP as a combinatorial optimization NP-hard problem.

We implemented our algorithm in MATLAB software with 50 bit parameters and maximum 200 iterations. The algorithm was tested with examples of TSP and the obtained values were compared with the solutions obtained by other methods in Table 1. This comparison shows that our algorithm has good performance. Simulation results indicate that PSO algorithm can increase the accuracy of the TSP network response and reduce training time. Table 1 shows the experimental results of the algorithm using the HC on TSPLIB instances. The first column contains the name of the sample, the second column contains the size of cities, for example, the third column and the fourth column show the best results from the TSPLIB and the results from the HC algorithm. Figure 6, shows algorithm converges after about 50 iterations. Figure 7 shows the output, for example Bays29 instance in TSPLIB. Finally, in Figure 8, the obtained route from the proposed algorithm is presented.

Acknowledgments

The authors would like to thank the anonymous referees for their helpful comments which improved the exposition of this paper.

Funding

Keivan Borna was partially supported by a grant from "National Elite Foundation of Iran" dedicated to the elite youth assistant professors [grant number 101048-15-3519].

Author details

Keivan Borna[1]

E-mail: borna@khu.ac.ir

ORCID ID: http://orcid.org/0000-0002-2941-6021

Razieh Khezri[2]

E-mail: raziehkhezri@gmail.com

ORCID ID: http://orcid.org/0000-0003-3807-4577

[1] Faculty of Mathematics and Computer Science, Kharazmi University, Tehran, Iran.

[2] Faculty of Engineering, Kharazmi University, Tehran, Iran.

References

Ai, T. J., & Kachitvichyanukul, V. (2008, November). Recent advances in adaptive particle swarm optimization algorithms. In *Proceedings of the Korea Institute of Industrial Engineering Conference*. Seoul.

Arumugam, M. S., & Rao, M. V. C. (2008). On the improved performances of the particle swarm optimization algorithms with adaptive parameters, cross-over operators and root mean square (RMS) variants for computing optimal control of a class of hybrid systems. *Applied Soft Computing, 8*, 324–336. http://dx.doi.org/10.1016/j.asoc.2007.01.010

Chen, W., Zhang, J., Chung, S. H., Zhong, W., Wu, W., & Shi, Y. (2010). A novel set-based particle swarm optimization method for discrete optimization problems. *IEEE Transactions on Evolutionary Computation, 14*, 278–300.

Gupta, S., & Panwar, P. (2013). Solving travelling salesman problem using genetic algorithm. *International Journal of Advanced Research in Computer Science and Software Engineering, 3*, 376–380.

Hu, X. (2006). *PSO tutorial*. Retrieved from www swarmintelligence.org/tutorials.php

Kachitvichyanukul, V. (2012). Comparison of three evolutionary algorithms: GA, PSO, and DE. *Industrial Engineering & Management Systems, 11*, 215–223.

Kennedy, J., & Eberhart, R. (2001). *Swarm intelligence* (1st ed.). San Diego, CA: Academic Press.

Kennedy, J., & Eberhart, R. C. (1995). Particle swarm optimization. In *Proceedings of the IEEE International Conference on Neural Networks* (Vol. 4, pp. 1942–1948), Perth. Piscataway, NJ: IEEE Service Center.

Labed, S., Gherboudj, A., & Chikhi, S. (2012). A modified hybrid particle swarm optimization algorithm for solving the traveling salesmen problem. *Journal of Theoretical and Applied Information Technology, 39*, 132–138.

Li, L., & Zhang, Y. (2007). An improved genetic algorithm for the traveling salesman problem. *Communications in Computer and Information Science, 2*, 208–216. http://dx.doi.org/10.1007/978-3-540-74282-1

Liao, Y. F., Yau, D. H., & Chen, Ch. L. (2012). Evolutionary algorithm to traveling salesman problems. *Computers and Mathematics with Applications, 64*, 788–797. http://dx.doi.org/10.1016/j.camwa.2011.12.018

Lin, S., & Kernighan, B. (1973). An effective heuristic algorithm for the traveling-salesman problem. *Operations Research, 21*, 498–516. http://dx.doi.org/10.1287/opre.21.2.498

Pang, S., Li, T., Dai, F., & Yu, M. (2013). Particle swarm optimization algorithm for multi-salesman problem with time and capacity constraints. *Applied Mathematics & Information Sciences, 6*, 2439–2444.

Pang, W., Wang, K. P., Zhou, Ch. G., & Dong, L. J. (2004). Fuzzy discrete particle swarm optimization for solving traveling salesman problem. In *Proceedings of the Fourth International Conference on Computer and Information Technology (CIT04)*. Jilin.

Shi, X. H., Liang, Y. C., Lee, H. P., Lu, C., & Wang, Q. X. (2007). Particle swarm optimization-based algorithms for TSP and generalized TSP. *Science Direct, 103*, 169–176.

Tasgetiren, M. F., Suganthan, P. N., & Pan, Q. K. (2007, July). A discrete particle swarm optimization algorithm for the generalized traveling salesman problem. In *GECCO07* (pp. 7–11). London.

van Hook, J., Sahin, F., & Arnavut, Z. (2008). *Application of particle swarm optimization for traveling salesman problem to lossless compression of color palette images*. Rochester, NY: Rochester Institute of Technology.

Xu, X. L., Cheng, X., Yang, Z. C., Yang, X., & Wang, W. L. (2013). Improved particle swarm optimization for traveling salesman problem. In *Proceedings 27th European Conference on Modelling and Simulation (ECMS)*. Ålesund.

Yan, X., Zhang, C., Luo, W., Li, W., Chen, W., & Liu, H. (2012). Solve traveling salesman problem using particle swarm optimization algorithm. *International Journal of Computer Science Issues, 9*, 264–271.

Zhang, D., Guan, Z., & Liu, X. (2007). An adaptive particle swarm optimization algorithm and simulation. *Proceedings of IEEE International Conference on Automation and Logistics, 2007*, 2399–2402.

2

On a mixed interpolation with integral conditions at arbitrary nodes

Srinivasarao Thota[1*] and Shiv Datt Kumar[1]

*Corresponding author: Srinivasarao Thota, Department of Mathematics, Motilal Nehru National Institute of Technology, Allahabad 211004, India

E-mail: srinithota@ymail.com

Reviewing editor: Lishan Liu, Qufu Normal University, China

Abstract: In this paper, we present a symbolic algorithm for a mixed interpolation of the form

$$a\cos kx + b\sin kx + \sum_{i=0}^{s-2} c_i x^i, \quad s \geq 2,$$

where $k > 0$ is a given parameter and the coefficients a, b, and $c_0, \ldots, c_{s-2}$ are determined by a given set of independent integral conditions at arbitrary nodes. Implementation of the proposed algorithm in Maple is described and sample computations are provided. This algorithm will help to implement the manual calculations in commercial packages such as Mathematica, Matlab, Singular, Scilab, etc.

Subjects: Applied Mathematics; Computer Mathematics; Mathematics & Statistics; Science

Keywords: mixed interpolation; integral conditions; symbolic algorithm

AMS subject classifications: 41A05 ; 65D05 ; 47A57

1. Introduction

The interpolation problem naturally arises in many applications, for example, the orbit problems, quantum mechanical problems, etc. The general form of a mixed interpolation problem is as follows (Coleman, 1998; Lorentz, 2000; Sauer, 1997): suppose we have a normed linear space $\mathcal{S}$, a finite linearly independent set $\Theta \subset \mathcal{S}$ of bounded functionals and an associated values $\Sigma = \{\alpha_\theta : \theta \in \Theta\} \subset \mathbb{R}$. Then the *mixed interpolation problem* is to find an approximation $\widetilde{f}_s(x) \in \mathcal{S}$ of the form

$$\widetilde{f}_s(x) = a\cos kx + b\sin kx + \sum_{i=0}^{s-2} c_i x^i, \quad s \geq 2, \tag{1}$$

such that

$$\Theta(\widetilde{f}_s) = \Sigma, \quad \text{i.e. } \theta\widetilde{f}_s = \alpha_\theta, \quad \theta \in \Theta. \tag{2}$$

ABOUT THE AUTHOR

Srinivasarao Thota completed his MSc in Mathematics from Indian Institute of Technology Madras, India. Now he is pursuing his PhD in Mathematics from Motilal Nehru National institute of Technology Allahabad, India. Srinivasarao Thota's area of research interest is Computer Algebra, precisely symbolic methods for ordinary differential equations. He attended and presented research papers in several national and international conferences.

PUBLIC INTEREST STATEMENT

We often come across a number of data points (obtained by sampling or experimentation) which represent the values of a function for a limited number of values of the independent variable, and the need to estimate the value of the function at other point of the independent variable. This may be achieved by interpolation. The interpolation problem naturally arises in many applications of science and engineering, for example, the orbit problems, solving differential and integral equations, quantum mechanical problems, etc. where we consider the *mixed interpolation* instead of the polynomial interpolation.

Here s is called the order of the interpolating function $\widetilde{f}_s(x)$. One can observe that, the interpolation problem given in Equations (1), (2) may have many solutions if there is no restriction on the dimension of the space. But our interest is to find the single interpolating function that must match with a finite number of conditions. Hence for a unique solution of the problem, one must have finite dimensional subspace Θ of $\mathcal{S}$ having dimension equal to the number of functionals.

The mixed interpolation problem, its formulation, and error estimation have been studied by several engineers and scientists with general nodes at uniformly spaced and arbitrary points on a chosen interval (see e.g. de Meyer, Vanthournout, & Vanden Berghe, 1990; de Meyer, Vanthournout, Vanden Berghe, & Vanderbauwhede, 1990; Chakrabarti & Hamsapriye, 1996; Coleman, 1998). In literature survey, we observe that there is no mixed interpolation algorithm available with integral conditions at arbitrary points on a chosen interval. Therefore, in this paper, we present a symbolic algorithm for the mixed interpolation with integral conditions using the algorithm presented by the authors in Thota and Kumar (2015). Indeed, we discuss a symbolic algorithm for mixed interpolation with a linearly independent set of the integral functionals/conditions at arbitrary nodes on a chosen interval. This is the first symbolic algorithm which deals with integral conditions. The rest of paper is organized as follows: Section 1.1 gives some definitions and basic concepts of the mixed interpolation, which are required to justify our proposed algorithm. Symbolic algorithm for the mixed interpolation with a finite linearly independent set of integral conditions is discussed in Section 2, the proposed algorithm for mixed interpolation is presented in Section 2.1 and some numerical examples are given in Section 2.2. Maple implementation of the proposed algorithm is presented in Section 3 with sample computations.

1.1. Preliminaries

In this section, we present some definitions and basic concepts of the mixed interpolation, which are required to justify our proposed algorithm.

Definition 1 A mixed interpolation problem is called *regular* for subspace $\mathcal{M}$ of linear space $\mathcal{S}$ with respect to Θ if the interpolation problem has a unique solution for each choice of values of $\Sigma \subset \mathbb{R}$ such that $\Theta(\widetilde{f}_s) = \Sigma$. Otherwise, the interpolation problem is called *singular.*

Definition 2 We call the triplet (M, Θ, Σ) an *interpolation problem,* where $M = \{\cos kx, \sin kx, 1, x, \dots, x^{s-2}\} \subset \mathcal{M}$ a basis for a finite dimensional space $\mathcal{S}$, and $\Theta \subset \mathcal{S}^*$ a finite linearly independent set of functionals with associated values $\Sigma \subset \mathbb{R}$.

If $\Sigma = \Theta\psi$, for $\psi \in \mathcal{S}$, then the interpolation problem (M, Θ, Σ) can be stated in a different way equivalently: Let $\Omega = \text{span}\{\theta{:}\theta \in \Theta\}$. Then $\Omega \subseteq \mathcal{S}^*$ and the interpolation problem is to find a $\widetilde{f}_s(x)$ such that $\Omega\widetilde{f}_s = \Omega\psi$ for given $\psi \in \mathcal{S}$. There is a connection between the regularity in terms of algebraic geometry and linear algebra as given in the following proposition.

Proposition 1 Let $M = \{m_0, \dots, m_t\}$ be a basis for $\mathcal{M}$, a finite dimensional subspace of $\mathcal{S}$, and $\Theta = \{\theta_0, \dots, \theta_s\}$ be a finite linearly independent subset of $\mathcal{S}^*$. Then the following statements are equivalent:

(i) The mixed interpolation problem is regular for $\mathcal{M}$ with respected to Θ.

(ii) $t = s$, and the matrix, so-called *evaluation matrix,*

$$\Theta M = \begin{pmatrix} \theta_0 m_0 & \cdots & \theta_0 m_t \\ \vdots & \ddots & \vdots \\ \theta_s m_0 & \cdots & \theta_s m_t \end{pmatrix} \in \mathbb{R}^{(s+1)\times(s+1)} \tag{3}$$

is regular. Denote the evaluation matrix ΘM by $\mathcal{E}$ for simplicity.

(iii) $\mathcal{S} = M \oplus \Theta^{\perp}$.

If we denote the integral condition by a symbol/operator A_x defined by $A_x \bullet = \int_p^x \bullet \, dx$, i.e. $A_x f(x) = \int_p^x f(x)\, dx$, for a fixed $p \in \mathbb{R}$, then the set of integral conditions is

$$\Theta = \{A_{x_0}, \dots, A_{x_s}\}, \tag{4}$$

where $x_0, \dots, x_s$ are arbitrary nodes. Now, the symbolic representation of the mixed interpolation problem (1), (2) is to find a function of the form (1) such that

$$A_{x_i} \tilde{f}_s = \alpha_{x_i}, \text{ where } A_{x_i} \in \Theta. \tag{5}$$

2. Symbolic algorithm for mixed interpolation

Consider the mixed interpolation problem defined in Section 1 for (M, Θ, Σ), where $M \subseteq \mathcal{M} \subset \mathcal{S}$, and $\Theta = \{\theta_0, \dots, \theta_s\}$ a finite set of integral conditions of the form (4). From Proposition (3), the mixed interpolation problem is regular with respect to linearly independent set Θ if and only if there exists a finite linearly independent set M of $\mathcal{S}$ such that the evaluation matrix $\mathcal{E}$ in (3) is regular.

2.1. Proposed symbolic algorithm

The mixed interpolation problem (M, Θ, Σ), i.e. $\tilde{f}_s(x) = a\cos kx + b\sin kx + \sum_{i=0}^{s-2} c_i x^i$ such that it satisfy $\Theta\tilde{f}_s = \Sigma$, can be expressed as a linear system

$$\mathcal{E}u = \sigma, \tag{6}$$

where $u = (a, b, c_0, \dots, c_{s-2})^T$, $\sigma = (\alpha_{\theta_0} \dots, \alpha_{\theta_s})^T$ and $\mathcal{E}$ is the evaluation matrix of Θ and M given by

$$\mathcal{E} = \begin{pmatrix} \frac{\sin kx_0}{k} & \frac{-\cos kx_0}{k} & x_0 & \frac{x_0^2}{2} & \cdots & \frac{x_0^{s-1}}{s-1} \\ \frac{\sin kx_1}{k} & \frac{-\cos kx_1}{k} & x_1 & \frac{x_1^2}{2} & \cdots & \frac{x_1^{s-1}}{s-1} \\ \vdots & \vdots & \vdots & \vdots & \ddots & \vdots \\ \frac{\sin kx_s}{k} & \frac{-\cos kx_s}{k} & x_s & \frac{x_s^2}{2} & \cdots & \frac{x_s^{s-1}}{s-1} \end{pmatrix} - \begin{pmatrix} \frac{\sin kp}{k} & \frac{-\cos kp}{k} & p & \frac{p^2}{2} & \cdots & \frac{p^{s-1}}{s-1} \\ \frac{\sin kp}{k} & \frac{-\cos kp}{k} & p & \frac{p^2}{2} & \cdots & \frac{p^{s-1}}{s-1} \\ \vdots & \vdots & \vdots & \vdots & \ddots & \vdots \\ \frac{\sin kp}{k} & \frac{-\cos kp}{k} & p & \frac{p^2}{2} & \cdots & \frac{p^{s-1}}{s-1} \end{pmatrix}$$
$$= \begin{pmatrix} \frac{\sin kx_0}{k} - \frac{\sin kp}{k} & \frac{\cos kp}{k} - \frac{\cos kx_0}{k} & x_0 - p & \frac{x_0^2}{2} - \frac{p^2}{2} & \cdots & \frac{x_0^{s-1}}{s-1} - \frac{p^{s-1}}{s-1} \\ \frac{\sin kx_1}{k} - \frac{\sin kp}{k} & \frac{\cos kp}{k} - \frac{\cos kx_1}{k} & x_1 - p & \frac{x_1^2}{2} - \frac{p^2}{2} & \cdots & \frac{x_1^{s-1}}{s-1} - \frac{p^{s-1}}{s-1} \\ \vdots & \vdots & \vdots & \vdots & \ddots & \vdots \\ \frac{\sin kx_s}{k} - \frac{\sin kp}{k} & \frac{\cos kp}{k} - \frac{\cos kx_s}{k} & x_s - p & \frac{x_s^2}{2} - \frac{p^2}{2} & \cdots & \frac{x_s^{s-1}}{s-1} - \frac{p^{s-1}}{s-1} \end{pmatrix}. \tag{7}$$

Remark If $p = 0$, then $\mathcal{E}$ in Equation (7) is given by

$$\mathcal{E} = \begin{pmatrix} \frac{\sin kx_0}{k} & \frac{1-\cos kx_0}{k} & x_0 & \frac{x_0^2}{2} & \cdots & \frac{x_0^{s-1}}{s-1} \\ \frac{\sin kx_1}{k} & \frac{1-\cos kx_1}{k} & x_1 & \frac{x_1^2}{2} & \cdots & \frac{x_1^{s-1}}{s-1} \\ \vdots & \vdots & \vdots & \vdots & \ddots & \vdots \\ \frac{\sin kx_s}{k} & \frac{1-\cos kx_s}{k} & x_s & \frac{x_s^2}{2} & \cdots & \frac{x_s^{s-1}}{s-1} \end{pmatrix}$$

Uniqueness of the solution is possible if and only if the evaluation matrix (7) is regular (non-singular). The simple form of the determinant of $\mathcal{E}$ is given by

$$\det \mathcal{E} = \frac{\prod_{i=0}^{s} x_i}{k^2(s-1)!} \prod_{k<j}(x_j - x_k) \begin{vmatrix} \sum_{i=0}^{s-1} \frac{\frac{\cos kx_i}{x_i}}{\prod_{j=0, j\neq i}^{s-1}(x_i - x_j)} & \sum_{i=0}^{s-1} \frac{\frac{\sin kx_i}{x_i}}{\prod_{j=0, j\neq i}^{s-1}(x_i - x_j)} \\ \sum_{i=0}^{s} \frac{\frac{\cos kx_i}{x_i}}{\prod_{j=0, j\neq i}^{s}(x_i - x_j)} & \sum_{i=0}^{s} \frac{\frac{\sin kx_i}{x_i}}{\prod_{j=0, j\neq i}^{s}(x_i - x_j)} \end{vmatrix}. \tag{8}$$

This simple form is obtained by performing the following steps:

I. Dividing i-th row by x_i in the determinant of $\mathcal{E}$ in Equation (7), we get

$$\det \mathcal{E} = \frac{\prod_{i=0}^{s} x_i}{k^2(s-1)!} \begin{vmatrix} \frac{\cos kx_0}{x_0} & \frac{\sin kx_0}{x_0} & 1 & x_0 & \cdots & x_0^{s-2} \\ \frac{\cos kx_1}{x_1} & \frac{\sin kx_1}{x_1} & 1 & x_1 & \cdots & x_1^{s-2} \\ \vdots & \vdots & \vdots & \vdots & \ddots & \vdots \\ \frac{\cos kx_s}{x_s} & \frac{\sin kx_s}{x_s} & 1 & x_s & \cdots & x_s^{s-2} \end{vmatrix}. \tag{9}$$

II. Subtract first row from the other $(i+1)$-th row, for $i = 1, 2, \dots s$, and divide $(i+1)$-th row by $x_i - x_0$ for $i = 1, 2, \dots s$, we get

$$\det \mathcal{E} = \frac{\prod_{i=0}^{s} x_i}{k^2(s-1)!} \prod_{k=1}^{s}(x_k - x_0) \begin{vmatrix} \frac{\cos kx_0}{x_0} & \frac{\sin kx_0}{x_0} & 1 & x_0 & \cdots & x_0^{s-2} \\ \frac{\frac{\cos kx_1}{x_1} - \frac{\cos kx_0}{x_0}}{x_1 - x_0} & \frac{\frac{\sin kx_1}{x_1} - \frac{\sin kx_0}{x_0}}{x_1 - x_0} & 0 & 1 & \cdots & x_1^{s-3} \\ \vdots & \vdots & \vdots & \vdots & \ddots & \vdots \\ \frac{\frac{\cos kx_s}{x_s} - \frac{\cos kx_0}{x_0}}{x_s - x_0} & \frac{\frac{\sin kx_s}{x_s} - \frac{\sin kx_0}{x_0}}{x_s - x_0} & 0 & 1 & \cdots & x_s^{s-3} \end{vmatrix}.$$

This reduces to a determinant of a matrix of order s similar to (9).

III. Repeating the step II finite number of times, we arrive at the simple form of $\det \mathcal{E}$ as in (8).

From the procedure given for simplification of the determinant of $\mathcal{E}$, we can construct the interpolating function $\widetilde{f}_s(x)$ for (M, Θ, Σ) in terms of evaluation matrix. The following theorem presents an algorithm to construct $\widetilde{f}_s(x)$. Denote $\mathcal{D} = \det(\mathcal{E})$ for simplicity.

THEOREM 1 *Let Θ be a finite set of integral conditions of the form $\Theta = \{A_{x_0}, \dots, A_{x_s}\}$ with associated values Σ and $M = \{\cos kx, \sin kx, 1, \dots, x^{s-2}\} \subset S$ be a finite linearly independent set such that the evaluation matrix $\mathcal{E}$ is regular. Then there exists unique interpolating function $\widetilde{f}_s(x)$ of the form (1), such that $\Theta\widetilde{f}_s = \Sigma$ as*

$$\widetilde{f}_s(x) = \sum_{k=1}^{s+1} \mathcal{D}^{-1}\mathcal{D}_k^1 \alpha_{\theta_{k-1}} \cos kx + \sum_{k=1}^{s+1} \mathcal{D}^{-1}\mathcal{D}_k^2 \alpha_{\theta_{k-1}} \sin kx + \sum_{l=0}^{s-2}\sum_{k=1}^{s+1} \mathcal{D}^{-1}\mathcal{D}_k^{l+3} \alpha_{\theta_{k-1}} x^l, \tag{10}$$

where $\mathcal{D}_i^j$ is the determinant of $\mathcal{E}_i^j$ obtained from $\mathcal{E}$ by replacing j-th column by the i-th unit vector.

Proof It is given that the evaluation matrix associated with Θ and M is regular, therefore there exists unique mixed interpolation. Suppose $\mathcal{D}_k^1$, $\mathcal{D}_k^2$ and $\mathcal{D}_k^{l+3}$ denote the determinants of the resultant matrix $\mathcal{E}$ after replacing 1st, 2nd, and lth columns by k-unit vector, respectively, for $l = 0, 1, \dots, s-2$, then the coefficients $a, b, c_0, \dots, c_{s-2}$ are determined uniquely using the *Cramer's rule*, as follows

$$\begin{aligned} a &= \sum_{k=1}^{s+1} \mathcal{D}^{-1}\mathcal{D}_k^1 \alpha_{\theta_{k-1}}, \\ b &= \sum_{k=1}^{s+1} \mathcal{D}^{-1}\mathcal{D}_k^2 \alpha_{\theta_{k-1}}, \\ c_l &= \sum_{k=1}^{s+1} \mathcal{D}^{-1}\mathcal{D}_k^{l+3} \alpha_{\theta_{k-1}}, \quad l = 0, 1, \dots, s-2. \end{aligned} \tag{11}$$

Now, the required interpolating function $\widetilde{f}_s(x)$ is the linear combination of elements of M with the coefficients $a, b, c_0, \dots, c_{s-2}$. Hence, we have

$$\widetilde{f}_s(x) = \sum_{k=1}^{s+1} \mathcal{D}^{-1}\mathcal{D}_k^1 \alpha_{\theta_{k-1}} \cos kx + \sum_{k=1}^{s+1} \mathcal{D}^{-1}\mathcal{D}_k^2 \alpha_{\theta_{k-1}} \sin kx + \sum_{l=0}^{s-2}\sum_{k=1}^{s+1} \mathcal{D}^{-1}\mathcal{D}_k^{l+3} \alpha_{\theta_{k-1}} x^l, \tag{12}$$

as stated. □

In general, it is very difficult to solve explicitly the linear system (6) for the coefficients $a, b, c_0, \ldots, c_{s-2}$ in terms of Σ at the interpolation points. However, we can express the coefficients of $\tilde{f}_s(x)$ in terms of evaluation matrix as given Theorem 4.

2.2. Examples

Now to verify the proposed algorithm in Theorem 4, we present some examples. We use *Maple*, the computer algebra software, for numerical computations in the following examples.

Example 2.1 Consider the integral conditions $\int_0^{0.1} f(x)dx = k_1$, $\int_0^{0.3} f(x)dx = k_2$, $\int_0^{0.5} f(x)dx = k_3$, $\int_0^{0.8} f(x)dx = k_4$ and $\int_0^{1.0} f(x)dx = k_5$, where k_i is constant, for $i = 1, 2, 3, 4, 5$. Now we construct $\tilde{f}_4(x) = a\cos kx + b\sin kx + c_0 + c_1x + c_2x^2$ such that $\tilde{f}_4(x)$ satisfies the given conditions. For simplicity, take $k = 1$. Here, $\Theta = \{A_{0.1}, A_{0.3}, A_{0.5}, A_{0.8}, A_{1.0}\}$, $M = \{\cos x, \sin x, 1, x, x^2\}$, and $\Sigma = \{k_1, k_2, k_3, k_4, k_5\}$. Following Theorem 4, we have the evaluation matrix

$$\mathcal{E} = \begin{pmatrix} 0.099833 & 0.004996 & 0.1 & 0.005 & 0.000333 \\ 0.295520 & 0.044664 & 0.3 & 0.045 & 0.009000 \\ 0.479426 & 0.122417 & 0.5 & 0.125 & 0.041667 \\ 0.717356 & 0.303293 & 0.8 & 0.320 & 0.170667 \\ 0.841471 & 0.459698 & 1.0 & 0.500 & 0.333333 \end{pmatrix},$$

$$\mathcal{D} = \det \mathcal{E} = 7.19735 \times 10^{-11};\ \mathcal{D}^{-1} = 1.3894 \times 10^{10},$$

$$\mathcal{D}_1^1 = \det \begin{pmatrix} 1 & 0.004996 & 0.1 & 0.005 & 0.000333 \\ 0 & 0.044664 & 0.3 & 0.045 & 0.009000 \\ 0 & 0.122417 & 0.5 & 0.125 & 0.041667 \\ 0 & 0.303293 & 0.8 & 0.320 & 0.170667 \\ 0 & 0.459698 & 1.0 & 0.500 & 0.333333 \end{pmatrix} = 0.15028 \times 10^{-5}$$

$$\mathcal{D}_2^1 = \det \begin{pmatrix} 0.099833 & 0 & 0.1 & 0.005 & 0.000333 \\ 0.295520 & 1 & 0.3 & 0.045 & 0.009000 \\ 0.479426 & 0 & 0.5 & 0.125 & 0.041667 \\ 0.717356 & 0 & 0.8 & 0.320 & 0.170667 \\ 0.841471 & 0 & 1.0 & 0.500 & 0.333333 \end{pmatrix} = -0.18396 \times 10^{-5}$$

$$\mathcal{D}_3^1 = \det \begin{pmatrix} 0.099833 & 0.004996 & 0 & 0.005 & 0.000333 \\ 0.295520 & 0.044664 & 0 & 0.045 & 0.009000 \\ 0.479426 & 0.122417 & 1 & 0.125 & 0.041667 \\ 0.717356 & 0.303293 & 0 & 0.320 & 0.170667 \\ 0.841471 & 0.459698 & 0 & 0.500 & 0.333333 \end{pmatrix} = 0.13131 \times 10^{-5}$$

$$\mathcal{D}_4^1 = \det \begin{pmatrix} 0.099833 & 0.004996 & 0.1 & 0 & 0.000333 \\ 0.295520 & 0.044664 & 0.3 & 0 & 0.009000 \\ 0.479426 & 0.122417 & 0.5 & 0 & 0.041667 \\ 0.717356 & 0.303293 & 0.8 & 1 & 0.170667 \\ 0.841471 & 0.459698 & 1.0 & 0 & 0.333333 \end{pmatrix} = -4.82523 \times 10^{-7}$$

$$\mathcal{D}_5^1 = \det \begin{pmatrix} 0.099833 & 0.004996 & 0.1 & 0.005 & 0 \\ 0.295520 & 0.044664 & 0.3 & 0.045 & 0 \\ 0.479426 & 0.122417 & 0.5 & 0.125 & 0 \\ 0.717356 & 0.303293 & 0.8 & 0.320 & 0 \\ 0.841471 & 0.459698 & 1.0 & 0.500 & 1 \end{pmatrix} = 1.31086 \times 10^{-7},$$

hence,

$$\sum_{k=1}^{5}\mathcal{D}_k^1\alpha_{\theta_{k-1}} = 0.15028\times10^{-5}k_1 - 0.18396\times10^{-5}k_2 + 0.13131\times10^{-5}k_3 - 4.82523\times10^{-7}k_4 + 1.31086\times10^{-7}k_5,$$

similarly,

$$\sum_{k=1}^{5}\mathcal{D}_k^2\alpha_{\theta_{k-1}} = 8.60525\times10^{-7}k_1 - 9.57686\times10^{-7}k_2 + 6.17919\times10^{-7}k_3 - 1.92581\times10^{-7}k_4 + 4.63585\times10^{-8}k_5,$$

$$\sum_{k=1}^{5}\mathcal{D}_k^3\alpha_{\theta_{k-1}} = -0.15011\times10^{-5}k_1 + 0.18389\times10^{-5}k_2 - 0.13128\times10^{-5}k_3 + 4.82459\times10^{-7}k_4 - 1.31072\times10^{-7}k_5,$$

$$\sum_{k=1}^{5}\mathcal{D}_k^4\alpha_{\theta_{k-1}} = -8.86346\times10^{-7}k_1 + 9.77076\times10^{-7}k_2 - 6.26828\times10^{-7}k_3 + 1.94676\times10^{-7}k_4 - 4.68155\times10^{-8}k_5$$

$$\sum_{k=1}^{5}\mathcal{D}_k^5\alpha_{\theta_{k-1}} = 8.52374\times10^{-7}k_1 - 0.10177\times10^{-5}k_2 + 7.11690\times10^{-7}k_3 - 2.55717\times10^{-7}k_4 + 6.88081\times10^{-8}k_5,$$

and the coefficients are given by

$$a = 20904.99k_1 - 25589.48k_2 + 18265.09k_3 - 6712.06k_4 + 1823.45k_5$$
$$b = 11970.22k_1 - 13321.75k_2 + 8595.47k_3 - 2678.87k_4 644.86k_5,$$
$$c_0 = -20881.23k_1 + 25580.00k_2 - 18261.10k_3 + 6711.16k_4 - 1823.26k_5,$$
$$c_1 = -12329.34k_1 + 13591.47k_2 - 8719.40k_3 + 2708.02k_4 - 651.22k_5,$$
$$c_2 = 11856.84k_1 - 14156.85k_2 + 9899.85k_3 - 3557.12k_4 + 957.14k_5.$$

Now the solution of the mixed interpolation (M, Θ, Σ) is

$$\begin{aligned}\widetilde{f}_4(x) = {} & (20904.99k_1 - 25589.48k_2 + 18265.09k_3 - 6712.06k_4 + 1823.45k_5)\cos x \\ & + (11970.22k_1 - 13321.75k_2 + 8595.47k_3 - 2678.87k_4 644.86k_5)\sin x \\ & - 20881.23k_1 + 25580.00k_2 - 18261.10k_3 + 6711.16k_4 - 1823.26k_5 \\ & + (-12329.34k_1 + 13591.47k_2 - 8719.40k_3 + 2708.02k_4 - 651.22k_5)x \\ & + (11856.84k_1 - 14156.85k_2 + 9899.85k_3 - 3557.12k_4 + 957.14k_5)x^2\end{aligned}$$

In particular, if we choose $k_i = i$, for $i = 1, 2, 3, 4, 5$, then

$a = 6790.30$, $b = 3621.97$, $c_0 = -6776.17$, $c_1 = -3728.64$, $c_2 = 3799.92$

and the solution of the interpolation (M, Θ, Σ) is

$$\widetilde{f}_4(x) = 6790.30\cos x + 3621.97\sin x - 6776.17 - 3728.64x + 3799.92x^2.$$

One can easily check in both the cases that $\Theta(\widetilde{f}_4) = \Sigma$.

Example 2.2 Suppose we have integral conditions $\int_0^{0.1} f(x)dx = 1$, $\int_0^{0.2} f(x)dx = 3$, $\int_0^{0.3} f(x)dx = 4$, $\int_0^{0.4} f(x)dx = 5$, $\int_0^{0.5} f(x)dx = 6$, $\int_0^{0.6} f(x)dx = 7$, $\int_0^{0.7} f(x)dx = 9$, $\int_0^{0.8} f(x)dx = 13$, $\int_0^{0.9} f(x)dx = 15$ and $\int_0^{1.0} f(x)dx = 16$. Now we construct $\widetilde{f}_9(x) = a\cos kx + b\sin kx + c_0 + c_1x + c_2x^2 + \cdots + c_7x^7$ such that $\widetilde{f}_9(x)$ satisfies the given conditions. For simplicity, take $k = 0.5$. In symbolic notations, we have $\Theta = \{A_{0.1}, A_{0.2}, A_{0.3}, A_{0.4}, A_{0.5}, A_{0.6}, A_{0.7}, A_{0.8}, A_{0.9}, A_{1.0}\}$, $M = \{\cos(0.5x), \sin(0.5x), 1, x, \ldots, x^7\}$ and $\Sigma = \{1, 3, 4, 5, 6, 7, 9, 13, 15, 16\}$. From Theorem 4, the coefficients are computed similar to Example 2.1 as follows

$$a = -1.496313140 \times 10^9, \quad b = 3.349193220 \times 10^{10},$$
$$c_0 = 1.496313072 \times 10^9, \quad c_1 = -1.674596380 \times 10^{10},$$
$$c_2 = -1.87067734 \times 10^8, \quad c_3 = 6.978924923 \times 10^8,$$
$$c_4 = 3.516587822 \times 10^6, \quad c_5 = -8.177983600 \times 10^6,$$
$$c_6 = -4.298813138 \times 10^5, \quad c_7 = 1.677402086 \times 10^5.$$

Now, the interpolating function $\widetilde{f}_9(x)$ is given by

$$\begin{aligned}\widetilde{f}_9(x) = &-1.496313140 \times 10^9 \cos(0.5x) + 3.349193220 \times 10^{10} \sin(0.5x)\\ &+ 1.496313072 \times 10^9 - 1.674596380 \times 10^{10}x - 1.87067734 \times 10^8 x^2\\ &+ 6.978924923 \times 10^8 x^3 + 3.516587822 \times 10^6 x^4 - 8.177983600 \times 10^6 x^5\\ &- 4.298813138 \times 10^5 x^6 + 1.677402086 \times 10^5 x^7.\end{aligned}$$

If we choose $k = 2$, then

$$\begin{aligned}\widetilde{f}_9(x) = &-3.85899899 \times 10^8 \cos(2x) + 2.91356330 \times 10^8 \sin(2x)\\ &+ 3.858998408 \times 10^8 - 5.82709230 \times 10^8 x - 7.71845620 \times 10^8 x^2\\ &+ 3.88781409 \times 10^8 x^3 + 2.560552184 \times 10^8 x^4 - 7.4670907 \times 10^7 x^5\\ &- 3.9114135 \times 10^7 x^6 + 1.208298237 \times 10^7 x^7.\end{aligned}$$

One can easily verify in both cases that $\Theta(\widetilde{f}_9) = \Sigma$.

The following section presents the implementation of the proposed algorithm in Maple.

3. Maple implementation

Maple implementation of the proposed algorithm is presented by creating different data types using the Maple package IntDiffOp implemented by Korporal, Regensburger, and Rosenkranz (2010). For displaying the operators, we have A for integral operator and E for evaluation operator as defined in IntDiffOp package, i.e. $A_x = E[x].A$.

The data type IntegralCondition(np) is created to represent the integral condition, where np is the node point.

```
with(IntDiffOp):
IntegralCondition := proc(np)
return BOUNDOP(EVOP(np,EVDIFFOP(0),EVINTOP(EVINTTERM(1,1))));
end proc:
```

The following producer EvaluationMatrix(IC) gives the evaluation matrix of the given M and Θ, where IC is the column matrix of the integral conditions.

```
EvaluationMatrix := proc (IC::Matrix)
local r,c,elts,fs;
r,c:=LinearAlgebra[Dimension](IC);
fs:=Matrix(1,r,[cos(k*x),sin(k*x),seq(x^(i-1),i=1..r-2)]);
elts:=seq(seq(ApplyOperator(IC[t,1],fs[1,j]),j=1..r), t=1..r);
```

```
return Matrix(r,r,[elts]);
end proc:
```

The procedure MixedInterpolation(IC,CM) is created to find the mixed interpolating function for (M, Θ, Σ), where CM is column matrix of the associated values of Σ.

```
MixedInterpolation := proc (IC::Matrix, CM::Matrix)
local r,c,fs,evm,invevm,approx;
r,c:=LinearAlgebra[Dimension](IC);
fs: Matrix(1,r,[cos(k*x),sin(k*x),seq(x^(i-1),i=1..r-2)]);
evm:=EvaluationMat(IC);
invevm:=1/evm; approx:=fs.invevm.CM;
return simplify(approx[1,1]);
end proc:
```

Example 3.1 Recall Example 2.1 for sample computations using Maple implementation.

```
> with(IntDiffOp):
> C1:=IntegralCondition(0.1); c1:=1;
C2:=IntegralCondition(0.3); c2:=2;
C3:=IntegralCondition(0.5); c3:=3;
C4:=IntegralCondition(0.8); c4:=4;
C5:=IntegralCondition(1.0); c5:=5;
```

C1: =E[.1].A

c1: =1

C2: =E[.3].A

c2: =2

C3: =E[.5].A

c3: =3

C4: =E[.8].A

c4: =4

C5: =E[1.0].A

c4: =5

```
> k:=1;
```

1

```
> C:=Matrix([[C1],[C2],[C3],[C4],[C5]]);
```

$$\begin{bmatrix} E[.1].A \\ E[.3].A \\ E[.5].A \\ E[.8].A \\ E[1.0].A \end{bmatrix}$$

```
CM:=Matrix([[c1],[c2],[c3],[c4],[c5]]);
```

$$\begin{bmatrix} 1 \\ 2 \\ 3 \\ 4 \\ 5 \end{bmatrix}$$

```
EvaluationMat(C);
```

$$\begin{bmatrix} 0.09983341665 & 0.004995834722 & 0.1 & 0.005 & 0.0003333 \\ 0.2955202067 & 0.04466351087 & 0.3 & 0.045 & 0.009000 \\ 0.4794255386 & 0.1224174381 & 0.5 & 0.125 & 0.041667 \\ 0.7173560909 & 0.3032932907 & 0.8 & 0.320 & 0.170667 \\ 0.8414709848 & 0.4596976941 & 1.0 & 0.500 & 0.333333 \end{bmatrix}$$

```
> MixedInterpolation(C,CM);
```

$$-6776.165565 - 3728.640530 * x + 6790.295165 * cos(x)$$
$$+ 3621.967910 * sin(x) + 3799.917488 * x^2$$

Acknowledgements
Authors thank the referees for useful suggestions in improving the presentation of the paper.

Funding
The authors received no direct funding for this research.

Author details
Srinivasarao Thota[1]
E-mail: srinithota@ymail.com
Shiv Datt Kumar[1]
E-mail: sdt@mnnit.ac.in
[1] Department of Mathematics, Motilal Nehru National Institute of Technology, Allahabad, 211004, India.

References

Chakrabarti, A. (1996). Hamsapriye: Derivation of a general mixed interpolation formula. *Journal of Computational and Applied Mathematics, 70*, 161–172.

Coleman, J. P. (1998). Mixed interpolation methods with arbitrary nodes. *Journal of Computational and Applied Mathematics, 92*, 69–83.

de Meyer, H., Vanthournout, J., & Vanden, G. (1990). Berghe: On a new type of mixed interpolation. *Journal of Computational and Applied Mathematics, 30*, 55–69.

de Meyer, H., Vanthournout, J., Vanden Berghe, G., & Vanderbauwhede, A. (1990). On the error estimation for a mixed type of interpolation. *Journal of Computational and Applied Mathematics, 32*, 407–415.

Korporal, A., Regensburger, G., & Rosenkranz, M. (2010). A Maple package for integro-differential operators and boundary problems. *ACM Communications in Computer Algebra, 44*, 120–122.

Lorentz, R. A. (2000). Multivariate Hermite interpolation by algebraic polynomials: A survey. *Journal of Computational and Applied Mathematics, 122*, 167–201.

Sauer, T. (1997). Polynomial interpolation, ideals and approximation order of refinable functions. *Proceedings American Mathematical Society, 130*, 3335–3347.

Thota, S., & Kumar, S. D. (2015). Symbolic method for polynomial interpolation with stieltjes conditions. *Proceedings of International Conference on Frontiers in Mathematics, 1*, 225–228.

3

Approximating solutions of nonlinear periodic boundary value problems with maxima

Bapurao C. Dhage[1*]
Corresponding author: Bapurao C.Dhage, Kasubai, Gurukul Colony, Dist. Latur, Ahmedpur 413515, Maharashtra, India
E-mail: bcdhage@gmail.com
Reviewing editor:Shaoyong Lai, Southwestern University of Finance and Economics, China

Abstract: In this paper we study a periodic boundary value problem of first order nonlinear differential equations with maxima and discuss the existence and approximation of the solutions. The main result relies on the Dhage iteration method embodied in a recent hybrid fixed point theorem of Dhage (2014) in a partially ordered normed linear space. At the end, we give an example to illustrate the applicability of the abstract results to some concrete periodic boundary value problems of nonlinear differential equations.

Subjects: Advanced Mathematics; Analysis - Mathematics; Applied Mathematics; Differential Equations; Mathematics & Statistics; Non-Linear Systems; Operator Theory; Science

Keywords: differential equations with maxima; Dhage iteration method; approximation of solutions

AMS Subject Classifications: 34A12; 34A45; 47H07; 47H10

1. Introduction

The study of fixed point theorems for the contraction mappings in partially ordered metric spaces is initiated by Ran and Reurings (2004) which is further continued by Nieto and Rodringuez-Lopez (2005) and applied to periodic boundary value problems of nonlinear first order ordinary differential equations for proving the existence results under certain monotonic conditions. Similarly, the study of hybrid fixed point theorems in a partially ordered metric space is initiated by Dhage (2013, 2014, 2015a) with applications to nonlinear differential and integral equation under weaker mixed conditions of nonlinearities. See Dhage (2015b, 2015c) and the references therein. In this paper we investigate the existence of approximate solutions of certain hybrid differential equations with maxima using the Dhage iteration method embodied in a hybrid fixed point theorem. We claim that the results of this paper are new to the theory of nonlinear differential equations with maxima.

ABOUT THE AUTHOR

The author of this paper is a nonlinear analyst always engaged in the investigation of new technique or method for studying the nonlinear equations in different abstract spaces under different situations. He has also a keen interest in the study of numerical or approximate solutions of nonlinear differential and integral equations. He deals with and claims that the periodic BVPs of first and second order ordinary nonlinear differential equations an easily be analyzed under minimum natural conditions for numerical or approximate and other qualitative aspects of the solutions.

PUBLIC INTEREST STATEMENT

Many of the natural and physical processes of the universe are governed by periodic boundary value problems of nonlinear differential equations. Therefore, the results of this paper are useful to scientists and mathematicians to describe some universal phenomena in a scientific manner for better conclusion. Again the Dhage iteration principle which has been used in this paper is a powerful technique for nonlinear equations and so other researchers of dynamic systems and applications may explore this new technique to tackle different nonlinear problems for qualitative analysis and applications.

Given a closed and bounded interval $J = [0, T]$ of the real line $\mathbb{R}$ for some $T > 0$, we consider the following hybrid differential equation (in short HDE) of first order periodic boundary value problems,

$$\begin{cases} x'(t) = f(t, x(t)) + g\left(t, \max_{0\le\xi\le t} x(\xi)\right), \\ x(0) = x(T), \end{cases} \tag{1.1}$$

for all $t \in J = [0, T]$ and $f, g : J \times \mathbb{R} \to \mathbb{R}$ are continuous functions.

By a solution of Equation (1.1) we mean a function $x \in C^1(J, \mathbb{R})$ that satisfies Equation (1.1), where $C^1(J, \mathbb{R})$ is the space of continuously differentiable real-valued functions defined on J.

Differential equations with maxima are often met in the applications, for instance in the theory of automatic control. Numerous results on existence and uniqueness, asymptotic stability as well as numerical solutions for such equations have been obtained. To name a few, we refer the reader to (Bainov & Hristova, 2011; Otrocol, 2014) and the references therein. The PBVP's of nonlinear first order ordinary differential equations have also been a topic of great interest since long time. The HDE (1.1) is a linear perturbation of first type of the PBVP of first order nonlinear differential equations. The details of different types of perturbation appears in Dhage (2010). The special cases of the HDE (1.1) are

$$\begin{cases} x'(t) = f(t, x(t)), \quad t \in J, \\ x(0) = x(T), \end{cases} \tag{1.2}$$

and

$$\begin{cases} x'(t) = g\left(t, \max_{0\le\xi\le t} x(\xi)\right), \quad t \in J, \\ x(0) = x(T). \end{cases} \tag{1.3}$$

The HDE (1.2) has already been discussed in the literature for different aspects of the solutions using usual Picard as well as Dhage iteration method. See Zeidler (1986) and Dhage and Dhage (2015a). Similarly, the HDE (1.3) has been studied earlier using Picard method. See Bainov, and Hristova (2011) and the references therein. Very recently, Dhage and Octrocol (2016) have initiated the study of initial value problems of first order ordinary nonlinear differential equations via new Dhage iteration method, however to the best of author's knowledge the HDE (1.3) is not discussed via Dhage iteration method. Therefore, the HDE (1.1) is new to the literature in the set up of Dhage iteration method. In this paper we discuss the HDE (1.1) for existence and approximation of the solutions via a new approach based upon Dhage iteration method which include the existence and approximation results for the HDEs (1.2) and (1.3) as special cases which are again new to the theory of differential equations.

In the following section we give some preliminaries and the key tool that will be used for proving the main result of this paper.

2. Preliminaries

Throughout this paper, unless otherwise mentioned, let $(E, \preceq, \|\cdot\|)$ denote a partially ordered normed linear space. Two elements x and y in E are said to be *comparable* if either the relation $x \preceq$ or $y \preceq x$ holds. A non-empty subset C of E is called a *chain* or *totally ordered* if all the elements of C are comparable. It is known that E is *regular* if $\{x_n\}$ is a nondecreasing (resp. nonincreasing) sequence in E such that $x_n \to x^*$ as $n \to \infty$, then $x_n \preceq x^*$ (resp. $x_n \succeq x^*$) for all $n \in \mathbb{N}$. The conditions guaranteeing the regularity of E may be found in Heikkilä and Lakshmikantham (1994) and the references therein.

We need the following definitions (see Dhage, 2013, 2014 and the references therein) in what follows.

Definition 2.1 A mapping $\mathcal{T}: E \to E$ is called *isotone* or *monotone nondecreasing* if it preserves the order relation $\preceq$, that is, if $x \preceq y$ implies $\mathcal{T}x \preceq \mathcal{T}y$ for all $x, y \in E$. Similarly, $\mathcal{T}$ is called *monotone nonincreasing* if $x \preceq y$ implies $\mathcal{T}x \succeq \mathcal{T}y$ for all $x, y \in E$. Finally, $\mathcal{T}$ is called *monotonic* or simply *monotone* if it is either monotone nondecreasing or monotone nonincreasing on E.

Definition 2.2 A mapping $\mathcal{T}: E \to E$ is called *partially continuous* at a point $a \in E$ if for $\epsilon > 0$ there exists a $\delta > 0$ such that $\|\mathcal{T}x - \mathcal{T}a\| < \epsilon$ whenever x is comparable to a and $\|x - a\| < \delta$. $\mathcal{T}$ called partially continuous on E if it is partially continuous at every point of it. It is clear that if $\mathcal{T}$ is partially continuous on E, then it is continuous on every chain C contained in E.

Definition 2.3 A non-empty subset S of the partially ordered Banach space E is called *partially bounded* if every chain C in S is bounded. An operator $\mathcal{T}$ on a partially normed linear space E into itself is called *partially bounded* if $\mathcal{T}(E)$ is a partially bounded subset of E. $\mathcal{T}$ is called *uniformly partially bounded* if all chains C in $\mathcal{T}(E)$ are bounded by a unique constant.

Definition 2.4 A non-empty subset S of the partially ordered Banach space E is called *partially compact* if every chain C in S is a relatively compact subset of E. A mapping $\mathcal{T}: E \to E$ is called *partially compact* if $\mathcal{T}(E)$ is a partially relatively compact subset of E. $\mathcal{T}$ is called *uniformly partially compact* if $\mathcal{T}$ is a uniformly partially bounded and partially compact operator on E. $\mathcal{T}$ is called *partially totally bounded* if for any bounded subset S of E, $\mathcal{T}(S)$ is a partially relatively compact subset of E. If $\mathcal{T}$ is partially continuous and partially totally bounded, then it is called *partially completely continuous* on E.

Remark 2.1 Suppose that $\mathcal{T}$ is a nondecreasing operator on E into itself. Then $\mathcal{T}$ is a partially bounded or partially compact if $\mathcal{T}(C)$ is a bounded or relatively compact subset of E for each chain C in E.

Definition 2.5 The order relation $\preceq$ and the metric d on a non-empty set E are said to be *compatible* if $\{x_n\}$ is a monotone sequence, that is, monotone nondecreasing or monotone nonincreasing sequence in E and if a subsequence $\{x_{n_k}\}$ of $\{x_n\}$ converges to x^* implies that the original sequence $\{x_n\}$ converges to x^*. Similarly, given a partially ordered normed linear space $(E, \preceq, \|\cdot\|)$, the order relation $\preceq$ and the norm $\|\cdot\|$ are said to be compatible if $\preceq$ and the metric d defined through the norm $\|\cdot\|$ are compatible. A subset S of E is called *Janhavi* if the order relation $\preceq$ and the metric d or the norm $\|\cdot\|$ are compatible in it. In particular, if $S = E$, then E is called a *Janhavi metric* or *Janhavi Banach space*.

Clearly, the set $\mathbb{R}$ of real numbers with usual order relation $\leq$ and the norm defined by the absolute value function $|\cdot|$ has this property. Similarly, the finite dimensional Euclidean space $\mathbb{R}^n$ with usual componentwise order relation and the standard norm possesses the compatibility property and so is a *Janhavi Banach space*.

Definition 2.6 An upper semi-continuous and monotone nondecreasing function $\psi: \mathbb{R}_+ \to \mathbb{R}_+$ is called a $\mathcal{D}$-function provided $\psi(0) = 0$. An operator $\mathcal{T}: E \to E$ is called partially nonlinear $\mathcal{D}$-contraction if there exists a $\mathcal{D}$-function ψ such that

$$\|\mathcal{T}x - \mathcal{T}y\| \leq \psi(\|x - y\|) \tag{2.1}$$

for all comparable elements $x, y \in E$, where $0 < \psi(r) < r$ for $r > 0$. In particular, if $\psi(r) = kr, k > 0$, $\mathcal{T}$ is called a partial Lipschitz operator with a Lischitz constant k and moreover, if $0 < k < 1$, $\mathcal{T}$ is called a partial linear contraction on E with a contraction constant k.

The Dhage iteration method embodied in the following applicable hybrid fixed point theorem of Dhage (2014) in a partially ordered normed linear space is used as a key tool for our work contained in this paper. The details of a Dhage iteration method is given in Dhage (2015b, 2015c), Dhage, Dhage, and Graef (2016) and the references therein.

THEOREM 2.1 (Dhage, 2014) Let $(E, \preceq, \|\cdot\|)$ be a regular partially ordered complete normed linear space such that every compact chain C of E is Janhavi. Let $\mathcal{A}, \mathcal{B}: E \to E$ be two nondecreasing operators such that

(a) $\mathcal{A}$ is partially bounded and partially nonlinear $\mathcal{D}$-contraction,

(b) $\mathcal{B}$ is partially continuous and partially compact, and

(c) there exists an element $x_0 \in E$ such that $x_0 \preceq \mathcal{A}x_0 + \mathcal{B}x_0$ or $x_0 \succeq \mathcal{A}x_0 + \mathcal{B}x_0$.Then the operator equation $\mathcal{A}x + \mathcal{B}x = x$ has a solution x^* in E and the sequence $\{x_n\}$ of successive iterations defined by $x_{n+1} = \mathcal{A}x_n + \mathcal{B}x_n$, $n = 0,1,\ldots,$ converges monotonically to x^*.

Remark 2.2 The condition that every compact chain of E is Janhavi holds if every partially compact subset of E possesses the compatibility property with respect to the order relation $\preceq$ and the norm $\|\cdot\|$ in it.

Remark 2.3 We remark that hypothesis (a) of Theorem 2.1 implies that the operator $\mathcal{A}$ is partially continuous and consequently both the operators $\mathcal{A}$ and $\mathcal{B}$ in the theorem are partially continuous on E. The regularity of E in above Theorem 2.1 may be replaced with a stronger continuity condition of the operators $\mathcal{A}$ and $\mathcal{B}$ on E which is a result proved in Dhage (2013, 2014).

3. Main results

In this section, we prove an existence and approximation result for the HDE (1.1) on a closed and bounded interval $J = [0, T]$ under mixed partial Lipschitz and partial compactness type conditions on the nonlinearities involved in it. We place the HDE (1.1) in the function space $C(J, \mathbb{R})$ of continuous real-valued functions defined on J. We define a norm $\|\cdot\|$ and the order relation $\leq$ in $C(J, \mathbb{R})$ by

$$\|x\| = \sup_{t\in J} |x(t)| \tag{3.1}$$

and

$$x \leq y \iff x(t) \leq y(t) \quad \text{for all} \quad t \in J. \tag{3.2}$$

Clearly, $C(J, \mathbb{R})$ is a Banach space with respect to above supremum norm and also partially ordered w.r.t. the above partially order relation $\leq$. It is known that the partially ordered Banach space $C(J, \mathbb{R})$ is regular and lattice so that every pair of elements of E has a lower and an upper bound in it. The following useful lemma concerning the Janhavi subsets of $C(J, \mathbb{R})$ follows immediately form the Arzelá-Ascoli theorem for compactness.

LEMMA 3.1 *Let $(C(J, \mathbb{R}), \leq, \|\cdot\|)$ be a partially ordered Banach space with the norm $\|\cdot\|$ and the order relation $\leq$ defined by (3.1) and (3.2) respectively. Then every partially compact subset of $C(J, \mathbb{R})$ is Janhavi.*

Proof The proof of the lemma is well-known and appears in the works of Dhage (2015b, 2015c), Dhage and Dhage (2014), Dhage et al. (2016) and so we omit the details. □

The following useful lemma is obvious and may be found in Dhage (2008) and Nieto (1997).

LEMMA 3.2 *For any function $\sigma \in L^1(J, \mathbb{R})$, x is a solution to the differential equation*

$$\left.\begin{array}{ll} x'(t) + \lambda x(t) = \sigma(t), & t \in J, \\ x(0) = x(T), & \end{array}\right\} \tag{3.3}$$

if and only if it is a solution of the integral equation

$$x(t) = \int_0^T G_\lambda(t, s)\,\sigma(s)\,ds \tag{3.4}$$

where,

$$G_\lambda(t,s) = \begin{cases} \frac{e^{\lambda s-\lambda t+\lambda T}}{e^{\lambda T}-1}, & \text{if} \quad 0 \le s \le t \le T, \\ \frac{e^{\lambda s-\lambda t}}{e^{\lambda T}-1}, & \text{if} \quad 0 \le t < s \le T. \end{cases} \tag{3.5}$$

Notice that the Green's function G_λ is continuous and nonnegative on $J \times J$ and therefore, the number

$$K_\lambda : = \max \{|G_\lambda(t,s)| \quad : \quad t,s \in [0,T]\}$$

exists for all $\lambda \in \mathbb{R}^+$. For the sake of convenience, we write $G_\lambda(t,s) = G(t,s)$ and $K_\lambda = K$.

Another useful result for establishing the main result is as follows.

LEMMA 3.3 *If there exists a differentiable function* $u \in C(J,\mathbb{R})$ *such that*

$$\left.\begin{aligned} &u'(t) + \lambda u(t) \le \sigma(t), \quad t \in J, \\ &u(0) \le u(T), \end{aligned}\right\} \tag{3.6}$$

for all $t \in J$, where $\lambda \in \mathbb{R}$, $\lambda > 0$ and $\sigma \in L^1(J,\mathbb{R})$, then

$$u(t) \le \int_0^T G(t,s)\,\sigma(s)\,ds, \tag{3.7}$$

for all $t \in J$, where $G(t,s)$ is a Green's function given by (3.5).

Proof Suppose that the function $u \in C(J,\mathbb{R})$ satisfies the inequalities given in (3.6). Multiplying the first inequality in (3.6) by $e^{\lambda t}$,

$$\left(e^{\lambda t}u(t)\right)' \le e^{\lambda t}\sigma(t).$$

A direct integration of above inequality from 0 to t yields

$$e^{\lambda t}u(t) \le u(0) + \int_0^t e^{\lambda s}\sigma(s)\,ds, \tag{3.8}$$

for all $t \in J$. Therefore, in particular,

$$e^{\lambda T}u(T) \le u(0) + \int_0^T e^{\lambda s}\sigma(s)\,ds. \tag{3.9}$$

Now $u(0) \le u(T)$, so one has

$$u(0)e^{\lambda T} \le u(T)e^{\lambda T}. \tag{3.10}$$

From (3.9) and (3.10) it follows that

$$e^{\lambda T}u(0) \le u(0) + \int_0^T e^{\lambda s}\sigma(s)\,ds \tag{3.11}$$

which further yields

$$u(0) \le \int_0^T \frac{e^{\lambda s}}{(e^{\lambda T}-1)}\sigma(s)\,ds. \tag{3.12}$$

Substituting (3.12) in (3.8) we obtain

$$u(t) \le \int_0^T G(t,s)\sigma(s)\,ds,$$

for all $t \in J$. This completes the proof. □

We need the following definition in what follows.

Definition 3.1 A function $u \in C^1(J, \mathbb{R})$ is said to be a lower solution of the Equation (1.1) if it satisfies

$$\begin{cases} u'(t) \leq f(t, u(t)) + g\left(t, \max_{0 \leq \xi \leq t} u(\xi)\right), \\ u(0) \leq u(T), \end{cases} \tag{$*$}$$

for all $t \in J$. Similarly, a differentiable function $v \in C^1(J, \mathbb{R})$ is called an upper solution of the HDE (1.1) if the above inequality is satisfied with reverse sign.

We consider the following set of assumptions in what follows:

(H_1) There exist constants $\lambda > 0, \mu > 0$ with $\lambda \geq \mu$ such that

$$0 \leq [f(t, x) + \lambda x] - [f(t, y) + \lambda y] \leq \mu(x - y)$$

for all $t \in J$ and $x, y \in \mathbb{R}$, $x \geq y$. Moreover, $\lambda K T < 1$.

(H_2) There exists a constant $M_g > 0$ such that $\|g(t, x)\| \leq M_g$, for all $t \in J$, $x \in \mathbb{R}$;

(H_3) $g(t, x)$ is nondecreasing in x for each $t \in J$.

(H_4) HDE (1.1) has a lower solution $u \in C^1(J, \mathbb{R})$.

Now we consider the following HDE

$$\begin{cases} x'(t) + \lambda x(t) = \tilde{f}(t, x(t)) + g\left(t, \max_{0 \leq \xi \leq t} u(\xi)\right), \\ x(0) = x(T), \end{cases} \tag{3.13}$$

for all $t \in J = [0, T]$, where $\tilde{f}(t, x) = f(t, x) + \lambda x, \quad \lambda > 0$.

Remark 3.1 A function $u \in C^1(J, \mathbb{R})$ is a solution of the HDE (3.13) if and only if it is a solution of the HDE (1.1) defined on J.

We also consider the following hypothesis in what follows.

(H_5) There exists a constant $M_{\tilde{f}} > 0$ such that $\left\|\tilde{f}(t, x)\right\| \leq M_{\tilde{f}}$ for all $t \in J$ and $x \in \mathbb{R}$.

LEMMA 3.4 *Suppose that the hypotheses (H_2), (H_3) and (H_5) hold. Then a function $x \in C(J, \mathbb{R})$ is a solution of the HDE (3.3) if and only if it is a solution of the nonlinear hybrid integral equation (in short HIE)*

$$x(t) = \int_0^T G(t, s)\tilde{f}(s, x(s))\, ds + \int_0^T G(t, s) g\left(s, \max_{0 \leq \xi \leq s} x(\xi)\right) ds, \tag{3.14}$$

for all $t \in J$.

THEOREM 3.1 Suppose that hypotheses $(H_1) - (H_5)$ hold. Then the HDE (1.1) has a solution x^* defined on J and the sequence $\{x_n\}$ of successive approximations defined by

$$
\begin{aligned}
x_0 &= u, \\
x_{n+1}(t) &= \int_0^T G(t,s)\widetilde{f}(s,x_n(s))\,ds \\
&\quad + \int_0^T G(t,s)g\left(s, \max_{0\le\xi\le s} x_n(\xi)\right) ds,
\end{aligned} \tag{3.15}
$$

for all $t \in J$, converges monotonically to x^*.

Proof Set $E = C(J, \mathbb{R})$. Then, in view of Lemma 3.1, every compact chain C in E possesses the compatibility property with respect to the norm $\|\cdot\|$ and the order relation $\le$ so that every compact chain C is Janhavi in E.

Define two operators $\mathcal{A}$ and $\mathcal{B}$ on E by

$$
\mathcal{A}x(t) = \int_0^T G(t,s)\widetilde{f}(s,x(s))\,ds, \quad t \in J, \tag{3.16}
$$

and

$$
\mathcal{B}x(t) = \int_0^T G(t,s)g\left(s, \max_{0\le\xi\le s} x(\xi)\right) ds, \quad t \in J. \tag{3.17}
$$

From the continuity of the integral, it follows that $\mathcal{A}$ and $\mathcal{B}$ define the operators $\mathcal{A}, \mathcal{B}: E \to E$. Applying Lemma (3.4), the HDE (1.1) is equivalent to the operator equation

$$
\mathcal{A}x(t) + \mathcal{B}x(t) = x(t), \quad t \in J.
$$

Now, we show that the operators $\mathcal{A}$ and $\mathcal{B}$ satisfy all the conditions of Theorem 2.1 in a series of following steps.

Step I: *$\mathcal{A}$ and $\mathcal{B}$ are nondecreasing on E.*

Let $x, y \in E$ be such that $x \ge y$. Then by hypothesis (H_1), we get

$$
\begin{aligned}
\mathcal{A}x(t) &= \int_0^T G(t,s)\widetilde{f}(s,x(s))\,ds \\
&\ge \int_0^T G(t,s)\widetilde{f}(s,y(s))\,ds \\
&= \mathcal{A}y(t),
\end{aligned}
$$

for all $t \in J$.

Next, we show that the operator $\mathcal{B}$ is also nondecreasing on E. Let $x, y \in E$ be such that $x \ge y$. Then $x(t) \ge y(t)$ for all $t \in J$. Since y is continuous on $[0, t]$, there exists a $\xi^* \in [a, t]$ such that $y(\xi^*) = \max_{a\le\xi\le t} y(\xi)$. By definition of $\le$, one has $x(\xi^*) \ge y(\xi^*)$. Consequently, we obtain

$$
\max_{a\le\xi\le t} x(\xi) = x(\xi^*) \ge y(\xi^*) = \max_{a\le\xi\le t} y(\xi).
$$

Now, using hypothesis (H_3), it can be shown that the operator $\mathcal{B}$ is also nondecreasing on E.

Step II: *$\mathcal{A}$ is partially bounded and partially contraction on E.*

Let $x \in E$ be arbitrary. Then by (H_5) we have

$$
\begin{aligned}
\|\mathcal{A}x(t)\| &\le \int_0^T G(t,s)\left\|\tilde{f}(s,x(s))\right\| ds \\
&\le M_{\tilde{f}} \int_0^T G(t,s)\, ds \\
&\le M_{\tilde{f}} K T,
\end{aligned}
$$

for all $t \in J$. Taking the supremum over t, we obtain $\|\mathcal{A}x(t)\| \le M_{\tilde{f}} K T$ and so, $\mathcal{A}$ is a bounded operator on E. This implies that $\mathcal{A}$ is partially bounded on E. Let $x, y \in E$ be such that $x \ge y$. Then by (H_1) we have

$$
\begin{aligned}
\|\mathcal{A}x(t) - \mathcal{A}y(t)\| &\le \left\| \int_0^T G(t,s)\left[\tilde{f}(s,x(s)) - \tilde{f}(s,y(s))\right] ds \right\| \\
&\le \int_0^T G(t,s)\mu \|x(s) - y(s)\|\, ds \\
&\le \int_0^T G(t,s)\lambda \|x(s) - y(s)\|\, ds \\
&\le \lambda \int_0^T G(t,s)\|x - y\|\, ds \\
&\le \lambda K T \|x - y\|,
\end{aligned}
$$

for all $t \in J$. Taking the supremum over t, we obtain $\|\mathcal{A}x - \mathcal{A}y\| \le L\|x - y\|$ for all $x, y \in E$ with $x \ge y$, where $L = \lambda K T < 1$. Hence $\mathcal{A}$ is a partially contraction on E and which also implies that $\mathcal{A}$ is partially continuous on E.

Step III: $\mathcal{B}$ is partially continuous on E.

Let $\{x_n\}_{n\in\mathbb{N}}$ be a sequence in a chain C such that $x_n \to x$, for all $n \in \mathbb{N}$. Then

$$
\begin{aligned}
\lim_{n\to\infty} \mathcal{B}x_n(t) &= \lim_{n\to\infty} \int_0^T G(t,s) g\left(s, \max_{0\le\xi\le s} x_n(\xi)\right) ds \\
&= \int_0^T G(t,s)\left[\lim_{n\to\infty} g\left(s, \max_{0\le\xi\le s} x_n(\xi)\right)\right] ds \\
&= \int_0^T G(t,s) g\left(s, \max_{0\le\xi\le s} x_n(\xi)\right) ds \\
&= \mathcal{B}x(t),
\end{aligned}
$$

for all $t \in J$. This shows that $\mathcal{B}x_n$ converges monotononically to $\mathcal{B}x$ pointwise on J.

Now we show that $\{\mathcal{B}x_n\}_{n\in\mathbb{N}}$ is an equicontinuous sequence of functions in E.

Let $t_1, t_2 \in J$ with $t_1 < t_2$. We have

$$
\begin{aligned}
\|\mathcal{B}x_n(t_2) - \mathcal{B}x_n(t_1)\| &= \left\| \int_0^T G(t_2,s) g\left(s, \max_{0\le\xi\le s} x_n(\xi)\right) ds \right. \\
&\qquad \left. - \int_0^T G(t_1,s) g\left(s, \max_{0\le\xi\le s} x_n(\xi)\right) ds \right\| \\
&\le \int_0^T \|G(t_2,s) - G(t_1,s)\| \left\| g\left(s, \max_{0\le\xi\le s} x_n(\xi)\right) ds \right\| \\
&\le M_g \int_0^T |G(t_2,s) - G(t_1,s)|\, ds \\
&\to 0 \quad \text{as} \quad t_2 \to t_1,
\end{aligned}
$$

uniformly for all $n \in \mathbb{N}$. This shows that the convergence $\mathcal{B}x_n \to \mathcal{B}x$ is uniform and hence $\mathcal{B}$ is partially continuous on E.

Step IV: $\mathcal{B}$ is partially compact operator on E.

Let C be an arbitrary chain in E. We show that $\mathcal{B}(C)$ is uniformly bounded and equicontinuous set in E. First we show that $\mathcal{B}(C)$ is uniformly bounded. Let $y \in \mathcal{B}(C)$ be any element. Then there is an element $x \in C$ such that $y = \mathcal{B}x$. By hypothesis (H_2)

$$\begin{aligned}\|y(t)\| &= \|\mathcal{B}x(t)\| \\ &= \left\|\int_0^T G(t,s)g\left(s, \max_{0\le\xi\le s} x(\xi)\right) ds\right\| \\ &\le \int_0^T G(t,s)\left\|g\left(s, \max_{0\le\xi\le s} x(\xi)\right)\right\| ds \\ &\le K\,T\,M_g = r,\end{aligned}$$

for all $t \in J$. Taking the supremum over t we obtain $\|y\| \le \|\mathcal{B}x\| \le r$, for all $y \in \mathcal{B}(C)$. Hence $\mathcal{B}(C)$ is uniformly bounded subset of E. Next we show that $\mathcal{B}(C)$ is an equicontinuous set in E. Let $t_1, t_2 \in J$, with $t_1 < t_2$. Then, for any $y \in \mathcal{B}(C)$, one has

$$\begin{aligned}\|y(t_2) - y(t_1)\| &= \|\mathcal{B}x(t_2) - \mathcal{B}x(t_1)\| \\ &= \left\|\int_0^T G(t_2,s)g\left(s, \max_{0\le\xi\le s} x(\xi)\right) ds \right.\\ &\quad \left. - \int_0^T G(t_1,s)g\left(s, \max_{0\le\xi\le s} x(\xi)\right) ds\right\| \\ &\le \int_0^T |G(t_2,s) - G(t_1,s)| \left|g\left(s, \max_{0\le\xi\le s} x(\xi)\right)\right| ds \\ &\le M_g \int_0^T |G(t_2,s) - G(t_1,s)|\, ds \\ &\to 0 \quad \text{as} \quad t_1 \to t_2\end{aligned}$$

uniformly for all $y \in \mathcal{B}(C)$. This shows that $\mathcal{B}(C)$ is an equicontinuous subset of E. So $\mathcal{B}(C)$ is a uniformly bounded and equicontinuous set of functions in E. Hence it is compact in view of Arzelá-Ascoli theorem. Consequently $\mathcal{B}: E \to E$ is a partially compact operator of E into itself.

Step V: u satisfies the inequality $u \le \mathcal{A}u + \mathcal{B}u$.

By hypothesis (H_4) the Equation (1.1) has a lower solution u defined on J. Then we have

$$\begin{cases} u'(t) & \le f(t,u(t)) + g\left(t, \max_{0\le\xi\le t} u(\xi)\right), \quad t \in J, \\ u(0) & \le u(T). \end{cases} \tag{3.18}$$

A direct application of lemma 3.3 yields that

$$u(t) \le \int_0^T G(t,s)\tilde{f}(s,u(s))ds + \int_0^T G(t,s)g\left(s, \max_{0\le\xi\le s} u(\xi)\right)ds, \tag{3.19}$$

for $t \in J$. From definitions of the operators $\mathcal{A}$ and $\mathcal{B}$ it follows that $u(t) \le \mathcal{A}u(t) + \mathcal{B}u(t)$, for all $t \in J$. Hence $u \le \mathcal{A}u + \mathcal{B}u$. Thus $\mathcal{A}$ and $\mathcal{B}$ satisfy all the conditions of Theorem 2.1 and we apply it to conclude that the operator equation $\mathcal{A}x + \mathcal{B}x = x$ has a solution. Consequently the integral equation and the Equation (1.1) has a solution x^* defined on J. Furthermore, the sequence $\{x_n\}_{n=0}^{\infty}$ of successive approximations defined by (3.5) converges monotonically to x^*. This completes the proof. □

Remark 3.2 The conclusion of Theorem 3.1 also remails true if we replace the hypothesis (H_4) with the following one.

(H_4') The HDE (1.1) has an upper solution $v \in C^1(J, \mathbb{R})$.

Remark 3.3 We note that if the PBVP (1.1) has a lower solution u as well as an upper solution v such that $u \le v$, then under the given conditions of Theorem 3.1 it has corresponding solutions x_* and x^* and these solutions satisfy $x_* \le x^*$. Hence they are the minimal and maximal solutions of the PBVP (1.1) in the vector segment $[u, v]$ of the Banach space $E = C^1(J, \mathbb{R})$, where the vector segment $[u, v]$ is a set in $C^1(J, \mathbb{R})$ defined by

$$[u, v] = \{x \in C^1(J, \mathbb{R}) \mid u \le x \le v\}.$$

This is because the order relation $\le$ defined by (3.2) is equivalent to the order relation defined by the order cone $\mathcal{K} = \{x \in C(J, \mathbb{R}) \mid x \ge \theta\}$ which is a closed set in $C(J, \mathbb{R})$.

In the following we illustrate our hypotheses and the main abstract result for the validity of conclusion.

Example 3.1 We consider the following HDE

$$\begin{cases} x'(t) = \arctan x(t) - x(t) + \tanh\left(\max_{0\le\xi\le t} x(\xi)\right), & t \in J = [0, 1], \\ x(0) = x(1). \end{cases} \tag{3.20}$$

Here $f(t, x) = \arctan x(t) - x(t)$ and $g(t, x) = \tanh x$. The functions f and g are continuous on $J \times \mathbb{R}$. Next, we have

$$0 \le \arctan x(t) - \arctan y(t) \le \frac{1}{\xi^2 + 1}(x - y),$$

for all $x, y \in \mathbb{R}, x > \xi > y$. Therefore $\lambda = 1 > \frac{1}{\xi^2+1} = \mu$. Hence the function f satisfies the hypothesis (H_1). Moreover, the function $\tilde{f}(t, x) = \arctan x(t)$ is bounded on $J \times \mathbb{R}$ with bound $M_{\tilde{f}} = \pi/2$, so that the hypothesis (H_5) is satisfied. The function g is bounded on $J \times \mathbb{R}$ by $M_g = 1$, so (H_2) holds. The function $g(t, x)$ is increasing in x for each $t \in J$, so the hypothesis (H_3) is satisfied. The HDE (3.20) has a lower solution $u(t) = -2\int_0^1 G(t, s)\, ds, t \in [0, 1]$, where $G(t, s)$ is a Green's function associated with the homogeneous PBVP

$$\left.\begin{aligned} &x'(t) + x(t) = 0, \quad t \in J, \\ &x(0) = x(1), \end{aligned}\right\} \tag{3.21}$$

given by

$$G(t, s) = \begin{cases} \frac{e^{s-t+1}}{e-1}, & \text{if} \quad 0 \le s \le t \le 1, \\ \frac{e^{s-t}}{e-1}, & \text{if} \quad 0 \le t < s \le 1. \end{cases}$$

Finally, $\lambda K T = \sup_{t,s\in J} G(t, s) < 1$. Thus all the hypotheses of Theorem 3.1 are satisfied and hence the HDE (3.11) has a solution x^* defined on J and the sequence $\{x_n\}_{n=0}^{\infty}$ defined by

$$\begin{aligned} x_0 &= -2\int_0^1 G(t, s)\, ds, \\ x_{n+1}(t) &= \int_0^1 G(t, s) \arctan x_n(s)\, ds \\ &\quad + \int_0^1 G(t, s) \tanh\left(\max_{0\le\xi\le s} x_n(\xi)\right) ds \end{aligned}$$

for each $t \in J$, converges monotonically to x^*.

Remark 3.4 Finally while concluding this paper, we mention that the study of this paper may be extended with appropriate modifications to the nonlinear hybrid differential equation with maxima,

$$\begin{cases} x'(t) = f\left(t, x(t), \max\limits_{a \le \xi \le t} x(\xi)\right) + g\left(t, x(t), \max\limits_{a \le \xi \le t} x(\xi)\right), \\ x(0) = x(T), \end{cases} \tag{3.22}$$

for all $t \in J = [a, b]$, where $f, g: J \times \mathbb{R} \times \mathbb{R} \to \mathbb{R}$ are continuous functions. When $g \equiv 0$, the differential Equation (3.12) reduces to the nonlinear differential equations with maxima,

$$\begin{cases} x'(t) = f\left(t, x(t), \max\limits_{a \le \xi \le t} x(\xi)\right), \quad t \in J, \\ x(0) = x(T), \end{cases} \tag{3.23}$$

which is new and could be studied for existence and uniqueness theorem via Picard iterations under strong Lipschitz condition. Therefore, the obtained results for differential Equation (3.12) with maxima via Dhage iteration method will include the existence and approximation results for the differential equation with maxima (3.13) under weak partial Lipschitz condition.

Acknowledgements
The author is thankful to the referee for pointing out some misprints/corrections for the improvement of this paper.

Funding
The author received no direct funding for this research.

Author details
Bapurao C. Dhage[1]
E-mail: bcdhage@gmail.com
[1] Kasubai, Gurukul Colony, Dist. Latur, Ahmedpur 413515, Maharashtra, India.

References

Bainov, D. D., & Hristova, S. (2011). *Differential equations with maxima*. New York, NY: Chapman & Hall/CRC Pure and Applied Mathematics.

Dhage, B. C. (2008). Periodic boundary value problems of first order Carathéodory and discontinuous differential equations. *Nonlinear Functional Analysis and its Applications, 13*, 323–352.

Dhage, B. C. (2010). Quadratic perturbations of periodic boundary value problems of second order ordinary differential equations. *Differential Equations & Applications, 2*, 465–486.

Dhage, B. C. (2013). Hybrid fixed point theory in partially ordered normed linear spaces and applications to fractional integral equations. *Differential Equations & Applications, 5*, 155–184.

Dhage, B. C. (2014). Partially condensing mappings in ordered normed linear spaces and applications to functional integral equations. *Tamkang Journal of Mathematics, 45*, 397–426.

Dhage, B. C. (2015a). Nonlinear $\mathcal{D}$-set-contraction mappings in partially ordered normed linear spaces and applications to functional hybrid integral equations. *Malaya Journal of Matematik, 3*, 62–85.

Dhage, B. C. (2015b). Operator theoretic techniques in the theory of nonlinear hybrid differential equations. *Nonlinear Analysis Forum, 20*, 15–31.

Dhage, B. C. (2015c). A new monotone iteration principle in the theory of nonlinear first order integro-differential equations. *Nonlinear Studies, 22*, 397–417.

Dhage, B. C., & Dhage, S. B. (2014). Approximating solutions of nonlinear first order ordinary differential equations. *GJMS Special Issue for Recent Advances in Mathematical Sciences and Applications-13, GJMS, 2*, 25–35.

Dhage, B. C., & Dhage, S. B. (2015a). Approximating solutions of nonlinear PBVPs of hybrid differential equations via hybrid fixed point theory. *Indian Journal of Mathematics, 57*, 103–119.

Dhage, B. C., & Dhage, S. B. (2015b). Approximating positive solutions of PBVPs of nonlinear first order ordinary quadratic differential equations. *Applied Mathematics Letters, 46*, 133–142.

Dhage, B. C., Dhage, S. B., & Graef, J. R. (2016). Dhage iteration method for initial value problems for nonlinear first order hybrid integrodifferential equations. *The Journal of Fixed Point Theory and Applications, 18*, 309–326. doi:10.1007/s11784-015-0279-3

Dhage, B. C., & Octrocol, D. (2016). Dhage iteration method for approximating solutions of nonlinear first order ordinary differential equations with maxima. *Fixed Point Theory, 17*(2).

Heikkilä, S., & Lakshmikantham, V. (1994). *Monotone iterative techniques for discontinuous nonlinear differential equations*. New York, NY: Marcel Dekker.

Nieto, J. J. (1997). Basic theory for nonresonance impulsive periodic problems of first order. *The Journal of Mathematical Analysis and Applications, 205*, 423–433.

Nieto, J. J., & Rodriguez-Lopez, R. (2005). Contractive mappings theorems in partially ordered sets and applications to ordinary differential equations. *Order, 22*, 223–239.

Otrocol, D. (2014). Systems of functional differential equations with maxima, of mixed type. *Electronic Journal of Qualitative Theory of Differential Equations, 2014*(5), 1–9.

Petruşel, A., & Rus, I. A. (2006). Fixed point theorems in ordered L-spaces. *Proceedings of the American Mathematical Society, 134*, 411–418.

Ran, A. C. M., & Reurings, M. C. (2004). A fixed point theorem in partially ordered sets and some applications to matrix equations. *Proceedings of the American Mathematical Society, 132*, 1435–1443.

Zeidler, E. (1986). *Nonlinear functional analysis and its applications, Vol. I: Fixed point theorems*. New York, NY: Springer.

4

On finite element approximation of system of parabolic quasi-variational inequalities related to stochastic control problems

Mohamed Amine Bencheikh Le Hocine[1,2], Salah Boulaaras[3,4*] and Mohamed Haiour[2]

Abstract: In this paper, an optimal error estimate for system of parabolic quasi-variational inequalities related to stochastic control problems is studied. Existence and uniqueness of the solution is provided by the introduction of a constructive algorithm. An optimally L^∞-asymptotic behavior in maximum norm is proved using the semi-implicit time scheme combined with the finite element spatial approximation. The approach is based on the concept of subsolution and discrete regularity.

Subjects: Advanced Mathematics; Applied Mathematics; Mathematics & Statistics; Science

Keywords: parabolic quasi-variational inequalities; Hamilton–Jacobi–Bellman equation; finite element methods; subsolutions method; L^∞-asymptotic behavior; orthogonal polynomials and special functions

1991 Mathematics subject classification: 35 R 35; 49 J 40

1. Introduction

We consider the following Parabolic Quasi-Variational Inequalities (PQVI):

$$\begin{cases} \dfrac{\partial u^i}{\partial t} + \mathbb{A}u^i - f^i \leq 0, \quad u^i \leq Mu^i, \\ \left(\dfrac{\partial u^i}{\partial t} + \mathbb{A}u^i - f^i\right)\left(u^i - Mu^i\right) = 0, \quad \text{in } \mathbb{Q}_T := \Omega \times]0, T[; \\ u^i\big|_{t=0} = u^i_0, \quad \forall i = 1, 2, \ldots, J, \ \text{in } \Omega; \\ u^i = 0, \quad \text{on } \sum_T :=]0, T[\times \Gamma, \end{cases} \tag{1.1}$$

ABOUT THE AUTHORS

Mohamed Amine Bencheick Le Hocine is an associate professor at Tamanarast University. He received his PhD on Numerical Analysis in January 2014 from University of Annaba, Algeria. He published more than 25 papers in international refereed journals.

Salah Boulaaras was born in 1985 in Algeria. He received his PhD in January 2012 He serves as an associate Professor at Qassim University, KSA. He published more than 25 papers in international refereed journals.

Mohamed Haiour is a full Professor at Annaba University. He received his PhD in Numerical Analysis in 2004 from the University of Annaba. He has more than 34 publications in refereed journal and conference papers.

PUBLIC INTEREST STATEMENT

The stationary and evolutionary free boundary problems are accomplished in some applications; for example, in stochastic control, their solution characterize the in mum of the cost function associated to an optimally controlled stochastic switching process without costs for switching and for the calculus of quasi-stationary state for the simulation of petroleum or gaseous deposit.

where Ω is a bounded convex domain in $\mathbb{R}^d$, $d \geq 1$ with smooth boundary Γ, and $\mathbb{Q}_T$ set in $\mathbb{R}^d \times \mathbb{R}$, $\mathbb{Q}_T = :\Omega \times [0, T]$ with $T < +\infty$, $\sum_T = :\Gamma \times [0, T]$, $\mathbb{A}^i$ are second order, uniformly elliptic operators of the form

$$\mathbb{A}^i = -\sum_{j,k=1}^{d} a^i_{jk}(x)\frac{\partial^2}{\partial x_j \partial x_k} + \sum_{j=1}^{d} b^i_j(x)\frac{\partial}{\partial x_j} + a^i_0(x), \tag{1.2}$$

where $\forall i = 1, ..., J, a^i_{jk}, b^i_j, a^i_0 \in C^2(\bar{\Omega}), x \in \bar{\Omega}, 1 \leq j, k \leq d$ are sufficiently smooth coefficients and satisfy the following conditions:

$$a^i_{jk}(x) = a^i_{kj}(x); \quad a^i_0(x) \geq \beta > 0, \quad \beta \text{ is a constant} \tag{1.3}$$

and

$$\sum\nolimits_{j,k=1}^{n} a^i_{jk}(x)\xi_j\xi_k \geq \gamma|\xi|^2; \quad \xi \in \mathbb{R}^d, \quad \gamma > 0, \quad x \in \bar{\Omega}. \tag{1.4}$$

f^i are given functions satisfying the following condition

$$f^i \in L^2(0, T, L^\infty(\Omega)) \cap C^1(0, T, H^{-1}(\Omega)), \text{ and } f^i \geq 0. \tag{1.5}$$

Mu^i represents the obstacle of stochastic control defined by:

$$Mu^i = k + u^{i+1} \tag{1.6}$$

where k is a strictly positive constant.

This problem arises in stochastic control problems. It also plays a fundamental role in solving the Hamilton–Jacobi–Bellman equation (Evans & Friedman, 1979; Lions & Menaldi, 1979).

In this paper, we are concerned with the numerical approximation in the L^∞ norm for the problem (1.1). From Lions and Menaldi (1979), we know that (1.1) can be approximated by the following system of parabolic quasi-variational inequalities (PQVIs): find a vector $U = (u^1, u^2, ..., u^M) \in (L^2(0, T, H^1_0(\Omega)))^J$ such that

$$\begin{cases} \frac{\partial}{\partial t}(u^i, v - u^i) + a^i(u^i, v - u^i) \geq (f^i, v - u^i), & \forall v \in H^1_0(\Omega); \\ u^i \leq k + u^{i+1}, \ v \leq k + u^{i+1}, & i = 1, 2, ..., J; \\ u^{J+1} = u^1; & \\ u^i(0) = u^i_0, & \end{cases} \tag{1.7}$$

where $a(u, v)$ is a continuous and noncoercive bilinear form associated with elliptic operator $\mathbb{A}$ defined as: for any $u, \ v \in H^1(\Omega)$

$$a(u, v) = \int_\Omega \left(\sum_{j,k=1}^{d} a_{jk}(x)\frac{\partial u}{\partial x_j}\frac{\partial v}{\partial x_k} + \sum_{k=1}^{d} b_k(x)\frac{\partial u}{\partial x_k}v + a_0(x)uv \right)dx \tag{1.8}$$

and $(.,.)$ is the inner product in $L^2(\Omega)$.

Next we give consideration to a discrete version of (1.1): let τ_h be a regular and quasi-uniform triangulation of Ω; $h > 0$ is the mesh size. Let also $\mathbb{V}_h$ be the finite element space consisting of continuous piecewise linear functions vanishing on Γ, $\{\varphi_i\}, i = 1, ..., m(h)$ the basis functions of $\mathbb{V}_h$, and r_h the usual restriction operator. We consider the fully discretized problem: find $U^n_h = (u^{1,n}_h, u^{2,n}_h, ..., u^{M,n}_h) \in (\mathbb{V}_h)^M$ such that for all $n = 1, 2, ..., N$

$$\begin{cases} \left(\dfrac{u_h^{i,n}-u_h^{i,n-1}}{\triangle t}, v_h - u_h^{i,n}\right) + a^i\left(u_h^{i,n}, v_h - u_h^{i,n}\right) \geq \left(f^{i,n}, v_h - u_h^{i,n}\right); \quad \forall v_h \in \mathbb{V}_h; \\ u_h^{i,n} \leq r_h\left(k + u_h^{i+1,n}\right), v_h \leq r_h\left(k + u_h^{i+1,n}\right); \\ u_h^{M+1,n} = u_h^{1,n}; \\ u_h^{i,n}(0) = u_{h,0}^{i,n}, \end{cases} \tag{1.9}$$

with $\triangle t := \frac{T}{N}; t_n = n \triangle t$ the time step, $f^{i,n} = f^i(t_n)$ and $u_{h,0}^{i,n}$ an appropriate approximation of u_0^i.

Error estimates for piecewise linear finite element approximations of parabolic variational and quasi-variational inequalities have been established in various papers (cf. e.g. Achdou, Hecht, & Pommier, 2008; Alfredo, 1987; Bencheikh Le Hocine, Boulaaras, & Haiour, 2016; Bensoussan & Lions, 1973; Berger & Falk, 1977; Boulaaras, Bencheikh Le Hocine, & Haiour, 2014; Diaz & Defonso, 1985; Scarpini & Vivaldi, 1977). More recently, Bencheikh Le Hocine and Haiour (2013) exploited the above arguments for system of parabolic quasi-variational inequalities, where they analyzed the semi-implicit Euler scheme with respect to the t- variable combined with a finite element spatial approximation and gave (for $d \geq 1$) the following L^{∞}-asymptotic behavior:

$$\|U_h(T,.) - U^{\infty}(.)\|_{\infty} \leq C\left(h^2|\log h|^4 + \left(\frac{1}{1+\beta\Delta t}\right)^n\right) \tag{1.10}$$

The quasi-optimal L^{∞}-asymptotic behavior ($d \geq 1$): for $\theta \geq \frac{1}{2}$

$$|U_h(T,.) - U^{\infty}(.)\|_{\infty} \leq C\left(h^2|\log h|^3 + \left(\frac{1}{1+\beta\theta\Delta t}\right)^n\right) \tag{1.11}$$

and for $\theta \in [0, \frac{1}{2}[$

$$\|U_h(T,.) - U^{\infty}(.)\|_{\infty} \leq C\left(h^2|\log h|^3 + \left(\frac{2Ch^2}{2Ch^2 + \beta\theta(1-2\theta)\rho(A)}\right)^n\right), \tag{1.12}$$

where $\rho(\mathbb{A}) = \min_{1\leq i\leq J}\left\|\rho\left(\mathbb{A}^i\right)\right\|_{\infty}$ is the spectral radius of the elliptic operator $\mathbb{A}$, has been obtained in Boulaaras and Haiour (2014).

In the current paper, we shall employ the concepts of subsolutions and discrete regularity (Bencheikh Le Hocine et al., 2016; Boulbrachene, 2014, 2015a, 2015b; Cortey-Dumont, 1987, 1985). More precisely, we use the characterization the continuous solution (resp. the discrete solution) as the maximum elements of the set of continuous subsolutions (resp. the maximum elements of the set of discrete subsolutions), in order to yield the following optimal L^{∞}-asymptotic behavior (for $d \geq 1$):

$$\|U_h(T,.) - U^{\infty}(.)\|_{\infty} \leq C\left(h^2|\log h|^2 + \left(\frac{1}{1+\beta\Delta t}\right)^n\right). \tag{1.13}$$

The paper is organized as follows. In Section 2, we present the continuous problem and study some qualitative properties. The discrete problem is proposed in Section 3. In Section 4, we derive an L^{∞}-error estimate of the approximation. The main result of the paper is presented in Section 5.

2. Statement of the continuous system

2.1. Existence and uniqueness

2.1.1. The time discretization

We discretize the problem (1.1) or (1.7) with respect to time by using the semi-implicit scheme. Therefore, we search a sequence of elements $u^{i,n} \in H_0^1(\Omega)$, $1 \leq i \leq J$, which approaches $u^i(t_n)$, $t_n = k\,\Delta t$, with initial data $u^{i,0} = u_{i,0}$.

Thus, we have for $n = 1, \ldots, N$

$$\begin{cases} \left(\dfrac{u^{i,n} - u^{i,n-1}}{\Delta t}, v - u^{i,n}\right) + a^i\left(u^{i,n}, v - u^{i,n}\right) \geq \left(f^{i,n}, v - u^{i,n}\right), & \forall v \in H_0^1(\Omega); \\ u^{i,n} \leq k + u^{i+1,n}, v \leq k + u^{i+1,n}; \\ u^{J+1,n} = u^{1,n}; \\ u^i(0) = u_0^i, \end{cases} \tag{2.1}$$

where

$$\Delta t = \frac{T}{N}. \tag{2.2}$$

By adding $\left(\dfrac{u^{i,n-1}}{\Delta t}, v - u^{i,n}\right)$ to both parties of the inequalities (2.1), we get

$$\begin{cases} a^i\left(u^{i,n}, v - u^{i,n}\right) + \dfrac{1}{\Delta t}\left(u^{i,n}, v - u^{i,n}\right) \geq \left(f^{i,n} + \dfrac{u^{i,n-1}}{\Delta t}, v - u^{i,n}\right); \\ u^{i,n} \leq k + u^{i+1,n}, \; v \leq k + u^{i+1,n}; \\ u^{J+1,n} = u^{1,n}; \\ u^i(0) = u_0^i. \end{cases} \tag{2.3}$$

The bilinear form $a(.,.)$, being noncoercive in $H_0^1(\Omega)$, there exist two constants $\alpha > 0$ and $\lambda > 0$ such that:

$$a(\varphi, \varphi) + \lambda\|\varphi\|_{L^2(\Omega)}^2 \geq \alpha\|\varphi\|_{H_0^1(\Omega)}^2 \quad \text{for all } \varphi \in H_0^1(\Omega). \tag{2.4}$$

Set

$$b(u, v) = a(u, v) + \lambda(u, v). \tag{2.5}$$

Then the bilinear form $b(.,.)$ is strongly coercive and therefore, the continuous the problem (2.3) reads as follows: find $U^n = \left(u^{1,n}, \ldots, u^{J,n}\right) \in \left(H_0^1(\Omega)\right)^J$ such that for all $n = 1, \ldots, N$

$$\begin{cases} b^i\left(u^{i,n}, v - u^{i,n}\right) \geq \left(f^{i,n} + \lambda u^{i,n-1}, v - u^{i,n}\right), & \forall v \in H_0^1(\Omega); \\ u^{i,n} \leq k + u^{i+1,n}, \; v \leq k + u^{i+1,n}; \\ u^{J+1,n} = u^{1,n}, \end{cases} \tag{2.6}$$

where

$$\begin{cases} b^i\left(u^{i,n}, v - u^{i,n}\right) = a^i\left(u^{i,n}, v - u^{i,n}\right) + \lambda\left(u^{i,n}, v - u^{i,n}\right), \\ \lambda = \dfrac{1}{\Delta t} > 0. \end{cases} \tag{2.7}$$

Remark 1 The problem (2.6) is called the coercive continuous problem of elliptic quasi-variational inequalities (QVI).

Notation 1 We denote by $u^{i,n} = \sigma\left(f^{i,n}; k + u^{i+1,n}\right)$ the solution of problem (2.6).

Let $U^0 = U_0 = \left(u_0^1, ..., u_0^J\right)$ be the solution of the following continuous equation:

$$b^i\left(u_0^i, v\right) = \left(f^i + \lambda u_0^i, v\right), \quad \forall v \in H_0^1(\Omega). \tag{2.8}$$

The existence and uniqueness of a continuous solution is obtained by means of Banach's fixed point theorem.

2.1.2. A fixed point mapping associated with continuous system (2.6)

Let $\mathbb{H}^+ = \prod_{i=1}^{J} L_+^\infty(\Omega)$, where $L_+^\infty(\Omega)$ is the positive cone of $L^\infty(\Omega)$. We introduce the following mapping:

$$\begin{aligned} &\mathbb{T}: \mathbb{H}^+ \longrightarrow \mathbb{H}^+, \\ &W \rightarrow \mathbb{T}W = \xi = \left(\xi^1, ..., \xi^J\right), \end{aligned} \tag{2.9}$$

where $\xi^i = \sigma\left(f^i + \lambda.w^i; k + \xi^{i+1}\right) \in H_0^1(\Omega)$ solves the following coercive system of QVI:

$$\begin{cases} b^i\left(\xi^i, v - \xi^i\right) \geq \left(f^i + \lambda.w^i, v - \xi^i\right); \\ \xi^i \leq k + \xi^{i+1}, \; v \leq k + \xi^{i+1}; \\ \xi^{J+1} = \xi^1. \end{cases} \tag{2.10}$$

THEOREM 1 *Under the preceding hypotheses and notations, the mapping $\mathbb{T}$ is a contraction in $\mathbb{H}^+$ with a contraction constant $\rho = \dfrac{1}{\beta\Delta t + 1}$. Therefore, $\mathbb{T}$ admits a unique fixed point which coincides with the solution of problem (2.6).*

Proof Boulbrachene, Haiour, and Chentouf (2002), taking $\lambda = \dfrac{1}{\Delta t}$, we have:

$$\left\|\mathbb{T}W - \mathbb{T}\widetilde{W}\right\|_\infty \leq \frac{1}{\beta\Delta t + 1}\left\|W - \widetilde{W}\right\|_\infty,$$

which completes the proof. □

The mapping $\mathbb{T}$ clearly generates the following iterative scheme.

2.2. A continuous iterative scheme

Starting from $U^0 = U_0$, the solution of Equation (2.8), we define the sequence:

$$U^n = \mathbb{T}U^{n-1}, \tag{2.11}$$

where U^n is a solution of the problem (2.6).

2.2.1. Geometrical convergence

In what follows, we shall establish the geometrical convergence of the proposed iterative scheme.

Proposition 1 Under conditions of Theorem 1, we have:

$$\max_{1 \leq i \leq J}\left\|u^{i,n} - u^{i,\infty}\right\|_\infty \leq \left(\frac{1}{\beta\Delta t + 1}\right)^n \max_{1 \leq i \leq J}\left\|u_0^i - u^{i,\infty}\right\|_\infty, \tag{2.12}$$

where U^∞ is the asymptotic solution of the problem of quasi-variational inequalities: find $U^\infty = \left(u^{1,\infty}, ..., u^{J,\infty}\right) \in \left(H_0^1(\Omega)\right)^J$ such that

$$\begin{cases} b^i\left(u^{i,\infty}, v - u^{i,\infty}\right) \geq \left(f^i + \lambda . u^{i,\infty}, v - u^{i,\infty}\right), & v \in H_0^1(\Omega); \\ u^{i,\infty} \leq k + u^{i+1,\infty}, \ v \leq k + u^{i+1,\infty}; \\ u^{J+1,\infty} = u^{1,\infty}. \end{cases} \tag{2.13}$$

Proof Under Theorem 1, we have for $n = 1$

$$\begin{aligned} \left\|u^{i,1} - u^{i,\infty}\right\|_\infty &= \left\|\mathbb{T}u_0^i - \mathbb{T}u^{i,\infty}\right\|_\infty \\ &\leq \left(\frac{1}{\beta \Delta t + 1}\right)\left\|u_0^i - u^{i,\infty}\right\|_\infty \end{aligned}$$

Now, we assume that

$$\left\|u^{i,n} - u^{i,\infty}\right\|_\infty \leq \left(\frac{1}{\beta \Delta t + 1}\right)^n \left\|u_0^i - u^{i,\infty}\right\|_\infty,$$

then

$$\begin{aligned} \left\|u^{i,n+1} - u^{i,\infty}\right\|_\infty &= \left\|\mathbb{T}u^{i,n} - \mathbb{T}u^{i,\infty}\right\|_\infty \\ &\leq \left(\frac{1}{\beta \Delta t + 1}\right)\left\|u^{i,n} - u^{i,\infty}\right\|_\infty. \end{aligned}$$

Thus,

$$\begin{aligned} \left\|u^{i,n+1} - u^{i,\infty}\right\|_\infty &\leq \left(\frac{1}{\beta \Delta t + 1}\right) \cdot \left(\frac{1}{\beta \Delta t + 1}\right)^n \left\|u_0^i - u^{i,\infty}\right\|_\infty \\ &\leq \left(\frac{1}{\beta \Delta t + 1}\right)^{n+1} \left\|u_0^i - u^{i,\infty}\right\|_\infty, \end{aligned}$$

which completes the proof. □

In what follows, we shall give monotonicity and Lipschitz dependence with respect to the right-hand sides and parameter k for the solution of system (2.6). These properties together with the notion of subsolution will play a fundamental role in the study the error estimate between the nth iterates of the continuous system (2.6) and its discrete counterpart.

2.3. A monotonicity property

Let k and $\tilde{k}$ be two parameters, $\left(f^{1,n}, ..., f^{J,n}\right)$ and $\left(\tilde{f}^{1,n}, ..., \tilde{f}^{J,n}\right)$ be two families of right-hand sides.

We denote $\left(u^{1,n}, ..., u^{J,n}\right)$ (resp. $\left(\tilde{u}^{1,n}, ..., \tilde{u}^{J,n}\right)$) the corresponding solution to system of quasi-variational inequalities (2.6) defined with $\left(f^{1,n}, ..., f^{J,n}; k\right)$. (resp. $\left(\tilde{f}^{1,n}, ..., \tilde{f}^{J,n}; \tilde{k}\right)$. Then, we have the following

LEMMA 1 *(cf. Boulbrachene et al., 2002) If $f^{i,n} \geq \tilde{f}^{i,n}$ and $k \geq \tilde{k}$, then*

$$u^{i,n} \geq \tilde{u}^{i,n}. \tag{2.14}$$

2.4. Lipschitz dependence with respect to the right-hand sides and the parameter k

Proposition 2 Under conditions of Lemma 1, we have

$$\max_{1\le i\le J}\left\|u^{i,n}-\tilde{u}^{i,n}\right\|_{\infty}\le C\max_{1\le i\le J}\left(\left|k-\tilde{k}\right|+\left\|f^{i,n}-\tilde{f}^{i,n}\right\|_{\infty}\right), \tag{2.15}$$

where C is a constant such that

$$a_0^iC\ge 1. \tag{2.16}$$

Proof Let

$$\phi^i=C\left(\left|k-\tilde{k}\right|+\left\|f^{i,n}-\tilde{f}^{i,n}\right\|_{\infty}\right).$$

Then, from (2.16) it is easy to see that

$$\begin{aligned}\tilde{f}^{i,n}&\le f^{i,n}+\left|k-\tilde{k}\right|+\left\|f^{i,n}-\tilde{f}^{i,n}\right\|_{\infty}\\&\le f^{i,n}+a_0^iC\left(\left|k-\tilde{k}\right|+\left\|f^{i,n}-\tilde{f}^{i,n}\right\|_{\infty}\right)\\&\le f^{i,n}+a_0^i\,\phi^i,\end{aligned}$$

and

$$\begin{aligned}\tilde{k}&\le k+C\left(\left|k-\tilde{k}\right|+\left\|f^{i,n}-\tilde{f}^{i,n}\right\|_{\infty}\right)\\&\le k+\phi^i.\end{aligned}$$

So, due to Lemma 1 it follows that

$$\begin{aligned}\sigma\left(\tilde{f}^{i,n};\tilde{k}+\tilde{u}^{i+1,n}\right)&\le\sigma\left(f^{i,n}+a_0^i\phi^i;k+\phi^i+u^{i+1,n}\right)\\&\le\sigma\left(f^{i,n};k+u^{i+1,n}\right)+\phi^i,\end{aligned}$$

hence

$$\sigma\left(\tilde{f}^{i,n};\tilde{k}+\tilde{u}^{i+1,n}\right)-\sigma\left(f^{i,n};k+u^{i+1,n}\right)\le\phi^i.$$

Interchanging the role of $f^{i,n}$ and $\tilde{f}^{i,n}$, k and $\tilde{k}$ we also get

$$\sigma\left(f^{i,n};k+u^{i+1,n}\right)-\sigma\left(\tilde{f}^{i,n};\tilde{k}+\tilde{u}^{i+1,n}\right)\le\phi^i.$$

Then

$$\left\|\sigma\left(f^{i,n};k+u^{i+1,n}\right)-\sigma\left(\tilde{f}^{i,n};\tilde{k}+\tilde{u}^{i+1,n}\right)\right\|_{\infty}\le C\left(\left|k-\tilde{k}\right|+\left\|f^{i,n}-\tilde{f}^{i,n}\right\|_{\infty}\right),$$

which completes the proof. □

2.5. Characterization of the solution of system (2.6) as the envelope of continuous subsolutions

Definition 1 $Z=(z^1,\dots,z^J)\in\left(H_0^1(\Omega)\right)^J$ is said to be a continuous subsolution for the system of quasi-variational inequalities (2.6) if

$$\begin{cases}b^i\left(z^i,v\right)\le\left(f^i+\lambda.z^i,v\right), & v\in H_0^1(\Omega);\\ z^i\le k+z^{i+1},\ v\ge 0;\\ z^{J+1}=z^1.\end{cases} \tag{2.17}$$

Notation 2 Let $\mathbb{X}$ denote the set of such subsolutions.

THEOREM 2 *(cf. Bensoussan & Lions, 1978) The solution of (2.6) is the least upper bound of the set $\mathbb{X}$.*

3. Statement of the discrete system

In this section we shall see that the discrete system below inherits all the qualitative properties of the continuous system, provided the discrete maximum principle assumption is satisfied. Their respective proofs shall be omitted, as they are very similar to their continuous analogues.

3.1. Spatial discretization

Let M_s, $1 \leq s \leq m(h)$ denote the vertex of the triangulation τ_h, and let ϕ_l, $1 \leq l \leq m(h)$, denote the functions of $\mathbb{V}_h$ which satisfies:

$$\phi_l(M_s) = \delta_{ls}, \quad 1 \leq l, s \leq m(h). \tag{3.1}$$

So that the function ϕ_l from a basis of $\mathbb{V}_h$. $\forall v_h \in L^2(0, T; H_0^1(\Omega)) \cap C(0, T; H_0^1(\bar{\Omega}))$

$$r_h v = \sum_{l=1}^{m(h)} v(M_l)\phi_l(x), \tag{3.2}$$

represents the interpolate of v over τ_h.

3.1.1. The discrete maximum principle (dmp)

Denote by $\mathbb{B}$ is the matrix with generic entries: $\forall\, i = 1, ..., J$

$$\mathbb{B}^i_{l,\, s} = b^i(\phi_l, \phi_s) = a^i(\phi_l, \phi_s) + \lambda \int_\Omega \phi_l\, \phi_s \, dx, \quad 1 \leq l, s \leq m(h). \tag{3.3}$$

LEMMA 2 *(cf. Cortey-Dumont, 1983) The matrix $\mathbb{B}$ is an M-matrix.*

3.2. Existence and uniqueness

The discrete problem of PQVI consists of seeking $U_h = (u_h^1, ..., u_h^J) \in (\mathbb{V}_h)^M$ such that

$$\begin{cases} \frac{\partial}{\partial t}\left(u_h^i, v_h - u_h^i\right) + a^i\left(u_h^i, v_h - u_h^i\right) \geq \left(f^i, v_h - u^i\right), & \forall v_h \in \mathbb{V}_h; \\ u_h^i \leq r_h\left(k + u_h^{i+1}\right), \; v_h \leq r_h\left(k + u_h^{i+1}\right); \\ u_h^{J+1} = u_h^1; \\ u_h^i(0) = u_{0h}^i, \end{cases} \tag{3.4}$$

or equivalently,

$$\begin{cases} b^i\left(u_h^{i,n}, v_h - u_h^{i,n}\right) \geq \left(f^{i,n} + \lambda . u_h^{i,n}, v_h - u_h^{i,n}\right); \\ u_h^{i,n} \leq r_h\left(k + u_h^{i+1,n}\right), \; v_h \leq r_h\left(k + u_h^{i+1,n}\right); \\ u_h^{J+1,n} = u_h^{1,n}. \end{cases} \tag{3.5}$$

Notation 3 We denote by $u_h^{i,n} = \sigma_h\left(f^{i,n}; r_h\left(k + u_h^{i+1,n}\right)\right)$ the solution of system (3.5).

Let $U_h^0 = U_{0h} = (u_{0h}^1, ..., u_{0h}^M)$ be the solution of the following discrete equation:

$$b^i\left(u_{0h}^i, v_h\right) = \left(f^i + \lambda u_{0h}^i, v_h\right), \quad \forall v_h \in \mathbb{V}_h. \tag{3.6}$$

3.2.1. A fixed point mapping associated with discrete problem (3.5)
We consider the following mapping :

$$\begin{aligned} &\mathbb{T}_h : \mathbb{H}^+ \longrightarrow (\mathbb{V}_h)^J, \\ &W \mapsto \mathbb{T}_h W = \xi_h = (\xi_h^1, \dots, \xi_h^J), \end{aligned} \tag{3.7}$$

where $\xi_h^i \in \mathbb{V}_h$ is a solution of the following coercive system of QVI:

$$\begin{cases} b^i\left(\xi_h^i, v_h - \xi_h^i\right) \geq \left(f^i + \lambda . w^i, v_h - \xi_h^i\right), \quad v_h \in \mathbb{V}_h; \\ \xi_h^i \leq r_h\left(k + \xi_h^{i+1}\right),\ v \leq r_h\left(k + \xi_h^{i+1}\right); \\ \xi_h^{J+1} = \xi_h^1. \end{cases} \tag{3.8}$$

THEOREM 3 *Under the dmp and the preceding hypotheses and notations, the mapping $\mathbb{T}_h$ is a contraction in $\mathbb{H}^+$ with a rate of contraction $\rho = \dfrac{1}{\beta\Delta t + 1}$. Therefore, $\mathbb{T}_h$ admits a unique fixed point which coincides with the solution of system (3.5).*

Proof It is very similar to that of the continuous case. □

3.3. A discrete iterative scheme

Starting from $U_h^0 = U_{0h}$, the solution of Equation (3.6), we define the sequence:

$$U_h^n = \mathbb{T} U_h^{n-1}, \quad n = 1, \dots, N, \tag{3.9}$$

where U_h^n is a solution of the problem (3.5).

3.3.1. Geometrical convergence

Proposition 3 Under the *dmp* and Theorem 3, we have :

$$\|U_h^n - U_h^\infty\|_\infty \leq \left(\frac{1}{\beta\Delta t + 1}\right)^n \left\|U_h^0 - U_h^\infty\right\|_\infty. \tag{3.10}$$

where U_h^∞ is the asymptotic solution of the problem of quasi-variational inequalities: find $U_h^\infty = \left(u_h^{1,\infty}, \dots, u_h^{J,\infty}\right) \in (\mathbb{V}_h)^J$ such that

$$\begin{cases} b^i\left(u_h^{i,\infty}, v_h - u_h^{i,\infty}\right) \geq \left(f + \lambda\, u_h^{i,\infty}, v_h - u_h^{i,\infty}\right), \quad v_h \in \mathbb{V}_h; \\ u_h^{i,\infty} \leq r_h\left(k + u_h^{i+1,\infty}\right),\ v_h \leq r_h\left(k + u_h^{i+1,\infty}\right); \\ u_h^{J+1,\infty} = u_h^{1,\infty}. \end{cases} \tag{3.11}$$

Proof It is very similar to that of the continuous case. □

3.4. A monotonicity property

Let $u_h^{i,n} = \sigma_h\left(f^{i,n}; k\right)$ (resp. $\tilde{u}_h^{i,n} = \sigma_h\left(\tilde{f}^{i,n}; \tilde{k}\right)$) the solution to (3.5).

LEMMA 3 *If $f^{i,n} \geq \tilde{f}^{i,n}$, and $k \leq \tilde{k}$ then*

$$u_h^{i,n} \geq \tilde{u}_h^{i,n}. \tag{3.12}$$

3.5. Lipschitz dependence with respect to the right-hand sides and parameter k

Proposition 4 Under *dmp* and conditions of Lemma 3, we have

$$\max_{1\leq i\leq J}\left\|u^{i,n} - \tilde{u}^{i,n}\right\|_\infty \leq C \max_{1\leq i\leq J}\left(\left|k - \tilde{k}\right| + \left\|f^{i,n} - \tilde{f}^{i,n}\right\|_\infty\right), \tag{3.13}$$

where C is a constant such that

$$a_0 C \geq 1. \tag{3.14}$$

Proof It is very similar to that of the continuous case. □

3.6. Characterization of the solution of problem (3.5) as the envelope of discrete subsolutions

Definition 2 $Z_h = (z_h^1, ..., z_h^M) \in (\mathbb{V}_h)^J$ is said to be a discrete subsolution for the system of quasi-variational inequalities (3.5) if

$$\begin{cases} b^i\left(z_h^i, \varphi_s\right) \leq \left(f^i + \lambda . z_h^i, \varphi_s\right), & \forall s, s = 1, ..., m(h); \\ z_h^i \leq r_h\left(k + z_h^{i+1}\right), \ \varphi_s \geq 0; \\ z_h^{J+1} = z_h^1. \end{cases} \tag{3.15}$$

Notation 4 Let $\mathbb{X}_h$ be the set of such subsolutions.

THEOREM 4 *Under the dmp, the solution of (3.5) is the least upper bound of the set* $\mathbb{X}_h$.

3.7. The discrete regularity

A discrete solution U_h^n of a system of quasi-variational inequalities is regular in the discrete sense if it satisfies:

THEOREM 5 *There exists a constant C independent of k and h such that*

$$\left|b^i\left(u_h^{i,n}, \varphi_s\right)\right| \leq C\|\varphi_s\|_{L^1(\Omega)}, \quad s = 1, ..., m(h). \tag{3.16}$$

Moreover, there exists a family of right-hand sides $\left\{g_{(h)}^{i,n}\right\}_{h>0}$ bounded in $(L^\infty(\Omega))^J$ such that

$$\left\|g_{(h)}^{i,n}\right\|_\infty \leq C \tag{3.17}$$

and

$$b^i\left(u_h^{i,n}, v_h\right) = \left(g_{(h)}^{i,n}, v_h\right), \ v_h \in \mathbb{V}_h. \tag{3.18}$$

Let $u_{(h)}^{i,n}$ be the corresponding continuous counterpart of (3.18), that is

$$b^i\left(u_{(h)}^{i,n}, v\right) = \left(g_{(h)}^{i,n}, v\right), \quad v \in H_0^1(\Omega), \tag{3.19}$$

then, there exists a constant C independent of k and h such that

$$\left\|u_{(h)}^{i,n}\right\|_{W^{2,P}(\Omega)} \leq C, \tag{3.20}$$

and

$$\left\|u_{(h)}^{i,n} - u_h^{i,n}\right\|_\infty \leq Ch^2|\log h|^2. \tag{3.21}$$

Proof We adapt [.]. □

Remark 2 This new concept of "discrete regularity", introduced in Berger and Falk (1977), Cortey-Dumont (1985) (see also Boulbrachene and Cortey-Dumont, 2009; Boulbrachene, 2015b), can be regarded as the discrete counterpart of the lewy-Stampacchia regularity estimate $\left\|A^i u\right\|_\infty \le C$ extended to the variational form through the $L^\infty - L^1$ duality. It plays a major role in deriving the optimal error estimate as it permits to regularize the discrete obstacle "$k + u_h^{i+1}$" with $W^{2,P}(\Omega)$ regular ones.

4. Finite element error analysis

This section is devoted to demonstrate that the proposed method is optimally accurate in L^∞. We first introduce the following two auxiliary systems :

4.1. Definition of two auxiliary sequences of elliptic variational inequalities

4.1.1. A discrete sequence of variational inequalities

We define the sequence $\left\{\bar{U}_h^n\right\}_{n\ge1}$ such that $\bar{U}_h^n = \left(\bar{u}_h^{1,n}, ..., \bar{u}_h^{J,n}\right)$ solves the discrete system of variational inequalities (VI):

$$\begin{cases} b^i\left(\bar{u}_h^{i,n},\ v - \bar{u}_h^{i,n}\right) \ge \left(f^{i,n} + \lambda.u^{i,n-1},\ v_h - \bar{u}_h^{i,n}\right), & v_h \in \mathbb{V}_h; \\ \bar{u}_h^{i,n} \le r_h\left(k + u^{i+1,n-1}\right),\ v_h \le r_h\left(k + u^{i+1,n-1}\right), & \end{cases} \tag{4.1}$$

where $U^n = \left(u^{1,n}, ..., u^{J,n}\right)$ is the solution of the continuous problem (2.6).

Proposition 5 There exists a constant C independent of h, $\triangle t$ and k such that

$$\max_{1\le i\le J}\left\|\bar{u}_h^{i,n} - u^{i,n}\right\|_\infty \le Ch^2\left|\log h\right|^2. \tag{4.2}$$

Proof Since $\bar{u}_h^{i,n} = \sigma_h\left(f^{i,n}; r_h\left(k + u^{i+1,n-1}\right)\right)$ is the approximation of $u^{i,n} = \sigma\left(f^{i,n}; k + u^{i+1,n-1}\right)$. So, making use of Cortey-Dumont (1985), we get the desired result. □

4.1.2. A continuous sequence of variational inequalities

We define the sequence $\left\{\bar{U}_{(h)}^n\right\}_{n\ge1}$ such that $\bar{U}_{(h)}^n = \left(\bar{u}_{(h)}^{1,n}, ..., \bar{u}_{(h)}^{J,n}\right)$ solves the continuous system of variational inequalities (VI):

$$\begin{cases} b^i\left(\bar{u}_{(h)}^{i,n},\ v - \bar{u}_{(h)}^{i,n}\right) \ge \left(f^{i,n} + \lambda.u_h^{i,n-1},\ v - \bar{u}_{(h)}^{i,n}\right), & v \in H_0^1(\Omega); \\ \bar{u}_{(h)}^{i,n} \le k + u_{(h)}^{i+1,n-1},\ v \le k + u_{(h)}^{i+1,n-1}, & \end{cases} \tag{4.3}$$

where $U_h^n = \left(u_h^{1,n}, ..., u_h^{M,n}\right)$ is the solution of the discrete problem (3.5), and $U_{(h)}^n = \left(u_{(h)}^{1,n}, ..., u_{(h)}^{M,n}\right)$ is the solution of Equation (3.19).

Proposition 6 There exists a constant C independent of h, k and $\triangle t$ such that

$$\max_{1\le i\le J}\left\|\bar{u}_{(h)}^{i,n} - u_h^{i,n}\right\|_\infty \le Ch^2\left|\log h\right|^2. \tag{4.4}$$

Proof We adapt Boulbrachene (2015b). □

LEMMA 4 *(cf. Nochetto & Sharp, 1988) There exists a constant C independent of h, k and Δt such that*

$$\max_{1\le i\le M}\left\|u_0^i - u_{h0}^i\right\|_\infty \le C\,h^2\left|\log h\right|. \tag{4.5}$$

4.1.3. Optimal L^∞-error estimates

Here, we shall estimate the error in the L^∞-norm between the n th iterates U^n and U_h^n defined in (2.11) and (3.9), respectively.

THEOREM 6 *Under the previous hypotheses, there exists a constant C independent of h , k and $\triangle t$ such that*

$$\|U^n - U_h^n\|_\infty \le Ch^2|\log h|^2. \tag{4.6}$$

The proof is based on two Lemmas:

LEMMA 5 *There exists a sequence of discrete subsolutions $\alpha_h^n = \left(\alpha_h^{1,n},...,\alpha_h^{M,n}\right)$ such that*

$$\begin{cases} \alpha_h^{i,n} \le u_h^{i,n}, \qquad i = 1,...,J; \\ \text{and} \\ \max\limits_{1\le i\le J}\left\|\alpha_h^{i,n} - u^{i,n}\right\|_\infty \le Ch^2|\log h|^2, \end{cases} \tag{4.7}$$

where the constant C is independent of h, k and $\triangle t$.

Proof For $n = 1$, we consider the discrete system of variational inequalities

$$\begin{cases} b^i\left(\bar{u}_h^{i,1}, v_h - \bar{u}_h^{i,1}\right) \ge \left(f^{i,1} + \lambda u_0^i, v_h - \bar{u}_h^{i,1}\right), \quad v \in \mathbb{V}_h; \\ \bar{u}_h^{i,1} \le r_h\left(k + u_0^{i+1}\right),\ v_h \le r_h\left(k + u_0^{i+1}\right), \end{cases}$$

Then, as $\bar{u}_h^1$ is solution to a discrete variational inequalities, it is also a subsolution, i.e.

$$\begin{cases} b^i\left(\bar{u}_h^{i,1}, \varphi_s\right) \le \left(f^{i,1} + \lambda u_0^i, \varphi_s\right), \quad \forall\varphi_s; \\ \bar{u}_h^{i,1} \le r_h\left(k + u_0^{i+1}\right), \end{cases}$$

or

$$\begin{cases} b^i\left(\bar{u}_h^{i,1}, \varphi_s\right) \le \left(f^{i,1} + \lambda u_0^i - \lambda u_{0h}^i + \lambda u_{0h}^i, \varphi_s\right); \\ \bar{u}_h^{i,1} \le r_h\left(k + u_0^{i+1}\right). \end{cases}$$

Then

$$\begin{cases} b^i\left(\bar{u}_h^{i,1}, \varphi_s\right) \le \left(f^{i,1} + \lambda\left\|u_0^i - u_{0h}^i\right\|_\infty + \lambda u_{0h}^i, \varphi_s\right); \\ \bar{u}_h^{i,1} \le r_h\left(k + u_0^{i+1}\right) + r_h\left(k + u_0^{i+1}\right) - r_h\left(k + \bar{u}_{0h}^{i+1}\right). \end{cases}$$

It follows

$$\begin{cases} b^i\left(\bar{u}_h^{i,1}, \varphi_s\right) \le \left(f^{i,1} + \lambda\left\|u_0^i - u_{0h}^i\right\|_\infty + \lambda u_{0h}^i, \varphi_s\right); \\ \bar{u}_h^1 \le k + \left\|u_0^{i+1} - \bar{u}_{0h}^{i+1}\right\|_\infty + \bar{u}_{0h}^{i+1}. \end{cases}$$

Using (4.5), we have

$$\begin{cases} b^i\left(\bar{u}_h^{i,1}, \varphi_s\right) \le \left(f^{i,1} + C\,h^2|\log h| + \lambda u_{0,h}^i, \varphi_s\right); \\ \bar{u}_h^{i,1} \le k + C\,h^2|\log h| + \bar{u}_{0h}^{i+1}. \end{cases}$$

So, $\bar{u}_h^1$ is a discrete subsolution for the quasi-variational inequalities whose solution is $\bar{U}_h^{i,1} = \sigma_h\left(f^{i,1} + C\,h^2|\log h|; k + C\,h^2|\log h| + \bar{u}_{0h}^{i+1}\right)$. Then, as $u_h^{i,1} = \sigma_h\left(f^{i,1}; k + \bar{u}_{0h}^{i+1}\right)$; making use of Proposition 4, we have

$$\begin{aligned}\left\|\bar{U}_h^{i,1} - u_h^{i,1}\right\|_\infty &\le C\left(\left|k + C\,h^2|\log h| - k\right| + \left\|f^{i,1} + C\,h^2|\log h| - f^{i,1}\right\|_\infty\right)\\ &\le C\,h^2|\log h| + C\,h^2|\log h|\\ &\le C\,h^2|\log h|.\end{aligned}$$

Hence, making use of Theorem 4, we have

$$\bar{u}_h^{i,1} \le \bar{U}_h^{i,1} \le u_h^{i,1} + C\,h^2|\log h|.$$

Putting

$$\alpha_h^{i,1} = \bar{u}_h^{i,1} - C\,h^2|\log h|,$$

we get

$$\alpha_h^{i,1} \le u_h^{i,1},$$

and

$$\begin{aligned}\left\|\alpha_h^{i,1} - u^{i,1}\right\|_\infty &= \left\|\bar{u}_h^{i,1} - C\,h^2|\log h| - u^1\right\|_\infty\\ &\le \left\|\bar{u}_h^{i,1} - u^{i,1}\right\|_\infty + C\,h^2|\log h|.\end{aligned}$$

Using Proposition 5, we get

$$\begin{aligned}\left\|\alpha_h^{i,1} - u^{i,1}\right\|_\infty &\le C\,h^2|\log h|^2 + C\,h^2|\log h|\\ &\le C\,h^2|\log h|^2.\end{aligned}$$

For $n+1$, let us now assume that

$$\begin{cases}\alpha_h^{i,n} \le u_h^{i,n},\\ \text{and}\\ \left\|\alpha_h^{i,n} - u^{i,n}\right\|_\infty \le C\,h^2|\log h|^2,\end{cases}$$

and we consider the system

$$\begin{cases} b^i\left(\bar{u}_h^{i,n+1}, v_h - \bar{u}_h^{i,n+1}\right) \ge \left(f^{i,n} + \lambda u^{i,n}, v_h - \bar{u}_h^{i,n+1}\right);\\ \bar{u}_h^{i,n+1} \le r_h\left(k + u^{i+1,n}\right),\ v_h \le r_h\left(k + u^{i+1,n}\right).\end{cases}$$

Then

$$\begin{cases} b^i\left(\bar{u}_h^{i,n+1}, \varphi_s\right) \le \left(f^{i,n} + \lambda u^{i,n}, \varphi_s\right);\\ \bar{u}_h^{i,n+1} \le r_h\left(k + u^{i+1,n}\right),\end{cases}$$

or

$$\begin{cases} b^i\left(\bar{u}_h^{i,n+1}, \varphi_s\right) \le \left(f^{i,n} + \lambda u^{i,n} - \lambda\,\bar{u}_h^{i,n} + \lambda \bar{u}_h^{i,n}, \varphi_s\right);\\ \bar{u}_h^{i,n+1} \le r_h\left(k + u^{i+1,n}\right) + r_h\left(k + \bar{u}_h^{i+1,n}\right) - r_h\left(k + \bar{u}_h^{i+1,n}\right).\end{cases}$$

Then

$$\begin{cases} b^i\left(\bar{u}_h^{i,n+1}, \varphi_s\right) \le \left(f^{i,n} + \lambda\left\|u^{i,n} - \bar{u}_h^{i,n}\right\|_\infty + \lambda \bar{u}_h^{i,n}, \varphi_s\right); \\ \bar{u}_h^{i,n+1} \le k + \left\|u^{i+1,n} - \bar{u}_h^{i+1,n}\right\|_\infty + \bar{u}_h^{i+1,n}. \end{cases}$$

Using (4.2), we have

$$\begin{cases} b^i\left(\bar{u}_h^{i,n+1}, \varphi_s\right) \le \left(f^{i,n} + C\,h^2|\log h|^2 + \lambda \bar{u}_h^{i,n}, \varphi_s\right); \\ \bar{u}_h^{i,n+1} \le k + C\,h^2|\log h|^2 + \bar{u}_h^{i+1,n}. \end{cases}$$

So, $\bar{u}_h^{i,n+1}$ is a discrete subsolution for the quasi-variational inequalities whose solution is $\bar{U}_h^{i,n+1} = \sigma_h\left(f^{i,n} + C\,h^2|\log h|^2; k + C\,h^2|\log h|^2 + \bar{u}_h^{i+1,n}\right)$. Then, as $u_h^{i,n+1} = \sigma_h\left(f^{i,n}; k + u_h^{i+1,n}\right)$, making use of Proposition 4, we have

$$\begin{aligned} \left\|\bar{U}_h^{i,n+1} - u_h^{i,n+1}\right\|_\infty &\le C\left(\left|k + C\,h^2|\log h|^2 - k\right| + \left\|f^{i,n} + C\,h^2|\log h|^2 - f^{i,n}\right\|_\infty\right) \\ &\le C\,h^2|\log h|^2. \end{aligned}$$

Hence, applying Theorem 4, we get

$$\bar{u}_h^{i,n+1} \le \bar{U}_h^{i,n+1} \le u_h^{i,n+1} + C\,h^2|\log h|^2.$$

Putting

$$\alpha_h^{i,n+1} = \bar{u}_h^{i,n+1} - C\,h^2|\log h|^2,$$

we get

$$\alpha_h^{i,n+1} \le u_h^{i,n+1},$$

and

$$\begin{aligned} \left\|\alpha_h^{i,n+1} - u^{i,n+1}\right\|_\infty &= \left\|\bar{u}_h^{i,n+1} - C\,h^2|\log h|^2 - u^{n+1}\right\|_\infty \\ &\le \left\|\bar{u}_h^{i,n+1} - u^{i,n+1}\right\|_\infty + C\,h^2|\log h|^2. \end{aligned}$$

Using Proposition 5, we get

$$\left\|\alpha_h^{i,n+1} - u^{i,n+1}\right\|_\infty \le C\,h^2|\log h|^2,$$

which completes the proof. □

LEMMA 6 *There exists a sequence of continuous subsolutions* $\beta_{(h)}^n = \left(\beta_{(h)}^{1,n}, \ldots, \beta_{(h)}^{M,n}\right)$ *such that*

$$\begin{cases} \beta_{(h)}^{i,n} \le u^{i,n}, \qquad i = 1, \ldots, J; \\ \text{and} \\ \max\limits_{1 \le i \le J}\left\|\beta_{(h)}^{i,n} - u_h^{i,n}\right\|_\infty \le Ch^2|\log h|^2, \end{cases} \tag{4.8}$$

where the constant C is independent of h, k and $\triangle t$.

Proof For $n = 1$, we consider the system of variational inequalities

$$\begin{cases} b^i\left(\bar{u}^{i,1}_{(h)}, v - \bar{u}^{i,1}_{(h)}\right) \geq \left(f^{i,1} + \lambda u^i_{0h}, v - \bar{u}^{i,1}_{(h)}\right), \quad v \in H^1_0(\Omega); \\ \bar{u}^{i,1}_{(h)} \leq k + u^{i+1}_{0(h)}, \; v \leq k + u^{i+1}_{0(h)}, \end{cases}$$

Then, as $\bar{u}^{i,1}_{(h)}$ is solution to a continuous variational inequalities, it is also a subsolution, i.e.,

$$\begin{cases} b^i\left(\bar{u}^{i,1}_{(h)}, v\right) \leq \left(f^{i,1} + \lambda u^i_{0h}, v\right); \\ \bar{u}^{i,1}_{(h)} \leq k + u^{i+1}_{0(h)}, \end{cases}$$

or

$$\begin{cases} b^i\left(\bar{u}^{i,1}_{(h)}, v\right) \leq \left(f^{i,1} + \lambda u^i_{0h} - \lambda u^i_0 + \lambda u^i_0, v\right); \\ \bar{u}^{i,1}_{(h)} \leq k + u^{i+1}_{0(h)} + \left(k + u^{i+1}_{0h}\right) - \left(k + u^{i+1}_{0h}\right) \\ +\left(k + \bar{u}^{i+1}_{0(h)}\right) - \left(k + \bar{u}^{i+1}_{0(h)}\right). \end{cases}$$

Then

$$\begin{cases} b^i\left(\bar{u}^{i,1}_{(h)}, v\right) \leq \left(f^{i,1} + \lambda \left\| u^i_0 - u^i_{0h} \right\|_\infty + \lambda u^i_0, v\right); \\ \bar{u}^{i,1}_{(h)} \leq \left\| u^{i+1}_{0(h)} - u^{i+1}_{0h} \right\|_\infty + \left\| \bar{u}^{i+1}_{0(h)} - u^{i+1}_{0h} \right\|_\infty + \left(k + \bar{u}^{i+1}_{0(h)}\right). \end{cases}$$

Using (4.5), we have

$$\begin{cases} b^i\left(\bar{u}^{i,1}_{(h)}, v\right) \leq \left(f^{i,1} + C\, h^2 |\log h| + \lambda u^i_0, v\right); \\ \bar{u}^{i,1}_{(h)} \leq k + C\, h^2 |\log h| + \bar{u}^{i+1}_{0(h)}. \end{cases}$$

So, $\bar{u}^{1}_{(h)}$ is a continuous subsolution for the variational inequalities whose solution is $\bar{U}^{i,1}_{(h)} = \sigma\left(f^{i,1} + C\, h^2 |\log h|; k + C\, h^2 |\log h|^2 + \bar{u}^{i+1}_{0(h)}\right)$. Then, as $u^{i,1} = \sigma\left(f^{i,1}; k + u^{i+1}_0\right)$; making use of Proposition 2, we have

$$\begin{aligned} \left\| \bar{U}^{i,1}_{(h)} - u^{i,1} \right\|_\infty &\leq C\left(\left| k + C\, h^2 |\log h| - k \right| + \left\| f^{i,1} + C\, h^2 |\log h| - f^{i,1} \right\|_\infty\right) \\ &\leq C\, h^2 |\log h| + C\, h^2 |\log h| \\ &\leq C\, h^2 |\log h|. \end{aligned}$$

Hence, making use of Theorem 2, we have

$$\bar{u}^{i,1}_{(h)} \leq \bar{U}^{i,1}_{(h)} \leq u^{i,1} + C\, h^2 |\log h|.$$

Putting

$$\beta^{i,1}_{(h)} = \bar{u}^{i,1}_{(h)} - C\, h^2 |\log h|,$$

we get

$$\beta^{i,1}_{(h)} \leq u^{i,1},$$

and

$$\left\| \beta^{i,1}_{(h)} - u^{i,1}_h \right\|_\infty = \left\| \bar{u}^{i,1}_{(h)} - C\,h^2 |\log h| - u^1_h \right\|_\infty$$
$$\leq \left\| \bar{u}^{i,1}_{(h)} - u^{i,1}_h \right\|_\infty + C\,h^2 |\log h|.$$

Using Proposition 6, we get

$$\left\| \beta^{i,1}_{(h)} - u^{i,1}_h \right\|_\infty \leq C\,h^2 |\log h|^2 + C\,h^2 |\log h|$$
$$\leq C\,h^2 |\log h|^2.$$

For $n+1$, let us now assume that

$$\begin{cases} \beta^{i,n}_{(h)} \leq u^{i,n}; \\ \text{and} \\ \left\| \beta^{i,n}_{(h)} - u^{i,n}_h \right\|_\infty \leq C\,h^2 |\log h|^2, \end{cases}$$

and consider the system

$$\begin{cases} b^i\left(\bar{u}^{i,n+1}_{(h)}, v - \bar{u}^{i,n+1}_{(h)}\right) \geq \left(f^{i,n} + \lambda u^{i,n}_h, v - \bar{u}^{i,n+1}_{(h)}\right); \\ \bar{u}^{i,n+1}_{(h)} \leq k + u^{i+1,n}_{(h)},\ v \leq k + u^{i+1,n}_{(h)}. \end{cases}$$

Then

$$\begin{cases} b^i\left(\bar{u}^{i,n+1}_{(h)}, v\right) \leq \left(f^{i,n} + \lambda u^{i,n}_h, v\right); \\ \bar{u}^{i,n+1}_h \leq k + u^{i+1,n}_{(h)}, \end{cases}$$

or

$$\begin{cases} b^i\left(\bar{u}^{i,n+1}_{(h)}, v\right) \leq \left(f^{i,n} + \lambda u^{i,n}_h - \lambda\, \bar{u}^{i,n}_{(h)} + \lambda \bar{u}^{i,n}_{(h)}, v\right); \\ \bar{u}^{i,n+1}_{(h)} \leq \left(k + u^{i+1,n}_{(h)}\right) - \left(k + u^{i+1,n}_h\right) + \left(k + u^{i+1,n}_h\right) \\ +\left(k + \bar{u}^{i+1,n}_{(h)}\right) - \left(k + \bar{u}^{i+1,n}_{(h)}\right). \end{cases}$$

Then

$$\begin{cases} b^i\left(\bar{u}^{i,n+1}_{(h)}, v\right) \leq \left(f^{i,n} + \lambda \left\| u^{i,n}_h - \bar{u}^{i,n}_{(h)} \right\|_\infty + \lambda \bar{u}^{i,n}_{(h)}, v\right); \\ \bar{u}^{i,n+1}_{(h)} \leq \left\| u^{i+1,n}_h - \bar{u}^{i+1,n}_{(h)} \right\|_\infty + \left\| u^{i+1,n}_h - u^{i+1,n}_{(h)} \right\|_\infty + \left(k + \bar{u}^{i+1,n}_{(h)}\right). \end{cases}$$

Using (4.4), we have

$$\begin{cases} b^i\left(\bar{u}^{i,n+1}_{(h)}, v\right) \leq \left(f^{i,n} + C\,h^2 |\log h|^2 + \lambda \bar{u}^{i,n}_{(h)}, v\right); \\ \bar{u}^{i,n+1}_{(h)} \leq \left(C\,h^2 |\log h|^2 + k + \bar{u}^{i+1,n}_{(h)}\right). \end{cases}$$

So, $\bar{u}^{n+1}_{(h)}$ is a continuous subsolution for the quasi-variational inequalities whose solution is $\bar{U}^{i,n+1}_{(h)} = \sigma\left(f^{i,n} + C\,h^2 |\log h|^2; k + C\,h^2 |\log h|^2 + \bar{u}^{i+1,n}_{(h)}\right)$. Then, as $u^{i,n+1} = \sigma\left(f^{i,n}; k + u^{i+1,n}_h\right)$; making use of Proposition 2, we have

$$\left\| \bar{U}_h^{i,n+1} - u_h^{i,n+1} \right\|_\infty \le C\left(\left| k + C\,h^2 |\log h|^2 - k \right| + \left\| f^{i,n} + C\,h^2 |\log h|^2 - f^{i,n} \right\|_\infty \right)$$
$$\le C\,h^2 |\log h|^2.$$

Hence, applying Theorem 2, we get

$$\bar{u}_{(h)}^{i,n} \le \bar{U}_{(h)}^{i,n+1} \le u^{i,n+1} + C\,h^2 |\log h|^2.$$

Putting

$$\beta_{(h)}^{i,n+1} = \bar{u}_{(h)}^{i,n+1} - C\,h^2 |\log h|^2,$$

we get

$$\beta_{(h)}^{i,n+1} \le u^{i,n+1}$$

and

$$\left\| \beta_{(h)}^{i,n+1} - u_h^{i,n+1} \right\|_\infty = \left\| \bar{u}_{(h)}^{i,n+1} - C\,h^2 |\log h|^2 - u_h^{n+1} \right\|_\infty$$
$$\le \left\| \bar{u}_{(h)}^{i,n+1} - u_h^{i,n+1} \right\|_\infty + C\,h^2 |\log h|^2.$$

Using Proposition 6, we get

$$\left\| \beta_{(h)}^{i,n+1} - u_h^{i,n+1} \right\|_\infty \le C\,h^2 |\log h|^2,$$

which completes the proof. □

We are now in a position to prove the Theorem 6.

Proof Using (4.7), we have

$$u^{i,n} \le \alpha_h^{i,n} + C\,h^2 |\log h|^2$$
$$\le u_h^{i,n} + C\,h^2 |\log h|^2$$

thus

$$u^{i,n} - u_h^{i,n} \le C\,h^2 |\log h|^2$$

and using (4.8), we have

$$u_h^{i,n} \le \beta_{(h)}^{i,n} + C\,h^2 |\log h|^2$$
$$\le u^{i,n} + C\,h^2 |\log h|^2,$$

thus, we get

$$u_h^{i,n} - u^{i,n} \le C\,h^2 |\log h|^2.$$

Therefore,

$$\left\| u^{i,n} - u_h^{i,n} \right\|_\infty \le C\,h^2 |\log h|^2,$$

which completes the proof. □

5. L^∞-Asymptotic behavior for a finite element approximation

This section is devoted to the proof of main result of the present paper, where we prove the theorem of the asymptotic behavior in L^∞-norm for parabolic quasi-variational inequalities.

Now, we evaluate the variation in L^∞-norm between $u_h(T,.)$ the discrete solution calculated at the moment $T = n\,\Delta t$ and u^∞ the solution of system (2.13).

THEOREM 7 *(The main result) Under Propositions 1 and 3, and Theorem 6, the following inequality holds:*

$$\max_{1\le i\le M}\left\|u_h^i(T,.) - u^{i,\infty}(.)\right\|_\infty \le C\left(h^2|\log h|^2 + \left(\frac{1}{\beta\Delta t+1}\right)^N\right). \tag{5.1}$$

Proof We have

$$u_h^i = u_h^i(t,.) \text{ for all} t \in \left](n-1).\Delta t,\ n.\Delta t\right[,$$

thus

$$\begin{aligned}\left\|u_h^i(T,.) - u^{i,\infty}(.)\right\|_\infty &= \left\|u_h^{i,N} - u^{i,\infty}\right\|_\infty \\ &\le \left\|u_h^{i,N} - u_h^{i,\infty}\right\|_\infty + \left\|u_h^{i,\infty} - u^{i,\infty}\right\|_\infty.\end{aligned}$$

Indeed, combining estimates (2.12), (3.10), and (4.6), we get

$$\begin{aligned}\left\|u_h^i(T,.) - u^{i,\infty}\right\|_\infty &\le \left\|u_h^{i,N} - u_h^{i,\infty}\right\|_\infty + \left\|u_h^{i,\infty} - u^{i,\infty}\right\|_\infty \\ &\le \left\|u_h^{i,N} - u_h^{i,\infty}\right\|_\infty + \left\|u_h^{i,\infty} - u_h^{i,N}\right\|_\infty + \left\|u_h^{i,N} - u^{i,\infty}\right\|_\infty \\ &\le 2\left\|u_h^{i,N} - u_h^{i,\infty}\right\|_\infty + \left\|u^{i,\infty} - u^{i,N}\right\|_\infty + \left\|u^{i,N} - u_h^{i,N}\right\|_\infty.\end{aligned}$$

Using Propositions 1 and 3, we have

$$\left\|u^{i,\infty} - u^{i,N}\right\|_\infty \le \left(\frac{1}{\beta\Delta t+1}\right)^N \left\|u^{i,\infty} - u_0^i\right\|_\infty,$$

and for the discrete case

$$\left\|u_h^{i,\infty} - u_h^{i,N}\right\|_\infty \le \left(\frac{1}{\beta\Delta t+1}\right)^N \left\|u_h^{i,\infty} - u_{h0}^i\right\|_\infty,$$

Applying the previous results of Propositions 1, 3 and Theorem 6 we get

$$\begin{aligned}\left\|u_h^i(T,.) - u^{i,\infty}\right\|_\infty \le{}& 2\left(\frac{1}{\beta\Delta t+1}\right)^N \left\|u_h^{i,\infty} - u_{h0}^i\right\|_\infty + \left(\frac{1}{\beta\Delta t+1}\right)^N \left\|u^{i,\infty} - u_0^i\right\|_\infty \\ &+ Ch^2|\log h|^2\end{aligned}$$

Then, the following result can be deduced:

$$\left\|u_h^i(T,.) - u^{i,\infty}\right\|_\infty \le C\left(h^2|\log h|^2 + \left(\frac{1}{\beta\Delta t+1}\right)^N\right),$$

which completes the proof. □

COROLLARY 1 It can be seen that in the previous estimate (5.1), $\left(\frac{1}{\beta\Delta t+1}\right)^N$ tends to 0 when N approaches to $+\infty$. Therefore, the convergence order for the noncoercive elliptic system of quasi-variational inequalities related to stochastic control problems is

$$\max_{1\le i\le M}\left\|u_h^{i,\infty} - u^{i,\infty}\right\|_\infty \le Ch^2|\log h|^2. \tag{5.2}$$

Acknowledgements
The second author gratefully acknowledge Qassim University in Kingdom of Saudi Arabia and all authors would like to thank the anonymous referees for their careful reading and for relevant remarks/suggestions which helped them to improve the paper.

Funding
The authors received no direct funding for this research.

Author details
Mohamed Amine Bencheikh Le Hocine[1,2]
E-mail: kawlamine@gmail.com
Salah Boulaaras[3,4]
E-mail: saleh_boulaares@yahoo.fr
Mohamed Haiour[2]
E-mail: haiourm@yahoo.fr
[1] Tamanghesset University Center, B.P. 10034, Sersouf, Tamanghesset 11000, Algeria.
[2] LANOS Laboratory, Faculty of Sciences, Department of Mathematics, Badji Mokhtar University, B.P. 12, Annaba 23000, Algeria.
[3] Department of Mathematics, College of Sciences and Arts, Al-Ras, Qassim University, Buraydah, Kingdom of Saudi Arabia.
[4] Laboratory of Fundamental and Applied Mathematics of Oran (LMFAO), University of Oran 1, Ahmed Benbella, Algeria.

Citation information
Cite this article as: On finite element approximation of system of parabolic quasi-variational inequalities related to stochastic control problems, Mohamed Amine Bencheikh Le Hocine, Salah Boulaaras & Mohamed Haiour, *Cogent Mathematics* (2016), 3: 1251386.

References

Achdou, A., Hecht, F., & Pommier, D. (2008). A posteriori error estimates for parabolic variational inequalities. *Journal of Scientific Computing, 37*, 336–366.

Alfredo, F. (1987). L^∞-error estimate for an approximation of a parabolic variational inequality. *Numerische Mathematik, 50*, 557–565.

Bensoussan, A., & Lions, J. L. (1973). Contrôle impulsionnel et inéquations quasi-variationnelles d'évolution. *Note CRAS Paris, 276*, 1333–1338.

Bensoussan, A., & Lions, J. L. (1978). *Applications des inéquations variationnelles en controle stochastique*. Paris: Dunod.

Bencheikh Le Hocine, M. A., Boulaaras, S., & Haiour, M. (2016). An optimal L^∞-error estimate for an approximation of a parabolic variational inequality. *Numerical Functional Analysis and Optimization, 37*, 1–18.

Bencheikh Le Hocine, M. A., & Haiour, M. (2013). Algorithmic approach for the aysmptotic behavior of a system of parabolic quasi variational inequalities. *Applied Mathematics Sciences, 7*, 909–921.

Berger, A., & Falk, R. (1977). An error estimate for the truncation method for the solution of parabolic obstacle variational inequalities. *Mathematics of Computation., 31*, 619–628.

Boulaaras, S., Bencheikh Le Hocine, M. E. D. A., & Haiour, M. (2014). The finite element approximation in a system of parabolic quasi-variational inequalities related to management of energy production with mixed boundary condition. *Computational Mathematics and Modeling, 25*, 530–543.

Boulaaras, S., & Haiour, M. (2014). The theta time scheme combined with a finite element spatial approximation in the evolutionary Hamilton-Jacobi-Bellman equation with linear source terms. *Computational Mathematics and Modeling, 25*, 423–438.

Boulbrachene, M. (2014). Optimal L^∞-error estimate for a system of elliptic quasi-variational inequalities with noncoercive operators. *Advances in Applied Mathematics* (Springer Proceedings in Mathematics & Statistics), *87*, 89–96.

Boulbrachene, M. (2015a). On the finite element approximation of variational inequalities with noncoercive operators. *Numerical Functional Analysis and Optimization, 36*, 1107–1121.

Boulbrachene, M. (2015b). On the finite element approximation of the impulse control quasivariational inequality. In A. H. Siddiqi, P. Manchanda, & R. Bhardwaj (Eds.), *Mathematical Models, Methods and Applications. Industrial and Applied Mathematics* (pp. 107–126). Singapore: Springer.

Boulbrachene, M., & Cortey-Dumont, P. (2009). Optimal L^∞-error estimate of a finite element method for Hamilton—Jacobi—Bellman equations. *Numerical Functional Analysis and Optimization, 30*, 421–435.

Boulbrachene, M., Haiour, M., & Chentouf, B. (2002). On a noncoercive system of quasi-variational inequalities related to stochastic. *Journal of Inequalities in Pure and Applied Mathematics, 3*, 1–14.

Cortey-Dumont, P. (1987). Sur l'analyse numerique des equations de Hamilton-Jacobi-Bellman. *Mathematical Methods in the Applied Sciences, 9*, 198–209.

Cortey-Dumont, P. (1985). On the finite element approximation in the L^∞-norm of variational inequalities with nonlinear operators. *Numerische Mathematik, 47*, 45–57.

Cortey-Dumont, P. (1985). Sur les inéquations variationnelles opérateur non coercif. *Modelisation Mathematique et Analyse Numerique, 19*, 195–212.

Cortey-Dumont, P. (1983). Contribution a l'approximation des inequations variationnelles en norme L^∞. *Comptes Rendus de l'Acadmie des Sciences - Series I - Mathematics, 17*, 753–756.

Diaz, I., & Defonso, J. (1985). On a Fully non-linear parabolic equation and the asymptotic behavior of its solution. *Journal of Mathematical Analysis and Applications, 15*, 144–168.

Evans, L. C., & Friedman, A. (1979). Optimal stochastic switching and the Dirichlet Problem for the Bellman equations. *Transactions of the American Mathematical Society, 253*, 365–389.

Lions, P. L., & Menaldi, J. L. (1979). Optimal control of stochastic integrals and Hamilton Jacobi Bellman equations (Part I). *SIAM Control and Optimization, 20*, 58–81.

Nochetto, R. H. (1988). Sharp L^∞-error estimates for semilinear elliptic problems with free boundaries. *Numerische Mathematik, 54*, 243–255.

Scarpini, F., & Vivaldi, M. A. (1977). Evaluation de l'erreur d'approximation pour une inéquation parabolique relative aux convexes d épendant du temps. *Applied Mathematics & Optimization, 4*, 121–138.

5

Nonlinear least squares algorithm for identification of hazards

Robert E. White[1]*
*Corresponding author: Department of Mathematics, Box 8205, North Carolina State University Raleigh, NC 27695- 8205, USA
E-mail: white@math.ncsu.edu
Reviewing editor: Yong Hong Wu, Curtin University of Technology, Australia

Abstract: Given observations of selected concentrations one wishes to determine unknown intensities and locations of the sources for a hazard. The concentration of the hazard is governed by a steady-state nonlinear diffusion–advection partial differential equation and the best fit of the data. The discretized version leads to a coupled nonlinear algebraic system and a nonlinear least squares problem. The coefficient matrix is a nonsingular *M*-matrix and is not symmetric. Iterative methods are compositions of nonnegative least squares and Picard/Newton methods, and a convergence proof is given. The singular values of the associated least squares matrix are important in the convergence proof, the sensitivity to the parameters of the model, and the location of the observation sites.

Subjects: Applied Mathematics; Inverse Problems; Mathematics & Statistics; Science

Keywords: advection–diffusion; impulsive sources; Schur complement; nonnegative least squares; nonlinear; singular values

AMS subject classifications: 35K60; 65H10; 93B40; 93E24

1. Introduction

The paper is a continuation of the work in White (2011). The first new result is a convergence proof of the algorithm to approximate a solution to a nonlinear least square problem. A second new result is a sensitivity analysis of the solution as a function of the model parameters, measured data, and observation sites. Here, the singular value decomposition of the least squares matrix plays an important role.

A convergence proof is given for the algorithm to approximate the solution of a coupled nonlinear algebraic system and a nonnegative least squares problem, see lines (9–11) in this paper and in White (2011). These discrete models evolve from the continuous models using the

ABOUT THE AUTHOR

Professor Robert E. White has published numerous articles on numerical analysis including approximate solutions of partial differential equations, numerical linear algebra, and parallel algorithms. The most recent work is on hazard identification given observation data. He has authored three textbooks. The second edition of *Computational Mathematics: Models, Methods and Analysis with MATLAB and MPI* will be published in the fall of 2015 by CRC Press/Taylor and Francis.

PUBLIC INTEREST STATEMENT

Chemical or biological hazards can move by diffusion or fluid flow. The goal of the research is to make predictions about the location and intensities of the hazards based on the down stream location of observations sites. Mathematical models of the diffusion and flow are used to extrapolate from the observations data sites to unknown upstream locations and intensities of the hazards. The convergence of the iterative process for these extrapolations is studied. The sensitivities of the calculations, because of variations of the model parameters, observation data, and location of the observation sites, are also studied.

advection–diffusion PDE in Equation (1) (see Pao, 1992). In contrast to the continuous models in Andrle and El Badia (2015), Hamdi (2007), and Mahar and Datta (1997), this analysis focuses on the linear and semilinear algebraic systems. In Hamdi (2007), the steady-state continuous linear model requires observations at all of the down stream portions of the boundary. In Andrle and El Badia (2015), the continuous linear velocity free model where the intensities of the source term are time dependent requires observations at the boundary over a given time interval. In both these papers, the Kohn–Vogelius objective function is used for the symmetric models in the identification problems.

Here and in White (2011) we assume the coefficient matrix associated with the steady-state discretized partial differential equation in Equation (1) is an *M*-matrix and may not be symmetric, which includes coefficient matrices from upwind finite difference schemes for the advection–diffusion PDE. The least squares matrix *C*(:, *ssites*), see Equations (6–8), is an $k \times l$ matrix where $k > l$ and k and l are the number of observation and source sites, respectively. The rank and singular values (see Meyer, 2000, section 5.12), of *C*(:, *ssites*) determines whether of not the observation and source sites are located so that the intensities can be accurately computed.

Four examples illustrate these methods. The first two examples in Section 3 are for $n = 2$ and $n = 3$ unknowns, and they show some of the difficulties associated with the nonlinear problem. Sections 4 and 5 contain the convergence proof. Examples three and four in Section 6 are applications of the 1D and 2D versions of the steady-state advection–diffusion PDE. Sensitivity of the computed solutions due to variation of the model parameters, the data and the relative location of the source and observation sites is illustrated. The connection with the sensitivity and the singular values of the least squares matrix is established.

2. Problem formulation

Consider a hazardous substance with sources from a finite number of locations. The sources are typically located at points in a plane and can be modeled by delta functionals. The hazard is described as concentration or density by a function of space and time, $u(x, y, t)$. This is governed by the advection–diffusion PDE

$$u_t - \nabla \bullet D\nabla u + v \bullet \nabla u + d_r u = f(u) + S \quad (1)$$

where S is a source term, D is the diffusion, v is the velocity of the medium, d_r is the decay rate, and $f(u)$ is the nonlinear term such as in logistic growth models. The source term will be a finite linear combination of delta functionals

$$S = \sum a_i \delta(x - \hat{x}_i) \quad (2)$$

where the coefficients a_i are the intensities and the locations $\hat{x}_i$ are possibly unknown points in the line or plane. The source coefficients should be nonnegative, which is in contrast with impulsive culling where the coefficient of the delta functionals are negative and have the form $-c_i u(x_i)$ (see White, 2009).

We will assume the source sites and the observation sites do not intersect. The reason for this is the ability to measure concentrations most likely allows one to measure the intensities at the same site.

Identification problem: Given *data* for *u*(*osites*) at a number of given observation sites, *osites*, determine the intensities (a_i) and locations ($\hat{x}_i$) at source sites, *ssites*, so that

$\|data - u(osites)\|$ is suitably small.

2.1. Linear least squares

Since the governing PDE is to be discretized, we first consider the corresponding linear discrete problem

$Au = d.$

The coefficient matrix A is derived using finite differences with upwind finite differences on the velocity term. Therefore, we assume A is a nonsingular M-matrix (see Berman & Plemmons, 1994, chapter 6 or Meyer, 2000, section 7.10). The following approach finds the solution in one least squares step. The coefficient matrix is $n \times n$ and nodes are partitioned into three ordered sets, whose order represents a reordering of the nodes:

osites observe sites
ssites source sites and
rsites remaining sites.

The *discrete identification* problem is given data *data* at *osites*, find *d(ssites)* such that

$Au = d$ such that $u(osites) = data.$

In general, the reordered matrix has the following 2×2 block structure with $other = [ssites \quad rsites]$

$$A = \begin{bmatrix} a & e \\ f & b \end{bmatrix} \tag{3}$$

where $a = A(osites, osites), e = A(osites, other), f = A(other, osites)$ and $b = A(other, other)$.

Assumptions of this paper:

(1) A is an M-matrix so that A and a have inverses.

(2) $\#(osites) = k$, and $\#(ssites) = l < k$ so that $n = k + l + \#(rsites)$.

(3) $d = [0 \quad d_1^T]^T$ and the only nonzero terms in d_1 are at the nodes in *ssites*, that is, $d \equiv [0 \quad d_1(ssites)^T \quad 0]^T = [0 \quad z^T \quad 0]^T$.

Multiply Equation (3) by a block elementary matrix (as in assumptions 1 and 2)

$$\begin{bmatrix} I_k & 0 \\ -fa^{-1} & I_{n-k} \end{bmatrix} \begin{bmatrix} a & e \\ f & b \end{bmatrix} \begin{bmatrix} u_0 \\ u_1 \end{bmatrix} = \begin{bmatrix} I_k & 0 \\ -fa^{-1} & I_{n-k} \end{bmatrix} \begin{bmatrix} 0 \\ d_1 \end{bmatrix} \tag{4}$$

$$\begin{bmatrix} a & e \\ 0 & \widehat{b} \end{bmatrix} \begin{bmatrix} u_0 \\ u_1 \end{bmatrix} = \begin{bmatrix} 0 \\ d_1 \end{bmatrix} \tag{5}$$

where $\widehat{b} \equiv b - fa^{-1}e$. Solve Equation (5) for u_1 and then $u_0 = -a^{-1}e(\widehat{b})^{-1}d_1$. Define

$$d_1 \equiv [d_1(ssites)^T \quad 0]^T \text{ and } C \equiv -a^{-1}e(\widehat{b})^{-1}. \tag{6}$$

The computed approximations of the observed *data* are in u_0 and the source data are in $z = d_1(ssites)$. This gives a *least squares* problem for z

$$data = C(:, ssites)z. \tag{7}$$

Since a is $k \times k$, e is $k \times (n-k)$, and $\hat{b}$ is $(n-k) \times (n-k)$, the matrix C is $k \times (n-k)$ and the *least squares matrix* $C(:, ssites)$ is $k \times l$ where $k > l$. The least squares problem in (7) has a unique solution if the columns of $C(:, ssites)$ are linearly independent ($C(:, ssites)z = 0$ implies $z = 0$).

Impose the nonnegative condition on the components of the least squares solution. That is, consider finding $z \geq 0$ such that

$$r(z)^T r(z) = \min_{y \geq 0} r(y)^T r(y) \text{ where } r(z) \equiv data - C(:, ssites)z \tag{8}$$

If the matrix $C(:, ssites)$ has full column rank, then the *nonnegative least squares* problem (8) has a unique solution (see Bjorck, 1996, section 5.2). The nonnegative least squares solution can be computed using the MATLAB command lsqnonneg.m (see MathWorks, 2015).

2.2. Least squares and nonlinear term

Consider a *nonlinear* variation of $Au = d$

$$Au = d(z) + \hat{d}(u) \tag{9}$$

where $d(z) = \begin{bmatrix} 0 & z^T & 0 \end{bmatrix}^T$ (as in assumption 3) and $\hat{d}(u) = [\hat{d}_i(u_i)]$.

Use the reordering in (3) and repeat the block elementary matrix transformation in (4) and (5) applied to the above. Using the notation $\hat{d}(u) = [\hat{d}_0(u)^T \quad \hat{d}_1(u)^T]^T$ one gets

$$\begin{bmatrix} a & e \\ 0 & \hat{b} \end{bmatrix} \begin{bmatrix} u_0 \\ u_1 \end{bmatrix} = \begin{bmatrix} I_k & 0 \\ -fa^{-1} & I_{n-k} \end{bmatrix} \left(\begin{bmatrix} 0 \\ d_1 \end{bmatrix} + \begin{bmatrix} \hat{d}_0(u) \\ \hat{d}_1(u) \end{bmatrix} \right)$$
$$= \begin{bmatrix} 0 \\ d_1 \end{bmatrix} + \begin{bmatrix} \hat{d}_0(u) \\ -fa^{-1}\hat{d}_0(u) + \hat{d}_1(u) \end{bmatrix}.$$

Solve for u_1 and then for u_0

$$u_0 = a^{-1}\hat{d}_0(u) - a^{-1}e(\hat{b})^{-1}\left(d_1 + (-fa^{-1}\hat{d}_0(u) + \hat{d}_1(u))\right)$$
$$= g(u) + Cd_1$$

where $C \equiv -a^{-1}e(\hat{b})^{-1}$ and $g(u) \equiv a^{-1}\hat{d}_0(u) + C(-fa^{-1}\hat{d}_0(u) + \hat{d}_1(u))$.

This leads to a *nonlinear least squares* problem for nonnegative z

$$data - g(u) = C(:, ssites)z. \tag{10}$$

The solution of the nonnegative least squares problem is input to the nonzero components in d, that is, $d(ssites) = z$. The *coupled problem* from (9) and (10) is to find $z \geq 0$ and u so that

$$data - g(u) = C(:, ssites)z \text{ and } Au = d(z) + \hat{d}(u). \tag{11}$$

3. Two algorithms for the coupled problem

If the nonnegative least squares problem has a unique solution $z = H(u)$ given a suitable u, then we can write (11) as

$$Au = d(H(u)) + \hat{d}(u),$$

or as a fixed point

$u = A^{-1}(d(H(u)) + \widehat{d}(u)) \equiv G(u).$

The following algorithm is a composition of nonnegative least squares and a Picard update to form one iteration step. Using additional assumptions we will show this is contractive and illustrate linear convergence. Example 3.2 is a simple implementation with $n = 3$, and in Section 6 Example 6.1 uses the 1D steady-state version of the model in (1) and Example 6.2 uses the 2D steady-state model in (1).

Algorithm 1. NLS-Picard Method for (11)
choose nonnegative u^0
for $m = 0, mmax$
solve the nonnegative least squares problem
$data - g(u^m) = C(:, ssites)z^{m+1}$
solve the linear problem
$Au^{m+1} = d(z^{m+1}) + \widehat{d}(u^m)$
test for convergence
end for-loop

The following algorithm uses a combination of nonnegative least squares and Newton like updates. Define $F(z, u)$ and $F_u(z, u)$ as

$F(z, u) \equiv Au - d(z) - \widehat{d}(u)$ and $F_u(z, u) \equiv A - 0 - \widehat{d}_u(u)$

where $\widehat{d}_u(u) \equiv [(\widetilde{d}_i)'(u_i)]$ is the diagonal matrix with components $(\widetilde{d}_i)'(u_i)$.

The matrix $F_u(z, u)$ is not the full derivative matrix of $F(z, u)$ because it ignores the dependence of z on u. Choose $\lambda > 0$ so that $F_u + \lambda I$ has an inverse.

Algorithm 2. NLS-Newton Method for (11)
choose nonnegative u^0 and $\lambda > 0$
for $m = 0, mmax$
solve the nonnegative least squares problem
$data - g(u^m) = C(:, ssites)z^{m+1}$
solve the linear problem
$Au^{m+1/2} = d(z^{m+1}) + \widehat{d}(u^m)$
compute $F(z^{m+1}, u^{m+1/2}) \equiv Au^{m+1/2} - d(z^{m+1}) - \widehat{d}(u^{m+1/2})$
$= \widehat{d}(u^m) - \widehat{d}(u^{m+1/2})$
compute $F_u(z^{m+1}, u^{m+1/2}) \equiv A - 0 - \widehat{d}_u(u^{m+1/2})$
solve the linear problem
$(F_u(z^{m+1}, u^{m+1/2}) + \lambda I)\ \Delta u = F(z^{m+1}, u^{m+1/2})$
$u^{m+1} = u^{m+1/2} - \Delta u$
test for convergence
end for-loop

Variations of the NLS-Newton algorithm include using over relaxation, ω, at the first linear solve and using damping, α, on the second linear solve in the Newton update:

$u^{m+1/2} = (1 - \omega)u^m + \omega u^{m+1/2}$ and
$u^{m+1} = u^{m+1/2} - \alpha \Delta u.$

Appropriate choices of w, α and λ can accelerate convergence.

The calculations recorded in Table 4 and Figure 4 in White (2011), illustrate the NLS-Newton algorithm for the 1D steady-state problem with logistic growth term $\widehat{d}(u) = f(u) = c(100 - u)u$ and variable growth rate c. The larger the c parameter resulted in larger concentrations. The intensities at the three source sites were identified. However, the number of iterations of the NLS-Newton algorithm increased as the c parameter increased. The algorithm did start to fail for c larger than 0.0100.

The lack of convergence is either because the associated fixed point problem does not have a contractive mapping or because the solutions become negative. The following example with $n = 2$, nonzero source term and nonsymmetric A illustrates the difficulty of solving a semilinear algebraic problem where the solution is required to be positive.

Example 3.1 Let $n = 2$ and use $f_i(u_i) = c(100 - u_i)u_i$. Equation (9) has the form

$$\begin{bmatrix} 1 & 0 \\ -\varepsilon & 1 \end{bmatrix}\begin{bmatrix} u_0 \\ u_1 \end{bmatrix} = \begin{bmatrix} 0 \\ z \end{bmatrix} + \begin{bmatrix} f_0(u_0) \\ f_1(u_1) \end{bmatrix}.$$

The first equation is $u_0 = c(100 - u_0)u_0$ whose solution is either $u_0 = 0$ or $u_0 = 100 - 1/c > 0$. Put the nonzero solution into the second equation $-\varepsilon(100 - 1/c) + u_1 = z + c(100 - u_1)u_1$ and solve for u_1. If $\varepsilon(100 - 1/c) + z > 0$, then the second equation is $u_1 = c(100 - u_1)u_1 + \varepsilon(100 - 1/c) + z$ and will have a positive solution.

The next example with $n = 3$, given *data* at the first and second nodes and a source term at the third node illustrates the coupled problem in (11). This simple example can be solved both by-hand calculations and the NLS-Picard algorithm, and more details are given in Appendix 1.

Example 3.2 Let the data be given at the first and second nodes

$$data = \begin{bmatrix} 2.9711 \\ 5.4971 \end{bmatrix}.$$

Let the matrix A and nonlinear terms be given by system

$$\begin{bmatrix} 3 & 0 & -1 \\ 0 & 3 & -2 \\ -2 & -2 & 4 \end{bmatrix}\begin{bmatrix} u_1 \\ u_2 \\ u_3 \end{bmatrix} = \begin{bmatrix} 0 \\ 0 \\ z \end{bmatrix} + \begin{bmatrix} cu_1(10 - u_1) \\ cu_2(10 - u_2) \\ cu_3(10 - u_3) \end{bmatrix}.$$

The submatrices of A are

$$a = \begin{bmatrix} 3 & 0 \\ 0 & 3 \end{bmatrix}, e = \begin{bmatrix} -1 \\ -2 \end{bmatrix}, f = \begin{bmatrix} -2 & -2 \end{bmatrix} \text{ and } b = [4].$$

Then one easily computes

$$\hat{b} = b - fa^{-1}e = [2] \text{ and } C = -a^{-1}e\hat{b}^{-1} = (1/6)\begin{bmatrix} 1 \\ 2 \end{bmatrix}.$$

The $g(u)$ in the nonlinear least square Equation (11) is

$$g(u) = c\begin{bmatrix} (4/9)u_1(10 - u_1) + (1/6)u_3(10 - u_3) + (1/9)u_2(10 - u_2) \\ (5/9)u_2(10 - u_2) + (2/6)u_3(10 - u_3) + (2/9)u_1(10 - u_1) \end{bmatrix}.$$

The calculation with the NLS-Picard algorithm for this example with $n = 3$ in White (2015, testlsnonlc.m) confirms both the exact solution for $c = 8/100 = 0.0800$ and convergence for $c < 0.1667$, which are given in Appendix 1. The number of iterations needed for convergence increases as c increases, and convergence fails for $c = 0.3000$. Both the exact and NLS-Picard calculations show $z > 0$ for $c \leq 0.1975$ and $z = 0$ for $c \geq 0.1976$. The outputs for five values of $c = 0.08{:}0.04{:}0.24$

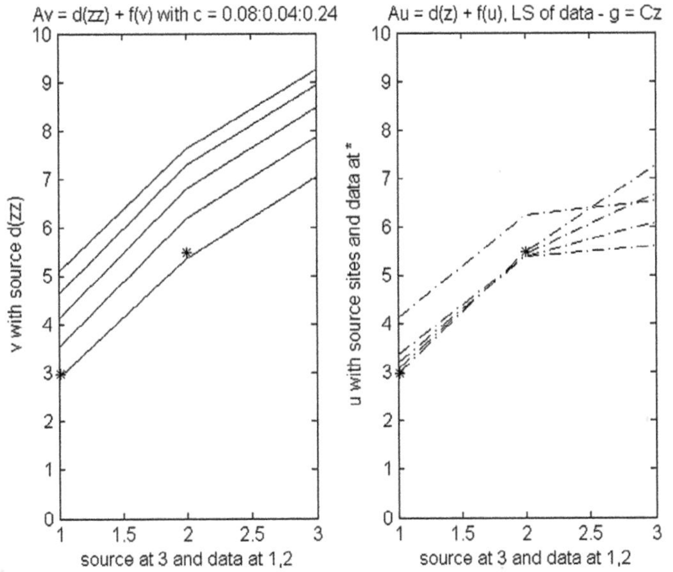

Figure 1. NLS-Picard algorithm for n = 3.

are given in Figure 1. The left graphs indicate the five solutions of (10) for fixed $z = zz = 10$ and increasing c. The two "*" are the given *data*, which are from the solution of (10) with $c = 0.0800$ and 5% error. The right graphs are the converged solutions of (11) for $c = 0.08{:}0.04{:}0.20$.

4. Nonnegative least squares problem

The nonnegative least squares problem in (10) for $z \geq 0$ has several forms

$$R(z)^T R(z) = \min_{y\geq 0} R(y)^T R(y) \text{ where } R(z) \equiv data - g(u) - C(:, ssites)z.$$

This may be written as

$$R(z)^T R(z) = (data - g(u))^T (data - g(u)) - 2J(z) \tag{12}$$

where

$$J(z) \equiv \frac{1}{2} z^T C(:, ssites)^T C(:, ssites)z - z^T C(:, ssites)^T (data - g(u)).$$

If $C(:, ssites)$ has full column rank, then the matrix $C(:, ssites)^T C(:, ssites)$ is symmetric positive definite (SPD). $J(z)$ is the quadratic functional associated with the linear system (normal equations)

$$0 = r(z) \equiv C(:, ssites)^T (data - g(u)) - C(:, ssites)^T C(:, ssites)z$$

When the nonnegative condition is imposed on $z \geq 0$ and the matrix is SPD, then the following are equivalent (see Cryer, 1971):

$J(z) = \min_{y\geq 0} J(y)$ (minimum quadratic functional),

$0 \geq r(z)^T (y - z)$ for all $y \geq 0$ (variational inequality) and

$0 = r(z)^T z$ and $0 \geq r(z)$ (linear complementarity problem).

Any solution of a variational inequality is unique and depends continuously on the right-hand side. The next theorem is a special case of this.

THEOREM 4.1 *Consider the nonnegative least squares problem in (10). If $C(:, ssites)$ has full column rank, then there is only one nonnegative solution for each u. Let $z = H(u)$ be the solution for each u in*

S where S is a bounded set of nonnegative n-vectors. Moreover, if $\|\hat{d}(u) - \hat{d}(v)\| \leq \hat{K}\|u - v\|$*, then there is a constant* C_1 *such that*

$$\|C(:, ssites)(H(u) - H(v))\| \leq C_1\|u - v\|$$

Proof Let z and w be solutions of (10). The variational inequalities for z with $y = w$, and for w with $y = z$ are

$$0 \geq r(z)^T(w - z) \text{ and } 0 \geq r(w)^T(z - w).$$

Add these to get a contradiction for the case $z - w$ is not a zero vector

$$0 \geq (z - w)^T C(:, ssites)^T C(:, ssites)(z - w) > 0.$$

In order to show the continuity, use the above with $z = H(u)$ and $w = H(v)$:

$$0 \geq [C(:, ssites)^T(data - g(u)) - C(:, ssites)^T C(:, ssites)H(u)]^T(H(v) - H(u))$$
$$0 \geq [C(:, ssites)^T(data - g(v)) - C(:, ssites)^T C(:, ssites)H(v)]^T(H(u) - H(v)).$$

Add these to obtain for $B \equiv C(:, ssites)^T C(:, ssites)$

$$(H(v) - Hu))^T B(H(v) - H(u)) \leq -(g(v) - g(u))^T C(:, ssites)(H(v) - H(u)).$$

Use the Cauchy inequality

$$\|C(:, ssites)(H(v) - H(u))\|^2 \leq \|g(v) - g(u)\|\,\|C(:, ssites)(H(v) - H(u))\|.$$

By the definition of g and the assumption on d we have for some C_1 □

$$\|C(:, ssites)(H(v) - H(u))\| \leq C_1\|v - u\|.$$

The solution of the variational problem for fixed u has the form $z = H(u)$. The assumption that $C(:, ssites)$ has full column rank implies there is a positive constant c_0 such that $c_0^2 w^T w \leq w^T C(:, ssites)^T C(:, ssites)w$. This and the above theorem give the following

$$c_0\|H(v) - H(u)\| \leq \|C(:, ssites)(H(v) - H(u))\| \leq C_1\|v - u\|. \quad (13)$$

Although in Example 3.2 with $n = 3$ one can estimate c_0 and C_1, generally these constants are not easily approximated. However, c_0 can be estimated by the smallest singular value of the least squares matrix.

5. Convergence proof of the NLS-Picard algorithm

Let the assumptions in the previous theorem hold so that (12) is true for all $u, v \in S$. The mapping $G(u) \equiv A^{-1}(d(H(u)) + \hat{d}(u))$ may not give $G(u) \in S$! This appears to be dependent on the particular problem and properties of $\hat{d}(u)$. If the bound is chosen so that $\hat{d}(u)$ is also nonnegative, then assumption (1) implies $A^{-1} \geq 0$ and hence $G(u) \geq 0$. The least squares condition requires the solution to be "close" to the given *data* at the *osites*, which suggests the $G(u)$ should remain bounded. The following theorem gives general conditions on the problem.

THEOREM 5.1 *Let the assumptions of Theorem 4.1 hold for* $u, v \in S$. *Assume there is a solution to the coupled problem (11),* $u^* \in S$. *Let* c_0 *and* C_1 *be from (12). If*

$$\hat{r} \equiv \|A^{-1}\|(C_1/c_0 + \hat{K}) < 1,$$

then the NLS-Picard algorithm will converge to this solution of (11).

Proof Let $u^* = G(u^*)$ and $u^{m+1} = G(u^m)$.

$$\begin{aligned}\left\|u^* - u^{m+1}\right\| &= \|G(u^*) - G(u^m)\| \\ &= \left\|A^{-1}(d(H(u^*) - d(H(u^m)) + A^{-1}(\hat{d}(u^*) - \hat{d}(u^m))\right\| \\ &\leq \left\|A^{-1}\|(C_1/c_0)\|u^* - u^m\| + \|A^{-1}\|\hat{K}\|u^* - u^m\right\| \\ &= \left\|A^{-1}\|(C_1/c_0 + \hat{K})\|u^* - u^m\right\| \\ &= \hat{r}\|u^* - u^m\| \\ &\vdots \\ &\leq \hat{r}^{m+1}\|u^* - u^0\|.\end{aligned}$$

Since $\hat{r} < 1$, this implies convergence □

6. Applications and sensitivity analysis

Both the NLS-Picard and NLS-Newton methods converge linearly, that is, the errors at the next iteration are bounded by a contractive constant, $\hat{r} < 1$, times the error from the current iteration. However, the contractive constant for the NLS-Newton algorithm is significantly smaller than the contractive constant for the NLS-Picard algorithm, and this results in fewer iterations steps for the NLS-Newton algorithm. The calculations in the next two examples can be done by either algorithm. The relevance of the singular values of the least squares matrix to the sensitivity of the calculations with variations in the data and the source and observation sites is demonstrated.

Example 6.1 Consider the steady-state 1D model in (1). The following calculations were done by the MATLAB code in White (2015, poll1dlsnonla2.m) and with seven observation sites, three source sites, and $n = 160$. The differential Equation (1) was discretized by the upwind finite difference approximations, and the sources terms were the intensities times the approximation of the delta functionals

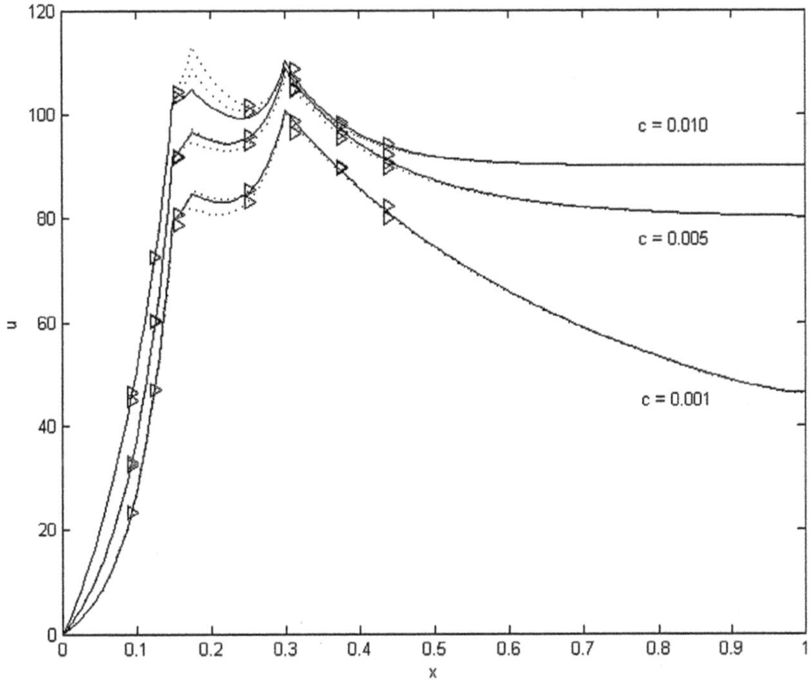

Figure 2. NLS-Newton algorithm with variable c.

$d(ssites) = [a_1 \quad a_2 \quad a_3]^T / dx$

where initially $d \equiv zeros(n, 1)$. In order to check the accuracy of the finite difference model, calculations were done with $n = 160, 320$ and 480, which gave similar results as reported below for $n = 160$. The condition number (ratio of the largest and smallest singular values) of the least squares matrix controls the relative errors in the computed least squares problem. The condition numbers for the $n = 160, 320$, and 480 are about the same at 17.0170, 16.5666, and 16.4146, respectively.

For $c = 0.010$ the NLS-Picard algorithm did not converge, but the NLS-Newton algorithm converged in 92 steps. The solid lines in Figure 2 are with no random error in the *data*, and the dotted lines are from *data* with 5% random error. For $c = 0.005$ the NLS-Picard algorithm converged in 100 steps with $\hat{r} \approx .83$, and the NLS-Newton algorithm converged in 19 steps with $\hat{r} \approx .41$. If w is changed from 1.0 to 1.1, then the NLS-Newton algorithm converges in 16 steps with $\hat{r} \approx .28$. As c decreases, the iterations required for convergence and $\hat{r}$ decrease.

The dotted lines indicate some uncertainty in the numerical solutions, which can be a function of the physical parameters and the location of the observation sites relative to the source sites. If there is no error in the data, the intensities of the sources are in the vector

$$z = \begin{bmatrix} 4.0000 & 1.0000 & 2.0000 \end{bmatrix}.$$

Use 100 computations with the $c = 0.001$ and 5% random errors. The means and standard deviations of the computed intensities at the three source sites are

$$mean(z) = \begin{bmatrix} 4.0357 & 0.9437 & 2.0187 \end{bmatrix} \text{ and}$$
$$std(z) = \begin{bmatrix} 0.2570 & 0.3631 & 0.1375 \end{bmatrix}.$$

The standard deviation of the intensities at the center source in Figure 2 is large relative to its mean value. The large computed least squares errors are a result of some relatively small singular values in the singular value decomposition of the least squares matrix

$$C(:, ssites) = U\Sigma V^T$$

where the singular values σ_i are the diagonal components of Σ; U is 7×7, Σ is 7×3 and V is 3×3.

In this example, the third singular value is small

$$\sigma = \begin{bmatrix} 0.2882 & 0.0916 & 0.0169 \end{bmatrix}.$$

The least square solution of (10) is given by the pseudo inverse of the least squares matrix times $data - g(u) \equiv \hat{d}$

$$V\Sigma^{\dagger}U^T\hat{d} = v_1\, u_1^T\hat{d}/\sigma_1 + v_2\, u_2^T\hat{d}/\sigma_2 + v_3\, u_3^T\hat{d}/\sigma_3.$$

Because σ_3 is relatively small, any errors in $\hat{d}$ will be amplified as well as the components of

$$v_3 = \begin{bmatrix} 0.5778 & -0.7882 & 0.2121 \end{bmatrix}^T.$$

This suggests the second component, the center source, of least squares solution will have significant errors. The errors can be decreased if the percentage random error is smaller or by alternative location of the observation sites. In the 1D model this is not too difficult to remedy. However, in the 2D model this is more challenging.

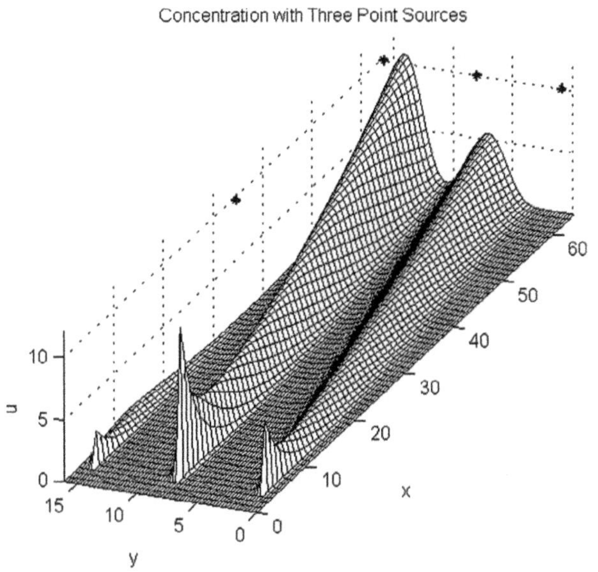

Figure 3. Three sources and four observations.

Example 6.2 Consider the steady-state 2D model in (1) with boundary conditions equal to zero up stream and zero normal derivative down stream. The calculations in Figure 3 were done by the MATLAB code in White (2015, testlsnonlf2da3.m) using NLS-Picard and with four variable observation sites and three fixed source sites. The three fixed sources are to the left near $x = 0$, and the four observation sites are indicated by the symbol "*" above the site. The intensities times the approximation of the delta functionals is

$$d(ssites) = [a_1 \ a_2 \ a_3]^T/(dx * dy)$$

where initially $d \equiv zeros(nn, 1)$ and $nn = (nx + 1) * (ny + 1)$. If there is no random error in the *data*, then the computed source will be

$$\left[\ 8.0000 \quad 16.0000 \quad 4.0000 \ \right].$$

The numerical experiments involve varying the location of the observation site at $(x, 16)$ where $x = L - \Delta L$ and varying the y-component of the velocity, *vely*. The velocity term in (1) is $(velx, vely) = (1.00, 0.10)$. The base calculation in Figure 3 uses $\Delta L = 30$ and $vely = 0.10$ along with 5% random error in the data and $c = 0.0004$ growth coefficient in the nonlinear term. The singular values of the least squares matrix and the mean and standard deviations of the intensities of the three computed sources are recorded for 100 computations.

$\Delta L = 30$ and $vely = 0.10$:

$$\sigma = \left[\ 0.0472 \quad 0.0300 \quad 0.0046 \ \right]$$

$$mean(z) = \left[\ 7.9947 \quad 16.0341 \quad 4.0040 \ \right] \text{ and}$$

$$std(z) = \left[\ 0.2523 \quad 0.4966 \quad 0.1451 \ \right].$$

Changing the *y*-component of the velocity can cause the concentration to be moved away from the observation sites and cause more uncertainty in the calculations, which is indicated by larger standard deviations and smaller singular values of the least squares matrix. Change $vely = 0.10$ to $vely = 0.15$ and $vely = 0.05$.

$\Delta L = 30$ and $vely = 0.15$:

$\sigma = \begin{bmatrix} 0.0424 & 0.0302 & 0.0002 \end{bmatrix}$

$mean(z) = \begin{bmatrix} 7.9562 & 16.034 & 23.6939 \end{bmatrix}$ and

$std(z) = \begin{bmatrix} 0.2399 & 0.5479 & 30.7650 \end{bmatrix}$.

Here, the third singular value has significantly decreased and can cause failure of the NLS-Picard algorithm or increased computation errors because of the variation in the data.

$\Delta L = 30$ and $vely = 0.05$:

$\sigma = \begin{bmatrix} 0.0853 & 0.0004 & 0.0001 \end{bmatrix}$

$mean(z) = \begin{bmatrix} 7.7883 & 16.6030 & 3.9778 \end{bmatrix}$ and

$std(z) = \begin{bmatrix} 0.5744 & 2.0884 & 0.1167 \end{bmatrix}$.

In this case the second and third singular values of the least squares matrix decreased, and the standard deviation of the second source increased.

Changing the location of the third observation site can also cause more uncertainty in the calculations, which is indicated by larger standard deviations and smaller singular values of the least squares matrix. Change $\Delta L = 30$ to $\Delta L = 20$ and $\Delta L = 10$ and keep $vely = 0.10$.

$\Delta L = 20$ and $vely = 0.10$:

$\sigma = \begin{bmatrix} 0.0472 & 0.0300 & 0.0005 \end{bmatrix}$

$mean(z) = \begin{bmatrix} 8.0012 & 16.0350 & 4.5229 \end{bmatrix}$ and

$std(z) = \begin{bmatrix} 0.2350 & 0.5321 & 4.5265 \end{bmatrix}$.

Here, the third singular value has significantly decreased and can cause failure of the NLS-Picard algorithm or increased computation errors because of the variation in the data. The standard deviation of the third source has significantly increased.

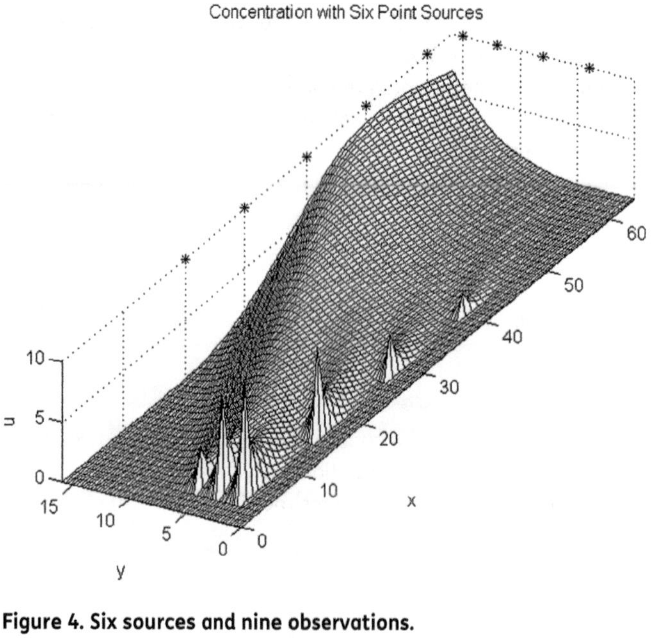

Figure 4. Six sources and nine observations.

$\Delta L = 10$ and $vely = 0.10$:

$$\sigma = \begin{bmatrix} 0.0472 & 0.0320 & 0.0000396 \end{bmatrix}$$
$$mean(z) = \begin{bmatrix} 8.0005 & 15.9137 & 238.9531 \end{bmatrix} \text{ and}$$
$$std(z) = \begin{bmatrix} 0.2379 & 0.5007 & 396.3124 \end{bmatrix}.$$

In this case the third singular values of the least squares matrix have dramatically decreased, and the standard deviation of the third source is very large relative to the mean.

The calculation in Figure 4 has six source sites (near the axes) and nine observation sites (down stream and below the "*") (White, 2015, testlsnonlf2da6.m) uses NLS-Picard. Here the *vely* is larger with velocity the equal to (1.00, 0.30), and the random error in the data is smaller and equal to 1%:

$$\sigma = \begin{bmatrix} 0.0782 & 0.0612 & 0.0459 & 0.0304 & 0.0178 & 0.0047 \end{bmatrix}$$
$$mean(z) = \begin{bmatrix} 23.9404 & 16.0215 & 8.0135 & 3.9869 & 16.1539 & 7.9334 \end{bmatrix} \text{ and}$$
$$std(z) = \begin{bmatrix} 0.8512 & 0.4408 & 0.2064 & 0.0549 & 0.9046 & 0.2879 \end{bmatrix}.$$

The source closest to the origin is the most difficult to identify; with one percent error in the data the standard deviation is 0.8512 and with five percent error this goes up to 4.2348. This happens despite the relatively close distribution of the singular values from 0.0782 to 0.0047 for a condition number equal to 16.7658.

7. Summary

In order to determine locations and intensities of the source sites from data at the observation sites, there must more observations sites than source sites and the observation sites must be more chosen so that the least squares matrix $C(:, ssites)$ has full column rank. Furthermore, the singular values in the singular value decomposition of the least squares matrix are important in the convergence proof and the location of the observation sites.

Measurement errors in the observations as well as uncertain physical parameters can contribute to significant variation in the computed intensities of the sources. Multiple computations with varying these should be done, and the means and standard deviations should be noted. Large standard deviations from the mean indicate a lack of confidence in the computations. In this case, one must adjust the observation sites, which can be suggested by inspection of the smaller singular values for the least squares matrix and the corresponding columns in V of the singular value decomposition.

Funding
No external funding. Some of this research was done before retirement at North Carolina State University.

Author details
Robert E. White[1]
E-mail: white@math.ncsu.edu
[1] Department of Mathematics, Box 8205, North Carolina State University, Raleigh, NC 27695-8205, USA.

References

Andrle, M., & El Badia, A. (2015). On an inverse problem. Application to a pollution detection problem, II. *Inverse Problems in Science and Engineering, 23*, 389–412.

Berman, A., & Plemmons, R. J. (1994). *Nonnegative matrices in the mathematical sciences*. Philadelphia, PA: SIAM.

Bjorck, A. (1996). *Numerical methods for least squares problems*. Philadelphia, PA: SIAM.

Cryer, C. W. (1971). The solution of a quadratic programming problem using systematic over ralaxation. *SIAM Journal on Control and Optimization, 9*, 385–392.

Hamdi, A. (2007). Identification of point sources in two-dimensional advection-diffusion-reaction equations: Application to pollution sources in a river. *Stationary case, Inverse Problems in Science and Engineering, 15*, 855–870.

Mahar, P. S., & Datta, B. (1997). Optimal monitoring network and ground-water-pollution source identification. *Journal of Water Resources Planning and Management, 199*, 199–2007.

MathWorks. (2015). (123, pp. 199–207) Retrieved from http://www.mathworks.com

Meyer, C. D. (2000). *Matrix analysis and applied linear algebra*. Philadelphia, PA: SIAM.

Pao, C. V. (1992). *Nonlinear parabolic and elliptic equations*. New York, NY: Plenum Press.

White, R. E. (2009). Populations with impulsive culling: Identification and control. *International Journal of Computer Mathematics, 86*, 2143–2164.

White, R. E. (2011). Identification of hazards with impulsive sources. *International Journal of Computer Mathematics, 88*, 762–780.

White, R. E. (2015). *MATLAB codes for hazard identification.* Retrieved from http://www4.ncsu.edu/eos/users/w/white/www/white/hazardid/hazardid.htm

Appendix 1

Details for Example 3.2 with $n = 3$

The least square problem in (11) can be solved for nonnegative $z = H(u)$

$$\begin{aligned} z = {} & (6/5)(data(1) + 2data(2)) \\ & - (16/15)cu_1(10 - u_1) \\ & - (22/15)cu_2(10 - u_2) \\ & - cu_3(10 - u_3). \end{aligned}$$

Next, consider the system in (11). The first two equations give the first and second unknowns in terms of the third unknown

$$u_1 = \frac{-(3 - c10) + \sqrt{(3 - c10)^2 + 4cu_3}}{2c} \text{ and}$$
$$u_2 = \frac{-(3 - c10) + \sqrt{(3 - c10)^2 + 8cu_3}}{2c}.$$

Insert the formulas for z, u_1, and u_2 into the third equation in the system to get a nonlinear problem for a single unknown u_3 and the single equation

$$\begin{aligned} & \sqrt{(3 - c10)^2 + 4cu_3} + 2\sqrt{(3 - c10)^2 + 8cu_3} \\ & = 3(3 - c10) + 2c(data(1) + 2data(2)). \end{aligned}$$

When $c = 8/100$, this can be solved by Newton's method to give $u_3 = 7.2526$. Then solve for the first two unknowns and finally solve for z

$$u_1 = 2.9748, u_2 = 5.4952 \text{ and } z = 10.4764.$$

In the above example, we were able to explicitly solve for nonnegative z in terms of the components of u. The problem $Au = d(H(u)) + \hat{d}(u)$ is

$$\begin{bmatrix} 3 & 0 & -1 \\ 0 & 3 & -2 \\ -2 & -2 & 4 \end{bmatrix} \begin{bmatrix} u_1 \\ u_2 \\ u_3 \end{bmatrix} = \begin{bmatrix} cu_1(10 - u_1) \\ cu_2(10 - u_2) \\ D(u_1, u_2) \end{bmatrix}$$

where

$$\begin{aligned} D(u_1, u_2) \equiv {} & (6/5)(data(1) + 2data(2)) \\ & - (16/15)cu_1(10 - u_1) \\ & - (22/15)cu_2(10 - u_2). \end{aligned}$$

The equivalent fixed point problem is $u = A^{-1}(d(H(u)) + \hat{d}(u))$

$$\begin{bmatrix} u_1 \\ u_2 \\ u_3 \end{bmatrix} = (1/18) \begin{bmatrix} 8 & 2 & 3 \\ 4 & 10 & 6 \\ 6 & 6 & 9 \end{bmatrix} \begin{bmatrix} cu_1(10 - u_1) \\ cu_2(10 - u_2) \\ D(u_1, u_2) \end{bmatrix} \equiv G(u).$$

Expand the matrix-vector product to get

$$G(u) \approx \begin{bmatrix} f_1(.26) + f_2(-.13) + 2.8 \\ f_1(-.13) + f_2(.07) + 5.6 \\ f_1(-.20) + f_2(-.40) + 8.4 \end{bmatrix} \text{where } f_i \equiv cu_i(10 - u_i).$$

Assume u, v are nonnegative and bounded and in

$$S \equiv \{u | u = \begin{bmatrix} u_1 & u_2 & u_3 \end{bmatrix}^T, 0 \le u_i \le 10, i = 1, 2, 3\}.$$

Then $0 \le f_i \le 25c$ and since $z \ge 0, G(u) \ge 0$. If $c \le 1$, then $G(u) < 10$ and G maps S into S.

The contraction mapping theorem requires $G(u)$ to be contractive, that is, $\|G(u) - G(v)\|_\infty \le r\|u - v\|_\infty$ where $r < 1$.

One can approximate the differences

$$\Delta f_i \equiv cu_i(10 - u_i) - cv_i(10 - v_i)$$
$$\|\Delta f_i\| \le c10\|u_i - v_i\|.$$

Then it is possible to estimate r as a function of c

$$\begin{aligned} \|G(u) - G(v)\|_\infty &\le \left\| (1/18) \begin{bmatrix} 8 & 2 & 3 \\ 4 & 10 & 6 \\ 6 & 6 & 9 \end{bmatrix} \begin{bmatrix} \Delta f_1 \\ \Delta f_2 \\ D(u_1, u_2) - D(v_1, v_2) \end{bmatrix} \right\|_\infty \\ &\le (1/18) \left\| \begin{bmatrix} \Delta f_1(8 + 3(-16/15)) + \Delta f_2(2 + 3(-22/15)) \\ \Delta f_1(4 + 6(-16/15)) + \Delta f_2(10 + 6(-22/15)) \\ \Delta f_1(6 + 9(-16/15)) + \Delta f_2(6 + 9(-22/15)) \end{bmatrix} \right\|_\infty \\ &\le c10(10.8/18)\|u - v\|_\infty, \end{aligned}$$

Let $r = c(108/18) < 1$ and require $c < 1/6 = 0.1667$.

6

Annihilating-ideal graphs with independence number at most four

S. Visweswaran[1]* and Jaydeep Parejiya[1]
*Corresponding author: S. Visweswaran, Department of Mathematics, Saurashtra University, Rajkot 360 005, India
E-mail: s_visweswaran2006@yahoo.co.in
Reviewing editor: Jonas Hartwig, Iowa State University, USA

Abstract: Let R be a commutative non-domain ring with identity and let $\mathbb{A}(R)^*$ denote the set of all nonzero annihilating ideals of R. Recall that the annihilating-ideal graph of R, denoted by $\mathbb{AG}(R)$, is an undirected simple graph whose vertex set is $\mathbb{A}(R)^*$ and distinct vertices I, J are joined by an edge in this graph if and only if $IJ = (0)$. The aim of this article was to classify commutative rings R such that the independence number of $\mathbb{AG}(R)$ is less than or equal to four.

Subjects: Arts; Arts & Humanities; Mathematics & Statistics; Science

Keywords: annihilating ideal; the annihilating-ideal graph; independence number; maximal N-prime of (0); special principal ideal ring

2010 Mathematics subject classifications: 13A15; 05C25

1. Introduction

The rings considered in this article are commutative with identity and which are not integral domains. The concept of associating a ring with a graph and investigating the interplay between the ring theoretic properties of rings under consideration and the graph theoretic properties of the graphs associated with them was initiated by Beck (1988). In Beck (1988), I. Beck was mainly interested in colorings. The work of I. Beck inspired a lot of research activity in the area of associating graphs with algebraic structures and exploring the influence of certain graph theoretic parameters on the algebraic structure of the considered algebraic objects. Let R be a ring. The concept of *zero-divisor graph* of R, denoted by $\Gamma(R)$, was introduced and studied by Anderson and Livingston (1999). Recall from Anderson and Livingston (1999) that $\Gamma(R)$ is an undirected simple graph, whose vertex set is $Z(R)^*$, where $Z(R)$ is the set of all zero-divisors of R and $Z(R)^* = Z(R)\backslash\{0\}$ and two distinct vertices $x, y \in Z(R)^*$ are joined by an edge in this graph if and only if $xy = 0$. During the last two decades several mathematicians have contributed to the area of zero-divisor graphs in commutative ring, to mention a few, refer Anderson, Frazier, Lauve, and Livingston (2001), Anderson and Livingston (1999), Anderson and Naseer (1993), Axtell, Coykendall and Stickles (2005), Lucas (2006), Smith

ABOUT THE AUTHORS

S. Visweswaran is serving as a professor in the Department of Mathematics, Saurashtra University, Rajkot, India. His research area is Commutative Ring Theory.

Jaydeep Parejiya is a lecturer in the Department of Mathematics, Government Polytechnic, Rajkot. He has registered for his PhD in the Department of Mathematics, Saurashtra University. His research interest is in Commutative Ring Theory.

PUBLIC INTEREST STATEMENT

The research work carried out by I. Beck in the year 1988 inspired a lot of researchers to investigate the interplay between graph theory and ring theory. The basic purpose of this research was to study the structure of commutative rings with the help of annihilating-ideal graphs of rings. Indeed, in this article, we focused our study on the independence number of annihilating-ideal graphs of commutative rings. The outcome of this study is that we are able to classify all commutative rings whose annihilating-ideal graph has independence number at most four.

(2003). For an excellent and clear exposition of the work done in the area of zero-divisor graphs in commutative rings, the reader is referred to the following survey article Anderson, Axtell and Stickles (2011).

Let R be a ring. Recall from Behboodi and Rakeei (2011a) that an ideal I of R is said to be an *annihilating ideal* if $Ir = (0)$ for some $r \in R\backslash\{0\}$. The concept of the *annihilating-ideal graph* of R, denoted by $\mathbb{AG}(R)$, was introduced in Behboodi and Rakeei (2011a) by M. Behboodi and Z. Rakeei. Recall form Behboodi and Rakeei (2011a) that $\mathbb{AG}(R)$ is an undirected simple graph whose vertex set is $\mathbb{A}(R)^*$, where $\mathbb{A}(R)$ is the set of all annihilating ideals of R and $\mathbb{A}(R)^* = \mathbb{A}(R)\backslash\{(0)\}$, and two distinct vertices I, J are joined by an edge in this graph if and only if $IJ = (0)$. The interplay between the ring theoretic properties of R and the graph theoretic properties of $\mathbb{AG}(R)$ was very well investigated in Behboodi and Rakeei (2011a, 2011b) and several interesting theorems were proved in Behboodi and Rakeei (2011a, 2011b) on $\mathbb{AG}(R)$ indicating the effect of certain graph theoretic parameters on the structure of R. Moreover, the annihilating-ideal graph of a commutative ring was also studied by several others, to mention a few, the reader is referred to Aalipour et al. (2014), Aalipour, Akbari, Nikandish, Nikmehr, and Shaivesi (2012), Hadian (2012).

The graphs considered in this article are undirected. Let $G = (V, E)$ be a simple graph. We denote the *complement* of a graph G by G^c and we denote the *complete graph* on n vertices by K_n. Recall from Balakrishnan and Ranganathan (2000, Definition 1.1.4) that a vertex u is a *neighbor* of v in G, if there is an edge of G joining u and v. A *clique* of G is a complete subgraph of G (Balakrishnan & Ranganathan, 2000, Definition 1.2.2). If the size of the cliques of a graph G is bounded, then the *clique number* of G, denoted by $\omega(G)$, is the largest positive integer n such that G contains a clique on n vertices (Balakrishnan & Ranganathan, 2000, p. 185). If G contains a clique on n vertices for all $n \geq 1$, then we set $\omega(G) = \infty$.

Let $G = (V, E)$ be a graph. A *vertex coloring* of G is a map $f: V \to S$, where S is a set of distinct colors and a vertex coloring f is said to be *proper*, if adjacent vertices of G receive distinct colors of S: that is, if u, v are adjacent in G, then $f(u) \neq f(v)$ (Balakrishnan & Ranganathan, 2000, p. 129). Recall from Balakrishnan and Ranganathan (2000, Definition 7.1.3) that the *chromatic number* of G, denoted by $\chi(G)$, is the minimum number of colors needed for a proper vertex coloring of G. It is well known that $\omega(G) \leq \chi(G)$.

Let $G = (V, E)$ be a graph. Recall from Balakrishnan and Ranganathan (2000, Definition 5.1.1) that a subset S of V is called *independent* if no two vertices of G are adjacent in G. $S \subseteq V$ is a *maximum independent set* of G if G has no independent set S' with $|S'| > |S|$. The number of vertices in a maximum independent set of G is called the *independence number* of G and is denoted by $\alpha(G)$ (Balakrishnan & Ranganathan, 2000, Definition 5.1.4). It is well known that for any simple graph G, $\alpha(G) = \omega(G^c)$ (Balakrishnan & Ranganathan, 2000, p. 186).

The clique number and chromatic number of zero-divisor graphs of commutative rings have been studied by several researchers Anderson et al. (2001), Anderson and Naseer (1993), Beck (1988), Smith (2003). A good account of the work done on the clique number and chromatic number of the zero-divisor graphs of commutative rings has been given in Anderson et al. (2011). Let $n \in \{1, 2, 3\}$. Rings R such that $\omega(\Gamma(R)) = n$ as determined by Beck (1988), and by Anderson and Naseer (1993) were listed in (2011). Moreover, Smith (2003) has classified all finite commutative nonlocal rings R such that $\omega(\Gamma(R)) = 4$. Section 3 of Visweswaran (2011) contains some results on the clique number of $(\Gamma(R))^c$. The study of the clique number and the chromatic number of the annihilating-ideal graph of a commutative ring was carried out in Aalipour et al. (2012), Behboodi and Rakeei (2011b). Let $n \in \{1, 2, 3, 4\}$. Inspired by the above-mentioned works, in this article, we try to classify commutative rings R such that $\omega((\mathbb{AG}(R))^c) = n$. We are also interested to determine the least integer $m \geq 2$

with $\omega((\mathbb{AG}(R))^c) = m < \chi((\mathbb{AG}(R))^c)$. Observe that $\omega((\mathbb{AG}(R))^c) = \alpha(\mathbb{AG}(R))$. As is suggested by the referee, we focus our study on classifying rings R such that $\alpha(\mathbb{AG}(R)) \in \{1, 2, 3, 4\}$.

It is useful to recall the following results from commutative ring theory that we use in this article. Let I be an ideal of a ring R with $I \neq R$. A prime ideal $\mathfrak{p}$ of R is said to be a *maximal N-prime* of I, if $\mathfrak{p}$ is maximal with respect to the property of being contained in $Z_R(R/I) = \{r \in R | rx \in I \text{ for some } x \in R\backslash I\}$ (Heinzer & Ohm, 1972). Thus a prime ideal $\mathfrak{p}$ of R is a maximal N-prime of (0) if $\mathfrak{p}$ is maximal with respect to the property of being contained in $Z(R)$. Observe that $S = R\backslash Z(R)$ is a multiplicatively closed subset of R. Let $x \in Z(R)$. Then $Rx \cap S = \emptyset$. Hence, it follows from Zorn's lemma and (Kaplansky, 1974, Theorem 1) that there exists a maximal N-prime $\mathfrak{p}$ of (0) in R such that $x \in \mathfrak{p}$. Therefore, we obtain that $Z(R) = \cup_{\alpha\in\Lambda}\mathfrak{p}_\alpha$, where $\{\mathfrak{p}_\alpha\}_{\alpha\in\Lambda}$ is the set of all maximal N-primes of (0) in R.

Recall that a principal ideal ring is a *special principal ideal ring* (SPIR) if it has a unique prime ideal. If R is a SPIR with $\mathfrak{m}$ as its only prime ideal, then we denote it using the notation $(R, \mathfrak{m})$ is a SPIR.

We say that a graph G satisfies (C) if G does not contain any infinite clique. Let R be a ring. In this article, we often use some of the results that were proved in Visweswaran and Patel (2015) on rings R such that $(\mathbb{AG}(R))^c$ satisfies (C). Let R be a ring with at least two maximal N-primes of (0). It is proved in Visweswaran and Patel (2015, Theorem 3.1) that $(\mathbb{AG}(R))^c$ satisfies (C) if and only if $R \cong R_1 \times R_2 \times \cdots \times R_n$ as rings for some $n \geq 2$, where $(R_i, \mathfrak{m}_i)$ is a local ring which admits only a finite number of ideals for each $i \in \{1, 2, \ldots, n\}$, if and only if $\omega((\mathbb{AG}(R))^c) < \infty$. Moreover, for a ring R with exactly one maximal N-prime of (0), it is not known whether the conditions that $(\mathbb{AG}(R))^c$ satisfies (C) and $\omega((\mathbb{AG}(R))^c) < \infty$ are equivalent. Motivated by Visweswaran and Patel (2015, Theorem 3.1), we propose to find the precise characterization of rings R, at least for smaller values of $\alpha(\mathbb{AG}(R))$. In Section 2 of this article, we classify rings R such that $\alpha(\mathbb{AG}(R)) = n$, where $n \in \{1, 2\}$. In Section 3, we focus our study on classifying rings R such that $\alpha(\mathbb{AG}(R)) = 3$. We devote Section 4 of this article on the problem of classifying rings R such that $\alpha(\mathbb{AG}(R)) = 4$.

We denote the nilradical of a ring R by *nil(R)*. A ring R with a unique maximal ideal is referred to as quasilocal and a ring R with only a finite number of maximal ideals is referred to as semiquasilocal. A Noetherian quasilocal (respectively, a semiquasilocal) ring R is referred to as local (respectively, semilocal). We use $|A|$ to denote the cardinality of a set A.

2. Classification of rings R such that $\alpha(\mathbb{AG}(R)) \in \{1, 2\}$

We start this section with the following lemma.

LEMMA 2.1 *Let R be a ring which admits at least n maximal N-primes of (0) with $n \geq 3$. Then $\alpha(\mathbb{AG}(R)) \geq n$.*

Proof The conclusion of the lemma holds if $\mathbb{AG}(R)$ contains an infinite independent set. Hence, we can assume that $\mathbb{AG}(R)$ does not admit any infinite independent set. In such a case, we know from Visweswaran and Patel (2015, Theorem 3.1) (the statement of this theorem is already stated in the introduction) that R is necessarily Artinian. Therefore, each proper ideal of R is an annihilating ideal. Let $\{\mathfrak{m}_1, \mathfrak{m}_2, \mathfrak{m}_3, \ldots, \mathfrak{m}_n\}(n \geq 3)$ be a subset of the set of all maximal ideals R. Let $i \in \{1, 2, 3, \ldots, n\}$. Let $A_i = \{1, 2, 3, \ldots, n\}\backslash\{i\}$. Since any two distinct maximal ideals R are not comparable under the inclusion relation, it follows from Prime avoidance lemma (Atiyah & Macdonald, 1969, Proposition 1.11(i)) that $\mathfrak{m}_i \not\subseteq \cup_{j\in A_i}\mathfrak{m}_j$. Hence, for each $i \in \{1, 2, 3, \ldots, n\}$, there exists $x_i \in \mathfrak{m}_i$ but $x_i \notin \cup_{j\in A_i}\mathfrak{m}_j$. It is clear that $Rx_i \neq Rx_j$ for all distinct $i, j \in \{1, 2, 3, \ldots, n\}$. Let $i, j \in \{1, 2, 3, \ldots, n\}$, $i \neq j$. Since $n \geq 3$, there exists $k \in \{1, 2, 3, \ldots, n\}\backslash\{i, j\}$. Observe that $x_i, x_j \notin \mathfrak{m}_k$ and hence, $x_ix_j \neq 0$. It is evident from the above discussion that $\{Rx_i | i \in \{1, 2, 3, \ldots, n\}\}$ is an independent set of $\mathbb{AG}(R)$. This proves that $\alpha(\mathbb{AG}(R)) \geq n$. □

In this section, our interest is to classify rings R such that $\alpha(\mathbb{AG}(R)) \in \{1, 2\}$. In view of Visweswaran and Patel (2015, Theorem 3.1), we assume in the hypothesis of many of the auxillary results we prove in this section that R is a finite direct product of rings.

LEMMA 2.2 *Let $n \geq 2$ and let $(R_i, \mathfrak{m}_i)$ be a quasilocal ring for each $i \in \{1,2,\ldots,n\}$ such that $\mathfrak{m}_i$ is an annihilating ideal for each i. Let $R = R_1 \times R_2 \times \cdots \times R_n$ be their direct product. Then the following hold:*

(i) Let $k \geq 1$. If $\alpha(\mathbb{AG}(R_i)) \geq k$ for some $i \in \{1,2,\ldots,n\}$, then $\alpha(\mathbb{AG}(R)) \geq k+1$. In particular, if $\mathfrak{m}_i \neq (0)$ for some $i \in \{1,2,\ldots,n\}$, then $\alpha(\mathbb{AG}(R)) \geq 2$.

(ii) If $\mathfrak{m}_i \neq (0)$ and $\mathfrak{m}_j \neq (0)$ for some distinct $i,j \in \{1,2,\ldots,n\}$, then $\alpha(\mathbb{AG}(R)) \geq 4$. If in addition, either $\mathfrak{m}_i^2 \neq (0)$ or $\mathfrak{m}_j^2 \neq (0)$, then $\alpha(\mathbb{AG}(R)) \geq 5$.

(iii) If $dim_{R_i/\mathfrak{m}_i}(\mathfrak{m}_i/\mathfrak{m}_i^2) \geq 2$ for some $i \in \{1,2,\ldots,n\}$, then $\alpha(\mathbb{AG}(R)) \geq 5$.

(iv) Let $n \geq 3$. If $\mathfrak{m}_i \neq (0)$ for some $i \in \{1,2,3,\ldots,n\}$, then $\alpha(\mathbb{AG}(R)) \geq 5$.

Proof

(i) Without loss of generality, we can assume that $\alpha(\mathbb{AG}(R_1)) \geq k$. Let $\{I_{11},\ldots,I_{1k}\}$ be an independent set of $\mathbb{AG}(R_1)$. Let $I_i = I_{1i} \times R_2 \times (0) \times \cdots \times (0)$ for each $i \in \{1,\ldots,k\}$ and $I_{k+1} = (0) \times R_2 \times (0) \times \cdots \times (0)$. It is clear that $\{I_1, I_2 \ldots, I_{k+1}\}$ is an independent set of $\mathbb{AG}(R)$. This shows that $\alpha(\mathbb{AG}(R)) \geq k+1$. If $\mathfrak{m}_i \neq (0)$ for some $i \in \{1,2,\ldots,n\}$, then $\alpha(\mathbb{AG}(R_i)) \geq 1$ and hence, $\alpha(\mathbb{AG}(R)) \geq 2$.

(ii) Without loss of generality, we can assume that $\mathfrak{m}_1 \neq (0)$ and $\mathfrak{m}_2 \neq (0)$. Let $I_1 = \mathfrak{m}_1 \times R_2 \times (0) \times \cdots \times (0), I_2 = R_1 \times (0) \times (0) \times \cdots \times (0), I_3 = R_1 \times \mathfrak{m}_2 \times (0) \times \cdots \times (0)$, and $I_4 = \mathfrak{m}_1 \times \mathfrak{m}_2 \times (0) \times \cdots \times (0)$. It is clear that $\{I_1, I_2, I_3, I_4\}$ is an independent set of $\mathbb{AG}(R)$. Hence, $\alpha(\mathbb{AG}(R)) \geq 4$. We can assume without loss of generality that $\mathfrak{m}_1^2 \neq (0)$. Let I_1, I_2, I_3, I_4 be as in as above and let $I_5 = \mathfrak{m}_1 \times (0) \times (0) \times \cdots \times (0)$. Note that the $\{I_1, I_2, I_3, I_4, I_5\}$ is an independent set of $\mathbb{AG}(R)$. Therefore, $\alpha(\mathbb{AG}(R)) \geq 5$.

(iii) Without loss of generality, we can assume that $dim_{R_1/\mathfrak{m}_1}(\mathfrak{m}_1/\mathfrak{m}_1^2) \geq 2$. Then there exist elements $x, y \in \mathfrak{m}_1$ such that $\{x + \mathfrak{m}_1^2, y + \mathfrak{m}_1^2\}$ is linearly independent over $R_1/\mathfrak{m}_1$. Let $I_1 = \mathfrak{m}_1 \times R_2 \times (0) \times \cdots \times (0), I_2 = R_1 x \times R_2 \times (0) \times \cdots \times (0), I_3 = R_1 y \times R_2 \times (0) \times \cdots \times (0)$, $I_4 = R_1(x+y) \times R_2 \times (0) \times \cdots \times (0)$, and $I_5 = (0) \times R_2 \times (0) \times \cdots \times (0)$. Note that $\{I_1, I_2, I_3, I_4, I_5\}$ is an independent set of $\mathbb{AG}(R)$. Therefore, $\alpha(\mathbb{AG}(R)) \geq 5$.

(iv) We are assuming that $n \geq 3$. Without loss of generality, we can assume that $\mathfrak{m}_1 \neq (0)$. Let $I_1 = \mathfrak{m}_1 \times R_2 \times (0) \times \cdots \times (0), I_2 = \mathfrak{m}_1 \times R_2 \times R_3 \times (0) \times \cdots \times (0), I_3 = (0) \times R_2 \times (0) \times \cdots \times (0), I_4 = (0) \times R_2 \times R_3 \times \cdots \times (0)$, and $I_5 = R_1 \times R_2 \times (0) \times \cdots \times (0)$. Observe that $\{I_1, I_2, I_3, I_4, I_5\}$ is an independent set of $\mathbb{AG}(R)$. This shows that $\alpha(\mathbb{AG}(R)) \geq 5$. □

LEMMA 2.3 *Let $n \geq 4$ and let R_i be a ring for each $i \in \{1,2,\ldots,n\}$. Let $R = R_1 \times R_2 \times R_3 \times R_4 \times \cdots \times R_n$ be their direct product. Then $\alpha(\mathbb{AG}(R)) \geq 6$.*

Proof Let $I_1 = R_1 \times (0) \times (0) \times (0) \times \cdots \times (0), I_2 = R_1 \times R_2 \times (0) \times (0) \times \cdots \times (0), I_3 = R_1 \times (0) \times R_3 \times (0) \times \cdots \times (0), I_4 = R_1 \times R_2 \times R_3 \times (0) \times \cdots \times (0), I_5 = R_1 \times R_2 \times (0) \times R_4 \times \cdots \times (0)$, *and* $I_6 = R_1 \times (0) \times R_3 \times R_4 \times \cdots \times (0)$. *Observe that* $I_i \in A(R)^*$ *for each* $i \in \{1,2,3,4,5,6\}$ *and* $\{I_1, I_2, I_3, I_4, I_5, I_6\}$ *is an independent set of* $\mathbb{AG}(R)$. *This proves that* $\alpha(\mathbb{AG}(R)) \geq 6$. □

We next proceed to characterize rings R such that $\alpha(\mathbb{AG}(R)) = 1$. It follows from Lemma 2.1 that such rings R can admit at most two maximal N-primes of (0). In Propositions 2.4 and 2.6, we classify rings R such that $\alpha(\mathbb{AG}(R)) = 1$. In view of Visweswaran and Patel (2015, Theorem 3.1), whenever a ring R admits at least two maximal N-primes of (0) with $\alpha(\mathbb{AG}(R)) < \infty$, we assume that R is an Artinian ring.

Proposition 2.4 Let R be an Artinian ring which admits exactly two maximal ideals. Then the following statements are equivalent:

(i) $\alpha(\mathbb{AG}(R)) = 1$.

(ii) $R \cong \mathbb{F}_1 \times \mathbb{F}_2$ as rings, where $\mathbb{F}_i$ is a field for each $i \in \{1, 2\}$.

Proof (*i*) $\Rightarrow$ (*ii*) Let $\{\mathfrak{m}_1, \mathfrak{m}_2\}$ denote the set of all maximal ideals of R. Then $\mathfrak{m}_1 + \mathfrak{m}_2 = R$. Hence, there exist $a \in \mathfrak{m}_1$ and $b \in \mathfrak{m}_2$ such that $a + b = 1$. It is clear that $a \notin \mathfrak{m}_2$ and $b \notin \mathfrak{m}_1$. Let $x \in \mathfrak{m}_1 \cap \mathfrak{m}_2$. Since R is Artinian, any proper ideal of R is an annihilating ideal. Observe that $Rx, Ra, Rb \in \mathbb{A}(R)$, $Rx \neq Ra$ and $Rx \neq Rb$. It follows from $\alpha(\mathbb{AG}(R)) = 1$ that $ax = bx = 0$. Since $a + b = 1$, we get that $x = 0$. This shows that $\mathfrak{m}_1 \cap \mathfrak{m}_2 = (0)$. Hence, it follows from the Chinese remainder theorem (Atiyah & Macdonald, 1969, Proposition 1.10(ii) and (iii)) that the mapping $f{:}R \to R/\mathfrak{m}_1 \times R/\mathfrak{m}_2$ defined by $f(r) = (r + \mathfrak{m}_1, r + \mathfrak{m}_2)$ is an isomorphism of rings. Thus with $\mathbb{F}_i = R/\mathfrak{m}_i$ for each $i \in \{1, 2\}$, we obtain that $\mathbb{F}_1, \mathbb{F}_2$ are fields and $R \cong \mathbb{F}_1 \times \mathbb{F}_2$ as rings.

(*ii*) $\Rightarrow$ (*i*) This is obvious. □

Remark 2.5 Let R be a ring. Let $a, b \in R$ be such that $ab \neq 0$. If $Ra \subseteq Rb$, then $b^2 \neq 0$.

Proof This is obvious. □

We state Visweswaran and Patel (2015, Remark 3.5(ii)) here as we use it in the proof of Proposition 2.6. Let R be a ring which admits $\mathfrak{p}$ as its unique maximal N-prime of (0). If $(\mathbb{AG}(R))^c$ satisfies (*C*) and $p^2 \neq 0$ for some $p \in \mathfrak{p}$, then R is necessarily a local Artinian ring with $\mathfrak{p}$ as its unique maximal ideal.

Proposition 2.6 Let R be a ring which admits $\mathfrak{p}$ as its unique maximal N-prime of (0). Then the following statements are equivalent:

(i) $\alpha(\mathbb{AG}(R)) = 1$.

(ii) Either $\mathfrak{p}^2 = (0)$, or $(R, \mathfrak{p})$ is a SPIR with $\mathfrak{p}^3 = (0)$ but $\mathfrak{p}^2 \neq (0)$.

Proof (*i*) $\Rightarrow$ (*ii*) Observe that $Z(R) = \mathfrak{p}$. Suppose that $\mathfrak{p}^2 \neq (0)$. Then there exist $p_1, p_2 \in \mathfrak{p}$ such that $p_1p_2 \neq 0$. Hence, $(Rp_1)(Rp_2) \neq (0)$. As $\alpha(\mathbb{AG}(R)) = 1$, it follows that $Rp_1 = Rp_2$. Therefore, from Remark 2.5, we obtain that $p_1^2 \neq 0$ and $p_2^2 \neq 0$. It follows from Visweswaran and Patel (2015, Remark 3.5(ii)) that R is a local Artinian ring with $\mathfrak{p}$ as its unique maximal ideal. Hence, $\mathfrak{p} \in A(R)^*$. From $\mathfrak{p}(Rp_1) \neq (0)$, we obtain that $\mathfrak{p} = Rp_1$. As $\mathfrak{p} = Rp_1 \neq Rp_1^2$, it follows that $\mathfrak{p}^3 = (Rp_1)(Rp_1^2) = (0)$. Hence, it follows from (*iii*) $\Rightarrow$ (*i*) of (Atiyah & Macdonald, 1969, Proposition 8.8) that $\{\mathfrak{p}, \mathfrak{p}^2\}$ is the set of all nonzero proper ideals of R. Therefore, $(R, \mathfrak{p})$ is a SPIR with $\mathfrak{p}^2 \neq (0)$ but $\mathfrak{p}^3 = (0)$.

(*ii*) $\Rightarrow$ (*i*) If $\mathfrak{p}^2 = (0)$, then $IJ = (0)$ for all $I, J \in \mathbb{A}(R)$. Otherwise, $(R, \mathfrak{p})$ is a SPIR with $\{\mathfrak{p}, \mathfrak{p}^2\}$ as its set of all nonzero proper ideals and $\mathfrak{p}^3 = (0)$. Therefore, $\alpha(\mathbb{AG}(R)) = 1$. □

Proposition 2.7 Let $T = S \times \mathbb{F}$, where $(S, \mathfrak{m})$ is a SPIR and $\mathbb{F}$ is a field. Let $n \geq 2$ be the least integer with $\mathfrak{m}^n = (0)$. Then $\alpha(\mathbb{AG}(T)) = \chi((\mathbb{AG}(T))^c) = n$.

Proof Let $n = 2$. Then $\mathbb{A}(T)^* = \{(0) \times \mathbb{F}, \mathfrak{m} \times (0), \mathfrak{m} \times \mathbb{F}, S \times (0)\}$. It is clear that $(\mathbb{AG}(T))^c$ is the path $(0) \times \mathbb{F} - \mathfrak{m} \times \mathbb{F} - S \times (0) - \mathfrak{m} \times (0)$. Therefore, $\alpha(\mathbb{AG}(T)) = \chi((\mathbb{AG}(T))^c) = 2$. So, we can assume that $n \geq 3$. We consider two cases.

Case(i). $n = 2k$ is even

Note that $k \geq 2$. Let $\mathcal{A} = \{\mathfrak{m}^i \times (0) | i \in \{1, \dots, n-1\}\} \cup \{S \times (0)\}$, $\mathcal{B} = \{\mathfrak{m}^j \times \mathbb{F} | j \in \{1, \dots, n\}\}$. It is clear that $\mathbb{A}(T)^* = \mathcal{A} \cup \mathcal{B}$. Let $i \in \{1, \dots, k\}$ and let $I_i = \mathfrak{m}^i \times (0)$. Let $j \in \{1, \dots, k-1\}$ and let $J_j = \mathfrak{m}^j \times \mathbb{F}$. Observe that $W = \{I_i | i \in \{1, \dots, k\}\} \cup \{J_j | j \in \{1, \dots, k-1\}\} \cup \{S \times (0)\}$ is an independent set of $\mathbb{AG}(T)$. Since W contains exactly $n = 2k$ elements, it follows that $\alpha(\mathbb{AG}(T)) \geq n$. We next show that there exists a proper vertex coloring of $(\mathbb{AG}(T))^c$ that makes use of n colors. Let $\{c_1, c_2, \dots c_k, c_{k+1}, \dots, c_{2k}\}$ be a set of n distinct colors. We now color the vertices of $(\mathbb{AG}(T))^c$ as follows: Let us assign the color c_i to $I_i = \mathfrak{m}^i \times (0)$ for each $i \in \{1, \dots, k\}$. Let the color c_{k+j} be assigned to $J_j = \mathfrak{m}^j \times \mathbb{F}$ for each $j \in \{1, \dots, k-1\}$ and color the vertex $S \times (0)$ using c_{2k}. We next assign colors to the vertices of $(\mathbb{AG}(T))^c$ which are not in W. Let us assign the color c_i to $\mathfrak{m}^{2k-i} \times \mathbb{F}$ for each $i \in \{1, \dots, k\}$. Let us assign the color c_{k+j} to $\mathfrak{m}^{2k-j} \times (0)$ for each $j \in \{1, \dots, k-1\}$. Let the color c_{2k} be assigned to $(0) \times \mathbb{F}$. It is easy to verify that the above-described assignment of colors using n colors is indeed a proper vertex coloring of $(\mathbb{AG}(T))^c$. Thus $\chi((\mathbb{AG}(T))^c) \leq n \leq \alpha(\mathbb{AG}(T)) \leq \chi((\mathbb{AG}(T))^c)$. Therefore, $\alpha(\mathbb{AG}(T)) = \chi((\mathbb{AG}(T))^c) = n$.

Case(ii). $n = 2k + 1$ is odd

Observe that $k \geq 1$. Note that $\{I_i = \mathfrak{m}^i \times (0) | i \in \{1, \dots, k\}\} \cup \{J_i = \mathfrak{m}^i \times \mathbb{F} | i \in \{1, \dots, k\}\} \cup \{S \times (0)\}$ is an independent set of $\mathbb{AG}(T)$. Hence, $\alpha(\mathbb{AG}(T)) \geq 2k + 1 = n$. Let $\{c_1, \dots, c_k, \dots, c_{2k}, c_{2k+1}\}$ be a set of n distinct colors. Let us now assign colors to the vertices of $(\mathbb{AG}(T))^c$ as follows: Let us assign the color c_i to I_i for each $i \in \{1, \dots, k\}$. Let us assign the color c_{k+i} to J_i for each $i \in \{1, \dots, k\}$. Let the color c_{2k+1} be assigned to $S \times (0)$. Let the color c_i be assigned to $\mathfrak{m}^{n-i} \times \mathbb{F}$ for each $i \in \{1, \dots, k\}$. Let the color c_{k+i} be assigned to $\mathfrak{m}^{n-i} \times (0)$ for each $i \in \{1, \dots, k\}$. Let the color c_{2k+1} be assigned to $(0) \times \mathbb{F}$. It is easy to show that the above-described vertex coloring of $(\mathbb{AG}(T))^c$ using n colors is in fact a proper coloring. Thus $\chi((\mathbb{AG}(T))^c) \leq n \leq \alpha(\mathbb{AG}(T)) \leq \chi((\mathbb{AG}(T))^c)$. Therefore, $\alpha(\mathbb{AG}(T)) = \chi((\mathbb{AG}(T))^c) = n$. □

Proposition 2.8 Let R be an Artinian ring which admits exactly two maximal ideals. Then the following statements are equivalent:

(i) $\alpha(\mathbb{AG}(T)) = 2$.

(ii) $R \cong S \times \mathbb{F}$ as rings, where $(S, \mathfrak{m})$ is a SPIR with $\mathfrak{m} \neq (0)$ but $\mathfrak{m}^2 = (0)$ and $\mathbb{F}$ is a field.

Proof (*i*) ⇒ (*ii*) It follows from (Atiyah & Macdonald, 1969, Theorem 8.7) that $R \cong R_1 \times R_2$ as rings, where $(R_i, \mathfrak{m}_i)$ is a local Artinian ring for each $i \in \{1, 2\}$. Since $\alpha(\mathbb{AG}(R_1 \times R_2)) = 2$, it follows that at least one between R_1 and R_2 cannot be a field. Without loss of generality, we can assume that R_1 is not a field. Moreover, we obtain from Lemma 2.2(ii) that R_2 must be a field. Furthermore, it follows from Lemma 2.2(iii) and (Atiyah & Macdonald, 1969, Proposition 2.8) that $\mathfrak{m}_1$ is principal. Thus $(R_1, \mathfrak{m}_1)$ is a SPIR. It is now clear from Proposition 2.7 that $\mathfrak{m}_1^2 = (0)$. With $S = R_1, \mathfrak{m} = \mathfrak{m}_1$, and $\mathbb{F} = R_2$, we obtain that $(S, \mathfrak{m})$ is a SPIR with $\mathfrak{m} \neq (0)$ but $\mathfrak{m}^2 = (0)$, $\mathbb{F}$ is a field, and $R \cong S \times \mathbb{F}$ as rings.

(*ii*) ⇒ (*ii*) This follows immediately from Proposition 2.7. □

For the sake of convenient reference, we state Visweswaran and Patel (2015, Lemmas 2.1 and 2.2), which we use in the proof of Lemma 2.9. Let R be a ring. If $(\mathbb{AG}(R))^c$ satisfies (C), then $nil(R) = \cap_{\alpha \in \Lambda} \mathfrak{p}_\alpha$, where $\{\mathfrak{p}_\alpha\}_{\alpha \in \Lambda}$ is the set of all maximal N-primes of (0) in R Visweswaran and Patel (2015, Lemma 2.1). If $(\mathbb{AG}(R))^c$ satisfies (C), then $nil(R) \in \mathbb{A}(R)$ Visweswaran and Patel (2015, Lemma 2.2).

LEMMA 2.9 *Let R be a ring which admits $\mathfrak{p}$ as its unique maximal N-prime of (0). If $\alpha(\mathbb{AG}(R)) = 2$, then $\mathfrak{p}$ is principal.*

Proof We know from Visweswaran and Patel (2015, Lemmas 2.1 and 2.2) that $\mathfrak{p} = nil(R)$ and $\mathfrak{p} \in \mathbb{A}(R)$. Suppose that $\mathfrak{p}$ is not principal. Observe that any independent set of $\mathbb{AG}(R)$ containing exactly two elements must contain $\mathfrak{p}$ as a member. Let $\{\mathfrak{p}, J\}$ be an independent set of $\mathbb{AG}(R)$. From $\mathfrak{p}J \neq (0)$, it follows that $\mathfrak{p}^2 \neq (0)$. Hence, there exist $p_1, p_2 \in \mathfrak{p}$ such that $p_1 p_2 \neq 0$. Therefore, $(Rp_1)(Rp_2) \neq (0)$. Since $\mathfrak{p} \neq Rp_i$ for each $i \in \{1, 2\}$ and $\alpha(\mathbb{AG}(R)) = 2$, it follows that $Rp_1 = Rp_2$. Therefore, we obtain from Remark 2.5 that $p_1^2 \neq 0$ and $p_2^2 \neq 0$. Let $p \in \mathfrak{p} \backslash Rp_1$. Since $\mathfrak{p} \notin \{Rp, Rp_1\}$, it follows that $p_1 p = 0$. Observe that $\{\mathfrak{p}, Rp_1, R(p_1 + p)\}$ is an independent set of $\mathbb{AG}(R)$. This is in contradiction to the assumption that $\alpha(\mathbb{AG}(R)) = 2$. Therefore, $\mathfrak{p}$ is principal. □

Using Visweswaran and Patel (2015, Remark 3.5(ii)), Lemma 2.9, and (2015, Proposition 3.7), it is not hard to prove Proposition 2.10. We state Visweswaran and Patel (2015, Proposition 3.7) for the sake of convenience. Let $(R, \mathfrak{m})$ be a SPIR with $\mathfrak{m}^2 \neq (0)$. Let $n \geq 3$ be the least integer with $\mathfrak{m}^n = (0)$. Then $\omega((\mathbb{AG}(R))^c) = \chi((\mathbb{AG}(R))^c) = [n/2]$, where $[n / 2]$ is the integral part of $n / 2$.

Proposition 2.10 Let R be a ring which admits $\mathfrak{p}$ as its unique maximal N-prime of (0). Then the following statements are equivalent:

(i) $\alpha(\mathbb{AG}(R)) = 2$.

(ii) $(R, \mathfrak{p})$ is a SPIR with either $\mathfrak{p}^4 = (0)$ but $\mathfrak{p}^3 \neq (0)$ or $\mathfrak{p}^5 = (0)$ but $\mathfrak{p}^4 \neq (0)$.

3. Classification of rings R such that $\alpha(\mathbb{AG}(R)) = 3$

The aim of this section was to classify rings R such that $\alpha(\mathbb{AG}(R)) = 3$. It follows from Lemma 2.1 that such rings R can admit at most three maximal N-primes of (0). We use *(ii)* ⇒ *(iii)* of Visweswaran and Patel (2015, Theorem 3.2) in the proof of Proposition 3.1. The statement of *(ii)* ⇒ *(iii)* of Visweswaran and Patel (2015, Theorem 3.2) is as follows: Let $n \geq 2$ and let $\mathbb{F}_i$ be a field for each $i \in \{1, 2, 3, \ldots, n\}$. Let $R = \mathbb{F}_1 \times \mathbb{F}_2 \times \cdots \times \mathbb{F}_n$. Then $\omega((\mathbb{AG}(R))^c) = \chi((\mathbb{AG}(R))^c) = 2^{n-1} - 1$.

Proposition 3.1 Let R be an Artinian ring which admits exactly three maximal ideals. Then the following statements are equivalent:

(i) $\alpha(\mathbb{AG}(R)) = 3$.

(ii) $R \cong \mathbb{F}_1 \times \mathbb{F}_2 \times \mathbb{F}_3$ as rings, where $\mathbb{F}_i$ is a field for each $i \in \{1, 2, 3\}$.

Proof It follows from (Atiyah & Macdonald, 1969, Theorem 8.7) that $R \cong R_1 \times R_2 \times R_3$ as rings, where $(R_i, \mathfrak{m}_i)$ is a local Artinian ring. From $\alpha(\mathbb{AG}(R_1 \times R_2 \times R_3)) = 3$, we obtain from Lemma 2.2(iv) that R_i is a field for each $i \in \{1, 2, 3\}$. With $\mathbb{F}_i = R_i$ for each $i \in \{1, 2, 3\}$, we obtain that $\mathbb{F}_i$ is a field and $R \cong \mathbb{F}_1 \times \mathbb{F}_2 \times \mathbb{F}_3$ as rings.

(ii) ⇒ *(i)* This is an immediate corollary to *(ii)* ⇒ *(iii)* of Visweswaran and Patel (2015, Theorem 3.2). □

Proposition 3.2 Let R be an Artinian ring with exactly two maximal ideals. Then the following statements are equivalent:

(i) $\alpha(\mathbb{AG}(R)) = 3$.

(ii) $R \cong S \times \mathbb{F}$ as rings, where $(S, \mathfrak{m})$ is a SPIR with $\mathfrak{m}^2 \neq (0)$ but $\mathfrak{m}^3 = (0)$ and $\mathbb{F}$ is a field.

Proof *(i)* ⇒ *(ii)* From (Atiyah & Macdonald, 1969, Theorem 3.1), we obtain that $R \cong R_1 \times R_2$ as rings, where $(R_i, \mathfrak{m}_i)$ is a local Artinian ring for each $i \in \{1, 2\}$. From $\alpha(\mathbb{AG}(R_1 \times R_2)) = 3$, it follows that at least one between R_1 and R_2 cannot be a field. Without loss of generality, we can assume that R_1 is not a field. Observe that we obtain from Lemma 2.2(ii) that R_2 must be a field. Moreover, it follows from Lemma 2.2(iii) and (Atiyah & Macdonald, 1969, Proposition 2.8) that $\mathfrak{m}_1$ is principal. Hence, $(R_1, \mathfrak{m}_1)$ is a SPIR. Furthermore, we obtain from Proposition 2.7 that $\mathfrak{m}_1^2 \neq (0)$ but $\mathfrak{m}_1^3 = (0)$. With $S = R_1, \mathfrak{m} = \mathfrak{m}_1$, and $\mathbb{F} = R_2$, it follows that $R \cong S \times \mathbb{F}$ as rings, where $(S, \mathfrak{m})$ is a SPIR with $\mathfrak{m}^2 \neq (0)$ but $\mathfrak{m}^3 = (0)$ and $\mathbb{F}$ is a field.

(ii) ⇒ *(i)* This follows from Proposition 2.7. □

Let R be a ring which admits a unique maximal N-prime of (0). We next proceed to classify such rings R for which $\alpha(\mathbb{AG}(R)) = 3$. We need several prelimary results to obtain the required classification. We state and prove them in the form of several lemmas.

LEMMA 3.3 *Let R be a ring which admits $\mathfrak{p}$ as its unique maximal N-prime of (0). If $\alpha(\mathbb{AG}(R)) = 3$, then $p^2 \neq 0$ for some $p \in \mathfrak{p}$.*

Proof It follows from Visweswaran and Patel (2015, Lemmas 2.1 and 2.2) that $\mathfrak{p} = nil(R) \in \mathbb{A}(R)$. Let $\{I, J, K\}$ be an independent set of $\mathbb{AG}(R)$. From $IJ \neq (0)$, it follows that $\mathfrak{p}^2 \neq (0)$. If $\mathfrak{p}$ is principal, then it is clear that $p^2 \neq 0$ for some $p \in \mathfrak{p}$. So we can assume that $\mathfrak{p}$ is not principal. From $\mathfrak{p}^2 \neq (0)$, it follows that there exist $p_1, p_2 \in \mathfrak{p}$ such that $p_1p_2 \neq 0$. We claim that either $p_1^2 \neq 0$ or $p_2^2 \neq 0$. Suppose that $p_1^2 = p_2^2 = 0$. Then it follows from Remark 2.5 that $Rp_1 \not\subseteq Rp_2$ and $Rp_2 \not\subseteq Rp_1$. Hence, $R(p_1 + p_2) \notin \{Rp_1, Rp_2\}$. Note that $\{Rp_1, Rp_2, R(p_1 + p_2), \mathfrak{p}\}$ is an independent set of $\mathbb{AG}(R)$. This is in contradiction to the assumption that $\alpha(\mathbb{AG}(R)) = 3$. Therefore, either $p_1^2 \neq 0$ or $p_2^2 \neq 0$. □

It follows from Lemma 3.3 and Visweswaran and Patel (2015, Remark 3.5(ii)) that if a ring R which admits $\mathfrak{p}$ as its unique maximal N-prime of (0) is such that $\alpha(\mathbb{AG}(R)) = 3$, then R is necessarily a local Artinian ring with $\mathfrak{p}$ as its unique maximal ideal.

LEMMA 3.4 *Let $(R, \mathfrak{m})$ be a local Artinian ring with $\mathfrak{m}^2 \neq (0)$. If $\alpha(\mathbb{AG}(R)) \leq 4$, then $\mathfrak{m}$ is generated by at most two elements.*

Proof If $\mathfrak{m}$ requires more than two generators, then $n = dim_{R/\mathfrak{m}}(\mathfrak{m}/\mathfrak{m}^2) \geq 3$.. Let $\{m_i | i \in \{1, 2, 3, \ldots, n\}\} \subseteq \mathfrak{m}$ be such that $\{m_i + \mathfrak{m}^2 | i \in \{1, 2, 3, \ldots, n\}\}$ is a basis of $\mathfrak{m}/\mathfrak{m}^2$ as a vector space over $R/\mathfrak{m}$. Then it follows from (Atiyah & Macdonald, 1969, Proposition 2.8) that $\mathfrak{m} = \sum_{i=1}^{n} Rm_i$. From $\mathfrak{m}^2 \neq (0)$, it follows that either $m_i^2 \neq 0$ for some $i \in \{1, 2, 3, \ldots, n\}$ or $m_im_j \neq 0$ for some distinct $i, j \in \{1, 2, 3, \ldots, n\}$.

Case(i). $m_i^2 \neq 0$ for some $i \in \{1, 2, 3, \ldots, n\}$

Without loss of generality, we can assume that $m_1^2 \neq 0$. Note that $\{Rm_1, Rm_1 + Rm_2, Rm_1 + Rm_3, \mathfrak{m}\}$ is an independent set of $\mathbb{AG}(R)$. If either $m_1m_2 \neq 0$ or $m_1m_3 \neq 0$, then $\{Rm_1, Rm_1 + Rm_2, Rm_1 + Rm_3, Rm_2 + Rm_3, \mathfrak{m}\}$ is an independent set of $\mathbb{AG}(R)$. This is impossible since by hypothesis, $\alpha(\mathbb{AG}(R)) \leq 4$. Hence, $m_1m_2 = m_1m_3 = 0$. Note that $\{Rm_1, R(m_1 + m_2), Rm_1 + Rm_2, Rm_1 + Rm_3, \mathfrak{m}\}$ is an independent set of $\mathbb{AG}(R)$. This is impossible.

Case(ii). $m_im_j \neq 0$ for some distinct $i, j \in \{1, 2, 3, \ldots, n\}$

Without loss of generality, we can assume that $m_1m_2 \neq 0$. The impossibility of Case(i) implies that $m_1^2 = m_2^2 = 0$. Observe that $\{Rm_1, Rm_2, R(m_1 + m_2), Rm_1 + Rm_2, \mathfrak{m}\}$ is an independent set of $\mathbb{AG}(R)$. This is impossible.

This shows that $\mathfrak{m}$ is generated by at most two elements. □

Proposition 3.5 Let $(R, \mathfrak{m})$ be a local Artinian ring with $\mathfrak{m}^2 \neq (0)$. If $\mathfrak{m}$ is principal, then the following statements are equivalent:

(i) $\alpha(\mathbb{AG}(R)) = 3$.

(ii) $(R, \mathfrak{m})$ *is a SPIR with either* $\mathfrak{m}^6 = (0)$ *but* $\mathfrak{m}^5 \neq (0)$ *or* $\mathfrak{m}^7 = (0)$ *but* $\mathfrak{m}^6 \neq (0)$.

Proof The proof of this proposition follows immediately from *(iii)* ⇒ *(i)* of (Atiyah & Macdonald, 1969, Proposition 8.8) and Visweswaran and Patel (2015, Proposition 3.7). □

Let $R, \mathfrak{p}$ be as in the statement of Lemma 3.3. We next assume that $\mathfrak{p}$ is not principal and try to classify rings R in order that $\alpha(\mathbb{AG}(R)) = 3$. Initially, we derive several necessary conditions for $\alpha(\mathbb{AG}(R)) = 3$.

LEMMA 3.6 *Let $(R, \mathfrak{m})$ be a local Artinian ring . If $\mathfrak{m}$ is not principal and $\alpha(\mathbb{AG}(R)) = 3$, then $\mathfrak{m}^3 = (0)$.*

Proof We know from Lemma 3.4 that there exist $m_1, m_2 \in \mathfrak{m}$ such that $\mathfrak{m} = Rm_1 + Rm_2$. If $m_1^2 m_2 \neq 0$ and $m_2^2 m_1 \neq 0$, then we obtain that $\{Rm_1, Rm_2, Rm_1m_2, \mathfrak{m}\}$ is an independent set of $\mathbb{AG}(R)$. This contradicts the assumption that $\alpha(\mathbb{AG}(R)) = 3$. Hence, either $m_1^2 m_2 = 0$ or $m_2^2 m_1 = 0$. Without loss of generality, we can assume that $m_1^2 m_2 = 0$. We assert that $m_1 m_2^2 = 0$. This is clear if $m_1 m_2 = 0$. If $m_1 m_2 \neq 0$, then $\{Rm_1, Rm_2, \mathfrak{m}\}$ is an independent set of $\mathbb{AG}(R)$. Since $R(m_1 + m_2) \notin \{Rm_1, Rm_2, \mathfrak{m}\}$ and $\alpha(\mathbb{AG}(R)) = 3$, it follows that either $R(m_1 + m_2)Rm_1 = (0)$ or $R(m_1 + m_2)Rm_2 = (0)$. Therefore, either $(m_1 + m_2)m_1 = 0$ or $(m_1 + m_2)m_2 = 0$. From $m_1^2 m_2 = 0$, it follows that $m_1 m_2^2 = 0$. Thus $m_1^2 m_2 = m_1 m_2^2 = 0$. If $m_1^3 \neq 0$, then $\{Rm_1, Rm_1^2, R(m_1 + m_2), \mathfrak{m}\}$ is an independent set of $\mathbb{AG}(R)$. This is impossible since by assumption, $\alpha(\mathbb{AG}(R)) = 3$. Therefore, $m_1^3 = 0$. Similarly, we obtain that $m_2^3 = 0$. This proves that $\mathfrak{m}^3 = (0)$. □

Remark 3.7 Let $(R, \mathfrak{m})$ be a local Artinian ring. Suppose that $\mathfrak{m}$ is not principal. If $\alpha(\mathbb{AG}(R)) = 3$, then there exist $x, y \in \mathfrak{m}$ such that $\mathfrak{m} = Rx + Ry$ with $xy = 0$.

Proof The proof of this remark is contained in the proof of Lemma 3.6. □

LEMMA 3.8 *Let $(R, \mathfrak{m})$ be a local Artinian ring. Suppose that $\mathfrak{m}$ is not principal. If $\alpha(\mathbb{AG}(R)) = 3$, then $|R/\mathfrak{m}| \leq 3$ and moreover, $\mathfrak{m}^2$ is principal.*

Proof It is proved in Lemma 3.6 that $\mathfrak{m}^3 = (0)$. We know from Remark 3.7 that there exist $x, y \in \mathfrak{m}$ such that $\mathfrak{m} = Rx + Ry$ and $xy = 0$. Hence, $\mathfrak{m}^2 = Rx^2 + Ry^2$. Since $\mathfrak{m}^2 \neq (0)$, it follows that either $x^2 \neq 0$ or $y^2 \neq 0$. Without loss of generality, we can assume that $x^2 \neq 0$. Note that $\{Rx, R(x+y), \mathfrak{m}\}$ is an independent set of $\mathbb{AG}(R)$. Let $r \in R\backslash\mathfrak{m}$ be such that $r - 1 \notin \mathfrak{m}$. Then $R(x + ry) \notin \{Rx, R(x+y), \mathfrak{m}\}$. Since $\alpha(\mathbb{AG}(R)) = 3$ and $(x + ry)x = x^2 \neq 0$, it follows that $R(x+y)R(x+ry) = (0)$. This implies that $x^2 + ry^2 = 0$. Let $s \in R\backslash\mathfrak{m}$ be such that $s - 1 \notin \mathfrak{m}$. Then $x^2 + sy^2 = 0$. Hence, $(r - s)y^2 = 0$. If $r - s \notin \mathfrak{m}$, then we obtain $y^2 = 0$ and so from $x^2 + ry^2 = 0$, it follows that $x^2 = 0$. This is a contradiction. Therefore, $r - s \in \mathfrak{m}$. This proves that $|R/\mathfrak{m}| \leq 3$.

As in the previous paragraph, $\mathfrak{m} = Rx + Ry$ with $xy = 0$ but $x^2 \neq 0$. Moreover, $\mathfrak{m}^3 = (0)$. Now $\mathfrak{m}^2 = Rx^2 + Ry^2$. If $y^2 = 0$, then $\mathfrak{m}^2 = Rx^2$ is principal. Suppose that $y^2 \neq 0$. Observe that $\{Ry, R(x+y), \mathfrak{m}\}$ is an independent set of $\mathbb{AG}(R)$. Note that $(y + x^2)y = y^2 \neq 0$ and $(y + x^2)(x + y) = y^2 \neq 0$. Since $\alpha(\mathbb{AG}(R)) = 3$, it follows that $R(y + x^2) = Ry$. Hence, there exists a unit $u \in R$ such that $y = u(y + x^2)$. This implies that $(1 - u)y = ux^2$. Therefore, $u - 1 \in \mathfrak{m}$. Let $u = 1 + m$ for some $m \in \mathfrak{m}$. Therefore, $y = (1 + m)(y + x^2) = y + x^2 + my$. Let $m = ax + by$ for some $a, b \in R$. Then $y = y + x^2 + by^2$. Thus $x^2 + by^2 = 0$. Since $x^2 \neq 0$, it follows that $b \notin \mathfrak{m}$. Hence, $Ry^2 \subseteq Rx^2$ and so $\mathfrak{m}^2 = Rx^2 + Ry^2 = Rx^2$ is principal.

Indeed, in the case $|R/\mathfrak{m}| = 3$, we verify that $x^2 = y^2$. Note that $\{Rx, R(x+y), \mathfrak{m}\}$ is an independent set of $\mathbb{AG}(R)$. Since $\alpha(\mathbb{AG}(R)) = 3$ and $R(x - y) \notin \{Rx, R(x+y), \mathfrak{m}\}$, it follows that $R(x+y)R(x-y) = (0)$. This proves that $x^2 = y^2$. □

LEMMA 3.9 *Let $(R, \mathfrak{m})$ be a local Artinian ring . Suppose that $\mathfrak{m}$ is not principal. If $\alpha(\mathbb{AG}(R)) = 3$, then $|R| \in \{16, 81\}$.*

Proof Since $\mathfrak{m}$ is not principal, it follows from Lemma 3.4 that $dim_{R/\mathfrak{m}}(\mathfrak{m}/\mathfrak{m}^2) = 2$. We know from Lemma 3.6 that $\mathfrak{m}^3 = (0)$. From Lemma 3.8, we know that $|R/\mathfrak{m}| \leq 3$ and $\mathfrak{m}^2$ is principal. As $\mathfrak{m}^2$ is an one-dimensional vector space over $R/\mathfrak{m}$ and $|R/\mathfrak{m}| \in \{2, 3\}$, it follows that $|\mathfrak{m}^2| \in \{2, 3\}$. Since $\mathfrak{m}/\mathfrak{m}^2$ is a two-dimensional vector space over $R/\mathfrak{m}$, it follows that $|\mathfrak{m}/\mathfrak{m}^2| \in \{4, 9\}$. Hence, $|\mathfrak{m}| \in \{8, 27\}$ and therefore, $|R| \in \{16, 81\}$. □

For any prime number p and $n \geq 1$, we denote by $\mathbb{F}_{p^n}$, the finite field containing exactly p^n elements . For any $n \geq 2$, we denote by $\mathbb{Z}_n$, the ring of integers modulo n.

Remark 3.10 With the help of theorems proved by Corbas and Williams (2000a), Belshoff and Chapman (2007, p. 475) listed (up to isomorphism of rings) all finite commutative rings with identity which are local and of order 16 and there are 21 such rings. In this remark, with the help of the list given in Belshoff and Chapman (2007, p. 475), we list below (up to isomorphism of rings) all finite local rings $(R, \mathfrak{m})$ of order 16 such that $m^2 \neq 0$ for some $m \in \mathfrak{m}$, $\mathfrak{m}^3 = (0)$, $|R/\mathfrak{m}| = 2$, $|\mathfrak{m}/\mathfrak{m}^2| = 4$, and $|\mathfrak{m}^2| = 2$.

(i) $\mathbb{F}_2[x,y]/(x^3, xy, y^2)$

(ii) $\mathbb{F}_2[x,y]/(x^2 - y^2, xy)$

(iii) $\mathbb{Z}_4[x,y]/(x^2 - 2, xy, y^2, 2x)$

(iv) $\mathbb{Z}_4[x,y]/(x^2 - 2, xy, y^2 - 2, 2x)$

(v) $\mathbb{Z}_4[x]/(2x, x^3)$

(vi) $\mathbb{Z}_4[x]/(x^2 - 2x)$

(vii) $\mathbb{Z}_8[x]/(2x, x^2)$

(viii) $\mathbb{Z}_8[x]/(2x, x^2 - 4)$.

From Corbas and Williams (2000b), it is known that there are exactly (up to isomorphism of rings) 24 finite commutative rings with identity which are local and of order 81. We next list some finite local rings $(R, \mathfrak{m})$ of order 81 such that $m^2 \neq 0$ for some $m \in \mathfrak{m}$, $\mathfrak{m}^3 = (0)$, $|R/\mathfrak{m}| = 3$, $|\mathfrak{m}/\mathfrak{m}^2| = 9$, and $|\mathfrak{m}^2| = 3$.

(a) $\mathbb{F}_3[x,y]/(x^3, xy, y^2)$

(b) $\mathbb{F}_3[x,y]/(x^2 - y^2, xy)$

(c) $\mathbb{F}_3[x,y]/(x^2, y^2)$

(d) $\mathbb{Z}_9[x,y]/(x^2 - 3, xy, y^2, 3x)$

(e) $\mathbb{Z}_9[x,y]/(x^2 - 3, xy, y^2 - 3, 3x)$

(f) $\mathbb{Z}_9[x,y]/(x^2, xy - 3, y^2)$

(g) $\mathbb{Z}_9[x]/(3x, x^3)$

(h) $\mathbb{Z}_9[x]/(x^2)$

(i) $\mathbb{Z}_9[x]/(x^2 - 3x)$

(j) $\mathbb{Z}_{27}[x]/(3x, x^2)$

(k) $\mathbb{Z}_{27}[x]/(3x, x^2 - 9)$

(l) $\mathbb{Z}_{27}[x]/(3x, x^2 - 18)$

We verify in Example 3.12 that each one of the finite local ring R of order 16 mentioned in (i) to (viii) in Remark 3.10 satisfies $\alpha(\mathbb{AG}(R)) = 3$. We use Lemma 3.11 to verify Example 3.12.

LEMMA 3.11 *Let* $(R, \mathfrak{m})$ *be a local Artinian ring such that* $\mathfrak{m}$ *is not principal,* $\mathfrak{m} = Ra + Rb$ *for some* $a, b \in \mathfrak{m}$ *with* $ab = 0$ *but* $a^2 \neq 0$, $\mathfrak{m}^3 = (0)$, $|R/\mathfrak{m}| = 2$, *and* $\mathfrak{m}^2 = \{0, a^2\}$. *Then* $\alpha(\mathbb{AG}(R)) = \chi((\mathbb{AG}(R))^c) = 3$.

Proof It is clear that $|\mathfrak{m}| = 8$ and $|R| = 16$. Let $A = \{0, 1\}$. Note that $\mathfrak{m} = \{xa + yb + za^2 | x, y, z$ vary over $A\}$. Observe that $\{Ra, R(a+b), \mathfrak{m}\}$ is an independent set of $\mathbb{AG}(R)$. Hence, $\alpha(\mathbb{AG}(R)) \geq 3$. We next verify that $\chi((\mathbb{AG}(R))^c) = 3$.

We first determine the set of all nonzero proper ideals of R. Let I be any nonzero proper ideal of R. If $I \subseteq \mathfrak{m}^2 = Ra^2$, then it is clear that $I = \mathfrak{m}^2 = Ra^2$. Suppose that $I \not\subseteq \mathfrak{m}^2$. Then there exists $xa + yb + za^2 \in I$ for some $x, y, z \in A$ with at least one between x and y is equal to 1. We consider the following cases.

Case(i). $x = 1$

In this case, it follows from $ab = a^3 = 0$ that $a^2 = (a + yb + za^2)a \in I$. As $\mathfrak{m}^2 \subset I$, we get that $dim_{R/\mathfrak{m}}(I/\mathfrak{m}^2) = 1$ or 2. If $dim_{R/\mathfrak{m}}(I/\mathfrak{m}^2) = 2$, then $I = \mathfrak{m}$. If $dim_{R/\mathfrak{m}}(I/\mathfrak{m}^2) = 1$, then I is principal and indeed $I \in \{Ra, R(a+b)\}$.

Case(ii). $x = 0$

In this case, $b + za^2 \in I$. Let $C = R(b + za^2)$. Then $C \subseteq I$. Note that R / C is local with $\mathfrak{m}/C$ as its unique maximal ideal. As $\mathfrak{m}/C$ is principal and $(\mathfrak{m}/C)^3 = (0 + C)$, it follows from *(iii)* $\Rightarrow$ *(i)* of (Atiyah & Macdonald, 1969, Proposition 8.8) that $\{(\mathfrak{m}/C)^i | i \in \{1, 2, 3\}\}$ is the set of all proper ideals of R / C. Therefore, we obtain that $I \in \{\mathfrak{m}, R(b + a^2), Rb, Rb + Ra^2\}$.

Observe that either $b^2 = 0$ or $b^2 \neq 0$. If $b^2 = 0$, then we claim that $a^2 \notin Rb$. For if $a^2 \in Rb$, then $a^2 = rb$ for some $r \in \mathfrak{m}$. As $r = r_1a + r_2b$ for some $r_1, r_2 \in R$, it follows that $a^2 = (r_1a + r_2b)b = r_1(ab) + r_2b^2 = 0$. This is a contradiction. Therefore, $a^2 \notin Rb$. In such a case, it follows from the above discussion that the set of all nonzero proper ideals of R equals $\{Ra, Rb, R(a+b), R(b + a^2), Rb + Ra^2, Ra^2, \mathfrak{m}\}$. As $b\mathfrak{m} = (0)$ and $\mathfrak{m}^3 = (0)$, the ideals $Rb, R(b + a^2), Rb + Ra^2, Ra^2$ are isolated vertices of $(\mathbb{AG}(R))^c$. Thus $(\mathbb{AG}(R))^c$ is the union of the cycle Γ:$Ra - R(a+b) - \mathfrak{m} - Ra$ of length 3 and the isolated vertices. Hence, $\chi((\mathbb{AG}(R))^c) = 3$. If $b^2 \neq 0$, then as $\mathfrak{m}^2 = \{0, a^2\}$, it follows that $b^2 = a^2$. In this case, it is clear that the set of all nonzero proper ideals of R equals $\{Ra, Rb, R(a+b), Ra^2, \mathfrak{m}\}$. Observe that $(\mathbb{AG}(R))^c$ is the union of the cycles Γ_1:$Ra - R(a+b) - \mathfrak{m} - Ra$, Γ_2:$Rb - R(a+b) - \mathfrak{m} - Rb$, each of length 3, and the isolated vertex Ra^2. Note that $R(a+b) - \mathfrak{m}$ is the edge common to both Γ_1 and Γ_2 and Ra, Rb are not adjacent in $(\mathbb{AG}(R))^c$. Now it is clear that $\chi((\mathbb{AG}(R))^c) = 3$.

Thus $3 \leq \alpha(\mathbb{AG}(R)) \leq \chi((\mathbb{AG}(R))^c) = 3$. *Therefore,* $\alpha(\mathbb{AG}(R))) = \chi((\mathbb{AG}(R))^c) = 3$. □

Example 3.12 With the help of Lemma 3.11, we now verify that each one of the ring R mentioned in (i) to (*viii*) of Remark 3.10 satisfies $\alpha(\mathbb{AG}(R)) = \chi((\mathbb{AG}(R))^c) = 3$.

(I) Let $T = \mathbf{F}_2[x, y]$ and I be the ideal of T given by $I = (x^3, xy, y^2)$. The ring mentioned in (i) is $R = T/I$ and it satisfies the hypotheses of Lemma 3.11 with $\mathfrak{m} = Ra + Rb$, where $a = x + I$ and $b = y + I$.

(II) Let $T = \mathbb{F}_2[x, y]$ and I be the ideal of T given by $I = (x^2 - y^2, xy)$. The ring mentioned in (ii) is $R = T/I$ and it satisfies the hypotheses of Lemma 3.11 with $\mathfrak{m} = Ra + Rb$, where $a = x + I$ and $b = y + I$.

(III) Let $T = \mathbb{Z}_4[x, y]$ and I be the ideal of T given by $I = (x^2 - 2, xy, y^2, 2x)$. The ring mentioned in (iii) is $R = T/I$ and it satisfies the hypotheses of Lemma 3.11 with $\mathfrak{m} = Ra + Rb$, where $a = x + I$ and $b = y + I$.

(IV) Let $T = \mathbb{Z}_4[x, y]$ and I be the ideal of T given by $I = (x^2 - 2, xy, y^2 - 2, 2x)$. The ring mentioned in (iv) is $R = T/I$ and it satisfies the hypotheses of Lemma 3.11 with $\mathfrak{m} = Ra + Rb$, where $a = x + I$ and $b = y + I$.

(V) Let $T = \mathbb{Z}_4[x]$ and I be the ideal of T given by $I = (2x, x^3)$. The ring mentioned in (v) is $R = T/I$ and it satisfies the hypotheses of Lemma 3.11 with $\mathfrak{m} = Ra + Rb$, where $a = x + I$ and $b = 2 + I$.

(VI) Let $T = \mathbb{Z}_4[x]$ and I be the ideal of T given by $I = (x^2 - 2x)$. The ring mentioned in (vi) is $R = T/I$ and it satisfies the hypotheses of Lemma 3.11 with $\mathfrak{m} = Ra + Rb$, where $a = x + I$ and $b = x - 2 + I$.

(VII) Let $T = \mathbb{Z}_8[x]$ and I be the ideal of T given by $I = (2x, x^2)$. The ring mentioned in (*vii*) is $R = T/I$ and it satisfies the hypotheses of Lemma 3.11 with $\mathfrak{m} = Ra + Rb$, where $a = 2 + I$ and $b = x + I$.

(VIII) Let $T = \mathbb{Z}_8[x]$ and I be the ideal of T given by $I = (2x, x^2 - 4)$. The ring mentioned in (*viii*) is $R = T/I$ and it satisfies the hypotheses of Lemma 3.11 with $\mathfrak{m} = Ra + Rb$, where $a = x + I$ and $b = 2 + I$. It follows immediately from Lemma 3.11 that each one of the ring R mentioned in (i) to (*viii*) of Remark 3.10 satisfies $\alpha(\mathbb{AG}(R)) = \chi((\mathbb{AG}(R))^c) = 3$.

Let $(R, \mathfrak{m})$ be a finite local ring such that $\mathfrak{m}$ is not principal and $|R| = 81$. Suppose that $\alpha(\mathbb{AG}(R)) = 3$. Then we know from Lemma 3.3 that $m^2 \neq 0$ for some $m \in \mathfrak{m}$. We know from Lemma 3.6 that $\mathfrak{m}^3 = (0)$. Moreover, we know from Remark 3.7 that there exist $a, b \in \mathfrak{m}$ such that $\mathfrak{m} = Ra + Rb$ with $ab = 0$. As $\mathfrak{m}^2 \neq (0)$, we can assume that $a^2 \neq 0$. Note that it follows from the proof of Lemma 3.8 that $|R/\mathfrak{m}| = 3$, $a^2 = b^2$, and $\mathfrak{m}^2 = Ra^2$. In Example 3.14, we provide some examples of finite local rings $(R, \mathfrak{m})$ of order 81 such that $\alpha(\mathbb{AG}(R)) = \chi(\mathbb{AG}(R))^c) = 3$. We use of Lemma 3.13 to verify Example 3.14.

LEMMA 3.13 *Let $(R, \mathfrak{m})$ be a local Artinian ring such that $\mathfrak{m}$ is not principal, but there exist $a, b \in R$ with $\mathfrak{m} = Ra + Rb$ and $ab = 0$. If $|R/\mathfrak{m}| = 3$, $a^2 = b^2 \neq 0$, then $\alpha(\mathbb{AG}(R))) = \chi((\mathbb{AG}(R))^c) = 3$.*

Proof It follows from $\mathfrak{m} = Ra + Rb$, $a^2 = b^2$, and $ab = 0$ that $\mathfrak{m}^2 = Ra^2 + Rb^2 + Rab = Ra^2$ and $\mathfrak{m}^3 = (0)$. From $|R/\mathfrak{m}| = 3$, we obtain that $|\mathfrak{m}^2| = 3$ and so $\mathfrak{m}^2 = \{0, a^2, 2a^2\}$. Moreover, it follows from the given hypotheses that $|\mathfrak{m}| = 27$. Let $A = \{0, 1, 2\}$. It is then clear that $\mathfrak{m} = \{xa + yb + za^2 | x, y, z \text{ vary over } A\}$. Let I be any nonzero proper ideal of R. If $I \subseteq \mathfrak{m}^2$, then it is clear that $I = \mathfrak{m}^2$. Suppose that $I \nsubseteq \mathfrak{m}^2$. Then there exists an element $r = xa + yb + za^2 \in I$ with $x, y, z \in A$ such that at least one between x and y is different from 0. Then it follows that $a^2 \in I$ and so $\mathfrak{m}^2 \subset I$. Hence, we obtain that either $dim_{R/\mathfrak{m}}(I/\mathfrak{m}^2) = 1$ or 2. If $dim_{R/\mathfrak{m}}(I/\mathfrak{m}^2) = 2$, then $I = \mathfrak{m}$. If $dim_{R/\mathfrak{m}}(I/\mathfrak{m}^2) = 1$, then $I = Rr$. In this case, it is not hard to show that $I \in \{Ra, R(a + b), R(a + 2b), Rb\}$. This proves that the set of all nonzero proper ideals of R equals $\{Ra, Rb, R(a + b), R(a + 2b), Ra^2, \mathfrak{m}\}$. Note that $\{Ra, R(a + b), \mathfrak{m}\}$ is an independent set of $\mathbb{AG}(R)$. Therefore, $\alpha(\mathbb{AG}(R)) \geq 3$. We next verify that $\chi((\mathbb{AG}(R))^c) \leq 3$. Let $\{c_1, c_2, c_3\}$ be a set of three distinct colors. Since $ab = 0$, Ra and Rb are not adjacent in $(\mathbb{AG}(R))^c$. As $(a + b)(a + 2b) = a^2 + 2b^2 = a^2 + 2a^2 = 0$, it follows that $R(a + b)$ and $R(a + 2b)$ are not adjacent in $(\mathbb{AG}(R))^c$. From $\mathfrak{m}^3 = (0)$, it is clear that Ra^2 is an isolated vertex of $(\mathbb{AG}(R))^c$. Observe that $(\mathbb{AG}(R))^c$ is the union of the cycles $\Gamma_1: Ra - \mathfrak{m} - R(a + b) - Ra, \Gamma_2: Ra - \mathfrak{m} - R(a + 2b) - Ra$, the edges $e_1: Rb - \mathfrak{m}$, $e_2: Rb - R(a + b)$, $e_3: Rb - R(a + 2b)$, and the isolated vertex Ra^2. Let us assign the color c_1 to Ra, Rb, and Ra^2, color c_2 to $\mathfrak{m}$, and the color c_3 to $R(a + b)$ and $R(a + 2b)$. It is easy to see that the above assignment of colors is indeed a proper coloring of the vertices of $(\mathbb{AG}(R))^c$. Hence, $\chi((\mathbb{AG}(R))^c) \leq 3$. Therefore, $3 \leq \alpha(\mathbb{AG}(R)) \leq \chi((\mathbb{AG}(R))^c) \leq 3$. This proves that $\alpha(\mathbb{AG}(R)) = \chi((\mathbb{AG}(R))^c) = 3$. □

Example 3.14 With the help of Lemma 3.13, we provide some examples of finite local rings $(R, \mathfrak{m})$ with $|R| = 81$ such that $\alpha(\mathbb{AG}(R)) = \chi((\mathbb{AG}(R))^c) = 3$.

(A) Let $T = \mathbb{F}_3[x, y]$ and I be the ideal of T given by $I = (x^2 - y^2, xy)$. Let $R = T/I$. Observe that R satisfies the hypotheses of Lemma 3.13 with $\mathfrak{m} = Ra + Rb$, where $a = x + I$ and $b = y + I$.

(B) Let $T = \mathbb{Z}_9[x, y]$ and I be the ideal of T given by $I = (x^2 - 3, xy, y^2 - 3, , 3x)$. Let $R = T/I$. It is clear that R satisfies the hypotheses of Lemma 3.13 with $\mathfrak{m} = Ra + Rb$, where $a = x + I$ and $b = y + I$.

(C) Let $T = \mathbb{Z}_{27}[x]$ and I be the ideal of T given by $I = (3x, x^2 - 9)$. Then $R = T/I$ satisfies the hypotheses of Lemma 3.13 with $\mathfrak{m} = Ra + Rb$, where $a = x + I$ and $b = 3 + I$.It follows immediately from Lemma 3.13 that each one of the ring R mentioned in (A) to (C) above satisfies $\alpha(\mathbb{AG}(R)) = \chi((\mathbb{AG}(R))^c) = 3$.

4. Classification of rings *R* such that $\alpha(\mathbb{AG}(R)) = 4$

In this section we try to classify rings R such that $\alpha(\mathbb{AG}(R)) = 4$. It follows from Lemma 2.1 that such a ring R can have at most four maximal N-primes of (0). Lemma 4.1 provides the precise number of maximal N-primes of (0) for a ring R with $\alpha(\mathbb{AG}(R)) = 4$.

LEMMA 4.1 *Let R be a ring such that* $\alpha(\mathbb{AG}(R)) = 4$. *Then either R has a unique maximal N-prime of (0) or has exactly two maximal N-primes of (0).*

Proof We know from Lemma 2.1 that R can admit at most four maximal N-primes of (0). Suppose to the contrary that R has exactly n maximal N-primes of (0) with $n \in \{3, 4\}$. Then we know from *(i)* ⇒ *(ii)* of Visweswaran and Patel (2015, Theorem 3.1) that $R \cong R_1 \times R_2 \times \cdots \times R_n$ as rings with $n \in \{3, 4\}$, where $(R_i, \mathfrak{m}_i)$ is a local ring which admits only a finite number of ideals for each $i \in \{1, 2, \ldots, n\}$. Hence, if $n = 4$, then we know from Lemma 2.3 that $\alpha(\mathbb{AG}(R)) \geq 6$. This is in contradiction to the assumption that $\alpha(\mathbb{AG}(R)) = 4$. Thus $n = 4$ is impossible. If $n = 3$ and $\mathfrak{m}_i \neq (0)$ for some $i \in \{1, 2, 3\}$, then we know from Lemma 2.2(v) that $\alpha(\mathbb{AG}(R)) \geq 5$. Moreover, if $n = 3$ and R_i is a field for each $i \in \{1, 2, 3\}$, then it follows from *(ii)* ⇒ *(iii)* of Visweswaran and Patel (2015, Theorem 3.2) that $\alpha(\mathbb{AG}(R)) = 3$. Thus $n = 3$ is also impossible. Therefore, either R has a unique maximal N-prime of (0) or has exactly two maximal N-primes of (0). □

Proposition 4.3 characterizes rings R such that R has exactly two maximal N-primes of (0) satisfying the property that $\alpha(\mathbb{AG}(R)) = 4$. We know from Visweswaran and Patel (2015, Theorem 3.1) that such rings are necessarily Artinian. We use Example 4.2 in the proof of Proposition 4.3.

Example 4.2 Let $i \in \{1, 2\}$ and $(R_i, \mathfrak{m}_i)$ be a SPIR such that $\mathfrak{m}_i \neq (0)$ but $\mathfrak{m}_i^2 = (0)$ for each i. Let $R = R_1 \times R_2$. Then $\alpha(\mathbb{AG}(R)) = \chi((\mathbb{AG}(R))^c) = 4$.

Proof It is clear that the vertex set of $(\mathbb{AG}(R))^c$ equals $\{v_1 = R_1 \times (0), v_2 = R_1 \times \mathfrak{m}_2, v_3 = \mathfrak{m}_1 \times \mathfrak{m}_2, v_4 = \mathfrak{m}_1 \times R_2, v_5 = (0) \times R_2, v_6 = \mathfrak{m}_1 \times (0), v_7 = (0) \times \mathfrak{m}_2\}$. Observe that the subgraph of $(\mathbb{AG}(R))^c$ induced on $\{v_1, v_2, v_3, v_4\}$ is a clique. Moreover in $(\mathbb{AG}(R))^c$, the set of all neighbors of v_5 equals $\{v_2, v_3, v_4, v_7\}$, the set of all neighbors of v_6 equals $\{v_1, v_2\}$, and the set of all neighbors of v_7 equals $\{v_4, v_5\}$. It follows from the above description of $(\mathbb{AG}(R))^c$ that $\alpha(\mathbb{AG}(R)) = \chi((\mathbb{AG}(R))^c) = 4$. □

Proposition 4.3 Let R be an Artinian ring which admits exactly two maximal ideals. Then the following statements are equivalent:

(i) $\alpha(\mathbb{AG}(R)) = 4$.

(ii) Either $R \cong S \times \mathbb{F}$ as rings, where $(S, \mathfrak{m})$ is a SPIR with $\mathfrak{m}^3 \neq (0)$ but $\mathfrak{m}^4 = (0)$ and $\mathbb{F}$ is a field, or $R \cong R_1 \times R_2$ as rings, where $(R_i, \mathfrak{m}_i)$ is a SPIR with $\mathfrak{m}_i \neq (0)$ but $\mathfrak{m}_i^2 = (0)$ for each $i \in \{1, 2\}$ .Moreover, if (i) or (ii) holds, then $\chi((\mathbb{AG}(R))^c) = 4$.

Proof We know from (Atiyah & Macdonald, 1969, Theorem 8.7) $R \cong R_1 \times R_2$ as rings, where $(R_i, \mathfrak{m}_i)$ is a local Artinian ring for each $i \in \{1, 2\}$. Since $\alpha(\mathbb{AG}(R)) = 4$, it is clear that at least one between R_1 and R_2 cannot be a field. Moreover, it follows from Lemma 2.2(iii) and (Atiyah & Macdonald, 1969, Proposition 2.8) that $\mathfrak{m}_i$ is principal for each $i \in \{1, 2\}$. Suppose that R_1 is not a field whereas R_2 is a field. Let $S = R_1$, $\mathfrak{m} = \mathfrak{m}_1$, and $\mathbb{F} = R_2$. Then $R \cong S \times \mathbb{F}$ as rings, where $(S, \mathfrak{m})$ is a SPIR and $\mathbb{F}$ is a field. From $\alpha(\mathbb{AG}(S \times \mathbb{F})) = 4$, it follows from Proposition 2.7 that $\mathfrak{m}^3 \neq (0)$ but $\mathfrak{m}^4 = (0)$ and moreover,

$\chi((\mathbb{AG}(R))^c) = 4$. Suppose that both R_1 and R_2 are not fields. Then $\mathfrak{m}_i \neq (0)$ for each $i \in \{1, 2\}$. Moreover, $(R_i, \mathfrak{m}_i)$ is a SPIR and as $\alpha(\mathbb{AG}(R_1 \times R_2)) = 4$, it follows from Lemma 2.2(ii) that $\mathfrak{m}_i^2 = (0)$ for each $i \in \{1, 2\}$. Moreover, in this case, it follows from Example 4.2 that $\chi((\mathbb{AG}(R))^c) = 4$.

(ii) $\Rightarrow$ *(i)* If $R \cong S \times \mathbb{F}$ as rings, where $(S, \mathfrak{m})$ is a SPIR with $\mathfrak{m}^3 \neq (0)$ but $\mathfrak{m}^4 = (0)$ and $\mathbb{F}$ is a field, then it follows from Proposition 2.7 that $\alpha(\mathbb{AG}(R)) = \chi((\mathbb{AG}(R))^c) = 4$. If $R \cong R_1 \times R_2$ as rings, where $(R_i, \mathfrak{m}_i)$ is a SPIR with $\mathfrak{m}_i \neq (0)$ but $\mathfrak{m}_i^2 = (0)$ for each $i \in \{1, 2\}$, then we obtain from Example 4.2 that $\alpha(\mathbb{AG}(R)) = \chi((\mathbb{AG}(R))^c) = 4$. □

We next try to classify rings R such that R admits exactly one maximal N-prime of (0) and $\alpha(\mathbb{AG}(R)) = 4$. Let $\mathfrak{p}$ denote the unique maximal N-prime of (0) in R. In Proposition 4.5, we present a classification of such rings R under the assumption that $p^2 = 0$ for each $p \in \mathfrak{p}$. We use *(ii)* $\Rightarrow$ *(i)* of Lemma 4.4 in the proof of Proposition 4.5.

LEMMA 4.4 *Let $(R, \mathfrak{m})$ be a local Artinian ring such that $\mathfrak{m}$ is not principal. Let $m_1, m_2 \in \mathfrak{m}$ be such that $\mathfrak{m} = Rm_1 + Rm_2$ with $m_1^2 = 0$, $m_2^2 = 0$ but $m_1 m_2 \neq 0$. The following statements are equivalent:*

(i) $\alpha(\mathbb{AG}(R)) = 4$.
(ii) $|R/\mathfrak{m}| \leq 3$.

Moreover, if either (i) or (ii) holds, then $|R| \in \{16, 81\}$ and $\chi((\mathbb{AG}(R))^c) = 4$.

Proof Note that $\mathfrak{m}^2 = Rm_1m_2$ and $\mathfrak{m}^3 = (0)$.

(i) $\Rightarrow$ *(ii)* Observe that $W = \{Rm_1, Rm_2, R(m_1 + m_2), \mathfrak{m}\}$ is an independent set of $\mathbb{AG}(R)$. If $|R/\mathfrak{m}| \geq 4$, then there exist $r_1, r_2 \in R\backslash\mathfrak{m}$ such that $\{r_1 - 1, r_2 - 1, r_1 - r_2\} \subseteq R\backslash\mathfrak{m}$. As $R(m_1 + r_im_2) \notin W$, $(m_1 + r_im_2)m_1 \neq 0$, $(m_1 + r_im_2)m_2 \neq 0$ for each $i \in \{1, 2\}$, and since $\alpha(\mathbb{AG}(R)) = 4$, it follows that $(m_1 + m_2)(m_1 + r_im_2) = 0$ for each $i \in \{1, 2\}$. This implies that $(r_i + 1)m_1m_2 = 0$ for each $i \in \{1, 2\}$ and so $(r_1 - r_2)m_1m_2 = 0$. This is impossible as $m_1m_2 \neq 0$ and $r_1 - r_2 \notin \mathfrak{m}$. Therefore, $|R/\mathfrak{m}| \leq 3$.

(ii) $\Rightarrow$ *(i)* Suppose that $|R/\mathfrak{m}| = 2$. Since $\mathfrak{m}^2 = Rm_1m_2$, it follows that $dim_{R/\mathfrak{m}}(\mathfrak{m}^2) = 1$ and so $|\mathfrak{m}^2| = 2$. As $dim_{R/\mathfrak{m}}(\mathfrak{m}/\mathfrak{m}^2) = 2$, we obtain that $|\mathfrak{m}/\mathfrak{m}^2| = 4$ and hence, $|\mathfrak{m}| = 8$. Therefore, $|R| = |\mathfrak{m}||R/\mathfrak{m}| = 16$. Let $A = \{0, 1\}$. Note that $\mathfrak{m} = \{am_1 + bm_2 + cm_1m_2 | a, b, c \in A\}$ and $R = \mathfrak{m} \cup \{1 + m | m \in \mathfrak{m}\}$. It is not hard to verify that the set of all nonzero proper ideals of R equals $\{Rm_1, Rm_2, R(m_1 + m_2), Rm_1m_2, \mathfrak{m}\}$. Since $W = \{Rm_1, Rm_2, R(m_1 + m_2), \mathfrak{m}\}$ is an independent set of $\mathbb{AG}(R)$, it follows that $\alpha(\mathbb{AG}(R)) \geq 4$. As $\mathfrak{m}^3 = (0)$, it is clear that Rm_1m_2 is an isolated vertex of $(\mathbb{AG}(R))^c$. Observe that $(\mathbb{AG}(R))^c$ is the union of the clique H, where H is the subgraph of $(\mathbb{AG}(R))^c$ induced on W with $|W| = 4$ and the isolated vertex Rm_1m_2. Hence, $\alpha(\mathbb{AG}(R)) = \chi((\mathbb{AG}(R))^c) = 4$.

Suppose that $|R/\mathfrak{m}| = 3$. Now $R/\mathfrak{m} = \{0 + \mathfrak{m}, 1 + \mathfrak{m}, 2 + \mathfrak{m}\}$. Let $B = \{0, 1, 2\}$. Note that $|\mathfrak{m}^2| = 3$, $|\mathfrak{m}/\mathfrak{m}^2| = 9$. Hence, $|\mathfrak{m}| = 27$ and $|R| = 81$. Observe that $\mathfrak{m} = \{am_1 + bm_2 + cm_1m_2 | a, b, c \in B\}$ and $R = \mathfrak{m} \cup \{1 + m | m \in \mathfrak{m}\} \cup \{2 + m | m \in \mathfrak{m}\}$. It is easy to verify that the set of all nonzero proper ideals of R equals $\{Rm_1, Rm_2, R(m_1 + m_2), R(m_1 + 2m_2), Rm_1m_2, \mathfrak{m}\}$. It is clear that the subgraph H_1 of $(\mathbb{AG}(R))^c$ induced on $\{Rm_1, Rm_2, R(m_1 + m_2), \mathfrak{m}\}$ is a clique on four vertices and the subgraph H_2 of $(\mathbb{AG}(R))^c$ induced on $|[Rm_1, Rm_2, R(m_1 + 2m_2), \mathfrak{m}\}$ is a clique on four vertices, and $(\mathbb{AG}(R))^c$ is the union of H_1, H_2, and the isolated vertex Rm_1m_2. Note that $(m_1 + m_2)(m_1 + 2m_2) = 3m_1m_2 \in \mathfrak{m}^3 = (0)$ and hence, $R(m_1 + m_2)$ and $R(m_1 + 2m_2)$ are not adjacent in $(\mathbb{AG}(R))^c$. Let $\{c_i | i \in \{1, 2, 3, 4\}\}$ be a set of four distinct colors. If we assign the color c_1 to Rm_1, color c_2 to Rm_2, color c_3 to $\mathfrak{m}$, and the color c_4 to the vertices $R(m_1 + m_2)$, $R(m_1 + 2m_2)$, and Rm_1m_2, then it is clear that the above assignment of colors is indeed a proper coloring of the vertices of $(\mathbb{AG}(R))^c$ and moreover, it is evident from the above discussion that $\alpha(\mathbb{AG}(R)) = \chi((\mathbb{AG}(R))^c) = 4$.

The moreover assertion is already verified in the proof of *(ii)* $\Rightarrow$ *(i)*. □

Proposition 4.5 Let R be a ring which admits $\mathfrak{p}$ as its unique maximal N-prime of (0). Suppose that $p^2 = 0$ for each $p \in P$. Then the following statements are equivalent:

(i) $\alpha(\mathbb{AG}(R)) = 4$.

(ii) R is necessarily a local Artinian with $\mathfrak{p}$ as its unique maximal ideal, $\mathfrak{p}$ is not principal but is two generated, $\mathfrak{p}^2 \neq (0)$, and $|R/\mathfrak{p}| = 2$.

Moreover, if either (i) or (ii) holds, then $|R| = 16$ and $\chi((\mathbb{AG}(R))^c) = 4$.

Proof *(i)* $\Rightarrow$ *(ii)* By hypothesis, $\alpha(\mathbb{AG}(R)) = 4$. Hence, it follows from Visweswaran and Patel (2015, Lemmas 2.1 and 2.2) that $\mathfrak{p} = nil(R) \in \mathbb{A}(R)$ and it is clear that $\mathfrak{p}^2 \neq (0)$. Therefore, there exist $p_1, p_2 \in \mathfrak{p}$ such that $p_1p_2 \neq 0$. We are assuming that $p^2 = 0$ for each $p \in P$. Hence, $\mathfrak{p}$ cannot be principal. Moreover, as $p_1p_2 \neq 0$, $p_1^2 = p_2^2 = 0$, it follows from Remark 2.5 that $Rp_1 \not\subseteq Rp_2$ and $Rp_2 \not\subseteq Rp_1$. Therefore, it follows that $R(p_1 + p_2)$ and Rp_i are not comparable under inclusion for each $i \in \{1, 2\}$. Note that $W = \{Rp_1, Rp_2, R(p_1 + p_2), Rp_1 + Rp_2\}$ is an independent set of $\mathbb{AG}(R)$. From $\alpha(\mathbb{AG}(R)) = 4$, it follows that $\mathfrak{p} \in W$ and hence, $\mathfrak{p} = Rp_1 + Rp_2$. It follows from $p_1^2 = p_2^2 = (p_1 + p_2)^2 = 0$ that $2p_1p_2 = 0$. As $p_1p_2 \neq 0$ and $\mathfrak{p} = Z(R)$, we obtain that $2 \in \mathfrak{p}$. Let $r \in R \backslash \mathfrak{p}$. Observe that $R(p_1 + rp_2)p_i \neq 0$ for each $i \in \{1, 2\}$. Moreover, if $r - 1 \notin \mathfrak{p}$, then $R(p_1 + rp_2) \notin W$ and $R(p_1 + p_2)R(p_1 + rp_2) = R(r + 1)p_1p_2 \neq 0$. Hence, $W \cup \{R(p_1 + rp_2)\}$ is an independent set of $\mathbb{AG}(R)$. This is impossible. Therefore, $r - 1 \in \mathfrak{p}$. This proves that $|R/\mathfrak{p}| = 2$. Therefore, $\mathfrak{p}$ is necessarily a maximal ideal of R and as $\mathfrak{p}^3 = (0)$, we obtain that R is a local Artinian ring with $\mathfrak{p}$ as its unique maximal ideal.

(ii) $\Rightarrow$ *(i)* If (ii) holds, then the local Artinian ring $(R, \mathfrak{p})$ satisfies the hypotheses of Lemma 4.4 and in addition $|R/\mathfrak{p}| = 2$. Hence, it follows from *(ii)* $\Rightarrow$ *(i)* of Lemma 4.4 that $\alpha(\mathbb{AG}(R)) = 4$.

If either (i) or (ii) holds, then again it follows from the proof of *(ii)* $\Rightarrow$ *(i)* of Lemma 4.4 that $|R| = 16$ and $\chi((\mathbb{AG}(R))^c) = 4$. □

We mention some examples in Example 4.6 to illustrate Lemma 4.4.

Example 4.6 With the help of Belshoff and Chapman (2007), Corbas and Williams (2000a, 2000b), we mention some examples of finite local rings R such that $|R| \in \{16, 81\}$ and $\alpha(\mathbb{AG}(R)) = \chi((\mathbb{AG}(R))^c) = 4$.

(i) Let $T = \mathbb{F}_2[x, y]$ and let I be the ideal of T given by $I = (x^2, y^2)$. Let $R = T/I$. Note that R is a local Artinian ring with $\mathfrak{m} = (x, y)/I$ as its unique maximal ideal and $(R, \mathfrak{m})$ satisfies the hypotheses of Lemma 4.4 with $m_1 = x + I, m_2 = y + I$ and moreover, $|R/\mathfrak{m}| = 2$. Hence, it follows from the proof of *(ii)* $\Rightarrow$ *(i)* of Lemma 4.4 that $\alpha(\mathbb{AG}(R)) = \chi((\mathbb{AG}(R))^c) = 4$. Furthermore, it is clear that $|R| = 16$ and $m^2 = 0 + I$ for each $m \in \mathfrak{m}$.

(ii) Let $T = \mathbb{Z}_4[x, y]$. Let I be the ideal of T given by $I = (x^2, xy - 2, y^2)$. Let $R = T/I$. Observe that R is a local Artinian ring with $\mathfrak{m} = (2, x, y)/I = (x + I, y + I)$ as its unique maximal ideal and the local Artinian ring $(R, \mathfrak{m})$ satisfies the hypotheses of Lemma 4.4 with $m_1 = x + I$ and $m_2 = y + I$. As $|R/\mathfrak{m}| = 2$, we obtain from the proof of *(ii)* $\Rightarrow$ *(i)* of Lemma 4.4 that $\alpha(\mathbb{AG}(R)) = \chi((\mathbb{AG}(R))^c) = 4$. It is clear that $|R| = 16$ and moreover, $m^2 = 0 + I$ for each $m \in \mathfrak{m}$.

(iii) Let $T = \mathbb{F}_3[x, y]$ and let I be the ideal of T given by $I = (x^2, y^2)$. Let $R = T/I$. Let $\mathfrak{m} = (x, y)/I = (x + I, y + I)$. It is clear that the local Artinian ring ring $(R, \mathfrak{m})$ satisfies the hypotheses of Lemma 4.4 with $m_1 = x + I$ and $m_2 = y + I$. Since $|R/\mathfrak{m}| = 3$, it follows from the proof of *(ii)* $\Rightarrow$ *(i)* of Lemma 4.4 that $\alpha(\mathbb{AG}(R)) = \chi((\mathbb{AG}(R))^c) = 4$. Note that $|R| = 81$.

(iv) Let $T = \mathbb{Z}_9[x, y]$ and let I be the ideal of T given by $I = (x^2, xy - 3, y^2)$. Let $R = T/I$. Observe that R is a local Artinian ring $\mathfrak{m} = (3, x, y)/I = (x + I, y + I)$ and $(R.\mathfrak{m})$ satisfies the hypotheses of Lemma 4.4 with $m_1 = x + I$ and $m_2 = y + I$. As $|R/\mathfrak{m}| = 3$, we obtain from the proof of *(ii)* $\Rightarrow$ *(i)* of Lemma 4.4 that $\alpha(\mathbb{AG}(R)) = \chi((\mathbb{AG}(R))^c) = 4$. It is clear that $|R| = 81$.

Let R be a ring which admits $\mathfrak{p}$ as its unique maximal N-prime of (0). Suppose that $p^2 \neq 0$ for some $p \in \mathfrak{p}$. If $\alpha(\mathbb{AG}(R)) = 4$, then we know from Visweswaran and Patel (2015, Remark 3.5(ii)) that R is a local Artinian ring with $\mathfrak{p}$ as its unique maximal ideal and moreover, we know from Lemma 3.4 that $\mathfrak{p}$ can be generated by at most two elements. In Proposition 4.7, we classify the local Artinian rings R such that $\alpha(\mathbb{AG}(R)) = 4$ under the assumption that $\mathfrak{p}$ is principal. In such a case, $(R, \mathfrak{p})$ is a SPIR.

Proposition 4.7 Let $(R, \mathfrak{m})$ be a SPIR. Then the following statements are equivalent:

(i) $\alpha(\mathbb{AG}(R)) = 4$.
(ii) Either $\mathfrak{m}^8 = (0)$ but $\mathfrak{m}^7 \neq (0)$ or $\mathfrak{m}^9 = (0)$ but $\mathfrak{m}^8 \neq (0)$.

Moreover, if (i) or (ii) holds, then $\chi((\mathbb{AG}(R))^c) = 4$.

Proof This follows immediately from Visweswaran and Patel (2015, Proposition 3.7). □

Let $(R, \mathfrak{m})$ be a local Artinian ring such that $\mathfrak{m}$ is not principal but $\mathfrak{m} = Rm_1 + Rm_2$ for some $m_1, m_2 \in \mathfrak{m}$. Our goal was to classify such local Artinian rings R satisfying the condition that $\alpha(\mathbb{AG}(R)) = 4$. First we assume that $m_1^2 \neq 0$, but $m_2^2 = m_1m_2 = 0$ and present the desired classification in Propositions 4.9 and 4.10. In Proposition 4.9, we assume that $m_1^3 \neq 0$ and in Proposition 4.10, we assume that $m_1^3 = 0$. We use Lemma 4.8 in the proof of Proposition 4.10.

LEMMA 4.8 *Let $(R, \mathfrak{m})$ be a local Artinian ring such that $\mathfrak{m}$ is not principal but $\mathfrak{m} = Rm_1 + Rm_2$. Suppose that $m_1^2 \neq 0$, whereas $m_2^2 = m_1m_2 = 0$. If $\alpha(\mathbb{AG}(R)) \leq 4$, then $|R/\mathfrak{m}| \leq 3$.*

Proof It is clear from the hypotheses that $\mathfrak{m}m_2 = (0)$. Suppose that $|R/\mathfrak{m}| > 3$. Then there exist $r_1, r_2 \in R$ such that $r_1 + \mathfrak{m} \neq r_2 + \mathfrak{m}$ and $r_1 + \mathfrak{m}, r_2 + \mathfrak{m} \notin \{0 + \mathfrak{m}, 1 + \mathfrak{m}\}$. Thus there exist $r_1, r_2 \in R\backslash\mathfrak{m}$ such that $r_i - 1 \notin \mathfrak{m}$ for each $i \in \{1, 2\}$ and $r_1 - r_2 \notin \mathfrak{m}$. As $m_1^2 \neq 0, m_2^2 = m_1m_2 = 0$, and $\mathfrak{m}$ is not principal, it follows that $\{Rm_1, R(m_1 + m_2), R(m_1 + r_1m_2), R(m_1 + r_2m_2), \mathfrak{m}\}$ is an independent set of $\mathbb{AG}(R)$. This implies that $\alpha(\mathbb{AG}(R)) \geq 5$ which contradicts the assumption that $\alpha(\mathbb{AG}(R)) \leq 4$. Therefore, $|R/\mathfrak{m}| \leq 3$. □

Proposition 4.9 Let $(R, \mathfrak{m})$ be a local Artinian such that $\mathfrak{m}$ is not principal but $\mathfrak{m} = Rm_1 + Rm_2$. Suppose that $m_2^2 = m_1m_2 = 0$. If $m_1^3 \neq 0$, then the following statements are equivalent:

(i) $\alpha(\mathbb{AG}(R)) = 4$.
(ii) $\mathfrak{m}^4 = (0)$ and $|R/\mathfrak{m}| = 2$.

Moreover, if (i) or (ii) holds, then $|R| = 32$ and $\chi((\mathbb{AG}(R))^c) = 4$.

Proof *(i) ⇒ (ii)* Note that $\mathfrak{m}m_2 = (0)$. Observe that $\{m_1 + \mathfrak{m}^2, m_2 + \mathfrak{m}^2\}$ is a basis of $\mathfrak{m}/\mathfrak{m}^2$ as a vector space over $R/\mathfrak{m}$. Therefore, the ideals $Rm_1, Rm_1^2, R(m_1 + m_2), R(m_1^2 + m_2), \mathfrak{m}$ are distinct. Since $m_1^3 \neq 0, m_2^2 = m_1m_2 = 0$, we obtain that $W = \{Rm_1, Rm_1^2, R(m_1 + m_2), \mathfrak{m}\}$ is an independent set of $\mathbb{AG}(R)$. If $\mathfrak{m}^4 \neq (0)$, then $m_1^4 \neq 0$. In such a case, $W \cup \{R(m_1^2 + m_2)\}$ is an independent set of $\mathbb{AG}(R)$. This implies that $\alpha(\mathbb{AG}(R)) \geq 5$ and this contradicts (i). Therefore, $\mathfrak{m}^4 = (0)$. We next prove that $|R/\mathfrak{m}| = 2$. If $|R/\mathfrak{m}| > 2$, then there exists $r \in R$ such that $r, r - 1 \in R\backslash\mathfrak{m}$. Then $W \cup \{R(m_1 + rm_2)\}$ is an independent set of $\mathbb{AG}(R)$. This is impossible as $\alpha(\mathbb{AG}(R)) = 4$. Therefore, $|R/\mathfrak{m}| = 2$. Note that $\mathfrak{m}^2 = Rm_1^2, \mathfrak{m}^3 = Rm_1^3$. Thus $dim_{R/\mathfrak{m}}(\mathfrak{m}^3) = dim_{R/\mathfrak{m}}(\mathfrak{m}^2/\mathfrak{m}^3) = 1$, and $dim_{R/\mathfrak{m}}(\mathfrak{m}/\mathfrak{m}^2) = 2$. Hence, $|\mathfrak{m}^3| = |\mathfrak{m}^2/\mathfrak{m}^3| = 2$, and $|\mathfrak{m}/\mathfrak{m}^2| = 4$. Therefore, $|\mathfrak{m}^2| = 4, |\mathfrak{m}| = 16$, and $|R| = 32$.

(ii) ⇒ (i) Let $A = \{0, 1\}$. Note that $\mathfrak{m} = \{am_1 + bm_2 + cm_1^2 + dm_1^3 | a, b, c, d \text{ vary over } A\}$. It can be easily shown that the set of all nonzero proper ideals of R equals $\{Rm_1, Rm_2, R(m_1 + m_2), Rm_1^2, Rm_1^3, R(m_1^2 + m_2), R(m_1^3 + m_2), Rm_1^2 + Rm_2, Rm_1^3 + Rm_2, \mathfrak{m}\}$. It is clear that $\{Rm_1, Rm_1^2, R(m_1 + m_2), \mathfrak{m}\}$ is an independent set of $\mathbb{AG}(R)$. Hence, $\alpha(\mathbb{AG}(R)) \geq 4$. We next verify that

$\chi((\mathbb{AG}(R))^c) \leq 4$. Let $\{c_1, c_2, c_3, c_4\}$ be a set of four distinct colors. Since $\mathfrak{m}m_2 = (0)$ and $\mathfrak{m}^4 = (0)$, it follows that the set of all isolated vertices of $(\mathbb{AG}(R))^c$ equals $\{Rm_2, Rm_1^3, R(m_1^3 + m_2), Rm_1^3 + Rm_2\}$. Observe that $R(m_1^2 + m_2), Rm_1^2 + Rm_2$ are not adjacent in $(\mathbb{AG}(R))^c$ and both are not adjacent to Rm_1^2 in $(\mathbb{AG}(R))^c$. Hence, if we assign the color c_1 to Rm_1, color c_2 to Rm_1^2, color c_3 to $R(m_1 + m_2)$, color c_4 to $\mathfrak{m}$, and the color c_2 to all the vertices in the set $\{R(m_1^2 + m_2), Rm_1^2 + Rm_2\} \cup$ the set of all isolated vertices of $(\mathbb{AG}(R))^c$, then it is clear that the above assignment of colors is a proper vertex coloring of $(\mathbb{AG}(R))^c$. Therefore, we obtain that $4 \leq \alpha(\mathbb{AG}(R)) \leq \chi((\mathbb{AG}(R))^c) \leq 4$ and so $\alpha(\mathbb{AG}(R)) = \chi((\mathbb{AG}(R))^c) = 4$.

The moreover assertion that $|R| = 32$ is already verified in the proof of *(i)* ⇒ *(ii)* and the assertion that $\chi((\mathbb{AG}(R))^c) = 4$ is verified in the proof of *(ii)* ⇒ *(i)*. □

Proposition 4.10 Let $(R, \mathfrak{m})$ be a local Artinian ring such that $\mathfrak{m}$ is not principal but $\mathfrak{m} = Rm_1 + Rm_2$ for some $m_1, m_2 \in \mathfrak{m}$. Suppose that $m_1^2 \neq 0$, whereas $m_2^2 = m_1 m_2 = 0$. If $m_1^3 = 0$, then the following statements are equivalent:

(i) $\alpha(\mathbb{AG}(R)) = 4$.

(ii) $|R/\mathfrak{m}| = 3$.

Moreover, if either (i) or (ii) holds, then $|R| = 81$ and $\chi((\mathbb{AG}(R))^c) = 4$.

Proof Note that $\mathfrak{m}^2 = Rm_1^2$ and $\mathfrak{m}^3 = (0)$.

(i) ⇒ *(ii)* We know from Lemma 4.8 that $|R/\mathfrak{m}| \leq 3$. If $|R/\mathfrak{m}| = 2$, then $\mathfrak{m}^2 = \{0, m_1^2\}$. In such a case, it follows from Lemma 3.11 that $\alpha(\mathbb{AG}(R)) = 3$. This contradicts (i). Therefore, $|R/\mathfrak{m}| = 3$.

Observe that $dim_{R/\mathfrak{m}}(\mathfrak{m}^2) = 1$ and $dim_{R/\mathfrak{m}}(\mathfrak{m}/\mathfrak{m}^2) = 2$. Hence, $|\mathfrak{m}^2| = 3, |\mathfrak{m}/\mathfrak{m}^2| = 9$ and so $|\mathfrak{m}| = 27$. Therefore, $|R| = |R/\mathfrak{m}||\mathfrak{m}| = 81$.

(ii) ⇒ *(i)* Note that $R/\mathfrak{m} = \{0 + \mathfrak{m}, 1 + \mathfrak{m}, 2 + \mathfrak{m}\}$. Observe that $\mathfrak{m} = \{am_1 + bm_2 + cm_1^2 | a, b, c$ vary over $\{0, 1, 2\}\}$. It is not hard to verify that the set of all nonzero proper ideals of R equals $\{Rm_1, Rm_2, R(m_1 + m_2), R(m_1 + 2m_2), Rm_1^2, R(m_1^2 + m_2), Rm_1^2 + Rm_2, R(m_1^2 + 2m_2), \mathfrak{m}\}$. Since $W = \{Rm_1, R(m_1 + m_2), R(m_1 + 2m_2), \mathfrak{m}\}$ is an independent set of $\mathbb{AG}(R)$, it follows that $\alpha(\mathbb{AG}(R)) \geq 4$. Since $\mathfrak{m}m_2 = (0)$ and $\mathfrak{m}^3 = (0)$, it follows that $A = \{Rm_2, Rm_1^2, R(m_1^2 + m_2), Rm_1^2 + Rm_2, R(m_1^2 + 2m_2)\}$ is the set of all isolated vertices of $(\mathbb{AG}(R))^c$. Note that $(\mathbb{AG}(R))^c$ is the union of H and A, where H is the subgraph of $(\mathbb{AG}(R))^c$ induced on W. It is clear from the above discussion that $\alpha(\mathbb{AG}(R)) = \chi((\mathbb{AG}(R))^c) = 4$.

The moreover assertion that $|R| = 81$ is already verified in the proof of *(i)* ⇒ *(ii)* and the assertion that $\chi((\mathbb{AG}(R))^c) = 4$ is verified in the proof of *(ii)* ⇒ *(i)*. □

In Example 4.11, we provide some examples to illustrate Propositions 4.9 and 4.10.

Example 4.11 With the help of theorems proved by Corbas and Williams (2000a, 2000b) and from the examples of rings of order 32 given in Belshoff and Chapman (2007), we give some examples of finite local rings $(R, \mathfrak{m})$ of order 32 such that $\mathfrak{m}$ satisfies the hypotheses of Proposition 4.9.

(i) Let $T = \mathbb{F}_2[x, y]$ and I be the ideal of T given by $I = (x^4, xy, y^2)$. Let $R = T/I$. Note that the unique maximal ideal $\mathfrak{m} = (x, y)/I = (x + I, y + I)$ of R is such that $\mathfrak{m}$ satisfies the hypotheses of Proposition 4.9 with $m_1 = x + I$ and $m_2 = y + I$, and moreover, $(R, \mathfrak{m})$ satisfies (ii) of Proposition 4.9.

(ii) Let $T = \mathbb{Z}_4[x, y]$ and $R = T/I$, where I is the ideal of T given by $I = (x^2 - 2, xy, y^2)$. Note that the unique maximal ideal $\mathfrak{m} = (2, x, y)/I = (x + I, y + I)$ of R satisfies the hypotheses of Proposition 4.9 with $m_1 = x + I, m_2 = y + I$, and moreover $(R, \mathfrak{m})$ also satisfies (ii) of Proposition 4.9.

(iii) Let $T = \mathbb{Z}_4[x,y]$. Let $R = T/I$, where I is the ideal of T given by $I = (x^3 - 2, xy, 2x, y^2)$. Note that the unique maximal ideal $\mathfrak{m} = (2,x,y)/I = (x+I, y+I)$ of R satisfies the hypotheses of Proposition 4.9 with $m_1 = x + I, m_2 = y + I$, and in addition $(R,\mathfrak{m})$ satisfies (ii) of Proposition 4.9.

(iv) Let $T = \mathbb{Z}_4[x,y]$ and $R = T/I$, where I is the ideal of T given by $I = (x^2 - 2x - 2, xy, y^2)$. Observe that the unique maximal ideal $\mathfrak{m} = (2,x,y)/I = (x+I, y+I)$ of R satisfies the hypotheses of Proposition 4.9 with $m_1 = x + I, m_2 = y + I$, and moreover $(R,\mathfrak{m})$ satisfies (ii) of Proposition 4.9.

(v) Let $T = \mathbb{Z}_4[x]$ and $R = T/I$, where I is the ideal of T given by $I = (2x, x^4)$. Note that the unique maximal ideal $\mathfrak{m} = (2,x)/I$ of R satisfies the hypotheses of Proposition 4.9 with $m_1 = x + I, m_2 = 2 + I$, and moreover, $(R,\mathfrak{m})$ satisfies (ii) of Proposition 4.9.Therefore, it follows from the proof of *(ii)* $\Rightarrow$ *(i)* of Proposition 4.9 that each one of the ring R mentioned in (i) to (v) above satisfies $\alpha((\mathbb{AG}(R)) = \chi((\mathbb{AG}(R))^c) = 4$.

Next with the help of Proposition 4.10, we give some examples of finite local rings $(R,\mathfrak{m})$ with $|R| = 81$ such that $\alpha(\mathbb{AG}(R)) = 4$.

(a) Let $T = \mathbb{F}_3[x,y]$ and $R = T/I$, where I is the ideal of T given by $I = (x^3, y^2, xy)$. The unique maximal ideal $\mathfrak{m} = (x,y)/I = (x+I, y+I)$ satisfies the hypotheses of Proposition 4.10 with $m_1 = x + I$ and $m_2 = y + I$.

(b) Let $T = \mathbb{Z}_9[x.y]$ and $R = T/I$, where I is the ideal of T given by $I = (x^2 - 3, xy, y^2, 3x)$. The unique maximal ideal $\mathfrak{m} = (3,x,y)/I = (x+I, y+I)$ satisfies the hypotheses of Proposition 4.10 with $m_1 = x + I$ and $m_2 = y + I$.

(c) Let $T = \mathbb{Z}_9[x]$ and $R = T/I$, where I is the ideal of T given by $I = (3x, x^3)$. The unique maximal ideal $\mathfrak{m} = (3,x)/I = (3+I, x+I)$ of R satisfies the hypotheses of Proposition 4.10 with $m_1 = x + I$ and $m_2 = 3 + I$.As $|R/\mathfrak{m}| = 3$, in each one of the ring R mentioned in (a) to (c) above, it follows from the proof of *(ii)* $\Rightarrow$ *(i)* of Proposition 4.10 that $\alpha(\mathbb{AG}(R)) = \chi((\mathbb{AG}(R))^c) = 4$.

Let $(R,\mathfrak{m})$ be a local Artinian ring such that $\mathfrak{m}$ is not principal but $\mathfrak{m} = Rm_1 + Rm_2$ for some $m_1, m_2 \in \mathfrak{m}$. We next focus on classifying such rings $(R,\mathfrak{m})$ in order that $\alpha(\mathbb{AG}(R)) = 4$ under the additional assumption that $m_1^2 \neq 0, m_2^2 \neq 0$, whereas $m_1 m_2 = 0$. The results regarding their classification are presented in Propositions 4.13, 4.16, and 4.18. We use Lemma 4.12 in the proof of Proposition 4.13.

LEMMA 4.12 *Let $(R,\mathfrak{m})$ be a local Artinian ring such that $\mathfrak{m}$ is not principal but $\mathfrak{m} = Rm_1 + Rm_2$. Suppose that $m_1^2 \neq 0, m_2^2 \neq 0$, whereas $m_1 m_2 = 0$. If $\alpha(\mathbb{AG}(R)) \leq 4$, then either $Rm_1^2 \subseteq Rm_2^2$ or $Rm_2^2 \subseteq Rm_1^2$.*

Proof Suppose that $Rm_1^2 \not\subseteq Rm_2^2$ and $Rm_2^2 \not\subseteq Rm_1^2$. If $Rm_1^2 \subseteq Rm_2$, then $m_1^2 = m_2 r$ for some $r \in R$. Note that r must be in $\mathfrak{m}$ and so $r = am_1 + bm_2$ for some $a, b \in R$. Hence, $m_1^2 = m_2(am_1 + bm_2) = bm_2^2$. This is in contradiction to the assumption that $Rm_1^2 \not\subseteq Rm_2^2$. Therefore, $Rm_1^2 \not\subseteq Rm_2$. Similarly, from the assumption that $Rm_2^2 \not\subseteq Rm_1^2$, it follows that $Rm_2^2 \not\subseteq Rm_1$. It follows from $\{m_1 + \mathfrak{m}^2, m_2 + \mathfrak{m}^2\}$ is a basis of $\mathfrak{m}/\mathfrak{m}^2$ as a vector space over $R/\mathfrak{m}$ and $Rm_2^2 \not\subseteq Rm_1$ that the ideals $Rm_1, R(m_1 + m_2), R(m_1 + m_2^2), Rm_1 + Rm_2^2, \mathfrak{m}$ are distinct. Moreover, it follows from $m_1^2 \neq 0, m_1 m_2 = 0$, and $m_1^2 + m_2^3 \neq 0$ that $\{Rm_1, R(m_1 + m_2), R(m_1 + m_2^2), Rm_1 + Rm_2^2, \mathfrak{m}\}$ is an independent set of $\mathbb{AG}(R)$. This implies that $\alpha(\mathbb{AG}(R)) \geq 5$ and this contradicts the hypothesis that $\alpha((\mathbb{AG}(R)) \leq 4$. Therefore, either $Rm_1^2 \subseteq Rm_2^2$ or $Rm_2^2 \subseteq Rm_1^2$. □

Proposition 4.13 Let $(R,\mathfrak{m})$ be a local Artinian ring such that $\mathfrak{m}$ is not principal but $\mathfrak{m} = Rm_1 + Rm_2$. Suppose that $m_1^2 \neq 0, m_2^2 \neq 0, m_1 m_2 = 0$, and moreover, $Rm_1^2 \neq Rm_2^2$. Then the following statements are equivalent:

(i) $\alpha(\mathbb{AG}(R)) = 4$.

(ii) Rm_1^2 and Rm_2^2 are comparable under the inclusion relation, $\mathfrak{m}^3 \neq (0), \mathfrak{m}^4 = (0)$, and $|R/\mathfrak{m}| = 2$. Moreover, if either (i) or (ii) holds, then $|R| = 32$ and $\chi((\mathbb{AG}(R))^c) = 4$.

Proof (*i*) ⇒ (*ii*) Since $\alpha(\mathbb{AG}(R)) = 4$, it follows from Lemma 4.12 that Rm_1^2 and Rm_2^2 are comparable under the inclusion relation. By hypothesis, $Rm_1^2 \neq Rm_2^2$. Hence, we can assume without loss of generality that $Rm_2^2 \subseteq Rm_1^2$ but $Rm_1^2 \not\subseteq Rm_2^2$. Thus $m_2^2 = rm_1^2$ for some $r \in \mathfrak{m}$. Let $r = am_1 + bm_2$ for some $a, b \in R$. Then $m_2^2 = m_1^2(am_1 + bm_2) = am_1^3$. From $m_2^2 \neq 0$, it follows that $m_1^3 \neq 0$ and so $\mathfrak{m}^3 \neq (0)$. From $m_2^2 = rm_1^2$ and $m_1m_2 = 0$, it follows that $m_2^3 = 0$. Hence, $\mathfrak{m}^3 = Rm_1^3$. It is now clear that $\mathfrak{m}^4 = (0)$ if and only if $m_1^4 = (0)$. Suppose that $m_1^4 \neq (0)$. Observe that $\{Rm_1, Rm_1^2, R(m_1 + m_2), Rm_1^2 + Rm_2, \mathfrak{m}\}$ is an independent set of $\mathbb{AG}(R)$. This implies that $\alpha(\mathbb{AG}(R)) \geq 5$ and this is a contradiction. Therefore, $\mathfrak{m}^4 = (0)$. If $|R/\mathfrak{m}| > 2$, then there exists $s \in R$ such that $s, s-1 \notin \mathfrak{m}$. Note that $\{Rm_1, Rm_1^2, R(m_1 + m_2), R(m_1 + sm_2), \mathfrak{m}\}$ is an independent set of $\mathbb{AG}(R)$. This contradicts (i). Therefore, $|R/\mathfrak{m}| = 2$.

Note that $dim_{R/\mathfrak{m}}(\mathfrak{m}^3) = 1$ and as $\mathfrak{m}^2 = Rm_1^2$, $dim_{R/\mathfrak{m}}(\mathfrak{m}^2/\mathfrak{m}^3) = 1$, and by hypothesis, $dim_{R/\mathfrak{m}}(\mathfrak{m}/\mathfrak{m}^2) = 2$. Hence, $|\mathfrak{m}^3| = 2$, $|\mathfrak{m}^2/\mathfrak{m}^3| = 2$, and $|\mathfrak{m}/\mathfrak{m}^2| = 4$. Thus $|\mathfrak{m}^2| = 4$, $|\mathfrak{m}| = 16$, and so $|R| = 32$.

(*ii*) ⇒ (*i*) We can assume without loss of generality that $Rm_2^2 \subseteq Rm_1^2$ but $Rm_1^2 \not\subseteq Rm_2^2$. It follows as in (*i*) ⇒ (*ii*) that $m_2^2 = um_1^3$ for some $u \in R$. From $\mathfrak{m}^4 = (0)$, it is clear that $u \notin \mathfrak{m}$ and hence, u is a unit in R. As $|R/\mathfrak{m}| = 2$, $u = 1 + m$ for some $m \in \mathfrak{m}$ and so $m_2^2 = m_1^3$. Note that $\mathfrak{m} = \{am_1 + bm_2 + cm_1^2 + dm_1^3 | a, b, c, d$ vary over $\{0, 1\}\}$.

It is easy to verify that the set of all nonzero proper ideals of R equals $\{Rm_1, Rm_2, R(m_1 + m_2), Rm_1^2, Rm_1^3, R(m_1^2 + m_2), Rm_1^2 + Rm_2, \mathfrak{m}\}$. Since $\{Rm_1, Rm_1^2, R(m_1 + m_2), \mathfrak{m}\}$ is an independent set of $\mathbb{AG}(R)$, it is clear that $\alpha(\mathbb{AG}(R)) \geq 4$. We next verify that $\chi((\mathbb{AG}(R))^c) \leq 4$. Let $\{c_1, c_2, c_3, c_4\}$ be a set of four distinct colors. Since $\mathfrak{m}^4 = (0)$, it is clear that Rm_1^3 is an isolated vertex of $(\mathbb{AG}(R))^c$. From $m_1m_2 = 0$ and $m_1^3 = m_2^2$, it follows that in $(\mathbb{AG}(R))^c$, Rm_1 and Rm_2 are not adjacent, $R(m_1 + m_2)$ and $R(m_1^2 + m_2)$ are not adjacent, and Rm_1^2 and $Rm_1^2 + Rm_2$ are not adjacent. If we assign the color c_1 to Rm_1 and Rm_2, color c_2 to $R(m_1 + m_2)$ and $R(m_1^2 + m_2)$, color c_3 to Rm_1^2 and $Rm_1^2 + Rm_2$, and the color c_4 to $\mathfrak{m}$ and Rm_1^3, then it is not hard to verify that the above assignment of colors is indeed a proper vertex coloring of $(\mathbb{AG}(R))^c$. The above discussion shows that $4 \leq \alpha(\mathbb{AG}(R)) \leq \chi((\mathbb{AG}(R))^c) \leq 4$. Therefore, $\alpha(\mathbb{AG}(R)) = \chi((\mathbb{AG}(R))^c) = 4$.

The moreover assertion that $|R| = 32$ is already verified in the proof of (*i*) ⇒ (*ii*) and the assertion that $\chi((\mathbb{AG}(R))^c) = 4$ is verified in the proof of (*ii*) ⇒ (*i*). □

We illustrate Proposition 4.13 with the help of some examples in Example 4.14.

Example 4.14 With the help of results from Belshoff and Chapman (2007) , Corbas and Williams (2000a, 2000b), we mention some examples of local rings $(R, \mathfrak{m})$ of order 32 satisfying the hypotheses of Proposition 4.13.

(i) Let $T = \mathbb{Z}_4[x, y]$ and I be the ideal of T given by $I = (x^3 - 2, xy, y^2 - 2)$. Let $R = T/I$. Note that the unique maximal ideal $\mathfrak{m} = (2, x, y)/I = (x + I, y + I)$ of R satisfies the hypotheses of Proposition 4.13 with $m_1 = x + I$ and $m_2 = y + I$. Moreover, observe that (ii) of Proposition 4.13 is also satisfied.

(ii) Let $T = \mathbb{Z}_4[x, y]$. Let I be the ideal of T given by $I = (x^2 - 2, xy, y^2 - 2x)$. Let $R = T/I$. The unique maximal ideal $\mathfrak{m} = (2, x, y)/I = (x + I, y + I)$ of R satisfies the hypotheses of Proposition 4.13 with $m_1 = x + I$ and $m_2 = y + I$. In addition, the local ring $(R, \mathfrak{m})$ also satisfies (ii) of Proposition 4.13.

(iii) Let $T = \mathbb{Z}_8[x]$ and $R = T/I$, where I is the ideal of T given by $I = (2x, x^3 - 4)$. The unique maximal ideal $\mathfrak{m} = (2, x)/I = (x + I, 2 + I)$ of R satisfies the hypotheses of Proposition 4.13 with $m_1 = x + I$ and $m_2 = 2 + I$. Moreover, the local ring $(R, \mathfrak{m})$ satisfies (ii) of Proposition 4.13.Therefore, it follows from the proof of (*ii*) ⇒ (*i*) of Proposition 4.13 that each one of the ring R mentioned above in (i) to (iii) satisfies $\alpha(\mathbb{AG}(R)) = \chi((\mathbb{AG}(R))^c) = 4$.

Let $(R, \mathfrak{m})$ be a local Artinian ring satisfying all the hypotheses of Proposition 4.13 except the hypothesis $Rm_1^2 \neq Rm_2^2$. That is, with the assumption that $Rm_1^2 = Rm_2^2$, in Propositions 4.16 and 4.18, we investigate on the desired classification. In Lemma 4.15, we provide a necessary condition on $|R/\mathfrak{m}|$ in order that $\alpha(\mathbb{AG}(R))) \leq 4$.

LEMMA 4.15 *Let $(R, \mathfrak{m})$ be a local Artinian ring such that $\mathfrak{m}$ is not principal but $\mathfrak{m} = Rm_1 + Rm_2$. Suppose that $m_1^2 \neq 0, m_1m_2 = 0$, and $Rm_1^2 = Rm_2^2$. If $\alpha(\mathbb{AG}(R)) \leq 4$, then $|R/\mathfrak{m}| \leq 5$.*

Proof Since R is local and $m_1^2 \neq 0$, it follows from $Rm_1^2 = Rm_2^2$ that $m_1^2 = um_2^2$ for some unit $u \in R$. From $m_1m_2 = 0$, it is now clear that $\mathfrak{m}^3 = (0)$. We consider the following cases:

Case(i). $2 \in \mathfrak{m}$

In this case, we show that $|R/\mathfrak{m}| \leq 4$. Suppose that $|R/\mathfrak{m}| > 4$. Then $|R/\mathfrak{m}| \geq 8$. Hence, we can find $r_1, r_2 \in R\backslash\mathfrak{m}$ such that $r_i - 1 \notin \mathfrak{m}$ for each $i \in \{1, 2\}$ and moreover, $r_1 + u, r_2 + u, r_1r_2 + u, r_1 - r_2 \in R\backslash\mathfrak{m}$. Observe that $\{Rm_1, R(m_1 + m_2), R(m_1 + r_1m_2), R(m_1 + r_2m_2), \mathfrak{m}\}$ is an independent set of $\mathbb{AG}(R)$ and hence, $\alpha(\mathbb{AG}(R)) \geq 5$. This contradicts the hypothesis that $\alpha(\mathbb{AG}(R)) \leq 4$. Therefore, $|R/\mathfrak{m}| \leq 4$.

Case(ii). $2 \notin \mathfrak{m}$ *but* $u - 1 \in \mathfrak{m}$

Note that $u = 1 + m$ for some $m \in \mathfrak{m}$ and so $m_1^2 = (1 + m)m_2^2$. From $\mathfrak{m}^3 = (0)$, we obtain that $m_1^2 = m_2^2$. In this case, we show that $|R/\mathfrak{m}| = 3$. From $2 \notin \mathfrak{m}$, it follows that $|R/\mathfrak{m}| \geq 3$. If $|R/\mathfrak{m}| > 3$, then there exists $r \in R\backslash\mathfrak{m}$ such that $r - 1, r + 1 \in R\backslash\mathfrak{m}$. Hence, $r^2 - 1 \in R\backslash\mathfrak{m}$. Observe that $\{Rm_1, R(m_1 + m_2), R(m_1 + rm_2), R(m_1 - rm_2), \mathfrak{m}\}$ is an independent set of $\mathbb{AG}(R)$. This implies that $\alpha(\mathbb{AG}(R)) \geq 5$ and this is a contradiction. Therefore, $|R/\mathfrak{m}| \leq 3$ and so $|R/\mathfrak{m}| = 3$.

Case(iii). $2 \notin \mathfrak{m}$ *and* $u - 1 \notin \mathfrak{m}$

In this case, we show that $|R/\mathfrak{m}| \leq 5$. Suppose that $|R/\mathfrak{m}| > 5$. Note that $1 + \mathfrak{m}, -1 + \mathfrak{m}, u + \mathfrak{m}, -u + \mathfrak{m} \in R/\mathfrak{m}$. Now there exists $r \in R\backslash\mathfrak{m}$ such that $r + \mathfrak{m} \notin \{1 + \mathfrak{m}, -1 + \mathfrak{m}, u + \mathfrak{m}, -u + \mathfrak{m}\}$. Note that $\{Rm_1, R(m_1 + um_2), R(m_1 - um_2), R(m_1 + rm_2), \mathfrak{m}\}$ is an independent set of $\mathbb{AG}(R)$. This is impossible since by hypothesis, $\alpha(\mathbb{AG}(R)) \leq 4$. Therefore, $|R/\mathfrak{m}| \leq 5$. □

Proposition 4.16 Let $(R, \mathfrak{m})$ be a local Artinian ring such that $\mathfrak{m}$ is not principal but $\mathfrak{m} = Rm_1 + Rm_2$. Suppose that $m_1^2 \neq 0, m_1m_2 = 0$, and $m_1^2 = m_2^2$. Then the following statements are equivalent:

(i) $\alpha(\mathbb{AG}(R)) = 4$.

(ii) $|R/\mathfrak{m}| = 4$.

Moreover, if either (i) or (ii) holds, then $|R| = 256$ and $\chi((\mathbb{AG}(R))^c) = 4$.

Proof It is clear that $\mathfrak{m}^2 = Rm_1^2$ and $\mathfrak{m}^3 = (0)$.

(i) ⇒ *(ii)* We know from the proof of Lemma 4.15 (see case(i) and case(ii) considered in the proof) that $|R/\mathfrak{m}| \leq 4$. Since $\alpha(\mathbb{AG}(R)) = 4$, it follows from Lemmas 3.11 and 3.13 that $|R/\mathfrak{m}| = 4$.

Note that $dim_{R/\mathfrak{m}}(\mathfrak{m}^2) = 1$ and $dim_{R/\mathfrak{m}}(\mathfrak{m}/\mathfrak{m}^2) = 2$. Hence, $|\mathfrak{m}^2| = 4, |\mathfrak{m}/\mathfrak{m}^2| = 16$. Therefore, $|\mathfrak{m}| = 64$ and so $|R| = |\mathfrak{m}||R/\mathfrak{m}| = 256$.

(ii) ⇒ *(i)* Let $r \in R\backslash\mathfrak{m}$ be such that $R/\mathfrak{m} = \{0 + \mathfrak{m}, 1 + \mathfrak{m}, r + \mathfrak{m}, (r + 1) + \mathfrak{m}\}$ with $r^2 + r + 1 \in \mathfrak{m}$. Let $A = \{0, 1, r, r + 1\}$. Observe that $\mathfrak{m} = \{am_1 + bm_2 + cm_1^2 | a, b, c \text{ vary over } A\}$. It is not hard to verify that the set of all nonzero proper ideals of R equals

$\{Rm_1, Rm_2, R(m_1 + m_2), R(m_1 + rm_2), R(m_1 + (r+1)m_2), Rm_1^2, \mathfrak{m}\}$. Note that $\{Rm_1, R(m_1 + m_2), R(m_1 + rm_2), \mathfrak{m}\}$ is an independent set of $\mathbb{AG}(R)$. Hence, $\alpha(\mathbb{AG}(R)) \geq 4$. We next verify that $\chi((\mathbb{AG}(R))^c) \leq 4$. As $\mathfrak{m}^3 = (0)$, it is clear that Rm_1^2 is an isolated vertex of $(\mathbb{AG}(R))^c$. From $m_1m_2 = 0$ and $m_1^2 + m_2^2 = 0$, it follows that in $(\mathbb{AG}(R))^c$, Rm_1 and Rm_2 are not adjacent, $R(m_1 + rm_2)$ and $R(m_1 + (r+1)m_2)$ are not adjacent. Let $\{c_1, c_2, c_3, c_4\}$ be a set of four distinct colors. Let us assign the color c_1 to Rm_1 and Rm_2, color c_2 to $R(m_1 + m_2)$, color c_3 to $R(m_1 + rm_2)$ and $R(m_1 + (r+1)m_2)$, and the color c_4 to $\mathfrak{m}$ and Rm_1^2. Then it is clear that the above assignment of colors is indeed a proper vertex coloring of $(\mathbb{AG}(R))^c$. This proves that $4 \leq \alpha(\mathbb{AG}(R)) \leq \chi((\mathbb{AG}(R))^c) \leq 4$. Therefore, $\alpha(\mathbb{AG}(R)) = \chi((\mathbb{AG}(R))^c) = 4$.

The moreover assertion that $|R| = 256$ is already verified in the proof of *(i)* ⇒ *(ii)* and the assertion that $\chi((\mathbb{AG}(R))^c) = 4$ is verified in the proof of *(ii)* ⇒ *(i)*. □

We illustrate Proposition 4.16 with the help of an example in Example 4.17.

Example 4.17 Let $T = \mathbb{F}_4[x, y]$. Let $R = T/I$, where I is the ideal of T given by $I = (x^2 - y^2, xy)$. Observe that the unique maximal ideal $\mathfrak{m} = (x, y)/I = (x + I, y + I)$ satisfies the hypotheses of Proposition 4.16 with $m_1 = x + I, m_2 = y + I$ and moreover, $|R/\mathfrak{m}| = 4$. Therefore, we obtain from the proof of *(ii)* ⇒ *(i)* of Proposition 4.16 that $\alpha(\mathbb{AG}(R)) = \chi((\mathbb{AG}(R))^c) = 4$.

Proposition 4.18 Let $(R, \mathfrak{m})$ be a local Artinian ring such that $\mathfrak{m}$ is not principal but $\mathfrak{m} = Rm_1 + Rm_2$ for some $m_1, m_2 \in \mathfrak{m}$. Suppose that $m_1^2 \neq 0, m_1m_2 = 0$, and $m_1^2 = um_2^2$ for some unit $u \in R$ with $u - 1 \notin \mathfrak{m}$. Then the following statements are equivalent:

(i) $\alpha(\mathbb{AG}(R)) = 4$.

(ii) $|R/\mathfrak{m}| \in \{3, 4, 5\}$. If $|R/\mathfrak{m}| = 5$, then $u + 1 \notin \mathfrak{m}$.

Moreover, if either (i) or (ii) holds, then $|R| \in \{81, 256, 625\}$ and $\chi((\mathbb{AG}(R))^c) = 4$

Proof Note that $\mathfrak{m}^2 = Rm_1^2$ and $\mathfrak{m}^3 = (0)$. We are assuming that $m_1^2 = um_2^2$ for some unit u in R such that $u - 1 \notin \mathfrak{m}$. Hence, it follows that $|R/\mathfrak{m}| \geq 3$.

(i) ⇒ *(ii)* It follows from Lemma 4.15 that $|R/\mathfrak{m}| \leq 5$. Therefore, $|R/\mathfrak{m}| \in \{3, 4, 5\}$.

Assume that $|R/\mathfrak{m}| = 5$. We prove that $u + 1 \notin \mathfrak{m}$. Suppose that $u + 1 \in \mathfrak{m}$. From $m_1^2 = um_2^2$, it follows that $m_1^2 = 4m_2^2 = (2m_2)^2$. Let $a = m_1, b = 2m_2$. Note that $\mathfrak{m} = Ra + Rb$ with $a^2 \neq 0, ab = 0$, and $a^2 = b^2$. In such a case, it follows from *(i)* ⇒ *(ii)* of Proposition 4.16 that $|R/\mathfrak{m}| = 4$. This is a contradiction. Hence, $u + 1 \notin \mathfrak{m}$.

Note that $dim_{R/\mathfrak{m}}(\mathfrak{m}^2) = 1$ and $dim_{R/\mathfrak{m}}(\mathfrak{m}/\mathfrak{m}^2) = 2$. Hence, $|R| = 81$ if $|R/\mathfrak{m}| = 3$, $|R| = 256$ if $|R/\mathfrak{m}| = 4$, and $|R| = 625$ if $|R/\mathfrak{m}| = 5$.

(ii) ⇒ *(i)* We first assume that $|R/\mathfrak{m}| = 3$. Note that $R/\mathfrak{m} = \{0 + \mathfrak{m}, 1 + \mathfrak{m}, 2 + \mathfrak{m}\}$. Let $A = \{0, 1, 2\}$. Observe that $u = 2 + m$ for some $m \in \mathfrak{m}$ and so $m_1^2 = 2m_2^2$. It is clear that $\mathfrak{m} = \{am_1 + bm_2 + cm_1^2 | a, b, c$ vary over $A\}$. It is easy to verify that the set of all nonzero proper ideals of R equals $\{Rm_1, Rm_2, R(m_1 + m_2), R(m_1 + 2m_2), Rm_1^2, \mathfrak{m}\}$. Observe that $\{Rm_1, R(m_1 + m_2), R(m_1 + 2m_2), \mathfrak{m}\}$ is an independent set of $\mathbb{AG}(R)$. Hence, $\alpha(\mathbb{AG}(R)) \geq 4$. We next verify that $\chi((\mathbb{AG}(R))^c)) \leq 4$. Since $\mathfrak{m}^3 = (0)$, Rm_1^2 is an isolated vertex of $(\mathbb{AG}(R))^c$. From $m_1m_2 = 0$, it follows that Rm_1 and Rm_2 are not adjacent in $(\mathbb{AG}(R))^c$. Let $\{c_1, c_2, c_3, c_4\}$ be a set of four distinct colors. Let us assign the color c_1 to Rm_1 and Rm_2, color c_2 to $R(m_1 + m_2)$, color c_3 to $R(m_1 + 2m_2)$, and the color c_4 to $\mathfrak{m}$ and Rm_1^2. It is clear that the above assignment of colors is indeed a proper vertex coloring of $(\mathbb{AG}(R))^c$. This proves that $4 \leq \alpha(\mathbb{AG}(R)) \leq \chi((\mathbb{AG}(R))^c) \leq 4$. Therefore, $\alpha(\mathbb{AG}(R)) = \chi((\mathbb{AG}(R))^c) = 4$.

Suppose that $|R/\mathfrak{m}| = 4$. In this case there exists $r \in R \backslash \mathfrak{m}$ such that $r^2 + r + 1 \in \mathfrak{m}$ and $R/\mathfrak{m} = \{0 + \mathfrak{m}, 1 + \mathfrak{m}, r + \mathfrak{m}, (r+1) + \mathfrak{m}\}$. Note that either $u = r + m$ for some $m \in \mathfrak{m}$ or $u = (r+1) + m$

for some $m \in \mathfrak{m}$. Hence, either $m_1^2 = rm_2^2$ or $m_1^2 = (r+1)m_2^2$. Observe that $r-(r+1)^2 \in \mathfrak{m}$ and $(r+1)-r^2 \in \mathfrak{m}$. Therefore, either $m_1^2 = ((r+1)m_2)^2$ or $m_1^2 = (rm_2)^2$. In the case $m_1^2 = ((r+1)m_2)^2$, we obtain with $a = m_1$ and $b = (r+1)m_2$ that $\mathfrak{m} = Ra + Rb, a^2 \neq 0, ab = 0$, and $a^2 = b^2$. Therefore, we obtain from the proof of (*ii*) $\Rightarrow$ (*i*) of Proposition 4.16 that $\alpha(\mathbb{AG}((R)) = \chi((\mathbb{AG}(R))^c) = 4$. If $m_1^2 = (rm_2)^2$, then the elements $a = m_1, c = rm_2$ are such that $\mathfrak{m} = Ra + Rc, a^2 \neq 0, ac = 0$, and $a^2 = c^2$. Hence, again it follows from the proof of (*ii*) $\Rightarrow$ (*i*) of Proposition 4.16 that $\alpha(\mathbb{AG}(R)) = \chi((\mathbb{AG}(R))^c) = 4$.

We next assume that $|R/\mathfrak{m}| = 5$. Then $R/\mathfrak{m} = \{0+\mathfrak{m}, 1+\mathfrak{m}, 2+\mathfrak{m}, 3+\mathfrak{m}, 4+\mathfrak{m}\}$. By hypothesis, $m_1^2 = um_2^2$ for some unit u in R such that $u-1, u+1 \notin \mathfrak{m}$. Hence, $R/\mathfrak{m} = \{0+\mathfrak{m}, 1+\mathfrak{m}, -1+\mathfrak{m}, u+\mathfrak{m}, -u+\mathfrak{m}\}$. Let $A = \{0, 1, -1, u, -u\}$. Note that $\mathfrak{m} = \{am_1 + bm_2 + cm_1^2 | a, b, c$ vary oner A$\}$. It is easy to show that the set of all nonzero proper ideals of R equals $\{Rm_1, Rm_2, R(m_1+m_2), R(m_1-m_2), R(m_1+um_2), R(m_1-um_2), Rm_1^2, \mathfrak{m}\}$. As $u^2 - u \notin \mathfrak{m}$, it follows that $\{Rm_1, R(m_1+um_2), R(m_1-um_2), \mathfrak{m}\}$ is an independent set of $\mathbb{AG}(R)$. Hence, $\alpha(\mathbb{AG}(R)) \geq 4$. We next verify that $\chi((\mathbb{AG}(R))^c) \leq 4$. Since $m_1m_2 = 0$, it follows that Rm_1 and Rm_2 are not adjacent in $(\mathbb{AG}(R))^c$. As $\mathfrak{m}^3 = (0)$, we obtain that Rm_1^2 is an isolated vertex of $(\mathbb{AG}(R))^c$. It follows from $m_1^2 = um_2^2$ that in $(\mathbb{AG}(R))^c$, $R(m_1+m_2)$ and $R(m_1-um_2)$ are not adjacent and $R(m_1-m_2)$ and $R(m_1+um_2)$ are not adjacent. Let $\{c_1, c_2, c_3, c_4\}$ be a set of four distinct colors. Let us assign the color c_1 to Rm_1 and Rm_2, color c_2 to $R(m_1+um_2)$ and $R(m_1-m_2)$, color c_3 to $R(m_1-um_2)$ and $R(m_1+m_2)$, and the color c_4 to $\mathfrak{m}$ and Rm_1^2. Note that the above assignment of colors is indeed a proper vertex coloring of $(\mathbb{AG}(R))^c$. This shows that $4 \leq \alpha(\mathbb{AG}(R)) \leq \chi((\mathbb{AG}(R))^c) \leq 4$. Therefore, $\alpha(\mathbb{AG}(R)) = \chi((\mathbb{AG}(R))^c) = 4$.

The moreover assertion $|R| \in \{81, 256, 625\}$ is already verified in the proof of (*i*) $\Rightarrow$ (*ii*) and the assertion that $\chi((\mathbb{AG}(R))^c) = 4$ is verified in the proof of (*ii*) $\Rightarrow$ (*i*). □

In Example 4.19, we illustrate Proposition 4.18 with the help of some examples.

Example 4.19

(i) Let $T = \mathbb{Z}_{27}[x]$ and I be the ideal of T given by $I = (3x, x^2 - 18)$. Let $R = T/I$. Note that the unique maximal ideal $\mathfrak{m} = (3, x)/I = (3+I, x+I)$ of R satisfies the hypotheses of Proposition 4.18 with $m_1 = x + I$ and $m_2 = 3 + I$. As $|R/\mathfrak{m}| = 3$, it follows from the proof of (*ii*) $\Rightarrow$ (*i*) of Proposition 4.18 that $\alpha(\mathbb{AG}(R)) = \chi((\mathbb{AG}(R))^c) = 4$.

(ii) Let $T = \mathbb{Z}_5[x, y]$ and I be the ideal of T given by $I = (x^2 - 2y^2, xy)$. Let $R = T/I$. Observe that the unique maximal ideal $\mathfrak{m} = (x, y)/I = (x+I, y+I)$ satisfies the hypotheses of Proposition 4.18 with $m_1 = x + I$ and $m_2 = y + I$. Since $m_1^2 = 2m_2^2$ and $|R/\mathfrak{m}| = 5$, it follows from the proof of (*ii*) $\Rightarrow$ (*i*) of Proposition 4.18 that $\alpha(\mathbb{AG}(R)) = \chi((\mathbb{AG}(R))^c) = 4$.

LEMMA 4.20 *Let $(R, \mathfrak{m})$ be a local Artinian ring such that $\mathfrak{m}$ is not principal but $\mathfrak{m} = Rm_1 + Rm_2$ for some $m_1, m_2 \in \mathfrak{m}$. Suppose that $m_1^2 \neq 0, m_2^2 = 0, m_1m_2 \neq 0$, and $m_1^2 + m_1m_2 \neq 0$. If $\alpha(\mathbb{AG}(R)) \leq 4$, then the following hold:*

(i) $m_1^2m_2 = 0$. Moreover, if $|R/\mathfrak{m}| \geq 3$, then $\mathfrak{m}^3 = (0)$.

(ii) $|R/\mathfrak{m}| \leq 4$.

Proof (i) Since $\{m_1 + \mathfrak{m}^2, m_2 + \mathfrak{m}^2\}$ is a basis of $\mathfrak{m}/\mathfrak{m}^2$ as a vector space over $R/\mathfrak{m}$, it follows that the ideals $Rm_1, Rm_2, R(m_1+m_2), \mathfrak{m}$ are distinct. Moreover, we obtain from the hypotheses on the elements m_1, m_2 that $W = \{Rm_1, Rm_2, R(m_1+m_2), \mathfrak{m}\}$ is an independent set of $\mathbb{AG}(R)$. We assert that $m_1^2m_2 = 0$. Suppose that $m_1^2m_2 \neq 0$. Then $Rm_1^2 \not\subseteq Rm_2$. For if $m_1^2 \in Rm_2$, then $m_1^2 \in \mathfrak{m}m_2$. Hence, $m_1^2 = (am_1 + bm_2)m_2$ for some $a, b \in R$. This implies that $m_1^2 = am_1m_2$ and so $m_1^2m_2 = am_1m_2^2 = 0$. Therefore, $Rm_1^2 \not\subseteq Rm_2$. In such a case, it is clear that $Rm_1^2 + Rm_2 \notin W$, and moreover, $W \cup \{Rm_1^2 + Rm_2\}$ is an independent set of $\mathbb{AG}(R)$. This is in contradiction to the hypothesis that $\alpha(\mathbb{AG}(R)) \leq 4$. Therefore, $m_1^2m_2 = 0$.

Suppose that $|R/\mathfrak{m}| \geq 3$. Then there exists $r \in R$ such that $r \notin \mathfrak{m}$ and $r - 1 \notin \mathfrak{m}$. Since

$W = \{Rm_1, Rm_2, R(m_1 + m_2), \mathfrak{m}\}$ is an independent set of $\mathbb{AG}(R)$ and as $R(m_1 + rm_2) \notin W$, it follows that either $m_1^2 + rm_1m_2 = 0$ or $m_1^2 + (r+1)m_1m_2 = 0$. Hence, $m_1^2 \in Rm_1m_2$ and from $m_1^2m_2 = 0$, we obtain that $m_1^3 = (0)$. Therefore, $\mathfrak{m}^3 = (0)$.

(ii) We consider two cases.

Case(I). $2 \in \mathfrak{m}$

If $|R/\mathfrak{m}| > 4$, then there exist $r, s \in R\backslash\mathfrak{m}$ such that $\{r-1, s-1, r-s, r-1-s\} \subseteq R\backslash\mathfrak{m}$. Note that $R(m_1 + rm_2) \notin W$ and as $\alpha(\mathbb{AG}(R)) \leq 4$, it follows that either $m_1^2 + rm_1m_2 = 0$ or $m_1^2 + (r+1)m_1m_2 = 0$. Similarly, it follows that either $m_1^2 + sm_1m_2 = 0$ or $m_1^2 + (s+1)m_1m_2 = 0$. Suppose that $m_1^2 + rm_1m_2 = 0$. Since $m_1m_2 \neq 0$ and as $r - s, r - (s+1) \in R\backslash\mathfrak{m}$, it follows that $m_1^2 + sm_1m_2$ cannot be 0 and $m_1^2 + (s+1)m_1m_2$ cannot be 0. Similarly, if $m_1^2 + (r+1)m_1m_2 = 0$, then $m_1^2 + sm_1m_2$ cannot be 0 and $m_1^2 + (s+1)m_1m_2$ cannot be 0. This is a contradiction. Therefore, $|R/\mathfrak{m}| \leq 4$.

Case(II). $2 \notin \mathfrak{m}$

Note that $R(m_1 - m_2) \notin W$ and as $\alpha(\mathbb{AG}(R)) \leq 4$, it follows that $W \cup \{R(m_1 - m_2)\}$ cannot be an independent set of $\mathbb{AG}(R)$. As $(m_1 - m_2)m_2 = m_1m_2 \neq 0, (m_1 - m_2)(m_1 + m_2) = m_1^2 \neq 0$, it follows that $(m_1 - m_2)m_1 = 0$. Thus $m_1^2 = m_1m_2$. We assert that $|R/\mathfrak{m}| = 3$. Suppose that $|R/\mathfrak{m}| > 3$. Then there exist $r, s \in R\backslash\mathfrak{m}$ such that $\{r-1, r+1, s-1, s+1, r-s\} \subseteq R\backslash\mathfrak{m}$. Then either $r + 2 \notin \mathfrak{m}$ or $s + 2 \notin \mathfrak{m}$. Without loss of generality, we can assume that $r + 2 \notin \mathfrak{m}$. Hence, $(r+1)m_1m_2 \neq 0$ and $(r+2)m_1m_2 \neq 0$. Observe that $W \cup \{R(m_1 + rm_2)\}$ is an independent set of $\mathbb{AG}(R)$. This is impossible. Therefore, $|R/\mathfrak{m}| = 3$. □

Proposition 4.21 Let $(R, \mathfrak{m})$ be a loccal Artinian ring satisfying the hypotheses mentioned in Lemma 4.20. If $|R/\mathfrak{m}| = 2$ and $\mathfrak{m}^3 = (0)$, then the following statements are equivalent:

(i) $\alpha(\mathbb{AG}(R)) = 4$.
(ii) $|R| = 32$.

Moreover, if (i) or (ii) holds, then $\chi((\mathbb{AG}(R))^c) = 4$.

Proof *(i)* ⇒ *(ii)* Note that from the given hypotheses on the elements m_1, m_2 of $\mathfrak{m}$, we obtain that $\mathfrak{m}^2 = Rm_1^2 + Rm_1m_2$. Since $\mathfrak{m}^3 = (0)$, $\mathfrak{m}^2$ is a vector space over $R/\mathfrak{m}$. We claim that $\{m_1^2, m_1m_2\}$ is linearly independent over $R/\mathfrak{m}$. Let $a, b \in R$ be such that $am_1^2 + bm_1m_2 = 0$. We first assert that at least one of $a, b \in \mathfrak{m}$. Suppose that $a \notin \mathfrak{m}$ and $b \notin \mathfrak{m}$. Since $|R/\mathfrak{m}| = 2$, it follows that $a = 1 + m, b = 1 + m'$ for some $m.m' \in \mathfrak{m}$. Now from $am_1^2 + bm_1m_2 = 0$ and $\mathfrak{m}^3 = (0)$, it follows that $m_1^2 + m_1m_2 = 0$. This is a contradiction. Thus either $a \in \mathfrak{m}$ or $b \in \mathfrak{m}$. If $a \in \mathfrak{m}$, then from $bm_1m_2 = 0$, it follows that $b \in \mathfrak{m}$. If $b \in \mathfrak{m}$, then from $am_1^2 = 0$, we obtain that $a \in \mathfrak{m}$. This shows that $\{m_1^2, m_1m_2\}$ is linearly independent over $R/\mathfrak{m}$. Therefore, $dim_{R/\mathfrak{m}}(\mathfrak{m}^2) = 2$. Note that $|\mathfrak{m}^2| = 4, |\mathfrak{m}/\mathfrak{m}^2| = 4$, and so $|\mathfrak{m}| = 16$. Hence, we obtain that $|R| = 32$.

(ii) ⇒ *(i)* It is clear that $|\mathfrak{m}| = 16$ and $|\mathfrak{m}^2| = 4$. Let $A = \{0, 1\}$. Observe that $\mathfrak{m} = \{am_1 + bm_2 + cm_1^2 + dm_1m_2 | a, b, c, d \text{ vary over } A\}$. It is not hard to verify that the set of all nonzero proper ideals of R equals $\{Rm_1, Rm_2, R(m_1 + m_2), R(m_1^2 + m_1m_2), R(m_2 + m_1^2), Rm_1^2, Rm_1m_2, Rm_1^2 + Rm_2, \mathfrak{m}^2, \mathfrak{m}\}$. Since $\{Rm_1, Rm_2, R(m_1 + m_2), \mathfrak{m}\}$ is an independent set of $\mathbb{AG}(R)$, it follows that $\alpha(\mathbb{AG}(R)) \geq 4$. We next verify that the vertices of $(\mathbb{AG}(R))^c$ can be properly colored using a set of four distinct colors. As $\mathfrak{m}^3 = (0)$, it follows that $A_1 = \{\mathfrak{m}^2, R(m_1^2 + m_1m_2), Rm_1m_2, Rm_1^2\}$ is the set of all isolated vertices of $(\mathbb{AG}(R))^c$. It follows from $m_2^2 = 0$ and $\mathfrak{m}^3 = (0)$ that no two members from $B = \{Rm_2, R(m_2 + m_1^2), Rm_1^2 + Rm_2\}$ are adjacent in $(\mathbb{AG}(R))^c$. Let $\{c_1, c_2, c_3, c_4\}$ be a set of four distinct colors. Let us assign the color c_1 to Rm_1, color c_2 to all the members from B, color c_3 to $R(m_1 + m_2)$, and the color c_4 to all the members from $\{\mathfrak{m}\} \cup A_1$. Observe that the above assignment of colors is indeed a proper vertex coloring of $(\mathbb{AG}(R))^c$. This proves that $4 \leq \alpha(\mathbb{AG}(R)) \leq \chi((\mathbb{AG}(R))^c) \leq 4$. Therefore, $\alpha(\mathbb{AG}(R)) = \chi((\mathbb{AG}(R))^c) = 4$.

The moreover assertion that $\chi((\mathbb{AG}(R))^c) = 4$ is verified in the proof of *(ii)* $\Rightarrow$ *(i)*. □

With the help of results from Belshoff and Chapman (2007), Corbas and Williams (2000a, 2000b), we now mention some examples to illustrate Proposition 4.21.

Example 4.22 (i) Let $T = \mathbb{Z}_2[x, y]$ and $R = T/I$, where I is the ideal of T given by $I = (x^3, x^2y, y^2)$. Note that $(R, \mathfrak{m})$ is a local Artinian ring with $\mathfrak{m} = (x, y)/I = (x + I, y + I)$. Observe that $\mathfrak{m}$ satisfies the hypotheses of Lemma 4.20 with $m_1 = x + I$ and $m_2 = y + I$. Moreover, $\mathfrak{m}^3 = (0)$ and $|R/\mathfrak{m}| = 2$. As $|R| = 32$, it follows from the proof of *(ii)* $\Rightarrow$ *(i)* of Proposition 4.21 that $\alpha(\mathbb{AG}(R)) = \chi((\mathbb{AG}(R))^c) = 4$.

(ii) Let $T = \mathbb{Z}_4[x]$ and I be the ideal of T given by $I = (2x^2, x^3)$. Let $R = T/I$. Note that $(R, \mathfrak{m})$ is a local Artinian ring with $\mathfrak{m} = (2, x)/I = (x + I, 2 + I)$ and moreover, $\mathfrak{m}$ satisfies the hypotheses of Lemma 4.21 with $m_1 = x + I$ and $m_2 = 2 + I$. Furthermore, $|R/\mathfrak{m}| = 2$ and $\mathfrak{m}^3 = (0)$. As $|R| = 32$, we obtain from the proof of *(ii)* $\Rightarrow$ *(i)* of Proposition 4.21 that $\alpha(\mathbb{AG}(R)) = \chi((\mathbb{AG}(R))^c) = 4$.

Let $(R, \mathfrak{m})$ be a local Artinian ring satisfying the hypotheses of Lemma 4.20. Suppose in addition that $|R/\mathfrak{m}| = 2$ and $\mathfrak{m}^3 \neq (0)$. In Propositions 4.24 and 4.26, we provide the classification of such rings R in order that $\alpha(\mathbb{AG}(R)) = 4$. We use Lemma 4.23 in the proof of Propositions 4.24 and 4.26.

LEMMA 4.23 *Let $(R, \mathfrak{m})$ be a local Artinian ring satisfying the hypotheses mentioned in Lemma 4.20. Suppose that $|R/\mathfrak{m}| = 2$, $\mathfrak{m}^3 \neq 0$, and $\alpha(\mathbb{AG}(R)) \leq 4$. Then $\mathfrak{m}^4 = (0)$. Moreover, if $m_1^3 \neq m_1m_2$, then $dim_{R/\mathfrak{m}}(\mathfrak{m}^2/\mathfrak{m}^3) = 2$.*

Proof Note that $W = \{Rm_1, Rm_2, R(m_1 + m_2), \mathfrak{m}\}$ is an independent set of $\mathbb{AG}(R)$. We know from Lemma 4.20 (i) that $m_1^2m_2 = 0$. As $m_2^2 = 0$, from $\mathfrak{m}^3 \neq (0)$, it follows that $m_1^3 \neq 0$ and to prove $\mathfrak{m}^4 = (0)$, it is enough to show that $m_1^4 = 0$. Suppose that $m_1^4 \neq 0$. Observe that $\{Rm_1, Rm_1^2, R(m_1 + m_2), Rm_1^2 + Rm_2, \mathfrak{m}\}$ is an independent set of $\mathbb{AG}(R)$. This is impossible since by hypothesis, $\alpha(\mathbb{AG}(R)) \leq 4$. Therefore, $\mathfrak{m}^4 = (0)$.

(ii) We now prove the moreover assertion of the lemma. Note that $\mathfrak{m}^2 = Rm_1^2 + Rm_1m_2$. We assert that $\{m_1^2 + \mathfrak{m}^3, m_1m_2 + \mathfrak{m}^3\}$ is linearly independent over $R/\mathfrak{m}$. Let $a, b \in R$ be such that $am_1^2 + bm_1m_2 \in \mathfrak{m}^3$. We assert that both a and b belong to $\mathfrak{m}$. First we verify that either $a \in \mathfrak{m}$ or $b \in \mathfrak{m}$. If $a \notin \mathfrak{m}$ and $b \notin \mathfrak{m}$, then $a = 1 + m, b = 1 + m'$ for some $m, m' \in \mathfrak{m}$. Therefore, $(1 + m)m_1^2 + (1 + m')m_1m_2 \in \mathfrak{m}^3$. This implies that $m_1^2 + m_1m_2 \in \mathfrak{m}^3$. Hence, $m_1^3 + m_1^2m_2 \in \mathfrak{m}^4 = (0)$ and from $m_1^2m_2 = 0$, it follows that $m_1^3 = 0$. This is impossible since $m_1^3 \neq 0$. Thus either $a \in \mathfrak{m}$ or $b \in \mathfrak{m}$. If $b \in \mathfrak{m}$, then we get that $am_1^2 \in \mathfrak{m}^3 = Rm_1^3$. As $m_1^2 \notin Rm_1^3$, it follows that $a \in \mathfrak{m}$. If $a \in \mathfrak{m}$, then we obtain that $bm_1m_2 \in \mathfrak{m}^3 = Rm_1^3$. If $b \notin \mathfrak{m}$, then $m_1m_2 = cm_1^3$ for some $c \in R\backslash\mathfrak{m}$. As $c \in 1 + \mathfrak{m}$, it follows that $m_1m_2 = m_1^3$. This contradicts the hypothesis that $m_1^3 \neq m_1m_2$. Hence, $b \in \mathfrak{m}$. This proves that $\{m_1^2 + \mathfrak{m}^3, m_1m_2 + \mathfrak{m}^3\}$ is linearly independent over $R/\mathfrak{m}$. Therefore, $dim_{R/\mathfrak{m}}(\mathfrak{m}^2/\mathfrak{m}^3) = 2$. □

Proposition 4.24 Let $(R, \mathfrak{m})$ be a local Artinian ring satisfying the hypotheses mentioned in Lemma 4.20. Suppose that $|R/\mathfrak{m}| = 2$, $\mathfrak{m}^3 \neq (0)$, and $m_1^3 = m_1m_2$. Then the following statements are equivalent:

(i) $\alpha(\mathbb{AG}(R)) = 4$.
(ii) $\mathfrak{m}^4 = (0)$ and $|R| = 32$.

Moreover, if (i) or (ii) holds, then $\chi((\mathbb{AG}(R))^c) = 4$.

Proof *(i)* $\Rightarrow$ *(ii)* We know from Lemma 4.20(i) that $m_1^2m_2 = 0$. We know from Lemma 4.23 that $\mathfrak{m}^4 = (0)$. Note that $\mathfrak{m}^2 = Rm_1^2 + Rm_1m_2 = Rm_1^2 + Rm_1^3 = Rm_1^2$. Observe that $\mathfrak{m}^3 = Rm_1^3$. Thus $dim_{R/\mathfrak{m}}(\mathfrak{m}^3) = dim_{R/\mathfrak{m}}(\mathfrak{m}^2/\mathfrak{m}^3) = 1$, and $dim_{R/\mathfrak{m}}(\mathfrak{m}/\mathfrak{m}^2) = 2$. Hence, $|\mathfrak{m}^3| = |\mathfrak{m}^2/\mathfrak{m}^3| = 2$, and $|\mathfrak{m}/\mathfrak{m}^2| = 4$. Thus $|\mathfrak{m}| = 16$ and so $|R| = 32$.

(ii) ⇒ *(i)* From $m_1^3 = m_1m_2$, $\mathfrak{m}^4 = (0)$, and $m_2^2 = 0$, it is clear that $\mathfrak{m}^2 = Rm_1^2, \mathfrak{m}^3 = Rm_1^3$. Observe that $\mathfrak{m} = \{am_1 + bm_2 + cm_1^2 + dm_1^3 | a, b, c, d$ vary over $\{0, 1\}\}$. It is not hard to verify that the set of all nonzero proper ideals of R equals $\{Rm_1, Rm_2, R(m_1 + m_2), R(m_1^2 + m_2), R(m_1^2 + m_2 + m_1m_2), Rm_1^2, Rm_1^3, Rm_1^2 + Rm_2, R(m_1^2 + m_2) + Rm_1^3, \mathfrak{m}\}$. As $\{Rm_1, Rm_2, R(m_1 + m_2), \mathfrak{m}\}$ is an independent set of $\mathbb{AG}(R)$, it follows that $\alpha(\mathbb{AG}(R)) \geq 4$. We next verify that $\chi((\mathbb{AG}(R))^c) \leq 4$.. Since $\mathfrak{m}^4 = (0)$, Rm_1^3 is an isolated vertex of $(\mathbb{AG}(R))^c$. As $m_1^2m_2 = 0$ and $m_2^2 = 0$, no two members from $A = \{Rm_2, Rm_1^2, R(m_1^2 + m_2), R(m_1^2 + m_2 + m_1m_2), Rm_1^2 + Rm_2, R(m_1^2 + m_2) + Rm_1^3\}$ are adjacent in $(\mathbb{AG}(R))^c$. Let $\{c_1, c_2, c_3, c_4\}$ be a set of four distinct colors. Let us assign the color c_1 to Rm_1, color c_2 to all the vertices from A, color c_3 to $R(m_1 + m_2)$, and the color c_4 to $\mathfrak{m}$ and Rm_1^3. It is now evident that the above assignment of colors is indeed a proper vertex coloring of $(\mathbb{AG}(R))^c$. Hence, it follows that $4 \leq \alpha(\mathbb{AG}(R)) \leq \chi((\mathbb{AG}(R))^c) \leq 4$. Therefore, $\alpha(\mathbb{AG}(R)) = \chi((\mathbb{AG}(R))^c) = 4$.

The moreover assertion that $\chi((\mathbb{AG}(R))^c) = 4$ is verified in the proof of *(ii)* ⇒ *(i)*. □

Wet mention an example in Example 4.25 from Belshoff and Chapman (2007) to illustrate Proposition 4.24.

Example 4.25 Let $T = \mathbb{Z}_4[x]$ and I be the ideal of T given by $I = (2x^2, x^3 - 2x)$. Let $R = T/I$. Let $\mathfrak{m} = (2, x)/I = (x + I, 2 + I)$. Note that $(R, \mathfrak{m})$ is a local Artinian ring and $\mathfrak{m}$ satisfies the hypotheses of Lemma 4.20 with $m_1 = x + I$ and $m_2 = 2 + I$. Moreover, $m_1^3 = m_1m_2$ and $|R/\mathfrak{m}| = 2$. As $\mathfrak{m}^4 = (0)$ and $|R| = 32$, it follows from the proof of *(ii)* ⇒ *(i)* of Proposition 4.24 that $\alpha(\mathbb{AG}(R)) = \chi((\mathbb{AG}(R))^c) = 4$.

Proposition 4.26 Let $(R, \mathfrak{m})$ be a local Artinian ring satisfying the hypotheses of Lemma 4.20. Suppose that $|R/\mathfrak{m}| = 2, m_1^3 \neq 0$, and $m_1^3 \neq m_1m_2$. Then the following statements are equivalent:

(i) $\alpha(\mathbb{AG}(R)) = 4$.

(ii) $m_1^2m_2 = 0, \mathfrak{m}^4 = (0)$, and $|R| = 64$.

Moreover, if (i) or (ii) holds, then $\chi((\mathbb{AG}(R))^c) = 4$.

Proof *(i)* ⇒ *(ii)* We know from Lemma 4.20(i) that $m_1^2m_2 = 0$. Moreover, we know from Lemma 4.23 that $\mathfrak{m}^4 = (0)$ and $dim_{R/\mathfrak{m}}(\mathfrak{m}^2/\mathfrak{m}^3) = 2$. Observe that $\mathfrak{m}^3 = Rm_1^3$. Thus $|\mathfrak{m}^3| = 2, |\mathfrak{m}^2/\mathfrak{m}^3| = 4$ and $|\mathfrak{m}/\mathfrak{m}^2| = 4$. Hence, $|\mathfrak{m}| = 32$ and so $|R| = 64$.

(ii) ⇒ *(i)* Note that $\mathfrak{m}^3 = Rm_1^3$ and so $|\mathfrak{m}^3| = 2$. From $|R| = 64, |R/\mathfrak{m}| = 2$, and $|\mathfrak{m}/\mathfrak{m}^2| = 4$, it follows that $|\mathfrak{m}| = 32$ and $|\mathfrak{m}^2| = 8$. As $\mathfrak{m}^2 = Rm_1^2 + Rm_1m_2$, we obtain that $\{m_1^2 + \mathfrak{m}^3, m_1m_2 + \mathfrak{m}^3\}$ is linearly independent over $R/\mathfrak{m}$. Let $A = \{0, 1\}$. Now it is clear that $\mathfrak{m} = \{am_1 + bm_2 + cm_1^2 + dm_1m_2 + em_1^3 | a, b, c, d, e$ vary over $A\}$. We now determine the set of all nonzero proper ideals of R. Let I be any nonzero proper ideal of R. Note that either $I \subseteq \mathfrak{m}^2$ or $I \not\subseteq \mathfrak{m}^2$. We first consider the case in which $I \subseteq \mathfrak{m}^2$. Since $\mathfrak{m}^2 = \{0, m_1^2, m_1^3, m_1^2 + m_1^3, m_1m_2, m_1^2 + m_1m_2, m_1^3 + m_1m_2, m_1^2 + m_1^3 + m_1m_2\}$, it follows that $I \in \{\mathfrak{m}^2 = Rm_1^2 + Rm_1m_2, Rm_1^2, Rm_1m_2, R(m_1^2 + m_1m_2), Rm_1^3, R(m_1^3 + m_1m_2), Rm_1^3 + Rm_1m_2\}$. We next consider the case in which $I \not\subseteq \mathfrak{m}^2$. Let $r \in I$ be such that $r \notin \mathfrak{m}^2$. Note that $r = am_1 + bm_2 + cm_1^2 + dm_1m_2 + em_1^3$ for some $a, b, c, d, e \in A$ with at least one between a and b equals 1. If $a = 1$, then it is easy to see that $\mathfrak{m}^2 \subset I$. Hence, either $dim_{R/\mathfrak{m}}(I/\mathfrak{m}^2) = 1$ or 2. If $dim_{R/\mathfrak{m}}(I/\mathfrak{m}^2) = 2$, then $I = \mathfrak{m}$. If $dim_{R/\mathfrak{m}}(I/\mathfrak{m}^2) = 1$, then $I = Rr$. In such a case, it is clear that $I \in \{Rm_1, R(m_1 + m_2)\}$. Suppose that $a = 0$ and $b = 1$. Note that $r = m_2 + cm_1^2 + dm_1m_2 + em_1^3$. Let us denote the ideal Rr by C. Observe that $R\ /\ C$ is a local Artinian principal ideal ring with $\mathfrak{m}/C$ as its unique maximal ideal. As $(\mathfrak{m}/C)^4 = (0 + C)$, it follows from *(iii)* ⇒ *(i)* of (Atiyah & Macdonald, 1969, Proposition 8.8) that $\{(\mathfrak{m}/C)^i | i \in \{1, 2, 3, 4\}\}$ is the set of all proper ideals of $R\ /\ C$. Therefore, $I \in \{C, C + \mathfrak{m}^2, C + \mathfrak{m}^3\}$. It is easy to verify that $I \in \{Rm_2, R(m_2 + m_1^2), R(m_2 + m_1^3), R(m_2 + m_1^2 + m_1m_2), Rm_2 + Rm_1^2, Rm_2 + Rm_1^3, R(m_2 + m_1^2) + Rm_1^3\}$. It follows from the above arguments that the set of all nonzero proper ideals of R equals $\{Rm_1, Rm_2, R(m_1 + m_2), \mathfrak{m} = Rm_1 + Rm_2, R(m_2 + m_1^2), R(m_2 + m_1^3), R(m_2 + m_1^2 + m_1m_2), Rm_2 + Rm_1^2, Rm_2 + Rm_1^3, R(m_2 + m_1^2) + Rm_1^3, Rm_1^2, Rm_1m_2, R(m_1^2 + m_1m_2), Rm_1^2 + Rm_1m_2 = \mathfrak{m}^2, R(m_1^3 + m_1m_2), Rm_1^3 + Rm_1m_2, Rm_1^3 = \mathfrak{m}^3\}$.

Since $\{Rm_1, Rm_2, R(m_1+m_2), \mathfrak{m}\}$ is an independent set of $\mathbb{AG}(R)$, it follows that $\alpha(\mathbb{AG}(R))) \geq 4$. We next verify that $\chi((\mathbb{AG}(R))^c) \leq 4$. Since $\mathfrak{m}^4 = (0)$, $m_2^2 = 0$, and $\mathfrak{m}(m_1m_2) = 0$, it is clear that the subgraph of $\mathbb{AG}(R)$ induced on $A_1 = \mathbb{A}(R)^* \backslash \{Rm_1, R(m_1+m_2), \mathfrak{m}\}$ is a clique. That is, no two members from A_1 are adjacent in $(\mathbb{AG}(R))^c$. Let $\{c_1, c_2, c_3, c_4\}$ be a set of four distinct colors. Let us assign the color c_1 to Rm_1, color c_2 to all the vertices from A_1, color c_3 to $R(m_1+m_2)$, and the color c_4 to $\mathfrak{m}$. Note that the above assignment of colors is indeed a proper vertex coloring of $(\mathbb{AG}(R))^c$. This proves that $4 \leq \alpha(\mathbb{AG}(R)) \leq \chi((\mathbb{AG}(R))^c) \leq 4$. Therefore, $\alpha(\mathbb{AG}(R)) = \chi((\mathbb{AG}(R))^c) = 4$. □

Example 4.27 illustrates Proposition 4.26.

Example 4.27 Let $T = \mathbb{Z}_2[x,y]$ and I be the ideal of T given by $I = (x^4, y^2, x^2y)$. Let $R = T/I$. Note that $(R, \mathfrak{m})$ is a local Artinian ring with $\mathfrak{m} = (x,y)/I = (x+I, y+I)$ satisfies the hypotheses of Lemma 4.20 with $m_1 = x + I$ and $m_2 = y + I$. Moreover, $|R/\mathfrak{m}| = 2$ and $m_1^3 \neq m_1m_2$. As $m_1^2m_2 = 0, \mathfrak{m}^4 = (0)$, and $|R| = 64$, it follows from the proof of *(ii)* ⇒ *(i)* of Proposition 4.26 that $\alpha(\mathbb{AG}(R)) = \chi((\mathbb{AG}(R))^c) = 4$.

Proposition 4.28 Let $(R, \mathfrak{m})$ be a local Artinian ring satisfying the hypotheses of Lemma 4.20. Suppose that $|R/\mathfrak{m}| = 3$. Then the following statements are equivalent:

(i) $\alpha(\mathbb{AG}(R)) = 4$.

(ii) $\mathfrak{m}^3 = (0)$ and $|R| = 81$.

Moreover, if (i) or (ii) holds, then $\chi((\mathbb{AG}(R))^c) = 4$.

Proof *(i)* ⇒ *(ii)* We know from the moreover part of Lemma 4.20(i) that $\mathfrak{m}^3 = (0)$. Also with $r = -1$, it follows from the proof of the moreover part of Lemma 4.20(i) that $m_1^2 = m_1m_2$. Thus $\mathfrak{m}^2 = Rm_1^2$ is an one-dimensional vector space over $R/\mathfrak{m}$. Hence, $|\mathfrak{m}^2| = 3$. Note that $|\mathfrak{m}/\mathfrak{m}^2| = 9$ and so $|\mathfrak{m}| = 27$. Therefore, $|R| = 81$.

(ii) ⇒ *(i)* From $|\mathfrak{m}/\mathfrak{m}^2| = 9, |\mathfrak{m}| = 27$, it is clear that $|\mathfrak{m}^2| = 3$. Hence, $Rm_1^2 = Rm_1m_2$. Since $\mathfrak{m}^3 = (0)$ and $m_1^2 + m_1m_2 \neq 0$, we obtain that $m_1^2 = m_1m_2$. With $A = \{0, 1, 2\}$, we have $\mathfrak{m} = \{am_1 + bm_2 + cm_1^2 | a, b, c$ vary over $A\}$. It is easy to verify that the set of all nonzero proper ideals of R equals $\{Rm_1, Rm_2, R(m_1+m_2), R(m_1+2m_2), Rm_1^2, \mathfrak{m}\}$. Since $\{Rm_1, Rm_2, R(m_1+m_2), \mathfrak{m}\}$ is an independent set of $\mathbb{AG}(R)$, it follows that $\alpha(\mathbb{AG}(R)) \geq 4$. We next verify that $\chi((\mathbb{AG}(R))^c) \leq 4$. As $\mathfrak{m}^3 = (0)$, Rm_1^2 is an isolated vertex of $(\mathbb{AG}(R))^c$. Observe that Rm_1 and $R(m_1 + 2m_2)$ are not adjacent in $(\mathbb{AG}(R))^c$. Let $\{c_1, c_2, c_3, c_4\}$ be a set of four distinct colors. Let us assign the color c_1 to Rm_1 and $R(m_1+2m_2)$, color c_2 to Rm_2, color c_3 to $R(m_1+m_2)$, and the color c_4 to $\mathfrak{m}$ and Rm_1^2. It is clear that the above assignment of colors is indeed a proper vertex coloring of $(\mathbb{AG}(R))^c$. This shows that $4 \leq \alpha(\mathbb{AG}(R)) \leq \chi((\mathbb{AG}(R))^c) \leq 4$. Therefore, $\alpha(\mathbb{AG}(R)) = \chi((\mathbb{AG}(R))^c) = 4$.

The moreover assertion that $\chi((\mathbb{AG}(R))^c) = 4$ is verified in the proof of *(ii)* ⇒ *(i)*. □

We illustrate Proposition 4.28 with the help of Example 4.29.

Example 4.29 Let $T = \mathbb{Z}_9[x]$ and I be the ideal of T given by $I = (x^2 - 3x)$. Let $R = T/I$. Note that with $\mathfrak{m} = (3,x)/I = (3+I, x+I)$, $(R, \mathfrak{m})$ is a local Artinian ring and it satisfies the hypotheses of Lemma 4.20 with $m_1 = x + I$ and $m_2 = 3 + I$. Moreover, $\mathfrak{m}^3 = (0)$, $|R/\mathfrak{m}| = 3$, and $|R| = 81$. Therefore, it follows from the proof of *(ii)* ⇒ *(i)* of Proposition 4.28 that $\alpha(\mathbb{AG}(R)) = \chi((\mathbb{AG}(R))^c) = 4$.

Proposition 4.30 Let $(R, \mathfrak{m})$ be a local Artinian ring satisfying the hypotheses of Lemma 4.20. Suppose that $|R/\mathfrak{m}| = 4$. Then the following statements are equivalent:

(i) $\alpha(\mathbb{AG}(R)) = 4$.

(ii) $\mathfrak{m}^3 = (0)$ and $|R| = 256$.

Moreover, if (i) or (ii) holds, then $\chi((\mathbb{AG}(R))^c) = 4$.

Proof (i) ⇒ (ii) We know from the moreover part of Lemma 4.20(i) that $\mathfrak{m}^3 = (0)$. From $|R/\mathfrak{m}| = 4$, it follows that $R/\mathfrak{m} = \{0+\mathfrak{m}, 1+\mathfrak{m}, r+\mathfrak{m}, (r+1)+\mathfrak{m}\}$, for some $r \in R\backslash\mathfrak{m}$ such that $r-1 \notin \mathfrak{m}$ and $r^2+r+1 \in \mathfrak{m}$. It follows from the proof of the moreover part of Lemma 4.20(i) that either $m_1^2 + rm_1m_2 = 0$ or $m_1^2 + (r+1)m_1m_2 = 0$. Hence, $dim_{R/\mathfrak{m}}(\mathfrak{m}^2) = 1$ and so $|\mathfrak{m}^2| = 4$. From $|\mathfrak{m}/\mathfrak{m}^2| = 16$, we obtain that $|\mathfrak{m}| = 64$. Therefore, $|R| = 256$.

(ii) ⇒ (i) As in the proof of (i) ⇒ (ii), we can assume that $R/\mathfrak{m} = \{0+\mathfrak{m}, 1+\mathfrak{m}, r+\mathfrak{m}, (r+1)+\mathfrak{m}\}$. Now it is clear that $|\mathfrak{m}| = 64$ and $|\mathfrak{m}^2| = 4$. Therefore, $Rm_1^2 = Rm_1m_2$. From $m_1^2 + m_1m_2 \neq 0$, it follows that either $m_1^2 + rm_1m_2 = 0$ or $m_1^2 + (r+1)m_1m_2 = 0$. Without loss of generality, we can assume that $m_1^2 + rm_1m_2 = 0$. Let $A = \{0, 1, r, r+1\}$. Note that $\mathfrak{m} = \{am_1 + bm_2 + cm_1^2 | a, b, c$ vary over $A\}$. It is easy to verify that the set of all nonzero proper ideals of R equals $\{Rm_1, Rm_2, R(m_1+m_2), R(m_1+rm_2), R(m_1+(r+1)m_2), Rm_1^2, \mathfrak{m}\}$. Since $\{Rm_1, Rm_2, R(m_1+m_2), \mathfrak{m}\}$ is an independent set of $\mathbb{AG}(R)$, we obtain that $\alpha(\mathbb{AG}(R))) \geq 4$. We next verify that $\chi((\mathbb{AG}(R))^c) \leq 4$. As $\mathfrak{m}^3 = (0)$, it is clear that Rm_1^2 is an isolated vertex of $(\mathbb{AG}(R))^c$. It follows from $m_1^2 + rm_1m_2 = 0$ that in $(\mathbb{AG}(R))^c$, Rm_1 and $R(m_1+rm_2)$ are not adjacent and $R(m_1+m_2)$ and $R(m_1+(r+1)m_2)$ are not adjacent. Let $\{c_1, c_2, c_3, c_4\}$ be a set of four distinct colors. Let us assign the color c_1 to Rm_1 and $R(m_1+rm_2)$, color c_2 to Rm_2, color c_3 to $R(m_1+m_2)$ and $R(m_1+(r+1)m_2)$, and the color c_4 to $\mathfrak{m}$ and Rm_1^2. It is clear that the above assignment of colors is indeed a proper vertex coloring of $(\mathbb{AG}(R))^c$. This proves that $4 \leq \alpha(\mathbb{AG}(R))) \leq \chi((\mathbb{AG}(R))^c) \leq 4$. Therefore, $\alpha(\mathbb{AG}(R)) = \chi((\mathbb{AG}(R))^c) = 4$.

The moreover assertion that $\chi((\mathbb{AG}(R))^c) = 4$ is verified in the proof of (ii) ⇒ (i). □

In Example 4.31, we provide an example to illustrate Proposition 4.30.

Example 4.31 Let $T = \mathbb{F}_4[x,y]$ and let I be the ideal of T given by $I = (x^3, y^2, x^2 + \alpha xy)$, where $\mathbb{F}_4 = \{0, 1, \alpha, \alpha^2 = \alpha + 1\}$. Let $R = T/I$. Note that $\mathfrak{m} = (x,y)/I = (x+I, y+I)$ is such that $(R.\mathfrak{m})$ is a local Artinian ring and it satisfies the hypotheses of Lemma 4.20 with $m_1 = x + I$, and $m_2 = y + I$. Moreover, $|R/\mathfrak{m}| = 4$, $\mathfrak{m}^3 = (0)$, and $|R| = 256$. Therefore, we obtain from the proof of (ii) ⇒ (i) of Proposition 4.30 that $\alpha(\mathbb{AG}(R)) = \chi((\mathbb{AG}(R))^c) = 4$.

LEMMA 4.32 *Let $(R, \mathfrak{m})$ be a local Artinian ring such that $\mathfrak{m}$ is not principal, but $\mathfrak{m} = Rm_1 + Rm_2$, $m_1^2 \neq 0, m_2^2 \neq 0, m_1m_2 \neq 0, m_1^2 + m_1m_2 \neq 0$, and $m_2^2 + m_1m_2 \neq 0$. If $\alpha(\mathbb{AG}(R)) = 4$, then $\mathfrak{m}^5 = (0)$. Moreover, $\mathfrak{m}^3$ and $\mathfrak{m}^4$ are principal.*

Proof First we show that $\mathfrak{m}^5 = (0)$. By contrary, suppose that $\mathfrak{m}^5 \neq (0)$. Then either $\mathfrak{m}^4 m_1 \neq 0$ or $\mathfrak{m}^4 m_2 \neq 0$. Without loss of generality, we can assume that $\mathfrak{m}^4 m_1 \neq 0$. Note that $U = \{Rm_1, \mathfrak{m}, \mathfrak{m}^2, \mathfrak{m}^3\}$ is an independent set of $\mathbb{AG}(R)$. It is clear that $Rm_2, R(m_1+m_2) \notin U$. From $\alpha(\mathbb{AG}(R)) = 4$, $m_1m_2 \neq 0$, and $m_1^2 + m_1m_2 \neq 0$, it follows that $\mathfrak{m}^3 m_2 = \mathfrak{m}^3(m_1+m_2) = (0)$. This implies that $\mathfrak{m}^3 m_1 = (0)$ and so $\mathfrak{m}^3(Rm_1 + Rm_2) = \mathfrak{m}^4 = (0)$. This is a contradiction. Therefore, $\mathfrak{m}^5 = (0)$.

We next verify that $\mathfrak{m}^3$ is principal. It follows from the hypotheses on m_1, m_2 that $W = \{Rm_1, Rm_2, R(m_1+m_2), \mathfrak{m}\}$ is an independent set of $\mathbb{AG}(R)$. We claim that $m_1^2 \in Rm_2$. If $m_1^2 \notin Rm_2$, then $Rm_1^2 + Rm_2 \notin W$ and moreover, $W \cup \{Rm_1^2 + Rm_2\}$ is an independent set of $\mathbb{AG}(R)$. This is in contradiction to the assumption that $\alpha(\mathbb{AG}(R)) = 4$. Hence, $m_1^2 \in Rm_2$ and so $m_1^2 = am_2$ for some $a \in \mathfrak{m}$. From $\mathfrak{m} = Rm_1 + Rm_2$, it follows that $m_1^2 \in Rm_1m_2 + Rm_2^2$. Therefore, $\mathfrak{m}^2 = Rm_1m_2 + Rm_2^2$. Similarly, we obtain that $m_2^2 \in Rm_1$ and so $\mathfrak{m}^2 = Rm_1m_2 + Rm_1^2$. Note that $\mathfrak{m}^3 = \mathfrak{m}^2 m_1 + \mathfrak{m}^2 m_2$. We first verify that $\mathfrak{m}^2 m_1$ is principal. It is clear that $\mathfrak{m}^2 m_1 = Rm_1^3 + Rm_1^2 m_2$. If either $m_1^3 = 0$ or $m_1^2 m_2 = 0$, then it follows that $\mathfrak{m}^2 m_1$ is principal. Suppose that $m_1^3 \neq 0$ and $m_1^2 m_2 \neq 0$. Then $\{Rm_1, Rm_1^2, Rm_2, \mathfrak{m}\}$ is an independent set of $\mathbb{AG}(R)$. It follows from $\alpha(\mathbb{AG}(R)) = 4$ that $m_1^2(m_1+m_2) = 0$. Hence, $m_1^3 + m_1^2 m_2 = 0$. This proves that $\mathfrak{m}^2 m_1$ is principal. Similarly, it can be shown that $\mathfrak{m}^2 m_2$ is principal. From $\mathfrak{m}^3 = \mathfrak{m}^2 m_1 + \mathfrak{m}^2 m_2$, it follows that $\mathfrak{m}^3$ is principal if either $\mathfrak{m}^2 m_1 = (0)$ or $\mathfrak{m}^2 m_2 = (0)$. If $\mathfrak{m}^2 m_1 \neq (0)$ and $\mathfrak{m}^2 m_2 \neq (0)$, then $\{Rm_1, Rm_2, \mathfrak{m}, \mathfrak{m}^2\}$ is an independent set of $\mathbb{AG}(R)$. It follows from $\alpha(\mathbb{AG}(R)) = 4$ that $(m_1+m_2)\mathfrak{m}^2 = (0)$. Hence, we obtain that $\mathfrak{m}^2 m_1 = \mathfrak{m}^2 m_2$ and therefore, $\mathfrak{m}^3 = \mathfrak{m}^2 m_1$ is principal.

We next show that $\mathfrak{m}^4$ is principal.. Now $\mathfrak{m}^3 = Ry$ for some $y \in \mathfrak{m}^3$. Hence, $\mathfrak{m}^4 = Rym_1 + Rym_2$. If either $ym_1 = 0$ or $ym_2 = 0$, then it is clear that $\mathfrak{m}^4$ is principal. Suppose that $ym_1 \neq 0$ and $ym_2 \neq 0$. In such a case, $\{Rm_1, Rm_2, Ry, \mathfrak{m}\}$ is an independent set of $\mathbb{AG}(R)$. Since $\alpha(\mathbb{AG}(R)) = 4$, we obtain that $y(m_1 + m_2) = 0$. Hence, $\mathfrak{m}^4 = Rym_1 + Rym_2$ is principal. □

Let $(R, \mathfrak{m})$ be a local Artinian ring satisfying the hypotheses of Lemma 4.32 and if in addition, suppose that $\mathfrak{m}^2$ is not principal. In Lemma 4.33, we provide some necessary conditions in order that $\alpha(\mathbb{AG}(R)) = 4$.

LEMMA 4.33 *Let $(R, \mathfrak{m})$ be a local Artinian ring satisfying the hypotheses of Lemma 4.32. In addition, suppose that $\mathfrak{m}^2$ is not principal. If $\alpha(\mathbb{AG}(R)) = 4$, then the following hold:*

(i) $|R/\mathfrak{m}| \leq 3$.
(ii) $\mathfrak{m}^4 = (0)$.

Proof It is clear from the hypotheses that $W = \{Rm_1, Rm_2, R(m_1 + m_2), \mathfrak{m}\}$ is an independent set of $\mathbb{AG}(R)$. It is noted in the proof of Lemma 4.32 (see the second paragraph of its proof) that $m_1^2 \in Rm_2, m_2^2 \in Rm_1$ and $\mathfrak{m}^2 = Rm_1m_2 + Rm_2^2 = Rm_1m_2 + Rm_1^2$.

(i) Let $r \in R\backslash\mathfrak{m}$ be such that $r - 1 \notin \mathfrak{m}$. Then $R(m_1 + rm_2) \notin W$. Since $\alpha(\mathbb{AG}(R)) = 4$, it follows that $R(m_1 + rm_2)$ must be adjacent to at least one member of W in $\mathbb{AG}(R)$. As $\mathfrak{m}^2$ is not principal by assumption, it follows that $R(m_1 + m_2)R(m_1 + rm_2) = (0)$. This implies that $m_1^2 + (r + 1)m_1m_2 + rm_2^2 = 0$. If $s \in R\backslash\mathfrak{m}$ is such that $s - 1 \notin \mathfrak{m}$, then a similar argument yields that $m_1^2 + (s + 1)m_1m_2 + sm_2^2 = 0$. Hence, we arrive at $(r - s)m_1m_2 + (r - s)m_2^2 = 0$. Since $\mathfrak{m}^2 = Rm_1m_2 + Rm_2^2$ is not principal, it follows that $r - s \in \mathfrak{m}$. This proves that $|R/\mathfrak{m}| \leq 3$.

(ii) We first show that $m_1^4 = 0$. Suppose that $m_1^4 \neq 0$. As $m_1^2 \in Rm_2$, it follows that $m_1^2m_2 \neq 0$. Note that $U = \{Rm_1, Rm_1^2, Rm_2, \mathfrak{m}\}$ is an independent set of $\mathbb{AG}(R)$. As $R(m_1 + m_2) \notin U$ and since $\alpha(\mathbb{AG}(R)) = 4$, it follows from the hypotheses on m_1, m_2 that $m_1^2(m_1 + m_2) = 0$. From the assumption that $m_1^4 \neq 0$, it follows that $m_1^3m_2 \neq 0$ and moreover, $m_1^4 = -m_1^3m_2 = m_1^2m_2^2$. This implies that $U \cup \{Rm_1m_2\}$ is an independent set of $\mathbb{AG}(R)$. This is in contradiction to the assumption that $\alpha(\mathbb{AG}(R)) = 4$. Therefore, $m_1^4 = 0$. Similarly, it follows that $m_2^4 = 0$. We next verify that $m_1^3m_2 = 0$. Suppose that $m_1^3m_2 \neq 0$. Then U is an independent set of $\mathbb{AG}(R)$. From $\alpha(\mathbb{AG}(R)) = 4$, it follows that $(m_1 + m_2)m_1^2 = 0$. This implies as before that $0 = m_1^4 = -m_1^3m_2 = m_1^2m_2^2$. Thus $m_1^3m_2 = 0$. Similarly, it can be shown that $m_1m_2^3 = 0$. If $m_1^2m_2^2 \neq 0$, then we obtain that $\{Rm_1, Rm_2, Rm_1m_2, \mathfrak{m}\}$ is an independent set of $\mathbb{AG}(R)$. It follows from $\alpha(\mathbb{AG}(R)) = 4$ that $(m_1 + m_2)m_1m_2 = 0$. This implies that $m_1^2m_2^2 = 0$ since $m_1^3m_2 = 0$. This proves that $\mathfrak{m}^4 = (0)$. □

With the hypotheses on $(R, \mathfrak{m})$ as in Lemma 4.33, in Proposition 4.34, we provide a classification of rings R such that $\alpha(\mathbb{AG}(R)) = 4$ under the additional assumptions that $\mathfrak{m}^2$ is not principal and $\mathfrak{m}^3 = (0)$.

Proposition 4.34 Let $(R, \mathfrak{m})$ be a local Artinian ring satisfying the hypotheses of Lemma 4.33. In addition, suppose that $\mathfrak{m}^2$ is not principal and $\mathfrak{m}^3 = (0)$. Then the following statements are equivalent:

(i) $\alpha(\mathbb{AG}(R)) = 4$.
(ii) $\mathfrak{m}^2 = Rm_1^2 + Rm_1m_2 = Rm_2^2 + Rm_1m_2$, and $|R/\mathfrak{m}| \leq 3$.

Moreover, in the case when $|R/\mathfrak{m}| = 2$, either $m_1^2 = m_2^2$ or m_1^2, m_2^2, and $m_1m_2 \in R(m_1 + m_2)$. If $|R/\mathfrak{m}| = 3$, then $m_1^2 = m_2^2$ and $m_1^2, m_1m_2 \in R(m_1 + m_2) \cap R(m_1 - m_2)$.Moreover, if (i) or (ii) holds, then $|R| = 32$ when $|R/\mathfrak{m}| = 2$ and $|R| = 243$ when $|R/\mathfrak{m}| = 3$. Furthermore, $\chi((\mathbb{AG}(R))^c) = 4$.

Proof (*i*) ⇒ (*ii*) It is already noted in the first paragraph of the proof of Lemma 4.33 that $W = \{Rm_1, Rm_2, R(m_1 + m_2), \mathfrak{m}\}$ is an independent set of $\mathbb{AG}(R)$ and moreover, it is shown there that $\mathfrak{m}^2 = Rm_1^2 + Rm_1m_2 = Rm_2^2 + Rm_1m_2$. And it follows from Lemma 4.33(i) that $|R/\mathfrak{m}| \leq 3$.

Suppose that $|R/\mathfrak{m}| = 2$ and $m_1^2 \neq m_2^2$. In such a case, as $\mathfrak{m}^3 = (0)$, it follows that $(m_1 + m_2)^2 = m_1^2 + m_2^2 \neq 0$. Thus if $m_1^2 \notin R(m_1 + m_2)$, then we obtain that $W \cup \{R(m_1 + m_2) + Rm_1^2\}$ is an independent set of $\mathbb{AG}(R)$. This is in contradiction to the assumption that $\alpha(\mathbb{AG}(R)) = 4$. Hence, $m_1^2 \in R(m_1 + m_2)$. Similarly, it follows that $m_2^2, m_1m_2 \in R(m_1 + m_2)$.

Suppose that $|R/\mathfrak{m}| = 3$. As $\mathfrak{m}^2 = Rm_1^2 + Rm_1m_2 = Rm_2^2 + Rm_1m_2$ is not principal, it follows that $m_1^2 - m_1m_2 \neq 0$ and $m_2^2 - m_1m_2 \neq 0$. If $m_1^2 \neq m_2^2$, then $W \cup \{R(m_1 - m_2)\}$ is an independent set of $\mathbb{AG}(R)$. This contradicts the assumption that $\alpha(\mathbb{AG}(R)) = 4$. Therefore, $m_1^2 = m_2^2$. Note that $(m_1 + m_2)^2 = 2(m_1^2 + m_1m_2) \neq 0$. Thus if $m_1^2 \notin R(m_1 + m_2)$, then $W \cup \{R(m_1 + m_2) + Rm_1^2\}$ is an independent set of $\mathbb{AG}(R)$. This is a contradiction. Therefore, we obtain that $m_1^2 \in R(m_1 + m_2)$. It follows from a similar argument that $m_1m_2 \in R(m_1 + m_2)$. Using the fact that $\{Rm_1, Rm_2, R(m_1 - m_2), \mathfrak{m}\}$ is an independent set of $\mathbb{AG}(R)$, it follows as argued above that $m_1^2, m_1m_2 \in R(m_1 - m_2)$.

(*ii*) ⇒ (*i*) Suppose that $|R/\mathfrak{m}| = 2$. Since $\mathfrak{m}^3 = (0)$, $\mathfrak{m}^2$ is a vector space over $R/\mathfrak{m}$. From $\mathfrak{m}^2 = Rm_1^2 + Rm_1m_2$ and $\mathfrak{m}^2$ is not principal, it follows that $|\mathfrak{m}^2| = 4$. Note that $|\mathfrak{m}/\mathfrak{m}^2| = 4$. Hence, $|\mathfrak{m}| = 16$ and so $|R| = 32$. Let $A = \{0, 1\}$. Observe that $\mathfrak{m} = \{am_1 + bm_2 + cm_1^2 + dm_1m_2 | a, b, c, d \text{ vary over } A\}$. If $m_1^2 = m_2^2$, then with $a = m_1, b = m_1 + m_2$, we get that $\mathfrak{m} = Ra + Rb$ and moreover, $a^2 \neq 0, ab = m_1^2 + m_1m_2 \neq 0$, whereas $b^2 = 0$ and $a^2 + ab = m_1m_2 \neq 0$. Hence, we obtain from the proof of (*ii*) ⇒ (*i*) of Proposition 4.21 that $\alpha(\mathbb{AG}(R)) = \chi((\mathbb{AG}(R))^c) = 4$. So we can assume that $m_1^2 \neq m_2^2$. Then $m_1^2 \in R(m_1 + m_2), m_2^2 \in R(m_1 + m_2)$, and $m_1m_2 \in R(m_1 + m_2)$. As the subgraph H of $(\mathbb{AG}(R))^c$ induced on $\{Rm_1, Rm_2, R(m_1 + m_2), \mathfrak{m}\}$ is a clique, it follows that $\alpha(\mathbb{AG}(R)) \geq 4$. We next verify that $\chi((\mathbb{AG}(R))^c) \leq 4$. Note that as $\mathfrak{m}^3 = (0)$, any nonzero ideal I of R with $I \subseteq \mathfrak{m}^2$ is an isolated vertex of $(\mathbb{AG}(R))^c$. Let A_1 be the set of all isolated veertices of $(\mathbb{AG}(R))^c$. It can be easily verified that the set of all nonzero proper ideals B of R with $B \not\subseteq \mathfrak{m}^2$ equals $\{Rm_1, Rm_2, R(m_1 + m_2), \mathfrak{m}\}$. Hence, $(\mathbb{AG}(R))^c$ is the union of H and A_1. It is now clear that $\alpha(\mathbb{AG}(R)) = \chi((\mathbb{AG}(R))^c) = 4$.

Suppose that $|R/\mathfrak{m}| = 3$. As $\mathfrak{m}^2$ is a two-dimensional vector space over $R/\mathfrak{m}$, it follows that $|\mathfrak{m}^2| = 9$. Observe that $|\mathfrak{m}/\mathfrak{m}^2| = 9$ and so $|\mathfrak{m}| = 81$. Therefore, $|R| = 243$. Let $A = \{0, 1, 2\}$. Note that $\mathfrak{m} = \{am_1 + bm_2 + cm_1^2 + dm_1m_2 | a, b, c, d \text{ vary over } A\}$. Since $\{Rm_1, Rm_2, R(m_1 + m_2), \mathfrak{m}\}$ is an independent set of $\mathbb{AG}(R)$, it follows that $\alpha(\mathbb{AG}(R)) \geq 4$. We next verify that $\chi((\mathbb{AG}(R))^c) \leq 4$. As $\mathfrak{m}^3 = (0)$, each nonzero ideal I of R with $I \subseteq \mathfrak{m}^2$ is an isolated vertex of $(\mathbb{AG}(R))^c$. Let A_1 be the set of all isolated vertices of $(\mathbb{AG}(R))^c$. It is easy to verify that the set of all proper nonzero ideals of R which are not contained in $\mathfrak{m}^2$ equals $\{Rm_1, Rm_2, R(m_1 + m_2), R(m_1 - m_2), \mathfrak{m}\}$. From $m_{1z}^2 = m_2^2$, it is clear that $R(m_1 + m_2)$ and $R(m_1 - m_2)$ are not adjacent in $(\mathbb{AG}(R))^c$. Let $\{c_1, c_2, c_3, c_4\}$ be a set of four distinct colors. Let us assign the color c_1 to Rm_1, color c_2 to Rm_2, color c_3 to $R(m_1 + m_2)$ and $R(m_1 - m_2)$, and the color c_4 to $\mathfrak{m}$ and all the vertices from A_1. The above assignment of colors is indeed a proper vertex coloring of $(\mathbb{AG}(R))^c$. This proves that $4 \leq \alpha(\mathbb{AG}(R)) \leq \chi((\mathbb{AG}(R))^c) \leq 4$. Therefore, $\alpha(\mathbb{AG}(R)) = \chi(\mathbb{AG}(R))^c) = 4$.

The moreover assertion regarding $|R|$ is verified in the proof of (*i*) ⇒ (*ii*) and the assertion that $\chi((\mathbb{AG}(R))^c) = 4$ is verified in the proof of (*ii*) ⇒ (*i*). □

We illustrate Proposition 4.34 with the help of some examples in Example 4.35.

Example 4.35 (i) Let $T = \mathbb{Z}_8[x]$ and $R = T/I$, where I is the ideal of T given by $I = (4x, x^2)$. Note that R is a local Artinian ring with $\mathfrak{m} = R(2 + I) + R(x + I)$ as its unique maximal ideal. Observe that with $m_1 = 2 + I, m_2 = x + 2 + I$, it is clear that $\mathfrak{m} = Rm_1 + Rm_2$. Moreover, $m_1^2 = m_2^2 = 4 + I \neq 0 + I$, $m_1m_2 = 2x + 4 + I \neq 0 + I, m_1^2 + m_1m_2 = m_2^2 + m_1m_2 = 2x + I \neq 0 + I., \mathfrak{m}^2 = Rm_1^2 + Rm_1m_2$ is not principal, $\mathfrak{m}^3 = (0 + I)$, and $|R/\mathfrak{m}| = 2$. Now it follows from the proof of (*ii*) ⇒ (*i*) of Proposition 4.34 that $\alpha(\mathbb{AG}(R)) = \chi((\mathbb{AG}(R))^c) = 4$. This example is found in Belshoff and Chapman (2007, p. 479).

(ii) Let $T = \mathbb{Z}_8[x]$ and $R = T/I$, where I is the ideal of T given by $I = (4x, x^2 - 2x - 4)$. Note that R is a local Artinian ring with $\mathfrak{m} = R(2+I) + R(x+I)$ as its unique maximal ideal. Let $m_1 = 2 + I$ and $m_2 = x + I$. It is clear that $\mathfrak{m} = Rm_1 + Rm_2, m_1^2 = 4 + I \neq 0 + I, m_2^2 = x^2 + I \neq 0 + I$, $m_1m_2 = 2x + I \neq 0 + I$, $m_1^2 + m_1m_2 = x^2 + I \neq 0 + I$, $m_2^2 + m_1m_2 = 4 + I \neq 0 + I$. Moreover, note that $\mathfrak{m}^2 = Rm_1^2 + Rm_1m_2 = Rm_2^2 + Rm_1m_2$ is not principal, $\mathfrak{m}^3 = (0 + I)$, $m_1^2 \neq m_2^2$, but $m_1^2, m_2^2, m_1m_2 \in R(m_1 + m_2)$, and $|R/\mathfrak{m}| = 2$. It follows from the proof of *(ii)* $\Rightarrow$ *(i)* of Theorem 4.34 that $\alpha(\mathbb{AG}(R)) = \chi((\mathbb{AG}(R))^c) = 4$. This example is found in Belshoff and Chapman (2007, p. 479).

Let $(R, \mathfrak{m})$ be a local Artinian ring satisfying the hypotheses of Lemma 4.32.. Suppose that $\mathfrak{m}^4 = (0)$ but $\mathfrak{m}^3 \neq (0)$ and $\mathfrak{m}^2$ is principal. In Propositon 4.37, we classify such rings R in order that $\alpha(\mathbb{AG}(R)) = 4$. Lemma 4.36 determines $|R/\mathfrak{m}|$ in order that $\alpha(\mathbb{AG}(R)) \leq 4$.

LEMMA 4.36 *Let $(R, \mathfrak{m})$ be a local Artinian ring satisfying the hypotheses of Lemma 4.32. Suppose that $\mathfrak{m}^2$ is principal and $\mathfrak{m}^3 \neq (0)$. If $\alpha(\mathbb{AG}(R)) \leq 4$, then $|R/\mathfrak{m}| = 2$.*

Proof Assume that $\alpha(\mathbb{AG}(R)) \leq 4$. We know from Lemma 4.32 that $\mathfrak{m}^5 = (0)$. Moreover, it is shown in the proof of Lemma 4.32 (see the second paragraph of iits proof) that $Rm_1^2 \subseteq Rm_2$ and $Rm_2^2 \subseteq Rm_1$ and using them, it is verified there that $\mathfrak{m}^2 = Rm_1^2 + Rm_1m_2 = Rm_2^2 + Rm_1m_2$. Observe that $\mathfrak{m}^2 = Rm_1^2 + Rm_1m_2 = (Rm_1 + Rm_2)m_1 = \mathfrak{m}m_1$. Similarly, it follows from $\mathfrak{m}^2 = Rm_2^2 + Rm_1m_2$ that $\mathfrak{m}^2 = \mathfrak{m}m_2$. Hence, $\mathfrak{m}^3 = \mathfrak{m}^2\mathfrak{m} = \mathfrak{m}^2m_1 = Rm_1^3 + Rm_1^2m_2 = \mathfrak{m}m_1^2$ and $\mathfrak{m}^3 = \mathfrak{m}^2\mathfrak{m} = \mathfrak{m}^2m_2 = Rm_2^3 + Rm_1m_2^2 = \mathfrak{m}m_2^2$. It follows from $Rm_1^2 \subseteq Rm_2^2 + Rm_1m_2$ that $Rm_1^3 \subseteq Rm_1m_2^2 + Rm_1^2m_2$ and therefore, we obtain that $\mathfrak{m}^3 = Rm_1^2m_2 + Rm_1m_2^2 = \mathfrak{m}m_1m_2$. From $\mathfrak{m}^3 \neq (0)$, it is clear that $\mathfrak{m}^2 \neq \mathfrak{m}^3$ and $\mathfrak{m}^3 \neq \mathfrak{m}^4$. It follows from $\mathfrak{m}^3 = \mathfrak{m}m_1^2 = \mathfrak{m}m_2^2 = \mathfrak{m}m_1m_2$ that $m_1^2, m_1m_2, m_2^2 \in \mathfrak{m}^2 \backslash \mathfrak{m}^3$. By assumption, $\mathfrak{m}^2$ is principal. Let $m \in \mathfrak{m}^2 \backslash \{0\}$ be such that $\mathfrak{m}^2 = Rm$. It now follows that there exist units $u, v \in R$ such that $m_2^2 = um_1^2$ and $m_1m_2 = vm_1^2$. Therefore, we obtain that there exist units $u_1, u_2, u_3 \in R$ such that $m_2^3 = u_1m_1^3, m_1^2m_2 = u_2m_1^3$, and $m_1m_2^2 = u_3m_1^3$. Thus $m_1^3, m_2^3, m_1^2m_2, m_1m_2^2 \in \mathfrak{m}^3 \backslash \{0\}$.

We next verify that $|R/\mathfrak{m}| = 2$. It follows from $m_1^2m_2, m_2^2m_1 \in R\backslash\{0\}$ that $U = \{Rm_1, Rm_2, Rm_1m_2, \mathfrak{m}\}$ is an independent set of $\mathbb{AG}(R)$. Observe that for any $r \in R\backslash\mathfrak{m}$, $R(m_1 + rm_2) \notin U$. Since $\alpha(\mathbb{AG}(R)) \leq 4$, it follows that $U \cup \{R(m_1 + rm_2)\}$ cannot form an independent set of $\mathbb{AG}(R)$. Therefore, $R(m_1 + rm_2)m_1m_2 = (0)$. Let $r, s \in R\backslash\mathfrak{m}$. It follows from $m_1^2m_2 + rm_1m_2^2 = 0 = m_1^2m_2 + sm_1m_2^2$ that $(r - s)m_1m_2^2 = 0$. From $m_1m_2^2 \neq 0$, we obtain that $r - s \in \mathfrak{m}$. This proves that $|R/\mathfrak{m}| = 2$. □

Proposition 4.37 Let $(R, \mathfrak{m})$ be a local Artinian ring satisfying the hypotheses of Lemma 4.32. Suppose that $\mathfrak{m}^2$ is principal, $\mathfrak{m}^4 = (0)$ but $\mathfrak{m}^3 \neq (0)$. Then the following statements are equivalent:

(i) $\alpha(\mathbb{AG}(R)) = 4$.

(ii) $|R/\mathfrak{m}| = 2$ and there exist $a, b \in \mathfrak{m}$ such that $\mathfrak{m} = Ra + Rb$ with $a^2 \neq 0, b^2 = 0, ab \neq 0, a^2 + ab \neq 0, a^2b = 0, ab = a^3$, and $|R| = 32$.

Moreover, if (i) or (ii) holds, then $\chi((\mathbb{AG}(R))^c) = 4$.

Proof *(i)* $\Rightarrow$ *(ii)* We know from Lemma 4.36 that $|R/\mathfrak{m}| = 2$. Moreover, we know from the proof of Lemma 4.36 that there exist units $u, v \in R$ such that $m_1m_2 = um_1^2$ and $m_1m_2 = vm_2^2$. It follows from $|R/\mathfrak{m}| = 2$ that if w is any unit in R, then $w \in 1 + \mathfrak{m}$. Hence, $u = 1 + m$ for some $m \in \mathfrak{m}$ and so $m_1^2 + m_1m_2 = (1 + u)m_1^2 = (2 + m)m_1^2 \in \mathfrak{m}^3$. Similarly, it follows that $m_2^2 + m_1m_2 \in \mathfrak{m}^3$. Moreover, it is noted in the proof of Lemma 4.36 that there exist units $u_1, u_2, u_3 \in R$ such that $m_2^3 = u_1m_1^3, m_1^2m_2 = u_2m_1^3, m_1m_2^2 = u_3m_1^3$. Thus $\mathfrak{m}^3 = Rm_1^3$. It follows from $\mathfrak{m}^4 = (0)$ and $|R/\mathfrak{m}| = 2$ that if $y_1, y_2 \in \mathfrak{m}^3 \backslash \{0\}$, then $y_1 = y_2$. Therefore, $m_1^2 + m_1m_2 = m_2^2 + m_1m_2$ and so $m_1^2 = m_2^2$. Moreover, $m_1^3 = m_2^3 = m_1^2m_2 = m_1m_2^2$. Let $a = m_1$ and $b = m_1 + m_2$. Observe that $\mathfrak{m} = Ra + Rb$. Note that $a^2 = m_1^2 \neq 0$, $b^2 = 2(m_1^2 + m_1m_2) \in \mathfrak{m}^4 = (0)$, $ab = m_1^2 + m_1m_2 \neq 0$, $a^2 + ab = m_1^2 + m_1^3 \neq 0$, $a^2b = m_1^3 + m_1^2m_2 \in \mathfrak{m}^4 = (0)$, and $ab = m_1^2 + m_1m_2 = m_1^3 = a^3$. We now verify that $|R| = 32$. Observe that $dim_{R/\mathfrak{m}}(\mathfrak{m}^3) = dim_{R/\mathfrak{m}}(\mathfrak{m}^2/\mathfrak{m}^3) = 1$, and $dim_{R/\mathfrak{m}}(\mathfrak{m}/\mathfrak{m}^2) = 2$. Therefore,

$|\mathfrak{m}^3| = |\mathfrak{m}^2/\mathfrak{m}^3| = 2$ and $|\mathfrak{m}/\mathfrak{m}^2| = 4$. Thus $|\mathfrak{m}| = 16$ and so $|R| = 32$.

(ii) $\Rightarrow$ *(i)* If (ii) holds, then it is clear that $(R, \mathfrak{m})$ with $\mathfrak{m} = Ra + Rb$ satisfies the hypotheses of Proposition 4.24 and (ii) of Proposition 4.24. Therefore, it follows from *(ii)* $\Rightarrow$ *(i)* of Proposition 4.24 that $\alpha(\mathbb{AG}(R)) = 4$.

The moreover assertion that $\chi((\mathbb{AG}(R))^c) = 4$ follows from the proof of *(ii)* $\Rightarrow$ *(i)* of Proposition 4.24. □

In Example 4.38, we mention an example to illustrate Proposition 4.37.

Example 4.38 Let $T = \mathbb{Z}_4[x]$ and $R = T/I$, where I is the ideal of T given by $I = (2x^2, x^3 - 2x)$. Observe that R is a local Artinian ring with $\mathfrak{m} = R(x + I) + R(x + 2 + I)$ as its unique maximal ideal. Note that $(R, \mathfrak{m})$ satisfies the hypotheses of Lemma 4.32 with $m_1 = x + I$ and $m_2 = x + 2 + I$. Moreover, it is clear that $\mathfrak{m}^2 = Rm_1^2$ is principal, $\mathfrak{m}^3 \neq (0)$, and $\mathfrak{m}^4 = (0)$. Furthermore, $(R, \mathfrak{m})$ satisfies (ii) of Proposition 4.37 with $a = x + I$ and $b = 2 + I$. Therefore, we obtain from *(ii)* $\Rightarrow$ *(i)* of Proposition 4.37 that $\alpha(\mathbb{AG}(R)) = 4$, and it follows from the moreover part of Proposition 4.37 that $\chi((\mathbb{AG}(R))^c) = 4$. This example is found in Belshoff and Chapman (2007) and is already mentioned in this article (see Example 4.25).

Acknowledgements

We are very much thankful to the referee for a careful reading of our article and for many valuable and useful suggestions. We are very much thankful to Professor Jonas Hartwig for the support.

Funding

The authors received no direct funding for this research.

Author details

S. Visweswaran[1]

E-mail: s_visweswaran2006@yahoo.co.in

Jaydeep Parejiya[1]

E-mail: parejiyajay@gmail.com

[1] Department of Mathematics, Saurashtra University, Rajkot 360 005, India.

References

Aalipour, G., Akbari, S., Behboodi, M., Nikandish, R., Nikmehr, M. J., & Shaveisi, F. (2014). The classification of the annihilating-ideal graphs of commutative rings. *Algebra Colloquium, 21*, 249. doi:10.1142/S1005386714000200

Aalipour, G., Akbari, S., Nikandish, R., Nikmehr, M. J., & Shaivesi, F. (2012). On the coloring of the annihilating-ideal graph of a commutative ring. *Discrete Mathematics, 312*, 2620–2625.

Anderson, D. F., Axtell, M. C., & Stickles, Jr., J. A., (2011). Zero-divisor graphs in commutative rings. In M. Fontana, S. E. Kabbaj, B. Olberding, & I. Swanson (Eds.), *Commutative algebra, Noetherian and non-Noetherian perspectives* (pp. 23–45). New York, NY: Springer-Verlag.

Anderson, D. F., Frazier, A., Lauve, A., & Livingston, P. S. (2001). The zero-divisor graph of a commutative ring II. *Lecture Notes in Pure and Applied Mathematics, 220*, 61–72.

Anderson, D. F., & Livingston, P. S. (1999). The zero-divisor graph of a commutative ring. *Journal of Algebra, 217*, 434–447.

Anderson, D. D., & Naseer, M. (1993). Beck's coloring of a commutative ring. *Journal of Algebra, 159*, 500–514.

Atiyah, M. F., & Macdonald, I. G. (1969). *Introduction to commutative algebra*. Reading, MA: Addison-Wesley.

Axtell, M., Coykendall, J., & Stickles, J. (2005). Zero-divisor graphs of polynomial and power series over commutative rings. *Communications in Algebra, 33*, 2043–2050.

Balakrishnan, R., & Ranganathan, K. (2000). *A textbook of graph theory* (Universitext). New York, NY: Springer.

Beck, I. (1988). Coloring of commutative rings. *Journal of Algebra, 116*, 208–226.

Behboodi, M., & Rakeei, Z. (2011a). The annihilating-ideal graph of commutative rings I. *Journal of Algebra and Applications, 10*, 727–739.

Behboodi, M., & Rakeei, Z. (2011b). The annihilating-ideal graph of commutative rings II. *Journal of Algebra and Applications, 10*, 741–753.

Belshoff, R., & Chapman, J. (2007). Planar zero-divisor graphs. *Journal of Algebra, 316*, 471–480.

Corbas, B., & Williams, G. D. (2000a). Rings of order p^5 I, Nonlocal rings. *Journal of Algebra, 231*, 677-690.

Corbas, B., & Williams, G. D. (2000b). Rings of order p^5 II, Local rings. *Journal of Algebra, 231*, 691–704.

Hadian, M. (2012). Unit action and geometric zero-divisor ideal graph. *Communications in Algebra, 40*, 2920–2930.

Heinzer, W., & Ohm, J. (1972). On the Noetherian-like rings of E.G. Evans. *Proceedings of the American Mathematical Society, 34*, 73–74.

Kaplansky, I. (1974). *Commutative rings*. Chicago, IL: University of Chicago Press.

Lucas, T. G. (2006). The diameter of a zero-divisor graph. *Journal of Algebra, 301*, 173–193.

Smith, N. O. (2003). Planar zero-divisor graphs. *Journal of Commutative Rings, 2*, 177–186.

Visweswaran, S. (2011). Some properties of the complement of the zero-divisor graph of a commutative ring. *ISRN Algebra, 2011*, 24 p., Article ID 59104.

Visweswaran, S., & Patel, H. D. (2015). On the clique number of the complement of the annihilating ideal graph of a commutative ring. *Contributions to Algebra and Geometry*. doi:10.1007s13366-015-0247-5

7

On norm equivalence between the displacement and velocity vectors for free linear dynamical systems

Ludwig Kohaupt[1*]

*Corresponding author: Ludwig Kohaupt, Department of Mathematics, Beuth University of Technology Berlin, Luxemburger Str. 10, D-13353 Berlin, Germany

E-mail: kohaupt@beuth-hochschule.de

Reviewing editor: Song Wang, Curtin University, Australia

Abstract: As the main new result, under certain hypotheses, for free vibration problems, the norm equivalence of the displacement vector $y(t)$ and the velocity vector $\dot{y}(t)$ is proven. The pertinent inequalities are applied to derive some two-sided bounds on $y(t)$ and $\dot{y}(t)$ that are known so far only for the state vector $x(t) = [y^T(t), \dot{y}^T(t)]^T$. Sufficient algebraic conditions are given such that norm equivalence between $y(t)$ and $\dot{y}(t)$ holds, respectively, does not hold, as the case may be. Numerical examples illustrate the results for vibration problems of n degrees of freedom with $n \in \{1,2,3,4,5\}$ by computing the mentioned algebraic conditions and by plotting the graphs of $y(t)$ and $\dot{y}(t)$. Some notations and definitions of References Kohaupt (2008b, 2011) are necessary and are therefore recapitulated. The paper is of interest to Mathematicians and Engineers.

Subjects: Applied Mathematics; Computer Mathematics; Engineering Technology; Engineering Mathematics; Science; Technology

Keywords: initial value problem; free vibration problem; state-space description; two-sided bounds; sufficient algebraic conditions; norm equivalence between displacement and velocity

ABOUT THE AUTHOR

Ludwig Kohaupt received the equivalent to the master's degree (Diplom-Mathematiker) in Mathematics in 1971 and the equivalent to the PhD (Dr.phil.nat.) in 1973 from the University of Frankfurt/Main. From 1974 until 1979, Kohaupt was a teacher in Mathematics and Physics at a Secondary School. During that time (from 1977 until 1979), he was also an auditor at the Technical University of Darmstadt in Engineering Subjects, such as Mechanics, and especially Dynamics. From 1979 until 1990, he joined the Mercedes-Benz car company in Stuttgart as a computational engineer, where he worked in areas such as Dynamics (vibration of car models), Cam Design, Gearing, and Engine Design. Then, in 1990, Kohaupt combined his preceding experiences by taking over a professorship at the Beuth University of Technology Berlin (formerly known as TFH Berlin). He retired on 01 April 2014.

PUBLIC INTEREST STATEMENT

Under certain conditions, the norm equivalence of the displacement vector $y(t)$ and the velocity vector $\dot{y}(t)$ for free linear dynamical systems is derived. Hereby, a relation of the form $c_0\|y(t)\| \le \|\dot{y}(t)\| \le c_1\|y(t)\|,\ t \ge t_1$, is understood with positive constants c_0 and c_1. As a consequence, under norm equivalence, one has that $\lim_{t\to 0} y(t) = 0$ is equivalent to $\lim_{t\to 0} \dot{y}(t) = 0$ and that boundedness of $y(t)$ is equivalent to boundedness of $\dot{y}(t)$.

1. Introduction

In free vibration problems with one degree of freedom and mild damping, the displacement as well as the velocity have zeros in any sufficiently large interval. But, with increasing dimension, it is likely that not all components of the displacement or of the velocity are zero simultaneously, in other words, it is increasingly likely with increasing dimension n that $y(t) \neq 0,\ t \geq t_1$, and $\dot{y}(t) \neq 0,\ t \geq t_1$, for sufficiently large t_1. Then, the question arises as to whether an inequality of the form $c_0\|y(t)\| \leq \|\dot{y}(t)\| \leq c_1\|y(t)\|,\ t \geq t_1$, can be proven for sufficiently large t_1; this property, if it is valid, will be called *norm equivalence between* $y(t)$ *and* $\dot{y}(t)$.

Now, the contents of this paper will be outlined.

In Section 2, the state-space description $\dot{x} = Ax,\ x(t_0) = x_0$, of the dynamical problem $M\ddot{y} + B\dot{y} + Ky = 0,\ y(t_0) = y_0,\ \dot{y}(t_0) = \dot{y}_0$ is given where M, B, and K are the mass, damping, and stiffness matrices, as the case may be, and where $y(t)$ is the displacement vector, y_0 is the initial displacement, and $\dot{y}_0$ is the initial velocity.

In Section 3, under certain hypotheses, the above-mentioned norm equivalence between $y(t)$ and $\dot{y}$ is proven for diagonalizable system matrix A, and in Section 4, the same is done for general system matrix A.

The pertinent norm inequalities between $y(t)$ and $\dot{y}$ are applied in Section 5 to improve Kohaupt (2011, Theorems 12 and 16). In both sections, also sufficient algebraic conditions are established that guarantee the validity, respectively, invalidity of norm equivalence of $y(t)$ and $\dot{y}$. In Section 6, numerical examples illustrate the results for vibration problems of n degrees of freedom for $n \in \{1,2,3,4,5\}$. More precisely, in Section 6.1, the mentioned algebraic conditions are computed and the graphs of $\|y(t)\|$ and $\|\dot{y}(t)\|$ are plotted showing that, in the examples, for $n \in \{1,2\}$ there is no norm equivalence and that for $n \in \{3,4,5\}$ there is norm equivalence; in Section 6.2, for $n = 4$, a case with $\nu_{x_0}[A] < \nu[A]$ is illustrated by graphs, where $\nu_{x_0}[A]$ is the spectral abscissa of matrix A with respect to x_0 and $\nu[A]$ is the spectral abscissa of A; in Section 6.3, for $n = 2$, a model with non-diagonalizable matrix A is constructed and analyzed in detail. Section 7 contains computational aspects, and in Section 8, conclusions are drawn. The non-cited references [1], [2], [6], and [7] are given because they may be useful to the reader.

2. The state-space description of $M\ddot{y} + B\dot{y} + Ky = 0,\ y(t_0) = y_0,\ \dot{y}(t_0) = \dot{y}_0$

Let $M, B, K \in \mathbb{R}^{n\times n}$ and $y_0, \dot{y}_0 \in \mathbb{R}^n$. Further, let M be regular. The matrices M, B, and K are the mass, damping, and stiffness matrices, as the case may be; y_0 is the initial displacement and $\dot{y}_0$ is the initial velocity. We study the initial value problem

$$M\ddot{y} + B\dot{y} + Ky = 0,\ y(t_0) = y_0,\ \dot{y}(t_0) = \dot{y}_0,$$

where $y(t)$ is the sought displacement and $z(t) = \dot{y}(t)$ is the associated velocity.

2.1. State-space description

Let

$$x := \begin{bmatrix} y \\ z \end{bmatrix} = \begin{bmatrix} y \\ \dot{y} \end{bmatrix},\quad x_0 := \begin{bmatrix} y_0 \\ z_0 \end{bmatrix} = \begin{bmatrix} y_0 \\ \dot{y}_0 \end{bmatrix},$$

and

$$A = \left[\begin{array}{c|c} 0 & E \\ \hline -M^{-1}K & -M^{-1}B \end{array}\right];$$

x is called *state vector* and A is called *system matrix*. Herewith, the above second-order initial value problem is equivalent to the first-order initial value problem of double size,

$$\dot{x} = A\,x,\ x(t_0) = x_0. \tag{1}$$

In the sequel, we need only the special form of $x(t)$.

3. Norm equivalence inequalities for diagonalizable matrix A

To show the norm equivalence between $y(t)$ and $\dot{y}(t)$ for diagonalizable matrix A, is a very simple task.

First, we formulate some hypotheses and conditions.

3.1. Hypotheses and conditions for diagonalizable matrix A

(H1) $m = 2n$ and $A \in \mathbb{R}^{m \times m}$,

(H2) $T^{-1}AT = J = diag(\lambda_k)_{k=1,\dots,m}$, where $\lambda_k = \lambda_k(A),\ k = 1,\dots,m$ are the eigenvalues of A,

(H3) $\lambda_i = \lambda_i(A) \neq 0,\ i = 1,\dots,m$,

(HS) the eigenvectors $p_1,\dots,p_n;\bar{p}_1,\dots,\bar{p}_n$ form a basis of $\mathbb{C}^{m \times m}$.

Remark Let (H1) be fulfilled and let $Ap = \lambda p$. Then, we have $A\overline{p} = \overline{\lambda}\overline{p}$, where the bar denotes the complex conjugate. So, together with (λ, p), also $(\overline{\lambda}, \overline{p})$ is a solution of the eigenvalue problem $Ap = \lambda p$. But, if λ and p would be real, then p and $\bar{p}$ would not be linearly independent. This situation cannot happen when hypothesis (HS) is supposed.

Remark In the sequel, when the special hypothesis (HS) is chosen, we do this in order to be specific in the construction of a solution basis, used already in Kohaupt (2008b, 2011). Other cases such as $A \in \mathbb{R}^{3\times3}$ can be handled in a similar manner, however.

Hypothesis (H4) defined in Kohaupt (2008b, 2011) is not need here.

As a preparation to the derivation of the norm equivalence of the displacement and velocity vectors, we collect some definitions, respectively, notations and representations for the solution vector $x(t)$ from Kohaupt (2011).

3.2. Representation of the basis $x_k^{(r)}(t), x_k^{(i)}(t),\ k = 1,\dots,n$

Under the hypotheses (H1), (H2), and (HS), from Kohaupt (2011), we obtain the following *real basis functions* for the ODE $\dot{x} = A\,x$:

$$
\boxed{\begin{aligned}
x_k^{(r)}(t) &= e^{\lambda_k^{(r)}(t-t_0)}\left[\cos \lambda_k^{(i)}(t-t_0)p_k^{(r)} - \sin \lambda_k^{(i)}(t-t_0)p_k^{(i)}\right],\\
x_k^{(i)}(t) &= e^{\lambda_k^{(r)}(t-t_0)}\left[\sin \lambda_k^{(i)}(t-t_0)p_k^{(r)} + \cos \lambda_k^{(i)}(t-t_0)p_k^{(i)}\right],
\end{aligned}} \tag{2}
$$

$k = 1,\dots,n$, where

$$\lambda_k = \lambda_k^{(r)} + i\lambda_k^{(i)} = Re\,\lambda_k + iIm\,\lambda_k,$$

$$p_k = p_k^{(r)} + ip_k^{(i)} = Re\,p_k + iIm\,p_k,$$

$k = 1,\dots,m = 2n$ are the decompositions of λ_k and p_k into their real and imaginary parts. As in Kohaupt (2011), the indices are chosen such that $\lambda_{n+k} = \overline{\lambda}_k, p_{n+k} = \overline{p}_k,\ k = 1,\dots,n$.

3.3. The spectral abscissa of A with respect to the initial vector $x_0 \in \mathbb{R}^n$

Let $u_k^*,\ k = 1,\dots,m = 2n$ be the eigenvectors of A^* corresponding to the eigenvalues $\overline{\lambda}_k,\ k = 1,\dots,m = 2n$. Under (H1), (H2), and (HS), the solution $x(t)$ of (1) has the form

$$x(t) = \sum_{k=1}^{m=2n} c_{1k}p_k e^{\lambda_k(t-t_0)} = \sum_{k=1}^{n}\left[c_{1k}p_k e^{\lambda_k(t-t_0)} + c_{2k}\bar{p}_k e^{\overline{\lambda}_k(t-t_0)}\right] \tag{3}$$

with uniquely determined coefficients $c_{1k},\ k = 1,\dots,m = 2n$. Using the relations

$$c_{2k} = c_{1,n+k} = \bar{c}_{1k}, \quad k = 1, \dots, n, \tag{4}$$

(see Kohaupt, 2008b, Section 3.1 for the last relation), then according to Kohaupt (2008a), the *spectral abscissa of A with respect to the initial vector* $x_0 \in \mathbb{R}^n$ is given by

$$\begin{aligned} \nu_0 := \nu_{x_0}[A] := & \max_{k=1,\dots,m=2n} \{\lambda_k^{(r)}(A) \mid x_0 \not\perp u_k^*\} \\ = & \max_{k=1,\dots,m=2n} \{\lambda_k^{(r)}(A) \mid c_{1k} \neq 0\} \\ = & \max_{k=1,\dots,n} \{\lambda_k^{(r)}(A) \mid c_{1k} \neq 0\} \\ = & \max_{k=1,\dots,n} \{\lambda_k^{(r)}(A) \mid x_0 \not\perp u_k^*\} \end{aligned} \tag{5}$$

3.4. Index sets

In the sequel, we need the following index sets:

$$J_{\nu_0} := \{k_0 \in \mathbb{N} \mid 1 \leq k_0 \leq n \text{ and } \lambda_{k_0}^{(r)}(A) = \nu_0\} \tag{6}$$

and

$$\begin{aligned} J_{\nu_0}^- := & \{1, \dots, n\} \setminus J_{\nu_0} \\ = & \{k_0^- \in \mathbb{N} \mid 1 \leq k_0^- \leq n \text{ and } \lambda_{k_0^-}^{(r)}(A) < \nu_0\}. \end{aligned} \tag{7}$$

3.5. Appropriate representation of $x(t)$

We have

$$x(t) = \sum_{k=1}^{n} [c_k^{(r)} x_k^{(r)}(t) + c_k^{(i)} x_k^{(i)}(t)]$$

with

$$c_k^{(r)} = 2\, Re\, c_{1k}, \quad c_k^{(i)} = -2\, Im\, c_{1k}, \quad k = 1, \dots, n$$

(cf. Kohaupt, 2008b). Thus, due to (2),

$$x(t) = \sum_{k=1}^{n} e^{\lambda_k^{(r)}(t-t_0)} f_k(t) \tag{8}$$

with

$$\begin{aligned} f_k(t) := & c_k^{(r)} [\cos \lambda_k^{(i)}(t-t_0) p_k^{(r)} - \sin \lambda_k^{(i)}(t-t_0) p_k^{(i)}] \\ & + c_k^{(i)} [\sin \lambda_k^{(i)}(t-t_0) p_k^{(r)} + \cos \lambda_k^{(i)}(t-t_0) p_k^{(i)}], \\ & k = 1, \dots, n \end{aligned} \tag{9}$$

3.6. Appropriate representation of $bdy(t)$ and $\dot{y}(t)$

Let

$$p_k := \begin{bmatrix} q_k \\ r_k \end{bmatrix} \quad p_k^{(r)} := \begin{bmatrix} q_k^{(r)} \\ r_k^{(r)} \end{bmatrix}, \quad p_k^{(i)} := \begin{bmatrix} q_k^{(i)} \\ r_k^{(i)} \end{bmatrix}, \tag{10}$$

with $q_k, r_k \in \mathbb{C}^{m\times m}, q_k^{(r)}, r_k^{(r)}, q_k^{(i)}, r_k^{(i)} \in \mathbb{R}^n, k = 1, \dots, m = 2n$. Then, from (8), (9),

$$y(t) = \sum_{k=1}^{n} e^{\lambda_k^{(r)}(t-t_0)}\, g_k(t) \tag{11}$$

with

$$\begin{aligned} g_k(t) := {} & c_k^{(r)}\,[\cos \lambda_k^{(i)}(t-t_0)q_k^{(r)} - \sin \lambda_k^{(i)}(t-t_0)q_k^{(i)}] \\ & + c_k^{(i)}\,[\sin \lambda_k^{(i)}(t-t_0)q_k^{(r)} + \cos \lambda_k^{(i)}(t-t_0)q_k^{(i)}], \end{aligned} \tag{12}$$

$k = 1, \ldots, n$ as well as

$$z(t) = \dot{y}(t) = \sum_{k=1}^{n} e^{\lambda_k^{(r)}(t-t_0)}\, h_k(t) \tag{13}$$

with

$$\begin{aligned} h_k(t) := {} & c_k^{(r)}\,[\cos \lambda_k^{(i)}(t-t_0)r_k^{(r)} - \sin \lambda_k^{(i)}(t-t_0)r_k^{(i)}] \\ & + c_k^{(i)}\,[\sin \lambda_k^{(i)}(t-t_0)r_k^{(r)} + \cos \lambda_k^{(i)}(t-t_0)r_k^{(i)}], \end{aligned}$$

$k = 1, \ldots, n$

(14)

After these preparations, for the quantities $J_{v_0}, g_k(t), h_k(t)$, we formulate the following conditions:

There exists a $t_1 \geq t_0$ such that

$$(C_g(t \geq t_1)) \quad \sum_{k \in J_{v_0}} g_k(t) \neq 0, \; t \geq t_1 \geq t_0,$$

$$(C_h(t \geq t_1)) \quad \sum_{k \in J_{v_0}} h_k(t) \neq 0, \; t \geq t_1 \geq t_0.$$

For these conditions, there are sufficient algebraic conditions, as the case may be:

$(A_{g,1})$ $q_k^{(r)}, q_k^{(i)},\; k \in J_{v_0}$ are linearly independent,

$(A_{h,1})$ $r_k^{(r)}, r_k^{(i)},\; k \in J_{v_0}$ are linearly independent.

In the examples of Section 6, also the case occurs that the above conditions are not fulfilled. For this, we formulate the following conditions:

For every $t_1 \geq t_0$ there exists a $t \geq t_1$ such that

$$(\overline{C_g}(t \geq t_1)) \quad \sum_{k \in J_{v_0}} g_k(t) = 0,$$

$$(\overline{C_h}(t \geq t_1)) \quad \sum_{k \in J_{v_0}} h_k(t) = 0.$$

For these conditions, there are sufficient algebraic conditions, as the case may be (see Kohaupt, 2011):

$(\overline{A_{g,1}})$ $J_{v_0} = \{k_0\}$ and $q_{k_0}^{(r)}, q_{k_0}^{(i)}$ are linearly dependent,

$(\overline{A_{h,1}})$ $J_{v_0} = \{k_0\}$ and $r_{k_0}^{(r)}, r_{k_0}^{(i)}$ are linearly dependent.

Further, here and in the sequel, we denote by $\|\cdot\|$ any vector norm.

THEOREM 1 *(Norm equivalence of $y(t)$ and $\dot{y}(t)$ for diagonalizable matrix A)*

Let the hypotheses (H1), (H2), and (HS) as well as the conditions ($C_g(t \geq t_1)$), ($C_h(t \geq t_1)$) or the sufficient algebraic conditions ($A_{g,1}$), ($A_{h,1}$) be fulfilled. Then, there exist constants $c_0 > 0$ and $c_1 > 0$ such that

$$c_0\|y(t)\| \leq \|\dot{y}(t)\| \leq c_1\|y(t)\|, \; t \geq t_2,$$

for sufficiently large $t_2 \geq t_1 \geq t_0$.

Proof The proof follows immediately from Kohaupt (2011, Theorems 7 and 13) or Kohaupt (2011, Theorems 8 and 14). □

4. Norm equivalence inequalities for general matrix *A*

In this section, we prove the same statement for a general square matrix *A* as in Theorem 1 for a diagonalizable matrix *A*. This *cannot be deduced in a similar way as for Theorem 1*, that is, it cannot be done by Kohaupt (2011, Theorems 9 and 15) since they contain the factor $e^{\varepsilon(t-t_0)}$ on the right-hand side. Neither can it be done by Kohaupt (2011, Theorems 12 and 16) since they contain the factor $e^{\varepsilon(t-t_0)}$ on the right-hand side and the factor $e^{-\varepsilon(t-t_0)}$ on the left-hand side. Nevertheless, the same equivalence inequalities as in Theorem 1 hold true in the general case. The proof, however, is much more involved.

Again, first we formulate some hypotheses and conditions.

4.1. Hypotheses and conditions for general square matrix A

(H1') $m = 2n$ and $A \in \mathbb{R}^{m\times m}$,

(H2') $T^{-1}AT = J = diag(J_i(\lambda_i))_{i=1,\dots,r}$ where $J_i(\lambda_i) \in \mathbb{C}^{m_i\times m_i}$ are the canonical Jordan forms,

(H3') $\lambda_i = \lambda_i(A) \neq 0,\; i = 1,\dots,r,$

(HS') $r = 2\rho$, and the principal vectors $p_1^{(1)},\dots,p_{m_1}^{(1)};\dots;\; p_1^{(\rho)},\dots,p_{m_\rho}^{(\rho)};\dots;\; \bar{p}_1^{(1)},\dots,\bar{p}_{m_1}^{(1)};\dots;\; \bar{p}_1^{(\rho)},\dots,\bar{p}_{m_\rho}^{(\rho)}$ form a basis of $\mathbb{C}^{m\times m}$.

We mention that for the special hypothesis (HS') similar remarks hold as for (HS) in the case of diagonalizable matrices *A*.

Let ($H1'$), ($H2'$), and (HS') be fulfilled and $Ap_k^{(l)} = \lambda_l p_k^{(l)} + p_{k-1}^{(l)},\; k = 1,\dots,m_l,\; l = 1,\dots,r$, where the indices are chosen such that $\lambda_{\rho+l} = \bar{\lambda}_l,\; l = 1,\dots,\rho$ and $p_k^{(\rho+l)} = \bar{p}_k^{(l)},\; k = 1,\dots,m_l,\; l = 1,\dots,\rho$. The vectors $p_k^{(l)}$ are the principal vectors of stage k corresponding to the eigenvalue λ_l of *A*.

Hypothesis ($H4'$) defined in Kohaupt (2008b, 2011) is not needed here.

In the case of a general square matrix *A*, we also have to collect some definitions, respectively, notations and representations of $x(t)$ from Kohaupt (2008b, 2011).

4.2. Representation of the basis $x_k^{(l,r)}(t), x_k^{(l,i)}(t),\; k = 1,\dots,m_l,\; l = 1,\dots,\rho$

Under the hypotheses ($H1'$), ($H2'$), and (HS'), from Kohaupt (2008b) we obtain the following *real basis functions* for the ODE $\dot{x} = A\,x$:

$$
\boxed{
\begin{aligned}
x_k^{(l,r)}(t) &= e^{\lambda_l^{(r)}(t-t_0)}\left\{\cos\lambda_l^{(i)}(t-t_0)\left[p_1^{(l,r)}\frac{(t-t_0)^{k-1}}{(k-1)!}+\ldots+p_{k-1}^{(l,r)}(t-t_0)+p_k^{(l,r)}\right]\right.\\
&\quad\left.-\sin\lambda_l^{(i)}(t-t_0)\left[p_1^{(l,i)}\frac{(t-t_0)^{k-1}}{(k-1)!}+\ldots+p_{k-1}^{(l,i)}(t-t_0)+p_k^{(l,i)}\right]\right\},\\
x_k^{(l,i)}(t) &= e^{\lambda_l^{(r)}(t-t_0)}\left\{\sin\lambda_l^{(i)}(t-t_0)\left[p_1^{(l,r)}\frac{(t-t_0)^{k-1}}{(k-1)!}+\ldots+p_{k-1}^{(l,r)}(t-t_0)+p_k^{(l,r)}\right]\right.
\end{aligned}
}
\tag{15}
$$

$k=1,\ldots,m_l$, $l=1,\ldots,\rho$, where

$$p_k^{(l)}=p_k^{(l,r)}+i\,p_k^{(l,i)}$$

is the decomposition of $p_k^{(l)}$ into its real and imaginary part.

4.3. The spectral abscissa of A with respect to the initial vector $x_0 \in I\!R^n$

Let $u_k^{(l)^*}$, $k=1,\ldots,m_l$ be the principal vectors of stage k of A^* corresponding to the eigenvalue $\overline{\lambda}_l$, $l=1,\ldots,r=2\rho$. Under $(H1')$, $(H2')$, and (HS'), the solution $x(t)$ of (1) has the form

$$x(t)=\sum_{l=1}^{r=2\rho}\sum_{k=1}^{m_l}c_{1k}^{(l)}x_k^{(l)}(t)=\sum_{l=1}^{\rho}\sum_{k=1}^{m_l}[c_{1k}^{(l)}x_k^{(l)}(t)+c_{2k}^{(l)}\overline{x}_k^{(l)}(t)]. \tag{16}$$

with uniquely determined coefficients $c_{1k}^{(l)}$, $k=1,\ldots,m_l$, $l=1,\ldots,r=2\rho$. Using the relations

$$
\begin{aligned}
c_{1k}^{(l)} &= (x_0,u_k^{(l)^*}),\ k=1,\ldots,m_l,\ l=1,\ldots,\rho\\
c_{2k}^{(l)} &= c_{1k}^{(\rho+l)}=\overline{c}_{1k}^{(l)},\ l=1,\ldots,\rho
\end{aligned}
\tag{17}
$$

(see [Section 3.2] Kohaupt, 2008b for the last relation), then the *spectral abscissa of A with respect to the initial vector* $x_0 \in I\!R^n$ is

$$
\begin{aligned}
\nu_0 := \nu_{x_0}[A] &:= \max_{l=1,\ldots,r=2\rho}\left\{\lambda_l^{(r)}(A)\mid x_0 \not\perp M_{\overline{\lambda}_l(A^*)} := [u_1^{(l)^*},\ldots,u_{m_l}^{(l)^*}]\right\}\\
&= \max_{l=1,\ldots,r=2\rho}\left\{\lambda_l^{(r)}(A)\mid c_{1k}^{(l)}\neq 0 \text{ for at least one } k\in\{1,\ldots,m_l\}\right\}\\
&= \max_{l=1,\ldots,\rho}\left\{\lambda_l^{(r)}(A)\mid c_{1k}^{(l)}\neq 0 \text{ for at least one } k\in\{1,\ldots,m_l\}\right\}\\
&= \max_{l=1,\ldots,\rho}\left\{\lambda_l^{(r)}(A)\mid x_0 \not\perp M_{\overline{\lambda}_l(A^*)} = [u_1^{(l)^*},\ldots,u_{m_l}^{(l)^*}]\right\}
\end{aligned}
\tag{18}
$$

4.4. Index sets

For the sequel, we need the following index sets:

$$J_{\nu_0}:=\{l_0\in I\!N\mid 1\le l_0\le\rho \text{ and} \lambda_{l_0}^{(r)}(A)=\nu_0\} \tag{19}$$

and

$$
\begin{aligned}
J_{\nu_0}^{-} &:= \{1,\ldots,\rho\}\setminus J_{\nu_0}\\
&= \{l_0^{-}\in I\!N\mid 1\le l_0^{-}\le\rho \text{ and } \lambda_{l_0^{-}}^{(r)}(A)<\nu_0\}.
\end{aligned}
\tag{20}
$$

4.5. Appropriate representation of $x(t)$

We have

$$x(t) = \sum_{l=1}^{\rho} \sum_{k=1}^{m_l} [c_k^{(l,r)} x_k^{(l,r)}(t) + c_k^{(l,i)} x_k^{(l,i)}(t)]$$

with

$$c_k^{(l,r)} = 2\, Re\, c_{1k}^{(l)}, \quad c_k^{(l,i)} = -2\, Im\, c_{1k}^{(l)}, \quad k = 1, \dots, m_l,\ l = 1, \dots, \rho$$

(cf. Kohaupt, 2008b). Thus, due (18),

$$x(t) = \sum_{l=1}^{\rho} e^{\lambda_l^{(r)}(t-t_0)} \sum_{k=1}^{m_l} f_k^{(l)}(t) \tag{21}$$

with

$$\begin{aligned} f_k^{(l)}(t) := c_k^{(l,r)} & \left\{ \cos \lambda_l^{(i)}(t-t_0) \left[p_1^{(l,r)} \frac{(t-t_0)^{k-1}}{(k-1)!} + \dots + p_{k-1}^{(l,r)}(t-t_0) + p_k^{(l,r)} \right] \right. \\ & \left. - \sin \lambda_l^{(i)}(t-t_0) \left[p_1^{(l,i)} \frac{(t-t_0)^{k-1}}{(k-1)!} + \dots + p_{k-1}^{(l,i)}(t-t_0) + p_k^{(l,i)} \right] \right\} \\ + c_k^{(l,i)} & \left\{ \sin \lambda_l^{(i)}(t-t_0) \left[p_1^{(l,r)} \frac{(t-t_0)^{k-1}}{(k-1)!} + \dots + p_{k-1}^{(l,r)}(t-t_0) + p_k^{(l,r)} \right] \right. \\ & \left. + \cos \lambda_l^{(i)}(t-t_0) \left[p_1^{(l,i)} \frac{(t-t_0)^{k-1}}{(k-1)!} + \dots + p_{k-1}^{(l,i)}(t-t_0) + p_k^{(l,i)} \right] \right\} \end{aligned} \tag{22}$$

$k = 1, \dots, m_l,\ l = 1, \dots, \rho$

4.6. Appropriate representation of $y(t)$ ***and*** $\dot{y}(t)$

Set

$$p_k^{(l)} := \begin{bmatrix} q_k^{(l)} \\ r_k^{(l)} \end{bmatrix}, \quad p_k^{(l,r)} := \begin{bmatrix} q_k^{(l,r)} \\ r_k^{(l,r)} \end{bmatrix}, \quad p_k^{(l,i)}(t) := \begin{bmatrix} q_k^{(l,i)} \\ r_k^{(l,i)} \end{bmatrix}, \tag{23}$$

with $q_k^{(l)}, r_k^{(l)} \in \mathbb{C}^n, q_k^{(l,r)}, r_k^{(l,r)}, q_k^{(l,i)}, r_k^{(l,i)} \in \mathbb{R}^n, k = 1, \dots, m_l,\ l = 1, \dots, \rho$.

Then, from (24), (25)

$$y(t) = \sum_{l=1}^{\rho} e^{\lambda_l^{(r)}(t-t_0)} \sum_{k=1}^{m_l} g_k^{(l)}(t) \tag{24}$$

with

$$\begin{aligned} g_k^{(l)}(t) := c_k^{(l,r)} & \left\{ \cos \lambda_l^{(i)}(t-t_0) \left[q_1^{(l,r)} \frac{(t-t_0)^{k-1}}{(k-1)!} + \dots + q_{k-1}^{(l,r)}(t-t_0) + q_k^{(l,r)} \right] \right. \\ & \left. - \sin \lambda_l^{(i)}(t-t_0) \left[q_1^{(l,i)} \frac{(t-t_0)^{k-1}}{(k-1)!} + \dots + q_{k-1}^{(l,i)}(t-t_0) + q_k^{(l,i)} \right] \right\} \\ + c_k^{(l,i)} & \left\{ \sin \lambda_l^{(i)}(t-t_0) \left[q_1^{(l,r)} \frac{(t-t_0)^{k-1}}{(k-1)!} + \dots + q_{k-1}^{(l,r)}(t-t_0) + q_k^{(l,r)} \right] \right. \\ & \left. + \cos \lambda_l^{(i)}(t-t_0) \left[q_1^{(l,i)} \frac{(t-t_0)^{k-1}}{(k-1)!} + \dots + q_{k-1}^{(l,i)}(t-t_0) + q_k^{(l,i)} \right] \right\} \end{aligned} \tag{25}$$

$k = 1, \ldots, m_l$, $l = 1, \ldots, \rho$ as well as

$$z(t) = \dot{y}(t) = \sum_{l=1}^{\rho} e^{\lambda_l^{(r)}(t-t_0)} \sum_{k=1}^{m_l} h_k^{(l)}(t) \tag{26}$$

with

$$\begin{aligned} h_k^{(l)}(t) := c_k^{(l,r)} \Bigg\{ & \cos \lambda_l^{(i)}(t-t_0) \left[r_1^{(l,r)} \frac{(t-t_0)^{k-1}}{(k-1)!} + \ldots + r_{k-1}^{(l,r)}(t-t_0) + r_k^{(l,r)} \right] \\ & - \sin \lambda_l^{(i)}(t-t_0) \left[r_1^{(l,i)} \frac{(t-t_0)^{k-1}}{(k-1)!} + \ldots + r_{k-1}^{(l,i)}(t-t_0) + r_k^{(l,i)} \right] \Bigg\} \\ + c_k^{(l,i)} \Bigg\{ & \sin \lambda_l^{(i)}(t-t_0) \left[r_1^{(l,r)} \frac{(t-t_0)^{k-1}}{(k-1)!} + \ldots + r_{k-1}^{(l,r)}(t-t_0) + r_k^{(l,r)} \right] \\ & + \cos \lambda_l^{(i)}(t-t_0) \left[r_1^{(l,i)} \frac{(t-t_0)^{k-1}}{(k-1)!} + \ldots + r_{k-1}^{(l,i)}(t-t_0) + r_k^{(l,i)} \right] \Bigg\} \end{aligned} \tag{27}$$

$k = 1, \ldots, m_l$, $l = 1, \ldots, \rho$.

After these preparations, for the quantities J_{v_0}, $J_{v_0}^-$, $g_k^{(l)}(t)$, $h_k^{(l)}(t)$, we formulate the following conditions:

There exists a $t_1 \geq t_0$ such that

$$(C_g'(t \geq t_1)) \quad \sum_{k \in J_{v_0}} \sum_{k=1}^{m_l} g_k^{(l)}(t) \neq 0, \; t \geq t_1 \geq t_0,$$

$$(C_h'(t \geq t_1)) \quad \sum_{k \in J_{v_0}} \sum_{k=1}^{m_l} h_k^{(l)}(t) \neq 0, \; t \geq t_1 \geq t_0.$$

For these conditions, there are sufficient algebraic conditions, as the case may be (see Kohaupt, 2011). *However, the following sufficient conditions are not so stringent in that only conditions on components of eigenvectors are used and not on the set of components of all principal vectors.* The sufficient algebraic conditions read:

$(A_{g,1}')$ $q_1^{(l,r)}, q_1^{(l,i)}, l \in J_{v_0}$, are linearly independent,

$(A_{h,1}')$ $r_1^{(l,r)}, r_1^{(l,i)}, l \in J_{v_0}$, are linearly independent.

The above conditions are not always fulfilled. For this, we formulate the following conditions:

For every $t_1 \geq t_0$ there exists a $t \geq t_1$ such that

$$(\overline{C_g'}(t \geq t_1)) \quad \sum_{k \in J_{v_0}} \sum_{k=1}^{m_l} g_k^{(l)}(t) = 0,$$

$$(\overline{C_h'}(t \geq t_1)) \quad \sum_{k \in J_{v_0}} \sum_{k=1}^{m_l} h_k^{(l)}(t) = 0.$$

For these conditions, there are sufficient algebraic conditions, as the case may be, (see Kohaupt, 2011). *However, the following sufficient conditions are not so stringent in that we do not suppose on the algebraic multiplicity that* $m_{l_0} = 1$. The sufficient algebraic conditions read:

$(\overline{A'_{g,1}})$ $J_{v_0} = \{l_0\}$ and $q_1^{(l_0,r)}, q_1^{(l_0,i)}$ are linearly dependent,

$(\overline{A'_{h,1}})$ $J_{v_0} = \{l_0\}$ and $r_1^{(l_0,r)}, r_1^{(l_0,i)}$ are linearly dependent.

For the next lemma, we set:

$$Y(t) := \left\| \sum_{k \in J_{v_0}} \sum_{k=1}^{m_l} g_k^{(l)}(t) \right\|,$$

$$Z(t) := \left\| \sum_{k \in J_{v_0}} \sum_{k=1}^{m_l} h_k^{(l)}(t) \right\|.$$

The definition of the *spectral abscissa* $v_0 = v_{x_0}[A]$ *of matrix A with respect to the initial vector* x_0 can also be found in Kohaupt (2011).

LEMMA 2 *Let hypotheses (H1′), (H2′), and (HS′) be fulfilled. Then,*

$$\frac{1}{2} Y(t)\, e^{v_0(t-t_0)} \le \|y(t)\| \le 2\, Y(t)\, e^{v_0(t-t_0)}, t \ge t_1,$$

$$\frac{1}{2} Z(t)\, e^{v_0(t-t_0)} \le \|z(t)\| \le 2\, Z(t)\, e^{v_0(t-t_0)}, t \ge t_1.$$

for sufficiently large $t_1 \ge t_0$.

Proof We prove only the first relation. The second one is proven in a similar way. One has

$$y(t) = \sum_{l=1}^{\rho} e^{\lambda_l^{(r)}(t-t_0)} \sum_{k=1}^{m_l} g_k^{(l)}(t)$$

$$= e^{v_0(t-t_0)} \sum_{l \in J_{v_0}} \sum_{k=1}^{m_l} g_k^{(l)}(t) + \sum_{l \in J_{v_0}^-} e^{\lambda_l^{(r)}(t-t_0)} \sum_{k=1}^{m_l} g_k^{(l)}(t).$$

This implies

$$\|y(t)\| \ge e^{v_0(t-t_0)} \| \sum_{l \in J_{v_0}} \sum_{k=1}^{m_l} g_k^{(l)}(t)\| - \| \sum_{l \in J_{v_0}^-} e^{\lambda_l^{(r)}(t-t_0)} \sum_{k=1}^{m_l} g_k^{(l)}(t)\|$$

$$= e^{v_0(t-t_0)} \| \sum_{l \in J_{v_0}} \sum_{k=1}^{m_l} g_k^{(l)}(t)\| \left[1 - \frac{\| \sum_{l \in J_{v_0}^-} e^{\lambda_l^{(r)}(t-t_0)} \sum_{k=1}^{m_l} g_k^{(l)}(t)\|}{e^{v_0(t-t_0)} \| \sum_{l \in J_{v_0}} \sum_{k=1}^{m_l} g_k^{(l)}(t)\|} \right]$$

$$\ge e^{v_0(t-t_0)} \| \sum_{l \in J_{v_0}} \sum_{k=1}^{m_l} g_k^{(l)}(t)\| \cdot \frac{1}{2}$$

for sufficiently large $t_1 \ge t_0$ since the fraction in the bracket tends to zero. Further,

$$
\begin{aligned}
\|y(t)\| &\le e^{\nu_0(t-t_0)}\|\sum_{l\in J_{\nu_0}}\sum_{k=1}^{m_l} g_k^{(l)}(t)\| + \|\sum_{l\in J_{\nu_0}^-} e^{\lambda_l^{(r)}(t-t_0)}\sum_{k=1}^{m_l} g_k^{(l)}(t)\| \\
&= e^{\nu_0(t-t_0)}\|\sum_{l\in J_{\nu_0}}\sum_{k=1}^{m_l} g_k^{(l)}(t)\|\left[1+\frac{\|\sum_{l\in J_{\nu_0}^-} e^{\lambda_l^{(r)}(t-t_0)}\sum_{k=1}^{m_l} g_k^{(l)}(t)\|}{e^{\nu_0(t-t_0)}\|\sum_{l\in J_{\nu_0}}\sum_{k=1}^{m_l} g_k^{(l)}(t)\|}\right] \\
&\le e^{\nu_0(t-t_0)}\|\sum_{l\in J_{\nu_0}}\sum_{k=1}^{m_l} g_k^{(l)}(t)\|\cdot 2
\end{aligned}
$$

for sufficiently large $t_1 \ge t_0$, again since the fraction tends to zero. □

For the formulation of the next lemma, we introduce some abbreviations. So, we define

$$m_l' := \max_{k=1,\ldots,m_l}\left\{k \mid |c_k^{(l,r)}|^2 + |c_k^{(l,i)}|^2 > 0\right\} = \max_{k=1,\ldots,m_l}\left\{k \mid c_{1k}^{(l)} \ne 0\right\},\ l \in J_{\nu_0},$$

where the quantities $c_k^{(l,r)}, c_k^{(l,i)}$, and $c_{1k}^{(l)}$ are contained in each of the quantities $g_k^{(l)}(t)$, $h_k^{(l)}(t)$, and $f_{S,k}^{(l)}(t)$. This clearly implies

$$c_{1,m_l'}^{(l)} \ne 0,\ l \in J_{\nu_0}.$$

Further, define

$$m' := \max_{l\in J_{\nu_0}} m_l'.$$

and

$$J_{\nu_0}' := \{l \in J_{\nu_0} \mid m_l' = m'\} \subset J_{\nu_0}.$$

as well as

$$
\begin{aligned}
u(t) &:= \sum_{l\in J_{\nu_0}'} c_{m_l'}^{(l,r)}\,[\cos\lambda_l^{(i)}(t-t_0)q_1^{(l,r)} - \sin\lambda_l^{(i)}(t-t_0)q_1^{(l,i)}] \\
&\quad + c_{m_l'}^{(l,i)}\,[\sin\lambda_l^{(i)}(t-t_0)q_1^{(l,r)} + \cos\lambda_l^{(i)}(t-t_0)q_1^{(l,i)}], \\
v(t) &:= \sum_{l\in J_{\nu_0}'} c_{m_l'}^{(l,r)}\,[\cos\lambda_l^{(i)}(t-t_0)r_1^{(l,r)} - \sin\lambda_l^{(i)}(t-t_0)r_1^{(l,i)}] \\
&\quad + c_{m_l'}^{(l,i)}\,[\sin\lambda_l^{(i)}(t-t_0)r_1^{(l,r)} + \cos\lambda_l^{(i)}(t-t_0)r_1^{(l,i)}], \\
&\quad + c_{m_l'}^{(l,i)}\,[\sin\lambda_l^{(i)}(t-t_0)p_{S,1}^{(l,r)} + \cos\lambda_l^{(i)}(t-t_0)p_{S,1}^{(l,i)}], \\
\eta(t) &:= \|u(t)\|, \\
\zeta(t) &:= \|v(t)\|, \\
p(t) &:= p_{m'-1}(t) = \frac{(t-t_0)^{m'-1}}{(m'-1)!}.
\end{aligned}
$$

After these preparations, we are now in a position to state the following lemma.

LEMMA 3 *Let hypotheses (H1′), (H2′), and (HS′) be fulfilled. Then,*

$$\frac{1}{2}\,p(t)\,\eta(t) \le Y(t) \le 2\,p(t)\,\eta(t), t \ge t_1,$$

$$\frac{1}{2}\,p(t)\,\zeta(t) \le Z(t) \le 2\,p(t)\,\zeta(t), t \ge t_1.$$

for sufficiently large $t_1 \geq t_0$.

Proof We prove only the first relation. The second one is proven in a similar way. One has

$$\sum_{l\in J_{v_0}}\sum_{k=1}^{m_l} g_k^{(l)}(t) := \sum_{l\in J_{v_0}}\sum_{k=1}^{m_l} c_k^{(l,r)} \langle \Big\{ \cos\lambda_l^{(i)}(t-t_0)\left[q_1^{(l,r)}\frac{(t-t_0)^{k-1}}{(k-1)!}+\ldots+q_{k-1}^{(l,r)}(t-t_0)+q_k^{(l,r)}\right]$$

$$-\sin\lambda_l^{(i)}(t-t_0)\left[q_1^{(l,i)}\frac{(t-t_0)^{k-1}}{(k-1)!}+\ldots+q_{k-1}^{(l,i)}(t-t_0)+q_k^{(l,i)}\right]\Big\}$$

$$+c_k^{(l,i)}\Big\{\sin\lambda_l^{(i)}(t-t_0)\left[q_1^{(l,r)}\frac{(t-t_0)^{k-1}}{(k-1)!}+\ldots+q_{k-1}^{(l,r)}(t-t_0)+q_k^{(l,r)}\right]$$

$$+\cos\lambda_l^{(i)}(t-t_0)\left[q_1^{(l,i)}\frac{(t-t_0)^{k-1}}{(k-1)!}+\ldots+q_{k-1}^{(l,i)}(t-t_0)+q_k^{(l,i)}\right]\Big\}\rangle.$$

This delivers

$$\sum_{l\in J_{v_0}}\sum_{k=1}^{m_l} g_k^{(l)}(t) = \sum_{l\in J_{v_0}}\sum_{k=1}^{m_l'} g_k^{(l)}(t) = \sum_{l\in J_{v_0}} \langle c_1^{(l,r)}\Big\{\cos\lambda_l^{(i)}(t-t_0)\left[q_1^{(l,r)}\right]-\sin\lambda_l^{(i)}(t-t_0)\left[q_1^{(l,i)}\right]\Big\}$$

$$+c_1^{(l,i)}\Big\{\sin\lambda_l^{(i)}(t-t_0)\left[q_1^{(l,r)}\right]+\cos\lambda_l^{(i)}(t-t_0)\left[q_1^{(l,i)}\right]\Big\}$$

$$+c_2^{(l,r)}\Big\{\cos\lambda_l^{(i)}(t-t_0)\left[q_1^{(l,r)}\frac{(t-t_0)}{1!}+q_2^{(l,r)}\right]-\sin\lambda_l^{(i)}(t-t_0)\left[q_1^{(l,i)}\frac{(t-t_0)}{1!}+q_2^{(l,i)}\right]\Big\}$$

$$+c_2^{(l,i)}\Big\{\sin\lambda_l^{(i)}(t-t_0)\left[q_1^{(l,r)}\frac{(t-t_0)}{1!}+q_2^{(l,r)}\right]+\cos\lambda_l^{(i)}(t-t_0)\left[q_1^{(l,i)}\frac{(t-t_0)}{1!}+q_2^{(l,i)}\right]\Big\}$$

$$+\ldots$$

$$+c_{m_l'}^{(l,r)}\Big\{\cos\lambda_l^{(i)}(t-t_0)\left[q_1^{(l,r)}\frac{(t-t_0)^{m_l'-1}}{(m_l'-1)!}+\ldots+q_{m_l'-1}^{(l,r)}(t-t_0)+q_{m_l'}^{(l,r)}\right]$$

$$-\sin\lambda_l^{(i)}(t-t_0)\left[q_1^{(l,i)}\frac{(t-t_0)^{m_l'-1}}{(m_l'-1)!}+\ldots+q_{m_l'-1}^{(l,i)}(t-t_0)+q_{m_l'}^{(l,i)}\right]\Big\}$$

$$+c_{m_l'}^{(l,i)}\Big\{\sin\lambda_l^{(i)}(t-t_0)\left[q_1^{(l,r)}\frac{(t-t_0)^{m_l'-1}}{(m_l'-1)!}+\ldots+q_{m_l'-1}^{(l,r)}(t-t_0)+q_{m_l'}^{(l,r)}\right]$$

$$+\cos\lambda_l^{(i)}(t-t_0)\left[q_1^{(l,i)}\frac{(t-t_0)^{m_l'-1}}{(m_l'-1)!}+\ldots+q_{m_l'-1}^{(l,i)}(t-t_0)+q_{m_l'}^{(l,i)}\right]\Big\}\rangle.$$

We note that the terms containing the vectors $q_1^{(l,r)}$ and $q_1^{(l,r)}$ with $c_{m_l'}^{(l,r)} = c_{m'}^{(l,r)}$ and $c_{m_l'}^{(l,i)} = c_{m'}^{(l,i)}$, give us the function $u(t)$, and we mention that it has the factor $p(t)$, both defined above. The rest of the sum is denoted by $R(t)$; it can be estimated from above by polynomials of degree less than m_l'. So, we obtain

$$Y(t) = \left\|\sum_{l\in J_{v_0}}\sum_{k=1}^{m_l} g_k^{(l)}(t)\right\|$$

$$= \left\|\sum_{l\in J_{v_0}}\sum_{k=1}^{m_l'} g_k^{(l)}(t)\right\|$$

$$= \|p(t)u(t) + R(t)\|.$$

This entails, taking into account the definition of the function $\eta(t)$,

$$Y(t) = \|p(t)u(t)\,[1 + R(t)/p(t)u(t)]\| \geq p(t)\eta(t)(1 - \|R(t)\|/p(t)u(t)) \geq \frac{1}{2}p(t)\eta(t),$$

for sufficiently large $t_1 \geq t_0$ since the last fraction tends to zero as t tends to infinity. Similarly,

$$Y(t) = \|p(t)u(t)\,[1 + R(t)/p(t)u(t)]\| \leq p(t)\eta(t)(1 + \|R(t)\|/p(t)u(t)) \leq 2p(t)\eta(t),$$

for sufficiently large $t_1 \geq t_0$. □

The next lemma is also important for results in the sequel.

LEMMA 4 *Let hypotheses (H1′), (H2′), and (HS′) be fulfilled. If additionally the sufficient algebraic condition* $(A'_{g,1})$*, respectively,* $(A'_{h,1})$ *is satisfied, then*

$$\eta(t) \neq 0, \quad t \geq t_1,$$
$$\zeta(t) \neq 0, \quad t \geq t_1.$$

as the case may be, for sufficiently large $t_1 \geq t_0$.

On the other hand, if additionally the sufficient algebraic condition $(\overline{A'_{g,1}})$*, respectively,* $(\overline{A'_{h,1}})$ *is satisfied, then for every* $t_1 \geq t_0$ *there exists a* $t \geq t_1$ *such that*

$$\eta(t) = 0,$$
$$\zeta(t) = 0,$$

as the case may be, meaning correspondingly,

$$Y(t) = 0,$$
$$Z(t) = 0.$$

Proof We prove only the first relation. The second one is proven in a similar way. Assume that for all $t_1 \geq t_0$ there exists a $\tilde{t} \geq t_1$ such that $\eta(\tilde{t}) = 0$. Then, $u(\tilde{t}) = 0$ so that

$$\sum_{l \in J'_{\nu_0}} \Big\{ \Big[c^{(l,r)}_{m_l'} \cos \lambda_l^{(i)}(\tilde{t} - t_0) + c^{(l,i)}_{m_l'} \sin \lambda_l^{(i)}(\tilde{t} - t_0) \Big] q_1^{(l,r)}$$
$$+ \Big[-c^{(l,r)}_{m_l'} \sin \lambda_l^{(i)}(\tilde{t} - t_0) + c^{(l,i)}_{m_l'} \cos \lambda_l^{(i)}(\tilde{t} - t_0) \Big] q_1^{(l,i)} \Big\} = 0.$$

Now, due to $(A'_{g,1})$, the vectors $q_1^{(l,r)}, q_1^{(l,i)}, l \in J'_{\nu_0}$ are linearly independent. Therefore,

$$c^{(l,r)}_{m_l'} \cos \lambda_l^{(i)}(\tilde{t} - t_0) + c^{(l,i)}_{m_l'} \sin \lambda_l^{(i)}(\tilde{t} - t_0) = 0,$$
$$-c^{(l,r)}_{m_l'} \sin \lambda_l^{(i)}(\tilde{t} - t_0) + c^{(l,i)}_{m_l'} \cos \lambda_l^{(i)}(\tilde{t} - t_0) = 0,$$

$l \in J'_{\nu_0}$, or in matrix form,

$$\left[\begin{array}{cc} \cos \lambda_l^{(i)}(\tilde{t} - t_0) & \sin \lambda_l^{(i)}(\tilde{t} - t_0) \\ \hline -\sin \lambda_l^{(i)}(\tilde{t} - t_0) & \cos \lambda_l^{(i)}(\tilde{t} - t_0) \end{array} \right] \left[\begin{array}{c} c^{(l,r)}_{m_l'} \\ c^{(l,i)}_{m_l'} \end{array} \right] = \left[\begin{array}{c} 0 \\ 0 \end{array} \right],$$

$l \in J_{\nu_0'}$. From this, we conclude that

$$c^{(l,r)}_{m_l'} = c^{(l,i)}_{m_l'} = 0, \; l \in J'_{\nu_0},$$

or,

$$c^{(l)}_{1,m_l'} = 0, \; l \in J'_{\nu_0}.$$

This delivers a contradiction since we have seen above that $c^{(l)}_{1,m_l'} \neq 0$, $l \in J_{\nu_0}$. □

Now, we state the following corollary.

COROLLARY 5 *Let hypotheses (H1′), (H2′), and (HS′) be fulfilled.*

(i) *If, further, the conditions $(C'_g(t \geq t_1))$, $(C'_h(t \geq t_1))$ are satisfied, then*

$$\frac{1}{4}\frac{Z(t)}{Y(t)} \leq \frac{\|z(t)\|}{\|y(t)\|} \leq 4\frac{Z(t)}{Y(t)}, \; t \geq t_2,$$

and $Y(t) > 0$ and $Z(t) > 0$ for sufficiently large $t_2 \geq t_1 \geq t_0$.

(ii) *If, instead, the sufficient algebraic conditions $(A'_{g,1})$ and $(A'_{h,1})$ are fulfilled, then,*

$$\frac{1}{16}\frac{\zeta(t)}{\eta(t)} \leq \frac{1}{4}\frac{Z(t)}{Y(t)} \leq \frac{\|z(t)\|}{\|y(t)\|} \leq 4\frac{Z(t)}{Y(t)} \leq 16\frac{\zeta(t)}{\eta(t)}, \; t \geq t_1,$$

and $\eta(t) > 0$ and $\zeta(t) > 0$ for sufficiently large $t_1 \geq t_0$.

Proof This follows from Lemmas 2 to 4. □

The last corollary is the basis for the derivation of the following theorem that is the main theoretical result of this paper.

THEOREM 6 *(Norm equivalence of $y(t)$ and $\dot{y}(t)$; general square matrix A)*

Let hypotheses $(H1')$, $(H2')$, and (HS') be fulfilled.

(i) If, further, the conditions $(C'_g(t \geq t_1))$ and $(C'_h(t \geq t_1))$ are satisfied, then there exist constants $c_0 > 0$ and $c_1 > 0$ such that

$$c_0 \|y(t)\| \leq \|\dot{y}(t)\| = \|z(t)\| \leq c_1 \|y(t)\|, \; t \geq t_2,$$

for sufficiently large $t_2 \geq t_1 \geq t_0$.

(ii) If, instead, $(A'_{g,1})$ and $(A'_{h,1})$ hold, then the above equivalence inequalities are valid for $t_2 = t_1$.

Proof

(i) Due to Corollary 5, we have

$$\frac{1}{4}\frac{Z(t)}{Y(t)} \leq \frac{\|z(t)\|}{\|y(t)\|} \leq 4\frac{Z(t)}{Y(t)}, \; t \geq t_2,$$

for sufficiently large $t_2 \geq t_1 \geq t_0$. Now, $Y(t)$ and $Z(t)$ are positive for $t \geq t_2$. Thus, due to the periodicity and continuity of $Y(t)$ and $Z(t)$ the extreme values

$$Y_{min} := \min_{t \geq t_2} Y(t),$$

$$Z_{min} := \min_{t \geq t_2} Z(t),$$

$$Y_{max} := \max_{t \geq t_2} Y(t),$$

$$Z_{max} := \max_{t \geq t_2} Z(t)$$

exist and are positive. Therefore,

$$\frac{1}{4}\frac{Z_{min}}{Y_{max}} \leq \frac{\|z(t)\|}{\|y(t)\|} \leq 4\frac{Z_{max}}{Y_{min}}, \; t \geq t_2,$$

so that Theorem 6 follows with $c_0 = \frac{1}{4} Z_{min}/Y_{max}$ and $c_1 = 4Z_{max}/Y_{min}$.

(ii) Due to Corollary 5, we have

$$\frac{1}{16}\frac{\zeta(t)}{\eta(t)} \leq \frac{\|z(t)\|}{\|y(t)\|} \leq 16\frac{\zeta(t)}{\eta(t)}, \; t \geq t_1.$$

Now, $\eta(t)$ and $\zeta(t)$ are periodic and continuous as well as positive for sufficiently large $t_1 \geq t_0$. Thus, the extreme values

$\eta_{min} := \min_{t \geq t_1} \eta(t)$,

$\zeta_{min} := \min_{t \geq t_1} \zeta(t)$,

$\eta_{max} := \max_{t \geq t_1} \eta(t)$,

$\zeta_{max} := \max_{t \geq t_1} \zeta(t)$

exist and are positive. Therefore,

$$\frac{1}{16} \frac{\zeta_{min}}{\eta_{max}} \leq \frac{\|z(t)\|}{\|y(t)\|} \leq 16 \frac{\zeta_{max}}{\eta_{min}}, \; t \geq t_1,$$

so that Theorem 6 follows with $c_0 = \frac{1}{16} \zeta_{min}/\eta_{max}$ and $c_1 = 16\, \zeta_{max}/\eta_{min}$. □

5. Applications

As applications, we improve Kohaupt (2011, Theorems 12 and 16). The corresponding results are known so far only for $x(t)$ (cf. Kohaupt, 2011).

THEOREM 7 *(Improvement of* Kohaupt, 2011, *Theorem 12)*

Let hypotheses (H1′), (H2′), and (HS′) be fulfilled. Moreover, let $\psi(t)$ be defined by Kohaupt (2011, (41)). *If the conditions ($C_g'(t \geq t_1)$) and ($C_h'(t \geq t_1)$) are satisfied, then there exist constants $\eta_0 > 0$ and $\eta_1 > 0$ such that*

$$\eta_0 \|\psi(t)\| \leq \|y(t)\| \leq \eta_1 \|\psi(t)\|, \; t \geq t_1,$$

for sufficiently large $t_1 \geq t_0$. The same holds true if the sufficient algebraic conditions ($A_{g,1}'$) and ($A_{h,1}'$) hold.

Proof From Theorem 6 and the equivalence of norms in finite-dimensional spaces, it follows that

$$c_{0,\infty} \|y(t)\|_\infty \leq \|\dot{y}(t)\|_\infty \leq c_{1,\infty} \|y(t)\|_\infty, \; t \geq t_1. \tag{28}$$

Further,

$$\|y(t)\|_2 \leq \left(\|y(t)\|_2^2 + \|\dot{y}(t)\|_2^2 \right)^{1/2} = \|x(t)\|_2, \; t \geq t_0. \tag{29}$$

Moreover, using (28), we get

$$\begin{aligned} \|y(t)\|_\infty &= \frac{1}{2} \|y(t)\|_\infty + \frac{1}{2} \|y(t)\|_\infty \geq \frac{1}{2} \|y(t)\|_\infty + \frac{1}{2} \frac{1}{c_{1,\infty}} \|\dot{y}(t)\|_\infty \\ &\geq \min\{\frac{1}{2}, \frac{1}{2} \frac{1}{c_{1,\infty}}\} (\|y(t)\|_\infty + \|\dot{y}(t)\|_\infty) \\ &\geq \min\{\frac{1}{2}, \frac{1}{2} \frac{1}{c_{1,\infty}}\} \max\{\|y(t)\|_\infty, \|\dot{y}(t)\|_\infty\} \\ &= \min\{\frac{1}{2}, \frac{1}{2} \frac{1}{c_{1,\infty}}\} \|x(t)\|_\infty, \end{aligned} \tag{30}$$

$t \geq t_1$. Due to the equivalence of norms in finite-dimensional spaces, from (29) and (30), we infer that there exist constants $\gamma_0 > 0$ and $\gamma_1 > 0$ such that

$$\gamma_0 \|x(t)\| \leq \|y(t)\| \leq \gamma_1 \|x(t)\|, \tag{31}$$

$t \geq t_1$, for sufficiently large t_1. By (31) and Kohaupt (2011, Theorem 6), the proof follows. □

Further, we have

THEOREM 8 *(Improvement of* Kohaupt, 2011, *Theorem 16) Let hypotheses* (H1′), (H2′), *and* (HS′) *be fulfilled. Moreover, let* $\psi(t)$ *be defined by* Kohaupt (2011, (41)). *If the conditions* $(C_g'(t \geq t_1))$ *and* $(C_h'(t \geq t_1))$ *are satisfied, then there exist constants* $\zeta_0 > 0$ *and* $\zeta_1 > 0$ *such that*

$$\zeta_0 \, \|\psi(t)\| \leq \|z(t)\| = \|\dot{y}(t)\| \leq \zeta_1 \, \|\psi(t)\| \, , \; t \geq t_1,$$

for sufficiently large $t_1 \geq t_0$*. The same holds true if the sufficient algebraic conditions* $(A_{g,1}')$ *and* $(A_{h,1}')$ *hold.*

Proof The proof is similar to that of Theorem 7 and is therefore omitted. □

6. Numerical examples

In this section, we illustrate the obtained results by examples.

We consider the multi-mass vibration model in Figure 1 for $n \in \{1, 2, 3, 4, 5\}$.

The associated initial value problem is given by

$$M\ddot{y} + B\dot{y} + Ky = 0, \quad y(0) = y_0, \; \dot{y}(0) = \dot{y}_0$$

where $y = [y_1, \ldots, y_n]^T$ and

$$M = \begin{bmatrix} m_1 & & & & \\ & m_2 & & & \\ & & m_3 & & \\ & & & \ddots & \\ & & & & m_n \end{bmatrix},$$

$$B = \begin{bmatrix} b_1 + b_2 & -b_2 & & & & \\ -b_2 & b_2 + b_3 & -b_3 & & & \\ & -b_3 & b_3 + b_4 & -b_4 & & \\ & & \ddots & \ddots & \ddots & \\ & & & -b_{n-1} & b_{n-1} + b_n & -b_n \\ & & & & -b_n & b_n + b_{n+1} \end{bmatrix},$$

$$K = \begin{bmatrix} k_1 + k_2 & -k_2 & & & & \\ -k_2 & k_2 + k_3 & -k_3 & & & \\ & -k_3 & k_3 + k_4 & -k_4 & & \\ & & \ddots & \ddots & \ddots & \\ & & & -k_{n-1} & k_{n-1} + k_n & -k_n \\ & & & & -k_n & k_n + k_{n+1} \end{bmatrix},$$

or, in the *state-space description*

$$\dot{x}(t) = A\,x(t), \quad x(0) = x_0,$$

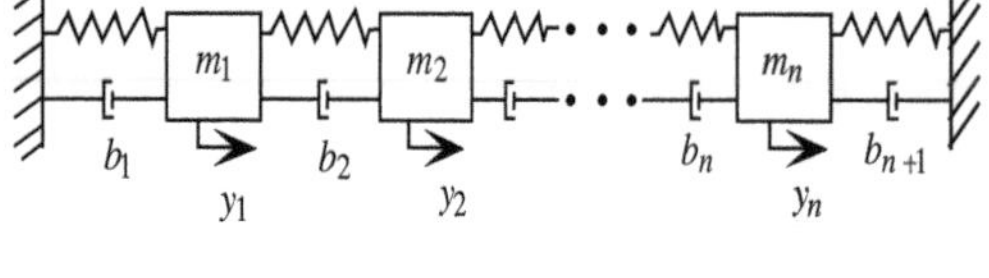

Figure 1. Multi-mass vibration model.

where the *state vector* x is given by $x = [y^T, z^T]^T$, $z = \dot{y}$, and

where the *system matrix* A has the form

$$A = \left[\begin{array}{c|c} 0 & E \\ \hline -M^{-1}K & -M^{-1}B \end{array}\right].$$

As in Kohaupt (2011), we specify the values as

$$m_j = 1, \quad j = 1, \ldots, n$$
$$k_j = 1, \quad j = 1, \ldots, n+1$$

and

$$b_j = \begin{cases} 1/2, & j \text{ even} \\ 1/4, & j \text{ odd.} \end{cases}$$

With the above numerical values, we have

$$M = E,$$

$$B = \begin{bmatrix} \frac{3}{4} & -\frac{1}{2} & & & \\ -\frac{1}{2} & \frac{3}{4} & -\frac{1}{4} & & \\ & -\frac{1}{4} & \frac{3}{4} & -\frac{1}{2} & \\ & & \ddots & \ddots & \ddots \\ & & -\frac{1}{4} & \frac{3}{4} & -\frac{1}{2} \\ & & & -\frac{1}{2} & \frac{3}{4} \end{bmatrix}$$

(if n is even), and

$$K = \begin{bmatrix} 2 & -1 & & & \\ -1 & 2 & -1 & & \\ & -1 & 2 & -1 & \\ & & \ddots & \ddots & \ddots \\ & & -1 & 2 & -1 \\ & & & -1 & 2 \end{bmatrix}.$$

Remark We mention that, in all examples, condition $(H3)$ resp. $(H3')$ is fulfilled, i.e., that all eigenvalues are different from zero. Therefore, the sufficient algebraic conditions $(A_{g,1})$ and $(A_{h,1})$ are equivalent (since then $r_1^{(k)} = \lambda_k q_1^{(k)}$, $k \in J_{v_0}$ (see Kohaupt, 2011)). The same holds true for $(A'_{g,1})$ and $(A'_{h,1})$, for $(\overline{A}_{g,1})$ and $(\overline{A}_{h,1})$, and for $(\overline{A}'_{g,1})$ and $(\overline{A}'_{h,1})$. So, we need only the first sufficient algebraic condition with index g, in each case. The stepsize in all figures is $\Delta t = 0.01$.

6.1. Illustration of the sufficient algebraic conditions

In this subsection, *we illustrate the sufficient algebraic conditions that guarantee the validity, respectively, invalidity of the equivalence inequalities*, as the case may be.

Remark In the following Examples 1–5, we have to consider the quantities $\tilde{u}_j = (Ux_0)_j = (x_0, u_j^*)$, $j = 1, \ldots, m = 2n$ because they play a role in the definition of $v_0 = v_{x_0}[A]$ (see Kohaupt, 2011). Due to the numbering $\lambda_{j+n}(A) = \overline{\lambda_j(A)} = \lambda_j(A^*)$, $j = 1, \ldots, n$, we have to study only the quantities $\tilde{u}_j$ for $j = 1, \ldots, n$ (and not for $j = 1, \ldots, m = 2n$), see also the definition of v_0 on this.

Example 1: $n = 1$. We choose

$y_0 = -1, \dot{y}_0 = 0.$

Here, $\tilde{u}_j = (Ux_0)_j \neq 0,\ j = 1$ and

$$\begin{aligned} \lambda_1(A) &= -0.37500000000000 + 1.36358901432946i, \\ \lambda_2(A) &= -0.37500000000000 - 1.36358901432946i = \overline{\lambda_1(A)} = \lambda_1(A^*). \end{aligned} \tag{32}$$

Thus,

Sufficient algebraic condition $(\overline{A_{g,1}})$:

$v_0 = v_{x_0}[A] = v[A] = Re\,\lambda_1(A) = -0.375.$

We have

$q_1^{(1,r)} = 0.55668288399531, \quad q_1^{(1,i)} = -0.15309310892395.$

Since $q_1^{(1,r)}, q_1^{(1,i)}$ are *linearly dependent*, the equivalence inequalities between $y(t)$ and $\dot{y}(t)$ do not hold. This is consistent with the fact that $|y(t)|$ and $|\dot{y}(t)|$*have zeros* (see Figures 2 and 3).

Example 2: $n = 2$. We choose

$y_0 = [-1, 1]^T, \dot{y}_0 = [0, 0]^T.$

Here, $\tilde{u}_j = (Ux_0)_j \neq 0,\ j = 1, 2$ and

$$\begin{aligned} \lambda_1(A) &= -0.62500000000000 + 1.61535599791501i, \\ \lambda_2(A) &= -0.12500000000000 + 0.99215674164922i, \\ \lambda_3(A) &= -0.62500000000000 - 1.61535599791501i = \overline{\lambda_1(A)} = \lambda_1(A^*), \\ \lambda_4(A) &= -0.12500000000000 - 0.99215674164922i = \overline{\lambda_2(A)} = \lambda_2(A^*). \end{aligned} \tag{33}$$

Thus,

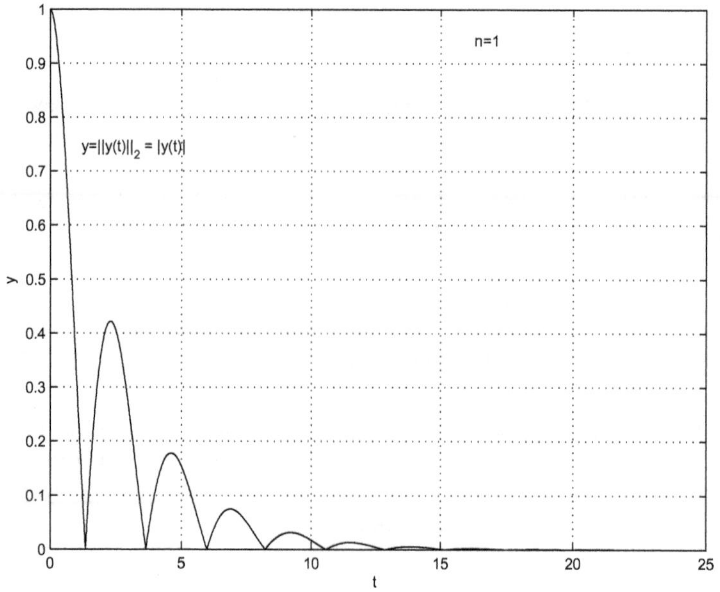

Figure 2. $y = |y(t)|$ **for** $n = 1$.

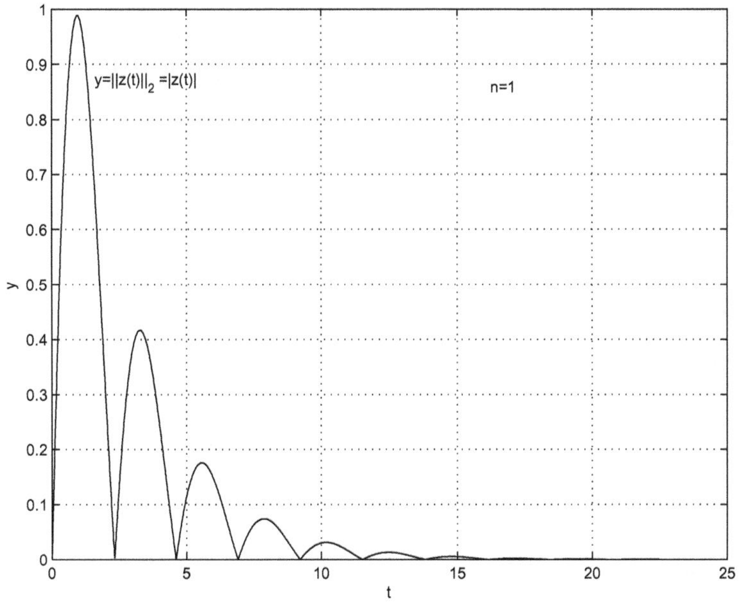

Figure 3. $y = |\dot{y}(t)|$ **for** $n = 1$.

$$\nu_0 = \nu_{x_0}[A] = \nu[A] = Re\,\lambda_2(A) = \max_{j=1,2} Re\,\lambda_j(A) = -0.125.$$

Sufficient algebraic condition $(\overline{A_{g,1}})$:

We have

$$q_1^{(2,r)} = \begin{bmatrix} 0.46392985110715 \\ 0.46392985110715 \end{bmatrix}, \qquad q_1^{(2,i)} = \begin{bmatrix} 0.18646472388014 \\ 0.18646472388014 \end{bmatrix}.$$

Since $q_1^{(2,r)}, q_1^{(2,i)}$ are *linearly dependent*, the equivalence inequalities between $y(t)$ and $\dot{y}(t)$ do not hold. This is consistent with the fact that $\|y(t)\|_2$ and $\|\dot{y}(t)\|_2$*have zeros* (see Figures 4 and 5).

Example 3: $n = 3$. *We choose*

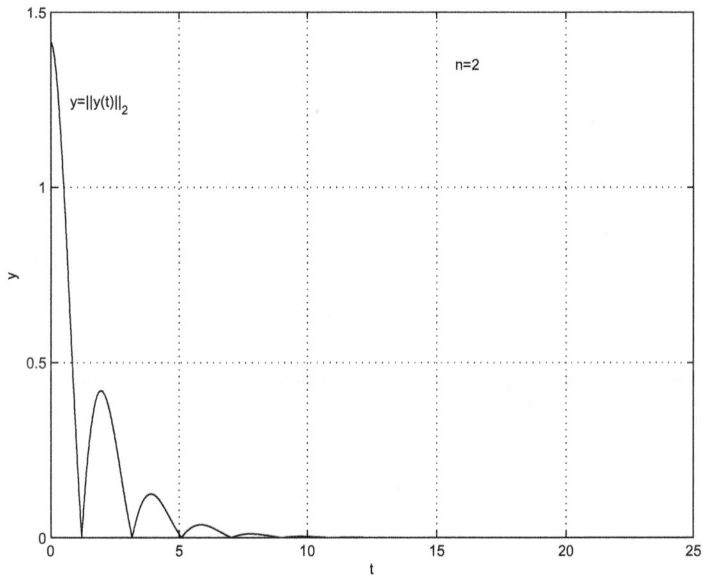

Figure 4. $y = \|y(t)\|_2$ **for** $n = 2$.

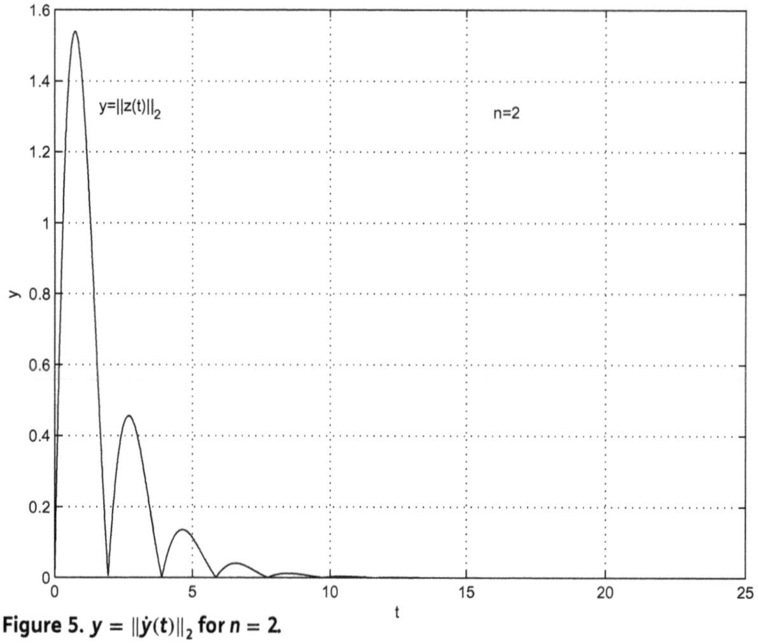

Figure 5. $y = \|\dot{y}(t)\|_2$ **for** $n = 2$.

$y_0 = [-1, 1, -1]^T, \dot{y}_0 = [0, 0, 0]^T$.

Here, $\tilde{u}_j = (Ux_0)_j \neq 0$, $j = 1, 2, 3$ and

$$\lambda_1(A) = -0.64018170840517 + 1.72238614772272i,$$
$$\lambda_2(A) = -0.37500000000000 + 1.36358901432946i,$$
$$\lambda_3(A) = -0.10981829159483 + 0.76176022151217i,$$
$$\lambda_4(A) = -0.64018170840517 - 1.72238614772272i = \overline{\lambda_1(A)} = \lambda_1(A^*),$$
$$\lambda_5(A) = -0.37500000000000 - 1.36358901432946i = \overline{\lambda_2(A)} = \lambda_2(A^*),$$
$$\lambda_6(A) = -0.10981829159483 - 0.76176022151217i = \overline{\lambda_3(A)} = \lambda_3(A^*).$$

Thus,

$$\nu_0 = \nu_{x_0}[A] = \nu[A] = Re\,\lambda_3(A) = \max_{j=1,2,3} Re\,\lambda_j(A) = -0.10981829159483.$$

Sufficient algebraic condition $(A_{g,1})$:

We have

$$q_1^{(3,r)} = \begin{bmatrix} 0.24265406168356 \\ 0.29298741809281 \\ 0.17263029735493 \end{bmatrix}, \qquad q_1^{(3,i)} = \begin{bmatrix} -0.32240386726516 \\ -0.47468024545176 \\ -0.35244526929766 \end{bmatrix}.$$

Since $q_1^{(3,r)}, q_1^{(3,i)}$ are *linearly independent*, the equivalence inequalities between $y(t)$ and $\dot{y}(t)$ hold. This is consistent with the fact that $\|y(t)\|_2$ and $\|\dot{y}(t)\|_2$ *do not have zeros* for $t > 0$ (see Figures 6 and 7).

Example 4: $n = 4$. We choose

$y_0 = [-1, 1, -1, 1]^T, \dot{y}_0 = [0, 0, 0, 0]^T$.

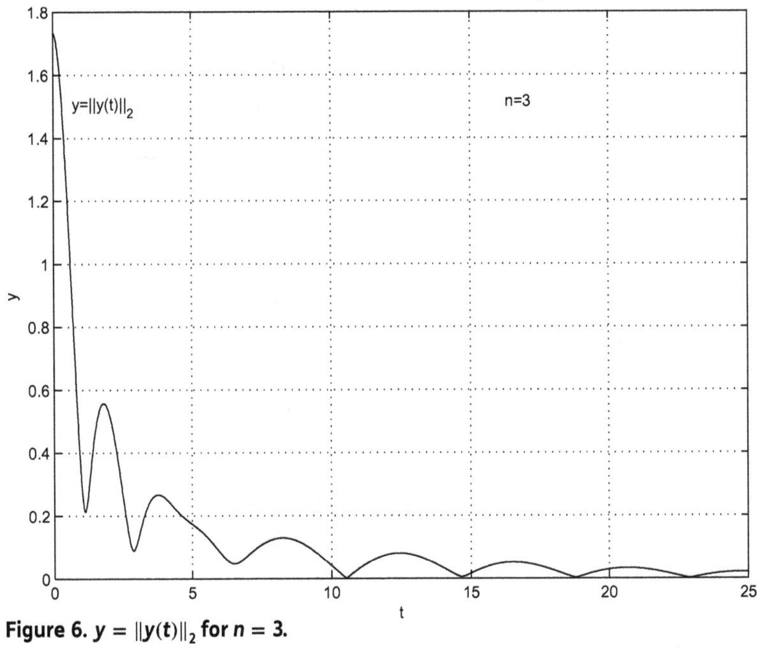

Figure 6. $y = \|y(t)\|_2$ **for** $n = 3$.

Here, $\tilde{u}_j = (Ux_0)_j \neq 0,\ j = 1, \dots, 4$ *is not true* since $\tilde{u}_4 = (Ux_0)_4 = (x_0, u_4^*) = 0$. We have

$$\lambda_1(A) = -0.68970367573270 + 1.76753133055006i,$$
$$\lambda_2(A) = -0.56419829475905 + 1.51175297583756i,$$
$$\lambda_3(A) = -0.18529632426730 + 1.16387666169148i,$$
$$\lambda_4(A) = -0.06080170524095 + 0.61674103415901i,$$
$$\lambda_5(A) = -0.68970367573270 - 1.76753133055006i = \overline{\lambda_1(A)} = \lambda_1(A^*),$$
$$\lambda_6(A) = -0.56419829475905 - 1.51175297583756i = \overline{\lambda_2(A)} = \lambda_2(A^*),$$
$$\lambda_7(A) = -0.18529632426730 - 1.16387666169148i = \overline{\lambda_3(A)} = \lambda_3(A^*),$$
$$\lambda_8(A) = -0.06080170524095 - 0.61674103415901i = \overline{\lambda_4(A)} = \lambda_4(A^*).$$

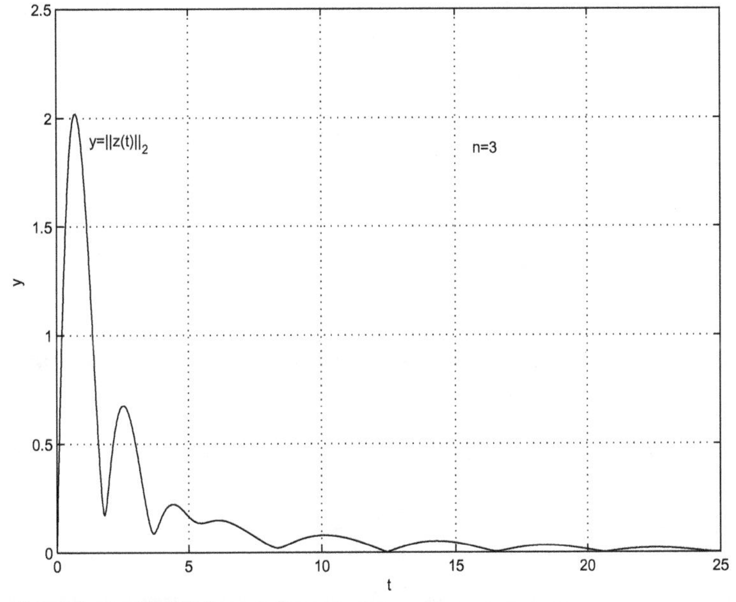

Figure 7. $y = \|\dot{y}(t)\|_2$ **for** $n = 3$.

Thus,

$$\nu_0 = \nu_{x_0}[A] \neq \nu[A] = Re\,\lambda_4(A) = \max_{j=1,\ldots,4} Re\,\lambda_j(A) = -0.06080170524095.$$

Since

$$\tilde{u}_3 = (Ux_0)_3 = (x_0, u_3^*) \neq 0,$$

it follows

$$\nu_0 = \nu_{x_0}[A] = Re\,\lambda_3(A) = \max_{j=1,\ldots,4} \{Re\,\lambda_j(A^*) \mid x_0 \not\perp u_j^*\}. = -0.18529632426730.$$

Sufficient algebraic condition $(A_{g,1})$:

We have

$$q_1^{(3,r)} = \begin{bmatrix} 0.02911851244640 \\ 0.04706992473723 \\ -0.04706992473723 \\ -0.02911851244640 \end{bmatrix}, \quad q_1^{(3,i)} = \begin{bmatrix} -0.38288215237183i \\ -0.24420344590968i \\ 0.24420344590968i \\ 0.38288215237183i \end{bmatrix}.$$

Since $q_1^{(3,r)}, q_1^{(3,i)}$ are *linearly independent*, the equivalence inequalities between $y(t)$ and $\dot{y}(t)$ hold. This is consistent with the fact that $\|y(t)\|_2$ and $\|\dot{y}(t)\|_2$ *do not have zeros* for $t > 0$ (see Figures 8 and 9).

Remark Here, we have a nontrivial example of a case with $\nu_{x_0}[A] < \nu[A]$.

Example 5: $n = 5$. *This model was often used before by the author. We choose*

$$y_0 = [-1, 1, -1, 1, -1]^T, \dot{y}_0 = [0, 0, 0, 0, 0]^T.$$

Here, $\tilde{u}_j = (Ux_0)_j \neq 0$, $j = 1, \ldots, 5$ and

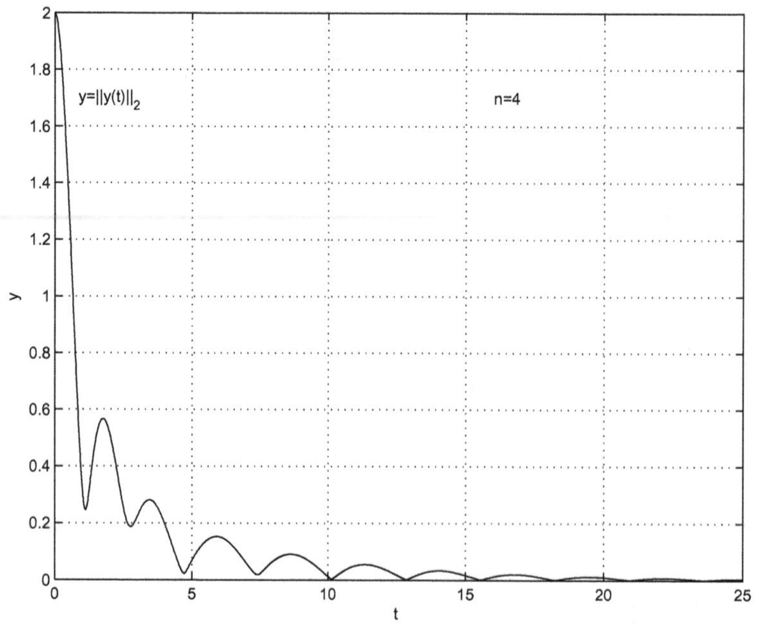

Figure 8. $y = \|y(t)\|_2$ **for** $n = 4$.

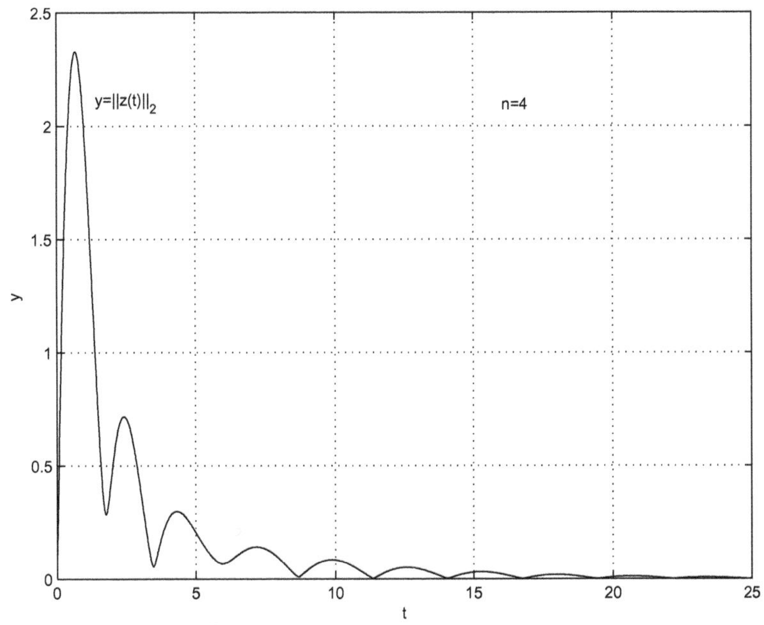

Figure 9. $y = \|\dot{y}(t)\|_2$ **for** $n = 4$.

$$\lambda_1(A) = -0.69976063878054 + 1.79598147815975i,$$
$$\lambda_2(A) = -0.56266837404074 + 1.61635870164386i,$$
$$\lambda_3(A) = -0.37500000000000 + 1.36358901432946i,$$
$$\lambda_4(A) = -0.18733162595926 + 0.99452168646559i,$$
$$\lambda_5(A) = -0.05023936121946 + 0.51637145071101i,$$
$$\lambda_6(A) = -0.69976063878054 - 1.79598147815975i = \overline{\lambda_1(A)} = \lambda_1(A^*),$$
$$\lambda_7(A) = -0.56266837404074 - 1.61635870164386i = \overline{\lambda_2(A)} = \lambda_2(A^*),$$
$$\lambda_8(A) = -0.37500000000000 - 1.36358901432946i = \overline{\lambda_3(A)} = \lambda_3(A^*),$$
$$\lambda_9(A) = -0.18733162595926 - 0.99452168646559i = \overline{\lambda_4(A)} = \lambda_4(A^*),$$
$$\lambda_{10}(A) = -0.05023936121946 - 0.51637145071101i = \overline{\lambda_5(A)} = \lambda_5(A^*).$$

Thus,

$$\nu_0 = \nu_{x_0}[A] = \nu[A] = Re\,\lambda_5(A) = \max_{j=1,\ldots,5} Re\,\lambda_j(A) = -0.05023936121946.$$

Sufficient algebraic condition $(A_{g,1})$:

We have

$$q_1^{(5,r)} = \begin{bmatrix} 0.17257779639348 \\ 0.31669429022046 \\ 0.36598767554684 \\ 0.31669429022046 \\ 0.19340987915336 \end{bmatrix}, \quad q_1^{(5,i)} = \begin{bmatrix} 0.19231277274243 \\ 0.31050187422113 \\ 0.35873345396061 \\ 0.31050187422113 \\ 0.16642068121818 \end{bmatrix}.$$

Since $q_1^{(5,r)}, q_1^{(5,i)}$ are *linearly independent*, the equivalence inequalities between $y(t)$ and $\dot{y}(t)$ hold. This is consistent with the fact that $\|y(t)\|_2$ and $\|\dot{y}(t)\|_2$ *do not have zeros* for $t > 0$ (see Figures 10 and 11).

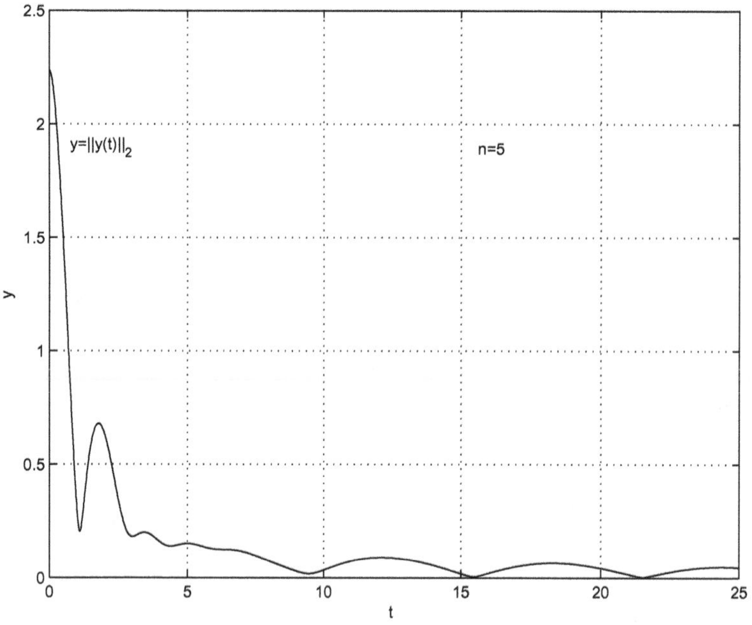

Figure 10. $y = \|y(t)\|_2$ **for** $n = 5$**.**

6.2. Illustration of a case with $\nu_{x_0}[A] < \nu[A]$

In most of the Examples 1–5 of Section 6.1, one has $\nu_{x_0}[A] = \nu[A]$. However, in *Example 4 of Section* 6.1, *we have seen that* $\nu_{x_0}[A] < \nu[A]$. *To illustrate this result, we employ Kohaupt* (2011, Theorems 7 and 13), where we restrict ourselves to the upper bounds $\|y(t)\|_2 \leq Y_{1,2}\, e^{\nu_0(t-t_0)}$ and $\|z(t)\|_2 \leq Z_{1,2}\, e^{\nu_0(t-t_0)}$ with the abbreviation $\nu_0 = \nu_{x_0}[A]$. For comparison reasons, however, first we plot the upper bounds $\|y(t)\|_2 \leq Y_{1,2}\, e^{\nu[A](t-t_0)}$ and $\|z(t)\|_2 \leq Z_{1,2}\, e^{\nu[A](t-t_0)}$.

We have

$$\nu[A] = Re\, \lambda_4(A) \doteq -0.060801,$$
$$\nu_{x_0}[A] = Re\, \lambda_3(A) \doteq -0.185296.$$

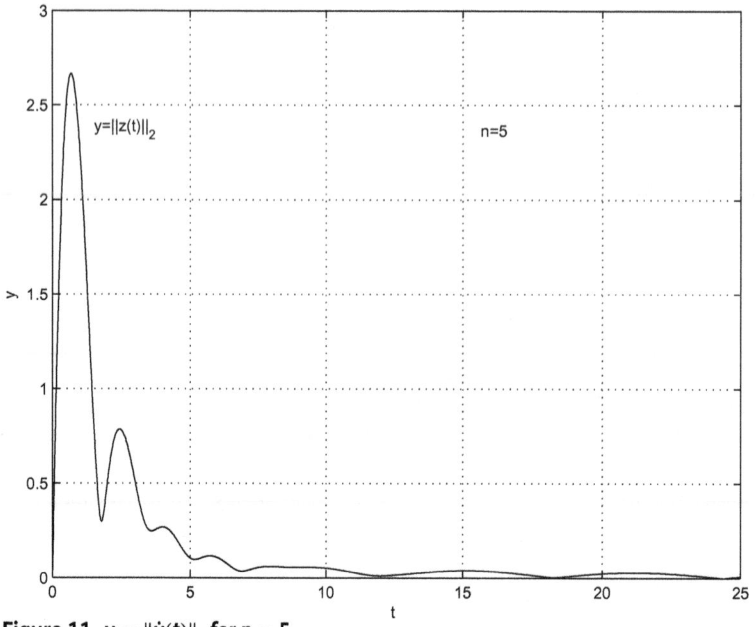

Figure 11. $y = \|\dot{y}(t)\|_2$ **for** $n = 5$**.**

In what follows, we give the point of contact $t_{s,u,2}$ between curve and upper bound as well as the optimal constants $Y_{1,2}$ and $Z_{1,2}$ computed by the differential calculus of norms.

For the upper bound $y = Y_{1,2}\, e^{\nu[A](t-t_0)}$, we obtain

$$t_{s,u,2} \doteq 0.017579,$$
$$Y_{1,2} \doteq 2.001064.$$

The curve $y = \|y(t)\|_2$ and its upper bound can be seen in Figure 12.

For the upper bound $y = Z_{1,2}\, e^{\nu[A](t-t_0)}$, we obtain

$$t_{s,u,2} \doteq 0.694699,$$
$$Z_{1,2} \doteq 2.426929.$$

The curve $y = \|z(t)\|_2$ and its upper bound can be seen in Figure 13.

For the upper bound $y = Y_{1,2}\, e^{\nu_0(t-t_0)}$, we obtain

$$t_{s,u,2} \doteq 0.0054810,$$
$$Y_{1,2} \doteq 2.010068.$$

The curve $y = \|y(t)\|_2$ and its upper bound can be seen in Figure 14.

For the upper bound $y = Z_{1,2}\, e^{\nu_0(t-t_0)}$, we obtain

$$t_{s,u,2} \doteq 0.730963,$$
$$Z_{1,2} \doteq 2.652107.$$

The curve $y = \|z(t)\|_2$ and its upper bound can be seen in Figure 15.

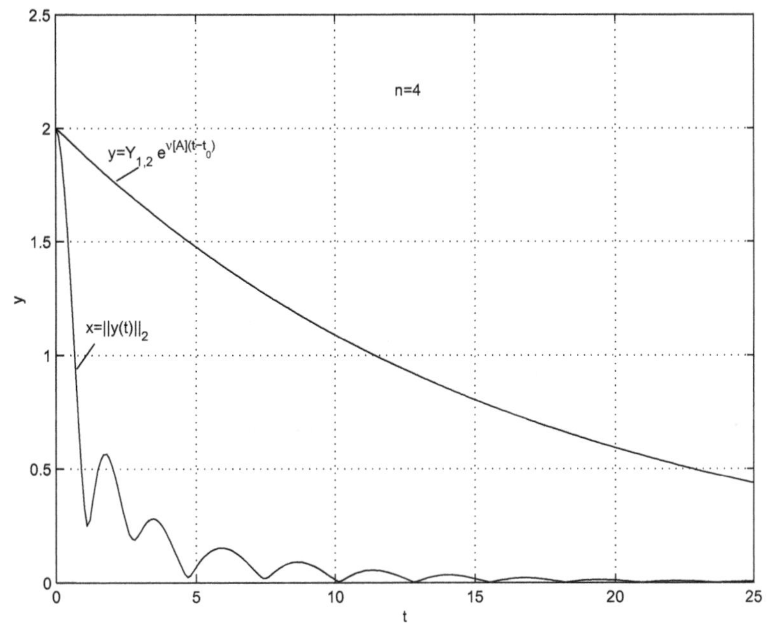

Figure 12. $y = \|y(t)\|_2$ **and upper bound** $y = Y_{1,2}\, e^{\nu[A](t-t_0)}$.

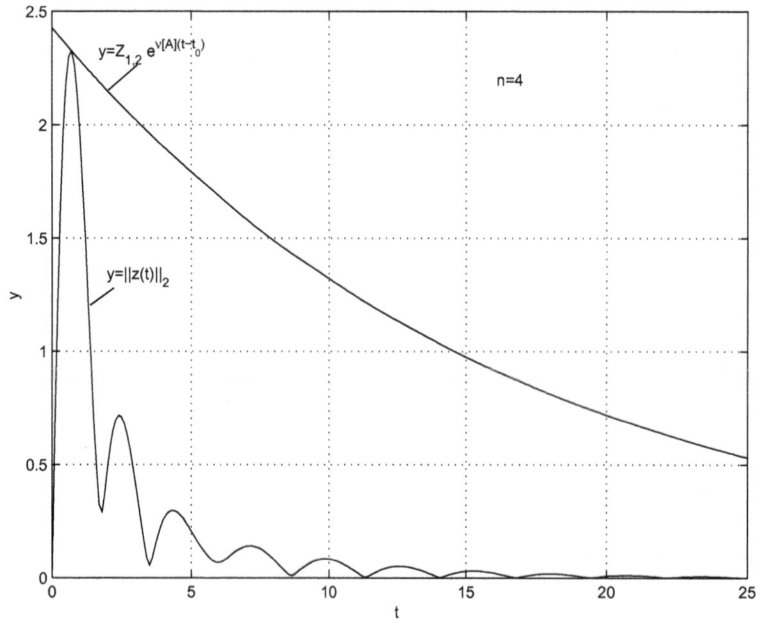

Figure 13. $y = \|y'(t)\|_2$ **and upper bound** $y = Z_{1,2}\, e^{\nu[A](t-t_0)}$.

Comparing the corresponding figures, it is evident that the spectral abscissa with respect to the initial vector x_0, i.e. $\nu_0 = \nu_{x_0}[A]$, has not only theoretical meaning, but sometimes also practical significance.

6.3. Illustration of a case with non-diagonalizable matrix A

In this subsection, we first construct an example with $n = 2$ degrees of freedom so that $A \in \mathbb{R}^{4\times 4}$ is not diagonalizable. The aim is then to apply Theorems 7 and 8, where we restrict ourselves to the upper bounds $\|y(t)\|_2 \le \eta_{1,2}\, \|\psi(t)\|_2$ and $\|z(t)\|_2 \le \zeta_{1,2}\, \|\psi(t)\|_2$.

(i) *Construction of a non-diagonalizable matrix*

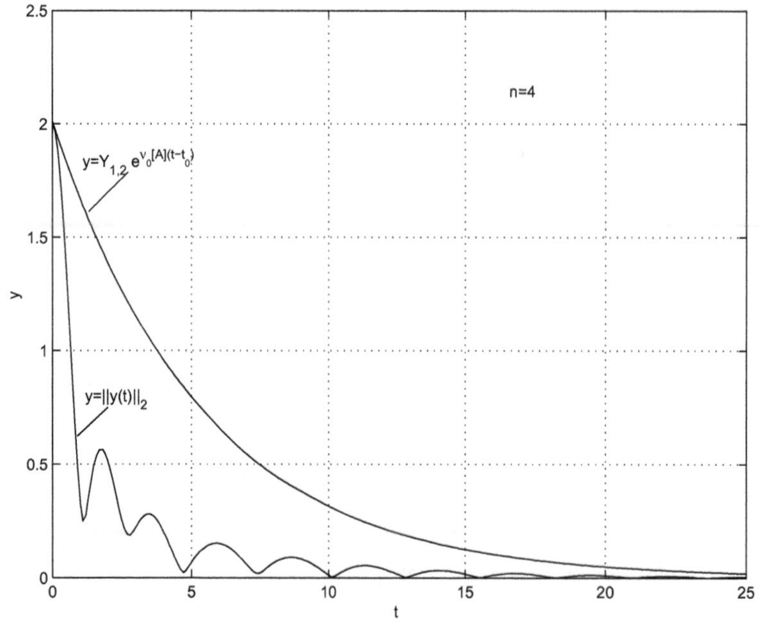

Figure 14. $y = \|y(t)\|_2$ **and upper bound** $y = Y_{1,2}\, e^{\nu_0(t-t_0)}$.

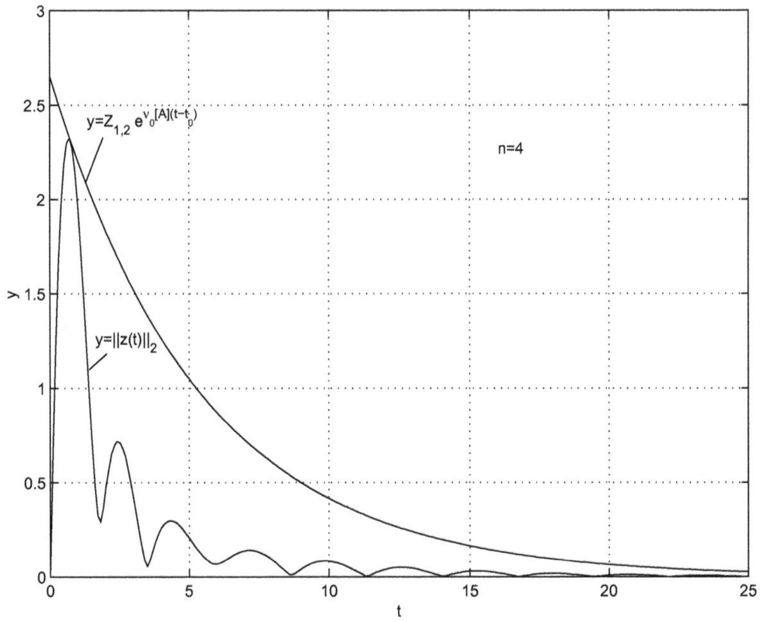

Figure 15. $y = \|\dot{y}(t)\|_2$ **and upper bound** $ly = Z_{1,2}\, e^{\nu_0(t-t_0)}$.

A In the case $n = 2$, we have

$$M = \left[\begin{array}{c|c} m_1 & 0 \\ \hline 0 & m_2 \end{array}\right],$$
$$B = \left[\begin{array}{c|c} b_1 + b_2 & -b_2 \\ \hline -b_2 & b_2 + b_3 \end{array}\right],$$
$$K = \left[\begin{array}{c|c} k_1 + k_2 & -k_2 \\ \hline -k_2 & k_2 + k_3 \end{array}\right],$$

so that the pertinent characteristic equation reads

$$|\lambda^2 M + \lambda B + K| = det \left[\begin{array}{c|c} \lambda^2 m_1 + \lambda(b_1 + b_2) + (k_1 + k_2) & \lambda(-b_2) - k_2 \\ \hline \lambda(-b_2) - k_2 & \lambda^2 m_2 + \lambda(b_2 + b_3) + (k_2 + k_3) \end{array}\right] = 0.$$

For the construction of a case with non-diagonalizable matrix *A*, we choose

$$b_2 = 0,\; m_2 = m_1 = 1,\; b_3 = b_1,\; k_3 = k_1.$$

Then,

$$\lambda^2 m_1 + \lambda b_1 + (k_1 + k_2) = s k_2 \quad \text{with} \quad s \in \{+1, -1\}.$$

Hence, with $m_1 = 1$,

$$\lambda = -\frac{b_1}{2} \pm \sqrt{(\frac{b_1}{2})^2 - k_1 - k_2 + s k_2}.$$

Now, in order to get one real solution, we set

$$k_1 := \left(\frac{b_1}{2}\right)^2.$$

This implies

$$\lambda = \begin{cases} -\frac{b_1}{2}, & s = +1, \\ -\frac{b_1}{2} \pm i\sqrt{2k_2}, & s = -1. \end{cases}$$

As numerical values for the quantities are not yet specified, we choose $b_1 = 1/4, k_2 = 1/2$. On the whole, this delivers the following data:

$m_1 = m_2 = 1;\ b_1 = 1/4,\ b_2 = 0,\ b_3 = 1/4;\ k_1 = 1/64 = 1/2^4,\ k_2 = 1/2,\ k_3 = 1/64 = 1/2^4,$

which leads to

$$M = \left[\begin{array}{c|c} m_1 & 0 \\ \hline 0 & m_2 \end{array}\right] = \left[\begin{array}{c|c} 1 & 0 \\ \hline 0 & 1 \end{array}\right],$$

$$B = \left[\begin{array}{c|c} b_1 + b_2 & -b_2 \\ \hline -b_2 & b_2 + b_3 \end{array}\right] = \left[\begin{array}{c|c} 0.25 & 0 \\ \hline 0 & 0.25 \end{array}\right],$$

$$K = \left[\begin{array}{c|c} k_1 + k_2 & -k_2 \\ \hline -k_2 & k_2 + k_3 \end{array}\right] = \left[\begin{array}{c|c} 1/64 + 1/2 & -1/2 \\ \hline -1/2 & 1/2 + 1/64 \end{array}\right] = \left[\begin{array}{c|c} 0.515625 & -0.5 \\ \hline -0.5 & 0.515625 \end{array}\right].$$

Now,

$$A = \left[\begin{array}{c|c} 0 & E \\ \hline -M^{-1}K & -M^{-1}B \end{array}\right].$$

The *jordan* routine of MATLAB gives $[V, J] = jordan(A)$ with

$$J = \begin{bmatrix} J_1(\lambda_1) & & \\ & J_2(\lambda_2) & \\ & & J_3(\lambda_3) \end{bmatrix} = \left[\begin{array}{c|c|cc} -0.125 + i & & & \\ \hline & -0.125 - i & & \\ \hline & & -0.125 & 1 \\ & & & -0.125 \end{array}\right]$$

and

$$V = [p_1, p_2, p_1^{(3)}, p_2^{(3)}] = \left[\begin{array}{c|c|c|c} 0.25 - 0.03125i & 0.25 + 0.03125i & 0.0625 & 0.5 \\ -0.25 + 0.03125i & -0.25 - 0.03125i & 0.0625 & 0.5 \\ 0.25390625i & -0.25390625i & -0.0078125 & 0 \\ -0.25390625i & 0.25390625i & -0.0078125 & 0 \end{array}\right].$$

Further, the Matlab command $[V_s, J_s] = jordan(A^*)$ delivers $J_s = J$. After rearranging the eigenvalues of A^* such that $\lambda_k(A^*) = \overline{\lambda_k(A)}$, $k = 1, 2, 3$, and calling the rearranged J_s now J_{A^*}, and the rearranged V_s now U^*, we obtain

$$J_{A^*} = \begin{bmatrix} J_1(\overline{\lambda_1}) & & \\ & J_2(\overline{\lambda_2}) & \\ & & J_3(\overline{\lambda_3}) \end{bmatrix} = \left[\begin{array}{c|c|cc} -0.125 - i & & & \\ \hline & -0.125 + i & & \\ \hline & & -0.125 & 1 \\ & & & -0.125 \end{array}\right]$$

and,

$$U^* = [u_1^*, u_2^*, u_1^{(3)^*}, u_2^{(3)^*}] = \left[\begin{array}{c|c|c|c} 0.25 + 0.03125i & 0.25 - 0.03125i & 0.0625 & 0.5 \\ -0.25 - 0.03125i & -0.25 + 0.03125i & 0.0625 & 0.5 \\ 0.25i & -0.25i & 0.5 & 0 \\ -0.25i & 0.25i & 0.5 & 0 \end{array}\right].$$

We have

$(\mathbf{p_1}, \mathbf{u_1^*}) \neq \mathbf{0}$	$(p_1, u_2^*) = 0$	$(p_1, u_1^{(3)^*}) = 0$	$(p_1, u_2^{(3)^*}) = 0$
$(p_2, u_1^*) = 0$	$(\mathbf{p_2}, \mathbf{u_2^*}) \neq \mathbf{0}$	$(p_2, u_1^{(3)^*}) = 0$	$(p_2, u_2^{(3)^*}) = 0$
$(p_1^{(3)}, u_1^*) = 0$	$(p_1^{(3)}, u_2^*) = 0$	$(p_1^{(3)}, u_1^{(3)^*}) = 0$	$(\mathbf{p_1^{(3)}}, \mathbf{u_2^{(3)^*}}) \neq \mathbf{0}$
$(p_2^{(3)}, u_1^*) = 0$	$(p_2^{(3)}, u_2^*) = 0$	$(\mathbf{p_2^{(3)}}, \mathbf{u_1^{(3)^*}}) \neq \mathbf{0}$	$(p_2^{(3)}, u_2^{(3)^*}) \neq 0$

The next step is to replace the principal vector of stage 2, $p_2^{(3)}$, by a principal vector of stage 2, $w_2^{(3)}$, with $(w_2^{(3)}, u_2^{(3)^*}) = 0$. Following the method of 2007, for this, we seek $w_2^{(3)}$ in the form

$$w_2^{(3)} = p_2^{(3)} + \alpha_1^{(3)} p_1^{(3)}.$$

From $(w_2^{(3)}, u_2^{(3)^*}) = 0$, we obtain $\alpha_1^{(3)} = -(p_2^{(3)}, u_2^{(3)^*})/(p_1^{(3)}, u_2^{(3)^*})$. Moreover, we normalize according to $\tilde{p}_1 = p_1/(p_1, u_1^*)$, $\tilde{p}_2 = p_2/(p_2, u_2^*)$, $\tilde{p}_1^{(3)} = p_1^{(3)}/(p_1^{(3)}, u_2^{(3)^*})$, $\tilde{p}_2^{(3)} = w_2^{(3)}/(w_2^{(3)}, u_1^{(3)^*})$, and rename $\tilde{p}_1, \tilde{p}_2, \tilde{p}_1^{(3)}, \tilde{p}_2^{(3)}$ to $p_1, p_2, p_1^{(3)}, p_2^{(3)}$, as the case may be. Then,

$(\mathbf{p_1}, \mathbf{u_1^*}) = \mathbf{1}$	$(p_1, u_2^*) = 0$	$(p_1, u_1^{(3)^*}) = 0$	$(p_1, u_2^{(3)^*}) = 0$
$(p_2, u_1^*) = 0$	$(\mathbf{p_2}, \mathbf{u_2^*}) = \mathbf{1}$	$(p_2, u_1^{(3)^*}) = 0$	$(p_2, u_2^{(3)^*}) = 0$
$(p_1^{(3)}, u_1^*) = 0$	$(p_1^{(3)}, u_2^*) = 0$	$(p_1^{(3)}, u_1^{(3)^*}) = 0$	$(\mathbf{p_1^{(3)}}, \mathbf{u_2^{(3)^*}}) = \mathbf{1}$
$(p_2^{(3)}, u_1^*) = 0$	$(p_2^{(3)}, u_2^*) = 0$	$(\mathbf{p_2^{(3)}}, \mathbf{u_1^{(3)^*}}) = \mathbf{1}$	$(p_2^{(3)}, u_2^{(3)^*}) = 0$

The numerical values of the new $p_1, p_2, p_1^{(3)}, p_2^{(3)}$ are:

$$[p_1, p_2, p_1^{(3)}, p_2^{(3)}] = \left[\begin{array}{c|c|c|c} 1 & 1 & 1 & 0 \\ -1 & -1 & 1 & 0 \\ -0.125 + i & -0.125 - i & -0.125 & 1 \\ 0.125 - i & 0.125 + i & -0.125 & 1 \end{array}\right] =: P.$$

(ii) *Complex basis functions*

Similar as in Kohaupt (2008b), we obtain as complex basis functions

$$\begin{aligned} x_1(t) &= p_1\, e^{\lambda_1(t-t_0)}, \\ x_2(t) &= p_2\, e^{\lambda_2(t-t_0)} = \overline{x}_1(t), \\ x_1^{(3)}(t) &= p_1^{(3)}\, e^{\lambda_3(t-t_0)}, \\ x_2^{(3)}(t) &= [p_1^{(3)}(t-t_0) + p_2^{(3)}]\, e^{\lambda_3(t-t_0)}. \end{aligned}$$

The general solution of $\dot{x} = Ax$ is given by

$$x(t) = c_{11}x_1(t) + \overline{c}_{11}\overline{x}_1(t) + c_1^{(3)}x_1^{(3)}(t) + c_2^{(3)}x_2^{(3)}(t),$$

where we prefer the usage of the double index for the first coefficient (c_{1k} with $k = 1$ in the notation of Kohaupt (2008b)). The boundary condition $x(t_0) = x_0$ is met for $t = t_0$, delivering

$$x_0 = c_{11}p_1 + \overline{c}_{11}\overline{p}_1 + c_1^{(3)}p_1^{(3)} + c_2^{(3)}p_2^{(3)}.$$

Scalar multiplication by the columns of U^* leads to

$$c_{11} = (x_0, u_1^*), \quad c_1^{(3)} = (x_0, u_2^{(3)^*}), \quad c_2^{(3)} = (x_0, u_1^{(3)^*}).$$

(iii) *Real basis functions*

As in Kohaupt (2008b), for the splitting in the real and imaginary parts, we set

$$p_k^{(l)} = p_k^{(l,r)} + i p_k^{(l,i)},$$
$$e^{\lambda_k(t-t_0)} = e^{(\lambda_k^{(r)}+i\lambda_k^{(i)})(t-t_0)} = e^{\lambda_k^{(r)}(t-t_0)}\{\cos\lambda_k^{(i)}(t-t_0) + i\sin\lambda_k^{(i)}(t-t_0)\},$$

$k = 1, \ldots, m_l; l = 1, \ldots, r$ where $r = 3$ and $m_1 = 1$, $m_2 = 1$, and $m_3 = 2$, and where we have set $p_k^{(1)} = p_k$, $k = 1, 2$, and so on. Then the solution with real basis is given by

$$x(t) = c_1^{(r)} x_1^{(r)}(t) + c_1^{(i)} x_1^{(i)}(t) + c_1^{(3,r)} x_1^{(3,r)}(t) + c_2^{(3,r)} x_2^{(3,r)}(t)$$

with

$$c_1^{(r)} = 2\,Re\{c_{11}\},$$
$$c_1^{(i)} = -2\,Im\{c_{11}\},$$

$$c_1^{(3,r)} = c_1^{(3)},$$
$$c_2^{(3,r)} = c_2^{(3)},$$

and with the real basis functions

$$x_1^{(r)}(t) = e^{\lambda_1^{(r)}(t-t_0)}\{\cos\lambda_1^{(i)}(t-t_0)p_1^{(r)} - \sin\lambda_k^{(i)}(t-t_0)p_1^{(i)}\},$$
$$x_1^{(i)}(t) = e^{\lambda_1^{(r)}(t-t_0)}\{\sin\lambda_1^{(i)}(t-t_0)p_1^{(r)} + \cos\lambda_k^{(i)}(t-t_0)p_1^{(i)}\},$$

$$x_1^{(3,r)}(t) = e^{\lambda_3^{(r)}(t-t_0)}\,p_1^{(3,r)},$$
$$x_2^{(3,r)}(t) = e^{\lambda_3^{(r)}(t-t_0)}\{p_1^{(3,r)}(t-t_0) + p_2^{(3,r)}\}.$$

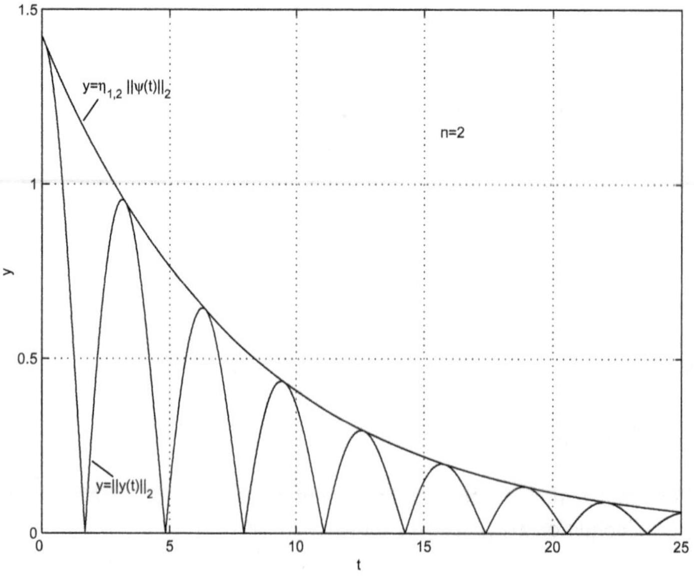

Figure 16. $y = \|y(t)\|_2$ **and upper bound** $y = \eta_{1,2}\,\|\psi(t)\|$.

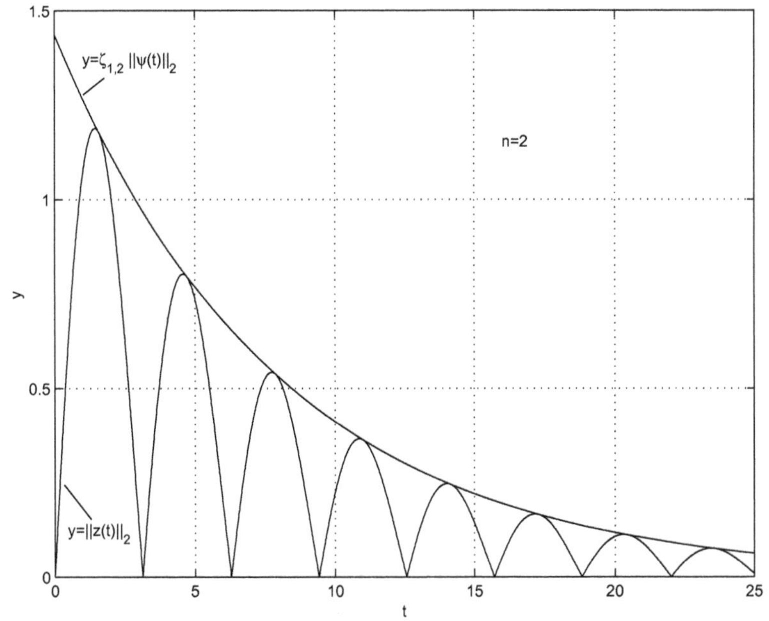

Figure 17. $y = \|\dot{y}(t)\|_2$ **and upper bound** $y = \zeta_{1,2}\,\|\cdot$

(iv) *Vector* $\psi(t)$

From Kohaupt (2011), we have

$$\psi_1(t) = (x_0, p_1)\, e^{\lambda_1^{(r)}(t-t_0)},$$
$$\psi_2(t) = (x_0, p_2)\, e^{\lambda_2^{(r)}(t-t_0)},$$
$$\psi_1^{(3)}(t) = (x_0, p_1^{(3)})\, e^{\lambda_3^{(r)}(t-t_0)}$$
$$\psi_2^{(3)}(t) = (x_0, p_1^{(3)}(t-t_0) + p_2^{(3)})\, e^{\lambda_3^{(r)}(t-t_0)},$$

and thus

$$\psi(t) = [\psi_1(t), \psi_2(t), \psi_1^{(3)}(t), \psi_2^{(3)}(t)]^T.$$

Remark Since $\psi_2(t) = \overline{\psi}_1(t)$, we could also use the vector $\psi(t)$ without component $\psi_2(t)$. Then merely the constants in the upper bounds would change.

(v) *Optimal upper bounds on* $y(t)$*and* $z(t) = \dot{y}(t)$

The displacement $y(t)$ and the velocity $\dot{y}(t)$ can be computed from $x(t) = [y^T(t), \dot{y}^T(t)]^T$. For comparison reasons, we have determined $x(t)$ also by $x(t) = e^{A(t-t_0)}x_0$ and obtained numerically identical results. The advantage of the representation of $x(t)$ by the real basis functions is that we get more insight into its vibration behavior than without it.

We restrict ourselves to the upper bounds $\|y(t)\|_2 \le \eta_{1,2}\|\psi(t)\|_2$ and $\|z(t)\|_2 \le \zeta_{1,2}\|\psi(t)\|_2$. As initial condition, we choose

$$y_0 = [-1, 1]^T;\ \dot{y}_0 = z_0 = [0, 0]^T.$$

In the sequel, we denote by $t_{s,u,2}$ the point of contact between the considered curve and optimal upper bound.

For the coefficients of the solution, we obtain

$$c = [c_{11}, \bar{c}_{11}, c_1^{(3)}, c_2^{(3)}]^T = [-0.5 + 0.0625i, -0.5 - 0.0625i, 0, 0]^T$$

and thus

$$c_1^{(r)} = 2\,Re\,c_{11} = -1,\ c_1^{(i)} = -2\,Im\,c_{11} = -0.125,\ c_1^{(3,r)} = c_1^{(3)} = 0,\ c_2^{(3,r)} = c_2^{(3)} = 0.$$

The curve $y = \|y(t)\|_2$ and its optimal upper bound $y = \eta_{1,2}\ \|\psi(t)\|$ can be seen in Figure 16. One has

$$t_{s,u,2} \doteq 0.124354,$$
$$\eta_{1,2} \doteq 0.503891.$$

The curve $y = \|z(t)\|_2 = \|\dot{y}(t)\|_2$ and its optimal upper bound $y = \zeta_{1,2}\ \|\psi(t)\|$ are drawn in Figure 17. One gets

$$t_{s,u,2} \doteq 1.570796,$$
$$\eta_{1,2} \doteq 0.507812.$$

Since $c_1^{(3)} = (x_0, u_2^{(3)^*}) = 0$ and $c_2^{(3)} = (x_0, u_1^{(3)^*}) = 0$,

it follows that the solution part corresponding to $\lambda_3(A)$ is suppressed. Thus, the solution behaves like a one-mass model with eigenvalues $\lambda_1(A)$ and $\overline{\lambda}_1(A)$. It is evident that the representation of the solution by the real basis functions offers much more insight into the vibration behavior than the representation $x(t) = e^{A\,(t-t_0)}x_0$ that does not allow such an interpretation. We mention that here the upper bounds $y = \eta_{1,2}\ \|\psi(t)\|$ and $y = \zeta_{1,2}\ \|\psi(t)\|$ are numerically identical with those of $y = Y_{1,2}\ e^{v[A](t-t_0)}$ and $y = Z_{1,2}\ e^{v[A](t-t_0)}$, as the case may be. The values $t_{s,u,2}$ and best constants $\eta_{1,2}$ are obtained by the differential calculus of norms.

7. Computational aspects

In this subsection, we say something about the used computer equipment and the computation time.

(i) As to the *computer equipment*, the following hardware was available: a Pentium D 940 (3.2 GHz), and 64 GB mass storage facility, and a 2048 MB DDR2-SDRAM 533 MHz (2x1024 MB) high-speed memory. As software package for the computations, we used 368-Matlab, Version 4.2.c; for the generation of the figures, Version 6.5, in order to be able to caption them; and for the *jordan* routine, likewise Version 6.5.

(ii) The *computation time* t of an operation was determined by the command sequence *t1=clock; operation; t=etime(clock,t1)*; it is put out in seconds rounded to two decimal places, by MATLAB. For example, to compute the points of contact and to generate the table of values $t, y(t), y_u(t), y_l(t),\ t = 0(0.01)25$ for Figure 16, we obtained $t_{16} = 2.69$ s.

8. Conclusion

In a one-mass vibration model with no or mild damping, the displacement $y(t)$ and the velocity $\dot{y}(t)$ cannot satisfy the equivalence relation $c_0\ \|y(t)\| \le \|\dot{y}(t)\| \le c_1\ \|y(t)\|,\ t \ge t_1$, for sufficiently large t_1 since $y(t) = 0$, respectively, $\dot{y}(t) = 0$ for some t occurs in any sufficiently large interval, which is not a disadvantage because then the lower bound for both functions is simply the time axis. On the other hand, for multi-mass vibration models, one can imagine that the case $y(t) \ne 0,\ \dot{y}(t) \ne 0,\ t \ge t_1$, occurs; the probability for this to happen increases intuitively with increasing dimension since then it will be unlikely that all components of $y(t)$ or $\dot{y}(t)$ will be zero simultaneously at any time. In the case $y(t) \ne 0,\ \dot{y}(t) \ne 0,\ t \ge t_1$, naturally the question of norm equivalence between the quantities $y(t)$ and $\dot{y}(t)$ arises. In this paper, sufficient conditions are given under which the norm equivalence of $y(t)$ and $\dot{y}(t)$ can be proven. Whereas the case of diagonalizable matrices A is simple to treat, the case of general square matrices needs much more effort. As application, improvements of some theorems of Kohaupt (2011) are presented. Moreover, the algebraic conditions for norm equivalence are illustrated for several examples of diagonalizable and non-diagonalizable matrices A, and their validity is underpinned by the graphs of $y = \|y(t)\|_2$ and $y = \|\dot{y}(t)\|_2$.

Acknowledgements
The author would like to thank the referees for evaluation of this paper and for suggesting some improvements that led to a better presentation.

Funding
The author received no direct funding for this research.

Author details
Ludwig Kohaupt[1]
E-mail: kohaupt@beuth-hochschule.de
[1] Department of Mathematics, Beuth University of Technology Berlin, Luxemburger Str. 10, D-13353 Berlin, Germany.

References

Coppel, W. A. (1965). *Stability and asymptotic behavior of differential equations*. Boston, MA: D.C. Heath.

Kohaupt, L. (2007). Construction of a biorthogonal system of principal vectors for the matrices A and A* with applications $\dot{x} = Ax$, $x\ to = x_0$. *Journal of Computational Mathematics and Optimization*, 3, 163–192.

Kohaupt, L. (2008a). Solution of the matrix eigenvalue problem $VA + A^*V = \mu V$ with applications to the study of free linear systems. *Journal of Computational and Applied Mathematics*, *213*, 142–165.

Kohaupt, L. (2008b). Solution of the vibration problem $M\ddot{Y} + B\dot{y} + Ky = 0$, $y(to) = y_{0,}$ $\dot{y}(to) = \dot{y}_0$ without the hypothesis $BM^{-1}K = KM^{-1}B$ or $B = \alpha M = \beta K$. *Applied Mathematical Sciences*, 2, 961–974.

Kohaupt, L. (2011). Two-sided bounds on the displacement *y(t)* and the velocity $\dot{y}(t)$ of the vibration system $M\ddot{Y} + B\dot{y} + Ky = 0$, $y(to) = y_{0,}$ $\dot{y}(to) = \dot{y}_0$, with application of the differential calculus of norms. *The Open Applied Mathematics Journal*, 5, 1–18.

Müller, P. C., & Schiehlen, W. O. (1985). *Linear vibrations*. Dordrecht: Martinus Nijhoff.

Thomson, W. T. (1971). *Theory of vibration with applications*. Prentice-Hall, NJ: Englewood Cliffs.

8

New exact solutions for the Khokhlov-Zabolotskaya-Kuznetsov, the Newell-Whitehead-Segel and the Rabinovich wave equations by using a new modification of the tanh-coth method

Şamil Akçağıl[1*] and Tuğba Aydemir[2]

*Corresponding author: Şamil Akçağıl, Faculty of Economics and Administrative Sciences, Bilecik Şeyh Edebali University, Bilecik, Turkey
E-mail: samilakcagil@hotmail.com
Reviewing editor: Song Wang, Curtin University, Australia

Abstract: The family of the tangent hyperbolic function methods is one of the most powerful method to find the solutions of the nonlinear partial differential equations. In the mathematical literature, there are a great deal of tanh-methods completing each other. In this article, the unified tanh-function method as a unification of the family of tangent hyperbolic function methods is introduced and implemented to find traveling wave solutions for three important physical models, namely the Khoklov–Zabolotskaya–Kuznetsov (KZK) equation, the Newell–Whitehead–Segel (NWS) equation, and the Rabinovich wave equation with nonlinear damping. Various exact traveling wave solutions of these physical structures are formally derived.

Subjects: Applied Mathematics; Mathematics & Statistics; Physical Sciences; Science

Keywords: the unified tanh-function method; the Khokhlov–Zabolotskaya–Kuznetsov (KZK) equation; the Newell–Whitehead–Segel (NWS) equation; the Rabinovich wave equation with nonlinear damping; traveling wave solution

1. Introduction

The (3+1) dimensional Zabolotskaya–Khokhlov (ZK) equation

$$\left(u_t + uu_x\right)_x + \gamma\Delta_y u + \theta\Delta_z u = 0 \tag{1}$$

ABOUT THE AUTHORS

Şamil Akçağıl received his PhD degree from Institute of Natural Sciences, Sakarya University, Turkey and he is an assistant professor in the Faculty of Economics and Administrative Sciences at Şeyh Edebali University in Turkey. His research interests include exact solutions of nonliner parabolic equations and higher order parabolic systems, traveling wave, soliton and trigonometric solutions of partial differential equations.

Tuğba Aydemir received his BSc degree from Hacettepe University, MSc degree from Sakarya University, and is currently a PhD scholar at Sakarya University. Her research areas are numerical and exact solution methods for nonlinear partial differential equations.

PUBLIC INTEREST STATEMENT

Over the past two decades, several expansion methods for finding solutions of nonlinear differential equations (NPDEs) have been proposed, developed, and extended. In the recent years, direct searching for exact solutions of NPDEs has become more and more attractive partly due to symbolic computation. One of the most effective direct methods to construct wave solutions of NPDEs is the family of the tanh-function methods. The first member of this family was introduced by Malfliet firstly and developed and used many researchers. The most known members of this family are the tanh-function method, the extended tanh-function method, the modified extended tanh-function method, and the complex tanh-function method. In this article, the authors have given a unification between these different tanh-function methods. Therefore, it can be obtained the solutions of different tanh-function methods using merely one method called the unified tanh-function method.

was proposed by Zabolotskaya and Khokhlov to describe the propagation of sound beam in a slightly nonlinear medium without dispersion or absorption (Zabolotskaya & Khokhlov, 1969). This equation enables to analyze the beam deformation associated with the nonlinear properties of the medium.

The ZK equation with a dissipative term may be written as

$$\left(u_t + uu_x + \lambda u_{xx}\right)_x + \gamma\Delta_y u + \theta\Delta_z u = 0, \tag{2}$$

where λ, γ and θ are some constants. This equation known as the (3+1) dimensional Khokhlov-Zabolotskaya-Kuznetsov (KZK) equation and derived by Kuznetsov which took into account of the thermoviscous term of adsorption (Kuznetsov, 1971).

The ZK and KZK equations have been investigated by many authors. Vinogradov and Vorob'ev (1976) investigated exact solutions of ZK equation using symmetries. Chowdhury and Nasker (1986) obtained the explicit structure for the generating function of Lie symmetries for the 3+1 dimensional Khokhlov-Zabolotskaya equation. Taniuti (1990) showed that systems of nonlinear evolutional equations are reducible to the Kadomtsev and Petviashvili equation and the Zabolotskaya-Khokhlov equation in the weakly dispersive and dissipative cases respectively, by means of an extension of the reductive perturbation method to quasi-one-dimensional propagation. Murakami (1990) presented N-traveling-wave solutions to this equation using the bilinear transformation method. Tajiri (1995) investigated similarity reductions of the Zabolotskaya-Khokhlov equation with a dissipative term to one-dimensional partial differential equations including the Burgers equation by means of Lie's method of infinitesimal transformation and obtained some similarity solutions of the ZK equation. Using the theory of nonclassical symmetry reductions, some traveling wave solutions of the dissipative Zabolotskaya-Khokhlov equation are obtained (Bruzon, Gandarias, Torrisi, & Tracinà, 2009).

The Newell-Whitehead-Segel (NWS) equation is a nonlinear parabolic partial differential equation and written as

$$u_t - ku_{xx} - au + bu^q = 0, \tag{3}$$

where a, b, k are real numbers , $k > 0$ is the coefficient of diffusion and q is a positive integer. The NWS equation models the interaction of the effect of the diffusion term with the nonlinear effect of the reaction term. This equation can be viewed as a generalization of the NWS equation which appeared in the investigation of fluid mechanics (Newell & Whitehead, 1969; Segel, 1969). The function u may be thought of as the distribution of temperature in an infinitely thin and long rod or as the flow velocity of a fluid in an infinitely long pipe with small diameter (Macías-Díaz & Ruiz-Ramírez, 2011). Besides, u is a function of the spatial variable x and the temporal variable t, with $x \in \mathbb{R}$ and $t \geq 0$.

The aplications of the NWS equation may be seen widely in mechanical and chemical engineering, ecology, biology, and bio-engineering. For more details, we refer the reader to Fisher (1937), FitzHugh (1955), Kastenberg and Chambré (1968), Nagumo, Arimoto, and Yoshizawa (1962) and references therein.

The NWS equation has been considered by many authors. For instance, Mací as-Díaz and Ruiz-Ramírez have proposed a finite-difference scheme to approximate the solutions of a generalization of the classical, one-dimensional Newell-Whitehead-Segel equation which is in the form

$$u_t - ku_{xx} - u + u^{2p+1} = 0, \tag{4}$$

where p is a positive integer (Macías-Díaz & Ruiz-Ramírez, 2011). Nourazar, Soori and Nazari-Golshan have obtained solutions of special cases of Equation (3) using the homotopy perturbation method.

They have solved this equation with $(a, b, k, q) = (2,3,1,2), (1,1,1,2), (1,1,1,4), (3,4,1,3)$ (Nourazar, Soori, Nazari-Golshan, 2011).

Rabinovich has considered how the establishment of self-oscillations takes place for explosion instability (Rabinovich, 1974). He has investigated such a mechanism using the example of medium described by the equation

$$-\beta u_{xxtt} - u_{tt} + \left(-\gamma u + u^2 - \alpha u^3\right)_t + \left(V + \delta u^2\right)u_{xx} = 0. \tag{5}$$

This equation describes electric signals in telegraph lines on the basis of the tunnel diode. In Korpusov (2011), setting $\beta = -1, \gamma = \alpha = \delta = 0$ and $V = 1$ in (Equation 5), Korpusov has considered the equation

$$u_{xxtt} - u_{tt} + u_t - \left(u^2\right)_t + u_{xx} = 0 \tag{6}$$

and named as "Rabinovih wave equation with nonlinear damping" . Also he has obtained sufficient conditions of the blow-up for Equation (6).

Over the last 20 years, several different hyperbolic tangent function method has been proposed for searching traveling wave solutions of nonlinear evolution equations. This technique was used by Huibin and Kelin (1990) first and then developed by Malfliet, Hereman, Fan, Senthilvelan, Wazwaz, and others since 1990. It has been used extensively in the literature to the present. The most common of these methods were the tanh-function method, the extended tanh-function method, the modified extended tanh-function method, and the complex tanh-function method (Wazwaz, 2006, 2007; Khuri, 2004).

In this article, a unification of the family of tangent hyperbolic function methods called the unified tanh-function method has been proposed. The other members of the family of hyperbolic function methods could overlook some type solutions or sometimes it can need any other member of this family to find all of the solutions. The advantage of this method is to give all type solutions within one method in a straightforward, concise and elegant manner without reproducing a lot of different forms of the same solution.

The rest of the paper is organized as follows: The unified tanh-function method is introduced in Section 2. The traveling wave solutions of (3+1) dimensional Khokhlov–Zabolotskaya–Kuznetsov (KZK) equation are obtained in Section 3. Equation (3) is considered and exact solutions of the generalized Newell-Whitehead-Segel (NWS) equation are obtained in Section 4. The new traveling wave, trigonometric, and solitary wave solutions of the Rabinovich wave equation are obtained in Section 5. Finally, our conclusions are summarized in Section 6.

2. The unified tanh-function method

The authors describe the unified tanh method for finding traveling wave solutions of nonlinear partial differential equations. Suppose that a nonlinear partial differential equation(NPDE), say in two independent variables x and t, is given by

$$P(u, u_t, u_x, u_{xt}, u_{tt}, u_{xx}, \ldots) = 0 \tag{7}$$

where $u(x,t)$ is an unknown function, P is a polynomial in $u = u(x,t)$, and its various partial derivatives, in which highest order derivatives and nonlinear terms are involved.

The summary of the unified tanh method can be presented in the following six steps:

Step 1: To find the traveling wave solutions of Equation (7), one uses the wave variable

$$u(x,t) = U(\xi), \xi = x - ct, \tag{8}$$

where the constant c is generally termed the wave velocity. Substituting Equation (8) into Equation (7), one obtains the following ordinary differential equation (ODE) in ξ (which illustrates a principal advantage of a traveling wave solution, i.e. a PDE is reduced to an ODE).

$$P(U, cU', U', cU'', c^2U'', U'', ...) = 0 \tag{9}$$

Step 2: If necessary one integrates Equation (9) as many times as possible and set the constants of integration to be zero for simplicity.

Step 3: Suppose the solution of nonlinear partial differential equation can be expressed by a polynomial in Y as follows:

$$u(\xi) = a_0 + \sum_{i=1}^{M} \left(a_i Y^i(\xi) + b_i Y^{-i}(\xi)\right) \tag{10}$$

where $Y = Y(\xi)$ satisfies the Riccati differential equation

$$Y'(\xi) = k^2 - Y^2(\xi), \tag{11}$$

where $Y' = \frac{dY}{d\xi}$, and a_i, b_i and k are constants. The general solution of Equation (11) as follows:

$$Y(\xi) = \begin{cases} \begin{cases} (a+ib)\tanh\left((a+ib)(\xi+\xi_0)\right) \\ (a+ib)\coth\left((a+ib)(\xi+\xi_0)\right) \end{cases}, k = a+ib \\ \frac{1}{\xi+\xi_0}, k = 0 \end{cases}. \tag{12}$$

If one takes $k = a$, then the first solutions group in (12) are $a\tanh\left(a(\xi+\xi_0)\right)$ and $a\coth\left(a(\xi+\xi_0)\right)$. On the other hand, if one takes $k = ib$, then the first solutions group in (12) are $-b\tan\left(b(\xi+\xi_0)\right)$ and $b\cot\left(b(\xi+\xi_0)\right)$. If the general solutions of Equation (11) are summed up, then one has

$$Y(\xi) = \begin{cases} \begin{cases} (a+ib)\tanh\left((a+ib)(\xi+\xi_0)\right) \\ (a+ib)\coth\left((a+ib)(\xi+\xi_0)\right) \end{cases}, k = a+ib \\ \begin{cases} a\tanh\left(a(\xi+\xi_0)\right) \\ a\coth\left(a(\xi+\xi_0)\right) \end{cases}, k = a \\ \begin{cases} -b\tan\left(b(\xi+\xi_0)\right) \\ b\cot\left(b(\xi+\xi_0)\right) \end{cases}, k = ib \\ \frac{1}{\xi+\xi_0}, k = 0 \end{cases}. \tag{13}$$

Step 4: The positive integer M can be accomplished by considering the homogeneous balance between the highest order derivatives and nonlinear terms appearing in Equation (3.3) as follows:

If one defines the degree of $u(\xi)$ as $D[u(\xi)] = M$, then the degree of other expressions is defined by

$$D\left[\frac{d^q u}{d\xi^q}\right] = M + q,$$

$$D\left[u^r\left(\frac{d^q u}{d\xi^q}\right)^s\right] = Mr + s(q+M).$$

Therefore, one gets the value of M in Equation (3.4).

Step 5: Substituting Equation (10) and (11) into Eq.(9) and collecting all terms with the same order of Y together, then setting each coefficient of this polynomial to zero yield a set of algebraic equations for a_i, b_i, c and k.

Step 6: Substituting a_i, b_i, c and k obtained in Step 5 into (10) and using the general solutions of Equation (11) in (12) or (13), one can obtain the explicit solutions of Equation (7) immediately depending on the value of k.

3. The (3+1) dimensional Khokhlov–Zabolotskaya–Kuznetsov (KZK) equation

The (3 + 1)-dimensional KZK equation reads:

$$u_{xt} + u_x^2 + uu_{xx} + \lambda u_{xxx} + \gamma u_{yy} + \theta u_{zz} = 0, \tag{14}$$

where λ, γ, and θ are real constants and $\lambda \neq 0$. We first substitute the wave variable $\xi = x + y + z - Vt$, V as the wave speed, with the wave transformation $u(x,t) = U(\mu\xi)$ into (14) and integrating once to obtain

$$(\theta + \gamma - V)U + \frac{1}{2}U^2 + \lambda U' = 0. \tag{15}$$

Using the balance process leads to $M = 1$. The tanh–coth method allows us to use the substitution

$$U(\mu\xi) = S(Y) = \sum_{k=0}^{1} a_k Y^k + \sum_{k=1}^{1} b_k Y^{-k} \tag{16}$$

Substituting (16) into (15), collecting the coefficients of each power of Y, setting each coefficient to zero we find a system of algebraic equations for a_0, a_1, b_1 and V in the following form:

$$\begin{aligned}
Y^2&: \quad a_1^2 - 2a_1\lambda\mu = 0\\
Y^1&: \quad 2a_1\theta + 2a_1\gamma - 2Va_1 + 2a_0a_1 = 0\\
Y^0&: \quad 2a_0\theta + 2a_0\gamma - 2Va_0 + 2a_1b_1 + a_0^2 + 2a_1\lambda\mu + 2b_1\lambda\mu = 0\\
Y^{-1}&: \quad 2b_1\theta + 2b_1\gamma - 2Vb_1 + 2a_0b_1 = 0\\
Y^{-2}&: \quad b_1^2 - 2b_1\lambda\mu = 0.
\end{aligned} \tag{17}$$

Solving the resulting system of algebraic equations, we find the following sets of solutions:

$$a_0 = -2\lambda\mu, \quad a_1 = 0, \quad b_1 = 2\lambda\mu, \quad V = \theta - 2\lambda\mu + \gamma \tag{18}$$

$$a_0 = 2\lambda\mu, \quad a_1 = 0, \quad b_1 = 2\lambda\mu, \quad V = \theta + 2\lambda\mu + \gamma \tag{19}$$

$$a_0 = -4\lambda\mu, \quad a_1 = 2\lambda\mu, \quad b_1 = 2\lambda\mu, \quad V = \theta - 4\lambda\mu + \gamma \tag{20}$$

$$a_0 = 2\lambda\mu, \quad a_1 = 2\lambda\mu, \quad b_1 = 0, \quad V = \theta + 2\lambda\mu + \gamma \tag{21}$$

$$a_0 = -2\lambda\mu, \quad a_1 = 2\lambda\mu, \quad b_1 = 0, \quad V = \theta - 2\lambda\mu + \gamma \tag{22}$$

$$a_0 = 4\lambda\mu, \quad a_1 = 2\lambda\mu, \quad b_1 = 2\lambda\mu, \quad V = \theta + 4\lambda\mu + \gamma \tag{23}$$

where μ is left as a free parameter. Consequently, using these values, we obtain following hyperbolic solutions, respectively:

$$u_1(x,t) = -2\lambda a + 2\lambda a \coth a\big(x + y + z - (\theta - 2\lambda a + \gamma)t\big) \tag{24}$$
$$u_2(x,t) = 2\lambda a + 2\lambda a \coth a\big(x + y + z - (\theta + 2\lambda a + \gamma)t\big) \tag{25}$$
$$\begin{aligned} u_3(x,t) = {} & -4\lambda a + 2\lambda a \tanh a(x + y + z - (\theta - 4a\lambda + \gamma)t) \\ & + 2\lambda a \coth a(x + y + z - (\theta - 4a\lambda + \gamma)t) \end{aligned} \tag{26}$$
$$u_4(x,t) = 2\lambda a + 2\lambda a \tanh a\big(x + y + z - (\theta + 2\lambda a + \gamma)t\big) \tag{27}$$
$$u_5(x,t) = -2\lambda a + 2\lambda a \tanh a\big(x + y + z - (\theta - 2\lambda a + \gamma)t\big) \tag{28}$$
$$\begin{aligned} u_6(x,t) = {} & 4\lambda a + 2\lambda a \tanh a(x + y + z - (\theta + 4\lambda a + \gamma)t) \\ & + 2\lambda a \coth a(x + y + z - (\theta + 4\lambda a + \gamma)t) \end{aligned} \tag{29}$$

where $\mu = a, a$ is a real constant. Using the hyperbolic identities $i\tanh(ix) = -\tan x$ and $i\coth(ix) = \cot x$, trigonometric solutions from the tanh-coth can be obtained method as follows:

$$u_7(x,t) = -2\lambda bi + 2\lambda b \cot b\big(x + y + z - (\theta - 2\lambda bi + \gamma)t\big) \tag{30}$$
$$u_8(x,t) = 2\lambda bi + 2\lambda b \cot b\big(x + y + z - (\theta + 2\lambda bi + \gamma)t\big) \tag{31}$$
$$\begin{aligned} u_9(x,t) = {} & -4\lambda bi - 2\lambda b \tan b\big(x + y + z - (\theta - 4\lambda bi + \gamma)t\big) \\ & + 2\lambda b \cot b\big(x + y + z - (\theta - 4\lambda bi + \gamma)t\big) \end{aligned} \tag{32}$$
$$u_{10}(x,t) = 2\lambda bi - 2\lambda b \tan b\big(x + y + z - (\theta + 2\lambda bi + \gamma)t\big) \tag{33}$$
$$u_{11}(x,t) = -2\lambda bi - 2\lambda b \tan b\big(x + y + z - (\theta - 2\lambda bi + \gamma)t\big) \tag{34}$$
$$\begin{aligned} u_{12}(x,t) = {} & 4\lambda bi - 2\lambda b \tan b\big(x + y + z - (\theta + 4\lambda bi + \gamma)t\big) \\ & + 2\lambda b \cot b\big(x + y + z - (\theta + 4\lambda bi + \gamma)t\big) \end{aligned} \tag{35}$$

where $\mu = ib, b$ is a real constant and $i = \sqrt{-1}$.

4. The Newell–Whitehead–Segel (NWS) equation

The Newell-Whitehead-Segel (NWS) equation is of the form

$$u_t - ku_{xx} - au + bu^q = 0, \tag{36}$$

where a, b, k are real numbers, $k > 0$ is the coefficient of diffusion, and q is a positive integer. Also, we assume that $q > 1$. Using the wave transformation $u(x,t) = U(\mu\xi)$ with wave variable $\xi = x - Vt$, Equation (36) will be converted to the ODE

$$-VU' - kU'' - aU + bU^q = 0. \tag{37}$$

Balancing the second term with the last term, we find $M + 2 = qM$ so that $M = \frac{2}{q-1}$. To get analytic closed solution, M should be an integer, hence we use the transformation

$$U = W^{\frac{1}{q-1}}. \tag{38}$$

Using (38) into (37) gives

$$-V(q-1)WW' - k(2-q)(W')^2 - k(q-1)WW'' - (q-1)^2 aW^2 + (q-1)^2 bW^3 = 0. \tag{39}$$

Balancing WW'' with W^3 gives $M = 2$. The tanh–coth method admits the use of the finite expansion

$$W(\mu\xi) = S(Y) = \sum_{i=0}^{2} a_i Y^i + \sum_{i=1}^{2} b_i Y^{-i} \tag{40}$$

Substituting Equation (40) into Equation (39), we obtain a system of algebraic equations for $a_0, a_1, a_2, b_1, b_2, \mu$ and V. Solving this system of equation, we obtain the following sets of solutions:

$$a_0 = a_2 = \frac{a}{4b}, a_1 = -\frac{2\mu V(q+1)}{b\left(q^2+2q-3\right)}, b_1 = b_2 = 0, V = \mp 2\sqrt{ak+k^2\mu^2}, \mu = \mp\frac{\sqrt{2ak(q+1)}(q-1)}{4k(q+1)} \tag{41}$$

$$a_0 = b_2 = \frac{a}{4b}, a_1 = a_2 = 0, b_1 = -\frac{2\mu V(q+1)}{b\left(q^2+2q-3\right)}, V = \mp 2\sqrt{ak+k^2\mu^2}, \mu = \mp\frac{\sqrt{2ak(q+1)}(q-1)}{4k(q+1)} \tag{42}$$

Consequently, using these values, we obtain following hyperbolic solutions, respectively:

$$w_1(x,t) = \frac{a}{4b} - \frac{2pV(q+1)}{b\left(q^2+2q-3\right)} \tanh p(x-Vt) + \frac{a}{4b}\tanh^2 p(x-Vt), \tag{43}$$

$$w_2(x,t) = \frac{a}{4b} - \frac{2pV(q+1)}{b\left(q^2+2q-3\right)} \coth p(x-Vt) + \frac{a}{4b}\coth^2 p(x-Vt), \tag{44}$$

where $\mu = p, p$ is a real constant. Using the hyperbolic identities $i\tanh(ix) = -\tan x$ and $i\coth(ix) = \cot x$, the trigonometric solutions from tanh-coth method can be obtained as follows:

$$w_3(x,t) = \frac{a}{4b} + \frac{2rV(q+1)}{b\left(q^2+2q-3\right)} \tan r(x-Vt) - \frac{a}{4b}\tan^2 r(x-Vt), \tag{45}$$

$$w_4(x,t) = \frac{a}{4b} - \frac{2rV(q+1)}{b\left(q^2+2q-3\right)} \cot r(x-Vt) - \frac{a}{4b}\cot^2 r(x-Vt), \tag{46}$$

where $\mu = ir, r$ is a real constant and $i = \sqrt{-1}$.

Recalling that $u = w^{\frac{1}{q-1}}$ we find the traveling wave solutions for the NWS equation in the following form:

$$u_1(x,t) = \left\{\frac{a}{4b} - \frac{2pV(q+1)}{b\left(q^2+2q-3\right)} \tanh p(x-Vt) + \frac{a}{4b}\tanh^2 p(x-Vt)\right\}^{\frac{1}{q-1}}, \tag{47}$$

$$u_2(x,t) = \left\{\frac{a}{4b} - \frac{2pV(q+1)}{b\left(q^2+2q-3\right)} \coth p(x-Vt) + \frac{a}{4b}\coth^2 p(x-Vt)\right\}^{\frac{1}{q-1}}, \tag{48}$$

$$u_3(x,t) = \left\{\frac{a}{4b} + \frac{2rV(q+1)}{b\left(q^2+2q-3\right)} \tan r(x-Vt) - \frac{a}{4b}\tan^2 r(x-Vt)\right\}^{\frac{1}{q-1}}, \tag{49}$$

$$u_4(x,t)=\left\{\frac{a}{4b}-\frac{2rV(q+1)}{b\left(q^2+2q-3\right)}\cot r(x-Vt)-\frac{a}{4b}\cot^2 r(x-Vt)\right\}^{\frac{1}{q-1}}. \tag{50}$$

5. The Rabinovich wave equation

The Rabinovich wave equation with nonlinear damping is given by

$$u_{xxtt}-u_{tt}+u_t-\left(u^2\right)_t+u_{xx}=0. \tag{51}$$

Using the wave variable $\xi = x - Vt$ in Equation (51), then integrating this equation and considering the integration constant to not be zero, we obtain

$$V^2U'''+\left(1-V^2\right)U'-VU+VU^2=0 \tag{52}$$

Balancing U^2 and U''' gives $M = 3$. Therefore, the solutions of (52) can be written in the form

$$U(\mu\xi)=S(Y)=\sum_{i=0}^{3}a_iY^i+\sum_{i=1}^{3}b_iY^{-i}. \tag{53}$$

Substituting (53) into (52), collecting the coefficients of each power of Y, setting each coefficient to zero, and solving the system of algebraic equations, we find sets of solutions in the following form:

Set 1.

$$\begin{gathered}\mu=\mp\frac{\sqrt{19V^2-19}}{38V}, b_3=b_2=b_1=0, a_3=\frac{15\mu\left(V^2-1\right)}{19V},\\ a_2=0, a_1=-\frac{45\mu\left(V^2-1\right)}{19V}, a_0=\frac{1}{2};\end{gathered} \tag{54}$$

Set 2.

$$\begin{gathered}\mu=\mp\frac{\sqrt{19V^2-19}}{38V}, a_3=a_2=a_1=0, b_3=\frac{15\mu\left(V^2-1\right)}{19V},\\ b_2=0, b_1=-\frac{45\mu\left(V^2-1\right)}{19V}, a_0=\frac{1}{2};\end{gathered} \tag{55}$$

Set 3.

$$\begin{gathered}\mu=\mp\frac{\sqrt{209-209V^2}}{38V}, b_3=b_2=b_1=0, a_3=-\frac{165\mu\left(V^2-1\right)}{19V},\\ a_2=0, a_1=\frac{135\mu\left(V^2-1\right)}{19V}, a_0=\frac{1}{2};\end{gathered} \tag{56}$$

Set 4.

$$\begin{gathered}\mu=\mp\frac{\sqrt{209-209V^2}}{38V}, a_3=a_2=a_1=0, b_3=-\frac{165\mu\left(V^2-1\right)}{19V},\\ b_2=0, b_1=\frac{135\mu\left(V^2-1\right)}{19V}, a_0=\frac{1}{2};\end{gathered} \tag{57}$$

Set 5.

$$\mu = \mp\frac{\sqrt{209-209V^2}}{76V}, a_2 = b_2 = 0, a_0 = \frac{1}{2}, b_3 = a_3 = -\frac{165\mu\left(V^2-1\right)}{76V},$$
$$a_1 = -\frac{495\left(V^2-1\right)^2}{23104\mu V^3}, b_1 = \frac{45\mu\left(V^2-1\right)}{76V}; \tag{58}$$

Set 6.

$$\mu = \mp\frac{\sqrt{19c^2-19}}{76V}, a_2 = b_2 = 0, a_0 = \frac{1}{2}, b_3 = a_3 = \frac{15\mu\left(V^2-1\right)}{76V},$$
$$a_1 = -\frac{135\left(V^2-1\right)^2}{23104\mu V^3}, b_1 = -\frac{135\mu\left(V^2-1\right)}{76V}. \tag{59}$$

Using these values, we obtain following hyperbolic solutions respectively:

$$u_1(x,t) = \frac{1}{2} + \frac{15\left(1-V^2\right)\sqrt{19V^2-19}}{722V^2}\left(3\tanh\left(\frac{\sqrt{19V^2-19}}{38V}(x-Vt)\right)\right.$$
$$\left.-\tanh^3\left(\frac{\sqrt{19V^2-19}}{38V}(x-Vt)\right)\right), \tag{60}$$

$$u_2(x,t) = \frac{1}{2} + \frac{15\left(1-V^2\right)\sqrt{19V^2-19}}{722V^2}\left(3\coth\left(\frac{\sqrt{19V^2-19}}{38V}(x-Vt)\right)\right.$$
$$\left.-\coth^3\left(\frac{\sqrt{19V^2-19}}{38V}(x-Vt)\right)\right), \tag{61}$$

where $V^2 > 1$;

$$u_3(x,t) = \frac{1}{2} - \frac{\left(1-V^2\right)\sqrt{209-209V^2}}{722V^2}\left(135\tanh\left(\frac{\sqrt{209-209V^2}}{38V}(x-Vt)\right)\right.$$
$$\left.-165\tanh^3\left(\frac{\sqrt{209-209c^2}}{38V}(x-Vt)\right)\right), \tag{62}$$

$$u_4(x,t) = \frac{1}{2} - \frac{\left(1-V^2\right)\sqrt{209-209V^2}}{722V^2}\left(135\coth\left(\frac{\sqrt{209-209V^2}}{38V}(x-Vt)\right)\right.$$
$$\left.-165\coth^3\left(\frac{\sqrt{209-209V^2}}{38V}(x-Vt)\right)\right), \tag{63}$$

where $V^2 < 1$;

$$u_5(x,t) = \frac{1}{2} - \frac{495\left(V^2-1\right)^2}{304V^2\sqrt{209-209V^2}} \tanh\left(\frac{\sqrt{209-209V^2}}{76c}(x-Vt)\right)$$
$$+ \frac{\left(V^2-1\right)\sqrt{209-209V^2}}{5776V^2}(-165\tanh^3\left(\frac{\sqrt{209-209V^2}}{76V}(x-Vt)\right)$$
$$+45\coth\left(\frac{\sqrt{209-209V^2}}{76V}(x-Vt)\right) - 165\coth^3\left(\frac{\sqrt{209-209V^2}}{76V}(x-Vt)\right)), \tag{64}$$

where $V^2 < 1$;

$$u_6(x,t) = \frac{1}{2} - \frac{135\left(V^2-1\right)^2}{304V^2\sqrt{19V^2-19}} \tanh\left(\frac{\sqrt{19V^2-19}}{76V}(x-Vt)\right)$$
$$+ \frac{\left(V^2-1\right)\sqrt{19V^2-19}}{5776V^2}(15\tanh^3\left(\frac{\sqrt{19V^2-19}}{76V}(x-Vt)\right)$$
$$-135\coth\left(\frac{\sqrt{19V^2-19}}{76V}(x-Vt)\right) + 15\coth^3\left(\frac{\sqrt{19V^2-19}}{76V}(x-Vt)\right)), \tag{65}$$

where $V^2 > 1$;

Using the hyperbolic identities $i\tanh(ix) = -\tan x$ and $i\coth(ix) = \cot x$, the trigonometric solutions from tanh-method can be obtained as follows:

$$u_7(x,t) = \frac{1}{2} + \frac{15\left(1-V^2\right)\sqrt{19-19V^2}}{722V^2}\left(-3\tan\left(\frac{\sqrt{19-19V^2}}{38V}(x-Vt)\right)\right.$$
$$\left.-\tan^3\left(\frac{\sqrt{19-19V^2}}{38V}(x-Vt)\right)\right), \tag{66}$$

$$u_8(x,t) = \frac{1}{2} + \frac{15\left(1-V^2\right)\sqrt{19-19V^2}}{722V^2}\left(3\cot\left(\frac{\sqrt{19-19V^2}}{38V}(x-Vt)\right)\right.$$
$$\left.+\cot^3\left(\frac{\sqrt{19-19V^2}}{38V}(x-Vt)\right)\right), \tag{67}$$

where $V^2 < 1$;

$$u_9(x,t) = \frac{1}{2} - \frac{\left(1-V^2\right)\sqrt{209V^2-209}}{722V^2}\left(-135\tan\left(\frac{\sqrt{209V^2-209}}{38V}(x-Vt)\right)\right.$$
$$\left.-165\tan^3\left(\frac{\sqrt{209V^2-209}}{38V}(x-Vt)\right)\right), \tag{68}$$

$$u_{10}(x,t) = \frac{1}{2} - \frac{\left(1-V^2\right)\sqrt{209V^2-209}}{722V^2}\left(135\cot\left(\frac{\sqrt{209V^2-209}}{38c}(x-Vt)\right)\right.$$
$$\left.+165\cot^3\left(\frac{\sqrt{209V^2-209}}{38V}(x-Vt)\right)\right), \tag{69}$$

where $V^2 > 1$;

$$u_{11}(x,t) = \frac{1}{2} - \frac{495\left(V^2-1\right)^2}{304V^2\sqrt{209V^2-209}}\tan\left(\frac{\sqrt{209V^2-209}}{76V}(x-Vt)\right) + \frac{\left(V^2-1\right)\sqrt{209V^2-209}}{5776V^2}\left(-165\tan^3\left(\frac{\sqrt{209V^2-209}}{76V}(x-Vt)\right) + 45\cot\left(\frac{\sqrt{209V^2-209}}{76V}(x-Vt)\right) + 165\cot^3\left(\frac{\sqrt{209c^2-209}}{76V}(x-Vt)\right)\right), \tag{70}$$

where $V^2 > 1$;

$$u_{12}(x,t) = \frac{1}{2} - \frac{135\left(V^2-1\right)^2}{304V^2\sqrt{19-19V^2}}\tan\left(\frac{\sqrt{19-19V^2}}{76V}(x-Vt)\right) + \frac{\left(V^2-1\right)\sqrt{19-19V^2}}{5776V^2}\left(15\tanh^3\left(\frac{\sqrt{19-19c^2}}{76V}(x-Vt)\right) - 135\coth\left(\frac{\sqrt{19-19V^2}}{76V}(x-Vt)\right) + 15\coth^3\left(\frac{\sqrt{19-19c^2}}{76V}(x-Vt)\right)\right), \tag{71}$$

where $V^2 < 1$.

6. Conclusion

In this paper, the (3+1) dimensional Khokhlov–Zabolotskaya–Kuznetsov (KZK), the Newell–Whitehead–Segel (NWS), and the Rabinovich wave equations were investigated using the unified tanh-function produced more general solutions in a straightforward, concise, and elegant manner. The reason why it is needed to give the unified tanh method is to give a unification for the tanh-function methods in the literature without reproducing a lot of different forms of the same solutions. Thus, the unified tanh method gives the solutions in a straightforward and brief way without requiring more effort. On the other hand, the obtained results clearly show the efficiency of the method used in this work. Throughout the entire study, Maple facilitates the tedious algebraic calculations.

Funding
The authors received no direct funding for this research.

Author details
Şamil Akçağıl[1]
E-mail: samilakcagil@hotmail.com
Tuğba Aydemir[2]
E-mail: tgb.aydemir@gmail.com
[1] Faculty of Economics and Administrative Sciences, Bilecik Şeyh Edebali University, Bilecik, Turkey.
[2] Institute of Natural Sciences, Sakarya University, Sakarya, Turkey.

References

Bruzon, M. S., Gandarias, M. L., Torrisi, M., & Tracinà, R. (2009). Some traveling wave solutions for the dissipative Zabolotskaya-Khokhlov equation. *Journal of Mathematical Physics, 50*, 103504.

Chowdhury, A. R., & Nasker, M. (1986). Towards the conservation laws and lie symmetries for the Khokhlov--Zabolotskaya equation in three dimensions. *Journal of Physics A, 19*, 1775.

Fisher, R. A. (1937). The wave of advance of advantageous genes. *Annals of Eugenics, 7*, 355–369.

FitzHugh, R. (1955). Mathematical models of threshold phenomena in the nerve membrane. *Bulletin of Mathematical Biology, 17*, 257–278.

Huibin, L., & Kelin, W. (1990). Exact solutions for two nonlinear equations. I, *Journal of Physics A: Mathematical and General, 23*, 3923.

Kastenberg, W. E., & Chambré, P. L. (1968). On the stability of nonlinear space-dependent reactor kinetics. *Nuclear Science and Engineering, 31*, 67–79.

Khuri, S. A. (2004). A complex tanh-function method applied to nonlinear equations of Schrödinger type. *Chaos, Solitons and Fractals, 20*, 1037–1040.

Korpusov, M. O. (2011). *Blow up in nonclassical nonlocal equations*. Moscow: URSS (in Russian).

Kuznetsov, V. P. (1971). Equations of nonlinear acoustics. *Soviet Physics-Acoustics, 16*, 467–470.

Macías-Díaz, J. E., & Ruiz-Ramírez, J. (2011). A non-standard symmetry-preserving method to compute bounded solutions of a generalized Newell-Whitehead-Segel equation. *Applied Numerical Mathematics, 61*, 630–640.

Murakami, Y. (1990). Obliquely interacting N traveling waves: Exact solutions of some two-dimensional nonlinear diffusion equation. *Journal of the Physical Society of Japan, 59*, 1–4.

Nagumo, J., Arimoto, S., & Yoshizawa, S. (1962). An active pulse transmission line simulating nerve axon. *Proceedings of the IRE, 50*, 2061–2070.

Newell, A. C., & Whitehead, J. A. (1969). Stability of stationary periodic structures for weakly supercritical convection and related problems. *Journal of Fluid Mechanics, 38*, 279–303.

Nourazar, S. S., Soori, M., & Nazari-Golshan, A. (2011). On the exact solution of Newell–Whitehead–Segel equation using the homotopy perturbation method. *Australian Journal of Basic and Applied Sciences, 5*, 1400–1411.

Rabinovich, M. I. (1974). Self-oscillations of distributed systems. *Radiophysics and Quantum Electronics, 17*, 361–385.

Segel, L. A. (1969). Distant side-walls cause slow amplitude modulation of cellular convection. *Journal of Fluid Mechanics, 38*, 203–224.

Tajiri, M. (1995). Similarity reductions of the Zabolotskaya--Khokhlov equation with a dissipative term. *Nonlinear Mathematical Physics, 2*, 392–397.

Taniuti, T. (1990). Reductive perturbation method for quasi one-dimensional nonlinear wave propagation I. *Wave Motion, 12*, 373–383.

Vinogradov, A. M., & Vorob'ev, E. M. (1976). Use of symmetries to find exact solutions of Zabolotskaya-Khokhlov equation. *Soviet Physics-Acoustics, 22*, 12–15.

Wazwaz, A. M. (2006). New solitary wave solutions to the modified forms of Degasperis–Procesi and Camass–Holm equations. *Applied Mathematics and Computation, 186*, 130–141.

Wazwaz, A. M. (2007). The extended tanh method for new solitons solutions for many forms of the fifth-order KdV equations. *Applied Mathematics and Computation, 184*, 1002–1014.

Zabolotskaya, E. A., & Khokhlov, R. V. (1969). Quasi-plane waves in the nonlinear acoustics of confined beams. *Soviet Physics-Acoustics, 15*, 35–40.

9

Relative contribution ratio: A quantitative metrics for multi-parameter analysis

Changtong Luo[1*], Zonglin Jiang[1], Chun Wang[1] and Zongmin Hu[1]

*Corresponding author: Changtong Luo, State Key Laboratory of High Temperature Gas Dynamics, Institute of Mechanics, Chinese Academy of Sciences, Beijing 100190, China

E-mail: luo@imech.ac.cn

Reviewing editor: Quanxi Shao, CSIRO, Australia

Abstract: In many applications, the objective function is determined by several parameters simultaneously. Properly assessing the relative contribution of each parameter can give the decision maker a better understanding of the problem. However, widely used assessing methods are qualitative or semi-quantitative. In this paper, a new concept, relative contribution ratio (RCR), is proposed. The concept follows the idea of proof by contradiction, and estimates the impact of absence of each parameter, based on the fact that the absence of a parameter with more contribution will bring more divergence. Based on surrogate models, a statistical method for calculating RCR is also presented. Numerical results indicate that RCR is capable of analyzing multi-parameter problems, regardless of whether they are linear or nonlinear.

Subjects: Applied Mathematics; Applied Physics; Mathematical Modeling; Mathematics & Statistics; Non-Linear Systems; Physical Sciences; Physics; Science; Statistics & Probability

Keywords: multi-parameter problem; quantitative assessment; data-driven modeling; impact of absence; relative contribution ratio

1. Introduction

Many parameters could affect the aerodynamic forces of hypersonic vehicles simultaneously. The most sensitive parameters include Mach number (of the free stream, determined by flight speed and altitude), Reynolds number (determined by free stream and characteristic length), and angle of attack, etc. (refer to Anderson, 2006 for more details).Proper evaluation of the relative contribution of each parameter to the aerodynamic coefficient is very important for its shape design and flight control. However, in this case, to assess a parameter's relative contribution is not easy. It is a non-linear, multi-parameter problem. In practical study, a number of easy and intuitive methods have been applied to indicate the relative sensitivity of an individual parameter. For example, to evaluate

ABOUT THE AUTHORS

The authors are from the group of Shock Wave and Detonation Physics (SWDP), under the supervision of Professor Zonglin Jiang. The research activities are concentrated on hypersonic aerodynamics, especially shock wave and detonation, as well as their applications by theoretical analysis, numerical simulation and physical experiment. The team has set up a large scale shock tunnel (JF-12) with long test duration (100–130 ms), and a hypervelocity shock-expansion tube (JF-16). This paper is motivated by a real-world application of hypersonic aerodynamics, and provides a quantitative metrics to assess the contribution of different parameters to the objective.

PUBLIC INTEREST STATEMENT

Motivated by a real-world application, a new metric, relative contribution ratio (RCR), is proposed. RCR uses a less-compressed projection for data processing, and more valuable information of the original data could be maintained. It provides a unique perspective on analyzing multi-parameter problems.

the contribution of each parameter to the dimensionless heat flux density around a hypersonic aircraft, the approach described in Table 1.

The result in Table 1 is easy to understand and it works fine for the qualitative analysis. Note that each of the sensitivity result in Table 1 is drawn by observing a series of data curves, on the assumption that the other parameters are fixed to some given values. If the other parameters are fixed at different values, the result may vary. This means such conclusions are drawn manually, and are inevitably subjective. Meanwhile, the sensitivity (marked by the number of stars) in Table 1 is quasi-quantitative, and it has a vague meaning to some extent.

Although the above method or something like that is widely used in practical applications, it can only provide qualitative (or at most quasi-quantitative) information to the decision maker. However, sometimes the qualitative result is not enough to make a further analysis. This motivates us to define a new concept, relative contribution ratio (RCR), to make it possible to quantitatively assess the contribution of an individual parameter to the objective value.

The rest of the paper is organized as follows. Pairwise correlation graph, the rudiment of RCR, is presented and discussed in Section 2. The concept of RCR is described in Section 3, and Section 4 provides a numerical computation of RCR based on surrogate models. Section 5 gives a real-world application of RCR. The concluding remarks are drawn in Section 6.

2. Foundation and observations

For a given multi-parameter problem $Y = f(X_1, X_2, \ldots, X_n)$, $X \in \Omega$, if the contribution of an individual parameter X_i is small, the change of X_i will not bring much variation to the objective values Y. Thus X_i and Y should be statistically uncorrelated, or the absolute value of the correlation coefficient will be very small. Based on this fact, we have suggested using a pairwise correlation graph to study multi-parameter problems, in which the data are projected onto a 2-D plane pairwise, and then the correlation coefficient between each parameter and the objective is determined based on data distribution on the 2-D plane. For example, consider a scalar valued problem with two parameters. Both of the parameters X_1 and X_2 could affect the value of objective Y. One needs to find the RCR of each parameter to the objective value. Suppose a set of 50 samples $\{(x_1^{(i)}, x_2^{(i)}, y^{(i)}), i = 1, 2, \ldots, 50\}$ has been obtained. To get the pairwise correlation graph, the 50 points are projected onto planes $X_1 - X_2$, $X_1 - Y$ and $X_2 - Y$, respectively, as shown in Figure 1. It is obvious that X_1 and X_2 are uncorrelated since their correlation ellipses are close to a circle. X_1 and Y are positively correlated, while X_2 and Y are inversely correlated since their correlation ellipses are both flat and the slopes of ellipse's semi-major axes are positive and negative, respectively. In fact, the exact relationship between the three variables is $Y = X_1/X_2$, where $(X_1, X_2) \in [1, 5]^2$ in this case.

Table 1. The sensitivity of each parameter to the dimensionless heat flux density around a hypersonic aircraft

Parameter	Influence on heat flux density	Degree of sensitivity
Static pressure	Little influence	☆☆☆
Static temperature	Medium influence, positively correlated	★★☆
Mach number	Small influence, positively correlated	★☆☆
Flight altitude	Medium influence, negatively correlated	★★☆
Angle of attack	Large influence, positively correlated	★★★
Model scale	Little influence	☆☆☆
Wall temperature	Small influence, negatively correlated	★☆☆

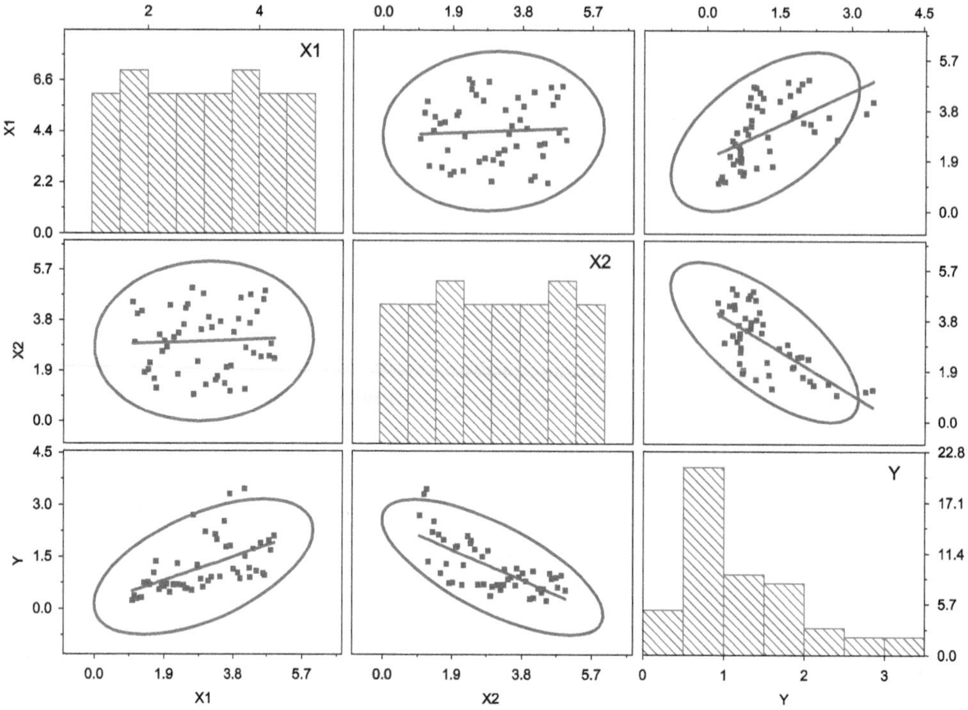

(a) Linearity dominated case

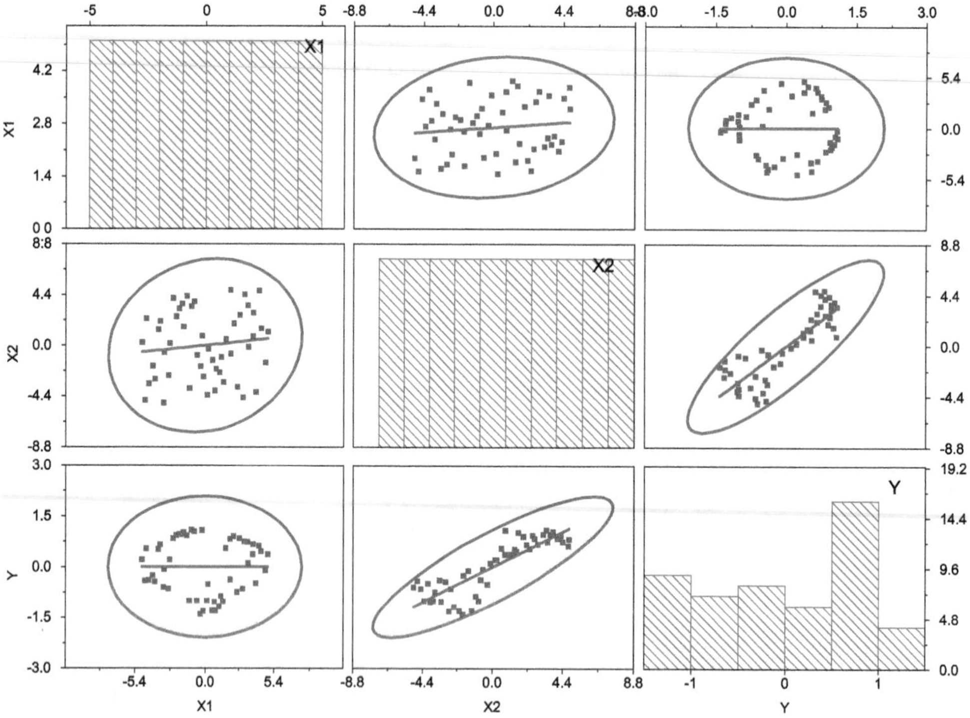

(b) Nonlinearity dominated case

Figure 1. An example of pairwise correlation graph.

In general, the proposed pairwise correlation graph can help to identify the qualitative impact of each parameter on the objective value, and can even give a good quantitative value to show the degree of its impact, provided that all of the other parameters have little impact. However, when the parameter and objective have a strong nonlinear relationship, the pair wise correlation graph cannot give helpful information. This can be illustrated by the following example. Suppose we have a set of 50 sample points randomly drawn from the nonlinear function $Y = \left(5 * X_2 + 0.2 * X_1^2\right)/\left(3 + {X_1}^2 + {X_2}^2\right)$ in the domain $(X_1, X_2) \in [-5, 5]^2$, and we try to detect the impact of each parameter $X_i (i = 1, 2)$ on the objective Y. The pairwise correlation graph is presented in Figure 1. It can be seen that the correlation ellipse of X_1 and Y is almost round, which means X_1 and Y are uncorrelated. This is not what we expect because X_1 and Y are actually correlated in the sense of nonlinear correlation. In other words, the pairwise correlation graph has failed to detect the desired correlation in this example.

Another drawback of the pairwise correlation graph is that it might give a misleading result. In fact, in many practical applications, the sample points could not be sampled evenly due to the limitations of experimental conditions. As a result, although the correlation ellipse looks very flat, the parameter and objective are not actually correlated.

Thus, for nonlinear problems with multiple parameters, we need some new concepts to quantitatively measure the relative contribution of each parameter to the objective.

3. Concept of RCR

3.1. Quick view of relevant concepts

As early as 1895, Pearson proposed a concept of correlation coefficient (Pearson, 1895). Although this concept is defined in 2-D space, it is still used to analyze multi-parameter problems in many practical applications. Pearson's correlation coefficient is strongly dependent on linearity. So Spearman (1904/2010) introduced a rank concept for correlation, which enables it to be capable of analyzing problems with monotone decreasing (or increasing) relationships. Thereafter, Kendall (1938) introduced another new concept of concordant and discordant, and made a further extension of correlation. Both Spearman and Kendall's correlation coefficients can depict part of the nonlinear relationship provided that there exists some partial ordering relations between the parameter and the objective. However, all of the above three correlation coefficients might fail to get the right correlation in general nonlinear cases. To address this problem, Wang, Shen, and Zhang (2005) proposed a nonlinear correlation measure, nonlinear correlation information entropy (NCIE), defined as $\mathrm{NCC}(X; Y) = H^r(X) + H^r(Y) - H^r(X, Y)$, where $H^r(X, Y)$ is the revised joint entropy of the two variables X and Y. Zheng, Shi, and Zhang (2012) proposed a new concept, generalized measure of correlation (GMC) as follows.

$$\{\mathrm{GMC}(Y|X),\ \mathrm{GMC}(X|Y)\} = \left\{1 - \frac{E(\{Y - E(Y|X)\}^2)}{\mathrm{var}(Y)},\ 1 - \frac{E(\{X - E(X|Y)\}^2)}{\mathrm{var}(X)}\right\}$$

Both NCIE and GMC can handle nonlinear correlation problems properly. However, essentially, both of the metrics are still defined in a 2-D space and using the two metrics it is difficult to analyze data with multiple parameters for their relative contributions. This motivates us to make a further extension of these concepts to n-D space.

3.2. Definition of relative ratio of contribution

Existing correlation coefficients are all defined in a 2-D space. To handle multi-parameter problems, one has to resort to dimensionality reduction, and project the data onto a 2-D plane pair by pair, as illustrated in Section 2. This could give misleading results, as discussed in Sections 2 and 3.1.

In our opinion, during the above projection process, the information contained in the data is over-compressed, and useful information might be lost. In our new concept, we try to define a less compressed projection process, so as to keep the valuable information as much as possible. That is, among the several parameters $X_1, X_2, \ldots, X_n$, to determine the contribution of parameter X_i, the sampled data are projected onto its complement space $(X_1, X_2, \ldots, X_{i-1}, X_{i+1}, \ldots, X_n) - Y$. The projection is mapped from $(n + 1)$-D space to n-D space $P: R^{n+1} \mapsto R^n$. Only one dimension is reduced during the projection. Thus, more information could be retained.

The parameter X_i will be absent after the projection process. It is obvious that the projected points will become more divergent if X_i has much contribution to the objective Y. Otherwise, the divergence will be little, and the projected points will converge to a curve (in 2-D), surface (in 3-D), or hypersurface (in k-D, $k \leq n$). To quantitatively measure its degree of convergence , we suggest using a surrogate model as the reference object. The surrogate model $m_i(X_1, X_2, \ldots, X_{i-1}, X_{i+1}, \ldots, X_n)$ is a data-driven model, determined by the projected points. The more divergent they are, the further they will deviate from the model. To illustrate the relationship between the relative contribution of a parameter and the divergence of projected data, we take a simple intuitive example as follows. Suppose we have a set of 200 sample points uniformly drawn from the rectangular region $[0, 5]^2$, and the objective function has an explicit expression $Y_1 = X_1 + 2X_2$, then we can get an illustrative result of each parameter's relative contribution to the 200 points $(x_1^{(k)}, x_2^{(k)}, y^{(k)})$, $k = 1, 2, \ldots, 200$ as follows. First, project these points onto plane $X_2 - Y_1$ and $X_1 - Y_1$ respectively, and then draw their data-driven models (see Figure 2(a) and (b)). It can be seen that the projected points are much more divergent when X_2 is absent, which means the parameter X_2 has more contribution to the objective Y than the parameter X_1. Of course, the actual RCR is known in this example, i.e. X_2 has double contribution than X_1. This example is used only for demonstration. In practical applications, the RCR is not so easy to observe in general.

If the problem involves only two parameters, X_1 and X_2, the divergence of the projected points can be easily shown with a scatter-point plot on a 2-D plane, as shown in Figure 2(a) and (b). Similarly, 3-D scatter-point plot can also be used to show the divergence of the projected points if there are only three influence parameters X_1, X_2 and X_3. However, scatter-point plot cannot help if the problem involves four or more influence parameters, which is usual in practical applications. So we suggest using an observation-prediction plot $(Y, m_i(X_1, X_2, \ldots, X_{i-1}, X_{i+1}, \ldots, X_n))$ to show the divergence of the projected points, where the observation denotes the objective value of samples, and the prediction denotes their predicted value with the data-driven model m_i. The more divergent the projected points are, the further they will deviate from the observation-prediction line segment (on the angle bisector of the first and third quadrants). For the above case, its observation-prediction figures are shown in Figure 3(a) and (b).

Based on these facts, the RCR of X_i to its objective function f can be defined as follows.

Definition Suppose the function $Y = f(X_1, X_2, \ldots, X_n)$ is continuous and bounded on the box-constrained domain Ω, where $f: \Omega \mapsto R$, $(X_1, X_2, \ldots, X_n) \in \Omega \subset R^n$. Let the subspace $S_{X_i} = (X_1, X_2, \ldots, X_{i-1}, X_{i+1}, \ldots, X_n, Y) = R^n$ be the orthogonal complement of X_i, the continuous region $P_{f, X_i} \subset S_{X_i}$ be the projection

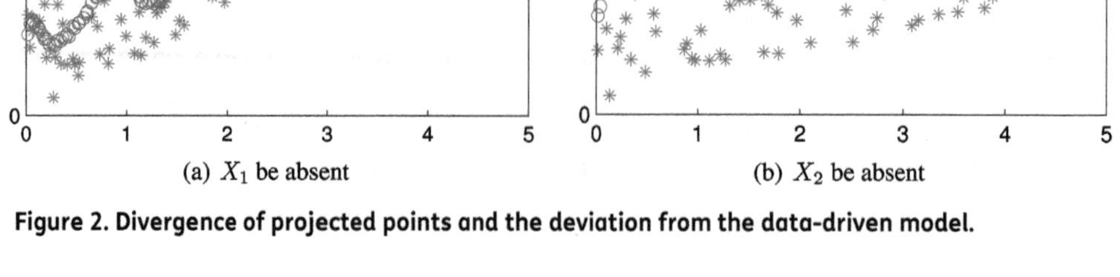

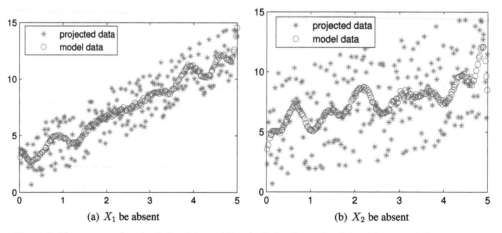

Figure 2. Divergence of projected points and the deviation from the data-driven model.

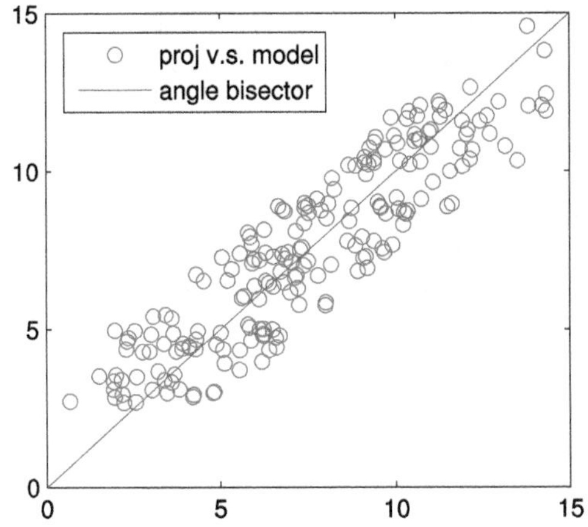

(a) X_1 be absent (b) X_2 be absent

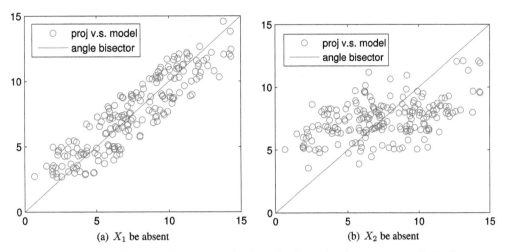

Figure 3. Divergence of projected points and the deviation from the observation-prediction line.

of the hypersuface $Y = f(X_1, X_2, \dots, X_n)$ onto the subspace S_{X_i}, the scalar V_{f,X_i} be the volume (or area in 2-D space) of P_{f,X_i} in its subspace, $i = 1, 2, \dots, n$. Then the RCR (RCR) of X_i to its objective function f is defined as $r_{X_i} = \frac{V_{f,X_i}}{\sum_{i=1}^{n} V_{f,X_i}}$.

In this definition, the volume/area of the projection reflects the divergence brought by the absence of parameter X_i. As a special case, when $n = 2$, the above definition has a geometric interpretation, which will be illustrated by some simple examples in Figure 4. The first two functions are linear and it is easy to get the volume of projection (the area of the projected parallelogram). From Figure 4(a), one can see that the area of the projection on the complemented subspace of X_2 (on the left) is twice

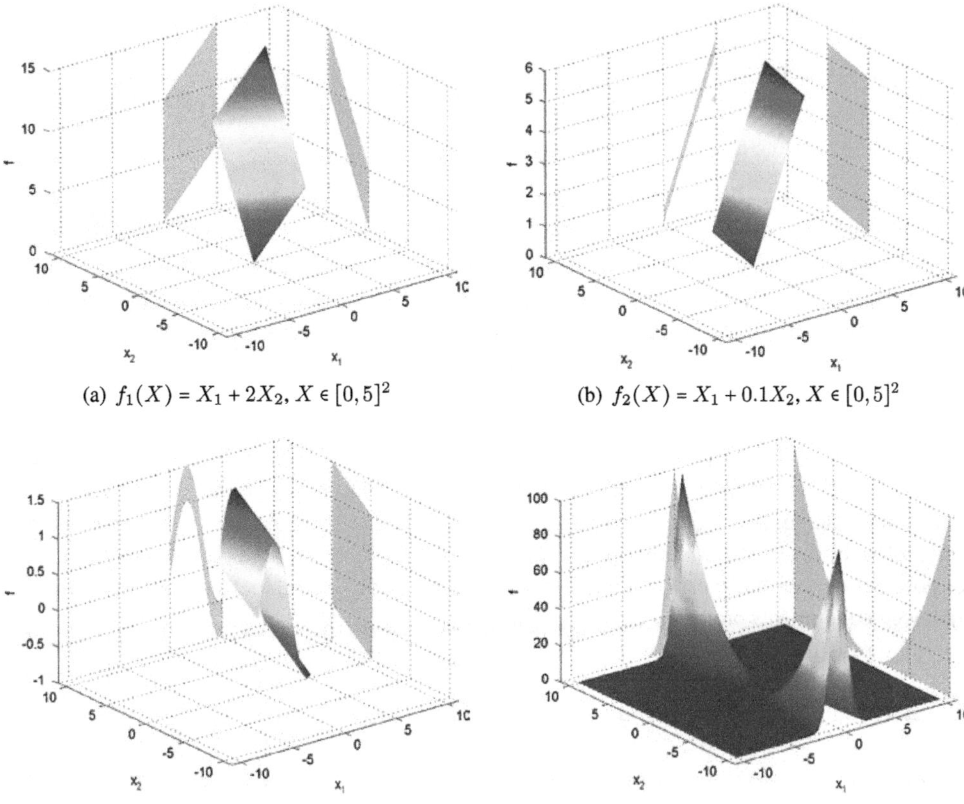

(a) $f_1(X) = X_1 + 2X_2$, $X \in [0,5]^2$

(b) $f_2(X) = X_1 + 0.1X_2$, $X \in [0,5]^2$

(c) $f_3(X) = \sin(X_1) + 0.1X_2$, $X \in [0,5]^2$

(d) $f_4(X) = \exp(-X_1^2 - X_2^{-2}) \cdot (X_1^2 + X_2^2)$, $X \in [-10,10]^2$

Figure 4. Geometric interpretation of RCR.

that of X_1 (on the left). So it is easy to get the RCR $r_{X_1} = 1/3$, and $r_{X_2} = 2/3$. Similarly, for the example in Figure 4(b), we have $r_{X_1} = 1/11$, and $r_{X_2} = 10/11$. The RCR is proportional to the product of its absolute coefficient and interval length.

As can be seen, the RCR of each parameter is easy to get if the problem is linear. However, it is not so easy to get the volume of projection when the problem is nonlinear (see Figure 4(c) and (d)), and the difficulty will increase as the problem involves more parameters (say, n is above 3). Therefore, special algorithms are needed to calculate RCR. To this end, a surrogate model-based method is proposed in the following section.

4. Numerical computation of RCR

Suppose the objective function has an explicit expression $Y = f(X_1, X_2, \dots, X_n)$, as examples in Figure 4, the RCR can be approximated by the following steps.

Step 1. (Random sampling) Randomly generate a sufficient number of sample points $(x_1^{(k)}, x_2^{(k)}, \dots, x_n^{(k)})$ within the given domain Ω, and calculate their corresponding objective values $f^{(k)}$, $k = 1, 2, \dots, K$. The sample data forms an $(n+1)$-by-K matrix, where each row is determined by a sample point, the first n columns indicate its parameter values, and the last column gives its objective values.

Step 2. (Subspace projecting) For each influence parameter X_i, remove its corresponding column for the $(n + 1)$-D data to make X_i absent. The projected points lie in space $(X_1, X_2, \dots, X_{i-1}, X_{i+1}, \dots, X_n) - Y$.

Step 3. (Data-driven modeling) Construct a surrogate model $Y = m_i(X_1, \dots, X_{i-1}, X_{i+1}, \dots, X_n)$ based on the projected points and their corresponding objective values $(x_1^{(k)}, \dots, x_{i-1}^{(k)}, x_{i+1}^{(k)}, \dots, x_n^{(k)})$ and $f^{(k)}$.

Step 4. (Residuals summarizing) Find the total residual

$$V_i = \sum_{k=1}^{K} \left| f^{(k)} - m_i(x_1^{(k)}, \dots, x_{i-1}^{(k)}, x_{i+1}^{(k)}, \dots, x_n^{(k)}) \right|.$$

Step 5. (Cycling) Repeat step 2 to step 4 until all total residuals V_i are obtained, $i = 1, 2, \dots, n$, and let the residual represent the volume of projection $V_{f,X_i} = V_i$ (since they are proportional to each other). Calculate and output the RCRs $r_{X_i} = \frac{V_{f,X_i}}{\sum_{i=1}^{n} V_{f,X_i}}$.

In the above steps, the surrogate modeling plays the most important role, in which the approximation models are constructed with a set of sample points. Although increasing the number of samples could help get better models, it will involve much higher computation costs. To enhance the stability and efficiency of the algorithm, the distribution of the samples should be as uniform as possible. Therefore, controlled sampling methods such as Latin hypercube sampling (Beachkofski & Grandhi, 2002) and orthogonal sampling (Steinberg & Lin, 2006) are preferred for sample generation.

After the sample generation and projection, one needs to choose a reliable method for data-driven modeling. There are many model construction methods, including classical linear/nonlinear fitting/interpolation, Kriging regression, radial basis function (RBF) interpolation/regression (Wendland, 2010), and parse matrix evolution (PME) (Luo & Zhang, 2012). For classical fitting/interpolation, the configuration of the model structure does not lead to a good approximation, especially in multidimensional space. RBF interpolation/regression and PME are distinguished for their good performance with fewer requirements on the number of sample points. Kriging regression is famous for its capability of noise-resistance. Note that the distribution of the projected points could be rugged in the subspace. Therefore, an improved version of Kriging regression, DACE (Lophaven, Nielsen, & Søndergaard, 2002), is recommended for the surrogate modeling to ensure its robustness.

For example, consider the problems in Figure 4 with the above method, randomly generate 100 sample points by Latin hypercube sampling, and use DACE for the model construction in the subspace, one can get each parameter's RCR as follows. $r_{X_1} = 0.33$, $r_{X_2} = 0.67$ for the first problem;

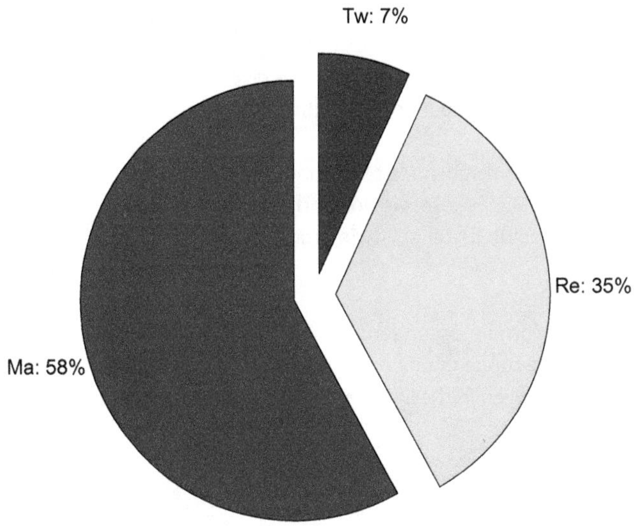

Figure 5. The RCR of *Ma, Re* and *Tw* to the axial force of an aircraft at hypersonic flight conditions.

$r_{X_1} = 0.09$, $r_{X_2} = 0.91$ for the second problem; $r_{X_1} = 0.83$, $r_{X_2} = 0.17$ for the third problem; And $r_{X_1} = 0.57, r_{X_2} = 0.43$ for the forth problem.

However, in most practical applications, no explicit function is available to describe the relationship between the influence parameters and the objective, and only some test data or simulation results could be obtained. Note that these sample data contain meaningful information that reflects their influence relationship. Therefore, again, we can use DACE to construct a surrogate model to represent the objective function before the first step. Then the RCR could be determined by following the above steps.

Note that DACE needs sufficient number of sample points to construct a surrogate model of high fidelity. This could be quite costly in practical applications. Therefore, in the case of small-sized samples (the amount of data is small relative to the number of influence parameters), we suggest using PME (Luo & Zhang, 2012) or radial basis function interpolation/regression (Wendland, 2010) to construct the surrogate model to approximate the underlying function.

5. A real-world application

As mentioned in Section 1, for a hypersonic aircraft, several parameters could affect its axial force coefficient C_A, including Mach number (*Ma*), Reynolds (*Re*) and wall temperature ratio ($\hat{T}_w$). It is of great importance to properly evaluate the relative influence ratio of each parameter for the aircraft design and the behavior control. Suppose we have got sufficient number of sample points for a given aircraft in a certain domain by wind tunnel tests, flight tests and validated CFD simulations, and the surrogate model has been deduced by PME (the surrogate modeling procedure is omitted here):

$$C_A = 0.029 + 0.907\left(\frac{1}{Ma^2} + \frac{1}{Re^{1/4}} + \frac{0.260}{\hat{T}_w}\right)$$

where the Mach number $Ma \in [5, 8]$, Reynolds $Re \in [3.8 \times 10^5, 4.8 \times 10^7]$, and wall temperature $T_w \in [60, 250.3]$ K. With the method described in the above section, the RCR of *Ma*, *Re* and $\hat{T}_w$ is 58, 35 and 7%, respectively (Figure 5).

6. Conclusion

Motivated by the real-world problem, to measure each parameter's relative contribution to the aerodynamic-force coefficient of a hypersonic vehicle, a new concept, RCR, has been presented. It considers the relative impact of absence of every parameter by projecting onto its orthogonal complement subspace. Thus, only one dimension is reduced, and more valuable information of the original data is maintained. This makes RCR capable of dealing with multi-parameter problems with linear or non-linear relations. RCR has provided an intuitive way to quantitatively assess different parameters' relative contribution to the aerodynamic coefficient of hypersonic vehicles, and it can also be used as a scientific metric for other multi-parameter problem analyses without any subjective prejudice.

Based on surrogate modeling, random sampling, subspace projecting, and data-driven modeling, a problem specific algorithm to calculate the RCR is also provided. The proposed algorithm has a good feature of global optimization and has shown its reliability in practice, which brings great convenience in the application of the algorithm.

The concept presented in this paper (RCR) is domain dependent. It is defined on a given domain (Ω), and the RCR value of a parameter will vary if the range of any parameter has changed. Therefore, this concept is easy to be extended to a local one, or even in the limit sense. These topics will be addressed in our future study.

Funding

This research has been supported by Innovation Grant of Chinese Academy of Sciences; the National Natural Science Foundation of China [grant number 90916028].

Author details

Changtong Luo[1]
E-mail: luo@imech.ac.cn
ORCID ID: http://orcid.org/0000-0002-6283-1817
Zonglin Jiang[1]
E-mail: zljiang@imech.ac.cn
Chun Wang[1]
E-mail: wangchun@imech.ac.cn
Zongmin Hu[1]
E-mail: huzm@imech.ac.cn
[1] State Key Laboratory of High Temperature Gas Dynamics, Institute of Mechanics, Chinese Academy of Sciences, Beijing 100190, China.

References

Anderson, Jr., J. (2006). *Hypersonic and high temperature gas dynamics*. Reston, VA: American Institute of Aerodynamics and Astronautics.

Beachkofski, B., & Grandhi, R. (2002). *Improved distributed hypercube sampling* (AIAA Paper Number 2002-1274). Reston, VA: The American Institute of Aeronautics and Astronautics.

Kendall, M. (1938). A new measure of rank correlation. *Biometrika, 30*, 81–89.

Lophaven, S. N., Nielsen, H., & Søndergaard, J. (2002). *DACE–A Matlab kriging toolbox* (pp. 1–26, IMM-REP-2002-12). Kongens Lyngby: Technical University of Denmark.

Luo, C. T., & Zhang, S.-L. (2012). Parse-matrix evolution for symbolic regression. *Engineering Applications of Artificial Intelligence, 25*, 1182–1193.

Pearson, K. (1895). Notes on regression and inheritance in the case of two parents. *Proceedings of the Royal Society of London, 58*, 240–242.

Spearman, C. (1904/2010). The proof and measurement of association between two things. *The American Journal of Psychology, 15*, 72–101; Reprinted by *International Journal of Epidemiology, 39*, 1137–1150.

Steinberg, D. M., & Lin, D. K. J. (2006). A construction method for orthogonal Latin hypercube designs. *Biometrika, 93*, 279–288.

Wang, Q., Shen, Y., & Zhang, J. (2005). A nonlinear correlation measure for multivariable data set. *Physica D: Nonlinear Phenomena, 200*, 287–295.

Wendland, H. (2010). *Scattered data approximation*. Cambridge: Cambridge University Press.

Zheng, S., Shi, N.-Z., & Zhang, Z. (2012). Generalized measures of correlation for asymmetry, nonlinearity, and beyond. *Journal of the American Statistical Association, 107*, 1239–1252.

10

Block-pulse functions approach to numerical solution of Abel's integral equation

Monireh Nosrati Sahlan[1]*, Hamid Reza Marasi[1] and Farzaneh Ghahramani[1]

*Corresponding author: Monireh Nosrati Sahlan, Technical Faculty, Department of Mathematics and Computer Science, University of Bonab, Bonab, Iran

E-mail: nosrati@bonabu.ac.ir

Reviewing editor: Yong Hong Wu, Curtin University of Technology, Australia

Abstract: This study aims to present a computational method for solving Abel's integral equation of the second kind. The introduced method is based on the use of Block-pulse functions (BPFs) via collocation method. Abel's integral equations as singular Volterra integral equations are hard and heavy in computation, but because of the properties of BPFs, as is reported in examples, this method is more efficient and more accurate than some other methods for solving this class of integral equations. On the other hand, the benefit of this method is low cost of computing operations. The applied method transforms the singular integral equation into triangular linear algebraic system that can be solved easily. An error analysis is worked out and applications are demonstrated through illustrative examples.

Subjects: Advanced Mathematics; Analysis - Mathematics; Integral Transforms & Equations; Mathematics & Statistics; Science

Keywords: Abel's integral equation; Block-pulse functions; collocation method

1. Introduction

The past two decades have been witnessing a strong interest among physicists, engineers, and mathematicians for the theory and numerical modeling of integral and integro-differential equations. These equations are solved analytically; see, for example, the excellent book by Mushkelishvili (1953), and the references therein. The generalized Abel's integral equation on a finite segment

ABOUT THE AUTHOR

Monireh Nosrati Sahlan is currently an associate professor at the Department of Mathematics and Computer Science, Technical Faculty, University of Bonab, Bonab, Iran. Nosrati Sahlan completed her PhD in 2013 from Iran University of Science and Technology, Tehran, Iran. She completed her MSc in Applied Mathematics at Iran University of Science and Technology, in 2007 and BSc in Mathematics at University of Shahid Madani Azerbaijan. Nosrati Sahlan has about ten years of research experience in various field of Applied Mathematics such as integral equations, integro-differential equations, wavelets, etc. She has published immense research papers in numerous fields and various international journals of repute like International Journal of Computer Mathematics, Communication in Nonlinear Science and Numerical Simulation, Computational and Applied Mathematics, etc. Her current research interest includes the numerical methods for the solutions of linear and nonlinear Abel's integral equations.

PUBLIC INTEREST STATEMENT

Abel's equation is one of the integral equations derived directly from a concrete problem of mechanics or physics (without passing through a differential equation). Historically, Abel's problem is the first one that led to the study of integral equations. The construction of high-order methods for the equations is, however, not an easy task because of the singularity in the weakly singular kernel. This class of equations (linear or nonlinear, of first kind or second kind) has applications in many fields of physics and experimental sciences: problems in mechanics, scattering theory, spectroscopy, stereology, seismology, and plasma physics lead to such equations.

appeared for the first time in the paper of Zeilon (1922). A comprehensive reference on Abel-type equations, including an extensive list of applications, can be found in Gorenflo and Vessella (1991) and Wazwaz (1997). The construction of high-order methods for the equations is, however, not an easy task because of the singularity in the weakly singular kernel. In fact, in this case the solution y is generally not differentiable at the endpoints of the interval, see Schneider (1979) and Vainikko and Pedas (1981), and due to this, to the best of the authors? knowledge the best convergence rate ever achieved remains only at polynomial order. For example, if we set uniform meshes with $n+1$ grid points and apply the spline method so for order m, then the convergence rate is only $O(n^{-2p})$ at most (Schneider, 1981; Graham, 1982), and it cannot be improved by increasing m. One way of remedying this is to introduce graded meshes. Then the rate is improved to $O(n^{-m})$ (Vainikko & Uba, 1981) which now depends on m, but still at polynomial order. Fettis (1964) proposed a numerical form of the solution to Abel equation by using the Gauss–Jacobi quadrature rule. Piessens and Verbaeten (1973) and Piessens (2000) developed an approximate solution to Abel equation by means of the Chebyshev polynomials of the first kind. Numerical solutions of weakly singular Volterra integral equations were introduced by many researchers, such as Baratella and Orsi (2004) and Abdou and Nasr (2003). Yanzhao, Min, Liping, and Yuesheng (2007) applied hybrid collocation method for solving these equations. Ishik, Sezer, and Gney (2011) used Bernstein series solution for solving linear integro-differential equations with weakly singular kernels. Wazwaz (2002) studied on singular initial value problems in the second-order ordinary differential equations. Yousefi (2006) applied Legendre wavelets to transform Abel integral equation to a algebraic system.

The aim of this work is to present a computational method for solving special case of singular Volterra integral equations of the second kind as named Abel's integral equation defined as

$$y(x) = f(x) - \int_0^x \frac{y(t)}{\sqrt{x-t}} dt \tag{1}$$

where $f \in L^2([0,T])$. Our method consists of reducing the given weakly singular integral equation to a set of algebraic equations by expanding the unknown function using block-pulse functions (BPFs) with unknown coefficients. Collocation method is utilized to evaluate the unknown coefficients. Because of orthogonality, disjointness and having completeness properties of these functions, the operational matrix of method is a sparse lower triangular matrix. Without loss of generality, we may consider $[0,T] = [0,1]$.

The paper is organized as follows: In the next section, we discuss BPFs, their key properties and function approximation by them. In Section 3, we give the description and development of the method for solving singular integral equation. Error analysis and convergence of the method is discussed in Section 4. In Section 5 for showing the efficiency of this method, some numerical examples are presented. Section 6 is devoted to the conclusion of this paper.

2. Block-pulse functions

BPFs are studied by many authors and applied for solving different problems, for example see Steffens (2006).

A k-set of BPFs over the interval $[0,T)$ is defined as

$$B_i(t) = \begin{cases} 1, & \frac{iT}{k} \le t < \frac{(i+1)T}{k} \\ 0, & \text{elsewhere} \end{cases} \tag{2}$$

$i = 0, 1, \ldots, k-1,$

with a positive integer value for k. In this paper, it is assumed that $T = 1$, so BPFs are defined over $[0,1)$. BPFs have some main properties, the most important of these properties are disjointness, orthogonality, and completeness.

(1) The disjointness property can be clearly obtained from the definition of BPFs

$$B_i(t)B_j(t) = \begin{cases} B_i(t), & i = j \\ 0, & i \neq j \end{cases} \quad i, j = 0, 1, \ldots, k-1 \tag{3}$$

(2) The orthogonality property of these functions is

$$\langle B_i(t), B_j(t) \rangle = \int_0^1 B_i(t)B_j(t)dt = \begin{cases} \frac{1}{k}, & i = j \\ 0, & i \neq j \end{cases} \quad i, j = 0, 1, \ldots, k-1 \tag{4}$$

(3) The third property is completeness. For every $y \in L^2[0, 1)$, when k approaches to the infinity, Parseval's identity holds, that is

$$\int_0^1 y^2(t)dt = \sum_{i=1}^{\infty} c_i^2 \|B_i(t)\|^2$$

where

$$c_i = k \int_0^1 f(t)B_i(t)dt \tag{5}$$

A function $y(t)$ defined over the interval $[0, 1)$ may be expanded by a k–set of BPFs as

$$y(t) \simeq y_k(t) = \sum_{i=0}^{k-1} c_i B_i(t) = \mathbf{C}^T \mathbf{B}(t) \tag{6}$$

where $c_i = k\langle y(t), B_i(t) \rangle$, and

$$\mathbf{C} = \left(c_0, c_1, \ldots, c_{k-1}\right)^T$$

and

$$\mathbf{B}(t) = \left(B_0(t), B_1(t), \ldots, B_{k-1}(t)\right)^T$$

where c_i are samples of y, for example $c_i = y(\frac{i}{k})$ for $i = 0, 1, \ldots, k-1$, and as a result there is no need for integration. The vector C is called the 1D-BPFs coefficient vector.

3. Numerical implementation

Consider the Abel's integral equation

$$y(x) = f(x) - \int_0^x \frac{y(t)}{\sqrt{x-t}} dt, \quad x \in [0, 1]$$

where $f \in L^2(\mathbb{R})$ is known and $y(t)$ is the unknown function to be determined. Now by substituting Equation 6 into Equation 1, we obtain

$$\begin{aligned} \mathbf{C}^T \mathbf{B}(x) &= f(x) - \int_0^x \frac{\mathbf{C}^T \mathbf{B}(t)}{\sqrt{x-t}} dt \\ &= f(x) - \mathbf{C}^T \int_0^x \frac{\mathbf{B}(t)}{\sqrt{x-t}} dt \end{aligned} \tag{7}$$

by evaluating Equation 7 at the collocation points $x_j = \frac{j-1/2}{k}, \quad j = 1, 2, \ldots, k$, we obtain

$$\mathbf{C}^T\mathbf{B}(x_j) = f(x_j) - \mathbf{C}^T \int_0^{x_j} \frac{\mathbf{B}(t)}{\sqrt{x_j - t}} dt \tag{8}$$

by considering $\mathbf{B}(x_j) = \mathbf{e}_j$ (the j-th column of identity matrix), we can rewrite Equation 8 as follows

$$c_j = f(x_j) - \mathbf{C}^T \int_0^{x_j} \frac{\mathbf{B}(t)}{\sqrt{x_j - t}} dt \tag{9}$$

Now for computing the unknown coefficients c_j, we introduce a recursive formula.

The unknown coefficient c_j satisfies the following recursive relation:

$$c_j = f(x_j) - \sum_{i=1}^{j-1} c_i \int_{\frac{i-1}{k}}^{\frac{i}{k}} \frac{1}{\sqrt{x_j - t}} dt - c_j \int_{\frac{j-1}{k}}^{\frac{j-1/2}{k}} \frac{1}{\sqrt{x_j - t}} dt \tag{10}$$

where

$$c_1 = f(x_1) - c_1 \int_0^{\frac{1}{2k}} \frac{1}{\sqrt{x_1 - t}} dt$$

The linear system of Equation 10 is a lower triangular system which can be solved easily by forward substitution with $O(k^2)$ operations. If we calculate a table of values of c_j, $j = 1, 2, \ldots, k$, then the coefficients c_j for every large k, can be calculated . The cost of calculating such table is relatively cheap. To prove this, fist note that

$$\begin{aligned}
\int_0^{x_j} \frac{\mathbf{B}(t)}{\sqrt{x_j - t}} dt &= \int_0^{\frac{j-1/2}{k}} \frac{(B_1(t), B_2(t), \ldots, B_k(t))^T}{\sqrt{x_j - t}} dt \\
&= \left(\int_0^{\frac{1}{k}} \frac{1}{\sqrt{x_j - t}} dt \right) . (1, 0, 0, \ldots, 0)^T \\
&+ \left(\int_{\frac{1}{k}}^{\frac{2}{k}} \frac{1}{\sqrt{x_j - t}} dt \right) . (0, 1, 0, \ldots, 0)^T \\
&\vdots \\
&+ \left(\int_{\frac{j-2}{k}}^{\frac{j-1}{k}} \frac{1}{\sqrt{x_j - t}} dt \right) . (0, \ldots, 0, 1, 0)^T + \left(\int_{\frac{j-1}{k}}^{\frac{j-1/2}{k}} \frac{1}{\sqrt{x_j - t}} dt \right) . (0, \ldots, 0, 1)^T
\end{aligned}$$

and in abstract form

$$\int_0^{x_j} \frac{\mathbf{B}(t)}{\sqrt{x_j - t}} dt =$$

$$\left(\int_0^{\frac{1}{k}} \frac{1}{\sqrt{x_j - t}} dt, \ldots, \int_{\frac{j-2}{k}}^{\frac{j-1}{k}} \frac{1}{\sqrt{x_j - t}} dt, \int_{\frac{j-1}{k}}^{\frac{j-1/2}{k}} \frac{1}{\sqrt{x_j - t}} dt \right)^T \tag{11}$$

Substituting Equation 11 in Equation 9 leads to Equation 10 and the proof is complete. □

4. Error analysis

In this section, we give an upper bound for the error of BPFs expansion. Assume that $y'(t) \in C[0,1]$, thus

$$\exists M > 0; \quad \forall t \in (0,1), \quad |y'(t)| \le M$$

and suppose $e_i(t)$ be the representation error of BPFs expansion in the subinterval $\left[\frac{i-1}{k}, \frac{i}{k}\right)$, that is,

$$\begin{aligned} e_i(t) &= c_i B_i(t) - y(t) \\ &= c_i - y(t) \end{aligned}$$

Using mean value theorem, we may proceed as follows

$$\begin{aligned} \|e_i\|^2 &= \int_{\frac{i-1}{k}}^{\frac{i}{k}} e_i^2(t)dt \\ &= \int_{\frac{i-1}{k}}^{\frac{i}{k}} (c_i - y(t))^2 dt \\ &= \left(\frac{i}{k} - (\frac{i-1}{k}))(c_i - y(\xi_1)\right)^2 \\ &= \frac{1}{k}(c_i - y(\xi_1))^2, \quad \xi_1 \in \left(\frac{i-1}{k}, \frac{i}{k}\right) \end{aligned} \tag{12}$$

For the coefficient c_i, we get

$$\begin{aligned} c_i &= k < y(t), B_i(t) > \\ &= k\int_{\frac{i-1}{k}}^{\frac{i}{k}} y(t)dt \\ &= k\left(\frac{i}{k} - \left(\frac{i-1}{k}\right)\right) y(\xi_2) \\ &= y(\xi_2), \quad \xi_2 \in \left(\frac{i-1}{k}, \frac{i}{k}\right) \end{aligned} \tag{13}$$

Substituting Equation 13 into Equation 12 and again using mean value theorem, we obtain

$$\begin{aligned} \|e_i\|^2 &= \frac{1}{k}\left(b_i - y(\xi_1)\right)^2 \\ &= \frac{1}{k}\left(y(\xi_2) - y(\xi_1)\right)^2 \\ &= \frac{1}{k}\left(\xi_2 - \xi_1\right)^2 y'^2(\xi) \quad (\xi_1 < \xi < \xi_2) \\ &\le \frac{1}{k^3} M^2 \end{aligned} \tag{14}$$

Now, for $i < j$, we have

$$\left[\frac{i-1}{k}, \frac{i}{k}\right) \cap \left[\frac{j-1}{k}, \frac{j}{k}\right) = \emptyset, \quad \Rightarrow \quad \int_0^1 e_i(t)e_j(t)dt = 0$$

Putting $e(t) = y_k(t) - y(t)$, we have

$$\begin{aligned}||e||^2 &= \int_0^1 e^2(t)dt \\ &= \int_0^1 \left(\sum_{i=1}^{k} e_i(t)\right)^2 dt \\ &= \int_0^1 \sum_{i=1}^{k} e_i^2(t)dt + 2\sum_{i<j}\int_0^1 e_i(t)e_j(t)dt \\ &= \sum_{i=1}^{k}\int_0^1 e_i^2(t)dt \\ &= \sum_{i=1}^{k} ||e_i||^2 \\ &\leq \frac{1}{k^2}M^2\end{aligned}$$

hence, $||e(t)|| = O(\frac{1}{k})$.

Remark It is clear that the approximation will be more accurate if k (the number of BPFs) is increased, thus for acheiving better results, using larger k is recommended.

5. Numerical examples

In this section, for showing the accuracy and efficiency of the described method we present some examples. The results for introduced method in this work in different scales of k are presented and compared with the results of some other methods.

Example 1 Consider the equation

$$y(x) = \frac{1}{\sqrt{x+1}} + \frac{\pi}{8} - \frac{1}{4}\arcsin\left(\frac{1-x}{1+x}\right) - \frac{1}{4}\int_0^x \frac{y(t)}{\sqrt{x-t}}dt$$

with the exact solution $y(x) = \frac{1}{\sqrt{x+1}}$. The solution for $y(x)$ is obtained by the method in Section 3 at the scales $k = 16, 32,$ and 64. In Table 1, the exact and approximate solutions of Example 1 both by our method and by Legendre wavelets method (Yousefi, 2006) in some arbitrary points are reported. Comparison with Legendre wavelets expansion, the method of this paper has more accuracy. As proved in Section 4, the error at the level $k = 64$ is smaller than the error at the levels $k = 16$ and $k = 32$.

L. W: Results by Legendre wavelets expansion.

In Figures 1 and 2, pointwise plots are the approximated solution of Example 1 (for $k = 32$ and $k = 64$, respectively) in some arbitrary points and the others are the plot of exact solution.

Table 1. Exact and approximate solutions of Example 1

	Approximate			L. W [19]	
x	$k = 16$	$k = 32$	$k = 64$	$k = 1, M = 5$	Exact
0	0.99734	0.999123	0.999993	0.999432	1
0.2	0.911748	0.912305	0.912873	0.91232	0.912871
0.4	0.848041	0.845156	0.845154	0.8453212	0.845154
0.6	0.788293	0.790527	0.790562	0.7905387	0.790569
0.8	0.746027	0.745361	0.745316	0.745342	0.745356
1	0.70423	0.70712	0.707103	0.707163	0.707107

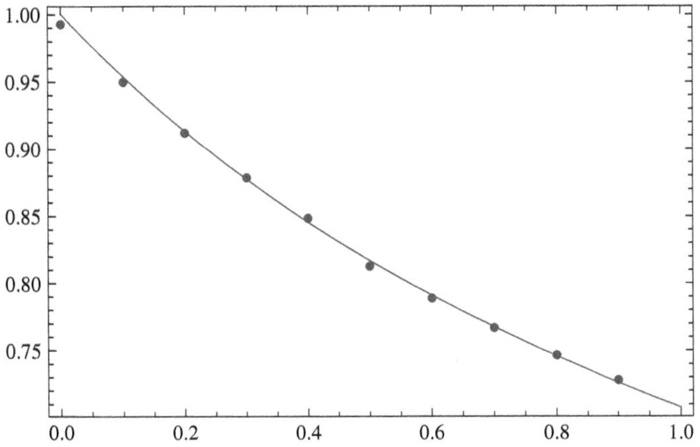

Figure 1. Exact and approximation solution of Example 1 in $k = 32$.

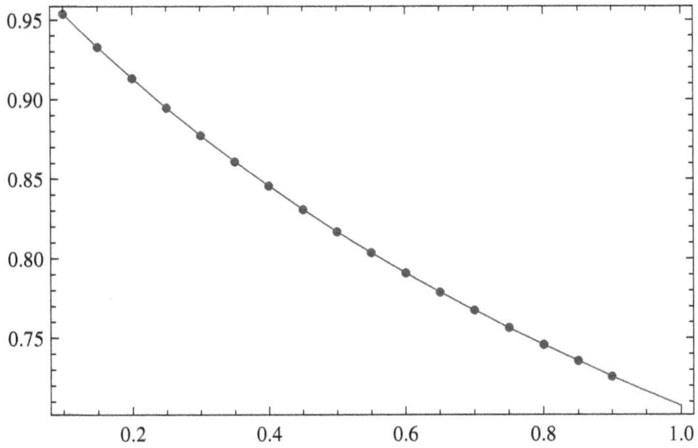

Figure 2. Exact and approximation solution of Example 1 in $k = 64$.

Example 2 Consider the equation

$$y(x) = -4\sqrt{x} + 4\sqrt{x}\ln(2) - 2\sqrt{x}\ln\left(\frac{1}{x}\right) + \ln(x) - \int_0^x \frac{y(t)}{\sqrt{x-t}}dt$$

with the exact solution $y(x) = \ln(x)$. The solution for $y(x)$ is obtained by the method in Section 3 at the scales $k = 16, 32$, and 64. In Table 2, we present the exact and approximate solutions of Example 2 both by our method and by Legendre wavelets method (Yousefi, 2006) in some arbitrary points. Comparison with Legendre wavelets expansion, the method of this paper has more accuracy. As proved in Section 4, the error at the level $k = 64$ is smaller than the error at the levels $k = 16$ and $k = 32$.

Table 2. Exact and approximate solutions of Example 2

	Approximate			L. W [19]	
x	$k = 16$	$k = 32$	$k = 64$	$k = 1, M = 5$	Exact
0.2	-1.609841	-1.60942	-1.60944	-1.60927	-1.60944
0.4	-0.916390	-0.916211	-0.916291	-0.916238	-0.916291
0.6	-0.51054	-0.510832	-0.510826	-0.51046	-0.510826
0.8	-0.223750	-0.223101	-0.223144	-0.223575	-0.223144
1	0.00042	0.000001	0	0.00013	0

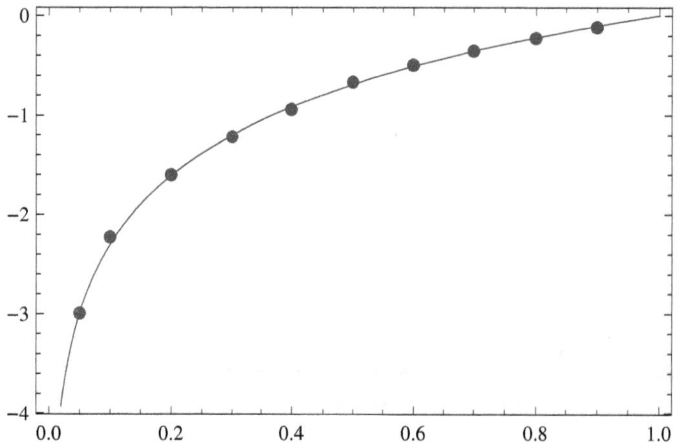

Figure 3. Exact and approximation solution of Example 2 in $k = 32$.

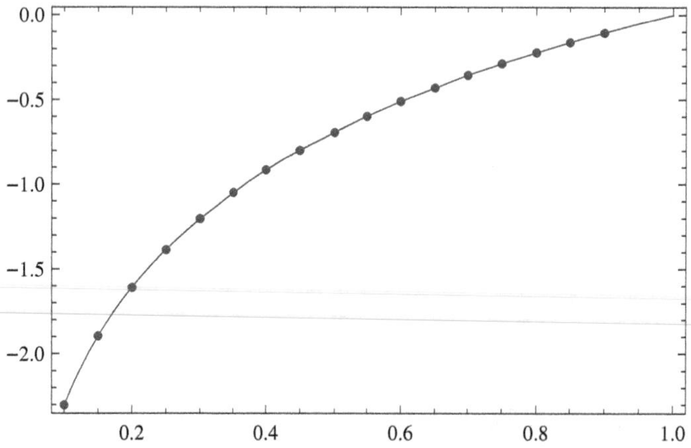

Figure 4. Exact and approximation solution of Example 2 in $k = 64$.

In Figures 3 and 4, pointwise plots are the approximated solution of Example 2 (for $k = 32$ and $k = 64$, respectively) in some arbitrary points and the others are the plot of exact solution. Obviously, there is less error between two plot for $k = 64$ rather than $k = 32$.

6. Conclusions

In the present paper, BPFs with the collocation method are applied to solve the Abel's integral equation. As for Legendre polynomials, Chebyshev polynomials and other generalized orthogonal polynomials, the calculation procedures are usually too tedious, although some recursive formula are available. The benefits of this method are low cost of setting up the equations and more accuracy and more efficiency of the solution than exiting methods for solving this class of equations. Also, the linear system of Equation 11 is a lower triangular system which can be easily solved by forward substitution with $O(k^2)$ operations, therefore, the count of operations is very low. The approach can be extended to nonlinear Abel integral equation and integro differential equation with little additional work. Further research along these lines is under progress and will be reported in due time.

Acknowledgements
The authors would like to thank University of Bonab for providing facilities and encouraging this work and also thank the anonymous reviewers of this paper for their careful reading, constructive comments, and nice suggestions which have improved the paper very much.

Funding
This work was supported by University of Bonab.

Author details
Monireh Nosrati Sahlan[1]
E-mail: nosrati@bonabu.ac.ir
Hamid Reza Marasi[1]
E-mail: hamidreza.marasi@gmail.com
Farzaneh Ghahramani[1]
E-mail: ghahremani9365@gmail.com
[1] Technical Faculty, Department of Mathematics and Computer Science, University of Bonab, Bonab, Iran.

References

Abdou, M. A., & Nasr, A. A. (2003). On the numerical treatment of the singular integral equation of the second kind. *Applied Mathematics and Computation, 146*, 373–380.

Baratella, P., & Orsi, A. P. (2004). A new approach to the numerical solution of weakly singular Volterra integral equations. *Journal of Computational and Applied Mathematics, 163*, 401–418.

Fettis, M. E. (1964). On numerical solution of equations of the Abel type. *Mathematics of Computation, 18*, 491–496.

Gorenflo, R., & Vessella, S. (1991). *Abel integral equations*. Lecture notes in mathematics (Vol. 1461). Berlin: Springer.

Graham, I. G. (1982). Galerkin methods for second kind integral equations with singularities. *Mathematics of Computation, 39*, 519–533.

Isik, O. R., Sezer, M., & Gney, Z. (2011). Bernstein series solution of a class of linear integro-differential equations with weakly singular kernel. *Applied Mathematics and Computation, 217*, 7009–7020.

Mushkelishvili, N. I. (1953). *Singular integral equations*. Groningen: Noordhoff.

Piessens, R. (2000). Computing integral transforms and solving integral equations using Chebyshev polynomial approximations. *Journal of Computational and Applied Mathematics, 121*, 113–124.

Piessens, R., & Verbaeten, P. (1973). Numerical solution of the Abel integral equation. *BIT, 13*, 451–457.

Schneider, C. (1979). Regularity of the solution to a class of weakly singular Fredholm integral equations of the second kind. *Integral Equation Operator Theory, 2*, 62–68.

Schneider, C. (1981). Product integration for weakly singular integral equations. *Mathematics of Computation, 36*, 207–213.

Steffens, K. G. (2006). *The history of approximation theory: From Euler to Brenstein*. Boston: Birkhauser. ISBN 0817643532.

Vainikko, G., & Pedas, A. (1981). The properties of solutions of weakly singular integral equations. *Journal of the Australian Mathematical Society Series B, 22*, 419–430.

Vainikko, G., & Uba, P. (1981). A piecewise polynomial approximation to the solution of an integral equation with weakly singular kernel. *Journal of the Australian Mathematical Society Series B, 22*, 431–438.

Wazwaz, A. M. (1997). *A first course in integral equations*. New Jersey: World Scientific Publishing Company.

Wazwaz, A. M. (2002). A new method for solving singular initial value problems in the second-order ordinary differential equations. *Applied Mathematics and Computation, 128*, 45–57.

Yanzhao, C., Min, H., Liping, L., & Yuesheng, X. (2007). Hybrid collocation methods for Fredholm integral equations with weakly singular kernels. *Applied Numerical Mathematics, 57*, 549–561.

Yousefi, S. A. (2006). Numerical solution of Abel integral equation by using Legendre wavelets. *Applied Mathematics and Computation, 175*, 574–580.

Zeilon, N. (1922). Sur quelques points de l'theorie de le equation integrale d'Abel [On some points of the theory of integral equation of Abel type]. *Arkiv för Matematik. Astronomi och Fysik, 18*, 1–19.

11

A detection for patent infringement suit via nanotopology induced by graph

M. Lellis Thivagar[1*], Paul Manuel[2] and V. Sutha Devi[1]

*Corresponding author: M. Lellis Thivagar, School of Mathematics, Madurai Kamaraj University, Madurai 625021, Tamil Nadu, India

E-mail: mlthivagar@yahoo.co.in.

Reviewing editor: Hari M. Srivastava, University of Victoria, Canada

Abstract: The aim of this paper was to generate nanotopological structure on the power set of vertices of simple digraphs using new definition neighbourhood of vertices on out linked of digraphs. Based on the neighbourhood we define the approximations of the subgraphs of a graph. A new nanotopological graph reduction to symbolic circuit analysis is developed in this paper. By means of structural equivalence on nanotopology induced by graph we have framed an algorithm for detecting patent infringement suit.

Subjects: Foundations & Theorems; Mathematics & Statistics; Science

Keywords: graph; neighbourhood; isomorphism; homeomorphism; electrical circuits

2010 AMS Subject classifications: 54B05; 54C05

1. Introduction

The theory of nanotopology proposed by Lellis Thivagar and Richard (2013a, 2013b), is an extension of set theory for the study of intelligent systems characterized by in sufficient and incomplete information. The purpose of the present work was to put a starting point for the nanotopological graph theory. Most real-life situations need some sort of approximation to fit mathematical models. The

ABOUT THE AUTHORS

M. Lellis Thivagar has published 210 research publications both in National and International journals to his credit. In his collaborative work, he has joined hands with intellectuals of high reputed persons internationally. He serves as a referee for 12 peer-reviewed international journals. At present he is the professor & chair person, School Of Mathematics, Madurai Kamaraj University.

Paul Manuel has published 114 research publications both in National and International journals to his credit. He is expertise in Graph Algorithms, Combinatorial chemistry and Grid computing and also reviewer of many prestigious professional bodies. Currently he is an Professor, Department of Information sciences, Kuwait University, Kuwait.

V. Sutha Devi is a research scholar of Mathematics under the guidance of M. Lellis Thivagar at the School of Mathematics, Madurai Kamaraj University, Madurai. She had 9 years of working experience as Assistant Professor of Mathematics. She has attended and presented two papers in international conferences. Four of her research papers are published/accepted in the reputed international peer-reviewed journals.

PUBLIC INTEREST STATEMENT

Lellis Thivagar introduced nanotopological space with respect to a subset X of an universe which is defined in terms of lower and upper approximations of X. The elements of a nanotopological space are called the nano-open sets. But certain nanoterms are satisfied simply to mean "very small". It originates from the Greek word "Nanos" which means "Dwarf" in its modern scientific sense, an order to magnititude—one billionth of something. Nanocar is an example. The topology recommended here is named so because of its size, since it has atmost five elements in it. The purpose of the present work was to put a starting point for the nanotopological graph theory. We hope these new results will further assist to comprehend the concept of nanotopological space in various applied fields.

beauty of using nanotopology in approximation is achieved via approximation for qualitative subgraphs without coding or using assumption. We believe that nanotopological graph structure will be an important base for modification of knowledge extraction of processing. In this section, we define graphical isomorphism (Diestel, 2010; Jensen & Shen, 2007) is a related task for deciding when two graphs with different specifications are structurally equivalent, that is whether they have the same pattern of connections. Nanohomeomorphism (Bonikowski, Bryniarski, & Wybraniec, 1998) between two nanotopological spaces are said to be topologically equivalent. Here, we are formalizing the structural equivalence of basic circuit of the chips from the graphs and their corresponding nanotopologies generated by them.

2. Preliminaries

This section represents a review of some fundamental notions related to nanotopology and graph theory.

Definition 2.1 (Lellis Thivagar & Richard, 2013a, 2013b): Let $\mathcal{U}$ be an universe. $\mathcal{R}$ be an equivalence relation on $\mathcal{U}$ and $\tau_R(X) = \{\mathcal{U}, \emptyset, L_R(X), U_R(X), B_R(X)\}$ where $X \subseteq \mathcal{U}$. $\tau_R(X)$ satisfies the following axioms:

(i) $\mathcal{U}$ and $\emptyset \in \tau_R(X)$.

(ii) The union of elements of any sub collection of $\tau_R(X)$ is in $\tau_R(X)$.

(iii) The intersection of the elements of any finite sub collection of $\tau_R(X)$ is in $\tau_R(X)$. That is, $\tau_R(X)$ forms a topology on $\mathcal{U}$ the nanotopology on $\mathcal{U}$ with respect to X. We call $(\mathcal{U}, \tau_R(X))$ as the nanotopological space. The elements of $\tau_R(X)$ are called nano-open sets.

Definition 2.2 (Bonikowski et al., 1998; Diestel, 2010): A graph G is an ordered pair of disjoint sets (*V*, *E*), where V is nonempty and *E* is a subset of unordered pairs of *V*. The vertices and edges of a graph G are the elements of *V* = *V*(*G*) and *E* = *E*(*G*), respectively. We say that a graph G is finite (resp. infinite) if the set *V*(*G*) is finite (resp.finite). The degree of a vertex $u \in V(G)$ is the number of edge in a graph contains a vertex u, then u is called an isolated point and so the degree of u is zero (Lellis Thivagar & Richard, 2013b). An edge which has the same vertex to ends is called a loop and the edge with distinct ends is called a link (Jensen & Shen, 2007).

Definition 2.3 (Bonikowski et al., 1998; Diestel, 2010): A graph is simple if it has no loops and no two of its links join the same pair of vertices. A graph which has no edge called a null graph. A graph which has no vertices is called a empty graph (Jensen & Shen, 2007; Lellis Thivagar & Richard, 2013b).

Definition 2.4 (Deseor & Kuh, 2009; Diestel, 2010): If *G*[*V*, *E*] is a directed graph and $u, v \in V$, then:

(i) u is invertex of v if $\overline{uv} \in E(G)$.

(ii) u is outvertex of v if $\overline{vu} \in E(G)$.

(iii) The indegree of a vertex 'v' is the number of vertices 'u' such that $\overline{uv} \in E(G)$.

(iv) The outdegree of a vertex 'v' is the number of vertices 'u' such that $\overline{vu} \in E(G)$.

Throughout this paper the word **graph** means **direct simple graph**.

3. Approximations via neighbourhood

In this section, we will define lower and upper approximation of subgraph H of a graph G[*V*, *E*]. Some properties of these concepts are studied.

Definition 3.1 Let G(*V*, *E*) be a graph, $v \in V(G)$. Then we define the neighbourhood of 'v' as follows, $N(v) = \{v\} \bigcup \{u \in V(G): \overline{vu} \in E(G)\}$.

Definition 3.2 Let G(*V*, *E*) be a graph, *H* is a subgraph of G and *N*(*v*) be neighbourhood of *v* in *V*. Then we define

(i) The lower approximation operation as follows: $L: P[V(G)] \to P[V(G)]$ such that, $L_N[V(H)] = \bigcup_{v \in V(G)} \{v | N(v) \subseteq V(H)\}$.

(ii) The upper approximation operation as follows: $U: P[V(G)] \to P[V(G)]$ such that, $U_N[V(H)] = \{N(v) : v \in V(H)\}$.

(iii) The boundary region is defined as $B_N[V(H)] = U_N[V(H)] - L_N[V(H)]$.

Definition 3.3 Let G be a graph, N(v) be neighbourhood of v in V and H be a subgraph of G, $\tau_N[V(H)] = \{V(G), \emptyset, L_N[V(H)], U_N[V(H)], B_N[V(H)]\}$ forms a topolgy on V(G) called the nanotopology on V(G) with respect to V(H). We call $[V(G), \tau_N[V(H)]]$ as the nanotopological space induced by a graph.

Example 3.4 Consider Figure 1.

Then $V(G) = \{V_1, V_2, V_3, V_4\}$ and $N(v_1) = \{V_1, V_2, V_3\}$, $N(v_2) = \{v_1, v_2, v_3\}$, $N(v_3) = \{v_3\}$, $N(v_4) = \{v_3, v_4\}$ and H be a subgraph of G, where $V(H) = \{V_2, V_3, V_4\}$, then $L_N[V(H)] = \{V_3, V_4\}$, $U_N[V(H)] = V(G)$, $B_N[V(H)] = \{V_1, V_2\}$. Therefore, the nanotopology induced by the graph is $\tau_N[V(H)] = \{V(G), \emptyset, \{V_3, V_4\}, \{V_1, V_2\}\}$ and let H be a subgraph of G, where $V(H) = \{V_1, V_2\}$ then $L_N[V(H)] = \{V_3\}$, $U_N[V(H)] = \{V_1, V_2, V_3\}$, $B_N[V(H)] = \{V_1, V_2\}$. Therefore, the nanotopology induced by the graph is $\tau_N[V(H)] = \{V(G), \emptyset, \{V_3\}, \{V_1, V_2, V_3\}, \{V_1, V_2\}\}$

THEOREM 3.5 *Let G[V, E] be a graph, H is a subgraph of G, then:*

(i) $L_N[V(H)] \subseteq V(H) \subseteq U_N[V(H)]$.

(ii) $L_N[V(G)] = V(G) = U_N[V(G)]$.

(iii) $L_N[\emptyset] = U_N[\emptyset] = \emptyset$.

THEOREM 3.6 *Let G[V, E] be a graph, H and K are two subgraphs of a graph G, then*

(a) If $V(H) \subseteq V(K)$ then $L_N[V(H)] \subseteq L_N[V(K)]$ and $U_N[V(H)] \subseteq U_N[V(K)]$.

(b) $L_N[V(H)] \cup L_N[V(K)] \subseteq L_N[V(H) \cup V(K)]$.

(c) $L_N[V(H) \cap V(K)] = L_N[V(H)] \cap L_N[V(K)]$.

(d) $U_N[V(H) \cup V(K)] = U_N[V(H)] \cup U_N[V(K)]$.

(e) $U_N[V(H) \cap V(K)] \subseteq U_N[V(H)] \cap U_N[V(K)]$.

Proof

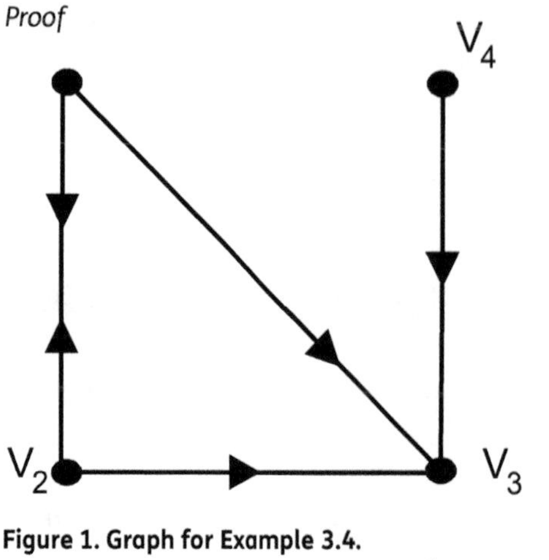

Figure 1. Graph for Example 3.4.

1

(a) Let $v \in L_N[V(H)]$. By definition of $L_N[V(H)]$, $N(v) \subseteq V(H)$, but $V(H) \subseteq V(K) \Rightarrow N(v) \subseteq V(H) \subseteq V(K)$ and hence $v \in L_N[V(K)]$. Since $v \in L_N[V(H)] \Rightarrow v \in L_N[V(K)]$. Therefore $L_N[V(H)] \subseteq L_N[V(K)]$. In a similar manner we can also prove that $U_N[V(H)] \subseteq U_N[V(K)]$.

(b) Since
$V[H] \subseteq V(H) \cup V(K),\ V[K] \subseteq V(H) \cup V(K),\ L_N[V(H)] \subseteq L_N[V(H) \cup V(K)],\ and\ L_N[V(K)] \subseteq L_N[V(H) \cup V(K)]$.
Therefore $L_N[V(H)] \cup L_N[V(K)] \subseteq L_N[V(H) \cup V(K)]$.

(c) Since $V(H) \cap V(K) \subseteq V(H),\ V(H) \cap V(K) \subseteq V(K),\ L_N[V(H) \cap V(K)] \subseteq L_N[V(H)]$ and $L_N[V(H) \cap V(K)] \subseteq L_N[V(K)]$. Therefore $L_N[V(H) \cap V(K)] \subseteq L_N[V(H)] \cap L_N[V(K)]$. Let $v \in L_N[V(H)] \cap L_N[V(K)] \Rightarrow v \in L_N[V(H)]\ and\ v \in L_N[V(K)]$. Hence by definition $N(v) \subseteq V(H)$ and $N(v) \subseteq V(K) \Rightarrow N(v) \subseteq V(H) \cap V(K)$. This means that $v \in L_N[V(H) \cap V(K)]$. Therefore $L_N[V(H)] \cup L_N[V(K)] \subseteq L_N[V(H) \cap V(K)]$. Hence, we conclude that $L_N[V(H)] \cap L_N[V(K)] = L_N[V(H) \cap V(K)]$.

(d) Since $V(H) \subseteq V(H) \cup V(K),\ V(K) \subseteq V(H) \cup V(K),\ U_N[V(H)] \subseteq U_N[V(H) \cup V(K)]$ and $U_N[V(K)] \subseteq U_N[V(H) \cup V(K)]$. Therefore $U_N[V(H)] \cup U_N[V(K)] \subseteq U_N[V(H) \cup V(K)]$. Let $v \in U_N[V(H) \cap V(K)]$, then by definition

$$x \in \bigcup\{N(v) : v \in [V(H) \cup V(K)]\} \Rightarrow x \in \bigcup\{N(v){:}v \in V(H)\}\ or\ x \in \bigcup\{N(v) : v \in V(K) \Rightarrow$$
$$x \in U_N[V(H)]\ or\ x \in U_N[V(K)] \Rightarrow x \in U_N[V(H)] \cup U_N[V(K)]$$

Therefore $U_N[V(H) \cup V(K)] \subseteq U_N[V(H)] \cup U_N[V(K)]$. Hence, we conclude that $U_N[V(H) \cup V(K)] = U_N[V(H)] \cup U_N[V(K)]$.

(e) Since $V(H) \cap V(K) \subseteq V(H),\ V(H) \cap V(K) \subseteq V(K),\ U_N[V(H) \cap V(K)] \subseteq U_N[V(H)]$ and $U_N[V(H) \cap V(K)] \subseteq U_N[V(K)]$. Therefore $U_N[V(H) \cap V(K)] \subseteq U_N[V(H)] \cap U_N[V(K)]$.□

Example 3.7 Consider Figure 2.

Then $V(G) = \{a, b, c, d, e\}$ and $N(a) = \{a, c\}$, $N(b) = \{a, b, c\}$, $N(c) = \{c, e\}$, $N(d) = \{a, d, e\}$. Table 1 shows the nanotopology of any subgraph H of a subgraph of G.

Remark 3.8 Let $G[V, E]$ be a graph, H and K are two subgraphs of G. Then from the examples 3.7 we can see some perception as follows:

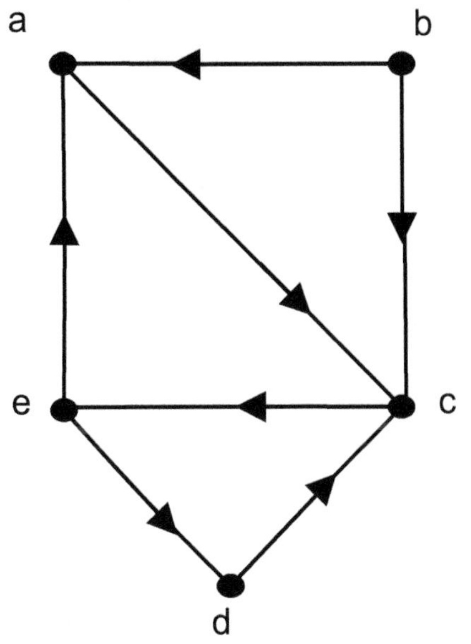

Figure 2. Graph for Example 3.7 and Remark 3.8.

Table 1. Nanotopology for the possible subgraphs of G

$V(H)$	$L_N[V(H)]$	$U_N[V(H)]$	$B_N[V(H)]$	$T_N[V(H)]$
$\{a\}$	$\emptyset$	$\{a,c\}$	$\{a,c\}$	$\{V(G),\emptyset,\{a,c\}\}$
$\{b\}$	$\emptyset$	$\{a,b,c\}$	$\{a,b,c\}$	$\{V(G),\emptyset,\{a,b,c\}\}$
$\{c\}$	$\emptyset$	$\{c,e\}$	$\{c,e\}$	$\{V(G),\emptyset,\{c,e\}\}$
$\{d\}$	$\emptyset$	$\{c,d\}$	$\{c,d\}$	$\{V(G),\emptyset,\{c,d\}\}$
$\{e\}$	$\emptyset$	$\{a,d,e\}$	$\{a,d,e\}$	$\{V(G),\emptyset,\{a,d,e\}\}$
$\{a,b\}$	$\emptyset$	$\{a,b,c\}$	$\{a,b,c\}$	$\{V(G),\emptyset,\{a,b,c\}\}$
$\{a,c\}$	$\{a\}$	$\{a,c,e\}$	$\{c,e\}$	$\{V(G),\emptyset,\{a\},\{a,c,e\},\{c,e\}\}$
$\{a,d\}$	$\emptyset$	$\{a,c,d\}$	$\{a,c,d\}$	$\{V(G),\emptyset,\{a,c,d\}\}$
$\{a,e\}$	$\emptyset$	$\{a,c,d,e\}$	$\{a,c,d,e\}$	$\{V(G),\emptyset,\{a,c,d,e\}\}$
$\{b,c\}$	$\emptyset$	$\{a,b,c,e\}$	$\{a,b,c,e\}$	$\{V(G),\emptyset,\{a,b,c,e\}\}$
$\{b,d\}$	$\emptyset$	$\{a,b,c,d\}$	$\{a,b,c,d\}$	$\{V(G),\emptyset,\{a,b,c,d\}\}$
$\{b,e\}$	$\emptyset$	$V(G)$	$V(G)$	$\{V(G),\emptyset\}$
$\{c,d\}$	$\{d\}$	$\{c,d,e\}$	$\{c,e\}$	$\{V(G),\emptyset,\{d\},\{c,d,e\},\{c,e\}\}$
$\{c,e\}$	$\{c\}$	$\{a,c,d,e\}$	$\{a,d,e\}$	$\{V(G),\emptyset,\{c\},\{a,c,d,e\},\{a,d,e\}\}$
$\{d,e\}$	$\emptyset$	$\{a,c,d,e\}$	$\{a,c,d,e\}$	$\{V(G),\emptyset,\{a,c,d,e\}\}$
$\{a,b,c\}$	$\{a,b\}$	$\{a,b,c,e\}$	$\{c,e\}$	$\{V(G),\emptyset,\{a,b\},\{a,b,c,e\},\{c,e\}\}$
$\{a,b,d\}$	$\emptyset$	$\{a,b,c,d\}$	$\{a,b,c,d\}$	$\{V(G),\emptyset,\{a,b,c,d\}\}$
$\{a,b,e\}$	$\emptyset$	$V(G)$	$V(G)$	$\{V(G),\emptyset\}$
$\{a,c,d\}$	$\{a,d\}$	$\{a,c,d,e\}$	$\{c,e\}$	$\{V(G),\emptyset,\{a,d\},\{a,c,d,e\},\{c,e\}\}$
$\{a,c,e\}$	$\{a,c\}$	$\{a,c,d,e\}$	$\{d,e\}$	$\{V(G),\emptyset,\{a,c\},\{a,c,d,e\},\{d,e\}\}$
$\{a,d,e\}$	$\{e\}$	$\{a,c,d,e\}$	$\{a,c,d\}$	$\{V(G),\emptyset,\{e\},\{a,c,d,e\},\{a,c,d\}\}$
$\{b,c,d\}$	$\{d\}$	$V(G)$	$\{a,b,c,e\}$	$\{V(G),\emptyset,\{d\},\{a,b,c,e\}\}$
$\{b,c,e\}$	$\{c\}$	$V(G)$	$\{a,d,e,d\}$	$\{V(G),\emptyset,\{c\},\{a,b,d,e\}\}$
$\{b,d,e\}$	$\emptyset$	$V(G)$	$V(G)$	$\{V(G),\emptyset\}$
$\{c,d,e\}$	$\{c,d\}$	$\{a,c,d,e\}$	$\{a,e\}$	$\{V(G),\emptyset,\{c,d\},\{a,c,d,e\},\{a,e\}\}$
$\{a,b,c,d\}$	$\{a,b,d\}$	$V(G)$	$\{c,e\}$	$\{V(G),\emptyset,\{a,b,d\},\{c,e\}\}$
$\{a,b,c,e\}$	$\{a,b,c\}$	$V(G)$	$\{d,e\}$	$\{V(G),\emptyset,\{a,b,c\},\{d,e\}\}$
$\{a,b,d,e\}$	$\{e\}$	$V(G)$	$\{a,b,c,e\}$	$\{V(G),\emptyset,\{e\},\{a,b,c,e\}\}$
$\{a,c,d,e\}$	$\{a,c,d,e\}$	$\{a,c,d,e\}$	$\emptyset$	$\{V(G),\emptyset,\{a,c,d,e\}\}$
$\{b,c,d,e\}$	$\{c,d\}$	$V(G)$	$\{a,b,e\}$	$\{V(G),\emptyset,\{c,d\},\{a,b,e\}\}$
$V(G)$	$V(G)$	$V(G)$	$\emptyset$	$\{V(G),\emptyset\}$
$\emptyset$	$\emptyset$	$\emptyset$	$\emptyset$	$\{V(G),\emptyset\}$

(i) $L[V(H)\cup V(K)] \not\subseteq L[V(H)]\cup L[V(K)]$, take $V(H)=\{a,b\}$ *and* $V(K)=\{c\}$.

(ii) $U[V(H)]\cap U[V(K)] \not\subseteq U[V(H)\cap V(K)]$, take $V(H)=\{a,d\}$ *and* $V(K)=\{a,e\}$.

(iii) $L[V(H)]^c \neq [U[V(H)]]^c$, take $V(H)=\{a\}$.

(iv) $U[V(H)]^c \neq [L[V(H)]]^c$, take $V(H)=\{a,b\}$.

(v) $U[U[V(H)]] \not\subseteq [U[V(H)]]$, take $V(H)=\{a\}$.

(vi) $U[V(H)] \not\subseteq L[U[V(H)]]$, take $V(H)=\{a,c\}$.

(vii) $L[U[V(H)]] \not\subseteq V(H)$, take $V(H)=\{b\}$.

(viii) $V(H) \not\subseteq U[L[V(H)]]$, take $V(H)=\{a\}$.

(ix) $U[L[V(H)]] \not\subseteq L[V(H)]$, take $V(H)=\{a,c\}$.

(x) $L[V(H)] \not\subseteq L[L[V(H)]]$, take $V(H) = \{a, c\}$.

THEOREM 3.9 *Let G[V, E], H is a subgraph of G, then* $U[L[V(H)]] \subseteq V(H) \subseteq L[U[V(H)]]$.

Proof Let $x \in U[L[V(H)]] \Rightarrow$ there exists a $v \in L[V(H)]$ such that $\overline{vx} \in E[G]$, therefore $x \in N(v) \subseteq V(H)$.

Now, since $x \in V(H)$, then $N(x) \subseteq U[V(H)]$ implies, $x \in L[U[V(H)]]$. □

THEOREM 3.10 *Let G[V,E], H is a subgraph of G, then*

(i) $L[U[L[V(H)]]] = L[V(H)]$.
(ii) $U[L[U[V(H)]]] = U[V(H)]$.

Proof

(i) Let $x \in L[V(H)] \Rightarrow$ $N(x) \subseteq U[L[V(H)]]$. So $x \in L[U[L[V(H)]]]$ we know that $U[L[V(H)]] \subseteq V(H)$, implies $L[U[L[V(H)]]] = L[V(H)]$.
(ii) we know that $U[L[V(H)]] \subseteq V(H)$ implies $U[L[U[V(H)]]] \subseteq U[V(H)]$ we know that $V(H) \subseteq L[U[[V(H)]]$ implies $U[L[U[V(H)]]] = U[V(H)]$. □

4. Formalizing structural equivalence

Here we are formalizing the structural equivalence for the graphs and their corresponding nanotopologies generated by them.

Remark 4.1 In this section we define graphical isomorphism is a related task for deciding when two graphs with different specifications are structurally equivalent, that is whether they have the same pattern of connections. Nanohomeomorphism between two nanotopological spaces are said to be topologically equivalent. Here we are formalizing the structural equivalence for the graphs and their corresponding nanotopologies generated by them.

Definition 4.2 (Hsu & Lin, 2008) Two digraphs *G* and *H* are isomorphic if there is an isomorphism *f* between their underlying graphs that preserves the direction of each edge. That is, e is directed from *u* to *v* if and only if *f*(e) is directed from *f*(*u*) to *f*(*v*).

Definition 4.3 (Hsu & Lin, 2008) Two digraphs *C* and *D* are isomorphic if *D* can be obtained by relabelling the vertices of *C*, that is, if there is a bijection between the vertices of *C* and those of *D*, such that the arcs joining each pair of vertices in *C* agree in both number and direction with the arcs joining the corresponding pair of vertices in *D*.

Definition 4.4 Let $(\mathcal{U}, \tau_R(X))$ and $(\mathcal{V}, \tau_{R'}(Y))$ be nanotopological spaces, then the mapping $f: (\mathcal{U}, \tau_R(X)) \to (\mathcal{V}, \tau_R(Y))$ is said to be a nanocontinuous on $\mathcal{U}$ if the inverse image of every nano-open set in $\mathcal{V}$ is nano-open in $\mathcal{U}$.

Definition 4.5 Let $(\mathcal{U}, \tau_R(X))$ and $(\mathcal{V}, \tau_{R'}(Y))$ be a nanotopological spaces, then the mapping $f: (\mathcal{U}, \tau_R(X)) \to (\mathcal{V}, \tau_R(Y))$ is said to be a nanohomeomorphism if

(i) *f* is 1–1 and onto
(ii) *f* is nanocontinuous
(iii) *f* is nano-open

Example 4.6 Let G = [V,E] and G' = [V', E'] be two isomorphic graphs, where $V = \{v_1, v_2, v_3, v_4\}$, $E = \{(v_1, v_2), (v_1, v_4), (v_2, v_4), (v_4, v_3), (v_3, v_2)\}$, $V' = \{u_1, u_2, u_3, u_4\}$ and $E' = \{(u_1, u_3), (u_2, u_1), (u_3, u_2), (u_4, u_1), (u_4, u_3)\}$.

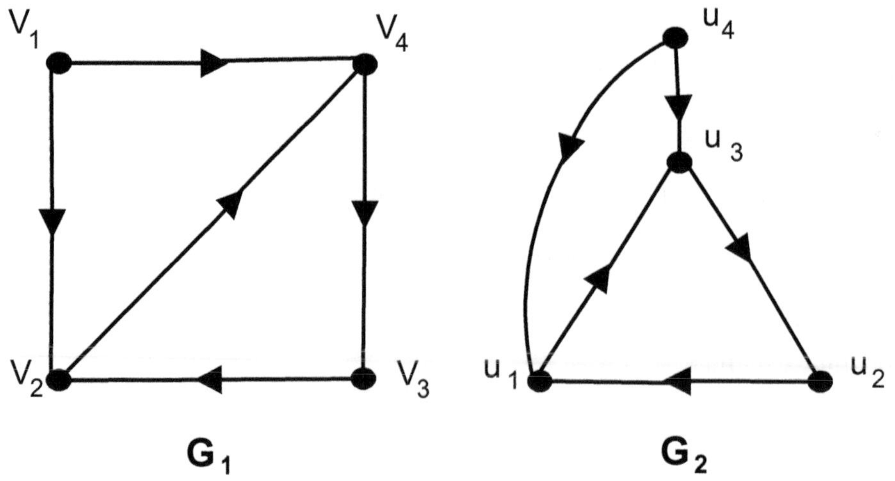

Figure 3. Isomorphic graphs.

Then there exists a function $f{:}V \to V'$ such that $f(v_1) = u_4, f(v_2) = u_1, f(v_3) = u_2, f(v_4) = u_3$. Let *H* be any subgraph of *G* and *V*(*H*) = $\{v_2, v_3\}$. Then the nanotopology generated by vertices of *V*(*H*) and *V*(*f*(*H*)) are $\tau_N[V(H)] = \{V(G), \emptyset, \{v_3\}, \{v_2, v_3, v_4\}, \{v_2, v_4\}\}$ and $\tau_N[f(V(H))] = \{V(G'), \emptyset, \{u_2\}, \{u_1, u_2, u_3\}, \{u_1, u_3\}\}$. Then the function $\phi : [V(G), \tau_N(V(H))] \to [V(G'), \tau_N(f(V(H))]$ is a homeomorphism (Figure 3).

THEOREM 4.7 *Let G = [V,E] and G' = [V',E'] be any two isomorphic graphs then there exists a homeomorphism* $\phi : [V(G), \tau_N(V(H))] \to [V(G'), \tau_N(f(V(H))]$ *for every subgraph H of G.*

Proof Since G and G' are isomorphic by defn. there is an isomorphism $f{:}\ V[G] \to V[G']$ between their uderlying graphs that preserves the direction of each edge and also *N*(*x*) = *N*(*f*(*x*)) $\forall x \in V(G)$. Suppose $[V(G), \tau_N(V(H))]$ and $[V(G'), \tau_N(f(V(H))]$ be the nanotopological space generated by *V*(*H*) and *f*(*V*(*H*)). Since f is a bijection clearly, it follows that ϕ is 1–1 and onto.

(i) To prove that ϕ is an open map. Let A be any nano-open set in $\tau_N(V(H))$, then $\phi(A)$ is nano-open since *N*(*x*) = *N*(*f*(*x*)) $\forall x \in A$.

(ii) To prove that ϕ is continuous. Let B be any nano-open set in $\tau_N(f(V(H))$, then $\phi^{-1}[B]$ is nano-open in $\tau_N[V(H)]$. Thus ϕ is a homeomorphism. □

5. Computer chip intellectual property rights

Based on the structural equivalence of graphs and the corresponding nanotopology induced by them, we have made an attempt to check whether the chip produced by a company have striking operational similarity produced by the another company.

Suppose that not long after Corporation $\mathcal{X}$ develops and markets a computer chip, it happens that the Corporation $\mathcal{Y}$ markets a chip with striking operational similarities. If Corporation $\mathcal{X}$ could prove that Corporation $\mathcal{Y}$'s circuit is merely a rearrangement of the Corporation $\mathcal{X}$ circuitry that is the circuitries are isomorphic], they might have the basis for a patent infringement suit.

Algorithm to detect patent infringement suit:

Step 1: Given the electrical circuit of the chips manufactured by two companies. An electrical network is an interconnection of electrical network elements such as resistances, capacitances, inductances, voltage and current sources, etc., We also assign reference direction by a directed edge results in the directed graph representing the network.

Step 2: Convert the electrical circuits C_1 and C_2 into graphs G_1 and G_2.

Step 3: Check whether G_1 and G_2 are isomorphic, and their corresponding nanotopologies induced from their vertices are homeomorphic.

Step 4: If $G_1 \cong G_2$ and $[V(G), \tau_N(V(H))] \approx [V(G'), \tau_N(f(V(H))]$ then the corresponding circuitries have striking operational similarities, and the company $\mathcal{X}$ can claim on the basis for a patent infringement suit.

Step 5: Otherwise, we can conclude that both the chip produced are entirely different.

Step 1: Consider the following basic circuit of the chip manufactured by two companies Corporation $\mathcal{X}$ and Corporation $\mathcal{Y}$. Using the above algorithm we can prove whether these two circuits have functional similarities via nanotopology induced by the vertices of its subgraphs (Figure 4).

Step 2: The graphs are good pictorial representations of circuits and capture all their structural characteristics. Transform the basic circuit C_1 and C_2 of the chip produced by Corporation $\mathcal{X}$ and Corporation $\mathcal{Y}$ into graphs $G_1 = [V_1, E_1]$ and $G_2 = [V_2, E_2]$, respectively (Figure 5).

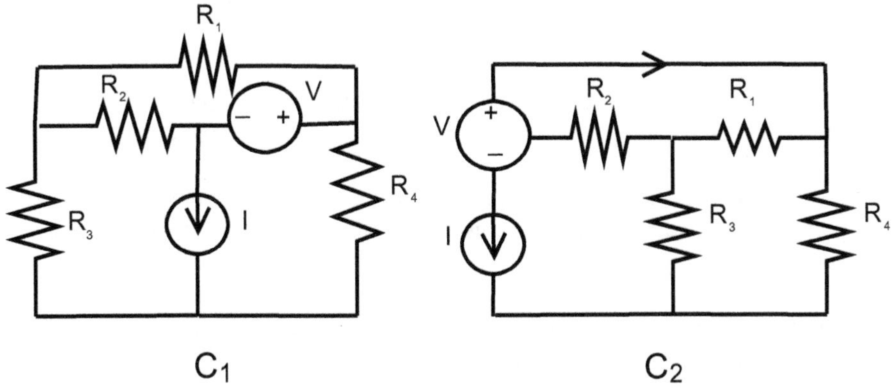

Figure 4. Electrical circuit of chips produced by *X* and *Y*.

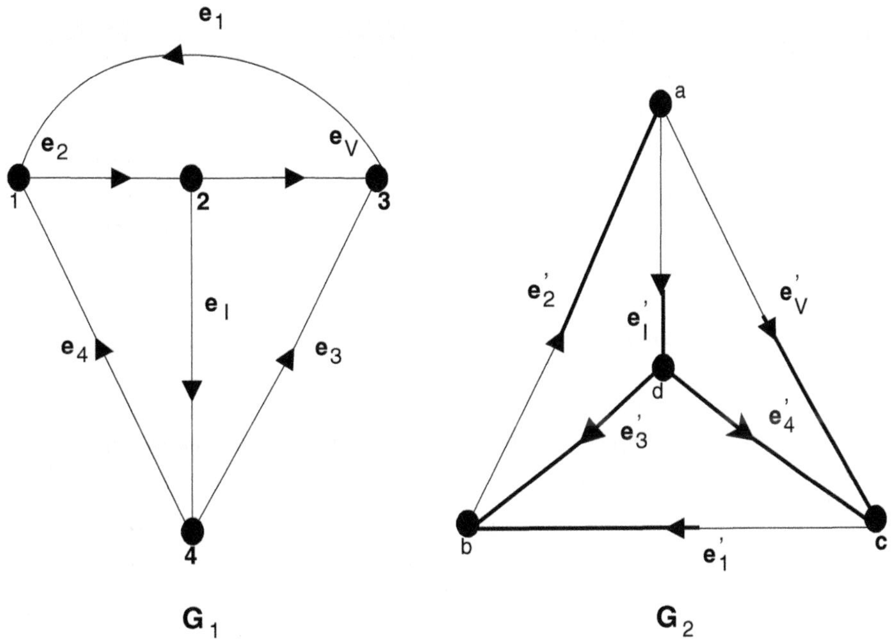

Figure 5. Graphs for circuit C_1 and circuit C_2.

Step 3: From the following graph we define a function $f\colon V_1 \to V_2$ such that f(1) = b, f(2) = a, f(3) = c, f(4) = d and clearly f is an isomorphism. Since G_2 can be obtained by relabelling the vertices of G_1, that is, f is a bijection between the vertices of G_1 and those of G_2, such that the arcs joining each pair of vertices in G_1 agree in both number and direction with the arcs joining the corresponding pair of vertices in G_2.

Then we also have to check ϕ:$[V(G), \tau_N(V(H))] \to [V(G'), \tau_N(f(V(H))]$ is a homeomorphism for every subgraph H of G.

Since f is a bijection clearly, it follows that ϕ is 1–1 and onto.

(i) To prove that ϕ is an open map.

Then the nanotopology generated by vertices of $V(H) = \{1,3\}$ and $V(f(H)) = \{b,c\}$ are $\tau_N[V(H)] = \{V(G_1), \emptyset, \{3\}, \{1,2,3\}, \{1,2\}\}$ and $\tau_N[f(V(H))] = \{V(G_2), \emptyset, \{c\}, \{a,b,c\}, \{a,b\}\}$.

Then the function

ϕ: $[V(G_1), \tau_N(V(H))] \to [V(G_2), \tau_N(f(V(H))]$ is a homeomorphism. This holds for every subgraph *H* of G_1 (Table 2).

Step 4: From the above process, we can conclude that the graph of the circuits and their corresponding nanotopologies generated by the vertices of the subgraphs are homeomorphic.

Step 5: Thus we can characterize that the chips manufactured by Corporation $\mathcal{Y}$ is just a rearrangement of Corporation $\mathcal{X}$ and also they have striking operational similarities and Corporation $\mathcal{X}$ can also claim for his patent infringement suit.

Observation: Using the above structural equivalence technique we can check whether two circuits are equivalent and we can also extend our theory in many industrial products for patent infringement suit.

Table 2. Nanotopolgy for *V*(*H*) and *f*(*V*(*H*))

V(H)	$\tau_N[V(H)]$	f[V(H)]	$\tau_N[f[V(H)]]$
$\{1\}$	$\{V(G_1), \emptyset, \{1,2\}\}$	$\{b\}$	$\{V(G_2), \emptyset, \{a,b\}\}$
$\{2\}$	$\{V(G_1), \emptyset, \{2,3,4\}\}$	$\{a\}$	$\{V(G_2), \emptyset, \{a,c,d\}\}$
$\{3\}$	$\{V(G_1), \emptyset, \{1,3\}\}$	$\{c\}$	$\{V(G_2), \emptyset, \{b,c\}\}$
$\{4\}$	$\{V(G_1), \emptyset, \{1,3,4\}\}$	$\{d\}$	$\{V(G_2), \emptyset, \{b,c,d\}\}$
$\{1,2\}\}$	$\{V(G_1), \emptyset, \{1\}, \{2,3,4\}\}$	$\{a,b\}$	$\{V(G_2), \emptyset, \{b\}, \{a,c,d\}$
$\{1,3\}$	$\{V(G_1), \emptyset, \{3\}, \{1,2,3\}, \{1,2\}\}$	$\{b,c\}$	$\{V(G_2), \emptyset, \{c\}, \{a,b,c\}, \{a,b\}\}$
$\{1,4\}$	$\{V(G_1), \emptyset\}$	$\{b,d\}$	$\{V(G_2), \emptyset\}$
$\{2,3\}$	$\{V(G_1), \emptyset\}$	$\{a,c\}$	$\{V(G_2), \emptyset\}$
$\{2,4\}$	$\{V(G_1), \emptyset\}$	$\{a,d\}$	$\{V(G_2), \emptyset\}$
$\{3,4\}$	$\{V(G_1), \emptyset, \{1,3,4\}\}$	$\{c,d\}$	$\{V(G_2), \emptyset, \{b,c,d\}\}$
$\{1,2,3\}$	$\{V(G_1), \emptyset, \{1,3\}, \{2,4\}\}$	$\{a,b,c\}$	$\{V(G_2), \emptyset, \{b,c\}, \{a,d\}\}$
$\{2,3,4\}$	$\{V(G_1), \emptyset, \{2\}, \{1,3,4\}\}$	$\{a,c,d\}$	$\{V(G_2), \emptyset, \{a\}, \{b,c,d\}\}$
$\{1,3,4\}$	$\{V(G_1), \emptyset, \{3,4\}, \{1,2\}\}$	$\{b,c,d\}$	$\{V(G_2), \emptyset, \{c,d\}, \{a,b\}, \{a,b\}\}$
$\{4,1,2\}$	$\{V(G_1), \emptyset, \{1\}, \{2,3,4\}\}$	$\{a,b,d\}$	$\{V(G_2), \emptyset, \{b\}, \{a,c,d\}\}$
$V(G_1)$	$\{V(G_1), \emptyset\}$	$V(G_2)$	$\{V(G_2), \emptyset\}$
$\emptyset$	$\{V(G_1), \emptyset\}$	$\emptyset$	$\{V(G_2), \emptyset\}$

6. Conclusion

The purpose of the present work was to put a starting point for the application of nanotopology via graph theory. We believe that nanotopological graph structure will be an important base for modification of knowledge extraction and processing.

Funding
The authors received no direct funding for this research.

Author details
M. Lellis Thivagar[1]
E-mail: mlthivagar@yahoo.co.in
Paul Manuel[2]
E-mail: pauldmanuel@gmail.com
V. Sutha Devi[1]
E-mail: vsdsutha@yahoo.co.in
[1] School of Mathematics, Madurai Kamaraj University, Madurai 625021, Tamil Nadu, India.
[2] Department of Information Science, College of Computing Sciences and Engineering, Kuwait University, Kuwait, Kuwait.

References

Bonikowski, Z., Bryniarski, E., & Wybraniec, U. (1998). Extensions and intentions in the rough set theory. *Information Sciences, 107*, 149–167.

Deseor, C. A., & Kuh, E. S. (2009). *Basic circuit theory*. Tata McGraw-Hill: Berkeley, CA.

Diestel, R. (2010). *Graph theory II*. Heidelberg: Springer-Verlag IV.

Hsu, L. H., & Lin, C. K. (2008). *Graph theory and interconnection networks*. CRC Press.

Jensen, R., & Shen, Q. (2007). Fuzzy-rough sets assisted attribute selection. *IEEE Transactions on Fuzzy System, 15*, 73–89.

Lellis Thivagar, M., & Richard, C. (2013a). On nano forms of weakly open sets. *International Journal of Mathematics and Statistics, 1*, 31–37. Retrieved from www.ijmsi.org [version 0.11e0111031037].

Lellis Thivagar, M., & Richard, C. (2013b). On nano continuity. *Journal of Mathematical Theory and Modelling, 3*, 32–37.

12

Two-sided bounds on some output-related quantities in linear stochastically excited vibration systems with application of the differential calculus of norms

L. Kohaupt[1*]

*Corresponding author: L. Kohaupt, Department of Mathematics, Beuth University of Technology Berlin, Luxemburger Str. 10, D-13353 Berlin, Germany

E-mail: kohaupt@beuth-hochschule.de

Reviewing editor: Cedric K.F. Yiu, Hong Kong Polytechnic University, Hong Kong

Abstract: A linear stochastic vibration model in state-space form, $\dot{x}(t) = Ax(t) + b(t),\ x(0) = x_0$, with output equation $x_S(t) = Sx(t)$ is investigated, where A is the system matrix and b(t) is the white noise excitation. The output equation $x_S(t) = Sx(t)$ can be viewed as a transformation of the state vector x(t) that is mapped by the rectangular matrix S into the output vector $x_s(t)$. It is known that, under certain conditions, the solution $x(t)$ is a random vector that can be completely described by its mean vector, $m_x(t) := m_{x(t)}$, and its covariance matrix, $P_x(t) := P_{x(t)}$. If matrix A is asymptotically stable, then $m_x(t) \rightarrow 0\ (t \rightarrow \infty)$ and $P_{x_S}(t) \rightarrow P_S\ (t \rightarrow \infty)$, where P_S is a positive (semi-)definite matrix. Similar results will be derived for some output-related quantities. The obtained results are of special interest to applied mathematicians and engineers.

Subjects: Applied Mathematics; Computer Mathematics; Dynamical Systems; Engineering & Technology; Mathematics & Statistics; Science; Technology

Keywords: linear stochastic vibration system excited by white noise with output equation; output-related mean vector; output-related covariance matrix; two-sided bounds; differential calculus of norms

AMS subject classifications: 34D05; 34F05; 65L05

ABOUT THE AUTHOR

Ludwig Kohaupt received the equivalent to the master's degree (Diplom-Mathematiker) in Mathematics in 1971 and the equivalent to the PhD (Dr.phil.nat.) in 1973 from the University of Frankfurt/Main. From 1974 until 1979, Kohaupt was a teacher in Mathematics and Physics at a Secondary School. During that time (from 1977 until 1979), he was also an auditor at the Technical University of Darmstadt in Engineering Subjects, such as Mechanics, and especially Dynamics. From 1979 until 1990, he joined the Mercedes-Benz car company in Stuttgart as a Computational Engineer, where he worked in areas such as Dynamics (vibration of car models), Cam Design, Gearing, and Engine Design. Then, in 1990, Dr. Kohaupt combined his preceding experiences by taking over a professorship at the Beuth University of Technology Berlin (formerly known as TFH Berlin). He retired on April 01, 2014.

PUBLIC INTEREST STATEMENT

When a dynamical system with solution vector x of length n describes an engineering problem, only a few components of x are needed, as a rule. But, nevertheless, the whole pertinent initial value problem must be solved. In order to obtain only the components of interest, one defines an output matrix, say S, that selects them from x by defining the new output vector $x_S := Sx$ showing its importance. This equation is called output equation. For example, if the engineer wants to apply only the first, second, and nth component, then one defines S as $S = [e_1, e_2, e_n]^T$ where e_i means the ith unit vector for $i = 1, 2, n$.

In the present paper, new two-sided estimates on the mean vector and covariance matrix pertinent to the output vector x_S in linear stochastically excited vibration systems are derived that parallel those associated with x obtained recently.

1. Introduction

In order to make the paper more easily readable for a large readership, we first introduce the notions of *output vector* and *output equation* common to engineers. When a dynamical system with solution vector x of length n describes an engineering problem, only a few components of x are needed, as a rule. But, nevertheless, the whole pertinent initial value problem must be solved. In order to obtain only the components of interest, one defines an output or transformation matrix, say S, that selects them from x by defining the output $x_S := Sx$. This equation is called output equation. For example, if the engineer wants to use only the first, second, and nth component, then one defines S as $S = [e_1, e_2, e_n]^T$ where e_i means the ith unit vector for $i = 1, 2, n$. In other words, by employing the output equation $x_S = Sx$, a subset of components can be selected from the whole set of degrees of freedom which is usually necessary in practice. Of course, one can also define S such that it forms linear combinations of components of x. Whereas, in the preceding paper Kohaupt (2015b), the whole vector x was analyzed, in the present paper, it is replaced by the output x_S. The given comments on x_S show why this is important.

In this paper, a linear stochastic vibration model of the form $\dot{x}(t) = Ax(t) + b(t),\ x(0) = x_0$, with output equation $x_S(t) = Sx(t)$ is investigated, where A is a real *system matrix, b(t) white noise excitation*, and x_0 an initial vector that can be completely characterized by its mean vector m_0 and its covariance matrix P_0. Likewise, the solution $x(t)$, also called *response*, is a random vector that can be described by its mean vector $m_x(t) := m_{x(t)}$, and its covariance matrix, $P_x(t) := P_{x(t)}$. For asymptotically stable matrices A, it is known that $m_x(t) \to 0\ (t \to \infty)$ and $P_x(t) \to P\ (t \to \infty)$, where P is a positive (semi-)definite matrix. Similarly, for the output or transformed quantity $x_S(t)$, one has $m_{x_S}(t) \to 0\ (t \to \infty)$ and $P_{x_S}(t) \to P_S\ (t \to \infty)$ with a positive (semi-)definite matrix P_S. The asymptotic behavior of $m_x(t)$ and $P_x(t) - P$ was studied in Kohaupt (2015b).

In this paper, we investigate the asymptotic behavior of $m_{x_S}(t)$ and $P_{x_S}(t) - P_S$. As appropriate norms for the investigation of this problem, again the Euclidean norm for $m_{x_S}(t)$ and the spectral norm for $P_{x_S}(t) - P_S$ is the respective natural choice; both norms are denoted by $\|\cdot\|_2$.

The *main new points* of the paper are

- the determination of two-sided bounds on $m_{x_S}(t)$ and $P_{x_S}(t) - P_S$,
- the derivation of formulas for the right norm derivatives $D_+^k \|P_{x_S}(t) - P_S\|_2,\ k = 0, 1, 2$, and
- the application of these results to the computation of the best constants in the two-sided bounds.
- Special attention is paid to conditions ensuring the positiveness of the constants in the lower bounds when S is only rectangular and not square regular.

The paper is structured as follows.

In Section 2, the linear stochastically excited vibration model with output equation is presented. Then, in Section 3, the transformed quantities $m_{x_S}(t)$ and $P_{x_S}(t) - P_S$ are determined from $m_x(t)$ and $P_x(t) - P$, respectively, by appropriate use of the output matrix S as transformation matrix. Section 4 derives two-sided bounds on $x_S(t) = Sx(t)$ with $\dot{x}(t) = Ax(t),\ x(0) = x_0$, as a preparation to derive two-sided bounds on $m_{x_S}(t)$ in Section 6. Section 5 determines two-sided bounds on $\Phi_S(t) := S\Phi(t)$ with $\dot{\Phi}(t) = A\Phi(t),\ \Phi(0) = E$, as a preparation to derive two-sided bounds on $P_{x_S}(t) - P_S$ in Section 7. Section 8 studies the local regularity of $P_{x_S}(t) - P_S$. Then in Section 9, as the main result, formulas for the right norm derivatives $D_+^k \|P_{x_S}(t) - P_S\|_2,\ k = 0, 1, 2$ are obtained. Section 10, for the specified data in the stochastically exited model, presents applications, where the differential calculus of norms is employed by computing the best constants in the new two-sided bounds on $m_{x_S}(t)$ and $P_{x_S}(t) - P_S$. In Section 11, conclusions are drawn. The Appendix A contains sufficient algebraic conditions that ensure the positiveness of the constants in the lower bounds when S is only rectangular and not square regular. Finally, we comment on the References. The author's papers on the differential calculus of norms are contained in Kohaupt (1999, 2001, 2002,2003, 2004a, 2004b, 2005, 2006, 2007a, 2007b, 2007c, 2008a, 2008b, 2008c, 2008d, 2009a, 2009b, 2009c, 2010a, 2010b, 2011, 2012, 2013, 2015a, 2015b). The articles Bhatia and Elsner (2003), Benner, Denißen, and Kohaupt (2013,2016), and Whidborne and Amer (2011) refer to some of the author's works. The publications Coppel (1965), Dahlquist (1959), Desoer and Haneda (1972), Hairer, Nørset, and Wanner (1993), Higueras and García-Celayeta (1999,2000), Hu and Hu (2000), Lozinskiĭ (1958), Pao (1973a,1973b), Söderlind and Mattheij (1985), Ström (1972,1975) contain subjects on the logarithmic norm which was the starting point of the author's development of the differential calculus of norms. The References Bickley and McNamee (1960), Kučera (1974), and Ma (1966) were important for the author's article on the equation $VA + A^*V = \mu V$ in Kohaupt (2008a). The publications Achieser and Glasman (1968), Heuser (1975), Kantorovich and Akilov (1982), Kato (1966), and Taylor (1958) are textbooks on functional analysis useful, for instance, in the proofs of the theorems in Section 5. The books Golub and van Loan (1989), Niemeyer and Wermuth (1987), and Stummel and Hainer (1980) contain chapters on Matrix Theory and Numerical Mathematics valuable in connection with the subject of the present paper. The books Müller and Schiehlen (1985), Thomson and Dahleh (1998), and Waller (1975) are on engineering dynamical systems. In paper Guyan (1965), a reduction method for stiffness and mass matrices is discussed, a method that is still in use nowadays. Last, but not least, Kloeden and Platen (1992) is a standard book on the numerical solution of stochastic differential equations.

2. The linear stochastically excited vibration system with output equation

In order to make the paper as far as possible self-contained, we summarize the known facts on linear stochastically excited systems. In the presentation, we closely follow the line of Müller and Schiehlen (1985, Sections 9.1 and 9.2).

So, let us depart from the *deterministic model in state-space form*

$$\dot{x}(t) = Ax(t) + b(t),\ t > 0,\ x(0) = x_0, \tag{1}$$

$$x_S(t) = Sx(t) \tag{2}$$

with *system matrix* $A \in \mathbb{R}^{n\times n}$, the *state vector* $x(t) \in \mathbb{R}^n$ and the *excitation vector* $b(t) \in \mathbb{R}^n,\ t \geq 0$, the *output matrix* $S \in \mathbb{R}^{l\times n}$, and the *output vector* $x_S(t)$. We call (2) *output equation*. It can be understood as a transformation making of $x(t)$ the *transformed quantity* $x_S(t)$ by applying the transformation matrix S to $x(t)$.

Now, we replace the deterministic excitation $b(t)$ by a *stochastic excitation* in the form of *white noise*. Thus, $b(t)$ can be completely described by the *mean vector* $m_b(t)$ and the *central correlation matrix* $N_b(t,\tau)$ with

$$\begin{aligned} m_b(t) &= 0, \\ N_b(t,\tau) &= Q\,\delta(t-\tau), \end{aligned} \tag{3}$$

where $Q = Q_b$ is the $n \times n$*intensity matrix* of the excitation and $\delta(t-\tau)$ the δ-function (more precisely, the δ-functional).

From the central correlation matrix, for $\tau = t$ one obtains the positive semi-definite *covariance matrix*

$$P_b(t) := N_b(t,t). \tag{4}$$

At this point, we mention that the definition of a real positive semi-definite matrix includes its symmetry.

When the excitation is white noise, the deterministic initial value problem (1) can be formally maintained as the theory of linear stochastic differential equations shows. However, the initial state x_0 must be introduced as Gaussian random vector,

$$x_0 \sim (m_0, P_0), \tag{5}$$

which is to be independent of the excitation; here, the sign $\sim$ means that the initial state x_0 is completely described by its mean vector m_0 and its covariance matrix P_0. More precisely: x_0 is a Gaussian random vector whose density function is completely determined by m_0 and P_0 alone.

The *stochastic response* of the system (1) is formally given by

$$x(t) = \Phi(t)x_0 + \int_0^t \Phi(t-\tau)b(\tau)d\tau, \tag{6}$$

where – besides the fundamental matrix $\Phi(t) = e^{At}$ and the initial vector x_0– a stochastic integral occurs.

It can be shown that the stochastic response $x(t)$ is a non-stationary Gauss–Markov process that can be described by the mean vector $m_x(t) := m_{x(t)}$ and the correlation matrix $N_x(t,\tau) := N_{(x(t),x(\tau))}$. For $\tau = t$, we get the covariance matrix $P_x(t) := P_{x(t)}$.

If the system is asymptotically stable, the properties of first and second order for the stochastic response $x(t)$ we need are given by

$$m_x(t) = \Phi(t)m_0, \tag{7}$$
$$P_x(t) = \Phi(t)(P_0 - P)\Phi^T(t) + P, \tag{8}$$

where the positive semi-definite $n \times n$ matrix P satisfies the *Lyapunov matrix equation*

$$AP + PA^T + Q = 0.$$

This is a special case of the matrix equation $AX + XB = C$, whose solution can be obtained by a method of Ma (1966). For the special case of diagonalizable matrices A and B, this is shortly described in Kohaupt (2015b, Appendix A.1).

For asymptotically stable matrices A, one has $\lim_{t\to\infty} \Phi(t) = 0$ and thus by (7) and (8),

$$\lim_{t\to\infty} m_x(t) = 0 \tag{9}$$

and

$$\lim_{t\to\infty} P_x(t) = P. \tag{10}$$

In Kohaupt (2015b), we have investigated the asymptotic behavior of $m_x(t)$ and $P_x(t) - P$.

In this paper, we want to derive formulas for $m_{x_s}(t)$ and $P_{x_s}(t)$ corresponding to those of (7) and (8) and study their asymptotic behavior. This will be done in the next five sections, that is, in Sections 3–7.

3. The output-related quantities $m_{x_s}(t)$ and $P_{x_s}(t)$

In this section, we determine the output-related quantities $m_{x_s}(t)$ and $P_{x_s}(t)$ from the corresponding quantities $m_x(t)$ and $P_x(t)$ by appropriate use of the output matrix S as the transformation matrix.

The results of this section are known to mechanical engineers, but are added for the sake of completeness, especially for mathematicians.

One obtains the following lemma.

LEMMA 1 *(Formulas for $m_{x_S}(t)$ and $P_{x_S}(t)$)*

Let $S \in \mathbb{R}^{l \times n}$ and $x(t)$ the solution vector of (1). Further, let $x_S(t)$ be given by (2), i.e.

$$x_S(t) = Sx(t).$$

Then, one has

$$m_{x_S}(t) = \Phi_S(t)m_0, \tag{11}$$

$$P_{x_S}(t) = SP_x(t)S^T = \Phi_S(t)(P_0 - P)\Phi_S^T(t) + P_S, \tag{12}$$

with

$$\Phi_S(t) := S\Phi(t) \tag{13}$$

and

$$P_S := SPS^T. \tag{14}$$

Proof

(i) One has

$$m_{x_S}(t) = E(x_S(t)) = E(Sx(t)) = S(E(x(t)) = Sm_x(t),$$

where here E denotes the expectation of a random vector. Using (7), this leads to (11).

(ii) Next, we show that, for the central *correlation matrices* $N_x(t,\tau)$ and $N_{x_S}(t,\tau)$, the identity

$$N_{x_S}(t,\tau) = SN_x(t,\tau)S^T \tag{15}$$

holds. This is because

$$\begin{aligned}
N_{x_S}(t,\tau) &= E\{[x_S(t) - m_{x_S}(t)][x_S(\tau) - m_{x_S}(\tau)]^T\} \\
&= E\{S[x(t) - m_x(t)][S(x(\tau) - m_x(\tau))]^T\} \\
&= E\{S[x(t) - m_x(t)][x(\tau) - m_x(\tau)]^T S^T\} \\
&= SE\{[x(t) - m_x(t)][x(\tau) - m_x(\tau)]^T\}S^T \\
&= SN_x(t,\tau)S^T.
\end{aligned}$$

Thus, (15) is proven. Setting $\tau = t$, this implies

$$P_{x_S}(t) = SP_x(t)S^T. \tag{16}$$

Taking into account (8), this leads to (12).

Remark: Let the system matrix A be asymptotically stable. Then, $\Phi(t) \to 0$, $(t \to \infty)$ and thus from (12) and (13),

$$\lim_{t\to\infty} \Phi_S(t) = 0$$

as well as

$$\lim_{t\to\infty} P_{x_S}(t) = P_S.$$ □

4. Two-sided bounds on $x_S(t) = Sx(t)$ with $\dot{x}(t) = Ax(t),\ x(t_0) = x_0$,

In this section, we discuss the deterministic case $x_S(t) = Sx(t)$ with $\dot{x}(t) = Ax(t),\ x(t_0) = x_0$, as a preparation for Section 6. There, two-sided bounds on $m_{x_S}(t)$ will be given based on those for $x_S(t)$ here.

For the positiveness of the constants in the lower bounds, we discuss two cases: the special case when matrix A is diagonalizable and the case of a general square matrix A.

Let $S \in \mathbb{C}^{l\times n}$ and

$$x_S(t) = Sx(t). \tag{17}$$

We obtain

THEOREM 2 *(Two-sided bound on $x_S(t) = Sx(t)$ by $e^{\nu_{x_0}[A](t-t_0)}$)*

Let $A \in \mathbb{C}^{n\times n}, 0 \neq x_0 \in \mathbb{C}^n$, and $x(t)$ be the solution of the initial value problem $\dot{x}(t) = Ax(t),\ x(t_0) = x_0$. Let $\|\cdot\|$ be any vector norm.

Then, there exists a constant $X_{S,0} \geq 0$ and for every $\varepsilon > 0$ a constant $X_{S,1}(\varepsilon) > 0$ such that

$$X_{S,0}\, e^{\nu_{x_0}[A](t-t_0)} \leq \|x_S(t)\| \leq X_{S,1}(\varepsilon)\, e^{(\nu_{x_0}[A]+\varepsilon)(t-t_0)},\ t \geq t_0, \tag{18}$$

where $\nu_{x_0}[A]$ is the spectral abscissa of A with respect to x_0.

If A is diagonalizable, then $\varepsilon = 0$ may be chosen, and we write $X_{S,1}$ instead of $X_{S,1}(\varepsilon = 0)$.

If S is square and regular, then $X_{S,0} > 0$.

Proof One has

$$0\,\|x(t)\| \leq \|x_S(t)\| \leq \|S\|\,\|x(t)\|. \tag{19}$$

Further, according to Kohaupt (2006, Theorem 8), there exists a constant $X_0 > 0$ and for every $\varepsilon > 0$ a constant $X_1(\varepsilon) > 0$ such that

$$X_0\, e^{\nu_{x_0}[A](t-t_0)} \leq \|x(t)\| \leq X_1(\varepsilon)\, e^{(\nu_{x_0}[A]+\varepsilon)(t-t_0)},\ t \geq t_0. \tag{20}$$

Combining (19) and (20) leads to (18) with $X_{S,0} = 0$.

Further, if S is square and regular, then instead of (19) we get

$$1/\|S^{-1}\|\,\|x(t)\| \leq \|x_S(t)\| \leq \|S\|\,\|x(t)\|. \tag{21}$$

Thus, apparently, $X_{S,0} = X_0/\|S^{-1}\| > 0$ can be chosen in (18). □

An interesting and important question is under what conditions the constant $X_{S,0}$ is positive when S is only rectangular, but not necessarily square and regular. To assert that $X_{S,0}$ is positive, additional conditions have to be imposed. We consider two cases.

Case 1: Diagonalizable matrix A In this case, we need the following *hypotheses on A* from Kohaupt (2011, Section 3.1).

(H1) $m = 2n$ and $A \in I\!R^{m \times m}$,

(H2) $T^{-1}AT = J = diag(\lambda_k)_{k=1,\dots,m}$, where $\lambda_k = \lambda_k(A)$, $k = 1, \dots, m$ are the eigenvalues of A,

(H3) $\lambda_i = \lambda_i(A) \neq 0,\ i = 1, \dots, m$,

(H4) $\lambda_i \neq \lambda_j,\ i \neq j,\ i,j = 1, \dots, m$,

(HS) the eigenvectors $p_1, \dots, p_n; \bar{p}_1, \dots, \bar{p}_n$ form a basis of $I\!C^m$.

As a preparation to the subsequent derivations, we collect some definitions resp. notations and representations for the solution vector $x(t)$ from Kohaupt (2006, 2011).

Representation of the basis $x_k^{(r)}(t), x_k^{(i)}(t),\ k = 1, \dots, n$

Under the hypotheses (*H1*), (*H2*), and (*HS*), from Kohaupt (2011), we obtain the following *real basis functions* for the ODE $\dot{x} = A\,x$:

$$\begin{aligned} x_k^{(r)}(t) &= e^{\lambda_k^{(r)}(t-t_0)}\left[\cos \lambda_k^{(i)}(t-t_0)p_k^{(r)} - \sin \lambda_k^{(i)}(t-t_0)p_k^{(i)}\right], \\ x_k^{(i)}(t) &= e^{\lambda_k^{(r)}(t-t_0)}\left[\sin \lambda_k^{(i)}(t-t_0)p_k^{(r)} + \cos \lambda_k^{(i)}(t-t_0)p_k^{(i)}\right], \end{aligned} \tag{22}$$

$k = 1, \dots, n$, where

$k = 1, \dots, m = 2n$ are the decompositions of λ_k and p_k into their real and imaginary parts. As in

$$\begin{aligned} \lambda_k &= \lambda_k^{(r)} + i\lambda_k^{(i)} = Re\,\lambda_k + i\,Im\,\lambda_k, \\ p_k &= p_k^{(r)} + ip_k^{(i)} = Re\,p_k + i\,Im\,p_k, \end{aligned}$$

Kohaupt (2011), the indices are chosen such that $\lambda_{n+k} = \bar{\lambda}_k, p_{n+k} = \bar{p}_k,\ k = 1, \dots, n$.

The spectral abscissa of A with respect to the initial vector $x_0 \in I\!R^n$ Let, $u_k^*,\ k = 1, \dots, m = 2n$ be the eigenvectors of A^* corresponding to the eigenvalues $\bar{\lambda}_k,\ k = 1, \dots, m = 2n$. Under (*H1*), (*H2*), and (*HS*), the solution $x(t)$ of (1) has the form

$$x(t) = \sum_{k=1}^{m=2n} c_{1k}p_k e^{\lambda_k(t-t_0)} = \sum_{k=1}^{n}\left[c_{1k}p_k e^{\lambda_k(t-t_0)} + c_{2k}\bar{p}_k e^{\bar{\lambda}_k(t-t_0)}\right] \tag{23}$$

with uniquely determined coefficients $c_{1k},\ k = 1, \dots, m = 2n$. Using the relations

$$c_{2k} = c_{1,n+k} = \bar{c}_{1k},\ k = 1, \dots, n, \tag{24}$$

(see Kohaupt, 2011, Section 3.1 for the last relation), then according to Kohaupt (2011), the *spectral abscissa of A with respect to the initial vector* $x_0 \in I\!R^n$ is given by

$$\begin{aligned} \nu_0 := \nu_{x_0}[A] := &\max_{k=1,\dots,m=2n} \{\lambda_k^{(r)}(A) \mid x_0 \not\perp u_k^*\} \\ = &\max_{k=1,\dots,m=2n} \{\lambda_k^{(r)}(A) \mid c_{1k} \neq 0\} \\ = &\max_{k=1,\dots,n} \{\lambda_k^{(r)}(A) \mid c_{1k} \neq 0\} \\ = &\max_{k=1,\dots,n} \{\lambda_k^{(r)}(A) \mid x_0 \not\perp u_k^*\} \end{aligned} \tag{25}$$

Index sets In the sequel, we need the following index sets:

$$J_{v_0} := \{k_0 \in \mathbb{N} | 1 \le k_0 \le n \text{ and } \lambda_{k_0}^{(r)}(A) = v_0\} \tag{26}$$

and

$$\begin{aligned} J_{v_0}^- &:= \{1, \dots, n\} \setminus J_{v_0} \\ &= \{k_0^- \in \mathbb{N} \mid 1 \le k_0^- \le n \text{ and } \lambda_{k_0^-}^{(r)}(A) < v_0\}. \end{aligned} \tag{27}$$

Appropriate representation of $x(t)$ We have

$$x(t) = \sum_{k=1}^{n} [c_k^{(r)} x_k^{(r)}(t) + c_k^{(i)} x_k^{(i)}(t)] \tag{28}$$

with

$$c_k^{(r)} = 2\,Re\, c_{1k}, \quad c_k^{(i)} = -2\,Im\, c_{1k}, \quad k = 1, \dots, n$$

(cf. Kohaupt, 2011). Thus, due to (28) and (22),

$$x(t) = \sum_{k=1}^{n} e^{\lambda_k^{(r)}(t-t_0)} f_k(t) \tag{29}$$

with

$k = 1, \cdots, n.$

$$\begin{aligned} f_k(t) := c_k^{(r)}\, &[\cos \lambda_k^{(i)}(t-t_0) p_k^{(r)} - \sin \lambda_k^{(i)}(t-t_0) p_k^{(i)}] \\ + c_k^{(i)}\, &[\sin \lambda_k^{(i)}(t-t_0) p_k^{(r)} + \cos \lambda_k^{(i)}(t-t_0) p_k^{(i)}], \end{aligned} \tag{30}$$

Appropriate representation of $y(t)$ *and* $\dot{y}(t)$*(needed in the Appendix)* Let

$$p_k := \begin{bmatrix} q_k \\ r_k \end{bmatrix} \quad p_k^{(r)} := \begin{bmatrix} q_k^{(r)} \\ r_k^{(r)} \end{bmatrix}, \quad p_k^{(i)} := \begin{bmatrix} q_k^{(i)} \\ r_k^{(i)} \end{bmatrix}, \tag{31}$$

with $q_k, r_k \in \mathbb{C}^n, q_k^{(r)}, r_k^{(r)}, q_k^{(i)}, r_k^{(i)} \in \mathbb{R}^n, k = 1, \dots, m = 2n$. Then, from (29), (30),

$$y(t) = \sum_{k=1}^{n} e^{\lambda_k^{(r)}(t-t_0)} g_k(t) \tag{32}$$

with

$$\begin{aligned} g_k(t) := c_k^{(r)}\, &[\cos \lambda_k^{(i)}(t-t_0) q_k^{(r)} - \sin \lambda_k^{(i)}(t-t_0) q_k^{(i)}] \\ + c_k^{(i)}\, &[\sin \lambda_k^{(i)}(t-t_0) q_k^{(r)} + \cos \lambda_k^{(i)}(t-t_0) q_k^{(i)}], \end{aligned} \tag{33}$$

$k = 1, \dots, n$ as well as

$$z(t) = \dot{y}(t) = \sum_{k=1}^{n} e^{\lambda_k^{(r)}(t-t_0)} h_k(t) \tag{34}$$

with

$$
\begin{aligned}
k &= 1, \ldots, n. \\
h_k(t) &:= c_k^{(r)} [\cos \lambda_k^{(i)}(t - t_0) r_k^{(r)} - \sin \lambda_k^{(i)}(t - t_0) r_k^{(i)}] \\
&\quad + c_k^{(i)} [\sin \lambda_k^{(i)}(t - t_0) r_k^{(r)} + \cos \lambda_k^{(i)}(t - t_0) r_k^{(i)}],
\end{aligned} \tag{35}
$$

Herewith, one obtains

$$
\begin{aligned}
\|x_S(t)\| = \|Sx(t)\| &= \| \sum_{k=1}^{n} e^{\lambda_k^{(r)}(t-t_0)} Sf_k(t) \| \\
&\geq \| \sum_{k \in J_{v_0}} e^{\lambda_k^{(r)}(t-t_0)} Sf_k(t) \| - \| \sum_{k \in J_{v_0}^-} e^{\lambda_k^{(r)}(t-t_0)} Sf_k(t) \| \\
&= \| \sum_{k \in J_{v_0}} Sf_k(t) \| \, e^{v_0(t-t_0)} - \| \sum_{k \in J_{v_0}^-} e^{\lambda_k^{(r)}(t-t_0)} Sf_k(t) \|, \quad t \geq t_0;
\end{aligned}
$$

for a corresponding estimate on $x(t)$, compare Kohaupt (2011, (10)).

Now, let

$$
\sum_{k \in J_{v_0}} Sf_k(t) \neq 0, \quad t \geq t_0. \tag{36}
$$

Then, similarly as in Kohaupt (2011, (12)),

$$
\| \sum_{k \in J_{v_0}} Sf_k(t) \| \geq \inf_{t \geq t_0} \| \sum_{k \in J_{v_0}} Sf_k(t) \| =: X_{S,v_0} > 0, \quad t \geq t_0. \tag{37}
$$

Together with (36), this entails

$$
\|x_S(t)\| \geq X_{S,0} \, e^{v_0(t-t_0)}, \quad t \geq t_1 \geq t_0 \tag{38}
$$

with

$$
X_{S,0} := \frac{X_{S,v_0}}{2} > 0
$$

for sufficiently large t_1. Thus, we obtain

THEOREM 3 *(Positiveness of the constant $X_{S,0}$ in lower bound if A diagonalizable)*

Let the hypoth.eses (H1), (H2), and (HS) for A be fulfilled, $0 \neq x_0 \in \mathbb{R}^m$, $S \in \mathbb{R}^{l \times m}$, A be diagonalizable as well as condition (37) be satisfied.

Then, there exists a positive constant $X_{S,0}$ such that

$$
X_{S,0} \, e^{v_{x_0}[A](t-t_0)} \leq \|x_S(t)\|, \; t \geq t_1 \geq t_0. \tag{39}
$$

for sufficiently large $t_1 \geq t_0$.

If $x_S(t) \neq 0$, $t \geq t_0$, then $t_1 = t_0$ can be chosen.

Proof The last statement is proven similarly as in the proof of Kohaupt (2011, Theorem 2). □

Remarks:

- As opposed to (37), the relation $\sum_{k\in J_{v_0}} f_k(t) \neq 0, \quad t \geq t_0$, in Kohaupt (2011, (11)) could be proven there and thus needed not be assumed.
- We mention that the quantities $f_k(t)$ depend on the initial vector x_0 through their coefficients $c_k^{(r)} c_k^{(i)}$ (Kohaupt, 2011, (8)). To stress this fact, one can write $f_k(t) = f_k(t, x_0)$ or $f_k(t) = f_{k,x_0}(t)$.

Case 2: General square matrix A In this case, we need the following *hypotheses on A* from Kohaupt (2011, Section 3.2).

(H1´) $m = 2n$ and $A \in \mathbb{R}^{m\times m}$,

(H2´) $T^{-1}AT = J = diag(J_i(\lambda_i))_{i=1,\ldots,r}$ where $J_i(\lambda_i) \in \mathbb{C}^{m_i\times m_i}$ are the canonical Jordan forms,

(H3´) $\lambda_i = \lambda_i(A) \neq 0,\ i = 1, \ldots, r,$

(H4´) $\lambda_i \neq \lambda_j,\ i \neq j,\ i,j = 1, \ldots, r,$

(H5´) $r = 2\rho$, and the principal vectors

$$p_1^{(1)}, \ldots, p_{m_1}^{(1)}; \ldots ; p_1^{(\rho)}, \ldots, p_{m_\rho}^{(\rho)}; \bar{p}_1^{(1)}, \ldots, \bar{p}_{m_1}^{(1)}; \ldots ; \bar{p}_1^{(\rho)}, \ldots, \bar{p}_{m_\rho}^{(\rho)}$$

form a basis of $\mathbb{C}^m$.In the case of a general square matrix A, we also have to collect some definitions resp. notations and representations of $x(t)$ from Kohaupt (2006,2011).

Representation of the basis $x_k^{(l,r)}(t), x_k^{(l,i)}(t),\ k = 1, \ldots, m_l,\ l = 1, \ldots, \rho$

Under the hypotheses (H1′), (H2′), and (HS′), from Kohaupt (2011) we obtain the following *real basis functions* for the ODE $\dot{x} = A\,x$:

$$\begin{aligned} x_k^{(l,r)}(t) &= e^{\lambda_l^{(r)}(t-t_0)} \Bigg\{ \cos \lambda_l^{(i)}(t-t_0) \left[p_1^{(l,r)} \frac{(t-t_0)^{k-1}}{(k-1)!} + \ldots + p_{k-1}^{(l,r)}(t-t_0) + p_k^{(l,r)} \right] \\ &\quad - \sin \lambda_l^{(i)}(t-t_0) \left[p_1^{(l,i)} \frac{(t-t_0)^{k-1}}{(k-1)!} + \ldots + p_{k-1}^{(l,i)}(t-t_0) + p_k^{(l,i)} \right] \Bigg\}, \\ x_k^{(l,i)}(t) &= e^{\lambda_l^{(r)}(t-t_0)} \Bigg\{ \sin \lambda_l^{(i)}(t-t_0) \left[p_1^{(l,r)} \frac{(t-t_0)^{k-1}}{(k-1)!} + \ldots + p_{k-1}^{(l,r)}(t-t_0) + p_k^{(l,r)} \right] \\ &\quad + \cos \lambda_l^{(i)}(t-t_0) \left[p_1^{(l,i)} \frac{(t-t_0)^{k-1}}{(k-1)!} + \ldots + p_{k-1}^{(l,i)}(t-t_0) + p_k^{(l,i)} \right] \Bigg\}, \end{aligned} \tag{40}$$

$k = 1, \ldots, m_l,\ l = 1, \ldots, \rho$, where

$$p_k^{(l)} = p_k^{(l,r)} + i\,p_k^{(l,i)}$$

is the decomposition of $p_k^{(l)}$ into its real and imaginary part.

The spectral abscissa of A with respect to the initial vector $x_0 \in \mathbb{R}^n$ Let $u_k^{(l)*}$, $k = 1, \ldots, m_l$ be the principal vectors of stage k of A^* corresponding to the eigenvalue $\bar{\lambda}_l$, $l = 1, \ldots, r = 2\rho$. Under $(H1')$, $(H2')$, and (HS'), the solution $x(t)$ of (1) has the form

$$x(t) = \sum_{l=1}^{r=2\rho} \sum_{k=1}^{m_l} c_{1k}^{(l)} x_k^{(l)}(t) = \sum_{l=1}^{\rho} \sum_{k=1}^{m_l} [c_{1k}^{(l)} x_k^{(l)}(t) + c_{2k}^{(l)} \bar{x}_k^{(l)}(t)]. \tag{41}$$

with uniquely determined coefficients $c_{1k}^{(l)}$, $k = 1, \ldots, m_l$, $l = 1, \ldots, r = 2\rho$. Using the relations

$$\begin{aligned} c_{1k}^{(l)} &= (x_0, u_k^{(l)*}),\ k = 1, \ldots, m_l,\ l = 1, \ldots, \rho \\ c_{2k}^{(l)} &= c_{1k}^{(\rho+l)} = \bar{c}_{1k}^{(l)},\ l = 1, \ldots, \rho \end{aligned} \tag{42}$$

(see Kohaupt, 2011, Section 3.2 for the last relation), then the *spectral abscissa of A with respect to the initial vector* $x_0 \in \mathbb{R}^n$ is

$$\begin{aligned} v_0 := v_{x_0}[A] :&= \max_{l=1,\ldots,r=2\rho} \{\lambda_l^{(r)}(A) \mid x_0 \not\perp M_{\bar{\lambda}_l(A^*)} := [u_1^{(l)*}, \ldots, u_{m_l}^{(l)*}]\} \\ &= \max_{l=1,\ldots,r=2\rho} \{\lambda_l^{(r)}(A) \mid c_{1k}^{(l)} \neq 0 \textit{ for at least one } k \in \{1, \ldots, m_l\}\} \\ &= \max_{l=1,\ldots,\rho} \{\lambda_l^{(r)}(A) \mid c_{1k}^{(l)} \neq 0 \textit{ for at least one } k \in \{1, \ldots, m_l\}\} \\ &= \max_{l=1,\ldots,\rho} \{\lambda_l^{(r)}(A) \mid x_0 \not\perp M_{\bar{\lambda}_l(A^*)} = [u_1^{(l)*}, \ldots, u_{m_l}^{(l)*}]\} \end{aligned} \tag{43}$$

Index sets For the sequel, we need the following index sets:

$$J_{v_0} := \{l_0 \in \mathbb{N} \mid 1 \le l_0 \le \rho \textit{ and } \lambda_{l_0}^{(r)}(A) = v_0\} \tag{44}$$

and

$$\begin{aligned} J_{v_0}^- :&= \{1, \ldots, \rho\} \setminus J_{v_0} \\ &= \{l_0^- \in \mathbb{N} \mid 1 \le l_0^- \le \rho \textit{ and } \lambda_{l_0^-}^{(r)}(A) < v_0\}. \end{aligned} \tag{45}$$

Appropriate representation of $x(t)$ We have

$$x(t) = \sum_{l=1}^{\rho} \sum_{k=1}^{m_l} [c_k^{(l,r)} x_k^{(l,r)}(t) + c_k^{(l,i)} x_k^{(l,i)}(t)] \tag{46}$$

with

$$c_k^{(l,r)} = 2\, Re\, c_{1k}^{(l)}, \quad c_k^{(l,i)} = -2\, Im\, c_{1k}^{(l)}, \quad k = 1, \ldots, m_l,\ l = 1, \ldots, \rho$$

(cf. Kohaupt, 2011). Thus, due (46),

$$x(t) = \sum_{l=1}^{\rho} e^{\lambda_l^{(r)}(t-t_0)} \sum_{k=1}^{m_l} f_k^{(l)}(t) \tag{47}$$

with

$$
\begin{aligned}
f_k^{(l)}(t) := c_k^{(l,r)} \Bigg\{ & \cos \lambda_l^{(i)}(t-t_0)\left[p_1^{(l,r)} \frac{(t-t_0)^{k-1}}{(k-1)!} + \ldots + p_{k-1}^{(l,r)}(t-t_0) + p_k^{(l,r)}\right] \\
& - \sin \lambda_l^{(i)}(t-t_0)\left[p_1^{(l,i)} \frac{(t-t_0)^{k-1}}{(k-1)!} + \ldots + p_{k-1}^{(l,i)}(t-t_0) + p_k^{(l,i)}\right]\Bigg\} \\
+ c_k^{(l,i)} \Bigg\{ & \sin \lambda_l^{(i)}(t-t_0)\left[p_1^{(l,r)} \frac{(t-t_0)^{k-1}}{(k-1)!} + \ldots + p_{k-1}^{(l,r)}(t-t_0) + p_k^{(l,r)}\right] \\
& + \cos \lambda_l^{(i)}(t-t_0)\left[p_1^{(l,i)} \frac{(t-t_0)^{k-1}}{(k-1)!} + \ldots + p_{k-1}^{(l,i)}(t-t_0) + p_k^{(l,i)}\right]\Bigg\}
\end{aligned} \tag{48}
$$

$k = 1, \ldots, m_l,\ l = 1, \ldots, \rho.$

Appropriate representation of $y(t)$ and $\dot{y}(t)$ (needed in the Appendix)

Set

$$
p_k^{(l)} := \begin{bmatrix} q_k^{(l)} \\ r_k^{(l)} \end{bmatrix}, \quad p_k^{(l,r)} := \begin{bmatrix} q_k^{(l,r)} \\ r_k^{(l,r)} \end{bmatrix}, \quad p_k^{(l,i)}(t) := \begin{bmatrix} q_k^{(l,i)} \\ r_k^{(l,i)} \end{bmatrix}, \tag{49}
$$

with $q_k^{(l)}, r_k^{(l)} \in \mathbb{C}^n, q_k^{(l,r)}, r_k^{(l,r)}, q_k^{(l,i)}, r_k^{(l,i)} \in \mathbb{R}^n, k = 1, \ldots, m_l,\ l = 1, \ldots, \rho.$

Then, from (47), (48)

$$
y(t) = \sum_{l=1}^{\rho} e^{\lambda_l^{(r)}(t-t_0)} \sum_{k=1}^{m_l} g_k^{(l)}(t) \tag{50}
$$

with

$$
\begin{aligned}
g_k^{(l)}(t) := c_k^{(l,r)} \Bigg\{ & \cos \lambda_l^{(i)}(t-t_0)\left[q_1^{(l,r)} \frac{(t-t_0)^{k-1}}{(k-1)!} + \ldots + q_{k-1}^{(l,r)}(t-t_0) + q_k^{(l,r)}\right] \\
& - \sin \lambda_l^{(i)}(t-t_0)\left[q_1^{(l,i)} \frac{(t-t_0)^{k-1}}{(k-1)!} + \ldots + q_{k-1}^{(l,i)}(t-t_0) + q_k^{(l,i)}\right]\Bigg\} \\
+ c_k^{(l,i)} \Bigg\{ & \sin \lambda_l^{(i)}(t-t_0)\left[q_1^{(l,r)} \frac{(t-t_0)^{k-1}}{(k-1)!} + \ldots + q_{k-1}^{(l,r)}(t-t_0) + q_k^{(l,r)}\right] \\
& + \cos \lambda_l^{(i)}(t-t_0)\left[q_1^{(l,i)} \frac{(t-t_0)^{k-1}}{(k-1)!} + \ldots + q_{k-1}^{(l,i)}(t-t_0) + q_k^{(l,i)}\right]\Bigg\}
\end{aligned} \tag{51}
$$

$k = 1, \ldots, m_l,\ l = 1, \ldots, \rho$

as well as

$$
z(t) = \dot{y}(t) = \sum_{l=1}^{\rho} e^{\lambda_l^{(r)}(t-t_0)} \sum_{k=1}^{m_l} h_k^{(l)}(t) \tag{52}
$$

with

$$
\begin{aligned}
h_k^{(l)}(t) := c_k^{(l,r)} \Bigg\{ & \cos \lambda_l^{(i)}(t-t_0)\left[r_1^{(l,r)}\frac{(t-t_0)^{k-1}}{(k-1)!}+\ldots+r_{k-1}^{(l,r)}(t-t_0)+r_k^{(l,r)}\right] \\
& -\sin \lambda_l^{(i)}(t-t_0)\left[r_1^{(l,i)}\frac{(t-t_0)^{k-1}}{(k-1)!}+\ldots+r_{k-1}^{(l,i)}(t-t_0)+r_k^{(l,i)}\right]\Bigg\} \\
+ c_k^{(l,i)} \Bigg\{ & \sin \lambda_l^{(i)}(t-t_0)\left[r_1^{(l,r)}\frac{(t-t_0)^{k-1}}{(k-1)!}+\ldots+r_{k-1}^{(l,r)}(t-t_0)+r_k^{(l,r)}\right] \\
& +\cos \lambda_l^{(i)}(t-t_0)\left[r_1^{(l,i)}\frac{(t-t_0)^{k-1}}{(k-1)!}+\ldots+r_{k-1}^{(l,i)}(t-t_0)+r_k^{(l,i)}\right]\Bigg\}
\end{aligned} \tag{53}
$$

$k = 1, \ldots, m_l,\ l = 1, \ldots, \rho.$

Now, let

$$\sum_{l \in J_{v_0}} \sum_{k=1}^{m_l} Sf_k^{(l)}(t) \neq 0, \quad t \geq t_0. \tag{54}$$

Then, similarly as in Kohaupt (2011, Section 3.2), there exists a constant $X_{S,0} > 0$ such that

$$\|x_S(t)\| \geq X_{S,0}\, e^{v_0(t-t_0)}, \quad t \geq t_1 \geq t_0 \tag{55}$$

for sufficiently large $t_1 \geq t_0$.

Thus, we obtain

THEOREM 4 *(Positiveness of the constant $X_{S,0}$ in lower bound if A general square)*

Let the hypotheses (*H1′*), (*H2′*), and (*HS′*) for *A* be fulfilled, $0 \neq x_0 \in I\!R^m$, $S \in I\!R^{l \times m}$, *A* be a general square matrix as well as condition (55) be satisfied.

Then, there exists a positive constant $X_{S,0}$ such that

$$X_{S,0}\, e^{v_{x_0}[A](t-t_0)} \leq \|x_S(t)\|,\ t \geq t_1 \geq t_0. \tag{56}$$

for sufficiently large $t_1 \geq t_0$.

If $x_S(t) \neq 0,\ t \geq t_0$, then $t_1 = t_0$ can be chosen.

Remark: Sufficient algebraic conditions for (37) resp. (55) will be given in the Appendix; they are independent of the initial vector x_0 and the time *t*.

5. Two-sided bounds on $\Phi_S(t) = S\Phi(t)$ with $\dot{\Phi}(t) = A\Phi(t)$, $\Phi(0) = E$,

In this section, we discuss the deterministic case $\Phi_S(t) = S\Phi(t)$ with $\dot{\Phi}(t) = A\Phi(t)$, $\Phi(0) = E$, as a preparation for Section 7. There, two-sided bounds on $P_{x_S}(t) - P_S = \Phi_S(t)(P_0 - P)\Phi_S^T(t)$ will be given based on those for $\Phi_S(t)$ here.

Moreover, for the positiveness of the constant in the lower bound, we discuss two cases: the special case when matrix *A* is diagonalizable and the case when *A* is general square.

We obtain

THEOREM 5 *(Two-sided bound on $P_{x_S}(t) - P_S$ based on $\|\Phi_S(t)\|_2^2$)*

Let $A \in \mathbb{R}^{n\times n}$, let $\Phi(t) = e^{At}$ be the associated fundamental matrix with $\Phi(0) = E$ where E is the identity matrix. Further, let $P_0, P \in \mathbb{R}^{n\times n}$ be the covariance matrices from Section 2.

Then,

$$q_0 \,\|\Phi_S(t)\|_2^2 \leq \|P_{x_S}(t) - P_S\|_2 \leq q_1 \,\|\Phi_S(t)\|_2^2,\ t \geq 0, \tag{57}$$

where

$$q_0 = \inf_{\|v\|_2=1} |((P_0 - P)v, v)| \tag{58}$$

and

$$q_1 = \sup_{\|v\|_2=1} |((P_0 - P)v, v)| = \|P_0 - P\|_2. \tag{59}$$

If $P_0 \neq P$, then $q_1 > 0$. If $P_0 - P$ is regular, then

$$q_0 = \|(P_0 - P)^{-1}\|_2^{-1} > 0. \tag{60}$$

Proof The proof follows from Kohaupt (2015b, Lemmas 1 and 2) with $C = P_0 - P$ and $\Psi = \Phi_S^*(t) = \Phi_S^T(t)$ as well as $\|\Psi^*(t)\|_2 = \|\Phi_S(t)\|_2$. □

Next, we have to derive two-sided bounds on $\|\Phi_S(t)\|_2$. For this, we write

$$S\Phi(t) = S[\varphi_1(t), \dots, \varphi_n(t)] = [S\varphi_1(t), \dots, S\varphi_n(t)], \tag{61}$$

where $\varphi_1(t), \dots, \varphi_n(t)$ are the columns of the fundamental matrix $\Phi(t)$, i.e.

$$\Phi(t) = [\varphi_1(t), \dots, \varphi_n(t)].$$

Now, $\dot{\Phi}(t) = A\Phi(t), \Phi(0) = E$, is equivalent to

$$\dot{\varphi}_j(t) = A\varphi_j(t), \varphi(0) = e_j. j = 1, \dots, n, \tag{62}$$

where e_j is the jth unit column vector.

The two-sided bounds on $\Phi_S(t) = S\Phi(t)$ can be done in any norm. Let the matrix norm $|\cdot|_\infty$ be given by

$$|B|_\infty = \max_{i,j=1,\dots,n} |B_{i,j}|,\ B = (B_{i,j}) \in \mathbb{C}^{n\times n}.$$

Then,

$$|\Phi_S(t)|_\infty = |S\Phi(t)|_\infty = \max_{j=1,\dots,n} \|S\varphi_j(t)\|_\infty. \tag{63}$$

Thus, the two-sided bound on $\Phi_S(t)$ has been reduced to two-sided bounds on $\|S\varphi_j(t)\|_\infty, j = 1, \dots, n$.

Similarly to Theorem 2, we obtain

THEOREM 6 *(Two-sided bound on $\Phi_S(t) = S\Phi(t)$ by $e^{\nu[A]t}$) Let $A \in \mathbb{C}^{n\times n}$ and $\Phi(t)$ be the fundamental matrix of A with $\Phi(0) = E$, i.e. let $\Phi(t)$ be the solution of the initial value problem $\dot{\Phi}(t) = A\Phi(t),\ \Phi(0) = E$ and $\Phi_S(t) = S\Phi(t)$.*

Then, there exists a constant $\varphi_{S,0} \geq 0$ and for every $\varepsilon > 0$ a constant $\varphi_{S,1}(\varepsilon) > 0$ such that

$$\varphi_{S,0}\, e^{v[A]t} \leq \|\Phi_S(t)\| \leq \varphi_{S,1}(\varepsilon)\, e^{(v[A]+\varepsilon)t},\ t \geq 0, \tag{64}$$

where $v[A]$ is the spectral abscissa of A.

If A is diagonalizable, then $\varepsilon = 0$ may be chosen, and we write $\varphi_{S,1}$ instead of $\varphi_{S,1}(\varepsilon = 0)$.

If S is square and regular, then $\varphi_{S,0} > 0$.

Proof From (18) and (63), there exist constants $\varphi_{S,0j} \geq 0$ and for every $\varepsilon > 0$ constants $\varphi_{S,1j}(\varepsilon) > 0$ such that

$$\varphi_{S,0j}\, e^{v_{e_j}[A]t} \leq \|S\varphi_j(t)\| \leq \varphi_{S,1j}(\varepsilon)\, e^{(v_{e_j}[A]+\varepsilon)t},\ t \geq 0. \tag{65}$$

Define

$$\varphi_{S,0} := \min_{j=1,\dots,n} \varphi_{S,0j}$$

and

$$\varphi_{S,1}(\varepsilon) := \max_{j=1,\dots,n} \varphi_{S,1j}(\varepsilon).$$

Then, taking into account (64) and the relation

$$\max_{j=1,\dots,n} v_{e_j}[A] = v[A] \tag{66}$$

(cf. Kohaupt, 2006, Proof of Theorem 8) as well as the equivalence of norms in finite-dimensional spaces, the two-sided bound (65) follows. The rest is clear from Theorem 2. □

Corresponding to Theorems 3 and 4, we obtain the following two theorems.

THEOREM 7 *(Positiveness of the constant $\varphi_{S,0}$ in lower bound if A diagonalizable) Let the hypotheses (H1), (H2), and (HS) for A be fulfilled, $S \in \mathbb{R}^{l\times m}$, A be diagonalizable as well as condition (37) be satisfied with $f_k(t) = f_{k,e_j}(t)$, $j = 1,\dots,m$.*

Then, there exists a positive constant $\varphi_{S,0}$ such that

$$\varphi_{S,0}\, e^{v[A]t} \leq \|\Phi_S(t)\|,\ t \geq t_1 \geq t_0. \tag{67}$$

for sufficiently large $t_1 \geq t_0$.

If $\Phi_S(t) \neq 0,\ t \geq t_0$, then $t_1 = t_0$ can be chosen.

THEOREM 8 *(Positiveness of the constant $\varphi_{S,0}$ in lower bound if A general square) Let the hypotheses (H1′), (H2′), and (HS′) for A be fulfilled, $S \in \mathbb{R}^{l\times m}$, A be a general square matrix as well as condition (55) be satisfied.*

Then, there exists a positive constant $\varphi_{S,0}$ such that

$$\varphi_{S,0}\, e^{v[A]t} \leq \|\Phi_S(t)\|,\ t \geq t_1 \geq t_0. \tag{68}$$

for sufficiently large $t_1 \geq t_0$.
If $\Phi_S(t) \neq 0,\ t \geq t_0$, then $t_1 = t_0$ can be chosen.

6. Two-sided bounds on $m_{x_S}(t)$

According to Equation (11), we have

$$m_{x_S}(t) = \Phi_S(t)m_0,\ t \geq 0.$$

Now, $x_S(t) = Sx(t) = S\Phi(t)x_0 = \Phi_S(t)x_0$ in Theorem 2. Assuming $m_0 \neq 0$ and choosing the Euclidean norm $\|\cdot\| = \|\cdot\|_2$ as well as m_0 instead of x_0, we therefore obtain from Theorem 2 for every $\varepsilon > 0$ the two-sided bound

$$\mu_{S,0}\, e^{\nu_{m_0}[A]t} \leq \|m_{x_S}(t)\|_2 \leq \mu_{S,1}(\varepsilon)\, e^{(\nu_{m_0}[A]+\varepsilon)t},\ t \geq 0, \tag{69}$$

for constants $\mu_{S,0} \geq 0$ and $\mu_{S,1}(\varepsilon) > 0$. Sufficient conditions for $\mu_{S,0} > 0$ are obtained by Theorems 3 and 4 when replacing there x_0 by m_0.

7. Two-sided bounds on $P_{x_S}(t) - P_S = \Phi_S(t)(P_0 - P)\Phi_S^T(t)$

Based on Theorems 5 and 6, we obtain

COROLLARY 9 (Two-sided bounds on $P_{x_S}(t) - P_S$ based on $e^{2\nu[A]t}$) Let $A \in \mathbb{R}^{n\times n}$, let $\Phi(t) = e^{At}$ be the associated fundamental matrix with $\Phi(0) = E$, where E is the identity matrix, as well as $S \in \mathbb{R}^{l\times n}$ and $\Phi_S(t) = S\Phi(t)$. Further, let $P_0, P \in \mathbb{R}^{n\times n}$ be the covariance matrices from Section 2.

Then, there exists a constant $p_{S,0} \geq 0$ and for every $\varepsilon > 0$ a constant $p_{S,1}(\varepsilon) > 0$ such that

$$p_{S,0}\, e^{2\nu[A]t} \leq \|P_{x_S}(t) - P_S\|_2 \leq p_{S,1}(\varepsilon)\, e^{2(\nu[A]+\varepsilon)t},\ t \geq 0. \tag{70}$$

If $P_0 - P$ and S are regular, then $p_{S,0} > 0$.

Remark: If $S \in \mathbb{R}^{l\times n}$ is not square regular, under additional conditions stated in Theorems 7 and 8, it can also be asserted that $p_{S,0} > 0$.

8. Local regularity of the function $\|P_{x_S}(t) - P_S\|_2$

We have the following lemma which states – loosely speaking – that for every $t_0 \geq 0$, the function $t \mapsto \|\Delta P_{x_S}(t)\|_2 := \|P_{x_S}(t) - P_S\|_2 := \|\Phi_S(t)(P_0 - P)\Phi_S^T(t)\|_2$ is real analytic in some right neighborhood $[t_0, t_0 + \Delta t_0]$.

LEMMA 10 *(Real analyticity of $t \mapsto \|P_{x_S}(t) - P_S\|_2$ on $[t_0, t_0 + \Delta t_0]$) Let $t_0 \in \mathbb{R}_0^+$. Then, there exists a number $\Delta t_0 > 0$ and a function $t \mapsto \widehat{\Delta P_{x_S}}(t)$, which is real analytic on $[t_0, t_0 + \Delta t_0]$ such that $\widehat{\Delta P_{x_S}}(t) = \|\Delta P_{x_S}(t)\|_2 = \|P_{x_S}(t) - P_S\|_2 = \|\Phi_S(t)(P_0 - P)\Phi_S^T(t)\|_2,\ t \in [t_0, t_0 + \Delta t_0]$.*

Proof Based on $\|\Delta P_{x_S}(t)\|_2 = \max\{|\lambda_{max}(\Delta P_{x_S}(t))|, |\lambda_{min}(\Delta P_{x_S}(t))|\}$, the proof is similar to that of Kohaupt (2002, Lemma 1). The details are left to the reader. □

9. Formulas for the norm derivatives $D_+^k \|P_{x_S}(t) - P_S\|_2,\ k = 0, 1, 2$

Let $A \in \mathbb{C}^{n\times n}$ and $C \in \mathbb{C}^{n\times n}$ with $C^* = C$. As in Kohaupt (2015b, Section 7), we set

$$\Psi(t) := \Phi(t)C\Phi^*(t),\ t \geq 0.$$

Let $S \in \mathbb{C}^{l\times n}$ and define

$$\Psi_S(t) := S\Psi(t)S^*,\ t \geq 0.$$

Then,

$$\Psi_S(t) := S\Phi(t)C\Phi^*(t)S^*,\ t \geq 0.$$

Similarly as in Kohaupt (2015b, Section 7), for $t_0 \in I\!R_0^+$,

$$\Psi_S(t) := S\Phi(t)\,C\,\Phi^*(t)S^* = \sum_{j=0}^{\infty} S\Phi(t_0)\,B_j\,\Phi^*(t_0)S^*\,\frac{(t-t_0)^j}{j!}$$

with

$$B_j = \sum_{k=0}^{j} \binom{j}{k} A^{*j-k}\,C\,A^k,$$

$j = 0,1,2,\ldots$, and thus

$$\Psi(t) = T_S^{(0)} + T_S^{(1)}(t-t_0) + T_S^{(2)}(t-t_0)^2 + \ldots$$

with

$$T_S^{(k)} = ST^{(k)}S^*,\ k = 0,1,2,\ldots,$$

where the quantities $T^{(k)},\ k = 0,1,2,\ldots$ are defined in Kohaupt (2015b, Section 7).

Consequently, one obtains the formulas for

$$D_+^k \|P_{x_S}(t) - P_S\|_2,\ k = 0,1,2,\ldots$$

from those for $D_+^k \|P_x(t) - P\|_2,\ k = 0,1,2,\ldots$ when replacing $T^{(k)}$ by $T_S^{(k)},\ k = 0,1,2,\ldots$.

10. Applications

In this section, we apply the new two-sided bounds on $\|P_{x_S}(t) - P_S\|_2$ obtained in Section 7 as well as the differential calculus of norms developed in Sections 8 and 9 to a linear stochastic vibration model with output equation for asymptotically stable system matrix and white noise excitation vector.

In Subsection 10.1, the stochastic vibration model as well as its state-space form is given, in Subsection 10.2 the transformation matrix S in chosen and in Section 10.3 the data are specified. In Section 10.4, the positiveness of the constants $X_{S,0}$ and $\varphi_{S,0}$ in the lower bounds is verified. In Section 10.5, computations with the chosen data are carried out, such as the computation of P and $P_0 - P$ as well as the computation of the curves $y = D_+^k \|P_{x_S}(t) - P_S\|_2,\ k = 0,1,2$ and of the curve $y = \|P_{x_S}(t) - P_S\|_2$ along with its best upper and lower bounds for the two ranges $t \in [0;5]$ and $t \in [5;26]$. In Section 10.6, computational aspects are shortly discussed.

10.1. The stochastic vibration model and its state-space form

Consider the multi-mass vibration model in Figure 1.

The associated initial-value problem is given by

$$M\ddot{y} + B\dot{y} + Ky = f(t),\quad y(0) = y_0,\ \dot{y}(0) = \dot{y}_0$$

where $y = [y_1,\ldots,y_n]^T$ and $f(t) = [f_1(t),\ldots,f_n(t)]^T$ as well as

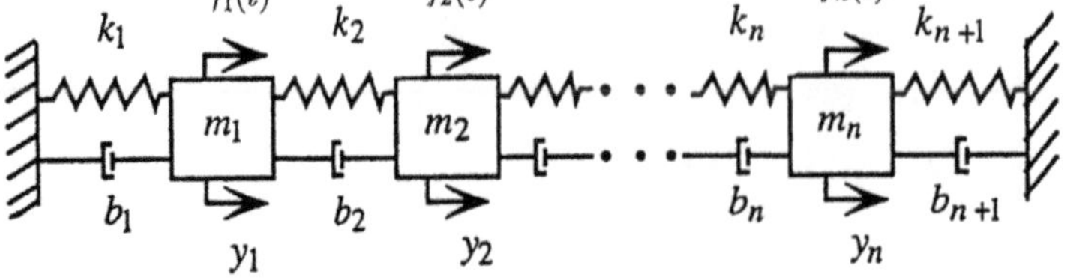

Figure 1. Multi-mass vibration model.

$$M = \begin{bmatrix} m_1 & & & & \\ & m_2 & & & \\ & & m_3 & & \\ & & \ddots & & \\ & & & & m_n \end{bmatrix},$$

$$B = \begin{bmatrix} b_1+b_2 & -b_2 & & & & \\ -b_2 & b_2+b_3 & -b_3 & & & \\ & -b_3 & b_3+b_4 & -b_4 & & \\ & \ddots & \ddots & \ddots & & \\ & & -b_{n-1} & b_{n-1}+b_n & -b_n & \\ & & -b_n & b_n+b_{n+1} & & \end{bmatrix},$$

$$K = \begin{bmatrix} k_1+k_2 & -k_2 & & & & \\ -k_2 & k_2+k_3 & -k_3 & & & \\ & -k_3 & k_3+k_4 & -k_4 & & \\ & \ddots & \ddots & \ddots & & \\ & & -k_{n-1} & k_{n-1}+k_n & -k_n & \\ & & -k_n & k_n+k_{n+1} & & \end{bmatrix}.$$

Here, y is the displacement vector, $f(t)$ the applied force, and M, B, and K are the mass, damping, and stiffness matrices, as the case may be.

In the state-space description, one obtains

$$\dot{x}(t) = A\,x(t) + b(t), \quad x(0) = x_0,$$

with $x = [y^T, z^T]^T$, $z = \dot{y}$, and $x_0 = [y_0^T, z_0^T]^T$, $z_0 = \dot{y}_0$, where the initial vector $x_0 = [y_0^T, z_0^T]^T$ is characterized by the *mean vector* m_0 and the *covariance matrix* P_0.

The *system matrix* A and the *excitation vector* $b(t)$ are given by

$$A = \left[\begin{array}{c|c} 0 & E \\ \hline -M^{-1}K & -M^{-1}B \end{array}\right], \qquad b(t) = \left[\begin{array}{c} 0 \\ \hline M^{-1}f(t) \end{array}\right],$$

The (symmetric positive semi-definite) intensity matrix $Q = Q_b$ is obtained from the (symmetric positive semi-definite) intensity matrix Q_f by

$$Q = Q_b = \left[\begin{array}{c|c} 0 & 0 \\ \hline 0 & M^{-1}Q_f M^{-1} \end{array}\right],$$

See Müller and Schiehlen (1985, (9.65)) relation in Kohaupt (2015b, Appendix A.5).

10.2. The transformation matrix S and the output equation $x_S(t) = Sx(t)$

We depart from the equation of motion in vector form, namely $M\ddot{y} + B\dot{y} + Ky = f(t)$, and rewrite it as

$$\ddot{y}_a(t) := \ddot{y} - M^{-1}f(t) = -M^{-1}K\,y(t) - M^{-1}B\,\dot{y}(t).$$

Following Müller and Schiehlen (1985, (9.56), (9.57)), for a one-mass model with base excitation, we call $\ddot{y}_a$ the *absolute acceleration* of our vibration system; it can be written as

$$\ddot{y}_a(t) = [-M^{-1}K, -M^{-1}B]\begin{bmatrix} y(t) \\ \dot{y}(t) \end{bmatrix} = Sx(t) = :x_S(t), \; t \geq 0,$$

with the *transformation matrix*

$$S = [-M^{-1}K, -M^{-1}B].$$

Our output equation therefore is

$$x_S(t) = Sx(t),$$

where here $S \in IR^{n\times 2n}$ is a rectangular, but not a square regular matrix.

10.3. Formulas for the norm derivatives $D_+^k\|P_{x_S}(t) - P_S\|_2$, $k = 0, 1, 2$

Let $A \in \mathbb{C}^{n\times n}$ and $C \in \mathbb{C}^{n\times n}$ with $C^* = C$. As in Kohaupt (2015b, Section 7), we set

$$\Psi(t) := \Phi(t)C\Phi^*(t), \; t \geq 0.$$

Let $S \in \mathbb{C}^{l\times n}$ and define

$$\Psi_S(t) := S\Psi(t)S^*, \; t \geq 0.$$

Then,

$$\Psi_S(t) := S\Phi(t)C\Phi^*(t)S^*, \; t \geq 0.$$

Similarly as in Kohaupt (2015b, Section 7), for $t_0 \in \mathbb{R}_0^+$,

$$\Psi_S(t) := S\Phi(t)\,C\,\Phi^*(t)S^* = \sum_{j=0}^{\infty} S\Phi(t_0)\,B_j\,\Phi^*(t_0)S^*\,\frac{(t-t_0)^j}{j!}$$

with

$$B_j = \sum_{k=0}^{j}\binom{j}{k} A^{*j-k}\,C\,A^k,$$

$j = 0, 1, 2, \ldots$, and thus

$$\Psi(t) = T_S^{(0)} + T_S^{(1)}(t-t_0) + T_S^{(2)}(t-t_0)^2 + \ldots$$

with

$$T_S^{(k)} = ST^{(k)}S^*, \; k = 0, 1, 2, \ldots,$$

where the quantities $T^{(k)}$, $k = 0, 1, 2, \ldots$ are defined in Kohaupt (2015b, Section 7).

Consequently, one obtains the formulas for

$$D_+^k\|P_{x_S}(t) - P_S\|_2, \; k = 0, 1, 2, \ldots$$

from those for $D_+^k\|P_x(t) - P\|_2$, $k = 0, 1, 2, \ldots$ when replacing $T^{(k)}$ by $T_S^{(k)}$, $k = 0, 1, 2, \ldots$.

10.4. Data for the model

As of now, we specify the values as

$$m_j = 1,\ j = 1, \ldots, n$$
$$k_j = 1,\ j = 1, \ldots, n + 1$$

and

$$b_j = \begin{cases} 1/2, & j \text{ even} \\ 1/4, & j \text{ odd.} \end{cases}$$

Then,

$$M = E$$

$$B = \begin{bmatrix} \frac{3}{4} & -\frac{1}{2} & & & & \\ -\frac{1}{2} & \frac{3}{4} & -\frac{1}{4} & & & \\ & -\frac{1}{4} & \frac{3}{4} & -\frac{1}{2} & & \\ & & \ddots & \ddots & \ddots & \\ & & -\frac{1}{4} & \frac{3}{4} & -\frac{1}{2} & \\ & & -\frac{1}{2} & \frac{3}{4} & & \end{bmatrix}$$

(if n is even), and

$$K = \begin{bmatrix} 2 & -1 & & & \\ -1 & 2 & -1 & & \\ & -1 & 2 & -1 & \\ & & \ddots & \ddots & \ddots \\ & & -1 & 2 & -1 \\ & & -1 & 2 & \end{bmatrix}.$$

We choose $n = 5$ in this paper so that the state-space vector $x(t)$ has the dimension $m = 2n = 10$.

For m_0, we take

$$m_0 = [m_{y_0}^T, m_{z_0}^T]^T$$

with

$$m_{y_0} = [-1, 1, -1, 1, -1]^T$$

and

$$m_{z_0} = \begin{cases} [0, 0, 0, 0, 0]^T & \text{(Case I)} \\ [-1, -1, -1, -1, -1]^T & \text{(Case II)} \end{cases}$$

similarly as in Kohaupt (2002) for y_0 and $\dot{y}_0$. For the 10×10 matrix P_0, we choose

$$P_0 = 0.01\,E.$$

The *white-noise force vector* $f(t)$ is specified as

$$f(t) = [0, \ldots, 0; f_n(t)]^T$$

so that its intensity matrix $Q_f \in IR^{n \times n}$ with $q_{f,nn} = :q$ has the form

$$Q_f = \left[\begin{array}{c|c} 0 & 0 \\ \hline 0 & q_{f,nn} \end{array}\right] = \left[\begin{array}{c|c} 0 & 0 \\ \hline 0 & q \end{array}\right] = q \left[\begin{array}{c|c} 0 & 0 \\ \hline 0 & 1 \end{array}\right] =: q\, E^{(n)}.$$

We choose

$q = 0.01.$

With $M = E$, this leads to (see Kohaupt, 2015b, Appendix A.5)

$$Q = Q_b = \left[\begin{array}{c|c} 0 & 0 \\ \hline 0 & Q_f \end{array}\right] = \left[\begin{array}{c|c} 0 & 0 \\ \hline 0 & q\,E^{(n)} \end{array}\right] = \left[\begin{array}{c|c} 0 & 0 \\ \hline 0 & q \end{array}\right] \in I\!R^{m\times m}.$$

10.5. Positiveness of the constants $X_{S,0}$ and $\varphi_{S,0}$ (resp. $p_{S,0}$)

i	$\lambda_i = \lambda_i(A)$	$\overline{\lambda}_i = \lambda_i(A^*)$
1	$-0.69976063878054 + 1.79598147815975i$	$-0.69976063878054 - 1.79598147815975i$
2	$-0.56266837404074 + 1.61635870164386i$	$-0.56266837404074 - 1.61635870164386i$
3	$-0.37500000000000 + 1.36358901432946i$	$-0.37500000000000 - 1.36358901432946i$
4	$-0.18733162595926 + 0.99452168646559i$	$-0.18733162595926 - 0.99452168646559i$
5	$-0.05023936121946 + 0.51637145071101i$	$-0.05023936121946 - 0.51637145071101i$

The eigenvalues of matrix A are given by

and

$\lambda_{5+i} = \overline{\lambda}_i,\ i = 1, \ldots, 5$

where the numbering is chosen such that $Im\,\lambda_i > 0,\ i = 1, \ldots, 5$. So,

$\lambda_i \neq \lambda_j,\ i \neq j,\ i,j = 1, \ldots, 10.$

$$p_5 = \left[\begin{array}{c} q_5 \\ \hline r_5 \end{array}\right] = \left[\begin{array}{c} 0.172578 + 0.192313i \\ 0.316694 + 0.310502i \\ 0.365988 + 0.358733i \\ 0.316694 + 0.310502i \\ 0.193410 + 0.166421i \\ \hline -0.107975 + 0.079453i \\ -0.176245 + 0.147932i \\ -0.203627 + 0.170963i \\ -0.176245 + 0.147932i \\ -0.095652 + 0.091510i \end{array}\right].$$

Thus, matrix A is diagonalizable. Further, conditions (H1)-(H4), and (HS) are fulfilled. Moreover, we have $J_{v_0} = \{5\}$ and

Therefore, q_5, $\bar{q}_5$ are linearly independent. Thus, by Lemma A.1 and Theorem 3 resp. Theorem 7, the constants $X_{S,0}$ and $\varphi_{S,0}$ are positive. Therefore, also the constant $p_{S,0}$ is positive.

10.6. Computations with the specified data

(i) *Bounds on $y = \Phi_S(t)m_0$ in the vector norm $\|\cdot\|_2$ Upper bounds* on $y = \Phi(t)m_0$ in the vector norm $\|\cdot\|_2$ for the two cases (I) and (II) of m_0 are given in Kohaupt (2002, Figures 2 and 3).

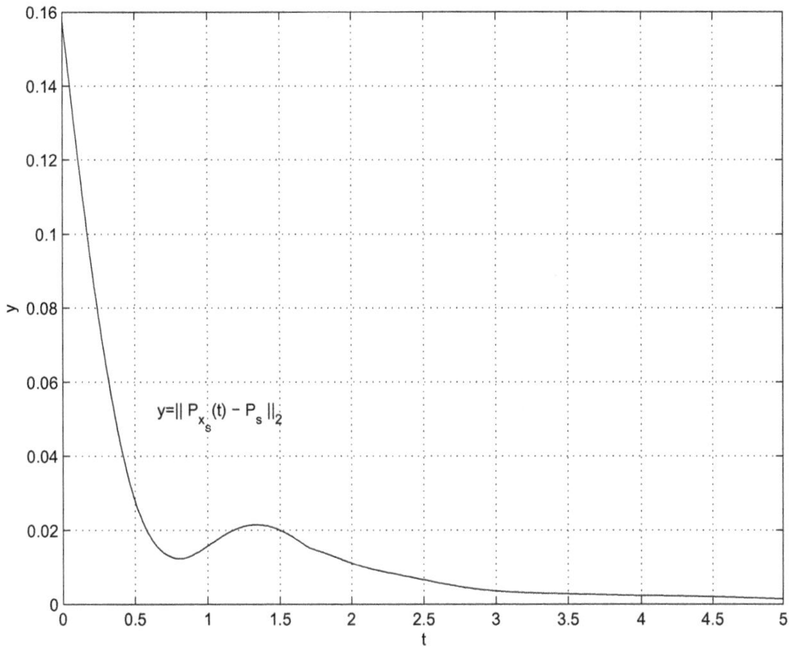

Figure 2. Curve $y = \|P_{x_s}(t) - P_S\|_2,\ 0 \le t \le 5,\ \Delta t = 0.01.$

There, we had a deterministic problem with $f(t) = 0$ and the solution vector $x(t) = \Phi(t)\,x_0$, where x_0 there had the same data as m_0 here. We mention that for the specified data, $v_{m_0}[A] = v[A] = \alpha$ in both cases (Kohaupt, 2006, p. 154) for a method to prove this. For the sake of brevity, we do not compute or plot the lower or upper bounds and thus the two-sided bounds on $y = \Phi_S(t)m_0$ but leave this to the reader.

(ii) *Computation of P and $P_0 - P$* The computation of these matrices was already done in Kohaupt (2015b, Subsection 3). There, we saw that P is symmetric and $P_0 - P$ symmetric and regular (but not positive definite). Matrix $P_0 - P$ is needed to compute the curve $y = \|P_{x_S}(t) - P_S\|_2 = \|\Phi_S(t)\,(P_0 - P)\,\Phi_S^T(t)\|_2$.

(iii) *Computation of the curves* $y = D_+^k\,\|P_{x_S}(t) - P_S\|_2 = D_+^k\,\|\Phi_S(t)\,(P_0 - P)\,\Phi_S^T(t)\|_2,\ k = 0, 1, 2$ The computation of $y = D_+^k\,\|P_{x_S}(t) - P_S\|_2, k = 0, 1, 2$ for the given data is done according to Section 9 with $C = P_0 - P$. The pertinent curves are illustrated in Figures 3–6. We have checked the results numerically by difference quotients. More precisely, setting

$$\Delta P_{x_S}(t) := P_{x_S}(t) - P_S,\ t > 0,$$

and

$$g(t) := \|\Delta P_{x_S}(t)\|_2 = \|P_{x_S}(t) - P_S\|_2,\ t > 0,$$

we have investigated the approximations

$$\delta_h g(t) := \frac{g(t+h) - g(t-h)}{2h} \approx D_+ g(t),\ t - h \ge 0,$$

and

$$\delta_{\frac{h}{2}}^2 g(t) := \delta_{\frac{h}{2}}\,(\delta_{\frac{h}{2}}\, g(t)) = \frac{g(t+h) - 2g(t) + g(t-h)}{h^2} \approx D_+^2 g(t),\ t - h \ge 0,$$

as well as

$$\delta_h Dg(t) := \frac{Dg(t+h) - Dg(t-h)}{2h} \approx D_+^2 g(t),\ t - h \ge 0.$$

For, e.g.

$$t = 2.5,$$
$$h = 10^{-5},$$

we obtain

$$D_+ g(t) = D_+ \|P_{x_S}(t) - P_S\|_2 = -0.00789413206599,$$
$$\delta_h g(t) = \delta_h \|P_{x_S}(t) - P_S\|_2 = -0.00789413206470,$$

as well as

$$D_+^2 g(t) = D^2 \|P_{x_S}(t) - P_S\|_2 = 0.00180394234645,$$
$$\delta_{\frac{h}{2}}^2 g(t) = \delta_{\frac{h}{2}}^2 \|P_x(t) - P\|_2 = 0.00180268994177,$$

and

$$D_+^2 g(t) = D^2 \|P_{x_S}(t) - P_S\|_2 = 0.00180394234645,$$
$$\delta_h D g(t) = \delta_h D \|P_{x_S}(t) - P_S\|_2 = 0.00180394235409,$$

so that the computational results for $y = D_+^k \|P_{x_S}(t) - P_S\|_2, k = 0, 1, 2$ with $t = 2.5$ are well underpinned by the difference quotients. As we see, the approximation of $D_+^2 g(t) = D_+^2 \|P_{x_S}(t) - P_S\|_2$ by $\delta_h D g(t)$ is much better than by $\delta_{\frac{h}{2}}^2 g(t)$, which was to be expected, of course.

(iv) *Bounds on* $y = P_{x_S}(t) - P_S = \Phi_S(t)(P_0 - P)\Phi_S^T(t)$ *in the spectral norm* $\|\cdot\|_2$ Let $\alpha := \nu[A]$ be the spectral abscissa of the system matrix A. With the given data, we obtain

$$\alpha := \nu[A] = -0.05023936121946 < 0$$

so that the system matrix A is asymptotically stable. The upper bound on $y = \|P_{x_S}(t) - P_S\|_2 = \|\Phi_S(t)(P_0 - P)\Phi_S^T(t)\|_2$ is given by $y = p_{S,1}(\varepsilon)\, e^{2(\alpha+\varepsilon)t}, t \geq 0$. Here, $\varepsilon = 0$ can be chosen since matrix A is diagonalizable. But, in the programs, we have chosen the machine precision $\varepsilon = eps = 2^{-52} \doteq 2.2204 \times 10^{-16}$ of MATLAB in order not to be bothered by this question. With $\varphi_{1,\varepsilon}(t) := p_{S,1}(\varepsilon)\, e^{2(\alpha+\varepsilon)t},\ t \geq 0$, the optimal constant $p_{S,1}(\varepsilon)$ in the upper bound is obtained by the two conditions

$$\begin{aligned} \|P_{x_S}(t_c) - P_S\|_2 &= \varphi_{1,\varepsilon}(t_c) = p_{S,1}(\varepsilon)\, e^{2(\alpha+\varepsilon)t_c}, \\ D_+ \|P_{x_S}(t_c) - P_S\|_2 &= \varphi'_{1,\varepsilon}(t_c) = 2(\alpha+\varepsilon)\,\varphi_{1,\varepsilon}(t_c), \end{aligned}$$

where t_c is the place of contact between the curves. This is a system of two nonlinear equations in the two unknowns t_c and $p_{S,1}(\varepsilon)$. By eliminating $\varphi_{1,\varepsilon}(t_c)$, this system is reduced to the determination of the zero of

$$D_+ \|P_{x_S}(t_c) - P_S\|_2 - 2(\alpha+\varepsilon)\|P_{x_S}(t_c) - P_S\|_2 = 0,$$

which is a single nonlinear equation in the single unknown t_c. For this, MATLAB routine *fsolve* was used. After t_c has been computed from the above equation, the best constant $p_{S,1}(\varepsilon)$ is obtained from

$$p_{S,1}(\varepsilon) = \|P_{x_S}(t_c) - P_S\|_2\, e^{-2(\alpha+\varepsilon)t_c}.$$

Numerical values for range [0;5] First, we consider the range [0;5]. From the initial guess $t_{c,0} = 1.4$, the computations deliver the values

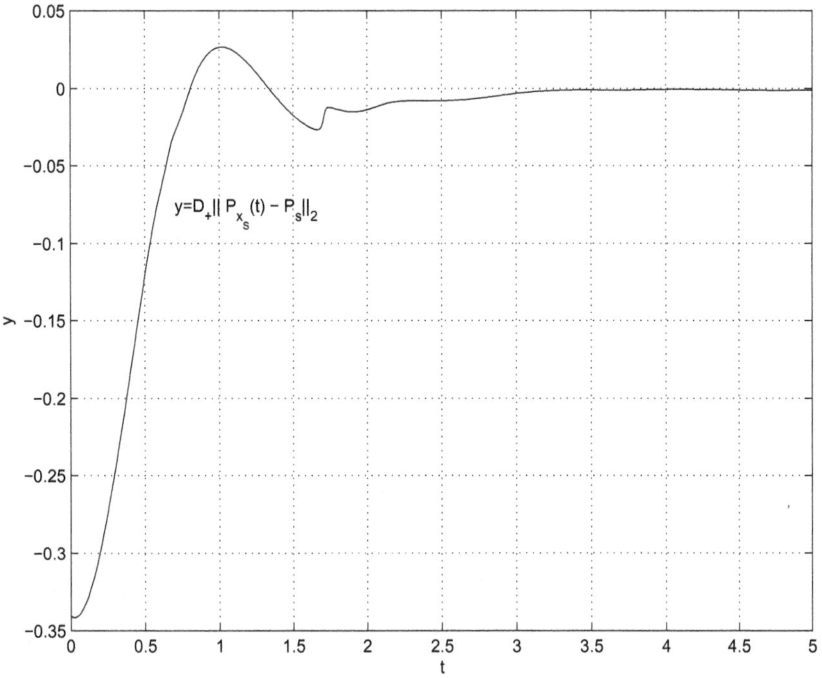

Figure 3. Right norm derivative $y = D_+ \|P_{x_s}(t) - P_S\|_2$, $0 \le t \le 5$, $\Delta t = 0.01$.

$t_c = 1.355984,$
$p_{S,1}(\varepsilon) = 0.024642.$

To compute the lower bound, we have to notice that the curve $y = \|P_{x_s}(t_c) - P_S\|_2$ has kinks like $|t|^{\frac{1}{2}}$ at $t = 0$. This is not seen in Figures 3-6 in the range [0;5], but in Figure 6 in the range [5;25]. Therefore, the point of contact t_s between the lower bound $y = M_{S,0}e^{2\alpha t}$ and the curve $y = \|P_{x_s}(t) - P_S\|_2$ cannot be determined by the calculus of norms, but must be computed from

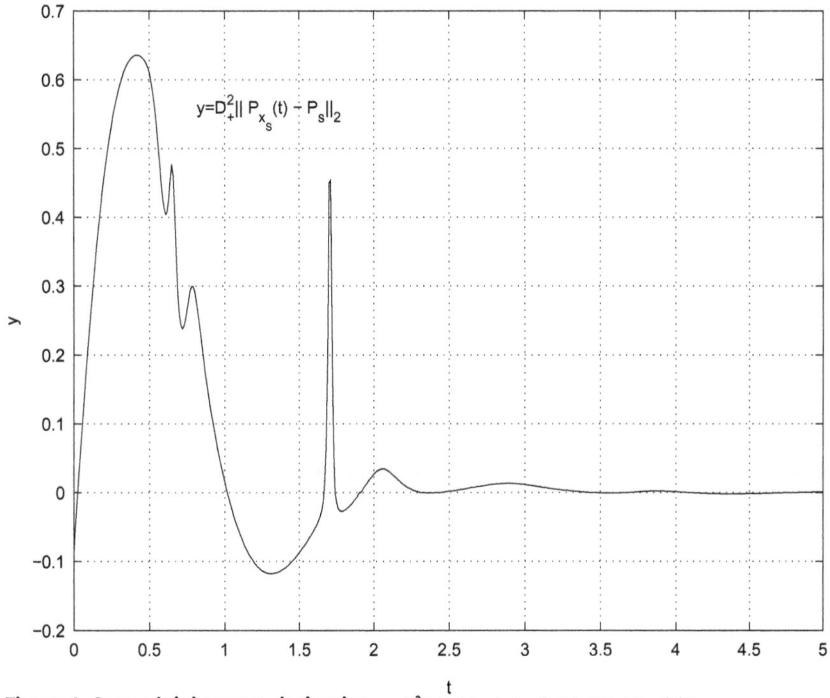

Figure 4. Second right norm derivative $y = D_+^2 \|P_{x_s}(t) - P_S\|_2$, $0 \le t \le 5$, $\Delta t = 0.01$.

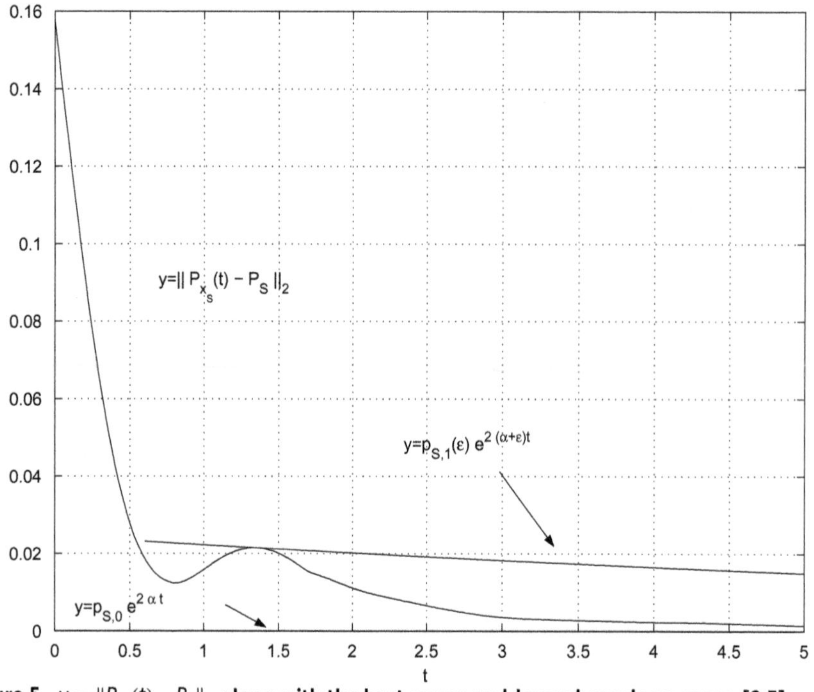

Figure 5. $y = \|P_{x_S}(t) - P_S\|_2$ **along with the best upper and lower bounds on range [0;5].**

$$t_s = \min_{j=1,2,\ldots} \|P_{x_S}(t_j) - P_S\|_2,$$

where $t_j, j = 1, 2, \ldots$ are the local minima of $y = \|P_{x_S}(t_c) - P_S\|_2$. In this way, with the initial guess $t_{s,0} = 3.0$, the results are

$$t_s = 17.152006,$$
$$p_{S,0} = 9.403735 \times 10^{-5}.$$

In Figure 5, the curve $y = \|P_{x_S}(t_c) - P_S\|_2$ along with the best upper and lower bounds are illustrated with stepsize $\Delta t = 0.01$. The upper bound is valid for $t \geq t_1 \doteq 1.172$.

Numerical values for range [5;25] On the rage [5;25], the two-sided bounds can be better adapted to the curve $y = \|P_{x_S}(t) - P_S\|_2$. From the initial guess $t_{c,0} = 14$, the computations deliver

$$t_c = 14.876956,$$
$$p_{S,1}(\varepsilon) = 0.00164024.$$

Further, with the initial guess $t_{s,0} = 25$, we obtain

$$t_s = 24.860534,$$
$$p_{S,0} = 3.548384.$$

In Figure 6, the curve $y = \|P_{x_S}(t) - P_S\|_2$ along with the best upper and lower bounds are illustrated with stepsize $\Delta t = 0.01$. The upper bound is valid for $t \geq t_1 \doteq 6.031$.

10.7. Computational aspects

In this subsection, we say something about the computer equipment and the computation time for some operations.

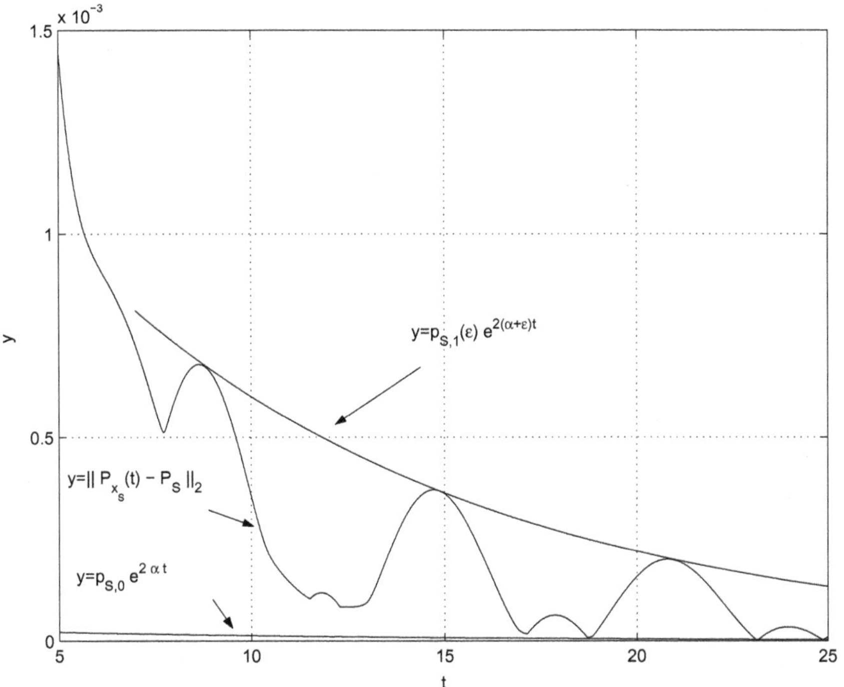

Figure 6. $y = \|P_{x_S}(t) - P_S\|_2$ **along with the best upper and lower bounds on range [5;25].**

(i) As to the *computer equipment*, the following hardware was available: an Intel Pentium D(3.20 GHz, 800 MHz Front-Side-Bus, 2x2MB DDR2-SDRAM with 533 MHz high-speed memories). As software package, we used MATLAB, Version 6.5.

(ii) The *computation time* t of an operation was determined by the command sequence $t_i = clock; operation; t = etime(clock, t_i);$ it is put out in seconds rounded to two decimal places by Matlab. For the computation of the eigenvalues of matrix A, we used the command $[XA, DA] = eig(A)$; the pertinent computation time is less than 0.01 s. To determine $\Phi(t) = e^{At}$, we employed Matlab routine *expm*. For the computation of the 501 values *t*, *y*, *yu*, *yl* in Figure 6, it took $t(\text{Table for Figure 5}) = 1.17s$. Here, t stands for the time value running from $t_0 = 0$ to $t_e = 25$ with stepsize $\Delta t = 0.1$; y stands for the value of $\|P_{x_S}(t) - P_S\|_2$, *yu* for the value of the best upper bound $p_{S,1}(\varepsilon)\, e^{2(\alpha+\varepsilon)t}$ and *yl* for the value of the lower bound $p_{S,0}\, e^{2\alpha t}$. For the computation of the 2501 values *t*, *y*, *yu*, *yl* in Figure 7, it took $t(\text{Table for Figure 6}) = 6.35s$.

11. Conclusion

In the present paper, a linear stochastic vibration system of the form $\dot{x}(t) = Ax(t) + b(t),\ x(0) = x_0$, with output equation $x_S(t) = Sx(t)$ was investigated, where A is the system matrix and $b(t)$ white noise excitation. The output equation $x_S(t) = Sx(t)$ is viewed as a transformation of the state vector $x(t)$ mapped by the rectangular matrix S into the output vector $x_S(t)$. If the system matrix A is asymptotically stable, then the mean vector $m_{x_S}(t)$ and the covariance matrix $P_{x_S}(t)$ both converge with $m_{x_S}(t) \to 0\ (t \to \infty)$ and $P_{x_S}(t) \to P_S\ (t \to \infty)$ for some symmetric positive (semi-)definite matrix P_S. This raises the question of the asymptotic behavior of both quantities. The pertinent investigations are made in the Euclidean norm $\|\cdot\|_2$ for $m_{x_S}(t)$ and in the spectral norm, also denoted by $\|\cdot\|_2$, for $P_{x_S}(t) - P_S$. The main new points are the derivation of two-sided bounds on both quantities, the determination of the right norm derivatives $D_+^k \|P_{x_S}(t) - P_S\|_2,\ k = 0, 1, 2$ and, as application, the computation of the best constants in the bounds. In the presentation, the author exhibits the relations between the quantities $m_x(t)$, $P_x(t) - P$, and the formulas for $D_+^k \|P_x(t) - P\|_2$, on the one hand, and the corresponding output-related quantities $m_{x_S}(t)$, $P_{x_S}(t) - P_S$, and $D_+^k \|P_{x_S}(t) - P_S\|_2$, on the other hand. As a result, we obtain that there is a close relationship between these quantities. Special attention is paid to the positiveness of the constants in the lower bounds if the transformation matrix is only rectangular and not necessarily square and regular. In the Appendix, a sufficient algebraic condition for the positiveness of the constants in the lower bounds is derived that is independent of the initial vector and the time variable. To make sure that the (new) formulas for $D_+^k \|P_{x_s}(t) - P_S\|_2$ are correct, we have checked them by various difference quotients. They underpin the correctness of the numerical values for the specified data.

The computation time to generate the last figure with a 10×10 matrix A is about 6 seconds. Of course, in engineering practice, much larger models occur. As in earlier papers, we mention that in this case engineers usually employ a method called condensation to reduce the size of the matrices.

We have shifted the details of the positiveness of the constants in the lower bounds to the Appendix in order to make the paper easier to comprehend.

The numerical values were given in order that the reader can check the results.

Altogether, the results of the paper should be of interest to applied mathematicians and particularly to engineers.

Acknowledgements
The author would like to give thanks to the anonymous referees for evaluating the paper and for comments that led to a better presentation of the paper.

Funding
The author received no direct funding for this research.

Author details
L. Kohaupt[1]
E-mail: kohaupt@beuth-hochschule.de
[1] Department of Mathematics, Beuth University of Technology Berlin, Luxemburger Str. 10, D-13353 Berlin, Germany.

References

Achieser, N. I., & Glasman, I. M. (1968). *Theorie der linearen Operatoren im Hilbert-Raum* [Theory of linear operators in Hilbert space]. Berlin: Akademie-Verlag.

Bhatia, R., & Elsner, L. (2003). Higher order logarithmic derivatives of matrices in the spectral norm. *SIAM Journal on Matrix Analysis and Applications, 25*, 662–668.

Benner, P., Denißen, J., & Kohaupt, L. (2013). Bounds on the solution of linear time-periodic systems. *Proceedings in Applied Mathematics and Mechanics, 13*, 447–448.

Benner, P., Denißen, J., & Kohaupt, L. (2016, January 12). *Trigonometric spline and spectral bounds for the solution of linear time-periodic systems* (Preprint MPIMD/16-1). Magdeburg: Max Planck Institute for Dynamics of Complex Technical Systems. Retrieved from https://protect-us.mimecast.com/s/oXA1BRUQvnpoto

Bickley, W. G., & McNamee, J. (1960). Matrix and other direct methods for the solution of linear difference equations. *Philosophical Transactions of the Royal Society of London: Series A, 252*, 69–131.

Coppel, W. A. (1965). *Stability and asymptotic behavior of differential equations*. Boston, MA: D.C. Heath.

Dahlquist, G. (1959). *Stability and error bounds in the numerical integration of ordinary differential equations*. Transactions of the Royal Institute of Technology, Stockholm, No. 130. Uppsala; Almqvist and Wiksells Boktryckeri AB.

Desoer, Ch. A., & Haneda, H. (1972). The measure of a matrix as a tool to analyse computer algorithms for circuit analysis. *IEEE Transaction on Circuit Theory, 19*, 480–486.

Golub, G. H., & van Loan, Ch F (1989). *Matrix computations*. Baltimore, MD: Johns Hopkins University Press.

Guyan, R. J. (1965). Reduction of stiffness and mass matrices. *AIAA Journal, 3*, 380.

Hairer, E., Nørset, S. P., & Wanner, G. (1993). *Solving ordinary differential equations I*. Berlin: Springer-Verlag.

Heuser, H. (1975). *Funktionalanalysis* [Functional analysis]. Stuttgart: B.G. Teubner.

Higueras, I., & García-Celayeta, B. (1999). Logarithmic norms for matrix pencils. *SIAM Journal on Matrix Analysis and Applications, 20*, 646–666.

Higueras, I., & García-Celayeta, B. (2000). How close can the logarithmic norm of a matrix pencil come to the spectral abscissa? *SIAM Journal on Matrix Analysis and Applications, 22*, 472–478.

Hu, G.-D., & Hu, G.-D. (2000). A relation between the weighted logarithmic norm of a matrix and the Lyapunov equation. *BIT, 40*, 606–610.

Kantorovich, L. V., & Akilov, G. P. (1982). *Funktional analysis*. Oxford: Pergamon Press.

Kato, T. (1966). *Perturbation theory for linear operators*. New York, NY: Springer.

Kloeden, P., & Platen, E. (1992). *Numerical solution of stochastic differential equations*. Berlin: Springer-Verlag.

Kohaupt, L. (1999). Second logarithmic derivative of a complex matrix in the Chebyshev norm. *SIAM Journal on Matrix Analysis and Applications, 21*, 382–389.

Kohaupt, L. (2001). Differential calculus for some p-norms of the fundamental matrix with applications. *Journal of Computational and Applied Mathematics, 135*, 1–21.

Kohaupt, L. (2002). Differential calculus for p-norms of complex-valued vector functions with applications. *Journal of Computational and Applied Mathematics, 145*, 425–457.

Kohaupt, L. (2003). Extension and further development of the differential calculus for matrix norms with applications. *Journal of Computational and Applied Mathematics, 156*, 433–456.

Kohaupt, L. (2004a). Differential calculus for the matrix norms $|\cdot|_1$ and $|\cdot|_\infty$ with applications to asymptotic bounds for periodic linear systems. *International Journal of Computer Mathematics, 81*, 81–101.

Kohaupt, L. (2004b). New upper bounds for free linear and nonlinear vibration systems with applications of the differential calculus of norms. *Applied Mathematical Modelling, 28*, 367–388.

Kohaupt, L. (2005). Illustration of the logarithmic derivatives by examples suitable for classroom teaching. *Rocky Mountain Journal of Mathematics, 35*, 1595–1629.

Kohaupt, L. (2006). Computation of optimal two-sided bounds for the asymptotic behavior of free linear dynamical systems with application of the differential calculus of norms. *Journal of Computational Mathematics and Optimization, 2*, 127–173.

Kohaupt, L. (2007a). New upper bounds for excited vibration systems with applications of the differential calculus of norms. *International Journal of Computer Mathematics, 84*, 1035–1057.

Kohaupt, L. (2007b). Short overview on the development of a differential calculus of norms with applications to vibration problems (in Russian). *Information Science and Control Systems, 13*, 21–32. ISSN 1814-2400.

Kohaupt, L. (2007c). Construction of a biorthogonal system of principal vectors of the matrices A and A^* with applications to the initial value problem $\dot{x} = Ax$, $x(t_0)=x_0$. *Journal of Computational Mathematics and Optimization, 3*, 163–192.

Kohaupt, L. (2008a). Solution of the matrix eigenvalue problem $VA + A^*V = \mu V$ with applications to the study of free linear systems. *Journal of Computational and Applied Mathematics, 213*, 142–165.

Kohaupt, L. (2008b). Biorthogonalization of the principal vectors for the matrices A and A^* with application to the computation of the explicit representation of the solution (t) of $\dot{x} = Ax$, $x(t_0)$ of . *Applied Mathematical Sciences, 2*, 961–974.

Kohaupt, L. (2008c). Solution of the vibration problem $M\ddot{y}$ $+By + Ky = 0$, $y(t_0) = y_0$, $y(t_0) = y_0$ without the hypothesis $BM^{-1}K = KM^{-1}B$ or $B = \alpha M +$ or βM . *Applied Mathematical Sciences, 2*, 1989–2024.

Kohaupt, L. (2008d). Two-sided bounds on the difference $R(t) = \Phi(t) - \Psi(t)$ between the continuous and discrete evolution as well as on $R(t)\,x_0 = \Phi(t) - \Psi(t)\,x_0$ with application of the differential calculus of norms. In M. P. Álvarez (Ed.), *Leading-edge applied mathematical modeling research* (pp. 319–340). New York, NY: Nova Science. ISBN 978-1-60021-977-1.

Kohaupt, L. (2009a, July 10–13). A short overview on the development of a differential calculus for norms with applications to vibration problems. In *The 2nd International Multi-Conference on Engineering and Technological Innovation* (Vol. II). Orlando, FL. ISBN-10: 1-934272-69-8, ISBN13: 978-1-934272-69-5

Kohaupt, L. (2009b). On an invariance property of the spectral abscissa with respect to a vector. *Journal of Computational Mathematics and Optimization, 5*, 175–180.

Kohaupt, L. (2009c). *Contributions to the determination of optimal bounds on the solution of ordinary differential equations with vibration behavior* (Habilitation Thesis, TU Freiberg, 91 pp.). Aachen: Shaker-Verlag.

Kohaupt, L. (2010). Two-sided bounds for the asymptotic behavior of free nonlinear vibration systems with application of the differential calculus of norms. *International Journal of Computer Mathematics, 87*, 653–667.

Kohaupt, L. (2010b, January). Phase diagram for norms of the solution vector of dynamical multi-degree-of-freedom systems. Lagakos, et al. (Eds.), *Recent advances in applied mathematics* (pp. 69–74, 27–29). American Conference on Applied Mathematics (American Math10), WSEAS Conference in Cambridge/USA at Harvard University. WSEAS Press. ISBN 978-960-474-150-2, ISSN 1790-2769.

Kohaupt, L. (2011). Two-sided bounds on the displacement $y(t)$ and the velocity $y(t)$ of the vibration problem $M\ddot{y}$ $+ By + Ky = 0$, $y(t_0) = y_0$, $y(t_0) = y_0$ with application of the differential calculus of norms. *The Open Applied Mathematics Journal, 5*, 1–18.

Kohaupt, L. (2012). Further investigations on phase diagrams for norms of the solution vector of multi-degree-of-freedom systems. *Applied Mathematical Sciences, 6*, 5453–5482. ISSN: 1312-885X.

Kohaupt, L. (2013). On the vibration-suppression property and monotonicity behavior of a special weighted norm for dynamical systems $\dot{x} = Ax$, $x(t_0)=x_0$. *Applied Mathematics and Computation, 222*, 307–330.

Kohaupt, L. (2015a). On norm equivalence between the displacement and velocity vectors for free linear dynamical systems. *Cogent Mathematics, 2*, 1095699 (33 p.).

Kohaupt, L. (2015b). Two-sided bounds on the mean vector and covariance matrix in linear stochastically excited vibration systems with application of the differential calculus of norms. *Cogent Mathematics, 2*, 1021603 (26 p).

Kučera, V. (1974). The matrix equation A X+X B = C. *SIAM Journal on Applied Mathematics, 26*, 15–25.

Lozinskiĭ, S. M. (1958). Error estimates for the numerical integration of ordinary differential equations I (in Russian). *Izvestija vysshikh uchebnykh zavedenij.Matematika, 5*, 52–90.

Ma, E.-Ch. (1966). A finite series solution of the matrix equation A X - X B = C. *SIAM Journal of Applied Mathematics, 14*, 490–495.

Müller, P. C., & Schiehlen, W. O. (1985). *Linear vibrations*. Dordrecht: Martinus Nijhoff.

Niemeyer, H., & Wermuth, E. (1987). *Lineare algebra* [Linear algebra]. Braunschweig: Vieweg.

Pao, C. V. (1973a). Logarithmic derivatives of a square matrix. *Linear Algebra and its Applications, 6*, 159–164.

Pao, C. V. (1973b). A further remark on the logarithmic derivatives of a square matrix. *Linear Algebra and its Applications, 7*, 275–278.

Söderlind, G., & Mattheij, R. M. M. (1985). Stability and asymptotic estimates in nonautonomous linear differential systems. *SIAM Journal on Mathematical Analysis, 16*, 69–92.

Ström, T. (1972). Minimization of norms and logarithmic norms by diagonal similarities. *Computing, 10*, 1–7.

Ström, T. (1975). On logarithmic norms. *SIAM Journal on Numerical Analysis, 10*, 741–753.

Stummel, F., & Hainer, K. (1980). *Introduction to numerical analysis*. Edinburgh: Scottish Academic Press.

Taylor, A. E. (1958). *Introduction to functional analysis*. New York, NY: Wiley.

Thomson, W. T., & Dahleh, M. D. (1998). *Theory of vibration with applications*. Upper Saddle River, NJ: Prentice-Hall.

Waller, H., & Krings, W. (1975). *Matrizenmethoden in der Maschinen- und Bauwerksdynamik* [Matrix methods in machine and building dynamics]. Mannheim: Bibliographisches Institut.

Whidborne, J. F., & Amer, N. (2011). Computing the maximum transient energy growth. *BIT Numerical Mathematics, 51*, 447–457.

Appendix 1

Algebraic conditions ensuring the positiveness of $X_{S,0}$ resp. $\varphi_{S,0}$ for $S = [-M^{-1}K, -M^{-1}B]$.
We discuss two cases, namely the case of a diagonalizable matrix A and the case of a general square matrix A.

The corresponding Lemmas A.1 and A.2 will deliver sufficient algebraic criteria for the positiveness of $X_{S,0}$ and $\varphi_{S,0}$, as the case may be, that are independent of the initial condition and the time, which is the important point.

The results are of interest on their own.

Case 1: Diagonalizable matrix A

Let the hypotheses (H1), (H2), and (HS) be fulfilled. Further, according to (37), we assume

$$\sum_{k \in J_{v_0}} Sf_k(t) \neq 0, \quad t \geq t_0, \tag{75}$$

with

$$f_k(t) = \begin{bmatrix} g_k(t) \\ h_k(t) \end{bmatrix}$$

so that

$$Sf_k(t) = -M^{-1}Kg_k(t) - M^{-1}Bh_k(t) = -M^{-1}[Kg_k(t) + Bh_k(t)], \; k \in J_{v_0}.$$

Thus, (37) resp. (72) is equivalent to

$$\sum_{k \in J_{v_0}} [Kg_k(t) + Bh_k(t)] \neq 0, \quad t \geq t_0. \tag{76}$$

We have the following

Sufficient condition for $\sum_{k \in J_{v_0}} [Kg_k(t) + Bh_k(t)] \neq 0, \quad t \geq t_0$:

$$\boxed{Kq_k^{(r)} + Br_k^{(r)},\; Kq_k^{(i)} + Br_k^{(i)},\; k \in J_{v_0},\ \textit{linearly independent}} \tag{77}$$

(see Kohaupt, 2011, Section 5.1 for a similar case).

LEMMA A.1 *(Some equivalences of the sufficient algebraic condition)*

Let the conditions (H1), (H2), (H3), and (HS) be fulfilled. Further, let $M, B, K \in IR^{n \times n}$ and M be regular.

Then, the following equivalences are valid:

$$Kq_k^{(r)} + Br_k^{(r)},\; Kq_k^{(i)} + Br_k^{(i)},\; k \in J_{v_0},\ \textit{linearly independent} \tag{78}$$

$$\Longleftrightarrow$$

$$Kq_k + Br_k,\; K\bar{q}_k + B\bar{r}_k,\; k \in J_{v_0},\ \textit{linearly independent} \tag{79}$$

$$\Longleftrightarrow$$

$$q_k\ \bar{q}_k,\ k \in J_{v_0},\ \textit{linearly independent} \tag{80}$$

$$\Longleftrightarrow$$

$$q_k^{(r)},\ q_k^{(i)},\ k \in J_{v_0},\ \textit{linearly independent} \tag{81}$$

Proof The equivalences (75) $\Longleftrightarrow$ (76) and (77) $\Longleftrightarrow$ (78) are clear. Further, since

$$r_k = \lambda_k q_k, \tag{82}$$

(76) is equivalent to

$$Kq_k + \lambda_k Bq_k,\ K\bar{q}_k + \bar{\lambda}_k B\bar{q}_k,\ k \in J_{v_0},\ \textit{linearly independent}. \tag{83}$$

Since

$$\lambda_k^2 Mq_k + \lambda_k Bq_k + Kq_k = 0,\quad \bar{\lambda}_k^2 M\bar{q}_k + \bar{\lambda}_k B\bar{q}_k + K\bar{q}_k = 0,\quad k \in J_{v_0},$$

(80) is equivalent to

$$-\lambda_k^2 Mq_k,\ -\bar{\lambda}_k^2 M\bar{q}_k,\ k \in J_{v_0},\ \textit{linearly independent.} \tag{84}$$

Since $\lambda_k \neq 0$ due to (H3) and M is regular by assumption, (81) is equivalent to (77). □

Case 2: General square matrix A Let the hypotheses $(H1')$, $(H2')$, $(H3')$, and (HS') be fulfilled. Further, according to (29), we assume

$$\sum_{l \in J_{v_0}} \sum_{k=1}^{m_l} Sf_k^{(l)}(t) \neq 0, \quad t \geq t_0, \tag{85}$$

with

$$f_k^{(l)}(t) = \begin{bmatrix} g_k^{(l)}(t) \\ h_k^{(l)}(t) \end{bmatrix}$$

so that

$$Sf_k^{(l)}(t) = -M^{-1}Kg_k^{(l)}(t) - M^{-1}Bh_k^{(l)}(t) = -M^{-1}[Kg_k^{(l)}(t) + Bh_k^{(l)}(t)],\ k = 1, \ldots, m_l,$$

$l \in J_{v_0}$. Thus, (55) resp. (72) is equivalent to

$$\sum_{l \in J_{v_0}} \sum_{k=1}^{m_l} [Kg_k^{(l)}(t) + Bh_k^{(l)}(t)] \neq 0, \quad t \geq t_0. \tag{86}$$

We have the following

Sufficient condition for $\sum_{l \in J_{v_0}} \sum_{k=1}^{m_l} [Kg_k^{(l)}(t) + Bh_k^{(l)}(t)] \neq 0, \quad t \geq t_0$:

$$\boxed{Kq_k^{(l,r)} + Br_k^{(l,r)},\ Kq_k^{(l,i)} + Br_k^{(l,i)},\ k = 1, \ldots, m_l,\ l \in J_{v_0},\ \textit{linearly independent}} \tag{87}$$

(see Kohaupt, 2011, Section 5.2 for a similar case).

LEMMA A.2 *(Some equivalences of the sufficient algebraic condition) Let the hypotheses* (H1′), (H2′), (H3′), *and* (HS′) *be fulfilled. Further, let* $M, B, K \in IR^{n\times n}$, *and M be regular.*

Then, the following equivalences are valid:

$$Kq_k^{(l,r)} + Br_k^{(l,r)},\ Kq_k^{(l,i)} + Br_k^{(l,i)},\ k = 1,\dots,m_l,\ l \in J_{v_0},\ \textit{linearly independent} \tag{88}$$

$\Longleftrightarrow$

$$Kq_k^{(l)} + Br_k^{(l)},\ K\bar{q}_k^{(l)} + B\bar{r}_k^{(l)},\ k = 1,\dots,m_l,\ l \in J_{v_0},\ \textit{linearly independent} \tag{89}$$

$\Longleftrightarrow$

$$q_k^{(l)}\ \bar{q}_k^{(l)},\ k = 1,\dots,m_l,\ l \in J_{v_0},\ \textit{linearly independent} \tag{90}$$

$\Longleftrightarrow$

$$q_k^{(l,r)},\ q_k^{(l,i)},\ k = 1,\dots,m_l,\ l \in J_{v_0},\ \textit{linearly independent} \tag{91}$$

Proof The equivalences (85) $\Longleftrightarrow$ (86) and (87) $\Longleftrightarrow$ (88) are clear.

Now we prove the equivalence of (86) and (87). From the relations

$$(A - \lambda_l E)p_k^{(l)} = p_{k-1}^{(l)} \tag{92}$$

with

$$p_k^{(l)} = \begin{bmatrix} q_k^{(l)} \\ r_k^{(l)} \end{bmatrix}, \tag{93}$$

$k = 1,\dots,m_l$, $l \in J_{v_0}$, in a first step, we derive associated relations for $q_k^{(l)}$ and $r_k^{(l)}$, $k = 1,\dots,m_l$, $l \in J_{v_0}$. Now, (89) means

$$\left[\begin{array}{c|c} 0 & E \\ \hline -M^{-1}K & -M^{-1}B \end{array}\right] \begin{bmatrix} q_k^{(l)} \\ r_k^{(l)} \end{bmatrix} = \lambda_l \begin{bmatrix} q_k^{(l)} \\ r_k^{(l)} \end{bmatrix} + \begin{bmatrix} q_{k-1}^{(l)} \\ r_{k-1}^{(l)} \end{bmatrix}, \tag{94}$$

that is,

$$\boxed{r_k^{(l)} = \lambda_l q_k^{(l)} + q_{k-1}^{(l)}} \tag{95}$$

$$-M^{-1}Kq_k^{(l)} - M^{-1}Br_k^{(l)} = \lambda_l r_k^{(l)} + r_{k-1}^{(l)}$$

or

$$\boxed{Kq_k^{(l)} + Br_k^{(l)} = -M[\lambda_l r_k^{(l)} + r_{k-1}^{(l)}]} \tag{96}$$

$k = 1,\dots,m_l$, $l \in J_{v_0}$. Based on (93) and the assumed regularity of M, we see that (86) is equivalent to

$$\lambda_l r_k^{(l)} + r_{k-1}^{(l)},\ \ \bar{\lambda}_l \bar{r}_k^{(l)} + \bar{r}_{k-1}^{(l)},\ k = 1,\dots,m_l,\ l \in J_{v_0},\ \textit{linearly independent.}$$

In the second step, we show the equivalence of (94) with the following condition:

$r_k^{(l)}\ \bar{r}_k^{(l)},\ k = 1, \dots, m_l,\ l \in J_{v_0},$ *linearly independent,* (97)

and then in the third step, the equivalence of (95) with (87).

Equivalence of (94) and (95):

(94) ⇒(95): So, let (94) be fulfilled. We write $r_k^{(l)}$ in the form

$$r_k^{(l)} = \lambda_l \tilde{r}_k^{(l)} + \tilde{r}_{k-1}^{(l)} \tag{98}$$

$k = 1, \dots, m_l,\ l \in J_{v_0}$, where the $\tilde{r}_k^{(l)}$ are also principal vectors of stage k corresponding to the eigenvalue λ_l. This is done as follows:

$$r_1^{(l)} = \lambda_l \tilde{r}_1^{(l)} + \tilde{r}_0^{(l)}$$

where $\tilde{r}_1^{(l)} = \frac{1}{\lambda_l} r_1^{(l)}$ is a principal vector of stage 1 (or eigenvector) and $\tilde{r}_0^{(l)} = 0$. Similarly,

$$r_2^{(l)} = \lambda_l \tilde{r}_2^{(l)} + \tilde{r}_1^{(l)}$$

where $\tilde{r}_2^{(l)} = \frac{1}{\lambda_l}(r_2^{(l)} - \tilde{r}_1^{(l)})$ is a principal vector of stage 2 corresponding to the eigenvalue λ_l.

Proceeding in this way, using induction, (96) is proven.

Therefore, apart from (94), also the following property must hold:

$r_k^{(l)} = \lambda_l \tilde{r}_k^{(l)} + \tilde{r}_{k-1}^{(l)},\ \bar{r}_k^{(l)} = \bar{\lambda}_l \bar{\tilde{r}}_k^{(l)} + \bar{\tilde{r}}_{k-1}^{(l)}\ k = 1, \dots, m_l,\ l \in J_{v_0},$ *linearly independent,* (99)

which proves (95).

(95) ⇒(94): Let (95) be fulfilled and

$$\sum_{l \in J_{v_0}} \sum_{k=1}^{m_l} \left\{ \alpha_k^{(l)}(\lambda_l r_k^{(l)} + r_{k-1}^{(l)}) + \beta_k^{(l)}(\bar{\lambda}_l \bar{r}_k^{(l)} + \bar{r}_{k-1}^{(l)}) \right\} = 0.$$

Fully written, we obtain with $r_0^{(l)} = 0$,

$$\begin{aligned} \sum_{l \in J_{v_0}} \Big\{ & \alpha_1^{(l)}(\lambda_l r_1^{(l)} + r_0^{(l)}) + \beta_1^{(l)}(\bar{\lambda}_l \bar{r}_1^{(l)} + \bar{r}_0^{(l)}) \\ & + \alpha_2^{(l)}(\lambda_l r_2^{(l)} + r_1^{(l)}) + \beta_2^{(l)}(\bar{\lambda}_l \bar{r}_2^{(l)} + \bar{r}_1^{(l)}) \\ & + \alpha_3^{(l)}(\lambda_l r_3^{(l)} + r_2^{(l)}) + \beta_3^{(l)}(\bar{\lambda}_l \bar{r}_3^{(l)} + \bar{r}_2^{(l)}) + \dots \\ & + \alpha_{m_l}^{(l)}(\lambda_l r_{m_l}^{(l)} + r_{m_l-1}^{(l)}) + \beta_{m_l}^{(l)}(\bar{\lambda}_l \bar{r}_{m_l}^{(l)} + \bar{r}_{m_l-1}^{(l)}) \Big\} \quad = 0 \end{aligned}$$

or regrouping

$$\begin{aligned} \sum_{l \in J_{v_0}} \Big\{ & (\alpha_1^{(l)} \lambda_l + \alpha_2^{(l)}) r_1^{(l)} + (\beta_1^{(l)} \bar{\lambda}_l + \beta_2^{(l)}) \bar{r}_1^{(l)} \\ & + (\alpha_2^{(l)} \lambda_l + \alpha_3^{(l)}) r_2^{(l)} + (\beta_2^{(l)} \bar{\lambda}_l + \beta_3^{(l)}) \bar{r}_2^{(l)} + \dots \\ & + (\alpha_{m_l-1}^{(l)} \lambda_l + \alpha_{m_l}^{(l)}) r_{m_l-1}^{(l)} + (\beta_{m_l-1}^{(l)} \bar{\lambda}_l + \beta_{m_l}^{(l)}) \bar{r}_{m_l}^{(l)} \\ & + (\alpha_{m_l}^{(l)} \lambda_l) r_{m_l}^{(l)} + (\beta_{m_l}^{(l)} \bar{\lambda}_l) \bar{r}_{m_l}^{(l)} \Big\} = 0 \end{aligned} \tag{100}$$

By assumption, from the last line, we get

$$\alpha^{(l)}_{m_l}\lambda_l = 0,\ \ \beta^{(l)}_{m_l}\bar{\lambda}_l = 0$$

or

$$\alpha^{(l)}_{m_l} = \beta^{(l)}_{m_l} = 0;$$

further,

$$\alpha^{(l)}_{m_l-1}\lambda_l + \alpha^{(l)}_{m_l} = 0,\ \ \beta^{(l)}_{m_l-1}\bar{\lambda}_l + \beta^{(l)}_{m_l} = 0,$$

leading to

$$\alpha^{(l)}_{m_l-1} = \beta^{(l)}_{m_l-1} = 0.$$

Continuing in this way, we ultimately obtain

$$\alpha^{(l)}_{k} = \beta^{(l)}_{k} = 0,\ k = 1,\ldots,m_l,\ l \in J_{v_0},$$

so that (94) is proven.

Further, because of the representation (92), then (95) is equivalent to

$$\lambda_l q^{(l)}_k + q^{(l)}_{k-1},\ \ \bar{\lambda}_l \bar{q}^{(l)}_k + \bar{q}^{(l)}_{k-1},\ k = 1,\ldots,m_l,\ l \in J_{v_0},\ \textit{linearly independent}. \tag{101}$$

Similarly as above, this is equivalent to (87).

On the whole, Lemma A.2 is proven. □

Alternative proof for the positiveness of $X_{S,0}$ resp. $\varphi_{S,0}$ when $S = [-M^{-1}K, -M^{-1}B]$

In the special case of $S = [-M^{-1}K, -M^{-1}B]$, there is an alternative proof for the positiveness of $X_{S,0}$. This alternative proof is simpler, but the foregoing one is applicable to more general forms of S.

We employ the vector resp. matrix norm $\|\cdot\|_2$ to obtain

$$\begin{aligned}\|x_S(t)\|_2^2 &= \|Sx(t)\|_2^2 = \|-M^{-1}Ky(t)\|_2^2 + \|-M^{-1}B\dot{y}(t)\|_2^2 \\ &\geq \|K^{-1}M\|_2^{-2}\|y(t)\|_2^2 + \|B^{-1}M\|_2^{-2}\|\dot{y}(t)\|_2^2 \\ &\geq X_{S,2,0}^2\|x(t)\|_2^2\end{aligned}$$

with

$$X_{S,2,0}^2 = \min\{\|K^{-1}M\|_2^{-2}, \|B^{-1}M\|_2^{-2}\}$$

so that

$$\|x_S(t)\|_2 \geq X_{S,2,0}\|x(t)\|_2.$$

Due to the equivalence of norms in finite-dimensional spaces, this entails that for every vector norm $\|\cdot\|$ one has

$$\|x_S(t)\| \geq X_{S,0}\|x(t)\|$$

with a positive constant $X_{S,0}$.

A similar proof for the positiveness of $\varphi_{S,0}$ is possible. This is left to the reader.

13

Gram–Schmidt–Fisher scoring algorithm for parameter orthogonalization in MLE

John Kwagyan[1*], Victor Apprey[1] and [†]George E. Bonney[1]

*Corresponding author: John Kwagyan, Design, Biostatistics & Population Studies & Department of Family Medicine, College of Medicine, Howard University, Washington, DC 20059, USA
E-mail: jkwagyan@howard.edu

Reviewing editor: Zudi Lu, University of Southampton, UK

Abstract: The estimation of parameters is a key component in statistical modelling and inference. However, parametrization of certain likelihood functions could lead to highly correlated estimates, causing numerical problems, mathematical complexities and difficulty in estimation or erroneous interpretation and subsequently inference. In statistical estimation, the concept of orthogonalization is familiar as a simplifying technique that allows parameters to be estimated independently and thus separates information from each other. We introduce a Fisher scoring iterative process that incorporates the Gram–Schmidt orthogonalization technique for maximum likelihood estimation. A finite mixture model for correlated binary data is used to illustrate the implementation of the method with discussion of application to oesophageal cancer data.

Subjects: Mathematics & Statistics; Medicine; Medicine, Dentistry, Nursing & Allied Health; Science

Keywords: correlated data; Fisher scoring algorithm; Gram–Schmidt orthogonalization; maximum likelihood estimation; orthogonal parameters

1. Introduction

The problem of estimating parameters is one of the key stages in fitting a statistical model to a set of data. Typically, the model will contain some parameters which are not of interest in themselves, but whose values affect the inferences that we make about the parameters of direct interest. Parametrization used when working with certain distributions could lead to high correlations of the maximum likelihood estimates. Maximization algorithms converge rapidly if the initial estimates are good, the likelihood function is well approximated by a quadratic in the neighbourhood of the parameter space and the information matrix is well conditioned, which means that the parameter estimates are not strongly intercorrelated. High intercorrelation of parameters causes numerical problems, and difficulty or erroneous interpretation in the parameter estimation. In statistical

ABOUT THE AUTHOR

Dr John Kwagyan is a mathematician and a public health and medical researcher. His research interests include mathematical and statistical modelling of correlated data, clinical trials, survival models, big data analytics, statistical genetics and pharmacokinetic & pharmacodynamics modeling. He is currently the director of Biostatistics, Epidemiology and Research Design, of the Georgetown-Howard University Center for Clinical and Translational Science, Howard University College of Medicine and adjunct professor in the Department of Mathematics, Howard University, Washington, DC, USA.

PUBLIC INTEREST STATEMENT

In statistical estimation, the concept of orthogonalization is simply a technique that allows parameters to be estimated independently, through the rotation of the parameter space. The paper introduces an iterative algorithm that utilizes the Fisher scoring process and incorporates the Gram–Schmidt orthogonalization technique for maximum likelihood estimation. The algorithm that we propose provides an exceedingly convenient method for multi-parameter statistical problems first to reduce numerical difficulties and second to improve accuracy in parameter estimation.

estimation, the concept of orthogonalization is familiar as a simplifying technique that allows parameters to be estimated independently, through rotation of the parameter space. Computationally, all that is required is that the original parameters should be computable from the new ones, and vice-versa. An injective transformation will therefore be desirable, though not necessary.

Ross (1970) gave a comprehensive discussion of techniques that can be used to reduce correlation in particular problems. Among them are sequential and nested maximizations. Kalbliesch and Sprott (1970) discuss methods aimed at eliminating nuisance parameters from the likelihood function so that inference can be made about only the parameters of interest. Amari (1982,1985) derived from a theoretical point of view, a general criteria for the existence and construction of orthogonal parameters for statistical models using differential geometry. Cox and Reid (1987) gave a more general procedure and covered the advantages in maximum likelihood estimation. The approach, though popular in theoretical statistics, is computationally impractical in many application situations. Willmot (1988) discussed orthogonal parametrization but only for a two-parameter family of discrete distributions. His method, however, does not allow for higher parametric problems. Hurlimann (1992) discusses the existence of orthogonal parameterization to the mean, characterized by a partial differential equation involving the mean, the variance and cummulant generating functions. Godambe (1991) deals with the problem of nuisance parameters, within a semi-parametric set-up which includes the class of distributions associated with generalized linear models. Their technique uses the optimum orthogonal estimating functions of Godambe and Thompson (1989). Bonney and Kissling (1986) applied the Gram–Schmidt orthogonalization (Clayton, 1971) to multinormal variates and presented an application in genetics. Kwagyan, Apprey and Bonney (2001) presented the idea of Gram–Schmidt parameter orthogonalization in genetic analysis. A major consequence of parameter orthogonalization is that the maximum likelihood estimate of one parameter is not affected or changes slowly with the misspecification of the other. The most direct interpreted consequence is that the maximum likelihood estimates of orthogonal coordinates are asymptotically independent.

The remainder of this paper is organized as follows. In Section 2, the disposition model for clustered binary data proposed by Bonney (1995,1998a) and further investigated by Kwagyan (2001) is introduced and used as a motivation. In Section 3, an overview of maximum likelihood estimation and parameter orthogonalization is then presented. Section 4 develops the proposed Gram–Schmidt parameter orthogonalization and iterative scheme for maximum likelihood estimation. In section Section 5, fitting algorithm of the disposition model is discussed with application to oesophageal cancer data in Chinese families. Finally, Section 6 wraps up with discussion of the methodology and outlines directions for further research.

2. Model for correlated binary data

Consider a sample of N groups, each of size $n_i, i = 1, \ldots, N$; and let $Y_i = (Y_{i1}, \ldots, Y_{in_i})^T$ denote the vector of binary outcomes for the ith group. It is postulated that the measures of the outcomes within a group are possibly correlated. Further suppose the jth subject in the ith group has $1 \times p$ individual-specific covariates $X_{ij} = (x_{ij1}, \ldots, x_{ijp})$ and let the ith group have group-specific covariates $Z_i = (z_1, \ldots, z_q)$. Let δ_{ij} denote the conditional probability of $Y_{ij} = 1$ given $Y_{ij'} = 1$; that is

$$\delta_{ij} = P(Y_{ij} = 1 | Y_{ij'} = 1), \quad j \neq j', \quad j, j' = 1, 2, \ldots, n.$$

We call δ_{ij} the individual disposition which is simply interpreted as the probability of the outcome on one unit given another unit from the same cluster has the attribute. This in essence is an indication of aggregation. Assume further that within the group, a pair of observations satisfy the relation

$$\frac{P(Y_{ij} = 1, Y_{ij'} = 1)}{P(Y_{ij} = 1)P(Y_{ij'} = 1)} = \frac{1}{\alpha_i}, \quad \alpha_i < 0, \quad j \neq j', \quad j, j' = 1, 2, \ldots, n,$$

where α_i is common for all pairs. Clearly, $\alpha_i = 1$ implies independence of the observations. Thus, α_i is a measure of the departure from independence and is called the relative disposition. With the above definitions, Bonney (1995,1998a), and from further investigation through a latent mixture formulation by Kwagyan (2001), has shown that the joint distribution for the N groups can be based on

$$L(\Theta) = \prod_{i=1}^{N} \left\{ (1-\alpha_i) \prod_{j=1}^{n_i} (1-y_{ij}) + \alpha_i \prod_{j=1}^{n_i} \delta_{ij}^{y_{ij}} \left(1-\delta_{ij}\right)^{1-y_{ij}} \right\} \tag{2.1}$$

The α_i and δ_{ij} are generally modelled as

$$\alpha_i = \frac{1+e^{[-\{M(Z_i)+D(Z_i)\}]}}{1+e^{-M(Z_i)}}, \delta_{ij} = \frac{1}{1+e^{-[M(Z_i)+D(Z_i)+W(X_{ij})]}}$$

where $M(Z_i)$ is function of mean effects, $D(Z_i)$ is a measure of within-group dependence and $W(X_{ij})$ a function describing the effect of the individual covariates. Typically, $M(Z_i)$, $D(Z_i)$ and $W(X_{ij})$ are modelled, respectively, as

$$\begin{aligned} M(Z_i) &= \lambda_0 + \lambda_1 Z_1 + \ldots + \lambda_p Z_p \\ D(Z_i) &= \gamma_0 + \gamma_1 Z_1 + \ldots + \gamma_q Z_q \\ W(X_{ij}) &= \beta_1 X_1 + \beta_2 X_2 + \ldots + \beta_r X_r \end{aligned}$$

where

$$\boldsymbol{\Theta}' = \{\boldsymbol{\Lambda}, \boldsymbol{\Gamma}, \boldsymbol{\beta}\}$$

and

$$\boldsymbol{\Lambda} = \gamma_0, \ldots, \gamma_q, \boldsymbol{\Gamma} = \lambda_0, \ldots, \lambda_q\}, \boldsymbol{\beta} = \{\beta_1, \ldots, \beta_r\}$$

are unknown parameters to be estimated. When data consist of a few large clusters or truncated or size-biased samples, Bonney (1998b) has shown that there is little or no information to separate the effects of $M(Z)$ and $D(Z)$. The estimates of the parameters tend to be highly correlated. Similar problems occur in other approaches as well. The popular estimating equations approach, GEE (Liang & Zeger, 1986), suffers the same problems when there are only a few large clusters (see discussion of Prentice, 1988).

3. Maximum likelihood estimation and parameter orthogonalization

There are different statistical methods for estimating parameters, but the approach most commonly used is that based on maximum likelihood estimation. Maximum likelihood estimates of parameters are those values of the parameters that make the likelihood function a maximum. Let $\mathbf{y} = (y_1, y_2, \ldots, y_n)$ be observed data from a population with a probability distribution $P(y; \boldsymbol{\theta})$ indexed by the vector of unknown parameters $\boldsymbol{\theta} = (\theta_1, \ldots, \theta_p)$. The likelihood function for $\boldsymbol{\theta}$ is the joint distribution

$$L(\boldsymbol{\theta}; y) = \prod_{i=1}^{n} P(y_i; \boldsymbol{\theta})$$

According to the likelihood principle, $\hat{\boldsymbol{\theta}}$ is regarded as the value of $\boldsymbol{\theta}$ which is most strongly supported by the observed data. In practice, $\hat{\boldsymbol{\theta}}$ is obtained by direct maximization of Log $L(\boldsymbol{\theta})$ or by solving the set of equations from the score function, $U(\boldsymbol{\theta})$,where

$$U(\boldsymbol{\theta}) = \frac{\partial \log L}{\partial \boldsymbol{\theta}} = 0$$

for which the Hessian matrix $H(\boldsymbol{\theta}) = (\frac{\partial^2 \log L}{\partial\theta\partial\theta^T})$ is negative definite. The matrix $I(\boldsymbol{\theta}) = E[-H(\boldsymbol{\theta})] = E(-\frac{\partial^2 \log L}{\partial\theta\partial\theta^T})$ is called *Fisher (expected) Information matrix* for $\boldsymbol{\theta}$ and its inverse, $\boldsymbol{\Omega}(\boldsymbol{\theta}) = [I(\boldsymbol{\theta})]^{-1}$ gives the asymptotic variances and covariances of the maximum likelihood estimates.

Suppose $\boldsymbol{\theta}$ is a p parameter vector that is partitioned into two vectors $\boldsymbol{\theta}_1$ and $\boldsymbol{\theta}_2$ of lengths p_1 and p_2, respectively, $p_1 + p_2 = p$. Cox and Reid (1987) define $\boldsymbol{\theta}_1$ to be orthogonal to $\boldsymbol{\theta}_2$ if the elements of the information matrix satisfy

$$E\left(\frac{\partial l}{\partial\theta_s}\frac{\partial l}{\partial\theta_t}\right) = E\left(-\frac{\partial^2 l}{\partial\theta_s\partial\theta_t}\right) = 0, \quad s = 1,\dots,p_1;\ t = p_1+1,\dots,p$$

If this holds for all $\boldsymbol{\theta}$ in the parameter space, it is sometimes called global orthogonality. If it holds at only one parameter value say θ^0, then $\boldsymbol{\theta}_1$ and $\boldsymbol{\theta}_2$ are said to be locally orthogonal at θ^0.

We now discuss Cox and Reid (1987) approach for the construction of orthogonal parameters. Suppose that initially the likelihood is specified in terms of $(\theta,\boldsymbol{\gamma}), \boldsymbol{\gamma} = (\gamma_1,\dots,\gamma_p)$ and let $l(\theta,\boldsymbol{\gamma})$ be the log-likelihood function. Assume θ is the parameter of interest and $\boldsymbol{\gamma}$ the set of nuisance parameters. We seek a transformation from $(\theta,\boldsymbol{\gamma})$ to a new set of orthogonal parameters $(\theta,\boldsymbol{\lambda})$, $\boldsymbol{\lambda} = (\lambda_1,\dots,\lambda_p)$. It is easiest to think of the original parameters $\boldsymbol{\gamma}$ as some function of the new parameters, $\boldsymbol{\lambda}$, that is

$$\boldsymbol{\gamma} = \boldsymbol{\gamma}(\theta,\boldsymbol{\lambda})$$

Then, the log-likelihood function can be expressed as

$$l^*(\theta,\boldsymbol{\lambda}) = l(\theta,\gamma_1(\theta,\lambda),\dots,\gamma_p(\theta,\lambda)),$$

where now l^* refers to the log-likelihood in the new parametrization. Taking derivatives of this equation with respect to the new parameters, we have by the chain rule;

$$\frac{\partial l^*}{\partial\theta} = \frac{\partial l}{\partial\theta} + \sum_{j=1}^{p}\frac{\partial l}{\partial\gamma_j}\frac{\partial\gamma_j}{\partial\theta}$$

and

$$\frac{\partial^2 l^*}{\partial\theta\partial\lambda_k} = \sum_{l}^{p}\frac{\partial^2 l}{\partial\theta\partial\gamma_l}\frac{\partial\gamma_l}{\partial\lambda_k} + \sum_{j}^{p}\sum_{l}^{p}\frac{\partial^2 l}{\partial\gamma_j\partial\gamma_l}\frac{\partial\gamma_l}{\partial\theta_k}\frac{\partial\gamma_j}{\partial\theta} + \sum_{l}^{p}\frac{\partial l}{\partial\gamma_l}\frac{\partial^2\gamma_l}{\partial\theta\partial\lambda_k} \tag{3.1}$$

The derivatives of $\boldsymbol{\gamma}$ are not functions of the data, and hence are constant with respect to expectation. Therefore, after taken expectations with respect to the distribution of the data indexed by the parameters $\{\theta,\boldsymbol{\gamma}\}$,the last term in Equation 3.1 is zero. If the parameters are orthogonal, then again from Equation 3.1,

$$\sum_{l=1}^{p}\frac{\partial\gamma_l}{\partial\lambda_k}\left(E\left\{\frac{\partial^2 l}{\partial\theta\partial\gamma_l}\right\} + \sum_{j=1}^{p}E\left\{\frac{\partial^2 l}{\partial\gamma_l\partial\gamma_j}\right\}\frac{\partial\gamma_j}{\partial\theta}\right) = 0.$$

so that the orthogonality equations are

$$\sum_{l=1}^{p}\frac{\partial\gamma_l}{\partial\lambda_k}\left(E\left\{\frac{\partial^2 l}{\partial\theta\partial\gamma_l}\right\} + \sum_{j=1}^{p}E\left\{\frac{\partial^2 l}{\partial\gamma_l\partial\gamma_j}\right\}\frac{\partial\gamma_j}{\partial\theta}\right) = 0, \quad k = 1,\dots,p.$$

We require the transformation from $(\theta,\boldsymbol{\gamma})$ to $(\theta,\boldsymbol{\lambda})$ to have a non-zero Jacobian; hence,

$$\sum_{j=1}^{p}E\left\{\frac{\partial^2 l}{\partial\gamma_l\partial\gamma_k}\right\}\frac{\partial\gamma_j}{\partial\theta} = -E\left\{\frac{\partial^2 l}{\partial\theta\partial\gamma_k}\right\}, \quad k = 1,\dots,p$$

This is a system of p differential equations which must be solved for $\boldsymbol{\gamma}(\theta, \boldsymbol{\lambda})$. In fact, since $\boldsymbol{\lambda}$ does not enter explicitly into the equations, the solution for γ_j can contain an arbitrary function of λ as the integrating constant. It is noted in the discussion of Cox and Reid that although it is sometimes theoretically possible to find a differential equation, simple explicit solutions of the differential equation were not feasible for the some models. There are also cases where explicit solutions are possible, but the original nuisance parameters could not be explicitly expressed in terms of the orthogonal parameter (Hills, 1987). In general, global orthogonalization can also not be achieved by this approach.

4. Gram–Schmidt parameter orthogonalization

The Gram–Schmidt orthogonalization process (Clayton, 1971) is equivalent to the linear transformation $\boldsymbol{\Theta} = (\theta_1, \dots, \theta_p)$ to $\Theta^* = (\theta_1^*, \dots, \theta_p^*)$ defined as:

$$\begin{aligned} \theta_1^* &= \theta_1 \\ \theta_2^* &= \theta_2 - b_{21}\theta_1 \\ &------- \\ \theta_j^* &= \theta_j - \sum_{k=1}^{j-1} b_{j(j-k)}\theta_{j-k},\ j = 2, \dots, p \end{aligned} \tag{4.1}$$

In linear regression set-up, θ_j^* is θ_j adjusted for $\theta_1, \dots, \theta_p$, and b_{jk}, $j = 2, \dots, p; k = 1, \dots, (j-1)$ are the multiple regression coefficients. Writing this using matrix notation, we have

$$\boldsymbol{\Theta}^* = \mathbf{B}\boldsymbol{\Theta}$$

where $\mathbf{B}$, the transformation matrix, is lower triangular with ones along the diagonal. The transformation matrix is chosen so that $\theta_1^*, \theta_2^*, \dots, \theta_p^*$ are mutually uncorrelated. The Jacobian of the transformation is unity. Suppose $\boldsymbol{\Omega}$ is the covariance matrix of Θ, then the covariance matrix of $\boldsymbol{\Theta}^*$, $\boldsymbol{\Omega}^* = B\Omega B^T$ is a diagonal matrix. *We recommend that the parameters be ordered in terms of interest. This ensures that the parameters of most interest are least affected by round-off errors.*

4.1. Evaluation of the transformation matrix

To evaluate the transformation matrix, $\mathbf{B}$, let $\boldsymbol{\Sigma} = (c_{ij})$, $i,j = 1, \dots, p$, where $c_{ij} = \mathrm{cov}(\theta_i, \theta_j) = \left[E(-\frac{\partial^2 \log L}{\partial\theta_i \partial\theta_j})\right]^{-1}$, are elements of the covariance matrix. The orthogonality relation, $c_{ij}^* = \mathrm{cov}(\theta_i^*, \theta_j^*) = 0\ (i \neq j)$ implies that for $i < j$,

$$\begin{aligned} 0 = c_{ij}^* &= \mathrm{cov}(\theta_i^*, \theta_j^*) \\ &= \mathrm{cov}(\theta_i - \sum_{k'=1}^{i-1} b_{i(i-k')}\theta_{i-k'},\ \theta_j - \sum_{k=1}^{j-1} b_{j(j-k)}\theta_{j-k}) \\ &= \mathrm{cov}(\theta_i, \theta_j) - \sum_{k=1}^{j-1} b_{j(j-k)}\mathrm{cov}(\theta_i, \theta_{j-k}) \\ &\quad - \sum_{k'=1}^{i-1} b_{i(i-k')}\left\{ \mathrm{cov}(\theta_{j-k'}, \theta_j) + \sum_{k=1}^{j-1} b_{j(j-k)}\mathrm{cov}(\theta_{i-k'}, \theta_{j-k}) \right\} \\ &= c_{ij} - \sum_{k=1}^{j-1} b_{j(j-k)}c_{i,j-k} - \sum_{k'=1}^{i-1} b_{i(i-k')}\left\{ c_{j-k',j} + \sum_{k=1}^{j-1} b_{j(j-k)}c_{i-k',j-k} \right\} \\ &= c_{ij} - \sum_{k=1}^{j-1} b_{j(j-k)}c_{i,j-k} - \sum_{k'=1}^{i-1} b_{i(i-k')}\left\{ c_{j-k',j}^* \right\} \\ &= c_{ij} - \sum_{k=1}^{j-1} b_{j(j-k)}c_{i,j-k},\ \text{since } c_{j-k',j}^* = 0 \end{aligned}$$

Thus, the system of linear equations to be solved for entries of the transformation matrix based on the covariance matrix is:

$$c_{ij} = \sum_{k=1}^{j-1} b_{j(j-k)} c_{i(j-k)}, i = 1, \ldots (j-1), \quad j = 2, \ldots, p. \tag{4.2}$$

Consequently, solving the system of linear equations (4.2), we obtain the elements of the transformation matrix as

$$b_{jk} = \sum_{r=1}^{j-1} c_{rj} I_{r(j-k)}, \; j = 2, \ldots, p; \quad k = 1, \ldots, (j-1). \tag{4.3}$$

where $I_{r(j-k)}$ are entries of the information matrix. The observed information matrix would be a good approximation of the expected information, if there is difficulty evaluating it.

For illustration, when $p = 4$, we have Gram-Schmidt orthogonalization process in matrix notation as,

$$\begin{pmatrix} \theta_1^* \\ \theta_2^* \\ \theta_3^* \\ \theta_4^* \end{pmatrix} = \begin{pmatrix} 1 & 0 & 0 & 0 \\ -b_{21} & 1 & 0 & 0 \\ -b_{31} & -b_{32} & 1 & 0 \\ -b_{41} & -b_{42} & -b_{43} & 1 \end{pmatrix} \begin{pmatrix} \theta_1 \\ \theta_2 \\ \theta_3 \\ \theta_4 \end{pmatrix}$$

The orthogonalization relationship of the parameters $(\theta_1^*, \theta_2^*, \theta_3^*, \theta_4^*)$ implies

$$\begin{aligned}
0 &= c_{12} - b_{21}c_{11} \\
0 &= c_{13} - b_{32}c_{12} - b_{31}c_{11} \\
0 &= c_{23} - b_{32}c_{22} - b_{31}c_{12} \\
0 &= c_{14} - b_{43}c_{13} - b_{42}c_{12} - b_{41}c_{11} \\
0 &= c_{24} - b_{43}c_{23} - b_{42}c_{22} - b_{41}c_{12} \\
0 &= c_{34} - b_{43}c_{33} - b_{42}c_{23} - b_{41}c_{13}
\end{aligned}$$

And so the system of linear equations to be solved for the elements of the transformation matrix is:

$$\left(\begin{array}{c|cc|ccc} c_{11} & 0 & 0 & 0 & 0 & 0 \\ \hline 0 & c_{11} & c_{12} & 0 & 0 & 0 \\ 0 & c_{12} & c_{22} & 0 & 0 & 0 \\ \hline 0 & 0 & 0 & c_{11} & c_{12} & c_{13} \\ 0 & 0 & 0 & c_{12} & c_{22} & c_{13} \\ 0 & 0 & 0 & c_{13} & c & c_{33} \end{array}\right) \left(\begin{array}{c} b_{21} \\ \hline b_{31} \\ b_{32} \\ \hline b_{41} \\ b_{42} \\ b_{43} \end{array}\right) = \left(\begin{array}{c} c_{12} \\ \hline c_{13} \\ c_{23} \\ \hline c_{14} \\ c_{24} \\ c_{34} \end{array}\right) \tag{4.4}$$

Let Q be the matrix of coefficients for the system of equations (4.4) Above; then, we note that Q is a patterned block diagonal matrix. Furthermore, let $D_r (r = 1, 2, 3)$, be the block diagonal of Q; then, in this illustration,

$$Q = \begin{pmatrix} D_1 & 0 & 0 \\ 0 & D_2 & 0 \\ 0 & 0 & D_3 \end{pmatrix}$$

where

$$D_1 = (c_{11}), D_2 = \begin{pmatrix} c_{11} & c_{12} \\ c_{12} & c_{22} \end{pmatrix}, \quad D_3 = \begin{pmatrix} c_{11} & c_{12} & c_{13} \\ c_{12} & c_{22} & c_{23} \\ c_{13} & c_{23} & c_{33} \end{pmatrix}$$

Thus, D_r is the covariance matrix of the first r parameters. It can easily be shown that D_r is symmetric and positive definite and so Q is non-singular. A unique solution thus exists for the system of linear *Equation (4.3)* and in general for *Equation (4.2)*. And so, the elements of the transformation matrix, **B**, can be obtained as

$$\left(\begin{array}{c} b_{21} \\ \hline b_{31} \\ b_{32} \\ \hline b_{41} \\ b_{42} \\ b_{43} \end{array}\right) = \left(\begin{array}{c|cc|ccc} c_{11} & 0 & 0 & 0 & 0 & 0 \\ \hline 0 & c_{11} & c_{12} & 0 & 0 & 0 \\ 0 & c_{12} & c_{22} & 0 & 0 & 0 \\ \hline 0 & 0 & 0 & c_{11} & c_{12} & c_{13} \\ 0 & 0 & 0 & c_{12} & c_{22} & c_{23} \\ 0 & 0 & 0 & c_{13} & c_{23} & c_{33} \end{array}\right)^{-1} \left(\begin{array}{c} c_{12} \\ \hline c_{13} \\ c_{23} \\ \hline c_{14} \\ c_{24} \\ c_{34} \end{array}\right)$$

or

$$\left(\begin{array}{c} b_{21} \\ \hline b_{31} \\ b_{32} \\ \hline b_{41} \\ b_{42} \\ b_{43} \end{array}\right) = \left(\begin{array}{c|cc|ccc} I_{11} & 0 & 0 & 0 & 0 & 0 \\ \hline 0 & I_{11} & I_{12} & 0 & 0 & 0 \\ 0 & I_{12} & I_{22} & 0 & 0 & 0 \\ \hline 0 & 0 & 0 & I_{11} & I_{12} & I_{13} \\ 0 & 0 & 0 & I_{12} & I_{22} & I_{23} \\ 0 & 0 & 0 & I_{13} & I_{23} & I_{33} \end{array}\right) \left(\begin{array}{c} c_{12} \\ \hline c_{13} \\ c_{23} \\ \hline c_{14} \\ c_{24} \\ c_{34} \end{array}\right)$$

where I_{ij} are the entries of the information matrix .

Having obtained $\boldsymbol{\Theta}^* = (\theta_1^*, \dots, \theta_p^*)$ the original parameters, $\boldsymbol{\Theta} = (\theta_1, \dots, \theta_p)$ can be obtained recursively as

$$\theta_1 = \theta_1^*$$

$$\theta_j = \theta_j^* + \sum_{k=1}^{j-1} b_{j(j-k)}\theta_{j-k}, \; j = 2, \dots, p$$

or writing this using matrix notation, we have

$$\boldsymbol{\Theta} = \mathbf{B}^{-1}\boldsymbol{\Theta}^*$$

4.2. Block orthogonalization

Let $\boldsymbol{\Theta}^T = \{\boldsymbol{\Lambda}, \boldsymbol{\Gamma}, \boldsymbol{\beta}\}$ be a set of parameters to be estimated where

$$\boldsymbol{\Lambda} = (\lambda_0, \lambda_1, \dots, \lambda_q)^T; \quad \boldsymbol{\Gamma} = (\gamma_0, \gamma_1, \dots, \gamma_p)^T; \quad \boldsymbol{\beta} = (\beta_1, \beta_{1,} \dots, \beta_r)^T$$

Suppose further that the set $\boldsymbol{\Theta}^T = \{\boldsymbol{\Lambda}, \boldsymbol{\Gamma}, \boldsymbol{\beta}\}$ is correlated. Then, we wish to find a new set $\boldsymbol{\Theta}^{*T} = \{\boldsymbol{\Lambda}^*, \boldsymbol{\Gamma}^*, \boldsymbol{\beta}^*\}$ through a linear transformation such that the vector of parameters in $\boldsymbol{\Theta}^*$ is mutually uncorrelated. We allow for correlation, if any, within each set of parameters in $\boldsymbol{\Omega}^*$.

Further suppose the vector $\boldsymbol{\beta}$ is the set of parameters of interest. Then, the Gram-Schmidt orthogonalization process computes the new set of parameters in terms of the original parameters as follows:

$$\boldsymbol{\beta}^* = \boldsymbol{\beta}$$
$$\boldsymbol{\Lambda}^* = \boldsymbol{\Lambda} - B_{21}\boldsymbol{\beta}$$
$$\boldsymbol{\Gamma}^* = \boldsymbol{\Gamma} - B_{31}\boldsymbol{\Lambda} - B_{32}\boldsymbol{\beta}$$

where B_{21}, B_{31} and B_{32} are matrices with dimensions $q \times r$, $p \times q$ and $p \times r$, respectively.

In matrix notation, we write

$$\begin{pmatrix} \boldsymbol{\beta}^* \\ \boldsymbol{\Lambda}^* \\ \boldsymbol{\Gamma}^* \end{pmatrix} = \begin{pmatrix} 1 & 0 & 0 \\ -B_{21} & 1 & 0 \\ -B_{31} & -B_{32} & 1 \end{pmatrix} \begin{pmatrix} \boldsymbol{\beta} \\ \boldsymbol{\Lambda} \\ \boldsymbol{\Gamma} \end{pmatrix}$$

or

$$\boldsymbol{\Theta}^* = \mathbf{B}\boldsymbol{\Theta}$$

where $\mathbf{B}$ is a lower triangular block matrix whose diagonal unit matrix is the transformation matrix chosen such that $\boldsymbol{\Lambda}^*, \boldsymbol{\Gamma}^*, \boldsymbol{\beta}^*$ are mutually uncorrelated and where $\boldsymbol{\Theta}^{*T}\boldsymbol{\Theta}$ is a block diagonal matrix. The Jacobian of the transformation is unity. The only way in which this procedure could break down would be if one of the vectors of $\boldsymbol{\Theta}$ is identically zero. From the method of formation of $\boldsymbol{\Theta}^*$, it is clear that it is a linear combination of the vectors in $\boldsymbol{\Theta}$. If $\boldsymbol{\Theta}$ is identically zero, this means that $\boldsymbol{\Theta}$ are linearly dependent, thus contradicting the assumption of independence. Extensions to more than three sets of vectors of parameters readily follow.

4.3. Gram–Schmidt–Fisher scoring algorithm

We introduce a modification of the Fisher scoring algorithm incorporating the Gram–Schmidt process to obtain an information matrix which is diagonal and thus ensuring the approximate (near) orthogonality and consequently the stability of the estimates of the new parameters. Since the transformation is linear and injective, the original parameters are readily obtained.

Let $l(\boldsymbol{\theta};\mathbf{y})$ be the log-likelihood in the original Parametrization; then, Fisher scoring algorithm is given by the iterative routine

$$\boldsymbol{\theta}_{m+1} = \boldsymbol{\theta}_m + [\mathbf{I}(\boldsymbol{\theta}_m)]^{-1}\mathbf{U}(\boldsymbol{\theta}_m) \qquad (4.5)$$

where $\mathbf{I}(\boldsymbol{\theta})$ is the expected information matrix and $\mathbf{U}(\boldsymbol{\theta})$ is the score function.

Suppose $\boldsymbol{\theta}$ is transformed to $\boldsymbol{\theta}^*$ through the Gram–Schmidt orthogonalization process. Let $\mathbf{B}= (b_{ij})$ be the matrix of transformation, defined as in *Equation (3.4)*. Then, since $\mathbf{B}$ is square and non-singular, we can write from *Equation (4.5)*.

$$\begin{aligned} \mathbf{B}\boldsymbol{\theta}_{m+1} &= \mathbf{B}\boldsymbol{\theta}_m + \mathbf{B}[\mathbf{I}(\boldsymbol{\theta}_m)]^{-1}[\mathbf{B}^T(\mathbf{B}^T)^{-1}]\mathbf{U}(\boldsymbol{\theta}_m) \\ \mathbf{B}\boldsymbol{\theta}_{m+1} &= \mathbf{B}\boldsymbol{\theta}_m + \{\mathbf{B}[\mathbf{I}(\boldsymbol{\theta}_m)]^{-1}\mathbf{B}^T\}[(\mathbf{B}^T)^{-1}\mathbf{U}(\boldsymbol{\theta}_m)] \\ \boldsymbol{\theta}^*_{m+1} &= \boldsymbol{\theta}^*_m + [\mathbf{I}(\boldsymbol{\theta}^*_m)]^{-1}\mathbf{U}(\boldsymbol{\theta}^*_m) \end{aligned} \qquad (4.6)$$

where

$$\boldsymbol{\theta}^*_m = \mathbf{B}\boldsymbol{\theta}_m$$
$$\mathbf{I}(\boldsymbol{\theta}^*_m) = \mathbf{B}[\mathbf{I}(\boldsymbol{\theta}_m)]^{-1}\mathbf{B}^T \text{ is asymptotically diagonal}$$
$$\mathbf{U}(\boldsymbol{\theta}^*_m) = (\mathbf{B}^T)^{-1}\mathbf{U}(\boldsymbol{\theta}_m)$$

We shall call *Equation (4.6)* the Gram–Schmidt–Fisher scoring algorithm.

4.3.1. Algorithmic process

The proposed Gram–Schmit–Fisher scoring algorithm is a *2-stage* iterative process that oscillates between Equations (4.3) and (4.6) until convergence and is described iteratively as follows:

1. Start with an initial estimate of the original parameter, $\boldsymbol{\theta}$, denoted by $\boldsymbol{\theta}^{(0)}$.
2. Estimate $\mathbf{B}$ at $\boldsymbol{\theta}^{(0)}$ from *Equation 4.3* that is $b_{jk} = \sum_{r=1}^{j-1} c_{rj} I_{r(j-k)}, \quad j = 2, \dots, p; \quad k = 1, \dots, (j-1)$.
3. Determine the initial estimate of the orthogonal parameterization, $\boldsymbol{\theta}^{*(0)}$ from *Equation 4.1*, i.e. $\theta_1^{*(0)} = \theta_1^{(0)}, \theta_j^{*(0)} = \theta_j^{(0)} - \sum_{k=1}^{j-1} b_{j(j-k)} \theta_{j-k}^{(0)}, j = 2, \dots, p.$
4. Update $\boldsymbol{\theta}^*$ to obtain a new value for $\boldsymbol{\theta}^{*(1)}$, that is $\boldsymbol{\theta}^{*(1)} = \boldsymbol{\theta}^{*(0)} + \theta^*$.
5. Update $\boldsymbol{\theta}$ to obtain a new value for $\boldsymbol{\theta}^{(1)}$, recursively as $\boldsymbol{\theta}^{(1)} = \mathbf{B}^{-1}\boldsymbol{\theta}^{*(1)}$.
6. Repeat steps 2 through 5 using $\boldsymbol{\theta}^{*(1)}$ to obtain $\boldsymbol{\theta}^{*(2)}$.
7. Stop when $|\boldsymbol{\theta}^{*(n-1)} - \boldsymbol{\theta}^{*(n)}| < \varepsilon$.

4.4. Example

We consider a sample problem which concerns inference about the difference between two exponential means. Let Y_1 and Y_2 be the independent exponential random variables with means ϕ and $(\phi + \psi)$, respectively. Then, the joint distribution is given by the function

$$f(y_1, y_2 | \phi, \psi) = \frac{1}{\phi(\phi + \psi)} \exp\left(-\left[\frac{y_1}{\phi} + \frac{y_2}{\phi + \psi}\right]\right)$$

The score vector is

$$\mathbf{U}(\phi, \psi) = \begin{pmatrix} \frac{\partial l}{\partial \phi} \\ \frac{\partial l}{\partial \psi} \end{pmatrix} = \begin{pmatrix} -\frac{n}{\phi} - \frac{n}{\phi+\psi} + \frac{\sum_{i=1}^{n} y_{1i}}{\phi^2} + \frac{\sum_{i=1}^{n} y_{2i}}{(\phi+\psi)^2} \\ -\frac{n}{\phi+\psi} + \frac{\sum_{i=1}^{n} y_{2i}}{(\phi+\psi)^2} \end{pmatrix}$$

The information matrix is

$$I_{\phi\psi} = \begin{pmatrix} i_{\phi\phi} & i_{\phi\psi} \\ i_{\phi\psi} & i_{\psi\psi} \end{pmatrix} = \begin{pmatrix} \frac{n}{(\phi+\psi)^2} & \frac{n}{(\phi+\psi)^2} \\ \frac{n}{(\phi+\psi)^2} & \frac{n}{\phi^2} + \frac{n}{(\phi+\psi)^2} \end{pmatrix}$$

and its inverse, the variance–covariance matrix, is

$$I^{\phi\psi} = \begin{pmatrix} i^{\phi\phi} & i^{\psi\phi} \\ i^{\psi\phi} & i^{\psi\psi} \end{pmatrix} = \begin{pmatrix} \frac{1}{n}\left(2\phi^2 + 2\phi\psi + \psi^2\right) & -\frac{1}{n}\phi^2 \\ -\frac{1}{n}\phi^2 & \frac{1}{n}\phi^2 \end{pmatrix}$$

4.4.1. Cox and Reid approach

Orthogonal parametrization, following Cox–Reid method, requires solving the differential equation

$$\left\{\frac{1}{(\phi + \psi)} + \frac{1}{\phi^2}\right\} \frac{\partial \phi}{\partial \psi} = -\frac{1}{\phi + \psi}$$

This can be solved by separation of variables, leading to $a(\lambda) = \phi(\psi + \phi)/(\psi + 2\phi)$, where $a(\lambda)$ is an arbitrary function of λ. Cox–Reid suggest setting $a(\lambda) = e^{\lambda}$ as a suitable choice. Clearly, this does not produce a unique solution for ϕ, regardless of the parametrization of $a(\lambda)$. Thus, different reparametrizations may lead to different modified likelihoods, so that a Cox–Reid estimator may not exist or there may be many of them.

4.4.2. Gram–Schmidt approach

The proposed Gram–Schmidt approach requires seeking a transformation (ψ, ϕ) to $(\psi, \lambda(\psi, \phi))$ such that $\lambda = \phi - b_{21}\psi$ and solving the equation

$i^{\phi\psi} = b_{21} i^{\psi\psi}$

From the variance-covariance matrix, we obtain

$$b_{21}(\phi, \psi) = -\frac{\phi^2}{\left(2\phi^2 + 2\phi\psi + \psi^2\right)} \Longrightarrow \lambda = \phi + \left[\frac{\phi^2}{\left(2\phi^2 + 2\phi\psi + \psi^2\right)}\right]\psi$$

Just like the Cox-Ried approach, it is impractical to obtain or express ϕ uniquely in terms of ψ and λ and subsequently formulate a modified approximate orthogonal joint distribution function. Therefore, one could proceed iteratively, using the proposed Gram-Schmidt-Fisher scoring algorithm.

5. Fitting the disposition model

We will present procedures for estimating the parameters in the correlated model *Equation (2.1)*. The calculations are standard, and so we will only outline the results. We write the likelihood of the joint distribution of the *i*th group as

$$L_i(Y_i; \boldsymbol{\theta}) = (1 - \alpha_i)\prod_{j=1}^{n_i}(1 - y_{ij}) + \alpha_i L_{0i}(\boldsymbol{\theta}|y_i)$$

where

$$L_{0i}(\boldsymbol{\theta}|y_i) = \prod_{j=1}^{n_i} \delta_{ij}^{y_{ij}}(1 - \delta_{ij})^{1-y_{ij}}$$

$$\delta_{ij}(\boldsymbol{\theta}) = \frac{1}{1 + \exp\{-[M(\mathbf{Z}_i) + D(\mathbf{Z}_i) + W(\mathbf{X}_{ij})]\}}$$

$$\alpha_i(\boldsymbol{\theta}) = \frac{1 + \exp[-(M(\mathbf{Z}_i) + D(\mathbf{Z}_i)]}{1 + \exp[-M(\mathbf{Z}_i)]}$$

Let

$$\Upsilon_{ij}(\boldsymbol{\theta}) = M(\mathbf{Z}_i) + D(\mathbf{Z}_i) + W(\mathbf{X}_{ij})$$

and define the following

$$\Upsilon_{ij}^{(1)} = \frac{\partial}{\partial\theta}\Upsilon_{ij}(\boldsymbol{\theta}) \text{ and } \Upsilon_{ij}^{(2)} = \frac{\partial^2}{\partial\boldsymbol{\theta}^T\partial\boldsymbol{\theta}}\Upsilon_{ij}(\boldsymbol{\theta})$$

The contribution of the i-th group to the log-likelihood is the term

$$\log L_i(\boldsymbol{\theta}|y_i) = \log\left[\{1 - \alpha(\boldsymbol{\theta})\}\prod(1 - y_{ij}) + \alpha(\boldsymbol{\theta})\, L_{0i}(\boldsymbol{\theta}|y_i)\right]$$

and the contribution to the score function is the term

$$\mathbf{U}_i = \frac{\partial}{\partial\boldsymbol{\theta}}\log L_i(\boldsymbol{\theta}) = A_i(\boldsymbol{\theta})\boldsymbol{\alpha}_i^* + D_i(\boldsymbol{\theta})\mathbf{U}_{0i}(\boldsymbol{\theta}|\mathbf{y}),$$

where

$$\alpha_i^*(\boldsymbol{\theta}|y) = \frac{\partial}{\partial\boldsymbol{\theta}}\log\alpha(\boldsymbol{\theta}) = \delta_{i0}(1-\alpha_i)\frac{\partial}{\partial\boldsymbol{\theta}}M_i(\mathbf{Z}) - (1-\delta_{i0})\frac{\partial}{\partial\boldsymbol{\theta}}D_i(\mathbf{Z})$$

$$\delta_{i0} = \frac{1}{1+\exp\{-[M(\mathbf{Z}_i)+D(\mathbf{Z}_i)]\}}$$

$$A_i(\boldsymbol{\theta}) = \alpha_i(\boldsymbol{\theta})\left[L_{0i}(\boldsymbol{\theta}|y) - \prod(1-y_{ij})\right]/L_i,$$

$$D_i(\boldsymbol{\theta}) = \frac{\alpha_i L_{0_i}}{L_i}$$

$$\mathbf{U}_{0i}(\boldsymbol{\theta}|y_i) = \frac{\partial}{\partial\boldsymbol{\theta}}\log L_{0i}(\boldsymbol{\theta}|y) = \sum_{j=1}^{n_i}(y_{ij}-\delta_{ij})\boldsymbol{\Upsilon}_{ij}^{(1)};$$

Setting $\mathbf{U}(\boldsymbol{\theta}) = \sum_{i=1}^{N}\mathbf{U}_i = \mathbf{0}$, we obtain the score equations. Closed-form solutions are not possible and so the equations are solved by iterative procedures to obtain the maximum likelihood estimates of the parameters.

The contribution of the i-th group to the Hessian matrix is the term

$$\mathbf{H}_i(\boldsymbol{\theta}) = \frac{\partial^2 l_i(\boldsymbol{\theta})}{\partial\boldsymbol{\theta}\partial\boldsymbol{\theta}^t} = \sum_{j=1}^{n_i}[(y_{ij}-\delta_{ij})\boldsymbol{\Upsilon}_{ij}^{(2)} - \delta_{ij}(1-\delta_{ij})\boldsymbol{\Upsilon}_{ij}^{(1)}\boldsymbol{\Upsilon}_{ij}^{(1)T}].$$

Estimates of the parameter vector can be obtained by the **Newton–Raphson iteration routine**, which is given by the updating the formula

$$\boldsymbol{\theta}_{s+1} = \boldsymbol{\theta}_s - [\mathbf{H}(\boldsymbol{\theta}_s)]^{-1}\mathbf{U}(\boldsymbol{\theta}_s)$$

where $\boldsymbol{\theta}_s$ is the estimate of the sth iteration.

The contribution of the i-th group to the Fisher information matrix is the term

$$\mathbf{I}_i(\boldsymbol{\theta}) = \alpha_i\mathbf{I}_{0i} + A_i\boldsymbol{\alpha}_i^*\boldsymbol{\alpha}^{*T} + D_i[\alpha^*\mathbf{U}_{0i}^T + \mathbf{U}_{0i}\alpha^{*T}] - D_i(1-\alpha_i)\mathbf{U}_{0i}\mathbf{U}_{0i}^T$$

where

$$\mathbf{I}_{0_i} = \sum_{j=1}^{n_i}\delta_{ij}(1-\delta_{ij})\boldsymbol{\Upsilon}_{ij}^{(1)}\boldsymbol{\Upsilon}_{ij}^{(1)T}$$

and where A_i, D_i and $\mathbf{U}_{0i}$ are evaluated at $\mathbf{y} = (y_1, y_2, \ldots, y_n) = \mathbf{0}$. The estimates can be alternatively obtained by the **Fisher scoring method** which is given by

$$\boldsymbol{\theta}_{s+1} = \boldsymbol{\theta}_s + [\mathbf{I}(\boldsymbol{\theta}_s)]^{-1}\mathbf{U}(\boldsymbol{\theta}_s)$$

The asymptotic variance-covariance matrix of the parameter estimates, $\mathbf{C}(\boldsymbol{\theta}) = [\mathbf{I}(\boldsymbol{\theta})]^{-1}$, is the inverse of the information matrix. Thus, the transformation matrix for use of the proposed **Gram–Schmidt–Fisher scoring algorithm** can be obtained as described from Equation 4.4. Specifically, the transformation matrix, a lower triangular matrix with ones along the diagonal, is $\mathbf{B} = (b_{jk})$, where $b_{jk} = \sum_{r=1}^{j-1} c_{rj}I_{r(j-k)}, j = 2, \ldots, p; k = 1, \ldots, (j-1)$, and where (c_{rj}) and $(I_{r(j-k)})$ are entries of the variance-covariance matrix, $\mathbf{C}(\boldsymbol{\theta})$, and the information matrix, $[\mathbf{I}(\boldsymbol{\theta})]$, respectively.

The parameter estimates can subsequently be obtained by the **Gram–Schmidt–Fisher scoring algorithm** given by

$$\boldsymbol{\theta}_{s+1}^* = \boldsymbol{\theta}_s^* + [\mathbf{I}(\boldsymbol{\theta}_s^*)]^{-1}\mathbf{U}(\boldsymbol{\theta}_s^*)$$

where

$$\boldsymbol{\theta}_s^* = \mathbf{B}\boldsymbol{\theta}_s;\ \mathbf{U}(\boldsymbol{\theta}_s^*) = (\mathbf{B}^T)^{-1}\mathbf{U}(\boldsymbol{\theta}_s);\ \mathbf{I}(\boldsymbol{\theta}_s^*) = \mathbf{B}[\mathbf{I}(\boldsymbol{\theta}_s)]^{-1}\mathbf{B}^T$$

5.1. Application to oesophageal cancer in Chinese families

This application involves the study of oesophageal cancer in 2951 nuclear families collected in Yangcheng County, Shanxi Province in China (Kwagyan, 2001). In this study, we consider as a group the nuclear family unit. The outcome variable is whether an individual is affected with oesophageal cancer or not. The objective of the study is to assess the presence and aggregation of oesophageal cancer in these families. Table 1 summarizes the distribution of number of affected individuals by family size. Of the 2951 families, 1580 (53%) had no affected individuals. The combined total number of individuals from the studied families was 14310, with mean $\pm$ sd age of 48.26 $\pm$ 18.17 years. Males comprise 56.4 and 25.4% indicated drinking alcohol.

The respondent within a family has correlated outcomes which are influenced in part or wholly by the group variables as well as the variables on the individual respondent. The main objective here is to assess the presence of familial aggregation of oesophageal cancer adjusting for measured risk factors: sex, age and alcohol consumption. Here, the model for the regression analysis of disposition is parametrization as

$$M(Z) = \lambda, \quad D(Z) = \gamma \text{ and } W(X) = \beta_1 * \text{ sex} + \beta_2 * \text{ alcohol} + \beta_3 * \text{ age}$$

In this application, the vector of parameters $\boldsymbol{\beta} = (\beta_1, \beta_2, \beta_3)$ is the set of parameters of interest. Computations are performed using the computer program we developed CORRDAT (Bonney, Kwagyan, Slater, & Slifker, 1997b), which was linked with the likelihood optimization software MULTIMAX (Bonney, Kwagyan, & Apprey, 1997a). Computations can also be accomplished in MATLAB. Table 2 gives estimates of the correlation matrices. The correlations between the original parameters are quite high compared to those of the orthogonal parameters. In particular, the correlation between λ and γ is -0.179; the correlation between λ and β_1 is -0.414; and that between λ and β_3 is high, -0.841. The correlations between the orthogonal parameters are near zero or nonexistent. The correlation between λ^* is and γ^* is -0.026; the correlation between λ^* and β_1^* is now low, 0.004 and that between λ^* and β_3^* is also low, 0.0188.

As expected, the orthogonal likelihood converged in fewer iterations than the non-orthogonal one—the orthogonal likelihood converged after 17 iterations; the non-orthogonal one converged

Table 1. Distribution of family size by number of affecteds

	Number of Affecteds (a)								
Family size (s)	**0**	**1**	**2**	**3**	**4**	**5**	**6**	**7**	**Total**
3	435	151	34	3					623
4	536	215	52	16	6				819
5	335	203	81	34	8	0			659
6	159	155	59	27	1	4	0		412
7	74	95	46	12	5	3	0	1	232
8	30	54	25	11	2	3	1	0	129
9	6	21	10	3	1	1	0	0	43
10	4	8	6	2	1	1	1	0	23
11	0	3	1	1	0	1	1	0	8
12	0	1	0	1	0	0	0	0	2
13	1	0	0	0	0	0	0	0	1
Total	1580	906	314	110	24	13	3	1	2951

Table 2. Correlation matrix from original and orthogonal parametrization. Fisher scoring algorithm used for original parametrization and Gram–Schmidt–Fisher scoring algorithm used of orthogonal parametrization

Original parametrization			Orthogonal parametrization		
	λ	γ		λ^*	γ^*
λ	1		λ^*	1	
γ	−0.179	1	γ^*	0.026	1
β_1	−0.414	−0.061	β_1^*	0.004	0.000
β_2	−0.086	−0.036	β_2^*	−0.016	0.001
β_3	−0.841	0.075	β_3^*	−0.188	0.024

Table 3. Regression analysis of disposition to oesophageal cancer. Fisher scoring algorithm used for original parametrization and Gram–Schmidt–Fisher scoring algorithm for orthogonal parametrization

Original parametrization		Orthogonal parametrization	
Parameter	**Estimates (SE)**	**Parameter**	**Estimates (SE)**
λ	−4.262(0.103)	λ^*	−1.873(0.028)
γ	0.577 (0.024)	γ^*	−0.008(0.038)
β_1	0.911 (0.056)	β_1^*	0.915 (0.054)
$\beta_2 \ldots$	−1.131(0.166)	β_2^*	−1.128(0.171)
β_3	0.039 (0.002)	β_3^*	0.038 (0.002)
log (Likelihood)	−5371.294	log (Likelihood)	−5377.876
No. of iterations	56	No. of iterations	27

after 56 iterations. Estimates of the parameters are summarized in Table 3. The maximum likelihood estimate of the relative dependence parameter, $\hat{\gamma} = 0.577$ with a corresponding asymptotic 95% confidence interval of (0.529, 0.625) suggests that there is significant familial aggregation of oesophageal cancer in the families sampled. Sex and age have a positive significance, while alcohol was negative. The results suggest that males are at a higher risk of getting oesophageal cancer than females and also that it is more prevalent in older people. The negative effect of alcohol seems to suggest that it has the propensity to lower the risk of oesophageal cancer in the Chinese population studied, perhaps if drank in moderation. In summary, we conclude that oesophageal cancer aggregates in the families sampled.

6. Conclusions

Parameter orthogonalization is used as an aid in computation, approximation, interpretation and elimination or reduction of the effect of nuisance parameters. The resulting algorithm that we have proposed based on the Gram-Schmidt orthogonalization process is computationally feasible. Unlike the approach of Cox–Reid which requires solving a system of differential equations to obtain orthogonality, the proposed method only requires solving a system of linear equations. Our approach has some similarities with the conjugate gradient algorithm, but is distinctly different from it. The conjugate gradient method is an optimization routine, whereas the method we have proposed is principally an approximate orthogonalization technique combined with a maximization algorithm to aid in parameter estimation. Amari (1985) claims that global orthogonalization is possible only in a special case. Our method allows for global orthogonalization, if the information matrix can be found or estimated. The approach we have proposed is based on exact calculations. The transformation is surjective, that is the original parameters can be sufficiently obtained. Clearly, the process can be cumbersome if a large number of parameters must be accurately estimated because of the inversion of the information matrix at every stage to obtain the covariance matrix and subsequently the transformation matrix. The advantages, however, are that convergence is generally rapid in iteration times, sure and accurate. Block parametrization of parameters would be desirable if interest is in sets of parameters and where the dimension of the parameter space is large. The work we have presented in this article is the first attempt to consider the use of Gram–Schmidt process for estimation of the parameters. It is possible, however, that closer scrutiny, practical considerations, numerical studies for numerical stability and properties, and simulation studies to evaluate and compare convergence times would suggest modifications and refinements to the methods we have discussed.

In conclusion, the algorithm that we have proposed provides an exceedingly convenient method for multi-parameter statistical problems first to reduce numerical difficulties and second improve accuracy in parameter estimation. The method would be efficient for use of function minimization in both linear and non-linear maximum likelihood estimations and particularly useful for small parameter space estimation problems.

Funding

The work was supported in part from NIH/NCATS [grant number UL1TR000101 previously UL1RR031975] and NIH/NIMHHD [grant number G12MD007597].

Author details

John Kwagyan[1]

E-mail: jkwagyan@howard.edu

Victor Apprey[1]

E-mail: vapprey@howard.edu

George E. Bonney[1]

E-mail: ge_bonney@howard.edu

[1] Design, Biostatistics & Population Studies & Department of Family Medicine, College of Medicine, Howard University, Washington, DC 20059, USA.

References

Amari, S. I. (1982). Differential geometry of curved exponential families- curvatures and information loss. *Annals of Statistics, 10*, 357–85.

Amari, S. I. (1985). *Differential geometry in statistics*. New York, NY: Springer Verlag.

Bonney, G. E., & Kissling, G. E. (1986). Gram-Schmidt orthogonalization of multinormal variates: Applications in genetics. *Biometrical Journal, 28*, 417–425.

Bonney, G. E. (1995). Some new results on regressive models in family studies. *Proceedings of the Biometrics Section, American Statistical Association*, 177–182.

Bonney, G. E. (1998a). *Regression analysis of disposition to correlated binary outcomes* (Scientific Report). Philadelphia, PA: Fox Chase Cancer Center.

Bonney, G. E. (1998b). *Regression analysis of disposition to correlated binary outcomes*. Unpublished Manuscript.

Bonney, G. E., Kwagyan, J., & Apprey, V. (1997). MULTIMAX-A computer package for MULTI-objective MAXimization with applications in genetics and epidemiology. *The American Journal of Human Genetics, 61*, 447.

Bonney, G. E., Kwagyan, J., Slater, E., & Slifker, M. (1997). CORRDAT-A computer package for CORRelated DATa. *The American Journal of Human Genetics, 61*, A194.

Cox, D. R., & Reid, N. (1987). Parameter orthogonality and approximate conditional inference. *Journal of the Royal Statistical Society: Series B, 49*, 1–39.

Cox, D. R., & Reid, N. (1989). On the stability of maximum likelihood estimators of orthogonal parameters. *Canada Journal of Statistics, 17*, 229–233.

Clayton, D. G. (1971). Gram-Schmidt orthogonalization. *Journal of the Royal Statistical Society: Series C (Applied Statistics), 20*, 335–338.

Godambe, V. P. (1991). Orthogonality of estimating functions and nuisance parameters. *Biometrika, 78*, 143–151.

Godambe, V. P., & Thompson, M. E. (1989). An extension of quasi-likelihood estimation (with discussion). *Journal of Statistical Planning and Inference, 22*, 137–72.

Hills, S. E. (1987). Parameter orthogonality and approximate conditional inference [Discussion]. *Journal of the Royal Statistical Society: Series B, 49*, 1–39.

Hurlimann, W. (1992). On parameter orthogonality of the mean. *Statistical Papers, 33*, 69–74.

Kalbliesch, J. D., & Sprott, D. A. (1970). Application of likelihood methods to models involving large numbers of parameters. *Journal of the Royal Statistical Society. Series B (Methodological), 32*, 175–208.

Kwagyan, J. (2001). *Further Investigation of the disposition Model for correlated binary outcomes* (PhD Thesis). Philadelphia, PA: Department of Statistics, Temple University.

Kwagyan, J., Apprey, V., & Bonney, G. E. (2001). Parameter orthogonalization in genetic analysis. *Genetic Epidemiology, 21*, 163IGES 059.

Liang, K. Y., & Zeger, S. L. (1986). Longitudinal data analysis using generalized linear models. *Biometrika, 73*, 13–22.

Prentice, R. L. (1988). Correlated binary regression with covariates specific to each binary observation. *Biometrics, 44*, 1088–1048.

Ross, G. J. S. (1970). The efficient use of function minimization in non-linear maximum-likelihood estimation. *Applied Statistics, 19*, 205–221.

Willmot, G. E. (1988). Parameter orthogonality for a family of discrete distributions. *The Journal of the Acoustical Society of America, 83*, 517–521.

Permissions

All chapters in this book were first published in CM, by Cogent OA; hereby published with permission under the Creative Commons Attribution License or equivalent. Every chapter published in this book has been scrutinized by our experts. Their significance has been extensively debated. The topics covered herein carry significant findings which will fuel the growth of the discipline. They may even be implemented as practical applications or may be referred to as a beginning point for another development.

The contributors of this book come from diverse backgrounds, making this book a truly international effort. This book will bring forth new frontiers with its revolutionizing research information and detailed analysis of the nascent developments around the world.

We would like to thank all the contributing authors for lending their expertise to make the book truly unique. They have played a crucial role in the development of this book. Without their invaluable contributions this book wouldn't have been possible. They have made vital efforts to compile up to date information on the varied aspects of this subject to make this book a valuable addition to the collection of many professionals and students.

This book was conceptualized with the vision of imparting up-to-date information and advanced data in this field. To ensure the same, a matchless editorial board was set up. Every individual on the board went through rigorous rounds of assessment to prove their worth. After which they invested a large part of their time researching and compiling the most relevant data for our readers.

The editorial board has been involved in producing this book since its inception. They have spent rigorous hours researching and exploring the diverse topics which have resulted in the successful publishing of this book. They have passed on their knowledge of decades through this book. To expedite this challenging task, the publisher supported the team at every step. A small team of assistant editors was also appointed to further simplify the editing procedure and attain best results for the readers.

Apart from the editorial board, the designing team has also invested a significant amount of their time in understanding the subject and creating the most relevant covers. They scrutinized every image to scout for the most suitable representation of the subject and create an appropriate cover for the book.

The publishing team has been an ardent support to the editorial, designing and production team. Their endless efforts to recruit the best for this project, has resulted in the accomplishment of this book. They are a veteran in the field of academics and their pool of knowledge is as vast as their experience in printing. Their expertise and guidance has proved useful at every step. Their uncompromising quality standards have made this book an exceptional effort. Their encouragement from time to time has been an inspiration for everyone.

The publisher and the editorial board hope that this book will prove to be a valuable piece of knowledge for researchers, students, practitioners and scholars across the globe.

List of Contributors

Keivan Borna
Faculty of Mathematics and Computer Science, Kharazmi University, Tehran, Iran

Razieh Khezri
Faculty of Engineering, Kharazmi University, Tehran, Iran

Srinivasarao Thota and Shiv Datt Kumar
Department of Mathematics, Motilal Nehru National Institute of Technology, Allahabad, 211004, India

Bapurao C. Dhage
Kasubai, Gurukul Colony, Dist. Latur, Ahmedpur 413515, Maharashtra, India

A. Mhlanga, C.P. Bhunu and S. Mushayabasa
Department of Mathematics, University of Zimbabwe, P.O. Box MP 167, Mount Pleasant, Harare, Zimbabwe

Robert E. White
Department of Mathematics, Box 8205, North Carolina State University Raleigh, NC 27695-8205, USA

S. Visweswaran and Jaydeep Parejiya
Department of Mathematics, Saurashtra University, Rajkot 360 005, India

Ludwig Kohaupt
Department of Mathematics, Beuth University of Technology Berlin,

Luxemburger Str. 10, D-13353 Berlin, Germany

Şamil Akçağıl
Faculty of Economics and Administrative Sciences, Bilecik Şeyh Edebali University, Bilecik, Turkey

Tuğba Aydemir
Institute of Natural Sciences, Sakarya University, Sakarya, Turkey

Changtong Luo, Zonglin Jiang, Chun Wang and Zongmin Hu
State Key Laboratory of High Temperature Gas Dynamics, Institute of Mechanics, Chinese Academy of Sciences, Beijing 100190, China

Monireh Nosrati Sahlan, Hamid Reza Marasi and Farzaneh Ghahramani
Department of Mathematics and Computer Science, University of Bonab, Bonab, Iran

M. Lellis Thivagar and V. Sutha Devi
School of Mathematics, Madurai Kamaraj University, Madurai 625021, Tamil Nadu, India

Paul Manuel
Department of Information Science, College of Computing Sciences and Engineering, Kuwait University, Kuwait, Kuwait

L. Kohaupt
Department of Mathematics, Beuth University of Technology Berlin, Luxemburger Str. 10, D-13353 Berlin, Germany

John Kwagyan, Victor Apprey and George E. Bonney
Department of Family Medicine, College of Medicine, Howard University, Washington, DC 20059, USA

Index